THE LUTHERAN HYMNARY

*Including the Symbols
of the Evangelical
Lutheran Church*

Published by AUGSBURG PUBLISHING HOUSE *Minneapolis*

Printed and manufactured in the United States of America
by Augsburg Publishing House, Minneapolis 15, Minnesota
F.54—8067

THE SYMBOLS OF THE
EVANGELICAL LUTHERAN
CHURCH

THE Evangelical Lutheran Church accepts without exception all the canonical books of the Old and New Testaments as a whole, and in all their parts, as the divinely inspired, revealed, and inerrant Word of God, and submits to this as the only infallible authority in all matters of faith and life.

It also accepts, without reservation, the symbolical books of the Evangelical Lutheran Church, not insofar as, but because they are the presentation and explanation of the pure doctrine of the Word of God and a summary of the faith of the Lutheran Church, as this has found expression in response to the exigencies arising from time to time.

(The Evangelical Lutheran Church, in agreement with the position of the Lutheran Church of Norway and Denmark, has officially accepted only the three Ecumenical Creeds, the Unaltered Augsburg Confession, and Luther's Small Catechism. This position does not imply that the Evangelical Lutheran Church in any way whatsoever rejects the remaining symbolical books of the Lutheran Church, as the constant reference to them in her theological literature amply testifies, but since the other symbolical books are not known to her constituency generally, it has not been deemed necessary to require formal subscription to the entire Book of Concord.)

The confessions of our Church which are here printed are recommended for earnest and prayerful study by every true member of our Church that we may truly know the faith once delivered to the saints and also know whereof we speak.

✠ J. A. Aasgaard

President of the Evangelical Lutheran Church

CONTENTS

The Three General Creeds

The Augsburg Confession

CHIEF ARTICLES OF FAITH

ARTICLES IN WHICH ARE RECOUNTED THE ABUSES CORRECTED

Luther's Small Catechism

The Three General Creeds

I. The Apostles' Creed

I BELIEVE in God, the Father Almighty, Maker of heaven and earth.

And in Jesus Christ, His only Son, our Lord; Who was conceived by the Holy Ghost, Born of the Virgin Mary; Suffered under Pontius Pilate, Was crucified, dead, and buried; He descended into hell; The third day He rose again from the dead; He ascended into heaven, And sitteth on the right hand of God the Father Almighty; From thence He shall come to judge the quick and the dead.

I believe in the Holy Ghost; The holy Christian Church, the communion of saints; The forgiveness of sins; The resurrection of the body; And the life everlasting. Amen.

II. The Nicene Creed

I BELIEVE in one God, the Father Almighty, Maker of heaven and earth, And of all things visible and invisible.

And in one Lord Jesus Christ, the only-begotten Son of God, Begotten of His Father before all worlds, God of God, Light of Light, Very God of Very God, Begotten, not made, Being of one substance with the Father; By whom all things were made; Who for us men, and for our salvation, came down from heaven, And was incarnate by the Holy Ghost of the Virgin Mary, And was made man; And was crucified also for us under Pontius Pilate. He suffered and was buried; And the third day He rose again, according to the Scriptures; And ascended into heaven, And sitteth on the right hand of the Father; And He shall come again with glory to judge both the quick and the dead; Whose kingdom shall have no end.

And I believe in the Holy Ghost, The Lord and Giver of life, Who proceedeth from the Father and the Son, who with the Father and the Son together is worshipped and glorified, Who spake by the Prophets. And I believe one holy Christian and Apostolic Church. I acknowledge one Baptism for the remission of sins; And I look for the Resurrection of the dead; And the Life of the world to come. Amen.

III. The Athanasian Creed

Written Against the Arians

WHOSOEVER will be saved, before all things it is necessary that he hold the true Christian faith.

Which faith except every one do keep whole and undefiled, without doubt he shall perish everlastingly.

And the true Christian faith is this: that we worship one God in Trinity, and Trinity in Unity;

Neither confounding the persons, nor dividing the substance.

For there is one person of the Father, another of the Son, and another of the Holy Ghost.

But the Godhead of the Father, of the Son, and of the Holy Ghost, is all one: the glory equal, the majesty coeternal.

Such as the Father is, such is the Son, and such is the Holy Ghost.

The Father uncreate, the Son uncreate, and the Holy Ghost uncreate.

The Father incomprehensible, the Son incomprehensible, and the Holy Ghost incomprehensible.

The Father eternal, the Son eternal, and the Holy Ghost eternal.

And yet they are not three Eternals, but one Eternal.

As also there are not three Uncreated, nor three Incomprehensibles, but one Uncreated, and one Incomprehensible.

So likewise the Father is almighty, the Son almighty, and the Holy Ghost almighty.

And yet they are not three Almighties, but one Almighty.

So the Father is God, the Son is God, and the Holy Ghost is God.

And yet they are not three Gods, but one God.

So likewise the Father is Lord, the Son Lord, and the Holy Ghost Lord.

And yet not three Lords, but one Lord.

For like as we are compelled by the Christian Verity to acknowledge every Person by Himself to be God and Lord;

So are we forbidden by the true Christian religion to say, There be three Gods, or three Lords.

The Father is made of none, neither created, nor begotten.

The Son is of the Father alone, not made, nor created, but begotten.

The Holy Ghost is of the Father, and of the Son; neither made, nor created, nor begotten, but proceeding.

So there is one Father, not three Fathers; one Son, not three Sons; one Holy Ghost, not three Holy Ghosts.

And in this Trinity none is afore, or after other; none is greater, or less than another.

But the whole three Persons are coeternal together, and co-equal:

So that in all things, as is aforesaid, the Unity in Trinity, and the Trinity in Unity, is to be worshipped.

He therefore that will be saved must thus think of the Trinity.

Furthermore, it is necessary to everlasting salvation that he also believe rightly the incarnation of our Lord Jesus Christ.

For the right faith is that we believe and confess that our Lord Jesus Christ, the Son of God, is God and Man;

God, of the substance of the Father, begotten before the worlds; and Man, of the substance of His mother, born in the world;

Perfect God, and perfect Man, of a reasonable soul and human flesh subsisting.

Equal to the Father, as touching His Godhead; and inferior to the Father, as touching His Manhood.

Who although He be God and Man, yet He is not two, but one Christ;

One; not by conversion of the Godhead into flesh, but by taking the Manhood into God;

One altogether; not by confusion of substance, but by unity of person.

For as the reasonable soul and flesh is one man, so God and Man is one Christ;

Who suffered for our salvation, descended into hell, rose again the third day from the dead.

He ascended into heaven; He sitteth on the right hand of the Father, God Almighty; from whence He shall come to judge the quick and the dead.

At whose coming all men shall rise again with their bodies, and shall give account for their own works.

And they that have done good shall go into life everlasting; and they that have done evil, into everlasting fire.

This is the true Christian faith, which, except a man believe faithfully, he cannot be saved.

The Augsburg Confession

Delivered to the Emperor, Charles V, at the
Diet of Augsburg, A.D. 1530

*"I will speak of thy testimonies also before kings, and will not be
ashamed"* (Psalm 119:46)

[This Translation is made from the Latin *Editio Princeps*, of 1530-31, the authority
of which, equally with that of the German *Editio Princeps*, surpasses all other known
Editions. It has been carefully prepared by a Joint Committee of The General Council,
The General Synod, The United Synod of the South, and The Joint Synod of Ohio, as
a Common Standard of The Augsburg Confession in English. The words in brackets
are inserted from the German *Editio Princeps*.]

Preface

MOST Invincible Emperor, Cæsar Augustus, most Clement Lord:
Inasmuch as Your Imperial Majesty has summoned a Diet of the
Empire here at Augsburg to deliberate concerning measures against the
Turk, that most atrocious, hereditary and ancient enemy of the Christian
name and religion, in what way effectually to withstand his furor and
assaults by strong and lasting military provision; and then also concerning
dissensions in the matter of our holy religion and Christian Faith, that
in this matter of religion the opinions and judgments of parties might be
heard in each other's presence, and considered and weighed among ourselves in charity, leniency and mutual kindness, to the end that the things
in the Scriptures which on either side have been differently interpreted or
misunderstood, being corrected and laid aside, these matters may be settled
and brought back to one perfect truth and Christian concord, that for the
future one pure and true religion may be embraced and maintained by us,
that as we all serve and do battle under one Christ, so we may be able
also to live in unity and concord in the one Christian Church. And inasmuch as we, the undersigned Electors and Princes, with others joined with
us, have been called to the aforesaid Diet, the same as the other Electors,
Princes and Estates, in obedient compliance with the Imperial mandate
we have come to Augsburg, and, what we do not mean to say as boasting,
we were among the first to be here.

SINCE then Your Imperial Majesty caused to be proposed to the Electors, Princes and others Estates of the Empire, also here at Augsburg at the very beginning of this Diet, among other things, that, by virtue of the Imperial Edict, the several Estates of the Empire should present their opinions and judgments in the German and Latin languages, after due deliberation, answer was given to Your Imperial Majesty, on the ensuing Wednesday, that on the next Friday the Articles of our Confession for our part would be presented.

WHEREFORE, in obedience to Your Imperial Majesty's wishes, we offer, in this matter of religion, the Confession of our preachers and of ourselves, showing what manner of doctrine from the Holy Scriptures and the pure Word of God has been up to this time set forth in our lands, dukedoms, dominions and cities, and taught in our churches. And if the other Electors, Princes and Estates of the Empire will present similar writings, to wit, in Latin and German, according to the said Imperial proposition, giving their opinions in this matter of religion, here before Your Imperial Majesty, our most clement Lord, we, with the Princes and friends aforesaid, are prepared to confer amicably concerning all possible ways and means, as far as may be honorably done, that we may come together, and, the matter between us on both sides being peacefully discussed without offensive strife, the dissension, by God's help, may be done away and brought back to one true accordant religion; for as we all serve and do battle under one Christ, we ought to confess the one Christ, and so, after the tenor of Your Imperial Majesty's Edict, everything be conducted according to the truth of God, which, with most fervent prayers, we entreat of God.

BUT, with regard to the other Electors, Princes and Estates, if they hold that this treatment of the matter of religion after the manner which Your Imperial Majesty has so wisely brought forward, namely with such mutual presentation of writings and calm conferring together among ourselves, should not proceed, or be unfruitful in results; we, at least, leave behind the clear testimony that we decline or refuse nothing whatever, allowed of God and a good conscience, which may tend to bring about Christian concord; as also Your Imperial Majesty and the other Electors and Estates of the Empire, and all who are moved by sincere love and zeal for religion, and who will give an impartial hearing to this matter, will graciously perceive and more and more understand from this our Confession.

YOUR Imperial Majesty also, not only once but often, graciously signified to the Electors, Princes and Estates of the Empire, and at the Diet of Spires held A. D. 1526, according to the form of Your Imperial instruction and commission given and prescribed, caused it to be stated and publicly proclaimed that Your Majesty, in dealing with this mattei of religion, for certain reasons which were alleged in Your Majesty's name, was not willing to decide and could not determine anything, but that Your Majesty would diligently use Your Majesty's office with the Roman Pontiff for the convening of a General Council, as the same was publicly set forth at greater length over a year ago at the last Diet which met at Spires. There Your Imperial Majesty, through His Highness Ferdinand, King of Bohemia and Hungary, our friend and clement Lord, as well as through the Orator and Imperial Commissioners, caused this, among other things, to be proclaimed: that Your Imperial Majesty had known of and pondered the resolution of Your Majesty's Representative in the Empire, and of the President and Imperial Counsellors, and the Legates from other Estates convened at Ratisbon, concerning the calling of a Council, and that this also was adjudged by Your Imperial Majesty to be of advantage; and because the matters to be adjusted between Your Imperial Majesty and the Roman Pontiff were nearing agreement and Christian reconciliation, Your Imperial Majesty did not doubt that the Roman Pontiff could be induced to hold a General Council; therefore Your Imperial Majesty himself signified that he would endeavor to secure the Chief Pontiff's consent together with Your Imperial Majesty to convene such General Council, and that letters to that effect would be publicly issued with all possible expedition.

IN the event, therefore, that the differences between us and the other parties in the matter of religion cannot be amicably and in charity settled here before Your Imperial Majesty, we offer this in all obedience, abundantly prepared to join issue and to defend the cause in such a general, free, Christian Council, for the convening of which there has always been accordant action and agreement of votes, in all the Imperial Diets held during Your Majesty's reign, on the part of the Electors, Princes and other Estates of the Empire. To this General Council, and at the same time to Your Imperial Majesty, we have made appeal in this greatest and gravest of matters even before this, in due manner and form of law. To this appeal, both to Your Imperial Majesty and to a Council, we still adhere, neither do we intend, nor would it be possible for us, to relinquish it by this or any other document, unless the matter between us and the other side, according to the tenor of the latest Imperial citation, can be amicably and charitably settled and brought to Christian accord, of which this also is our solemn and public testimony.

Chief Articles of Faith

Article I

OF GOD

OUR Churches, with common consent, do teach that the decree of the Council of Nicæa concerning the Unity of the Divine Essence and concerning the Three Persons, is true and to be believed without any doubting; that is to say, there is one Divine Essence which is called and which is God: eternal, without body, without parts, of infinite power, wisdom and goodness, the Maker and Preserver of all things, visible and invisible; and yet that there are three Persons, of the same essence and power, who also are co-eternal, the Father, the Son and the Holy Ghost. And the term "person" they use as the Fathers have used it, to signify, not a part or quality in another, but that which subsists of itself.

They condemn all heresies which have sprung up against this article, as the Manichæans, who assumed two principles [gods], one Good, and the other Evil; also the Valentinians, Arians, Eunomians, Mohammedans, and all such. They condemn also the Samosatenes, old and new, who contending that there is but one Person, sophistically and impiously argue that the Word and the Holy Ghost are not distinct Persons, but that "Word" signifies a spoken word, and "Spirit" [Ghost] signifies motion created in things.

Article II

OF ORIGINAL SIN

ALSO they teach that since the fall of Adam all men begotten according to nature are born with sin, that is, without the fear of God, without trust ·in God, and with concupiscence; and that this disease, or vice of origin, is truly sin, even now condemning and bringing eternal death upon those not born again through baptism and the Holy Ghost.

They condemn the Pelagians and others, who deny that the vice of origin is sin, and who, to obscure the glory of Christ's merit and benefits, argue that man can be justified before God by his own strength and reason.

Article III
OF THE SON OF GOD

ALSO they teach that the Word, that is, the Son of God, did take man's nature in the womb of the blessed Virgin Mary, so that there are two natures, the divine and the human, inseparably conjoined in one person, one Christ, true God and true man, who was born of the Virgin Mary, truly suffered, was crucified, dead and buried, that He might reconcile the Father unto us, and be a sacrifice, not only for original guilt, but for all actual sins of men. He also descended into hell, and truly rose again the third day; afterward He ascended into heaven, that He might sit on the right hand of the Father, and forever reign, and have dominion over all creatures, and sanctify them that believe in Him, by sending the Holy Ghost into their hearts, to rule, comfort and quicken them, and to defend them against the devil and the power of sin. The same Christ shall openly come again to judge the quick and the dead, etc., according to the Apostles' Creed.

Article IV
OF JUSTIFICATION

ALSO they teach that men cannot be justified before God by their own strength, merits or works, but are freely justified for Christ's sake through faith, when they believe that they are received into favor and that their sins are forgiven for Christ's sake, who, by His death, hath made satisfaction for our sins. This faith God imputes for righteousness in His sight, Rom. 3 and 4.

Article V
OF THE MINISTRY OF THE CHURCH

THAT we may obtain this faith, the office of teaching the Gospel and administering the sacraments was instituted. For, through the Word and sacraments, as through instruments, the Holy Ghost is given, who worketh faith where and when it pleaseth God in them that hear the Gospel, to wit, that God, not for our own merits, but for Christ's sake, justifieth those who believe that they are received into favor for Christ's sake.

They condemn the Anabaptists and others, who think that the Holy Ghost cometh to men without the external Word, through their own preparations and works.

Article VI
OF NEW OBEDIENCE

ALSO they teach that this faith is bound to bring forth good fruits, and that it is necessary to do good works commanded by God, because of God's will, but not that we should rely on those works to merit justification before God. For remission of sins and justification are apprehended by faith, as also the voice of Christ attests: "When ye shall have done all these things, say: We are unprofitable servants" [Luke 17:10]. The same is also taught by the Fathers. For Ambrose says: "It is ordained of God that he who believes in Christ, is saved; freely receiving remission of sins, without works, by faith alone."

Article VII
OF THE CHURCH

ALSO they teach that one holy Church is to continue for ever. The Church is the congregation of saints, in which the Gospel is rightly taught and the sacraments rightly administered. And to the true unity of the Church, it is enough to agree concerning the doctrine of the Gospel and the administration of the sacraments. Nor is it necessary that human traditions, rites, or ceremonies, instituted by men, should be everywhere alike. As Paul says: "One faith, one baptism, one God and Father of all," etc. [Eph. 4:5, 6].

Article VIII
WHAT THE CHURCH IS

ALTHOUGH the Church properly is the congregation of saints and true believers, nevertheless, since, in this life, many hypocrites and evil persons are mingled therewith, it is lawful to use the sacraments, which are administered by evil men according to the saying of Christ: "The Scribes and the Pharisees sit in Moses' seat," etc. [Matt. 23:2]. Both the sacraments and the Word are effectual by reason of the institution and commandment of Christ, notwithstanding they be administered by evil men.

They condemn the Donatists, and such like, who denied it to be lawful to use the ministry of evil men in the Church, and who thought the ministry of evil men to be unprofitable and of none effect.

Article IX
OF BAPTISM

OF Baptism they teach that it is necessary to salvation, and that through Baptism is offered the grace of God; and that children are to be baptized, who, being offered to God through Baptism, are received into His grace.

They condemn the Anabaptists, who allow not the baptism of children, and say that children are saved without Baptism.

Article X
OF THE LORD'S SUPPER

OF the Supper of the Lord they teach that the Body and Blood of Christ are truly present, and are distributed to those who eat in the Supper of the Lord; and they disapprove of those that teach otherwise.

Article XI
OF CONFESSION

OF confession they teach that private absolution ought to be retained in the churches, although in confession an enumeration of all sins is not necessary. For it is impossible, according to the Psalm: "Who can understand his errors?" [Ps. 19:12].

Article XII
OF REPENTANCE

OF repentance they teach that for those that have fallen after Baptism, there is remission of sins whenever they are converted; and that the Church ought to impart absolution to those thus returning to repentance.

Now repentance consists properly of those two parts: One is contrition, that is, terrors smiting the conscience through the knowledge of sin; the other is faith, which, born of the Gospel, or of absolution, believes that, for Christ's sake, sins are forgiven, comforts the conscience, and delivers it from terrors. Then good works are bound to follow, which are the fruits of repentance.

They condemn the Anabaptists, who deny that those once justified can lose the Holy Ghost. Also those who contend that some may attain to such perfection in this life, that they cannot sin. The Novatians also are condemned, who would not absolve such as had fallen after Baptism, though they returned to repentance. They also are rejected who do not teach that remission of sins cometh through faith, but command us to merit grace through satisfactions of our own.

Article XIII
OF THE USE OF THE SACRAMENTS

OF the use of the sacraments they teach that the sacraments were ordained, not only to be marks of profession among men, but rather to be signs and testimonies of the will of God toward us, instituted to awaken and confirm faith in those who use them. Wherefore we must so use the sacraments that faith be added to believe the promises which are offered and set forth through the sacraments.

They therefore condemn those who teach that the sacraments justify by the outward act, and do not teach that, in the use of the sacraments, faith which believes that sins are forgiven, is required.

Article XIV
OF ECCLESIASTICAL ORDER

OF ecclesiastical order they teach that no one should publicly teach in the Church or administer the sacraments, unless he be regularly called.

Article XV
OF ECCLESIASTICAL RITES

OF rites and usages in the Church they teach that those ought to be observed which may be observed without sin, and which are profitable unto tranquility and good order in the Church, as particular holydays, festivals, and the like.

Nevertheless, concerning such things, let men be admonished that consciences are not to be burdened, as though such observance were necessary to salvation. They are admonished also that human traditions instituted to propitiate God, to merit grace and to make satisfaction for sins, are opposed to the Gospel and the doctrine of faith. Wherefore vows and traditions concerning meats and days, etc., instituted to merit grace and to make satisfaction for sins, are useless and contrary to the Gospel.

Article XVI
OF CIVIL AFFAIRS

OF civil affairs they teach that lawful civil ordinances are good works of God, and that it is right for Christians to bear civil office, to sit as judges, to determine matters by the Imperial and other existing laws, to award just punishments, to engage in just wars, to serve as soldiers, to make legal contracts, to hold property, to make oath when required by the magistrates, to marry, to be given in marriage.

They condemn the Anabaptists, who forbid these civil offices to Christians. They condemn also those who do not place the perfection of the Gospel in the fear of God and in faith, but in forsaking civil offices; for the Gospel teaches an eternal righteousness of the heart. Meanwhile, it does not destroy the State or the family, but especially requires their preservation as the ordinances of God, and in such ordinances the exercise of charity. Therefore, Christians are necessarily bound to obey their own magistrates and laws, save only when commanded to sin, for then they ought to obey God rather than men [Acts 5:29].

Article XVII
OF CHRIST'S RETURN TO JUDGMENT

ALSO they teach that, at the consummation of the world, Christ shall appear for judgment, and shall raise up all the dead; He shall give to the godly and elect eternal life and everlasting joys, but ungodly men and the devils He shall condemn to be tormented without end.

They condemn the Anabaptists, who think that there will be an end to the punishments of condemned men and devils. They condemn also others, who are now spreading certain Jewish opinions that, before the resurrection of the dead, the godly shall take possession of the kingdom of the world, the ungodly being everywhere suppressed [exterminated].

Article XVIII
OF THE FREEDOM OF THE WILL

OF the freedom of the will they teach that man's will has some liberty for the attainment of civil righteousness, and for the choice of things subject to reason. Nevertheless, it has no power, without the Holy Ghost, to work the righteousness of God, that is, spiritual righteousness; since the natural man receiveth not the things of the Spirit of God [1 Cor. 2:14] but this righteousness is wrought in the heart when the Holy Ghost is received through the Word. These things are said in as many words by Augustine in his *Hypognosticon,* book iii: "We grant that all men have a certain freedom of will in judging according to [natural] reason; not such freedom, however, whereby it is capable, without God, either to begin, or much less to complete, aught in things pertaining to God, but only in works of this life, whether good or evil. 'Good,' I call those works which spring from the good in nature, that is, to have a will to labor in the field, to eat and drink, to have a friend, to clothe oneself, to build a house, to marry, to keep cattle, to learn divers useful arts, or whatsoever good pertains to this life, none of which things are without dependence on the providence of God; yea, of Him and through Him they are and have their beginning. 'Evil,' I call such works as to have a will to worship an idol, to commit murder," etc.

They condemn the Pelagians and others who teach that, without the Holy Ghost, by the power of nature alone, we are able to love God above all things; also to do the commandments of God as touching "the substance of the act." For, although nature is able in some sort to do the outward work (for it is able to keep the hands from theft and murder), yet it cannot work the inward motions, such as the fear of God, trust in God, chastity, patience, etc.

Article XIX
OF THE CAUSE OF SIN

OF the cause of sin they teach that although God doth create and preserve nature, yet the cause of sin is the will of the wicked, that is, of the devil and ungodly men; which will, unaided of God, turns itself from God, as Christ says [John 8:44]: "When he speaketh a lie, he speaketh of his own."

Article XX
OF GOOD WORKS

OUR teachers are falsely accused of forbidding good works. For their published writings on the Ten Commandments, and others of like import, bear witness that they have taught to good purpose concerning all estates and duties of life, as to what estates of life and what works in every calling be pleasing to God. Concerning these things preachers heretofore taught but little, and urged only childish and needless works, as particular holydays, particular fasts, brotherhoods, pilgrimages, services in honor of saints, the use of rosaries, monasticism, and such like. Since our adversaries have been admonished of these things, they are now unlearning them, and do not preach these unprofitable works as heretofore. Besides, they begin to mention faith, of which there was heretofore marvellous silence. They teach that we are justified not by works only, but they conjoin faith and works, and say that we are justified by faith and works. This doctrine is more tolerable than the former one, and can afford more consolation than their old doctrine.

Forasmuch, therefore, as the doctrine concerning faith, which ought to be the chief one in the Church, has lain so long unknown, as all must needs grant that there was the deepest silence in their sermons concerning the righteousness of faith, while only the doctrine of works was treated in the churches, our teachers have instructed the churches concerning faith as follows:

First, that our works cannot reconcile God or merit forgiveness of sins, grace and justification, but that we obtain this only by faith, when we believe that we are received into favor for Christ's sake, who alone has been set forth the Mediator and Propitiation [1 Tim. 2:5], in order that the Father may be reconciled through Him. Whoever, therefore, trusts that by works he merits grace, despises the merit and grace of Christ, and seeks a way to God without Christ, by human strength, although Christ has said of Himself: "I am the Way, the Truth and the Life" [John 14:6].

This doctrine concerning faith is everywhere treated by Paul [Eph. 2:8]: "By grace are ye saved through faith; and that not of yourselves; it is the gift of God, not of works," etc.

And lest any one should craftily say that a new interpretation of Paul has been devised by us, this entire matter is supported by the testimonies of the Fathers. For Augustine, in many volumes, defends grace and the righteousness of faith, over against the merits of works. And Ambrose, in his *De Vocatione Gentium,* and elsewhere, teaches to like effect. For in his *De Vocatione Gentium,* he says as follows: "Redemption by the Blood of Christ would become of little value, neither would the preeminence of man's works be superseded by the mercy of God, if justification, which is wrought through grace, were due to merits going before, so as to be, not the gift of a donor, but the reward due to the laborer."

But although this doctrine is despised by the inexperienced, nevertheless God-fearing and anxious consciences find by experience that it brings the greatest consolation, because consciences cannot be pacified through any works, but only by faith, when they are sure that, for Christ's sake, they have a gracious God. As Paul teaches [Rom. 5:1]: "Being justified by faith, we have peace with God." This whole doctrine is to be referred to that conflict of the terrified conscience; neither can it be understood apart from that conflict. Therefore, inexperienced and profane men judge ill concerning this matter, who dream that Christian righteousness is nothing but the civil righteousness of natural reason.

Heretofore consciences were plagued with the doctrine of works, nor did they hear any consolation from the Gospel. Some persons were driven by conscience into the desert, into monasteries, hoping there to merit grace by a monastic life. Some also devised other works whereby to merit grace and make satisfaction for sins. There was very great need to treat of and renew this doctrine of faith in Christ, to the end that anxious consciences should not be without consolation, but that they might know that grace and forgiveness of sins and justification are apprehended by faith in Christ.

Men are also admonished that here the term "faith" doth not signify merely the knowledge of the history, such as is in the ungodly and in the devil, but signifieth a faith which believes, not merely the history, but also the effect of the history—namely, this article of the forgiveness of sins, to wit, that we have grace, righteousness, and forgiveness of sins, through Christ.

Now he that knoweth that he has a Father reconciled to him through Christ, since he truly knows God, knows also that God careth for him, and calls upon God; in a word, he is not without God, as the heathen. For devils and the ungodly are not able to believe this article of the forgiveness of sins. Hence, they hate God as an enemy; call not upon Him; and expect no good from Him. Augustine also admonishes his readers concerning the word "faith," and teaches that the term "faith" is accepted in the Scriptures, not for knowledge such as is in the ungodly, but for confidence which consoles and encourages the terrified mind.

Furthermore, it is taught on our part that it is necessary to do good works, not that we should trust to merit grace by them, but because it is the will of God. It is only by faith that forgiveness of sins and grace are apprehended. And because through faith the Holy Ghost is received, hearts are renewed and endowed with new affections, so as to be able to bring forth good works. For Ambrose says: "Faith is the mother of a good will and right doing." For man's powers without the Holy Ghost are full of ungodly affections, and are too weak to do works which are good in God's sight. Besides, they are in the power of the devil, who impels men to divers sins, to ungodly opinions, to open crimes. This we may see in the philosophers, who, although they endeavored to live an honest life, could not succeed, but were defiled with many open crimes. Such is the feebleness of man, when he is without faith and without the Holy Ghost, and governs himself only by human strength.

Hence it may be readily seen that this doctrine is not to be charged with prohibiting good works, but rather the more to be commended, because it shows how we are enabled to do good works. For without faith, human nature can in no wise do the works of the First or of the Second Commandment. Without faith, it does not call upon God, nor expect anything from Him, nor bear the cross; but seeks and trusts in man's help. And thus, when there is no faith and trust in God, all manner of lusts and human devices rule in the heart. Wherefore Christ said [John 15:5]: "Without me ye can do nothing," and the Church sings:

"Without Thy power divine
In man there nothing is,
Naught but what is harmful."

Article XXI

OF THE WORSHIP OF SAINTS

OF the worship of saints they teach that the memory of saints may be set before us, that we may follow their faith and good works, according to our calling, as the Emperor may follow the example of David in making war to drive away the Turk from his country. For both are kings. But the Scripture teaches not the invocation of saints, or to ask help of saints, since it sets before us Christ, as the only Mediator, Propitiation, High-Priest and Intercessor. He is to be prayed to, and hath promised that He will hear our prayer; and this worship He approves above all, to wit, that in all afflictions He be called upon [1 John 2:1]: "If any man sin, we have an Advocate with the Father," etc.

This is about the sum of our doctrine, in which, as can be seen, there is nothing that varies from the Scriptures, or from the Church Catholic, or from the Church of Rome as known from its writers. This being the case, they judge harshly who insist that our teachers be regarded as heretics. The disagreement, however, is on certain abuses which have crept into the Church without rightful authority. And even in these, if there were some difference, there should be proper lenity on the part of bishops to bear with us by reason of the Confession which we have now drawn up; because even the Canons are not so severe as to demand the same rites everywhere, neither, at any time, have the rites of all churches been the same; although, among us, in large part, the ancient rites are diligently observed. For it is a false and malicious charge that all the ceremonies, all the things instituted of old, are abolished in our churches. But it has been a common complaint that some abuses were connected with the ordinary rites. These, inasmuch as they could not be approved with a good conscience, have been to some extent corrected.

Articles in Which Are Recounted the Abuses Corrected

INASMUCH then as our churches dissent in no article of the faith from the Church Catholic, but omit some abuses which are new, and which have been erroneously accepted by fault of the times, contrary to the intent of the Canons, we pray that Your Imperial Majesty would graciously hear both what has been changed, and also what were the reasons, in order that the people be not compelled to observe those abuses against their conscience. Nor should Your Imperial Majesty believe those who, in order to excite the hatred of men against our part, disseminate strange slanders among our people. Having thus excited the minds of good men, they have first given occasion to this controversy, and now endeavor, by the same arts, to increase the discord. For Your Imperial Majesty will undoubtedly find that the form of doctrine and of ceremonies with us, is not so intolerable as these ungodly and malicious men represent. Furthermore, the truth cannot be gathered from common rumors, or the revilings of our enemies. But it can readily be judged that nothing would serve better to maintain the dignity of worship, and to nourish reverence and pious devotion among the people, than that the ceremonies be rightly observed in the churches.

Article XXII
OF BOTH KINDS IN THE LORD'S SUPPER

TO the laity are given both kinds in the sacrament of the Lord's Supper, because this usage has the commandment of the Lord [in Matt. 26:27]: "Drink ye all of it"; where Christ has manifestly commanded concerning the cup that all should drink; and lest any man should craftily say that this refers only to priests, Paul [in 1 Cor. 11:27] recites an example from which it appears that the whole congregation did use both kinds. And this usage has long remained in the Church, nor is it known when, or by whose authority, it was changed; although Cardinal Cusanus mentions the time when it was approved. Cyprian in some places testifies that the Blood was given to the people. The same is testified by Jerome, who says: "The priests administer the Eucharist, and distribute the Blood of Christ to the people." Indeed, Pope Gelasius commands that the sacrament be not divided (*Dist.* ii, *De Consecratione, Cap. Comperimus*). Only custom, not so ancient, has it otherwise. But it is evident that any custom introduced against the commandments of God is not to be allowed, as the Canons witness (*Dist.* iii, *Cap. Veritate,* and the following chapters). But this custom has been received, not only against the Scripture, but also against the old Canons and example of the Church. Therefore if any preferred to use both kinds of the sacrament, they ought not to have been compelled with offence to their consciences to do otherwise.

And because the division of the sacrament does not agree with the ordinance of Christ we are accustomed to omit the procession, which hitherto has been in use.

Article XXIII

OF THE MARRIAGE OF PRIESTS

THERE has been common complaint concerning the examples of priests who were not chaste. For that reason also, Pope Pius is reported to have said that there were certain reasons why marriage was taken away from priests, but that there were far weightier ones why it ought to be given back; for so Platina writes. Since, therefore, our priests were desirous to avoid these open scandals, they married wives, and taught that it was lawful for them to contract matrimony. First, because Paul says [1 Cor. 7:2]: "To avoid fornication, let every man have his own wife." Also [9]: "It is better to marry, than to burn." Secondly, Christ says [Matt. 19:11]: "All men cannot receive this saying"; where He teaches that not all men are fit to lead a single life; for God created man for procreation [Gen. 1:28]. Nor is it in man's power, without a singular gift and work of God, to alter this creation. Therefore those that are not fit to lead a single life, ought to contract matrimony: For no man's law, no vow, can annul the commandment and ordinance of God. For these reasons the priests teach that it is lawful for them to marry wives. It is also evident that in the ancient Church, priests were married men. For Paul says [1 Tim. 3:2] that a bishop should be the husband of one wife. And in Germany, four hundred years ago, for the first time, the priests were violently compelled to lead a single life, who indeed offered such resistance that the Archbishop of Mayence, when about to publish the Pope's decree concerning this matter, was almost killed in the tumult raised by the enraged priests. And so harsh was the dealing in the matter, that not only were marriages forbidden for the time to come, but also existing marriages were torn asunder, contrary to all laws, divine and human, contrary even to the Canons themselves, made not only by the Popes, but by most celebrated councils.

Seeing, also, that, as the world is aging, man's nature is gradually growing weaker, it is well to guard that no more vices steal into Germany. Furthermore, God ordained marriage to be a help against human infirmity. The Canons themselves say that the old rigor ought now and then, in the latter times, to be relaxed because of the weakness of men; which it is to be devoutly wished were done also in this matter. And it is to be expected that the churches shall at length lack pastors, if marriage should be any longer forbidden.

But while the commandment of God is in force, while the custom of the Church is well known, while impure celibacy causes many scandals, adulteries, and other crimes deserving the punishments of just magistrates, yet it is a marvelous thing that in nothing is more cruelty exercised than against the marriage of priests. God has given commandment to honor marriage. By the laws of all well-ordered commonwealths, even among the heathen, marriage is most highly honored. But now men, and also priests, are cruelly put to death, contrary to the intent of the Canons, for no other cause than marriage. Paul [in 1 Tim. 4:3] calls that a doctrine of devils, which forbids marriage. This may now be readily understood when the law against marriage is maintained by such penalties.

But as no law of man can annul the commandment of God, so neither can it be done by any vow. Accordingly Cyprian also advises that women who do not keep the chastity they have promised should marry. His words are these [Book 1, Epistle xi]: "But if they be unwilling or unable to persevere, it is better for them to marry than to fall into the fire by their lusts; at least, they should give no offence to their brethren and sisters." And even the Canons show some leniency toward those who have taken vows before the proper age, as heretofore has generally been the case.

Article XXIV
OF THE MASS

FALSELY are our churches accused of abolishing the Mass; for the Mass is retained on our part, and celebrated with the highest reverence. All the usual ceremonies are also preserved, save that the parts sung in Latin are interspersed here and there with German hymns, which have been added to teach the people. For ceremonies are needed to this end alone, that the unlearned be taught. And not only has Paul commanded to use in the Church a language understood by the people [1 Cor. 14: 2, 9], but it has also been so ordained by man's law.

The people are accustomed to partake of the sacrament together, if any be fit for it, and this also increases the reverence and devotion of public worship. For none are admitted, except they be first proved. The people are also advised concerning the dignity and use of the sacrament, how great consolation it brings anxious consciences, that they may learn to believe God, and to expect and ask of Him all that is good. This worship pleases God; such use of the sacrament nourishes true devotion toward God. It does not, therefore, appear that the Mass is more devoutly celebrated among our adversaries, than among us.

But it is evident that for a long time it has been the public and most grievous complaint of all good men that Masses have been basely profaned and applied to purposes of lucre. For it is unknown how far this abuse obtains in all the churches, by what manner of men Masses are said only for fees or stipends, and how many celebrate them contrary to the Canons. But Paul severely threatens those who deal unworthily with the Eucharist, when he says [1 Cor. 11:27]: "Whosoever shall eat this bread, and drink this cup of the Lord unworthily, shall be guilty of the body and blood of the Lord." When, therefore, our priests were admonished concerning this sin, private Masses were discontinued among us, as scarcely any private Masses were celebrated except for lucre's sake.

Neither were the bishops ignorant of these abuses, and if they had corrected them in time, there would now be less dissension. Heretofore, by their own negligence, they suffered many corruptions to creep into the Church. Now, when it is too late, they begin to complain of the troubles of the Church, seeing that this disturbance has been occasioned simply by those abuses, which were so manifest that they could be borne no longer. Great dissensions have arisen concerning the Mass, concerning the sacrament. Perhaps the world is being punished for such long-continued profanations of the Mass as have been tolerated in the churches for so many centuries, by the very men who were both able and in duty bound to correct them. For, in the Ten Commandments, it is written (Exodus 20), "The Lord will not hold him guiltless that taketh his name in vain." But since the world began, nothing that God ever ordained seems to have been so abused for filthy lucre as the Mass.

There was also added the opinion, which infinitely increased private Masses, namely, that Christ, by His passion, had made satisfaction for original sin, and instituted the Mass wherein an offering should be made for daily sins, venial and mortal. From this has arisen the common opinion that the Mass taketh away the sins of the living and the dead, by the outward act. Then they began to dispute whether one Mass said for many were worth as much as special Masses for individuals, and this brought forth that infinite multitude of Masses. Concerning these opinions our teachers have given warning, that they depart from the Holy Scriptures and diminish the glory of the passion of Christ. For Christ's passion was an oblation and satisfaction, not for original guilt only, but also for all sins, as it is written to the Hebrews (10:10), "We are sanctified through the offering of Jesus Christ, once for all." Also, 10:14, "By one offering he hath perfected forever them that are sanctified." Scripture also teaches that we are justified before God through faith in Christ, when we believe that our sins are forgiven for Christ's sake. Now if the Mass take away the sins of the living and the dead by the outward act, justification comes of the work of Masses, and not of faith, which Scripture does not allow.

But Christ commands us [Luke 22:19], "This do in remembrance of me"; therefore the Mass was instituted that the faith of those who use the sacrament should remember what benefits it receives through Christ, and cheer and comfort the anxious conscience. For, to remember Christ, is to remember His benefits, and to realize that they are truly offered unto us. Nor is it enough only to remember the history, for this the Jews and the ungodly also can remember. Wherefore the Mass is to be used to this end, that there the sacrament [Communion] may be administered to them that have need of consolation; as Ambrose says: "Because I always sin, I am always bound to take the medicine."

Now, forasmuch as the Mass is such a giving of the sacrament, we hold one Communion every holyday, and also other days, when any desire the sacrament it is given to such as ask for it. And this custom is not new in the Church; for the Fathers before Gregory make no mention of any private Mass, but of the common Mass [the Communion] they speak very much. Chrysostom says that the priest stands daily at the altar, inviting some to the Communion and keeping back others. And it appears from the ancient Canons that some one celebrated the Mass from whom all the other presbyters and deacons received the Body of the Lord; for thus the words of the Nicene Canon say: "Let the deacons, according to their order, receive the Holy Communion after the presbyters, from the bishop or from a presbyter." And Paul [1 Cor. 11:33] commands concerning the Communion: "Tarry one for another," so that there may be a common participation.

Forasmuch, therefore, as the Mass with us has the example of the Church, taken from the Scripture and the Fathers, we are confident that it cannot be disapproved, especially since the public ceremonies are retained for the most part, like those hitherto in use; only the number of Masses differs, which, because of very great and manifest abuses, doubtless might be profitably reduced. For in olden times, even in churches most frequented, the Mass was not celebrated every day, as the Tripartite History

(Book 9, chapter 33) testifies: "Again in Alexandria, every Wednesday and Friday, the Scriptures are read, and the doctors expound them, and all things are done, except only the celebration of the Eucharist."

Article XXV

OF CONFESSION

CONFESSION in our churches is not abolished; for it is not usual to give the Body of the Lord, except to them that have been previously examined and absolved. And the people are most carefully taught concerning the faith and assurance of absolution, about which, before this time, there was profound silence. Our people are taught that they should highly prize the absolution, as being the voice of God, and pronounced by His command. The power of the Keys is commended, and we show what great consolation it brings to anxious consciences; that God requires faith to believe such absolution as a voice sounding from heaven, and that such faith in Christ truly obtains and receives the forgiveness of sins.

Aforetime, satisfactions were immoderately extolled; of faith and the merit of Christ, and the righteousness of faith, no mention was made; wherefore, on this point, our churches are by no means to be blamed. For this even our adversaries must needs concede to us that the doctrine concerning repentance has been most diligently treated and laid open by our teachers.

But of confession they teach that an enumeration of sins is not necessary, and that consciences be not burdened with anxiety to enumerate all sins, for it is impossible to recount all sins, as the Psalm testifies [19:13]: "Who can understand his errors?" Also Jeremiah [17:9]: "The heart is deceitful, who can know it?" But if no sins were forgiven, except those that are recounted, consciences could never find peace; for very many sins they neither see, nor can remember.

The ancient writers also testify that an enumeration is not necessary. For, in the Decrees, Chrysostom is quoted, who thus says: "I say not to thee that thou shouldest disclose thyself in public, nor that thou accuse thyself before others, but I would have thee obey the prophet who says: 'Disclose thy way before God.' Therefore confess thy sins before God, the true Judge, with prayer. Tell thine errors, not with the tongue, but with the memory of thy conscience." And the Gloss ("Of Repentance," Distinct. v, Cap. *Consideret*) admits that confession is of human right only. Nevertheless, on account of the great benefit of absolution, and because it is otherwise useful to the conscience, confession is retained among us.

Article XXVI
OF THE DISTINCTION OF MEATS

IT has been the general persuasion, not of the people alone, but also of such as teach in the churches, that making distinctions of meats, and like traditions of men, are works profitable to merit grace, and able to make satisfactions for sins. And that the world so thought, appears from this, that new ceremonies, new orders, new holydays, and new fastings were daily instituted, and the teachers in the churches did exact these works as a service necessary to merit grace, and did greatly terrify men's consciences, if they should omit any of these things. From this persuasion concerning traditions, much detriment has resulted in the Church.

First, the doctrine of grace and of the righteousness of faith has been obscured by it, which is the chief part of the Gospel, and ought to stand out, as the most prominent in the Church, that the merit of Christ may be well known, and that faith, which believes that sins are forgiven for Christ's sake, may be exalted far above works. Wherefore Paul also lays the greatest stress on this article, putting aside the law and human traditions, in order to show that the righteousness of the Christian is another than such works, to wit, the faith which believes that sins are freely forgiven for Christ's sake. But this doctrine of Paul has been almost wholly smothered by traditions, which have produced an opinion that, by making distinctions in meat and like services, we must merit grace and righteousness. In treating of repentance, there was no mention made of faith; all that was done was to set forth those works of satisfaction, and in these all repentance seemed to consist.

Secondly, these traditions have obscured the commandments of God; because traditions were placed far above the commandments of God. Christianity was thought to consist wholly in the observance of certain holydays, fasts and vestures. These observances had won for themselves the exalted title of being the spiritual life and the perfect life. Meanwhile the commandments of God, according to each one's calling, were without honor, namely, that the father brought up his family, that the mother bore children, that the prince governed the commonwealth—these were-accounted works that were worldly and imperfect, and far below those glittering observances. And this error greatly tormented devout consciences, which grieved that they were bound by an imperfect state of life, as in marriage, in the office of magistrate, or in other civil ministrations; on the other hand, they admired the monks and such like, and falsely imagined that the observances of such men were more acceptable to God.

Thirdly, traditions brought great danger to consciences; for it was impossible to keep all traditions, and yet men judged these observances to be necessary acts of worship. Gerson writes that many fell into despair, and that some even took their own lives, because they felt that they were not able to satisfy the traditions; and meanwhile they heard not the consolation of the righteousness of faith and grace.

We see that the summists and theologians gather the traditions together, and seek mitigations whereby to ease consciences, and yet they do not succeed in releasing them, but sometimes entangle consciences even more. And, with the gathering of these traditions, the schools and sermons have been so much occupied that they have had no leisure to touch upon Scripture, and to seek the more profitable doctrine of faith, of the cross, of hope, of the dignity of civil affairs, of consolation of sorely tried consciences. Hence Gerson, and some other theologians, have grievously complained that, by these strivings concerning traditions, they were prevented from giving attention to a better kind of doctrine. Augustine also forbids that men's consciences should be burdened with such observances, and prudently advises Januarius that he must know that they are to be observed as things indifferent; for these are his words.

Wherefore our teachers must not be looked upon as having taken up this matter rashly, or from hatred of the bishops, as some falsely suspect. There was great need to warn the churches of these errors, which had arisen from misunderstanding the traditions. For the Gospel compels us to insist in the churches upon the doctrine of grace, and of the righteousness of faith; which, however, cannot be understood, if men think that they merit grace by observances of their own choice.

Thus, therefore, they have taught that by the observance of human traditions we cannot merit grace, or be justified; and hence we must not think such observances necessary acts of worship.

They add hereunto testimonies of Scripture. Christ [Matt. 15:3] defends the Apostles who had not observed the usual tradition, which, however, seemed to pertain to a matter not unlawful, but indifferent, and to have a certain affinity with the purifications of the law, and says [9]: "In vain do they worship me with the commandments of men." He, therefore, does not exact an unprofitable service. Shortly after, He adds [11]: "Not that which goeth into the mouth, defileth a man." So also Paul [Rom. 14:17]: "The Kingdom of God is not meat and drink." Col. [2:16]: "Let no man therefore judge you in meat, or in drink, or in respect of an holyday, or of the Sabbath day"; also [v. 20, sq.]: "If ye be dead with Christ from the rudiments of the world, why, as though living in the world, are ye subject to ordinances, touch not, taste not, handle not?" And Peter says [Acts 15:10]: "Why tempt ye God, to put a yoke upon the neck of the disciples, which neither our fathers nor we were able to bear; but we believe that through the grace of the Lord Jesus Christ we shall be saved, even as they." Here Peter forbids to burden the consciences with many rites, either of Moses, or of others.

And in 1 Tim. [4:1, 3], Paul calls the prohibition of meats a doctrine of devils; for it is against the Gospel to institute or to do such works that by them we may merit grace, or as though Christianity could not exist without such service of God.

Here our adversaries cast up that our teachers are opposed to discipline and mortification of the flesh, as Jovinian. But the contrary may be learned from the writings of our teachers. For they have always taught concerning the cross that it behooves Christians to bear afflictions. This is the true, earnest and unfeigned mortification, to wit, to be exercised with divers afflictions, and to be crucified with Christ.

Moreover, they teach that every Christian ought to exercise and subdue himself with bodily restraints and labors, that neither plenty nor slothfulness tempt him to sin, but not that we may merit grace or make satisfaction for sins by such exercises. And such external discipline ought to be urged at all times, not only on a few and set days. So Christ commands [Luke 21:34]: "Take heed, lest your hearts be overcharged with surfeiting"; also [Matt. 17:21]: "This kind goeth not out but by prayer and fasting." Paul also says [1 Cor. 9:27]: "I keep under my body and bring it into subjection." Here he clearly shows that he was keeping under his body, not to merit forgiveness of sins by that discipline, but to have his body in subjection and fitted for spiritual things, and for the discharge of duty according to his calling. Therefore, we do not condemn fasting, but the traditions which prescribe certain days and certain meats, with peril of conscience, as though works of such kinds were a necessary service.

Nevertheless, very many traditions are kept on our part, which conduce to good order in the church, as the Order of Lessons in the Mass, and the chief holydays. But, at the same time, men are warned that such observances do not justify before God, and that, in such things, it should not be made sin, if they be omitted without scandal. Such liberty in human rites was not unknown to the Fathers. For in the East they kept Easter at another time than at Rome, and when, on account of this diversity, the Romans accused the Eastern Church of schism, they were admonished by others that such usages need not be alike everywhere. And Irenæus says: "Diversity concerning fasting does not destroy the harmony of faith." As also Pope Gregory intimates, in *Dist.* xii, that such diversity does not violate the unity of the Church. And in the Tripartite History, Book 9, many examples of dissimilar rites are gathered, and the following statement is made: "It was not the mind of the Apostles to enact rules concerning holydays, but to preach godliness and a holy life."

Article XXVII

OF MONASTIC VOWS

WHAT is taught, on our part, concerning monastic vows, will be better understood if it be remembered what has been the state of the monasteries, and how many things were daily done in those very monasteries, contrary to the Canons. In Augustine's time, they were free associations. Afterward, when discipline was corrupted, vows were everywhere added for the purpose of restoring discipline, as in a carefully planned prison. Gradually, many other observances were added besides vows. And these fetters were laid upon many before the lawful age, contrary to the Canons. Many also entered into this kind of life through ignorance, being unable to judge their own strength, though they were of sufficient age. Being thus ensnared, they were compelled to remain, even though some could have been freed by the provision of the Canons. And this was more the case in convents of women than of monks, although more consideration should have been shown the weaker sex. This rigor displeased many good men before this time, who saw that young men and maidens were thrown into convents for a living, and what unfortunate results came of this procedure, and what scandals were created, what snares were cast upon consciences! They were grieved that the authority of the Canons in so momentous a matter was utterly despised and set aside.

To these evils was added an opinion concerning vows, which, it is well known, in former times, displeased even those monks who were more thoughtful. They taught that vows were equal to Baptism: they taught that, by this kind of life, they merited forgiveness of sins and justification before God. Yea, they added that the monastic life not only merited righteousness before God, but even greater things, because it kept not only the precepts, but also the so-called "evangelical counsels."

Thus they made men believe that the profession of monasticism was far better than Baptism, and that the monastic life was more meritorious than that of magistrates, than the life of pastors and such like, who serve their calling in accordance with God's commands, without any man-made services. None of these things can be denied; for they appear in their own books.

What then came to pass in the monasteries? Aforetime, they were schools of theology and other branches profitable to the Church; and thence pastors and bishops were obtained. Now it is another thing. It is needless to rehearse what is known to all. Aforetime they came together to learn; now they feign that it is a kind of life instituted to merit grace and righteousness; yea, they preach that it is a state of perfection, and they put it far above all other kinds of life ordained of God.

These things we have rehearsed without odious exaggeration, to the end that the doctrine of our teachers, on this point, might be better under-stood. First, concerning such as contract matrimony, they teach, on our part, that it is lawful for all men who are not fitted for single life to con-tract matrimony, because vows cannot annul the ordinance and command-ment of God. But the commandment of God is [1 Cor. 7:2]: "To avoid fornication, let every man have his own wife." Nor is it the command-ment only, but also the creation and ordinance of God, which forces those to marry who are not excepted by a singular work of God, according to the text [Gen. 2:18]: "It is not good that the man should be alone." There-fore they do not sin who obey this commandment and ordinance of God. What objection can be raised to this? Let men extol the obligation of a vow as much as they list, yet shall they not bring to pass that the vow annuls the commandment of God. The Canons teach that the right of the superior is excepted in every vow; much less, therefore, are these vows of force which are against the commandments of God.

Now if the obligation of vows could not be changed for any cause whatever, the Roman Pontiffs could never have given dispensation; for it is not lawful for man to annul an obligation which is altogether divine. But the Roman Pontiffs have prudently judged that leniency is to be ob-served in this obligation, and therefore we read that many times they have dispensed from vows. The case of the King of Aragon who was called back from the monastery is well known, and there are also examples in our own times.

In the second place, why do our adversaries exaggerate the obligation or effect of a vow, when, at the same time, they have not a word to say of the nature of the vow itself, that it ought to be in a thing possible, free, and chosen spontaneously and deliberately? But it is not known to what extent perpetual chastity is in the power of man. And how few are there who have taken the vow spontaneously and deliberately! Young men and maidens, before they are able to judge, are persuaded, and sometimes even compelled, to take the vow. Wherefore it is not fair to insist so rigorously on the obligation, since it is granted by all that it is against the nature of a vow to take it without spontaneous and deliberate action.

Many canonical laws rescind vows made before the age of fifteen; for before that age there does not seem sufficient judgment in a person to decide concerning a perpetual life. Another Canon, granting even more liberty to the weakness of man, adds a few years, and forbids a vow to be made before the age of eighteen. But whether we followed the one or the other, the most part have an excuse for leaving the monasteries, be-cause most of them have taken vows before they reached these ages.

But, finally, even though the violation of a vow might be rebuked, yet it seems not forthwith to follow that the marriages of such persons ought to be dissolved. For Augustine denies that they ought to be dissolved, (XXVII Quæst. i, Cap. *Nuptiarum*); and his authority is not lightly to be esteemed, although other men afterwards thought otherwise.

But although it appears that God's command concerning marriage delivers many from their vows, yet our teachers introduce also another argument concerning vows, to show that they are void. For every service of God, ordained and chosen of men without the commandment of God to merit justification and grace, is wicked; as Christ says [Matt. 15:9]: "In vain they do worship me with the commandments of men." And Paul teaches everywhere that righteousness is not to be sought by our own observances and acts of worship, devised by men, but that it comes by faith to those who believe that they are received by God into grace for Christ's sake.

But it is evident that monks have taught that services of man's making satisfy for sins and merit grace and justification. What else is this but to detract from the glory of Christ and to obscure and deny the righteousness of faith? It follows, therefore, that the vows thus commonly taken have been wicked services, and consequently, are void. For a wicked vow, taken against the commandment of God, is not valid; for (as the Canon says) no vow ought to bind men to wickedness.

Paul says [Gal. 5:4]: "Christ is become of no effect unto you, whosoever of you are justified by the law; ye are fallen from grace." They, therefore, who want to be justified by their vows, are made void of Christ and fall from grace. For such as ascribe justification to vows, ascribe to their own works that which properly belongs to the glory of Christ. But it is undeniable that the monks have taught that, by their vows and observances, they were justified, and merited forgiveness of sins, yea, they invented still greater absurdities, saying that they could give others a share in their works. If any one should be inclined to enlarge on these things with evil intent, how many things could he bring together, whereof even the monks are now ashamed! Over and above this, they persuaded men that services of man's making were a state of Christian perfection. And is not this assigning justification to works? It is no light offence in the Church to set forth to the people a service devised by men, without the commandment of God, and to teach that such service justifies men. For the righteousness of faith in Christ, which chiefly ought to be in the Church, is obscured, when this wonderful worshipping of angels, with its show of poverty, humility and chastity, is cast before the eyes of men.

Furthermore, the precepts of God and the true service of God are obscured when men hear that only monks are in a state of perfection. For Christian perfection is to fear God from the heart, again to conceive great faith, and to trust that, for Christ's sake, we have a gracious God, to ask of God and assuredly to expect His aid in all things that, according to our calling, are to be borne; and meanwhile to be diligent in outward good works, and to serve our calling. In these things consist the true perfection and the true service of God. It does not consist in the unmarried life, or in begging, or in vile apparel. But the people conceive many pernicious opinions from the false commendations of monastic life. They hear unmarried life praised above measure; therefore they lead their married life with offence to their consciences. They hear that only beggars are perfect; therefore they keep their possessions and do business with offence to their consciences. They hear that it is an evangelical counsel not to avenge; therefore some in private life are not afraid to take revenge, for they hear that it is but a counsel, and not a commandment; while others judge that the Christian cannot properly hold a civil office, or be a magistrate.

There are on record examples of men who, forsaking marriage and the adminstration of the Commonwealth, have hid themselves in monasteries. This they call fleeing from the world, and seeking a kind of life which should be more pleasing to God. Neither did they see that God ought to be served in those commandments which He Himself has given, and not in commandments devised by men. A good and perfect kind of life is that which has for it the commandment of God. It is necessary to admonish men of these things. And before these times, Gerson rebuked this error concerning perfection, and testified that, in his day, it was a new saying that the monastic life is a state of perfection.

So many wicked opinions are inherent in the vows such as that they justify, that they constitute Christian perfection, that they keep the counsels and commandments, that they have works of supererogation. All these things, since they are false and empty, make vows null and void.

Article XXVIII
OF ECCLESIASTICAL POWER

THERE has been great controversy concerning the power of bishops, in which some have awkwardly confounded the power of the Church and the power of the sword. And from this confusion very great wars and tumults have resulted, while the Pontiffs, emboldened by the power of the Keys, not only have instituted new services and burdened consciences with reservation of cases, but have also undertaken to transfer the kingdoms of this world, and to take the Empire from the Emperor. These wrongs have long since been rebuked in the Church by learned and godly men. Therefore, our teachers, for the comforting of men's consciences, were constrained to show the difference between the power of the Church and the power of the sword, and taught that both of them, because of God's commandment, are to be held in reverence and honor, as among the chief blessings of God on earth.

But this is their opinion, that the power of the Keys, or the power of the bishops, according to the Gospel, is a power or commandment of God, to preach the Gospel, to remit and retain sins, and to administer sacraments. For with that commandment, Christ sends forth His Apostles [John 20:21 sqq.]: "As my Father hath sent me, even so send I you. Receive ye the Holy Ghost. Whose soever sins ye remit, they are remitted unto them; and whose soever sins ye retain, they are retained." Mark [16: 15]: "Go, preach the Gospel to every creature."

This power is exercised only by teaching or preaching the Gospel and administering the sacraments, according to the calling, either to many or to individuals. For thereby are granted, not bodily, but eternal things, as eternal righteousness, the Holy Ghost, eternal life. These things cannot come but by the ministry of the Word and the sacraments. As Paul says [Rom. 1:16]: "The Gospel is the power of God unto salvation to every one that believeth." Therefore, since the power of the Church grants eternal things, and is exercised only by the ministry of the Word, it does not interfere with civil government; no more than the art of singing interferes with civil government. For civil government deals with other things than does the Gospel; the civil rulers defend not souls, but bodies and bodily things against manifest injuries, and restrain men with the sword and bodily punishments in order to preserve civil justice and peace.

Therefore the power of the Church and the civil power must not be confounded. The power of the Church has its own commission, to teach the Gospel and to administer the sacraments. Let it not break into the office of another; let it not transfer the kingdoms of this world; let it not abrogate the laws of civil rulers; let it not abolish lawful obedience; let it not interfere with judgments concerning civil ordinances or contracts; let it not prescribe laws to civil rulers concerning the form of the Commonwealth. As Christ says [John 18:36]: "My kingdom is not of this world"; also [Luke 12:14]: "Who made me a judge or a divider over you?" Paul also says [Phil. 3:20]: "Our citizenship is in heaven"; [2 Cor. 10:4]: "The weapons of our warfare are not carnal; but mighty through God to the casting down of imaginations." After this manner, our teachers discriminate between the duties of both these powers, and command that both be honored and acknowledged as gifts and blessings of God.

If bishops have any power of the sword, that power they have, not as bishops, by the commission of the Gospel, but by human law, having received it of Kings and Emperors, for the civil administration of what is theirs. This, however, is another office than the ministry of the Gospel.

When, therefore, a question arises concerning the jurisdiction of bishops, civil authority must be distinguished from ecclesiastical jurisdiction. Again, according to the Gospel, or, as they say, according to Divine Law, to the bishops as bishops, that is, to those to whom has been committed the ministry of the Word and sacraments, no jurisdiction belongs, except to forgive sins, to discern doctrine, to reject doctrines contrary to the Gospel, and to exclude from the communion of the Church wicked men, whose wickedness is known, and this without human force, simply by the Word. Herein the congregations are bound by Divine Law to obey them, according to Luke 10:16: "He that heareth you, heareth me."

But when they teach or ordain anything against the Gospel, then the congregations have a commandment of God prohibiting obedience [Matt. 7:15]: "Beware of false prophets"; Gal. [1:8]: "Though an angel from heaven preach any other Gospel let him be accursed"; 2 Cor. [13:8]: "We can do nothing against the truth; but for the truth." Also [v. 10]: "The power which the Lord hath given me to edification, and not to destruction." So, also, the Canonical Laws command (II Q. vii, Cap. *Sacerdotes* and Cap. *Oves*). And Augustine (*Contra Petiliani Epistolam*): "Not even to Catholic bishops must we submit, if they chance to err, or hold anything contrary to the Canonical Scriptures of God."

If they have any other power or jurisdiction, in hearing and judging certain cases, as of matrimony or of tithes, they have it by human law. But where the ordinaries fail, princes are bound, even against their will, to dispense justice to their subjects, for the maintenance of peace.

Moreover, it is disputed whether bishops or pastors have the right to introduce ceremonies in the Church, and to make laws concerning meats, holydays and degrees, that is, orders of ministers, etc. They that claim this right for the bishops, refer to this testimony [John 16:12, 13]: "I have yet many things to say unto you, but ye cannot bear them now.—Howbeit when he, the Spirit of truth, is come, he will guide you into all truth." They also refer to the example of the Apostles, who commanded to abstain from blood and from things strangled [Acts 15:29]. They refer to the Sabbath Day, as having been changed into the Lord's Day, contrary to the Decalogue, as it seems. Neither is there any example whereof they make more than concerning the changing of the Sabbath Day. Great, say they, is the power of the Church, since it has dispensed with one of the Ten Commandments!

But, concerning this question, it is taught on our part (as has been shown above) that bishops have no power to decree anything against the Gospel. The Canonical Laws teach the same thing (*Dist.* ix). Now it is against Scripture to establish or require the observance of any traditions, to the end that, by such observance, we may make satisfaction for sins, or merit grace and righteousness. For the glory of Christ's merit is dishonored when, by such observances, we undertake to merit justification. But it is manifest that, by such belief, traditions have almost infinitely multiplied in the Church, the doctrine concerning faith and the righteousness of faith being meanwhile suppressed. For gradually more holydays were made, fasts appointed, new ceremonies and services in honor of saints instituted; because the authors of such things thought that, by these works, they were meriting grace. Thus, in times past, the Penitential Canons increased, whereof we still see some traces in the satisfactions.

Again, the authors of traditions do contrary to the command of God when they find matters of sin in foods, in days, and like things, and burden the Church with bondage of the law, as if there ought to be among Christians, in order to merit justification, a service like the Levitical, the arrangement of which God has committed to the Apostles and bishops. For thus some of them write; and the Pontiffs in some measure seem to be misled by the example of the Law of Moses. Hence are such burdens, as that they make it mortal sin, even without offence to others, to do manual labor on holydays, to omit the Canonical Hours, that certain foods defile the conscience, that fastings are works which appease God, that sin in a reserved case cannot be forgiven but by the authority of him who reserved it; whereas the Canons themselves speak only of the reserving of the ecclesiastical penalty, and not of the reserving of the guilt.

Whence have the bishops the right to lay these traditions upon the Church for the ensnaring of consciences, when Peter [Acts 15:10] forbids to put a yoke upon the neck of the disciples, and Paul says [2 Cor. 13:10] that the power given him was to edification, not to destruction? Why, therefore, do they increase sins by these traditions?

But there are clear testimonies which prohibit the making of such traditions, as though they merited grace or were necessary to salvation. Paul says [Col. 2:16]: "Let no man judge you in meat, or in drink, or in respect of an holyday, or ot the new moon, or of the Sabbath day"; vss. 20-23: "If ye be dead with Christ from the rudiments of the world, why, as though living in the world, are ye subject to ordinances (touch not; taste not; handle not, which all are to perish with the using); after the commandments and doctrines of men? which things have indeed a show of wisdom." Also in Titus [1:14] he openly forbids traditions: "Not giving heed to Jewish fables and commandments of men, that turn from the truth." And Christ [Matt. 15:14] says of those who require traditions: "Let them alone; they be blind leaders of the blind"; and He rebukes such services [v. 13]: "Every plant which my Heavenly Father hath not planted, shall be plucked up."

If bishops have the right to burden churches with infinite traditions, and to ensnare consciences, why does Scripture so often prohibit to make and to listen to traditions? Why does it call them "doctrines of devils" [1 Tim. 4:1]? Did the Holy Ghost in vain forewarn of these things?

Since, therefore, ordinances instituted as things necessary, or with an opinion of meriting grace, are contrary to the Gospel, it follows that it is not lawful for any bishop to institute or exact such services. For it is necessary that the doctrine of Christian liberty be preserved in the churches, namely, that the bondage of the Law is not necessary to justification, as it is written in the Epistle to the Galatians [5:1]: "Be not entangled again with the yoke of bondage." It is necessary that the chief article of the Gospel be preserved, to wit, that we obtain grace freely by faith in Christ, and not for certain observances or acts of worship devised by men.

What, then, are we to think of the Sunday and like rites in the house of God? To this we answer that it is lawful for bishops or pastors to make ordinances that things be done orderly in the Church, not that thereby we should merit grace or make satisfaction for sins, or that consciences be bound to judge them necessary services, and to think that it is a sin to break them without offence to others. So Paul ordains [1 Cor. 11:5] that women should cover their heads in the congregation; [1 Cor. 14:30] that interpreters of Scripture be heard in order in the church, etc.

It is proper that the churches should keep such ordinances for the sake of charity and tranquility, so far that one do not offend another, that all things be done in the churches in order, and without confusion; but so that consciences be not burdened to think that they be necessary to salvation, or to judge that they sin when they break them without offence to others; as no one will say that a woman sins who goes out in public with her head uncovered, provided only that no offence be given.

Of this kind is the observance of the Lord's Day, Easter, Pentecost, and like holydays and rites. For those who judge that, by the authority of the Church, the observance of the Lord's Day instead of the Sabbath Day was ordained as a thing necessary, do greatly err. Scripture has abrogated the Sabbath Day; for it teaches that, since the Gospel has been revealed, all the ceremonies of Moses can be omitted. And yet, because it was necessary to appoint a certain day, that the people might know when they ought to come together, it appears that the Church [the Apostles] designated the Lord's Day for this purpose; and this day seems to have been chosen all the more for this additional reason, that men might have an example of Christian liberty, and might know that the keeping neither of the Sabbath, nor of any other day, is necessary.

There are monstrous disputations concerning the changing of the law, the ceremonies of the new law, the changing of the Sabbath Day, which all have sprung from the false belief that there must needs be in the

Church a service like to the Levitical, and that Christ had given commission to the Apostles and bishops to devise new ceremonies as necessary to salvation. These errors crept into the Church when the righteousness of faith was not clearly enough taught. Some dispute that the keeping of the Lord's Day is not indeed of divine right; but in a manner so. They prescribe concerning holydays, how far it is lawful to work. What else are such disputations but snares of consciences? For although they endeavor to modify the traditions, yet the equity can never be perceived as long as the opinion remains that they are necessary, which must needs remain where the righteousness of faith and Christian liberty are disregarded.

The Apostles commanded to abstain from blood. Who doth now observe it? And yet they that do it not, sin not; for not even the Apostles themselves wanted to burden consciences with such bondage; but they forbade it for a time, to avoid offence. For, in any decree, we must consider what is the perpetual aim of the Gospel. Scarcely any Canons are kept with exactness, and, from day to day, many go out of use even with those who are the most zealous advocates of traditions. Neither can due regard be paid to consciences unless this equity be observed, that we know that the Canons are kept without holding them to be necessary, and that no harm is done consciences, even though traditions go out of use.

But the bishops might easily retain the lawful obedience of the people, if they would not insist upon the observance of such traditions as cannot be kept with a good conscience. Now they command celibacy; they admit none, unless they swear that they will not teach the pure doctrine of the Gospel. The churches do not ask that the bishops should restore concord at the expense of their honor; which, nevertheless, it would be proper for good pastors to do. They ask only that they would release unjust burdens which are new and have been received contrary to the custom of the Church Catholic. It may be that there were plausible reasons for some of these ordinances; and yet they are not adapted to later times. It is also evident that some were adopted through erroneous conceptions. Therefore, it would be befitting the clemency of the Pontiffs to mitigate them now; because such a modification does not shake the unity of the Church. For many human traditions have been changed in process of time, as the Canons themselves show. But if it be impossible to obtain a mitigation of such observances as cannot be kept without sin, we are bound to follow the Apostolic rule [Acts 5:29], which commands us to obey God rather than men. Peter [1 Pet. 5:3] forbids bishops to be lords, and to rule over the churches. Now it is not our design to wrest the government from the bishops, but this one thing is asked, namely, that they allow the Gospel to be purely taught, and that they relax some few observances which cannot be kept without sin. But if they make no concession, it is for them to see how they shall give account to God for having, by their obstinacy, caused a schism.

Conclusion

THESE are the Chief Articles which seem to be in controversy. For although we might have spoken of more abuses, yet, to avoid undue length, we have set forth the chief points, from which the rest may be readily judged. There have been great complaints concerning indulgences, pilgrimages, and the abuses of excommunication. The parishes have been vexed in many ways by the dealers in indulgences. There were endless contentions between the pastors and the monks concerning the parochial rites, confessions, burials, sermons on extraordinary occasions, and innumerable other things. Things of this sort we have passed over, so that the chief points in this matter, having been briefly set forth, might be the most readily understood. Nor has anything been here said or adduced to the reproach of any one. Only those things have been recounted, whereof we thought that it was necessary to speak, so that it might be understood that, in doctrine and ceremonies, nothing has been received on our part, against Scripture or the Church Catholic, since it is manifest that we have taken most diligent care that no new and ungodly doctrine should creep into our churches.

The above articles we desire to present in accordance with the edict of Your Imperial Majesty, so that our Confession should therein be exhibited, and a summary of the doctrine of our teachers might be discerned. If anything further be desired, we are ready, God willing, to present ampler information according to the Scriptures.

> JOHN, Duke of Saxony, Elector.
> GEORGE, Margrave of Brandenburg.
> ERNEST, Duke of Luneburg.
> PHILIP, Landgrave of Hesse.
> JOHN FREDERICK, Duke of Saxony.
> FRANCIS, Duke of Luneburg.
> WOLFGANG, Prince of Anhalt.
> SENATE and MAGISTRACY of Nuremburg.
> SENATE of Reutlingen.

Luther's Small Catechism

Part I

THE TEN COMMANDMENTS

*In the plain form in which the head of the family
shall teach them to his household*

THE INTRODUCTION

I am the Lord thy God.

THE FIRST COMMANDMENT

Thou shalt have no other gods before me.

What does this mean?

Answer: We should fear, love, and trust in God above all things.

THE SECOND COMMANDMENT

Thou shalt not take the name of the Lord thy God in
vain; for the Lord will not hold him guiltless that taketh
His name in vain.

What does this mean?

Answer: We should fear and love God so that we do not curse, swear,
conjure, lie, or deceive by His name, but call upon Him in every time of
need, and worship Him with prayer, praise, and thanksgiving.

THE THIRD COMMANDMENT

Remember the Sabbath day, to keep it holy.

What does this mean?

Answer: We should fear and love God so that we do not despise His
Word and the preaching of the same, but deem it holy, and gladly hear
and learn it.

THE FOURTH COMMANDMENT

Honor thy father and thy mother, that thy days may be long upon the land which the Lord thy God giveth thee.

What does this mean?

Answer: We should fear and love God so that we do not despise our parents and superiors, nor provoke them to anger, but honor, serve, obey, love, and esteem them.

THE FIFTH COMMANDMENT

Thou shalt not kill.

What does this mean?

Answer: We should fear and love God so that we do our neighbor no bodily harm nor cause him any suffering, but help and befriend him in every need.

THE SIXTH COMMANDMENT

Thou shalt not commit adultery.

What does this mean?

Answer: We should fear and love God so that we lead a chaste and pure life in word and deed, and that husband and wife love and honor each other.

THE SEVENTH COMMANDMENT

Thou shalt not steal.

What does this mean?

Answer: We should fear and love God so that we do not rob our neighbor of his money or property, nor bring them into our possession by unfair dealing or fraud, but help him to improve and protect his property and living.

THE EIGHTH COMMANDMENT

Thou shalt not bear false witness against thy neighbor.

What does this mean?

Answer: We should fear and love God so that we do not deceitfully belie, betray, backbite, nor slander our neighbor, but apologize for him, speak well of him, and put the most charitable construction on all that he does.

THE NINTH COMMANDMENT

Thou shalt not covet thy neighbor's house.

What does this mean?

Answer: We should fear and love God so that we do not seek by craftiness to gain possession of our neighbor's inheritance or home, nor obtain them under pretense of a legal right, but assist and serve him in keeping the same.

THE TENTH COMMANDMENT

Thou shalt not covet thy neighbor's wife, nor his manservant, nor his maidservant, nor his cattle, nor anything that is thy neighbor's.

What does this mean?

Answer: We should fear and love God so that we do not estrange or entice away our neighbor's wife, servants, or cattle, but seek to have them remain and discharge their duty to him.

THE CONCLUSION

What does God declare concerning all these commandments?
He says:

I the Lord thy God am a jealous God, visiting the iniquity of the fathers upon the children unto the third and fourth generation of them that hate me; and showing mercy unto thousands of them that love me and keep my commandments.

What does this mean?

Answer: God threatens to punish all who transgress these commandments. We should, therefore, fear His wrath, and in no wise disobey them. But He promises grace and every blessing to all who keep them. We should, therefore, love Him, trust in Him, and gladly keep His commandments.

Part II

THE CREED

*In the plain form in which the head of the family
shall teach it to his household*

THE FIRST ARTICLE

OF CREATION

I believe in God the Father Almighty, Maker of heaven and earth.

What does this mean?

Answer: I believe that God has created me and all that exists; that He has given and still preserves to me my body and soul, my eyes and ears, and all my members, my reason and all the powers of my soul, together with food and raiment, home and family, and all my property; that He daily provides abundantly for all the needs of my life, protects me from all danger, and guards and keeps me from all evil; and that He does this purely out of fatherly and divine goodness and mercy, without any merit or worthiness in me; for all which I am in duty bound to thank, praise, serve, and obey Him. This is most certainly true.

THE SECOND ARTICLE

OF REDEMPTION

And in Jesus Christ His only Son, our Lord; Who was conceived by the Holy Ghost, Born of the Virgin Mary; Suffered under Pontius Pilate, Was crucified, dead, and buried; He descended into hell; The third day He rose again from the dead; He ascended into heaven, And sitteth on the right hand of God the Father Almighty; From thence He shall come to judge the quick and the dead.

What does this mean?

Answer: I believe that Jesus Christ, true God, begotten of the Father from eternity, and also true Man, born of the Virgin Mary, is my Lord;

who has redeemed me, a lost and condemned creature, bought me and freed me from all sins, from death, and from the power of the devil; not with silver and gold, but with His holy and precious blood, and with His innocent sufferings and death; in order that I might be His own, live under Him in His kingdom, and serve Him in everlasting righteousness, innocence and blessedness; even as He is risen from the dead, and lives and reigns to all eternity. This is most certainly true.

THE THIRD ARTICLE

OF SANCTIFICATION

I believe in the Holy Ghost; The holy Christian Church, the communion of saints; The forgiveness of sins; The resurrection of the body; And the life everlasting. Amen.

What does this mean?

Answer: I believe that I cannot by my own reason or strength believe in Jesus Christ, my Lord, or come to Him; but the Holy Ghost has called me through the Gospel, enlightened me with His gifts, and sanctified and preserved me in the true faith; in like manner as He calls, gathers, enlightens, and sanctifies the whole Christian Church on earth, and preserves it in union with Jesus Christ in the one true faith; in which Christian Church He daily forgives abundantly all my sins, and the sins of all believers, and at the last day will raise up me and all the dead, and will grant everlasting life to me and to all who believe in Christ. This is most certainly true.

Part III

THE LORD'S PRAYER

*In the plain form in which the head of the family
shall teach it to his household*

❡

THE INTRODUCTION

Our Father who art in heaven.

What does this mean?

Answer: God thereby tenderly encourages us to believe that He is truly
our Father, and that we are truly His children, so that we may boldly
and confidently come to Him in prayer, even as beloved children come
to their dear father.

❡

THE FIRST PETITION

Hallowed be Thy Name.

What does this mean?

Answer: God's Name is indeed holy in itself; but we pray in this
petition that it may be hallowed also among us.

How is this done?

Answer: When the Word of God is taught in its truth and purity, and
we, as God's children, lead holy lives, in accordance with it. This grant
us, dear Father in heaven! But whoever teaches and lives otherwise than
as God's Word teaches, profanes the Name of God among us. From this
preserve us, heavenly Father!

❡

THE SECOND PETITION

Thy kingdom come.

What does this mean?

Answer: The kingdom of God comes indeed of itself, without our
prayer; but we pray in this petition that it may also come to us.

How is this done?

Answer: When our heavenly Father gives us His Holy Spirit, so that by His grace we believe His holy Word, and live a godly life here on earth, and in heaven for ever.

THE THIRD PETITION

Thy will be done on earth as it is in heaven.

What does this mean?

Answer: The good and gracious will of God is done indeed without our prayer; but we pray in this petition that it may also be done among us.

How is this done?

Answer: When God destroys and brings to naught every evil counsel and purpose of the devil, the world, and our own flesh, which would hinder us from hallowing His Name, and prevent the coming of His kingdom; and when He strengthens us and keeps us steadfast in His Word and in faith, even unto our end. This is His good and gracious will.

THE FOURTH PETITION

Give us this day our daily bread.

What does this mean?

Answer: God indeed gives daily bread to all men, even to the wicked, without our prayer; but we pray in this petition that He would lead us to acknowledge our daily bread as His gift, and to receive it with thanksgiving.

What is meant by daily bread?

Answer: Everything that is required to satisfy our bodily needs; such as food and raiment, house and home, fields and flocks, money and goods; pious parents, children and servants; godly and faithful rulers, good government; seasonable weather, peace and health; order and honor; true friends, good neighbors, and the like.

THE FIFTH PETITION

And forgive us our trespasses, as we forgive those who trespass against us.

What does this mean?

Answer: We pray in this petition that our heavenly Father would not regard our sins nor because of them deny our prayers; for we neither merit, nor deserve those things for which we pray; but that He would grant us all things through grace, even though we sin daily, and deserve nothing but punishment. And certainly we, on our part, will heartily forgive, and gladly do good to those who may sin against us.

THE SIXTH PETITION

And lead us not into temptation.

What does this mean?

Answer: God indeed tempts no one to sin; but we pray in this petition that God would so guard and preserve us, that the devil, the world, and our own flesh may not deceive us, nor lead us into error and unbelief, despair, and other great and shameful sins; but that, when so tempted, we may finally prevail and gain the victory.

THE SEVENTH PETITION

But deliver us from evil.

What does this mean?

Answer: We pray in this petition, as in a summary, that our heavenly Father would deliver us from all manner of evil, whether it affect the body or soul, property or reputation, and at last, when the hour of death shall come, grant us a blessed end, and graciously take us from this world of sorrow to Himself in heaven.

THE CONCLUSION

For Thine is the kingdom, and the power, and the glory, for ever and ever. Amen.

What does the word "Amen" mean?

Answer: It means that I should be assured that such petitions are acceptable to our heavenly Father, and are heard by Him; for He Himself has commanded us to pray in this manner, and has promised to hear us. Amen, amen, that is, Yea, yea, it shall be so.

Part IV

THE SACRAMENT OF BAPTISM

*In the plain form in which the head of the family
shall teach it to his household*

❧

I

What is Baptism?

Answer: Baptism is not simply water, but it is the water used according to God's command and connected with God's Word.

What is this Word of God?

Answer: It is the word of our Lord Jesus Christ, as recorded in the last chapter of Matthew:

"Go ye therefore, and make disciples of all the nations, baptizing them into the Name of the Father, and of the Son, and of the Holy Spirit."

❧

II

What gifts or benefits does Baptism bestow?

Answer: It works forgiveness of sins, delivers from death and the devil, and gives everlasting salvation to all who believe, as the word and promise of God declares.

What is this word and promise of God?

Answer: It is the word of our Lord Jesus Christ, as recorded in the last chapter of Mark:

"He that believeth and is baptized shall be saved; but he that believeth not shall be damned."

III

How can water do such great things?

Answer: It is not the water, indeed, that does such great things, but the Word of God connected with the water, and our faith which relies on that Word of God. For without the Word of God, it is simply water and no Baptism. But when connected with the Word of God, it is a Baptism, that is, a gracious water of life and a washing of regeneration in the Holy Ghost, as St. Paul says to Titus, in the third chapter:

"According to his mercy he saved us, by the washing of regeneration, and renewing of the Holy Ghost; which he shed on us abundantly through Jesus Christ our Savior; that being justified by his grace, we should be made heirs according to the hope of eternal life. This is a faithful saying."

IV

What does such baptizing with water signify?

Answer: It signifies that the old Adam in us, together with all sins and evil lusts, should be drowned by daily sorrow and repentance, and be put to death; and that the new man should daily come forth and rise, to live before God in righteousness and holiness for ever.

Where is it so written?

Answer: St. Paul, in the sixth chapter of the Epistle to the Romans, says:

"We are buried with Christ by baptism into death: that like as he was raised up from the dead by the glory of the Father, even so we also should walk in newness of life."

OF CONFESSION

What is confession?

Answer: Confession consists of two parts: the one is that we confess our sins; the other, that we receive absolution or forgiveness from the pastor as from God Himelf, in no wise doubting, but firmly believing, that our sins are thereby forgiven before God in heaven.

What sins should we confess?

Answer: Before God we should acknowledge ourselves guilty of all manner of sins, even of those of which we are not aware, as we do in the Lord's Prayer. To the pastor we should confess only those sins which we know and feel in our hearts.

What are such sins?

Answer: Here examine yourself in the light of the Ten Commandments, whether, as father or mother, son or daughter, master or servant, you have been disobedient, unfaithful, slothful, ill-tempered, unchaste, or quarrelsome, or whether you have injured any one by word or deed, stolen, neglected or wasted aught, or done any other evil.

Part V

THE SACRAMENT OF THE ALTAR

*In the plain form in which the head of the family
shall teach it to his household*

I

What is the Sacrament of the Altar?

Answer: It is the true Body and Blood of our Lord Jesus Christ, under the bread and wine, given unto us Christians to eat and to drink, as it was instituted by Christ Himself

Where is it so written?

Answer: The holy Evangelists, Matthew, Mark, and Luke, together with St. Paul, write thus:

"Our Lord Jesus Christ, in the night in which he was betrayed, took bread; and when he had given thanks, he brake it and gave it to his disciples, saying, Take, eat; this is my body, which is given for you; this do in remembrance of me."

"After the same manner also he took the cup, when he had supped, and when he had given thanks, he gave it to them, saying, Drink ye all of it; this cup is the new testament in my blood, which is shed for you, and for many, for the remission of sins; this do, as oft as ye drink it, in remembrance of me."

II

What is the benefit of such eating and drinking?

Answer: It is pointed out in these words:

"Given and shed for you for the remission of sins."

Through these words the remission of sins, life and salvation are given unto us in the sacrament; for where there is remission of sins, there is also life and salvation.

⸱

III

How can the bodily eating and drinking produce
such great benefits?

Answer: The eating and drinking, indeed, do not produce them, but the words:

"Given and shed for you for the remission of sins."

For besides the bodily eating and drinking, these words are the chief thing in the sacrament; and he who believes them, has what they say and declare, namely, the remission of sins.

⸱

IV

Who, then, receives the sacrament worthily?

Answer: Fasting and bodily preparation are indeed a good outward discipline, but he is truly worthy and well prepared who believes these words:

"Given and shed for you for the remission of sins."

But he who does not believe these words or who doubts them, is unworthy and unprepared; for the words: "For you," require truly believing hearts.

MORNING AND EVENING PRAYER

*In the plain form in which the head of the family
shall teach it to his household*

MORNING

In the morning, when thou risest thou shalt make the sign of the holy cross, and thou shalt say:

In the Name of the Father, and of the Son, and of the Holy Ghost. Amen.

Then, kneeling or standing, thou shalt say the Apostle's Creed and the Lord's Prayer.

Then mayest thou say this prayer:

I give thanks unto Thee, heavenly Father, through Jesus Christ Thy dear Son, that Thou hast protected me through the night from all danger and harm; and I beseech Thee to preserve and keep me, this day also, from all sin and evil; that in all my thoughts, words, and deeds, I may serve and please Thee. Into Thy hands I commend my body and soul, and all that is mine. Let Thy holy angel have charge concerning me, that the wicked one have no power over me. Amen.

And then shouldst thou go with joy to thy work, after a hymn, or the Ten Commandments, or whatever thy devotion may suggest.

EVENING

In the evening, when thou goest to bed, thou shalt make the sign of the holy cross, and thou shalt say:

In the Name of the Father, and of the Son, and of the Holy Ghost. Amen.

Then kneeling or standing, thou shalt say the Apostles' Creed and the Lord's Prayer.

Then mayest thou say this prayer:

I give thanks unto Thee, heavenly Father, through Jesus Christ, Thy dear Son, that Thou hast this day so graciously protected me, and I beseech Thee to forgive me all my sins, and the wrong which I have done, and by Thy great mercy defend me from all the perils and dangers of this night. Into Thy hands I commend my body and soul, and all that is mine. Let Thy holy angel have charge concerning me, that the wicked one have no power over me. Amen.

And then lie down in peace, and sleep.

BLESSING AND THANKSGIVING AT TABLE

In the plain form in which the head of the family shall teach them to his household

BEFORE MEAT

Before meat, the members of the family standing at the table reverently and with folded hands, there shall be said:

The eyes of all wait upon Thee, O Lord: and Thou givest them their meat in due season. Thou openest Thine hand, and satisfiest the desire of every living thing.

Then shall be said the Lord's Prayer, and after that this prayer:

O Lord God, heavenly Father, bless unto us these Thy gifts, which of Thy tender kindness Thou hast bestowed upon us, through Jesus Christ our Lord. Amen.

AFTER MEAT

After meat, all standing reverently and with folded hands, there shall be said:

O give thanks unto the Lord, for He is good; for His mercy endureth for ever. He giveth food to all flesh; He giveth to the beast his food, and to the young ravens which cry. He delighteth not in the strength of the horse; He taketh not pleasure in the legs of a man. The Lord taketh pleasure in them that fear Him: in those that hope in His mercy.

Then shall be said the Lord's Prayer and after that this prayer:

We give thanks unto Thee, O God, our Father, for all Thy benefits, through Jesus Christ, our Lord, who with Thee liveth and reigneth for ever and ever. Amen.

TABLE OF DUTIES

Certain Scripture passages for various holy orders and estates

BISHOPS, PASTORS AND PREACHERS

A bishop must be blameless, the husband of one wife, vigilant, sober of good behavior, given to hospitality, apt to teach; not given to wine, no striker, not greedy of filthy lucre; but patient, not a brawler, not covetous; one that ruleth well his own house, having his children in subjection with all gravity; not a novice, but holding fast the faithful Word as he hath been taught, that he may be able by sound doctrine both to exhort and to convince the gainsayers. 1 Tim. 3:2-6; Tit. 1:6-9.

WHAT DUTIES HEARERS OWE THEIR PASTORS

Even so hath the Lord ordained that they which preach the Gospel should live of the Gospel. 1 Cor. 9:14.

Let him that is taught in the Word communicate unto him that teacheth in all good things. Gal. 6:6.

Let the elders that rule well be counted worthy of double honor, especially they who labor in the word and doctrine. For the Scripture saith, Thou shalt not muzzle the ox that treadeth out the corn. And, The laborer is worthy of his reward. 1 Tim. 5:17-18.

Obey them that have the rule over you, and submit yourselves: for they watch for your souls, as they that must give account, that they may do it with joy, and not with grief: for that is unprofitable for you. Heb. 13:17.

MAGISTRATES

Let every soul be subject unto the higher powers. For there is no power but of God; the powers that be are ordained of God; for rulers are not a terror to good works, but to the evil. Wilt thou then not be afraid of the power? do that which is good, and thou shalt have praise of the same: for he is the minister of God to thee for good. But if thou do that which is evil, be afraid; for he beareth not the sword in vain; for he is the minister of God, a revenger to execute wrath upon him that doeth evil. Rom. 13:1-4.

WHAT DUTIES SUBJECTS OWE MAGISTRATES

Render therefore unto Caesar the things which are Caesar's. Matt. 22:21.

Let every soul be subject unto the higher powers, etc. Wherefore ye must needs be subject, not only for wrath, but also for conscience' sake. For, for this cause pay ye tribute also: for they are God's ministers, attending continually upon this very thing. Render therefore to all their dues: tribute to whom tribute is due; custom to whom custom; fear to whom fear; honor to whom honor. Rom. 13:1, 5-7.

I exhort therefore, that, first of all, supplications, prayers, intercessions, and giving of thanks, be made for all men; for kings and for all that are in authority, that we may lead a quiet and peaceable life in all godliness and honesty. I Tim. 2:1-2.

Put them in mind to be subject to principalities and powers, etc. Tit. 3:1.

Submit yourselves to every ordinance of man for the Lord's sake: whether it be to the king as supreme; or unto governors, as unto them that are sent, etc. I Pet. 2:13

HUSBANDS

Ye husbands, dwell with your wives, according to knowledge, giving honor unto the wife as unto the weaker vessel, and as being heirs together of the grace of life; that your prayers be not hindered. I Pet. 3:7.

And be not bitter against them. Col. 3:19.

WIVES

Wives, submit yourselves unto your own husbands, as unto the Lord. Even as Sarah obeyed Abraham, calling him lord: whose daughters ye are, as long as ye do well, and are not afraid with any amazement. Eph. 5:22; I Pet. 3:6.

PARENTS

Ye fathers, provoke not your children to wrath: but bring them up in the nurture and admonition of the Lord. Eph. 6:4.

CHILDREN

Children, obey your parents in the Lord: for this is right. Honor thy father and mother; which is the first commandment with promise; that it may be well with thee, and thou mayest live long on the earth. Eph. 6:1-3.

MALE AND FEMALE SERVANTS, AND LABORERS

Servants, be obedient to them that are your masters according to the flesh, with fear and trembling, in singleness of your heart, as unto Christ; not with eye-service, as men-pleasers; but as the servants of Christ, doing the will of God from the heart; with good will doing service, as to the Lord, and not to men: knowing that whatsoever good thing any man doeth the same shall he receive of the Lord, whether he be bond or free. Eph. 6:5-8.

MASTERS AND MISTRESSES

Ye masters, do the same thing unto them, forbearing threatening; knowing that your Master also is in heaven; neither is there respect of persons with him. Eph. 6:9; Col. 4:1.

YOUNG PERSONS, IN GENERAL

Likewise, ye younger, submit yourselves unto the elder. Yea, all of you be subject one to another, and be clothed with humility; for God resisteth the proud, and giveth grace to the humble. Humble yourselves therefore under the mighty hand of God, that he may exalt you in due time. I Pet. 5:5, 6.

WIDOWS

She that is a widow indeed, and desolate, trusteth in God, and continueth in supplications and prayer night and day; but she that liveth in pleasure is dead while she liveth. I Tim. 5:5, 6.

CHRISTIANS, IN GENERAL

Thou shalt love thy neighbor as thyself. Herein are comprehended all the commandments. Rom. 13:9, 10.

And persevere in prayer for all men. I Tim. 2:1, 2.

Let each his lesson learn, with care,
And all the household well shall fare.

THE LUTHERAN HYMNARY

PREFACE.

THE compilation of "The Lutheran Hymnary" is the work of a joint committee of twelve members, four of whom were appointed by the United Norwegian Lutheran Church, four by the Norwegian Lutheran Synod, and four by the Hauge's Lutheran Synod. Few changes in the personnel of the committee have been made during the four years in which it has been at work upon the hymnal.

The considerations which prompted the creation of the joint committee were, chiefly, the common need of an adequate and satisfactory English hymn book; the fact of a common faith and confession as well as a common inheritance of Lutheran hymnody; the probability of getting a better hymn book through united endeavor than by separate effort; and finally, the desirability of a common hymnary, especially in the event of a union of the Church bodies concerned.

Prior to the organization of the joint committee, the United Church had for some years, through a committee, been engaged in compiling a new English hymn book; the Norwegian Synod had been similarly engaged. Thus the joint committee, when it set out upon its work, had the result of the labors of these two individual committees to begin with. It also had, in "The Christian Hymns" of the Norwegian Synod and "The Church and Sunday School Hymnal" of the United Church, a nucleus for the proposed joint hymn book.

It has been the constant aim and effort of the committee to embody in "The Lutheran Hymnary" the best translations of German and Norwegian Lutheran hymns. Seventy-two hymns from the Norwegian and Danish, familiar to our Norwegian-Danish Church people, from Landstad's and the Synod hymn books, appear in this collection for the first time in English dress.

The Norwegian Lutheran Church of America has inherited a rich treasury of hymns and chorals from the Mother Church; and while the Norwegian-American Church would secure this treasure and transmit it to her children, it is also hoped that the hymns of Kingo, Grundtvig, Brorson, Landstad, Brun and others, rendered into English, may prove attractive to the English bodies of the Church of the Reformation, and eventually find a place in their hearts and hymnals.

Another feature of the present collection is its large number of distinctively Lutheran chorals. The committee has, in general, observed the principle of retaining the tune with which the hymn is associated. When, however, it has been found that a tune is lacking in churchliness or appropriateness for congregational singing, the committee has given the hymn a standard Lutheran choral. These chorals have survived the test of time and have proven their vitality and

Preface

intrinsic value by long and constant use in the homes and sanctuaries of the people of God.

Twenty German chorals are arranged in rhythmical meter; twenty have a melodic or countrapuntal setting. These special features the committee hopes will serve a purpose in discovering the wish of the Church regarding the rhythmical form and the melodic arrangement of Lutheran chorals.

It is hoped that the arrangement of the hymns according to Sunday texts of the church year, a feature familiar from our Norwegian hymn books, will prove a valuable aid in selecting appropriate hymns for the services, and, better than a mere topical index, serve to promote a general use of the hymns found in the hymnal.

It is due to add that, thanks to the very extensive hymnological library and hymnological knowledge and patient research of Rev. Carl Døving, late of New York City, and for the last year a member of the committee, many excellent translations of well-known German Lutheran hymns, translations made mostly by prominent English hymnologists, have been secured for "The Lutheran Hymnary"; these translations have not appeared in an English Lutheran hymn book before.

Grateful acknowledgment is made to the Concordia Publishing House of St. Louis, Mo., for permission to use the music of the second Morning and Evening Service.

Grateful acknowledgment is also due to the many who, either in an official capacity or personally, have rendered the committee valuable aid by suggestions, translations or criticisms. A true hymnal cannot be made to order; it is not an artificial production. It develops out of the consciousness of the Church itself. The committee has not felt that its duty was to make a new hymn book, but only to make out of the vast treasury of Lutheran hymnody such a collection of genuine Lutheran hymns and chorals as should satisfy the needs and meet the expectations of our Norwegian-American Lutheran Church people.

Finally, it is the prayer of the committee, that "The Lutheran Hymnary" may prove no small factor in the efforts made to unify the various Norwegian Lutheran Church bodies of our land.

THE COMMITTEE.

September, 1912

Table of Contents

Table of Contents

The Order of Morning Service

¶ *While a Prelude is being played, the Minister proceeds to the Altar and kneels before it. He remains in this position while an Assistant reads:*

1. THE OPENING PRAYER.

O Lord, our Maker, Redeemer, and Comforter, we are assembled in Thy presence to hear Thy holy word. We pray Thee so to open our hearts by Thy Holy Spirit, that through the preaching of Thy word we may be taught to repent of our sins, to believe on Jesus in life and in death, and to grow day by day in grace and holiness. Hear us for Christ's sake. Amen.

¶ *The Minister rises and stands facing the Altar.*

2. THE HYMN.

¶ *The contents of this Hymn may be determined by the season of the Church Year. On ordinary Sundays the Hymn may be a general Hymn of Prayer.*

3a. THE CONFESSION OF SIN.

¶ *The Minister, turning to the Congregation, shall say:*

Let us bow before the Lord and confess our sins.

¶ *Then the Minister, kneeling before the Altar, shall say:*

Almighty God, our Maker and Redeemer, we poor sinners confess unto Thee, that we are by nature sinful and unclean, and that we have sinned against Thee by thought, word and deed. Wherefore we flee for refuge to Thine infinite mercy, seeking and imploring Thy grace, for the sake of our Lord Jesus Christ. Amen.

Or:

O most merciful God, who hast given Thine only-begotten Son to die for us, have mercy upon us, and for His sake grant us remission of all our sins; and by Thy Holy Spirit increase in us true knowledge of Thee, and of Thy will, and true obedience to Thy word, to the end that by Thy grace we may come to everlasting life, through Jesus Christ, our Lord. Amen.

3b. THE KYRIE.

¶ *The Congregation shall sing or say:*

O God the Father in heav - en, have mer - cy up - on us!

O God the Son, Re-deemer of the world, have mercy up-on us!

O God the Holy Ghost, true Com-for-ter, have mer - cy up - on us!

7

The Order of Morning Service

3c. THE ABSOLUTION.

¶ *Then shall the Minister turn to the Congregation and say:*

Almighty God, our heavenly Father, hath had mercy upon us, and hath given His Only Son to die for us, and for His sake forgiveth us all our sins. To them that believe on His name, He giveth power to become the sons of God, and hath promised them His Holy Spirit. He that believeth, and is baptized, shall be saved. Grant this, Lord, unto us all.

4. THE GLORIA.

¶ *Then shall the Minister turn to the Altar and chant or say:*

¶ *On the three great Festivals the Congregation shall then sing the Hymn:*

"All glory be to God on high."

(*During Lent the Gloria may be omitted.*)

5. THE COLLECT.

¶ *The Congregation shall rise and stand until the Epistle is read.*
¶ *Then shall the Minister turn to the Congregation and chant:*

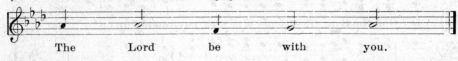

¶ *The Congregation shall sing:*

8

¶ *The Minister shall then chant:*

Let us all........... pray.

¶ *Then shall the Minister, turning to the Altar, chant the Collect for the day.*

¶ *The Collect ended, the Congregation shall sing:*

A - - - - - - - men.

6.   THE EPISTLE, OR LESSON.

¶ *The Minister, turning to the Congregation, shall read the Epistle for the day, announcing it as follows:*

The Epistle for (*here he shall name the day*) is written in the —— chapter of ——, beginning at the —— verse.

¶ *The Epistle ended, the Minister shall then say:*
Here endeth the Epistle (or Lesson).

7.   HYMN.

¶ *This hymn shall correspond to the Epistle or be a Hymn of Praise.*

8.   THE GOSPEL.

¶ *The Minister, turning to the Congregation, shall say:*
The holy Gospel is written in the —— chapter of St.——, beginning at the—— verse.

¶ *The Congregation shall here rise and remain standing until the Confession of Faith has been said.*

¶ *Then shall the Minister read the Gospel for the day.*

¶ *The Gospel ended, the Minister shall say:*
Here endeth the Gospel.

¶ *Then shall the Congregation sing:*

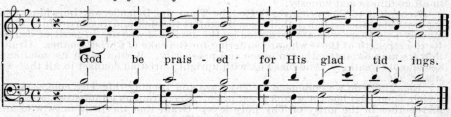

God be prais - ed for His glad tid - ings.

9.   THE CONFESSION OF FAITH.

¶ *The Minister shall say:*

Let us confess our holy Faith.

9

The Order of Morning Service

¶ *The Minister shall turn to the Altar and, together with the Congregation, he shall say*
THE APOSTLES' CREED.

I believe in God the Father Almighty, Maker of heaven and earth.

And in Jesus Christ, His only Son, our Lord; Who was conceived by the Holy Ghost, Born of the Virgin Mary: Suffered under Pontius Pilate, Was crucified, dead, and buried; He descended into hell; The third day He rose again from the dead; He ascended into heaven, And sitteth on the right hand of God the Father Almighty; From thence He shall come to judge the quick and the dead.

I believe in the Holy Ghost; The holy Christian Church, the Communion of Saints; The Forgiveness of sins; The Resurrection of the body; And the Life everlasting.

¶ *The Congregation shall sing*:

A - - - - - - - - - - - - - men.

10.   HYMN.

¶ *Then shall a hymn be sung, during which the Minister shall enter the pulpit.*

¶ *After the Hymn shall follow*

11a.   THE SERMON.

¶ *The Sermon shall close with the GLORIA PATRI:*

Glory be to the Father, and to the Son, and to the Holy Ghost: as it was in the beginning, is now, and ever shall be, world without end.   Amen.

11b.   THE GENERAL PRAYER.

Everlasting and merciful God, we beseech Thee in the Name of our Lord Jesus Christ:

Look in mercy upon Thy Church.   Protect it, and sanctify it by Thy truth. May Thy word be taught in its purity and Thy sacraments be rightly administered.   Grant unto Thy Church faithful pastors who shall declare Thy truth with power and shall live according to Thy will.   Send forth laborers into Thy harvest, and open the door of faith unto all the heathen and unto the people of Israel. In mercy remember the enemies of Thy Church and grant to them repentance unto life.

Let Thy protecting hand be over our nation and country and over all who travel by land or water.   Prosper what is good among us, and bring to naught every evil counsel and purpose.   Protect and bless Thy servants, the President of the United States, the Governor of this Commonwealth, our Judges and Magistrates, and all others in authority.   Fit them for their high calling by the gift of the Spirit of Thy wisdom and fear, that we may lead a quiet and peaceable life, in all godliness and honesty.

According to Thy promise, O God, be Thou the Defender of the widow and the Father of the orphan.   Relieve and comfort the sick and the sorrowful.   Graciously help those who are assaulted by the devil and who are in peril of death. Be the strength of those who are suffering for the sake of Christ's name.   Grant that we may dwell together in peace and prosperity.   Bestow upon us good and seasonable weather.   And bless us with upright Christian counsel in all that we undertake.

Especially do we commend to Thy care and keeping this Thy congregation which Thou hast bought with a great price.   Keep from us all offenses, and bind us together in the unity of Thy holy love.   Grant that the little ones who are baptized in Thy Name may be brought up in Thy fear.   (Bestow the power of renunciation and faith upon the hearts of the young who are to be confirmed in their baptismal covenant.*)   And at Thy Table give unto those who there commune with Thee peace and life everlasting.

*) The words enclosed in this parenthesis are to be used when a class is being prepared for confirmation

10

The Order of Morning Service

Be merciful, O God, unto all men, according to Thy great love in Christ Jesus. our Lord. And, when our final hour shall come, grant us a blessed departure from this world, and, on the last day, a resurrection to Thy glory. Amen.

¶ *Here special Supplications, Intercessions, and Prayers may be made.*

THE LORD'S PRAYER.

Our Father, who art in heaven; Hallowed be Thy name; Thy kingdom come; Thy will be done on earth, as it is in heaven; Give us this day our daily bread: And forgive us our trespasses, as we forgive those who trespass against us; And lead us not into temptation; But deliver us from evil: For Thine is the kingdom, and the power, and the glory, for ever and ever. Amen.

¶ *The Minister shall then say:*

The grace of the Lord Jesus Christ, and the love of God, and the communion of the Holy Ghost be with you all. Amen.

12 HYMN.

¶ *The Hymn ended, the Offerings may be gathered, during which an anthem may be sung or an interlude played.*

¶ *Holy Baptism shall then be administered before and after which a baptismal Hymn shall be sung.*

(The Catechisation of the Young may here take place. This shall begin and close with appropriate Hymns.)

13. HOLY COMMUNION.

¶ *When Holy Communion is to be celebrated, it shall be introduced with a COMMUNION HYMN or the following PREFACE.*

¶ *The Minister, turning to the Congregation, shall chant:*

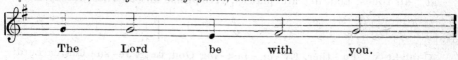

The Lord be with you.

¶ *The Congregation shall rise and sing:*

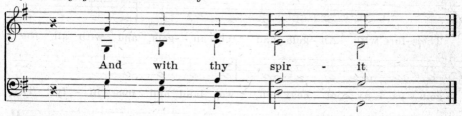

And with thy spir - it

¶ *The Minister:*

Lift up your hearts un - to the Lord......

¶ *The Congregation:*

We lift up our hearts un - to the Lord......

The Order of Morning Service

¶ *The Minister:*

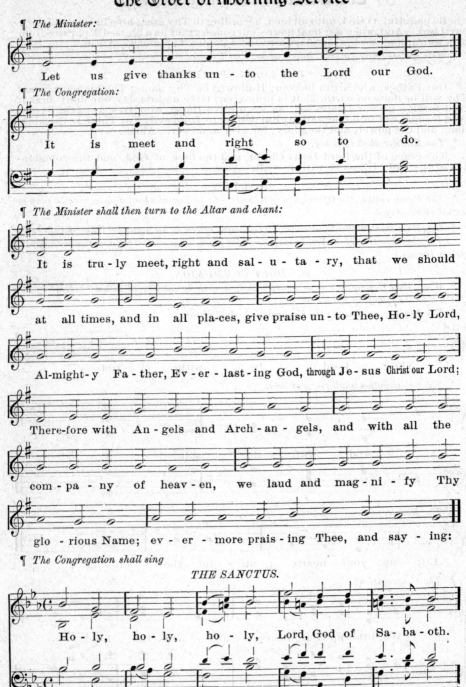

Let us give thanks un-to the Lord our God.

¶ *The Congregation:*

It is meet and right so to do.

¶ *The Minister shall then turn to the Altar and chant:*

It is tru-ly meet, right and sal-u-ta-ry, that we should at all times, and in all pla-ces, give praise un-to Thee, Ho-ly Lord, Al-might-y Fa-ther, Ev-er-last-ing God, through Je-sus Christ our Lord; There-fore with An-gels and Arch-an-gels, and with all the com-pa-ny of heav-en, we laud and mag-ni-fy Thy glo-rious Name; ev-er-more prais-ing Thee, and say-ing:

¶ *The Congregation shall sing*

THE SANCTUS.

Ho-ly, ho-ly, ho-ly, Lord, God of Sa-ba-oth.

12

The Order of Morning Service

Heaven and earth are full of Thy glo - - ry. Ho - - san - na in the high - est. Bless - ed is He that com - eth in the name of the Lord. Ho - - san · na in the high - est.

¶ *The Communicants shall gather about the Altar and remain standing, while the Minister, turning to the Congregation, shall say:*

14. *THE EXHORTATION BEFORE COMMUNION.*

Dear Friends in Christ! In order that you may receive this holy Sacrament worthily it becomes you diligently to consider what you must now believe and do. From the words of Christ: "This is my Body, which is given for you"; "This is my Blood, which is shed for you for the remission of sins"; you should believe that Jesus Christ is Himself present with His Body and Blood, as the words declare. From Christ's words, "For the remission of sins", you should, in the next place, believe that Jesus Christ bestows upon you His Body and Blood to confirm unto you the remission of all your sins. And, finally, you should do as Christ commands you when He says: "Take, eat"; "Drink ye all of it"; and, "This do in remembrance of me". If you believe these words of Christ, and do as He therein has commanded, then have you rightly examined yourselves and may worthily eat Christ's Body and drink His Blood for the remission of your sins. You should, also, unite in giving thanks to Almighty God, the Father of our Lord Jesus Christ, for so great a gift, and should love one another with a pure heart, and thus, with the whole Christian Church, have comfort and joy in Christ our Lord. To this end may God the Father grant you His grace; through the same, our Lord Jesus Christ. Amen.

¶ *Then shall the Minister say:*
Let us all pray.
¶ *The Communicants kneel.*

15. *THE LORD'S PRAYER.*

¶ *The Minister, turning to the Altar, shall chant:*

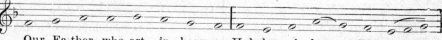

Our Fa - ther, who art in heav - en; Hal - low - ed be.... Thy name;

13

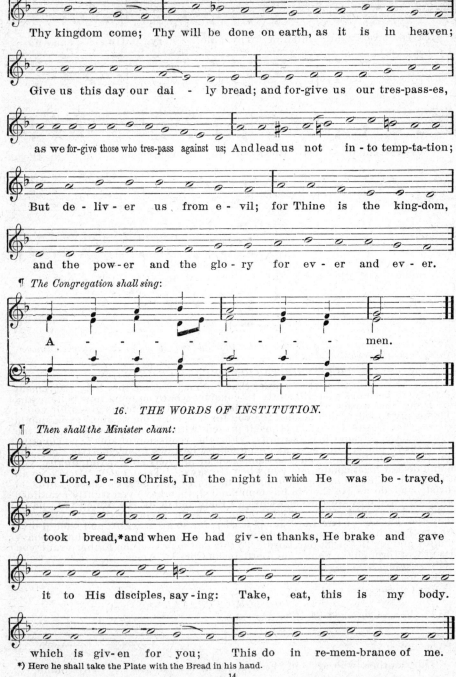

Thy kingdom come; Thy will be done on earth, as it is in heaven;

Give us this day our dai - ly bread; and for-give us our tres-pass-es,

as we for-give those who tres-pass against us; And lead us not in - to temp-ta-tion;

But de - liv - er us from e - vil; for Thine is the king-dom,

and the pow - er and the glo - ry for ev - er and ev - er.

¶ *The Congregation shall sing:*

A - - - - - - - - men.

16. THE WORDS OF INSTITUTION.

¶ *Then shall the Minister chant:*

Our Lord, Je - sus Christ, In the night in which He was be - trayed,

took bread,*and when He had giv - en thanks, He brake and gave

it to His disciples, say - ing: Take, eat, this is my body.

which is giv - en for you; This do in re-mem-brance of me.

*) Here he shall take the Plate with the Bread in his hand.

14

Af-ter the same manner, al-so, He took the cup, when He had supped,* and when

He had giv-en thanks, He gave it to them, say-ing: Drink ye all of it;

this cup is the New Tes-ta-ment in my blood,

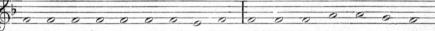

which is shed for you and for man-y for the re-mis-sion of sin;

this do, as oft as ye drink it, in re-mem-brance of me.

17. THE DISTRIBUTION.

¶ *Then shall the Minister give the Bread to the Communicants, saying to each one:*
This is the true Body of Christ.

¶ *He then gives the Cup to the Communicants, saying to each one:*
This is the true Blood of Christ.

¶ *A Communion Hymn is sung by the Congregation during the Distribution.*
¶ *The Distribution ended, the Minister, turning to the Communicants, shall say:*

Our crucified and risen Lord, Jesus Christ, who now hath bestowed upon you His holy Body and Blood, whereby He hath made full satisfaction for all your sins, strengthen and preserve you in the true faith unto everlasting life. Peace be with you. Amen.

18. A HYMN OF THANKSGIVING.

19. THE COLLECT OF THANKSGIVING.

¶ *The Minister, turning to the Congregation, shall chant:*

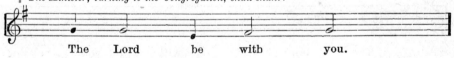

The Lord be with you.

¶ *The Congregation, standing, shall sing:*

And with thy spir - - it.

*) Here he shall take the cup in his hand.

The Order of Morning Service

¶ *The Minister shall chant:*

Let us give thanks and pray.

¶ *Then shall the Minister,* turning to the Altar, *chant:*

We thank Thee, Lord God Al-might-y, that Thou hast vouch-safed to re-fresh us with these Thy sal-u-ta-ry gifts; and we be-seech Thee, of Thy mer-cy, to strengthen us through the same, in faith to-ward Thee, in fer-vent love to-ward one an-oth-er; through Je-sus Christ, Thy Son, our Lord.

¶ *The Congregation shall sing:*

A - - - - - - - men.

20.   THE BENEDICTION.

¶ *The Minister,* turning to the Congregation, *shall chant:*

The Lord be with you.

¶ *The Congregation:*

And with thy spir-it.

The Order of Morning Service.

The Minister:

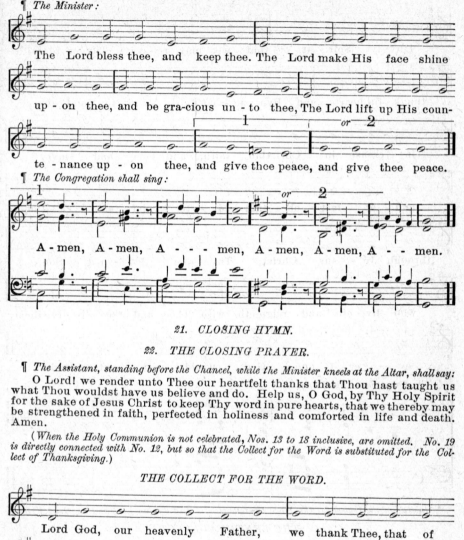

The Lord bless thee, and keep thee. The Lord make His face shine up-on thee, and be gra-cious un-to thee, The Lord lift up His coun-te-nance up-on thee, and give thee peace, and give thee peace.

The Congregation shall sing:

A-men, A-men, A---men, A-men, A-men, A--men.

21. CLOSING HYMN.

22. THE CLOSING PRAYER.

The Assistant, standing before the Chancel, while the Minister kneels at the Altar, shall say:

O Lord! we render unto Thee our heartfelt thanks that Thou hast taught us what Thou wouldst have us believe and do. Help us, O God, by Thy Holy Spirit for the sake of Jesus Christ to keep Thy word in pure hearts, that we thereby may be strengthened in faith, perfected in holiness and comforted in life and death. Amen.

(*When the Holy Communion is not celebrated, Nos. 13 to 18 inclusive, are omitted. No. 19 is directly connected with No. 12, but so that the Collect for the Word is substituted for the Collect of Thanksgiving.*)

THE COLLECT FOR THE WORD.

Lord God, our heavenly Father, we thank Thee, that of Thy great mer-cy Thou hast given us Thy ho-ly and blessed word by which Thou dost al-so a-mong us gath-er Thy Chris-tian Church. We hum-bly en-treat Thee, grant us Thy

The Order of Morning Service.

Ho - ly Spir - it, that we may re - ceive Thy word with

thank - ful hearts, and live ac - cord - ing there - to, and ev - er

in - crease in Christian faith, and hope, and love,

and at last ob - tain e - ter - nal sal - va - tion:

through Je - sus Christ, Thy be - lov - ed Son,

who liv - eth and reign-eth with Thee and the Ho - ly Ghost,

ev - er one God, world with - out end.

¶ *The Congregation shall sing:*

A - - - - - - - - men.

¶ *Instead of the Collect for the Word the following is used during Lent and on Good Friday.*

THE LENTEN COLLECT.

We thank Thee, Lord God the Father, that Thou didst give Thine on - ly-

be - got - ten Son, that whosoever believeth on Him shall not per-ish,

but have ev - er - last - ing life. We thank Thee, Lord Je-sus Christ,

The Order of Morning Service.

that Thou hast borne in Thy sacred body all our sins,

and by Thy blood hast blotted out all our trans - gres-sions.

We thank Thee, Lord the Ho-ly Ghost, that Thou hast wrought in our hearts

such faith, that we know nothing wherein to trust for sal-va - tion,

save Je - sus Christ and Him cru -ci - fied. Grant us, O God, Thy grace,

that we may perfectly believe that all our sins are for - giv - en,

for the sake of the passion and death of Je - sus Christ,

and so enlighten us by Thy Holy Spir - it, that, in the power

of our Redeem - er's death, we may day by day put off sin,

and nev - er for - sake the Lord Je - sus, until we see Him face

to face in life e - ter - nal. We ask it all in Christ's name.

¶ The Congregation shall sing:

A - - - - - - - men.

19

The Evening Service.

¶ *After a prelude upon the organ, during which the minister kneels before the Altar, the service shall be conducted in the following order:*

1. THE OPENING PRAYER,

as used at the Morning Service, shall be said by the Assistant. During the opening prayer the Minister shall kneel at the Altar.

2. A HYMN.

3. THE SERMON AND THE GENERAL PRAYER.

¶ *The sermon shall e preached upon the Epistle or the Lesson for the day. In the case that Epiphany occurs upon a Sunday, the Epistle or Lesson for Epiphany shall be used.*

¶ *On Good Friday, the sermon shall be based upon one of the following texts: During the Church Year in which the First Series is used, John 19 :31-42; during the Church Year in which the Second Series is used, Matthew 27 :51-66; during the Church Year in which the Third Series is used, Luke 23 :47-56.*

4. A HYMN.

5. THE COLLECT FOR THE WORD.

¶ *During Lent and on Good Friday the Passion Collect shall be said.*

6. THE BENEDICTION.

7. THE CLOSING HYMN.

8. THE CLOSING PRAYER,

as used at the Morning Service, shall be said by the Assistant, concluding with the Lord's Prayer.

The Order of Morning Service
or the Communion.

¶ *A Hymn of Invocation of the Holy Ghost may be sung.*

¶ *The Congregation shall rise, and the Minister, standing at the Altar, shall say:*

In the Name of the Father, and of the Son, and of the Holy Ghost.

¶ *The Congregation shall sing or say:*

A - - - - - - - - men.

¶ *Then shall be said the Confession of Sins, as here followeth:*

THE CONFESSION OF SINS.

Beloved in the Lord! Let us draw near with a true heart, and confess our sins unto God our Father, beseeching Him, in the Name of our Lord Jesus Christ, to grant us forgiveness.

¶ *Then, all kneeling or standing, shall be sung or said:*

¶ *Minister.*

Our help is in the Name of the Lord.

¶ *Congregation.*

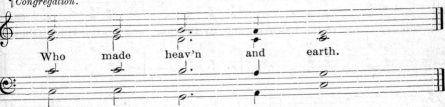

Who made heav'n and earth.

¶ *Minister.*

I said, I will confess my transgressions unto the Lord.

¶ *Congregation.*

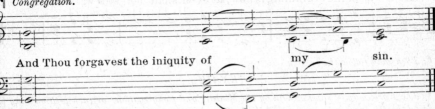

And Thou forgavest the iniquity of my sin.

¶ *Then shall the Minister say:*

Almighty God, our Maker and Redeemer, we poor sinners confess unto Thee. that we are by nature sinful and unclean, and that we have sinned against Thee by thought, word and deed. Wherefore we flee for refuge to Thine infinite mercy, seeking and imploring Thy grace, for the sake of our Lord Jesus Christ.

¶ *The Congregation shall say with the Minister:*

O most merciful God, who hast given Thine Only-begotten Son to die for us, have mercy upon us, and for His sake grant us remission of all our sins: and by Thy Holy Spirit increase in us true knowledge of Thee, and of Thy will, and true obedience to Thy word, to the end that by Thy grace we may come to everlasting life, through Jesus Christ, our Lord. Amen.

Morning Service

¶ *Then the Minister, standing, shall say:*

Almighty God, our heavenly Father, hath had mercy upon us, and hath given His Only Son to die for us, and for His sake forgiveth us all our sins. To them that believe on His name, He giveth power to become the sons of God, and hath promised them His Holy Spirit. He that believeth, and is baptized, shall be saved. Grant this, Lord, unto us all.

¶ *Then shall the Congregation sing or say:*

A - - - - - - - men.

¶ *Then, all standing to the close of the Collect, shall be sung or said the Introit for the day.*

THE INTROIT.

¶ *The Introit with the Gloria Patri may be sung by the Choir; or the Introit may be said by the Minister, and the Gloria Patri sung or said by the Congregation.*

¶ *Instead of the Introit a Psalm or Hymn may be used.*

GLORIA PATRI

Glo - ry be to the Fa-ther, and to the Son, and to the Ho-ly Ghost!

As it was in the beginning, is now, and ev-er shall be: world without end, A-men.

¶ *Then shall follow the*

KYRIE

¶ *The Kyrie may be sung or said by the Minister and Congregation, or each petition may be said by the Minister and sung or said by the Congregation in response.*

¶ *Congregation:*

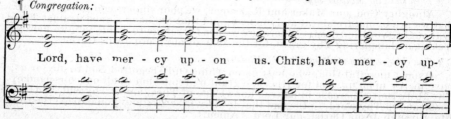

Lord, have mer - cy up - on us. Christ, have mer - cy up-

22

or the Communion

on us. Lord have mer - cy up - on us.

¶ *Then shall be sung the Gloria in Excelsis as here followeth. Instead of the Gloria in Excelsis, another Canticle or Hymn of Praise may be sung, except on Festival days, and when there is a Communion.*

GLORIA IN EXCELSIS.

¶ *The Minister shall say:*
Glory be to God on high.

' *Congregation:*

Glory be to .... God on high:
We praise Thee, we bless Thee, we.... wor - ship Thee,

And on earth.....................peace, good will toward men.
We glorify Thee, we give thanks to Thee for Thy great glory.

O Lord, God,....................... heav'n - ly King,
O Lord, the Only-be-gotten Son, Je - sus Christ;

God the................... Fa - ther Al - - - mighty.
O Lord God, Lamb of God Son of the Father.

23

Morning Service

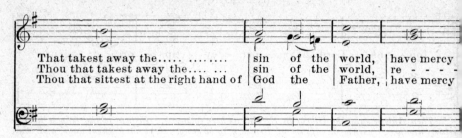

That takest away the..... .... | sin | of the | world, | have mercy
Thou that takest away the.... ... | sin | of the | world, | re - - -
Thou that sittest at the right hand of | God | the | Father, | have mercy

up - on | us. ‖ For Thou...................... only art | holy;
ceive our | prayer. ‖ Thou only, O Christ, with the Ho - ly | Ghost,
up - on | us. ‖

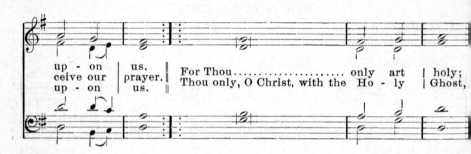

Thou................ .... | on - ly | art the | Lord.
Art most high in the | glory of | God the | Father. A - - men.

¶ *Then shall the Minister say:*

The Lord be with you.

¶ *The Congregation shall sing or say:*

And with thy spir - - - it.

¶ *The Minister shall say:*

Let us pray.

¶ *Then shall the Minister say the Collect for the Day.*

90

or the Communion

THE COLLECT.

¶ *The Collect ended, the Congregation shall sing or say:*

A - - - - - - - - - - - men.

¶ *Then shall the Minister read the Epistle for the Day. Other Scripture Lessons may be read before the Epistle, but the Epistle and Gospel for the Day shall always be read. The Minister shall announce the Epistle, saying:*

The Epistle for (*here he shall name the Day*) is written in the————Chapter of ————, beginning at the————Verse.

THE EPISTLE FOR THE DAY.

¶ *The Epistle ended, the Minister shall say:* Here endeth the Epistle.
¶ *Then shall the Hallelujah be sung or said, except in the Passion season.*

THE HALLELUJAH.

Hal - - le - - - lu - - - - jah!

¶ *Then shall the Minister announce the Gospel for the Day, saying:*
The Holy Gospel is written in the————Chapter of St.————beginning at the ————Verse.

¶ *The Congregation may sing or say:*

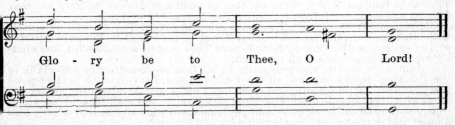

Glo - ry be to Thee, O Lord!

25

Morning Service

¶ *Then shall the Minister read*

THE GOSPEL FOR THE DAY.

¶ *The Gospel ended, the Minister shall say:* Here endeth the Gospel, *and the Congregation shall stand up, unless they have stood at the reading of the Gospel, and shall sing or say:*

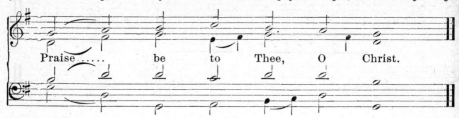

Praise...... be to Thee, O Christ.

¶ *Then shall be said or sung the Apostles' Creed.*

THE APOSTLES' CREED.

I believe in God the Father Almighty, Maker of heaven and earth.

And in Jesus Christ, His only Son, our Lord; Who was conceived by the Holy Ghost, Born of the Virgin Mary: Suffered under Pontius Pilate, Was crucified, dead, and buried; He descended into hell; The third day He rose again from the dead; He ascended into heaven, And sitteth on the right hand of God the Father Almighty; From thence He shall come to judge the quick and the dead.

I believe in the Holy Ghost; The holy Christian Church, the Communion of Saints; The Forgiveness of sins; The Resurrection of the body; And the Life everlasting. Amen.

¶ *Then may a Hymn be sung and the Minister shall go into the pulpit. After the Hymn shall follow the Sermon.*

THE SERMON.

¶ *The Sermon ended, the Congregation standing up, the Minister shall say:*

The peace of God, which passeth all understanding, keep your hearts and minds through Christ Jesus.

¶ *The Offerings shall be gathered and brought to the Minister, who shall place them on the Altar.*

¶ *Then shall the Minister make mention of any special petitions, intercessions or thanksgivings which may have been requested. He may also make mention of the death of any member of the Congregation.*

¶ *Then shall follow the General Prayer. The Prayer here following may be used; or, if there be no Communion, the Litany, or a selection from the Collects and Prayers, or any other suitable prayer. The Minister shall stand before the Altar.*

THE GENERAL PRAYER.

Almighty and most merciful God, the Father of our Lord Jesus Christ: We give Thee thanks for all Thy goodness and tender mercies, especially for the gift of Thy dear Son, and for the revelation of Thy will and grace; and we beseech Thee so to implant Thy Word in us, that in good and honest hearts, we may keep it, and bring forth fruit by patient continuance in well doing.

Most heartily we beseech Thee so to rule and govern Thy Church universal, with all its pastors and ministers, that it may be preserved in the pure doctrine of Thy saving word, whereby faith toward Thee may be strengthened, and charity increased in us toward all mankind.

Grant also health and prosperity to all that are in authority, especially to the President [and Congress] of the United States, the Governor [and Legislature] of this Commonwealth, and to all our Judges and Magistrates; and endue them with grace to rule after Thy good pleasure, to the maintenance of righteousness, and to the hinderance and punishment of wickedness, that we may lead a quiet and peaceable life, in all godliness and honesty.

May it please Thee also to turn the hearts of our enemies and adversaries, that they may cease their enmity, and be inclined to walk with us in meekness and in peace.

All who are in trouble, want, sickness, anguish of labor, peril of death, or any other adversity, especially those who are in suffering for Thy Name and for Thy truth's sake, comfort, O God, with Thy Holy Spirit, that they may receive and acknowledge their afflictions as the manifestation of Thy fatherly will.

And although we have deserved Thy righteous wrath and manifold punishments, yet, we entreat Thee, O most merciful Father, remember not the sins of our youth, nor our many transgressions; but out of Thine unspeakable goodness, grace and mercy, defend us from all harm and danger of body and soul. Preserve us from false and pernicious doctrine, from war and bloodshed, from plague and pestilence, from all calamity by fire and water, from hail and tempest, from failure of harvest and from famine, from anguish of heart and despair of Thy mercy, and from an evil death. And in every time of trouble, show Thyself a very present Help, the **Savior** of all men, and especially of them that believe.

Cause also the needful fruits of the earth to prosper, that we may enjoy them in due season. Give success to the Christian training of the young, to all lawful occupations on land and sea, and to all pure arts and useful knowledge; and crown them with Thy blessing.

¶ *Here special Supplications, Intercessions and Prayers may be made.*

These, and whatsoever other things Thou wouldest have us ask of Thee, O God, vouchsafe unto us for the sake of the bitter sufferings and death of Jesus Christ, Thine only Son, our Lord and **Savior,** who liveth and reigneth with Thee and the Holy Ghost, ever one God, world without end.

¶ *Then shall the Minister, and the Congregation with him, say the Lord's Prayer.*

THE LORD'S PRAYER.

Our Father, who art in heaven; Hallowed be Thy name; Thy kingdom come; Thy will be done on earth, as it is in heaven; Give us this day our daily bread; And forgive us our trespasses, as we forgive those who trespass against us; And lead us not into temptation; But deliver us from evil: For Thine is the kingdom, and the power, and the glory, for ever and ever. Amen.

¶ *Then shall be sung a Hymn.*

¶ *If there be no Communion, a Doxology may be sung, and the Minister, standing at the Altar, shall pronounce the Benediction, after which the Congregation shall offer silent prayer.*

THE BENEDICTION.

The Lord bless thee, and keep thee.
The Lord make His face shine upon thee, and be gracious unto thee.
The Lord lift up His countenance upon thee and give thee peace.

¶ *The Congregation shall sing or say :*

A - - men, A - - men, A - - men.

Morning Service

¶ *Whilst the Hymn is sung, the Minister shall go to the Altar, make ready the Communion vessels and prepare for the administration of the Holy Communion.*

¶ *The Hymn ended, the Congregation shall rise, and stand to the end of the Agnus Dei.*

THE PREFACE.

¶ *The Minister shall say:*

The Lord be with you.

¶ *The Congregation shall sing or say:*

And........ with thy........ spir - it.

¶ *Minister.* Lift up your hearts.

¶ *Congregation:*

We lift them up un - to the Lord.

¶ *Minister.* Let us give thanks unto the Lord our God.

¶ *Congregation:*

It is meet and right so to do.

¶ *Minister.* It is truly meet, right and salutary, that we should at all times and in all places, give thanks unto Thee, O Lord, Holy Father, Almighty Everlasting God.

Therefore with Angels and Archangels, and with all the company of heaven we laud and magnify Thy glorious name; evermore praising Thee, and saying

28

or the Communion

¶ *Then shall be said or sung the Sanctus.*

THE SANCTUS

Traditional

Ho - - ly, ho - - - ly, ho - ly, Lord, God of Sa - ba - oth;

Heav'n and earth are full of Thy glo - - ry; Ho - san - na, Ho -

Soli.
1st and 2nd Sop.

Alto

san - na, Ho-san - na in the high - est. Bless-ed is He,

Tutti. *Congregation:*

Blessed is He, Bless-ed is He that cometh in the name of the Lord.

Ho - san - na, Ho - san - na, Ho-san - na, in the high - - est.

29

¶ *Then may the Minister give this Exhortation.*

THE EXHORTATION.

Dearly Beloved! Forasmuch as we purpose to come to the Holy Supper of our Lord Jesus Christ, it becometh us diligently to examine ourselves, as St. Paul exhorteth us. For this Holy Sacrament hath been instituted for the special comfort and strengthening of those who humbly confess their sins, and who hunger and thirst after righteousness.

But if we thus examine ourselves, we shall find nothing in us but only sin and death, from which we can in no wise set ourselves free. Therefore our Lord Jesus Christ hath had mercy upon us and hath taken upon Himself our nature, that so He might fulfill for us the whole will and law of God, and for us and for our deliverance suffer death and all that we by our sins have deserved. And to the end that we should the more confidently believe this, and be strengthened by our faith in a cheerful obedience to His holy will, He hath instituted the Holy Sacrament of His Supper, in which He feedeth us with His Body, and giveth us to drink of His Blood.

Therefore whoso eateth of this bread, and drinketh of this cup, firmly believing the words of Christ, dwelleth in Christ, and Christ in him, and hath eternal life.

We should also do this in remembrance of Him, showing His death, that He was delivered for our offenses, and raised again for our justification, and rendering unto Him most hearty thanks for the same, take up our cross and follow Him, and according to His commandment, love one another even as He hath loved us. For we are all one bread and one body, even as we are all partakers of this one bread, and drink of this one cup.

¶ *Then the Minister, turning to the Altar, shall say:*

Let us pray.

Our Father, who art in heaven; Hallowed be Thy Name; Thy kingdom come; Thy will be done on earth, as it is in heaven; Give us this day our daily bread; And forgive us our trespasses, as we forgive those who trespass against us; And lead us not into temptation; But deliver us from evil:

¶ *Then shall the Congregation sing or say:*

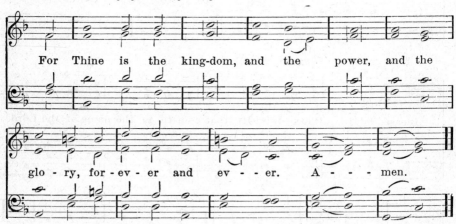

For Thine is the king-dom, and the power, and the glo-ry, for-ev-er and ev - - er. A - - - men.

¶ *Then shall the Minister say:*

Our Lord Jesus Christ, in the night in which He was betrayed, took bread;* and when He had given thanks He brake it and gave it to His disciples, saying: Take, eat; this is my Body, which is given for you; this do in remembrance of Me.

*) Here he shall take the Plate with the Bread in his hand.

or the Communion

After the same manner, also, He took the cup,* when He had supped, and when He had given thanks, He gave it to them, saying: Drink ye all of it; this cup is the New Testament in My Blood, which is shed for you, and for many, for the remission of sins; this do, as oft as ye drink it, in remembrance of Me.

¶ *Then shall the Minister say:*
The peace of the Lord be with you alway.

¶ *Then shall be sung or said the Agnus Dei, and the distribution shall begin.*

THE AGNUS DEI.

Braunschweig, 1528

O Christ, Thou Lamb of God, that tak-est a-way the sin of the world, have mer-cy up-on us! O Christ, Thou Lamb of God, that tak-est a-way the sin of the world, have mer-cy up-on us! O Christ, Thou Lamb of God, that tak-est a-way the sin of the world, grant us Thy peace. A- - - - - men.

*) Here he shall take the Cup in his hand.

31

Morning Service

¶ *When the Minister giveth the Bread he shall say:*

Take and eat, this is the true Body of Christ given for thee.

¶ *When he giveth the Cup he shall say:*

Take and drink, this is the true Blood of the New Testament, shed for thy sins.

¶ *In dismissing the Communicants, the Minister may say:*

The Body of our Lord Jesus Christ and His precious Blood strengthen and preserve you in the true faith unto everlasting life.

¶ *If the consecrated Bread or Wine be spent before all have communed, the Minister shall consecrate more, saying aloud so much of the words of institution as pertaineth to the element to be consecrated.*

¶ *When all have communed, the Minister shall reverently cover what remaineth of the Bread and Wine.*

¶ *Then, all standing, may be sung or said the Nunc Dimittis.*

THE NUNC DIMITTIS.

Pomeranian. 1535

1 Lord, now lettest Thou Thy servant de - - - - - part in peace: ac - cord - ing to Thy word.

2 For mine eyes have seen Thy salvation: which Thou hast pre - pared be - fore the face of all peo - ple.

3 A light to light - en the Gen - tiles, and the glo - ry of Thy peo - ple Is - ra - el.

4 Glo - ry | be to the Father, and......................
5 As it | was in the beginning, is now, and...........

to the Son: and to the Ho - ly Ghost.
ev - er shall be: world with - out end, A-men.

¶ *Then shall be said:*

THE THANKSGIVING.

¶ *Minister.* O give thanks unto the Lord, for He is good.

¶ *The Congregation shall sing or say:*

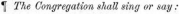

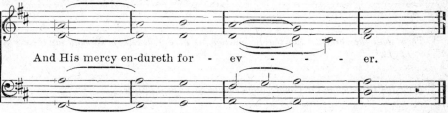

And His mercy en-dureth for - ev - - - - er.

¶ *Minister.*

We give thanks to Thee, Almighty God, that Thou hast refreshed us through this salutary gift; and we beseech Thee, that of Thy mercy Thou wouldst strength-en us through the same in faith towards Thee and in fervent love toward one an-other, through Jesus Christ, Thy dear Son, our Lord, who liveth and reigneth with Thee, and the Holy Ghost, ever one God, world without end.

¶ *The Congregation shall sing or say:*

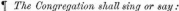

A - - - - - - - men.

Morning Service

Then may be sung or said the Benedicamus.

THE BENEDICAMUS.

¶ *Minister.* The Lord be with you.

¶ *Congregation:*

And with thy spir - - it.

¶ *Minister.* Bless we the Lord.

¶ *Congregation:*

Thanks be to God.

¶ *Then shall the Minister say the Benediction as here followeth, or he may say the words 2 Cor. 13 :14.*

¶ *After the Benediction the Congregation should offer silent prayer.*

THE BENEDICTION.

The Lord bless thee, and keep thee.
The Lord make His face shine upon thee, and be gracious unto thee.
The Lord lift up His countenance upon thee, and give thee peace.

¶ *The Congregation shall sing or say:*

A - men, A - - men.

Order of Evening Service, or Vespers

¶ *A Hymn of Invocation of the Holy Ghost, or another Hymn may be sung.*

¶ *Then shall be sung or said responsively the* VERSICLE *with the* GLORIA PATRI *as here followeth, all standing to the end of the Psalm.*

¶ *Versicle.* O Lord, open Thou my lips.

¶ *Congregation.*

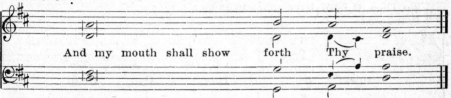

And my mouth shall show   forth   Thy   praise.

¶ *Versicle.* Make haste, O God, to deliver me.

¶ *Congregation.*

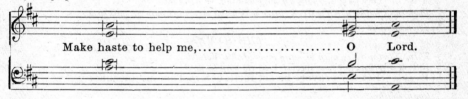

Make haste to help me,........................... O   Lord.

GLORIA PATRI.

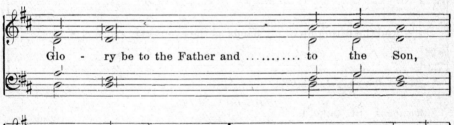

Glo - ry be to the Father and .... to   the   Son,

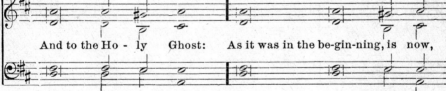

And to the Ho - ly   Ghost: As it was in the be-gin-ning, is now,

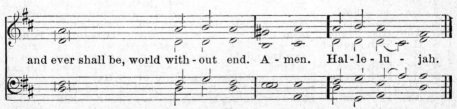

and ever shall be, world with-out end. A - men. Hal-le-lu - jah.

35

Evening Service, or Vespers

¶ *During the Passion Season the Hallelujah shall be omitted.*

THE PSALM.

¶ *Then shall be sung or said one or more Psalms. At the end of the Psalm the Gloria Patri shall be sung. An Antiphon may be used with each Psalm.*

THE LESSON.

¶ *The Scripture Lessons shall then be read, and after each Lesson may be sung or said:*
But Thou, O Lord, have mercy upon us.

¶ *Congregation:*

Thanks   be   to   Thee,   O   Lord!

¶ *After the Lessons a Responsory may be sung, or a hymn.*
¶ *Then may follow a SERMON, after which the Offerings may be gathered.*
¶ *Then shall be sung*

THE HYMN.

¶ *Then, all standing, may be sung or said this Versicle.*
¶ *But on Festival days, a special Versicle may be used.*
¶ *Versicle.* Let my prayer be set forth before Thee as incense:

¶ *Congregation:*

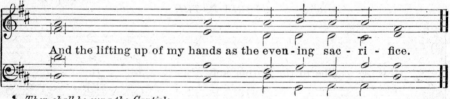

And the lifting up of my hands as the even-ing sac-ri-fice.

¶ *Then shall be sung the Canticle.*

THE CANTICLE.

¶ *Magnificat.* St. Luke. i.

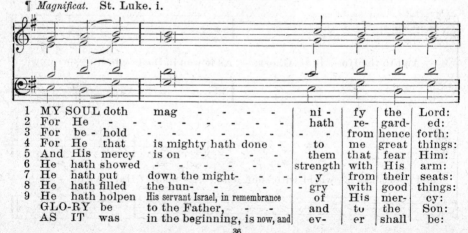

1	MY SOUL doth	mag - - - -		ni -	fy	the	Lord:
2	For He -	- - - - - - -		hath	re-	gard-	ed:
3	For be - hold	- - - - - - - -		- -	from	hence	forth:
4	For He that	is mighty hath done -		to	me	great	things:
5	And His mercy	is on - - - - -		them	that	fear	Him:
6	He hath showed	- - - - - -		strength	with	His	arm:
7	He hath put	down the might- - -		- y	from	their	seats:
8	He hath filled	the hun - - - - -		- gry	with	good	things:
9	He hath holpen	His servant Israel, in remembrance		of	His	mer-	cy:
	GLO-RY be	to the Father, - -		and	to	the	Son:
	AS IT was	in the beginning, is now, and		ev-	er	shall	be:

36

Evening Service, or Vespers

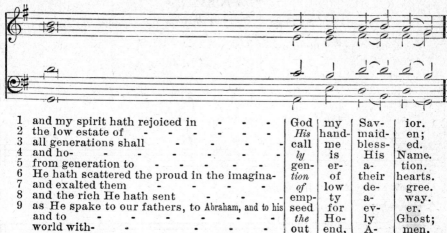

1	and my spirit hath rejoiced in - - -	God	my	Sav-	ior.
2	the low estate of - - - - - -	*His*	hand-	maid-	en;
3	all generations shall - - - -	call	me	bless-	ed.
4	and ho- - - - - - - - -	*ly*	is	His	Name.
5	from generation to - - - - -	gen-	er-	a-	tion.
6	He hath scattered the proud in the imagina-	*tion*	of	their	hearts.
7	and exalted them - - - -	*of*	low	de-	gree.
8	and the rich He hath sent - - -	emp-	ty	a-	way.
9	as He spake to our fathers, to Abraham, and to his	seed	for	a-	ev-	er.
	and to - - - - - - -	*the*	Ho-	ly	Ghost;
	world with- - - - - -	out	end,	A-	men.

Or the

NUNC DIMITTIS. St. Luke ii.

1	LORD, NOW	lettest Thou Thy servant	de-	part	in	peace:
2	For mine	eyes have seen - - -	Thy	sal-	va-	tion:
3	A light	to light- - - - -	en	the	Gen-	tiles:
	GLO - RY	be to the Father, - -	and	to	the	Son:
	AS IT	was in the beginning, is now, and	ev-	er	shall	be:

1	accord- - - - - - - -	*ing*	to	Thy	Word;
2	which Thou hast prepared before the face	*of*	all	peo-	ple;
3	and the glory of Thy - - -	peo-	ple	Isra-	el.
	and to - - - - - -	*the*	Ho-	ly	Ghost;
	world with- - - - - -	out	end.	A-	men.

¶ *An Antiphon may be sung with the Canticle.*

37

Evening Service, or Vespers

THE PRAYER.

¶ *Then shall be said the Prayers here following, or the Suffrages, the Litany, or other prayers.*

Lord, have mercy upon us.

¶ *Congregation:*

Lord, have mer — cy up — on us.

Christ, have mercy upon us.

¶ *Congregation:*

Christ, have mer — cy up — on us.

Lord, have mercy upon us.

¶ *Congregation.*

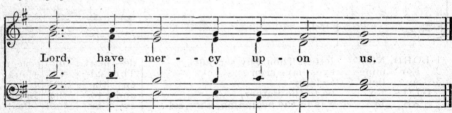

Lord, have mer — cy up — on us.

¶ *Then all shall say:*

Our Father, who art in heaven; Hallowed be Thy Name; Thy kingdom come; Thy will be done on earth, as it is in heaven; Give us this day our daily bread; And forgive us our trespasses, as we forgive those who trespass against us; And lead us not into temptation; But deliver us from evil: for Thine is the Kingdom, and the power, and the glory, for ever and ever. Amen.

¶ *Salutation.* The Lord be with you.

¶ *Congregation:*

And with thy spir — — — it.

Evening Service, or Vespers

Let us pray.

¶ *Then shall be said the COLLECT for the day; the Collect for the Sunday is said through-out the week following until Friday, but on Saturday the Collect for the following Sunday is said. Then may be said any other Collects and after that this COLLECT FOR PEACE. A Versicle may be used with the Collect.*

O God, from whom all holy desires, all good counsels, and all just works do proceed; Give unto Thy servants that peace which the world cannot give; that our hearts may be set to obey Thy commandments, and also that by Thee, we being defended from the fear of our enemies, may pass our time in rest and quietness; through the merits of Jesus Christ our Savior.

¶ *Congregation:*

A — — — — — — — — — — — — — — men.

¶ *Then may be sung or said the Benedicamus.*

THE BENEDICAMUS.

Bless we the Lord.

¶ *Congregation:*

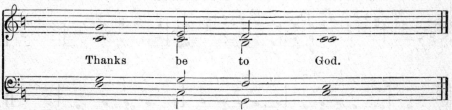

Thanks   be   to   God.

¶ *The service may end with the Benedicamus; or a Closing Hymn may be sung, after which may be said:*

The grace of the Lord Jesus Christ, and the love of God, and the commun-ion of the Holy Ghost, be with you all.

Congregation:

A — — men,   A — — men,   A — — . men.

¶ *At the close of the Service silent prayer should be offered.*

The Litany

¶ *Congregation.*

1 Lord, have mer-cy up-on us.
2 Christ, have mer-cy up-on us. 3 Lord, have mer-cy up-on us.

4 O Christ, hear us. O Christ, hear us.

5 O God the Father in heav - - en; have mer-cy up-on us.
6 O God the Son, Re - deem-er of the world; have mer-cy up-on us.

7 O God the Holy Ghost, true Com-for-ter; have mer-cy up-on us.

8 Be gra-cious un - to us. Spare us, good Lord.
9 Be gra-cious un - to us. Help us, good Lord.

The Litany

¶ *Minister.* From all sin;
From all error;
From all evil:

¶ *Congregation.*

10. Good Lord, de - - liv - - er us.

¶ *Minister.* From the crafts and assaults of the devil;
From sudden and evil death;
From pestilence and famine;
From war and bloodshed;
From sedition and rebellion;
From lightning and tempest;
From all calamity by fire and water;
And from everlasting death:

¶ *Congregation.*

11. Good Lord, de - - liv - - er us.

¶ *Minister.* By the mystery of Thy holy Incarnation;
By Thy holy Nativity;
By Thy Baptism, Fasting, and Temptation;
By Thine Agony and Bloody Sweat;
By Thy Cross and Passion;
By Thy precious Death and Burial;
By Thy glorious Resurrection and Ascension;
And by the coming of the Holy Ghost, the Comforter:

¶ *Congregation.*

12. Help us, good Lord.

The Litany

¶ *Minister.* In all time of our tribulation;
In all time of our prosperity;
In the hour of death;
And in the day of judgment:

¶ *Congregation.*

13 Help   us,   good   Lord.

¶ *Minister.* We poor sinners do beseech Thee;

¶ *Congregation.*

14 To   hear   us,   O   Lord   God.

¶ *Minister.*

And to lead and govern Thy holy Christian Church in the right way;
To preserve all pastors and ministers of Thy Church in the true knowledge
and understanding of Thy Word, and in holiness of life;
To put an end to all schisms and causes of offense;
To bring into the way of truth all such as have erred, and are deceived;
To beat down Satan under our feet;
To send faithful laborers into Thy harvest;
To accompany Thy Word with Thy Spirit and grace;
To raise up them that fall, and to strengthen such as do stand;
And to comfort and help the weak-hearted and the distressed:

¶ *Congregation.*

15 We   be-seech   Thee   to   hear   us,   good   Lord.

¶ *Minister.*

To give to all nations peace and concord;
To preserve our country from discord and contention;
To give to our nation perpetual victory over all its enemies;
To direct and defend our President, and all in authority;
And to bless and keep our magistrates, and all our people:

The Litany

¶ *Congregation.*

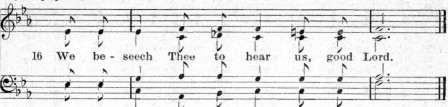

16 We be-seech Thee to hear us, good Lord.

¶ *Minister.*

To behold and succor all who are in danger, necessity, and tribulation;
To protect all who travel by land or water;
To preserve all women in the perils of childbirth;
To strengthen and keep all sick persons and young children;
To set free all who are innocently imprisoned;
To defend and provide for all fatherless children and widows;
And to have mercy upon all men:

¶ *Congregation.*

17 We be-seech Thee to hear us, good Lord.

¶ *Minister.*

To forgive our enemies, persecutors, and slanderers, and to turn their hearts;
To give and preserve to our use the fruits of the earth;
And graciously to hear our prayers:

¶ *Congregation.*

18 We be-seech Thee to hear us, good Lord.

¶ *Minister.* O Lord Jesus Christ, Son of God;

¶ *Congregation.*

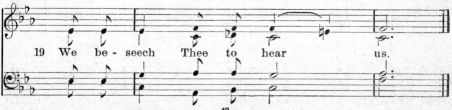

19 We be-seech Thee to hear us.

The Litany

20 O Lamb of God, that tak-est a-way the sin of the
21 O Lamb of God, that tak-est a-way the sin of the
22 O Lamb of God, that tak-est a-way the sin of the

world; Have mer-cy up-on us.
world; Have mer-cy up-on us.
world; Grant us Thy peace.

23 O Christ, hear us. O Christ, hear us.

24 Lord, have mercy up-on us.
25 Christ, have mercy up-on us. 26. Lord, have mercy up-on us.

A - - - - men.

Collects for the Church Year

The first Series of Collects is to be used with the first Service; the second Series, together with the Introits, to be used with the second or Common Service.

FIRST SUNDAY IN ADVENT.

The Collect.

Lord God, heavenly Father, we thank Thee, we bless and praise Thee forever, that Thou didst send Thy Son to rule over us poor sinners, who for our transgressions did justly deserve to remain in the bondage of sin and Satan, and didst give us in Him a meek and righteous King, who by His death became our Savior from sin and eternal death: We beseech Thee so to enlighten, govern and direct us by Thy Holy Spirit, that we may ever remain faithful to this righteous King and Savior, and not, after the manner of the world, be offended with His humble form and despised word, but, firmly believing in Him, obtain eternal salvation; through the same, Thy beloved Son, Jesus Christ, our Lord, who liveth and reigneth with Thee and the Holy Ghost, one true God, world without end. Amen.

Introit.

Unto Thee, O Lord, do I lift up my soul: O my God, I trust in Thee;
Let me not be ashamed: Let not mine enemies triumph over me;
Yea, let none that wait on Thee be ashamed.
Ps. Shew me Thy ways. O Lord: teach me Thy paths.
Glory be to the Father, &c.

The Collect.

Stir up, we beseech Thee, Thy power, O Lord, and come, that by Thy protection we may be rescued from the threatening perils of our sins, and saved by Thy mighty deliverance; who livest and reignest with the Father and the Holy Ghost, ever one God, world without end. Amen.

I. *Epistl* Rom. xiii: 11—14.   *Gospel*, Matt. xxi: 1—9.
II. *Lesson*, Rev. iii: 20—22.   *Gospel*, John xviii: 33—37.
III. *Lesson*, Jer. xxxi: 31—34.   *Gospel*, Luke iv: 16—22.

SECOND SUNDAY IN ADVENT.

The Collect.

Lord God, heavenly Father, who by Thy Son hast revealed to us that heaven and earth shall pass away, that our bodies shall rise again, and that we all shall appear before the judgment seat: We beseech Thee, keep us by Thy Holy Spirit in Thy word; establish us in the true faith, graciously defend us from sin and preserve us in all temptations, that our hearts may not be overcharged with surfeiting and drunkenness, and cares of this life, but that we may ever watch and pray and, trusting fully in Thy grace, await with joy the glorious coming of Thy Son, and at last obtain eternal salvation, through Thy beloved Son, Jesus Christ our Lord, who liveth and reigneth with Thee and the Holy Ghost, one true God, world without end. Amen.

Introit.

Daughter of Zion: behold thy salvation cometh. The Lord shall cause His glorious voice to be heard: and ye shall have gladness of heart.
Ps. Give ear, O Shepherd of Israel: Thou that leadest Joseph like a flock.
Glory be to the Father, &c.

Collects for the Church Year

The Collect.

Stir up our hearts, O Lord, to make ready the way of Thine only-begotten Son, so that by His coming we may be enabled to serve Thee with pure minds; who liveth and reigneth with Thee and the Holy Ghost, ever one God, world without end. Amen.

I. *Epistle*, Rom. xv: 4—9.   *Gospel*, Luke xxi: 25—36.
II. *Epistle*, Heb. x: 35—39.   *Gospel*, Luke xii: 35—40.
III. *Lesson*, Isa. xi: 1—5.   *Gospel*, Luke xvii: 20—30.

THIRD SUNDAY IN ADVENT.

The Collect.

Lord God, heavenly Father, who didst suffer Thy Son, our Lord Jesus Christ, to become man, and to come into the world, that He might destroy the works of the devil, deliver us poor offenders from sin and death, and give us everlasting life: We beseech Thee so to rule and govern our hearts by Thy Holy Spirit, that we may seek no other refuge than His word, and thus avoid all offense to which, by nature, we are inclined, in order that we may always be found among the faithful followers of Thy Son, Jesus Christ, and by faith in Him obtain eternal salvation, through the same, Thy beloved Son, Jesus Christ our Lord, who liveth and reigneth with Thee and the Holy Ghost, one true God, world without end. Amen.

Introit.

Rejoice in the Lord alway: and again I say, Rejoice.

Let your moderation be known unto all men: the Lord is at hand.

Be careful for nothing: but in everything by prayer and supplication with thanksgiving let your requests be made known unto God.

Ps. Lord, Thou hast been favorable unto Thy land: Thou hast brought back the captivity of Jacob.

Glory be to the Father, &c.

The Collect.

Lord, we beseech Thee, give ear to our prayers, and lighten the darkness of our hearts, by Thy gracious visitation; who livest and reignest with the Father and the Holy Ghost, ever one God, world without end. Amen.

I. *Epistle*, I Cor. iv: 1—5.   *Gospel*, Matt. xi: 2—10.
II. *Epistle*, II Pet. 1: 19—21.   *Gospel*, Matt. xi: 11—15.
III. *Lesson*, Mal. iii: 1—4.   *Gospel*, Luke iii: 1—6.

FOURTH SUNDAY IN ADVENT.

The Collect.

Lord God, heavenly Father, it is meet and right that we should give thanks unto Thee, that Thou hast given us a more glorious baptism than that of John the Baptist, and hast therein promised us the remission of sins, the Holy Spirit, and everlasting life through Thy Son, Jesus Christ: Preserve us, we beseech Thee, in such faith in Thy grace and mercy, that we may never doubt Thy promise, but be comforted by the same in all temptations: and grant us Thy Holy Spirit that we may renounce sin, and ever continue in the righteousness bestowed upon us in baptism, until by Thy grace we obtain eternal salvation, through the same, Thy beloved Son, Jesus Christ our Lord, who liveth and reigneth with Thee and the Holy Ghost, one true God, world without end. Amen.

Collects for the Church Year

Drop down, ye heavens, from above: and let the skies pour down righteousness:

Let the earth open: and bring forth salvation.

Ps. The heavens declare the glory of God: and the firmament sheweth His handiwork.

Glory be to the Father, &c.

The Collect.

Stir up, O Lord, we beseech Thee, Thy power, and come, and with great might succor us, that by the help of Thy grace whatsoever is hindered by our sins may be speedily accomplished, through Thy mercy and satisfaction; who livest and reignest with the Father and the Holy Ghost, ever one God, world without end. Amen.

I. *Epistle,* Phil. iv: 4—7.   *Gospel,* John i: 19—28.
II. *Epistle,* I John i: 1—7,   *Gospel,* John iii: 22—36.
III. *Epistle,* I Pet. i: 10—13.   *Gospel,* John v: 31—39.

CHRISTMAS.

The Collect.

Lord God, heavenly Father, we give thanks unto Thee, that of Thy mercy and compassion Thou didst suffer Thy dear Son to become incarnate, and didst through Him redeem us from sin and everlasting death: We beseech Thee, enlighten our hearts by Thy Holy Spirit, that we may ever be thankful for such grace, and comfort ourselves with the same in all tribulation and temptation, and at last obtain eternal salvation through the same, Thy beloved Son, Jesus Christ our Lord, who liveth and reigneth with Thee and the Holy Ghost, one true God, world without end. Amen.

Introit.

Unto us a Child is born, unto us a Son is given; and the government shall be upon His shoulder.

And His name shall be called Wonderful, Counsellor, the Mighty God: the Everlasting Father, the Prince of Peace.

Ps. O sing unto the Lord a new song: for He hath done marvellous things.

Glory be to the Father, &c.

The Collect.

Grant, we beseech Thee, almighty God, that the new birth of Thine only-begotten Son in the flesh may set us free who are held in the old bondage under the yoke of sin, through the same, Thy Son, Jesus Christ, our Lord, who liveth and reigneth with Thee and the Holy Ghost, ever one God, world without end. Amen.

Epistle, Heb. i: 1—5.   *Gospel,* Luke ii: 1—14.

ST. STEPHEN'S DAY.

The Collect.

O eternal and merciful God, our heavenly Father, who didst give such grace to Saint Stephen, that for the sake of Thy word and Thy dear Son he became the first martyr after the ascension of Christ, and with patience did make intercession for his persecutors: Grant us grace to endure patiently whatever Thy divine will appointeth, that we also may love our enemies and pray for them; through the same, Thy beloved Son, Jesus Christ our Lord, who liveth and reigneth with Thee and the Holy Ghost, one true God, world without end. Amen.

(To be used with II and III series of texts.)

Eternal and almighty God, heavenly Father, we thank Thee, that Thou hast revealed Thyself in Thine only-begotten Son, and hast sent Thy witnesses with Thy blessed word, whereby Thou dost call us into Thy kingdom: We beseech Thee, that Thou wouldst open our hearts by Thy Holy Spirit that we may not resist Thy gospel, but believe in Thine only-begotten Son, take up His cross and magnify His name, and at last obtain eternal salvation, through the same, Thy beloved Son, Jesus Christ our Lord, who liveth and reigneth with Thee and the Holy Ghost, one true God, world without end. Amen.

(The Introit is same as for Christmas Day.)

The Collect.

Grant, O Lord, that, in all our sufferings here upon earth for the testimony of Thy truth, we may steadfastly look up to heaven, and by faith behold the glory that shall be revealed; and, being filled with the Holy Ghost, may learn to love and bless our persecutors by the example of Thy first martyr Saint Stephen, who prayed for his murderers to Thee, O blessed Jesus, who standest at the right hand of God to succor all those who suffer for Thee, our only Mediator and Advocate. Amen.

I.	*Lesson*, Acts vi: 8—15 and 7: 45—60.	*Gospel*, Matt. xxiii: 34—39.
II.	*Lesson*, Isa. ix: 2—7.	*Gospel*, Luke ii: 15—20.
III.	*Epistle*, Tit. ii: 11—14.	*Gospel*, John i: 1—14.

SUNDAY AFTER CHRISTMAS.

The Collect.

O almighty and everlasting God, mercifully direct our ways, that we may walk in Thy law, and be made to abound in good works: through Thy beloved Son, Jesus Christ our Lord, who liveth and reigneth with Thee and the Holy Ghost, one true God, world without end. Amen.

Introit.

Thy testimonies are very sure: holiness becometh Thine house, O Lord, forever.

Thy throne is established of old: Thou art from everlasting.

Ps. The Lord reigneth, He is clothed with majesty: the Lord is clothed with strength, wherewith He hath girded Himself.

Glory be to the Father, &c.

The Collect.

Almighty and everlasting God, direct our actions according to Thy good pleasure, that in the name of Thy beloved Son, we may be made to abound in good works; through the same Jesus Christ our Lord, who liveth and reigneth with Thee and the Holy Ghost, ever one God, world without end. Amen.

I.	*Epistle*. Gal. iv: 1—7.	*Gospel*, Luke ii: 33—40.
II.	*Lesson*, Psalm xvi: 5—11.	*Gospel*, Luke ii: 25—32.
III.	*Epistle*, I Pet. ii: 4—10.	*Gospel*, Luke i: 68—75.

Collects for the Church Year

NEW YEAR.

The Collect.

O merciful and eternal God, heavenly Father, who didst cause Thy Son to endure circumcision and to be made subject to the law, that we might be redeemed from the curse of the law: We beseech Thee, grant us grace to become partakers of this redemption and thus obtain eternal salvation, through the same, Thy beloved Son, Jesus Christ our Lord, who liveth and reigneth with Thee and the Holy Ghost, one true God, world without end. Amen.

Introit.

O Lord, our Lord, how excellent is Thy name in all the earth: Who hast set Thy glory above the heavens. What is man that Thou art mindful of him: and the son of man that Thou visitest him?

Ps. Thou, O Lord, art our Father and our Redeemer: from everlasting is Thy name.

Glory be to the Father, &c.

The Collect.

O Lord God, who, for our sakes, hast made Thy blessed Son our Savior subject to the law, and caused Him to endure the circumcision of the flesh: Grant us the true circumcision of the spirit, that our hearts may be pure from all sinful desires and lusts; through the same, Thy Son, our Lord Jesus Christ, who liveth and reigneth with Thee and the Holy Ghost, ever one God, world without end. Amen.

Almighty and everlasting God, from whom cometh down every good and perfect gift: We give Thee thanks for all Thy benefits, temporal and spiritual, bestowed upon us in the year past, and we beseech Thee of Thy goodness, grant us a favorable and joyful year, defend us from all dangers and adversities, and send upon us the fullness of Thy blessing; through Jesus Christ, Thy Son, our Lord, who liveth and reigneth with Thee and the Holy Ghost, one true God, world without end. Amen.

I.	*Epistle*, Gal. iii: 23—29.	*Gospel*, Luke ii: 21.
II.	*Epistle*, Heb. xiii: 8—15.	*Gospel*, John i: 16—18.
III.	*Lesson*, Acts iv: 8—12.	*Gospel*, Luke xiii: 6—9.

SUNDAY AFTER NEW YEAR.

The Collect.

O Lord God, heavenly Father, who didst suffer Thy dear Son, Jesus Christ, to become a stranger and a sojourner in Egypt for our sakes, and didst lead Him safely home to His fatherland: Mercifully grant that we poor sinners, who are strangers and sojourners in this perilous world, may soon be called home to our true fatherland, the kingdom of heaven, where we shall live in eternal joy and glory; through the merits of Thy Son, Jesus Christ our Lord, who liveth and reigneth with Thee and the Holy Ghost, one true God, world without end. Amen.

(The Introit and second Collect are the same as for the Sunday after Christmas.)

I.	*Epistle*, Rom. iii: 19—22.	*Gospel*, Matt. ii: 19—23.
II.	*Lesson*, Acts iv: 23—31.	*Gospel*, Matt. ii: 13—18.
III.	*Lesson*, Is. xl: 27—31.	*Gospel*, Luke xii: 32—34

49

Collects for the Church Year

EPIPHANY.

The Collect.

Lord God, heavenly Father, who hast given us the light of Thy holy word, the guiding star, which leadeth us to the Christ-child: Send, we beseech Thee, Thy Holy Spirit into our hearts, that we may receive this light and make use of it unto our salvation, and that we, like the wise men, when they were seeking the star, may not be afraid because of any hardship or peril, but put all our trust in Thine only-begotten Son, Jesus Christ, our Lord, as our only Savior; devote our earthly possessions to the advancement of Thy kingdom, and in all things serve Him, Thine only-begotten Son, Jesus Christ, our Lord, who liveth and reigneth with Thee and the Holy Ghost, one true God, world without end. Amen.

Introit.

Behold the Lord, the Ruler hath come: and the kingdom, and the power, and the glory are in His hand.

Ps. Give the King Thy judgments, O God; and Thy righteousness unto the King's Son.

Glory be to the Father, &c.

The Collect.

O God, who, by the leading of a star, didst manifest Thy only-begotten Son to the Gentiles: Mercifully grant that we, who know Thee now by faith, may after this life have the fruition of Thy glorious Godhead; through the same, Thy Son, Jesus Christ our Lord, who liveth and reigneth with Thee and the Holy Ghost, ever one God, world without end. Amen.

I. *Lesson*, Is. lx: 1—6. *Gospel*, Matt. ii: 1—12.
II. *Epistle.* I Tim. iii: 14—16. *Gospel*, Matt. iv: 13—17.
III. *Lesson*, Is. xlix: 1—6. *Gospel*, Matt. xii: 15—21.

FIRST SUNDAY AFTER EPIPHANY.

The Collect.

Lord God, heavenly Father, who in mercy hast established the Christian home among us: We beseech Thee so to rule and direct our hearts, that we may be good examples to children and servants, and not offend them by word or deed, but faithfully teach them to love Thy Church and hear Thy blessed word. Give them Thy Spirit and grace, that this seed may bring forth good fruit, so that our homelife may conduce to Thy glory, honor and praise, to our own improvement and welfare, and give offense to no one; through the same, Thy beloved Son, Jesus Christ our Lord, who liveth and reigneth with Thee and the Holy Ghost, one true God, world without end. Amen.

Introit.

I saw also the Lord sitting upon a throne: high and lifted up.

And I heard the voice of a great multitude, saying, Hallelujah: for the Lord God Omnipotent reigneth.

Ps. Make a joyful noise unto the Lord, all ye lands: serve the Lord with gladness.

Glory be to the Father, &c.

The Collect.

O Lord, we beseech Thee mercifully to receive the prayers of Thy people who call upon Thee; and grant that they may both perceive and know what things hey ought to do, and also may have grace and power faithfully to fulfill the same; through Jesus Christ, Thy Son, our Lord, who liveth and reigneth with Thee and the Holy Ghost, ever one God, world without end. Amen.

I. *Epistle*, Rom. xii: 1—5.   *Gospel*, Luke ii. 42—52.
II. *Epistle*, Heb. ii; 11—16.   *Gospel*, John vii: 14—18.
III. *Epistle*, Eph. vi; 1—4.   *Gospel*, Mark x: 13—16.

SECOND SUNDAY AFTER EPIPHANY.

The Collect.

Lord God, heavenly Father, we thank Thee, that of Thy grace Thou hast instituted holy matrimony, in which Thou keepest us from unchastity, and other offenses: We beseech Thee to send Thy blessing upon every husband and wife, that they may not provoke each other to anger and strife, but live peaceably together in love and godliness, receive Thy gracious help in all temptations, and rear their children in accordance with Thy will; grant unto us all to walk before Thee, in purity and holiness, to put all our trust in Thee, and lead such lives on earth, that in the world to come we may have everlasting life, through the same, Thy beloved Son, Jesus Christ our Lord, who liveth and reigneth with Thee and the Holy Ghost, one true God, world without end. Amen.

Introit.

All the earth shall worship Thee: and shall sing unto Thee, O God.
They shall sing unto Thy name: O Thou Most Highest.
Ps. Make a joyful noise unto God, all ye lands: sing forth the honor of His name, make His praise glorious.
Glory be to the Father, &c.

The Collect.

Almighty and everlasting God, who dost govern all things in heaven and earth: Mercifully hear the supplications of Thy people, and grant us Thy peace all the days of our life; through Thy Son, Jesus Christ our Lord, who liveth and reigneth with Thee and the Holy Ghost, ever one God, world without end. Amen.

I. *Epistle*, Rom, xii: 6—16.   *Gospel*, John ii: 1—11.
II. *Epistle*, Eph. ii; 10—16.   *Gospel*, John iv: 4—26.
III. *Epistle*, I Cor. i: 26—31.   *Gospel*, Luke xix: 1—10.

THIRD SUNDAY AFTER EPIPHANY.

The Collect.

O almighty and everlasting God, mercifully look upon our infirmities, and in all dangers and necessities stretch forth Thy mighty hand, to defend us against our enemies; through Jesus Christ, Thy Son, who liveth and reigneth with Thee and the Holy Ghost, one true God, world without end. Amen.

Introit.

Worship Him, all ye His angels: Zion heard and was glad.
The daughters of Judah rejoiced: because of Thy judgments, O Lord.
Ps. The Lord reigneth, let the earth rejoice, let the multitude of isles be glad thereof.
Glory be to the Father, &c.

The Collect.

Almighty and everlasting God, mercifully look upon our infirmities, and in all our dangers and necessities stretch forth the right hand of Thy majesty, to

Collects for the Church Year

help and defend us; through Jesus Christ, our Lord, who liveth and reigneth with Thee and the Holy Ghost, ever one God, world without end. Amen.

I. *Epistle*, Rom. xii: 16—21. *Gospel*, Matt. viii: 1—13.
II. *Epistle*, Heb. xi: 1—10. *Gospel*, John iv: 27—42.
III. *Epistle*, II Cor. i: 3—11. *Gospel*, Mark i: 21—35.

FOURTH SUNDAY AFTER EPIPHANY.

The Collect.

Lord God, heavenly Father, who in Thy divine wisdom and fatherly goodness makest Thy children to bear the cross, and sendest divers afflictions upon us to subdue the flesh, and quicken our hearts unto faith, hope and unceasing prayer: We beseech Thee to have mercy upon us, and graciously deliver us out of our trials and afflictions, so that we may perceive Thy grace and fatherly help, and with all saints forever praise and worship Thee; through Thy dear Son, our Lord Jesus Christ, who liveth and reigneth with Thee and the Holy Ghost, one true God, world without end. Amen.

Introit.

(Same as for Third Sunday after Epiphany).

The Collect.

Almighty God, who knowest us to be set in the midst of so many and great dangers, that by reason of the frailty of our nature we cannot always stand upright: Grant to us such strength and protection as may support us in all dangers, and carry us through all temptations: through Jesus Christ, our Lord, who liveth and reigneth with Thee and the Holy Ghost, ever one God, world without end. Amen.

I. *Epistle*, Rom. xiii: 8—10. *Gospel*, Matt. viii: 23—27.
II. *Epistle*, Heb. xii: 1—3. *Gospel*, Matt. xxi: 18—22.
III. *Epistle*, II Tim. i: 7—10. *Gospel*, Matt. xiv: 22—33.

FIFTH SUNDAY AFTER EPIPHANY.

The Collect.

Lord God, heavenly Father, we thank Thee, that Thou hast sown the good seed, Thy holy word, in our hearts: We pray Thee that by Thy Holy Spirit Thou wilt cause this seed to grow and bring forth fruit, and defend us from the enemy, that he may not sow tares therein. Keep us from carnal security, help us in all temptations, and give us at last eternal salvation; through Thy beloved Son, who liveth and reigneth with Thee and the Holy Ghost, one true God, world without end. Amen.

Introit.

(Same as for Third Sunday after Epiphany).

The Collect.

O Lord, we beseech Thee to keep Thy Church and Household continually in Thy true religion; that they who do lean only upon the hope of Thy heavenly grace may evermore be defended by Thy mighty power; through Jesus Christ, Thy Son, our Lord, who liveth and reigneth with Thee and the Holy Ghost, ever one God, world without end. Amen.

I. *Epistle*, Col. iii: 12—17. *Gospel*, Matt. xiii: 24—30.
II. *Epistle*, I Cor. i: 10—18. *Gospel*, Matt. xiii: 31—35.
III. *Epistle*, Eph. iv: 11—16. *Gospel*, Mark iv: 26—29.

Collects for the Church Year

SIXTH SUNDAY AFTER EPIPHANY.

The Collect.

O merciful and everlasting God, heavenly Father: We thank Thee that Thou hast revealed unto us the glory of Thy Son, and let the light of Thy gospel shine upon us: We pray Thee, guide us by this light that we may walk diligently as Christians in all good works, ever be strengthened by Thy grace, and conduct our lives in all godliness; through the same, Thy beloved Son, Jesus Christ our Lord, who liveth and reigneth with Thee and the Holy Ghost, one true God, world without end. Amen.

Introit.

The lightnings lightened the world: the earth trembled and shook.

Ps. How amiable are Thy tabernacles, O Lord of Hosts: My soul longeth, yea, even fainteth for the courts of the Lord.

Glory be to the Father, &c.

The Collect

O God, who in the glorious transfiguration of Thy only-begotten Son hast confirmed the mysteries of the faith by the testimony of the fathers, and who, in the voice that came from the bright cloud, didst in a wonderful manner foreshow the adoption of sons; Mercifully vouchsafe to make us co-heirs with the King of His glory, and bring us to the enjoyment of the same; through the same, our Lord Jesus Christ, who liveth and reigneth with Thee and the Holy Ghost, ever one God, world without end. Amen.

Epistle, II Peter i: 12—18.   *Gospel,* Matt. xvii: 1—9.

SEPTUAGESIMA SUNDAY.

The Collect.

Lord God, heavenly Father, who through Thy holy word hast called us into Thy vineyard: Send, we beseech Thee, Thy Holy Spirit into our hearts, that we may labor faithfully in Thy vineyard, shun sin and all offense, obediently keep Thy word and do Thy will, and put our whole and only trust in Thy grace, which Thou hast bestowed upon us so plenteously through Thy Son Jesus Christ, that we may obtain eternal salvation through Him, who liveth and reigneth with Thee and the Holy Ghost, one true God, world without end. Amen.

Introit.

The sorrows of death compassed me; the sorrows of hell compassed me about.

In my distress, I called upon the Lord; and He heard my voice out of His temple.

Ps. I will love Thee, O Lord my Strength: the Lord is my Rock and my Fortress!

Glory be to the Father, &c.

The Collect.

O Lord, we beseech Thee favorably to hear the prayers of Thy people: That we, who are justly punished for our offenses, may be mercifully delivered by Thy goodness, for the glory of Thy name; through Jesus Christ, Thy Son, our Savior, who liveth and reigneth with Thee and the Holy Ghost, ever one God, world without end. Amen.

I.   *Epistle,* I Cor. ix: 24 to x: 5.   *Gospel,* Matt. xx: 1—16.
II. *Epistle,* I Cor. iii: 7—15.   *Gospel,* Matt. xix: 27—30.
III. *Epistle,* Phil. iii: 7—16.   *Gospel,* Matt. xxv: 14—30.

53

Collects for the Church Year

SEXAGESIMA SUNDAY.

The Collect.

Lord God, heavenly Father, we thank Thee, that through Thy Son Jesus Christ Thou hast sown Thy holy word among us: We pray that Thou wilt prepare our hearts by Thy Holy Spirit, that we may diligently and reverently hear Thy word, keep it in good hearts, and bring forth fruit with patience; and that we may not incline to sin, but subdue it by Thy power, and in all persecutions comfort ourselves with Thy grace and continual help, through Thy beloved Son, Jesus Christ, our Lord, who liveth and reigneth with Thee and the Holy Ghost, ever one God, world without end. Amen.

Introit.

Awake, why sleepest Thou, O Lord?: Arise, cast us not off forever. Wherefore hidest Thou Thy face: and forgettest our afflictions?
Our soul is bowed down to the dust: arise for our help and redeem us.
Ps. We have heard with our ears, O God: our fathers have told us what work Thou didst in their days.
Glory be to the Father, &c.

The Collect.

O God, who seest that we put not our trust in anything that we do: Mercifully grant, that by Thy power we may be defended against all adversity; through Jesus Christ, our Lord, who liveth and reigneth with Thee and the Holy Ghost, ever one God, world without end. Amen.

I. *Epistle,* II Cor. xii: 2—9.	*Gospel,* Luke viii: 4—15.
II. *Epistle,* I Cor. i: 20—25.	*Gospel,* John xii: 35—43.
III. *Epistle,* II Tim. iii: 14 to iv: 5.	*Gospel,* Matt. ix: 37 to x: 7.

QUINQUAGESIMA SUNDAY.

The Collect.

Lord God, heavenly Father, who didst manifest Thyself, with the Holy Ghost, in the fullness of grace at the baptism of Thy dear Son, and with Thy voice didst direct us to Him who hath borne our sins, that we might receive grace and the remission of sins: Keep us, we beseech Thee, in the true faith; and inasmuch as we have been baptized in accordance with Thy command, and the example of Thy dear Son, we pray Thee to strengthen our faith by Thy Holy Spirit, and lead us to everlasting life and salvation, through Thy beloved Son, Jesus Christ our Lord, who liveth and reigneth with Thee and the Holy Ghost, one true God, world without end. Amen.

Introit.

Be Thou my strong Rock: for an house of defense to save me.
Thou art my Rock and my Fortress: therefore for Thy name's sake lead me and guide me.
Ps. In Thee, O Lord, do I put my trust; let me never be ashamed: deliver me in Thy righteousness.
Glory be to the Father, &c.

Collects for the Church Year

The Collect.

O Lord, we beseech Thee, mercifully hear our prayers, and, having set us free from the bonds of sin, defend us from all evil; through Jesus Christ, Thy Son, our Lord, who liveth and reigneth with Thee and the Holy Ghost, ever one God, world without end. Amen.

I. *Epistle*, I Pet. iii: 18—22.   *Gospel*, Matt. iii: 13—17.
II. *Epistle*, Eph. v: 25—27.   *Gospel*, Luke xviii: 31—43.
III. *Lesson*, Is. liii: 1—7.   *Gospel*, John i: 29—34.

FIRST SUNDAY IN LENT.

The Collect.

Lord God, heavenly Father, inasmuch as the adversary doth continually afflict us, and as a roaring lion doth walk about, seeking to devour us: We beseech Thee for the sake of the suffering and death of Thy Son, Jesus Christ, to help us by the grace of the Holy Spirit, and to strengthen our hearts by Thy word, that our enemy may not prevail over us, but that we may evermore abide in Thy grace, and be preserved unto everlasting life; through the same, Thy beloved Son, Jesus Christ, our Lord, who liveth and reigneth with Thee and the Holy Ghost, one true God, world without end. Amen.

Introit.

He shall call upon me, and I will answer him: I will deliver him and honor him.

With long life will I satisfy him: and show him my salvation.

Ps. He that dwelleth in the secret place of the Most High: shall abide under the shadow of the Almighty.

Glory be to the Father, &c.

The Collect.

O Lord, mercifully hear our prayer, and stretch forth the right hand of Thy majesty to defend us from them that rise up against us, through Jesus Christ, Thy Son, our Lord, who liveth and reigneth with Thee and the Holy Ghost, ever one God, world without end. Amen.

I. *Epistle*, II Cor. vi: 1—10.   *Gospel*, Matt. iv: 1—11.
II. *Epistle*, I Pet. iv: 1—6.   *Gospel*, Matt. xvi: 21—23.
III. *Lesson*, Rev. xii: 9—11.   *Gospel*, Luke x: 17—20.

SECOND SUNDAY IN LENT,

The Collect.

Lord God, heavenly Father, grant us, we beseech Thee, by Thy Holy Spirit, that He may strengthen our hearts and confirm our faith and hope in Thy grace and mercy, so that, although we have reason to fear because of our conscience, our sin, and our unworthiness, we may nevertheless, with the woman of Canaan, hold fast to Thy grace, and in every trial and temptation find Thee a very present help and refuge, through Thy beloved Son, Jesus Christ our Lord, who liveth and reigneth with Thee and the Holy Ghost, one true God, world without end. Amen.

Collects for the Church Year

Introit.

Remember, O Lord, Thy tender mercies and Thy loving-kindnesses: for they have been ever of old.

Let not mine enemies triumph over me: God of Israel, deliver us out of all our troubles.

Ps. Unto Thee, O Lord, do I lift up my soul: O my God, I trust in Thee; let me not be ashamed.

Glory be to the Father, &c.

The Collect.

O God, who seest that of ourselves we have no strength: Keep us both outwardly and inwardly; that we may be defended from all adversities which may happen to the body, and from all evil thoughts which may assault and hurt the soul; through Jesus Christ, Thy Son, our Lord, who liveth and reigneth with Thee and the Holy Ghost, ever one God, world without end. Amen.

I.	*Epistle,* I Thess. iv: 1—7.	*Gospel,* Matt. xv: 21—28.
II.	*Lesson,* Is. xlii: 1—7.	*Gospel,* Luke vii: 36—50.
III.	*Lesson,* Rev. iii: 7—13.	*Gospel,* Mark ix: 17—29.

THIRD SUNDAY IN LENT.

The Collect.

Lord God, heavenly Father, who hast sent Thy Son, our Lord Jesus Christ, to take upon Himself our flesh, that He might overcome the devil, and defend us poor sinners against the adversary: We give thanks unto Thee for Thy merciful help, and we beseech Thee to attend us with Thy grace in all temptations, to preserve us from carnal security, and by Thy Holy Spirit to keep us in Thy word and Thy fear, that unto the end we may be delivered from the enemy, and obtain eternal salvation, through the same, Thy beloved Son, Jesus Christ our Lord, who liveth and reigneth with Thee and the Holy Ghost, one true God, world without end. Amen.

Introit.

Mine eyes are ever toward the Lord: for He shall pluck my feet out of the net.

Turn Thee unto me, and have mercy upon me: for I am desolate and afflicted.

Ps. Unto Thee, O Lord, do I lift up my soul: O my God, I trust in Thee; let me not be ashamed.

Glory be to the Father, &c.

The Collect.

We beseech Thee, almighty God, look upon the hearty desires of Thy humble servants, and stretch forth the right hand of Thy majesty to be our defense against all our enemies; through Jesus Christ, Thy Son, our Lord, who liveth and reigneth with Thee and the Holy Ghost, ever one God, world without end. Amen.

I.	*Epistle,* Eph. v: 1—9.	*Gospel,* Luke xi: 14—28.
II.	*Lesson,* Rev. ii: 1—7.	*Gospel,* Luke iv: 31—37.
III.	*Lesson,* Rev. ii: 8—11.	*Gospel,* Luke viii: 31—37.

Collects for the Church Year

FOURTH SUNDAY IN LENT.

The Collect.

Lord God, heavenly Father, who by Thy Son didst feed five thousand men in the desert with five loaves and two fishes: We beseech Thee to abide graciously also with us in the fullness of Thy blessing. Preserve us from avarice and the cares of this life, that we may seek first Thy kingdom and Thy righteousness, and in all things perceive Thy fatherly goodness, through Jesus Christ, who liveth and reigneth with Thee and the Holy Ghost, one true God world without end. Amen.

Introit.

Rejoice ye with Jerusalem, and be glad with her: all ye that love her. Rejoice for joy with her: all ye that mourn for her.
Ps. I was glad when they said unto me: Let us go into the house of the Lord.
Glory be to the Father, &c.

The Collect.

Grant, we beseech Thee, almighty God, that we, who for our evil deeds do worthily deserve to be punished, by the comfort of Thy grace may mercifully be relieved; through our Lord and Savior Jesus Christ, who liveth and reigneth with Thee and the Holy Ghost, ever one God, world without end. Amen.

I.	*Epistle,* Gal. iv: 21—31.	*Gospel,* John vi: 1—15.
II.	*Lesson,* Ps. lxxxiv: 2—5.	*Gospel,* John vi: 24—36.
III.	*Lesson,* Ex. xvi: 11—18.	*Gospel,* John vi: 52—65.

THE ANNUNCIATION OF THE VIRGIN MARY.

The Collect.

O almighty God, who of Thy great mercy didst cause Thy Son to be conceived by the Holy Ghost, and to become incarnate of the blessed virgin Mary according to the angel's annunciation: Grant us by Thy grace, that our sinful conception may be purified by His holy conception, through the same, Thy beloved Son, Jesus Christ, our Lord, who liveth and reigneth with Thee and the Holy Ghost, one true God, world without end. Amen.

Introit.

All the rich among the people shall entreat Thy favor.
She shall be brought unto the King in raiment of needle-work.
Her companions shall be brought unto Thee: with gladness and rejoicing.
Ps. My heart is inditing a good matter: I speak of the things which I have made touching the King.
Glory be to the Father, &c.

The Collect.

We beseech Thee, O Lord, pour Thy grace into our hearts; that, as we have known the incarnation of Thy Son, Jesus Christ, by the message of an angel, so by His cross and passion we may be brought into the glory of His resurrection· through the same Jesus Christ, our Lord. Amen.

I.	*Lesson,* Is. vii; 10—15.	*Gospel,* Luke i: 26—38.
II.	*Lesson,* Jer. xxxiii: 14—17.	*Gospel,* Luke i: 39—45.
III.	*Lesson,* Rev. xxi. 1—7.	*Gospel,* Luke i: 46—55.

Collects for the Church Year

PALM SUNDAY.

The Collect.

Almighty and everlasting God, who hast caused Thy beloved Son to take our nature upon Himself, that He might give all mankind the example of humility and suffer death upon the cross for our sins: Mercifully grant us a believing knowledge of this, and that, following the example of His patience, we may be made partakers of the benefits of His sacred passion and death, through the same, Thy beloved Son, Jesus Christ, our Lord, who liveth and reigneth with Thee and the Holy Ghost, one true God, world without end. Amen.

Introit.

Be not Thou far from me, O Lord: O my Strength, haste Thee to help me. Save me from the lion's mouth: and deliver me from the horns of the unicorns.

Ps. My God, my God, why hast Thou forsaken me?: Why art Thou so far from helping me?

Glory be to the Father, &c.

The Collect.

Almighty and everlasting God, who hast sent Thy Son, our Savior, Jesus Christ, to take upon Him our flesh, and to suffer death upon the cross, that all mankind should follow the example of His great humility: Mercifully grant that we may both follow the example of His patience, and also be made partakers of His resurrection; through the same, Jesus Christ, our Lord, who liveth and reigneth with Thee and the Holy Ghost, ever one God, world without end. Amen.

I.	*Epistle,* Phil. ii: 5—11.	*Gospel,* Matt. xxi: 1—9.	
II.	*Lesson,* Is. lxii: 10—12.	*Gospel,* John xii: 1—16.	
III.	*Lesson,* Is. liii: 10—12.	*Gospel,* John xii: 20—33.	

HOLY THURSDAY.

The Collect.

O Lord Jesus Christ, we thank Thee, that of Thine infinite mercy Thou hast instituted this Thy sacrament, in which we eat Thy body and drink Thy blood: Grant us, we beseech Thee, by Thy Holy Spirit, that we may not receive this gift unworthily, but that we may confess our sins, remember Thine agony and death, believe the forgiveness of sin, and day by day grow in faith and love, until we obtain eternal salvation through Thee, who livest and reignest with the Father and the Holy Ghost, one true God, world without end. Amen.

Introit.

God forbid that I should glory: save in the cross of our Lord Jesus Christ. In Him is salvation, life and resurrection from the dead: by Him we are redeemed and set at liberty.

Ps. God be merciful unto us and bless us: and cause His face to shine upon us.

Glory be to the Father, &c.

Collects for the Church Year

The Collect.

O Lord God, who hast left unto us in a wonderful sacrament a memorial of Thy passion: Grant, we beseech Thee, that we may so use this sacrament of Thy body and blood, that the fruits of Thy redemption may continually be manifest in us; Thou, who livest and reignest with the Father and the Holy Ghost, ever one God, world without end. Amen.

I. *Epistle,* I Cor. xi: 23—29. *Gospel,* Luke xxii: 14—20.
II. *Epistle,* I Cor. x: 16—17. *Gospel,* Matt. xxvi: 17—29.
III. *Lesson,* Acts. ii: 44—47. *Gospel,* John xiii: 1—15.

GOOD FRIDAY.

Introit.

Surely He hath borne our griefs and carried our sorrows: He was wounded for our transgressions, He was bruised for our iniquities.

All we like sheep have gone astray: and the Lord hath laid on Him the iniquity of us all.

Ps. Hear my prayer, O Lord: and let my cry come unto Thee.

Glory be to the Father, &c.

The Collect.

Almighty and everlasting God, who hast willed that Thy Son should bear for us the pains of the cross, that Thou mightest remove from us the power of the adversary; Help us to remember and give thanks for our Lord's passion that we may obtain remission of sin and redemption from everlasting death; through the same, our Lord Jesus Christ. Amen.

Lesson, Isa. lii: 13-liii: 12. *Gospel,* John xviii: 1-xix: 42, or The Passion History.

EASTER.

The Collect.

Lord God, heavenly Father, who didst deliver Thy Son for our offenses, and didst raise Him again for our justification: We beseech Thee, grant us Thy Holy Spirit, that He may rule and govern us according to Thy will; graciously keep us in the true faith; defend us from all sins, and after this life raise us unto eternal life, through the same, Thy beloved Son, who liveth and reigneth with Thee and the Holy Ghost, one true God, world without end. Amen.

Introit.

He is risen, Hallelujah!: Why seek ye the Living among the dead? Hallelujah!

Remember how He spake unto you, Hallelujah: the Son of Man must be crucified and the third day rise again. Hallelujah! Hallelujah!

Ps. Thou crownedst Him with glory and honor: Thou madest Him to have dominion over the works of Thy hands.

Glory be to the Father, &c.

The Collect.

Almighty God, who, through Thine only-begotten Son, Jesus Christ, hast overcome death, and opened unto us the gate of everlasting life: We humbly beseech Thee, that, as Thou dost put into our minds good desires, so by Thy

continual help we may bring the same to good effect; through Jesus Christ, ou
Lord, who liveth and reigneth with Thee and the Holy Ghost, ever one God
world without end. Amen.

    I. *Epistle*, I Cor. v: 7—8.   *Gospel*, Mark xvi: 1—7.
    II. *Epistle*, I Cor. xv: 12—21.   *Gospel*, Luke xxiv: 1—9.
    III. *Epistle*, Eph. i: 15—23.   *Gospel*, Matt. xxiii: 1—8.

EASTER MONDAY.

The Collect.

Lord God, heavenly Father, who didst reveal Thy Son to the two disciple
in the way to Emmaus: We beseech Thee to enlighten our hearts also by Th
word and by Thy Holy Spirit, that we may become established in the faitl
hold fast to Thy word, delight to speak thereof, and diligently meditate thereor
that although, according to the example of Christ, we must suffer much evil o
earth, we nevertheless may have and retain a sure comfort in Thy word, until
after this life, we shall be raised unto eternal life, through the same, Thy Son
who liveth and reigneth with Thee and the Holy Ghost, one true God, worl
without end. Amen.

    I. *Lesson*, Acts x: 34—41.   *Gospel*, Luke xxiv: 13—35.
    II. *Epistle*, II Cor. v: 14—21.   *Gospel*, John xx: 11—18.
    III. *Epistle*, I Pet. i: 17—23.   *Gospel*, Matt. xxviii: 9—15.

FIRST SUNDAY AFTER EASTER.

The Collect.

Lord God, heavenly Father, we thank Thee, that of Thine ineffable grace
for the sake of Thy Son, Thou hast given us the holy gospel, and hast institute
the holy sacraments, that through the same we may have comfort and forgive
ness of sin: We beseech Thee, grant us Thy Holy Spirit, that we may heartil
believe Thy word; and through the holy sacraments day by day establish ou
faith, until we at last obtain salvation through Jesus Christ our Lord, who liv
eth and reigneth with Thee and the Holy Ghost, one true God, world withou
end. Amen.

Introit.

As newborn babes: desire the sincere milk of the word.

Hear, O my people, and I will testify unto Thee: O Israel, if thou wil
hearken unto me.

Ps. Sing aloud unto God our strength: Make a joyful noise unto the Go
of Jacob.

Glory be to the Father, &c.

The Collect.

Grant, we beseech Thee, almighty God, that we who have celebrated th
solemnities of the Lord's resurrection, may, by the help of Thy grace, brin
forth the fruits thereof in our life and conversation; through the same, Jesu
Christ, Thy Son, our Lord; who liveth and reigneth with Thee and the Hol
Ghost, ever one God, world without end. Amen.

    I. *Epistle*, I John v: 4—12.   *Gospel*, John xx: 19—31.
    II. *Lesson*, Acts iii: 11—21.   *Gospel*, John xxi: 1—14.
    III. *Lesson*, Acts xiii: 26—39.   *Gospel*, Luke xxiv: 36—43.

Collects for the Church Year

SECOND SUNDAY AFTER EASTER.

The Collect.

Lord God, heavenly Father, who of Thy fatherly goodness hast been mindful of us poor, miserable sinners, and hast given Thy beloved Son to be our Shepherd, not only to nourish us by His word, but also to defend us from sin, death, and the devil: We beseech Thee, grant us Thy Holy Spirit, that, even as his Shepherd doth know us and succor us in every affliction, we also may know Him, and, trusting in Him, seek help and comfort in Him, from our hearts obey His voice, and obtain eternal salvation, through the same, Thy Son Jesus Christ, who liveth and reigneth with Thee and the Holy Ghost, one true God, world without end. Amen.

Introit.

The earth is full of the goodness of the Lord.
By the word of the Lord were the heavens made.
Ps. Rejoice in the Lord, O ye righteous: for praise is comely for the upright.
Glory be to the Father, &c.

The Collect.

God, who, by the humiliation of Thy Son, didst raise up the fallen world: grant unto Thy faithful ones perpetual gladness, and those whom Thou hast delivered from the danger of everlasting death, do Thou make partakers of eternal joys; through the same, Jesus Christ, our Lord, who liveth and reigneth with Thee and the Holy Ghost, ever one God, world without end. Amen.

I. *Epistle,* I Pet. ii: 21—25.   *Gospel,* John x. 11—16.
II. *Epistle,* I Pet. v: 1—4.   *Gospel,* John xxi: 15—25.
III. *Epistle,* Hebr. xiii: 20—21.   *Gospel,* John x: 1—10.

THIRD SUNDAY AFTER EASTER.

The Collect.

Lord God, heavenly Father, who of Thy fatherly goodness dost suffer Thy children to come under Thy chastening rod here on earth, that we may be like unto Thine only-begotten Son in suffering and hereafter in glory: We beseech Thee, comfort us in temptations and afflictions by Thy Holy Spirit, that we may not fall into despair, but that we may continually trust in Thy Son's promise, that our trials will endure but a little while, and will then be followed by eternal joy; that we thus, in patient hope, may overcome all evil, and at last obtain eternal salvation, through the same, Thy Son, Jesus Christ, our Lord, who liveth and reigneth with Thee and the Holy Ghost, one true God, world without end. Amen.

Introit.

Make a joyful noise unto God, all ye lands:
Sing forth the honor of His name; make His praise glorious.
Ps. Say unto God, how terrible art Thou in Thy works: through the greatness of Thy power shall Thine enemies submit themselves unto Thee.
Glory be to the Father, &c.

The Collect.

Almighty God, who showest to them that be in error the light of Thy truth, to the intent that they may return into the way of righteousness: Grant unto all them that are admitted into the fellowship of Christ's religion that they may eschew those things that are contrary to their profession, and follow all such things as are agreeable to the same: through our Lord, Jesus Christ, who liveth and reigneth with Thee and the Holy Ghost, ever one God, world without end. Amen.

I. *Epistle*, I Peter ii: 11—20.   *Gospel*, John xvi: 16—22.
II. *Epistle*, Hebr. iv: 14—16.   *Gospel*, John xvii: 1—8.
III. *Epistle*, I Peter i: 3—9.   *Gospel*, John xiv: 1—12.

FOURTH SUNDAY AFTER EASTER.

The Collect.

Lord God, heavenly Father, who didst through Thy Son promise us Thy Holy Spirit, that He should convince the world of sin, of righteousness, and of judgment: We beseech Thee, enlighten our hearts, that we may confess our sins, through faith in Christ obtain everlasting righteousness, and in all our trials and temptations retain this consolation, that Christ is Lord over the devil and death, and all things, and that He will graciously deliver us out of all our afflictions, and make us forever partakers of eternal salvation, through the same, Thy Son, Jesus Christ, our Lord, who liveth and reigneth with Thee and the Holy Ghost, one true God, world without end. Amen.

Introit.

O sing unto the Lord a new song: for He hath done marvellous things.

The Lord hath made known His salvation: His righteousness He hath openly showed in the sight of the heathen.

Ps. His right hand and His holy arm: hath gotten Him the victory.

Glory be to the Father, &c.

The Collect.

O God, who makest the minds of the faithful to be of one will: Grant unto Thy people that they may love what Thou commandest, and desire what Thou dost promise: that, among the manifold changes of this world, our hearts may there be fixed where true joys are to be found; through Jesus Christ, Thy Son, our Lord, who liveth and reigneth with Thee and the Holy Ghost, ever one God, world without end. Amen.

I. *Epistle*, James i: 17—21.   *Gospel*, John xvi: 5—15.
II. *Epistle*, Hebr. v: 1—10.   *Gospel*, John xvii: 9—17.
III. *Epistle*, I John iii: 19—24.   *Gospel*, John vii: 37—39.

FIFTH SUNDAY AFTER EASTER.

The Collect.

Lord God, heavenly Father, who through Thy Son didst promise us that whatsoever we ask in His name Thou wilt give us: We beseech Thee, keep us in Thy word, and grant us Thy Holy Spirit, that He may govern us according to Thy will; protect us from the power of the devil, from false doctrine and worship; also defend our lives against all danger; grant us Thy blessing and peace, that we may in all things perceive Thy merciful help, and both now and forever praise and glorify Thee as our gracious Father, through our Lord Jesus Christ, Thy Son, who liveth and reigneth with Thee and the Holy Ghost, one true God, world without end. Amen.

Collects for the Church Year

Introit.

With the voice of singing declare ye, and tell this: utter it even to the end
f the earth. Hallelujah!
The Lord hath redeemed His servant Jacob: Hallelujah! Hallelujah!
Ps. Make a joyful noise unto God, all ye lands: sing forth the honor of His
ame; make His praise glorious.
Glory be to the Father, &c.

The Collect.

O God, from whom all good things do come: Grant to us, Thy humble serv-
nts, that by Thy holy inspiration we may think those things that be right, and
y Thy merciful guiding may perform the same; through Jesus Christ, Thy
on, our Lord, who liveth and reigneth with Thee and the Holy Ghost, ever
ne God, world without end. Amen.

I.	*Epistle,* James i: 22—27.	*Gospel,* John xvi: 23—28.
II.	*Epistle,* Hebr. vii: 18—25.	*Gospel,* John xvii: 18—23.
III.	*Epistle,* James v: 16—20.	*Gospel,* Matt. vi: 5—13.

ASCENSION.

The Collect.

O Jesus Christ, Thou almighty Son of God, who art no longer in humiliation
ere on earth, but sittest at the right hand of Thy Father, Lord over all things:
Ve beseech Thee, send us Thy Holy Spirit; give Thy Church pious pastors, pre-
erve Thy word, control and restrain the devil and all who would oppress us:
ightily uphold Thy kingdom, until all Thine enemies shall have been put un-
er Thy feet, that we may hold the victory over sin, death, and the devil, through
hee, who livest and reignest with God the Father and the Holy Ghost, one true
od, world without end. Amen.

Introit.

Ye men of Galilee, why stand ye gazing up into heaven?: Hallelujah!
This same Jesus which is taken up from you into heaven, shall come in like
anner as ye have seen Him go into heaven: Hallelujah! Hallelujah!
Ps. O clap your hands, all ye people: shout unto God with the voice of triumph.
Glory be to the Father, &c.

The Collect.

Grant, we beseech Thee, almighty God, that like as we do believe Thy only
egotten Son, our Lord, Jesus Christ, to have ascended into the heavens, so may
e also in heart and mind thither ascend, and with Him continually dwell, who
veth and reigneth with Thee and the Holy Ghost, ever one God, world without
nd. Amen.

I.	*Lesson,* Acts i: 1—11.	*Gospel,* Mark xvi: 14—20.
II.	*Lesson,* Psalm cx: 1—7.	*Gospel,* John xvii: 24—26.
III.	*Epistle,* Eph. iv: 7—10.	*Gospel,* Luke xxiv: 44—53.

SIXTH SUNDAY AFTER EASTER.

The Collect.

Lord God, heavenly Father, we give thanks unto Thee, that through Thy
Ioly Spirit Thou hast appointed us to bear witness of Thy dear Son, our Lord
esus Christ: We beseech Thee, inasmuch as the world cannot endure such testi-

mony, and persecutes us in every way, grant us courage and comfort, that we may not be offended because of the cross, but continue steadfastly in Thy testimony, and be found always among those who know Thee and Thy Son, until we obtain eternal salvation through the same, Thy Son, Jesus Christ our Lord, who liveth and reigneth with Thee and the Holy Ghost, one true God, world without end. Amen.

Introit.

Hear, O Lord, when I cry with my voice: Hallelujah!

When Thou saidst, seek ye my face; my heart said unto Thee, Thy face, Lord, will I seek: Hide not Thy face from me. Hallelujah! Hallelujah!

Ps. The Lord is my Light, and my Salvation: whom shall I fear?

Glory be to the Father, &c.

The Collect.

Almighty, everlasting God: Make us to have always a devout will towards Thee, and to serve Thy majesty with a pure heart, through Thy Son, Jesus Christ, our Lord, who liveth and reigneth with Thee and the Holy Ghost, ever one God, world without end. Amen.

I. *Epistle*, I Peter iv: 7—11.	*Gospel*, John xv: 26—xvi: 4.	
II. *Lesson*, Act. i: 12—14.	*Gospel*, Luke xi: 5—13.	
III. *Epistle*, I Peter iii: 15—17.	*Gospel*, Luke xii: 4—12.	

PENTECOST.

The Collect.

O Lord Jesus Christ, Thou almighty Son of God: We beseech Thee, send Thy Holy Spirit into our hearts, through Thy word, that He may rule and govern us according to Thy will, comfort us in every temptation and misfortune, and defend us by Thy truth against every error, so that we may continue steadfast in the faith, increase in love and all good works, and firmly trusting in Thy grace, which through death Thou hast purchased for us, obtain eternal salvation, Thou who reignest, with the Father and the Holy Ghost, world without end. Amen.

Introit.

The Spirit of the Lord filleth the world: Hallelujah!

Let the righteous be glad; let them rejoice before God: yea, let them exceedingly rejoice. Hallelujah! Hallelujah!

Ps. Let God arise; let His enemies be scattered: let them also that hate Him flee before Him.

Glory be to the Father, &c.

The Collect.

O God, who didst teach the hearts of Thy faithful people, by sending to them the light of Thy Holy Spirit: Grant us by the same Spirit to have a right judgment in all things, and evermore to rejoice in His holy comfort: through our Lord Jesus Christ, Thy Son, who with Thee and the Holy Ghost liveth and reigneth, ever one God, world without end. Amen.

I. *Lesson*, Acts ii: 1—11.	*Gospel*, John xiv: 23—31.	
II. *Epistle*, Eph. ii: 17—22.	*Gospel*, John xv: 1—11.	
III. *Lesson*, Acts ii: 32—41.	*Gospel*, John xiv: 15—21.	

Collects for the Church Year

PENTECOST MONDAY.

The Collect.

Lord God, heavenly Father, who of Thy fatherly love hast given us Thy Son, that through faith in Him we may be saved: We beseech Thee, grant us Thy Holy Spirit in our hearts, that we may continue steadfast in such faith unto the end, and thus obtain everlasting salvation, through the same, Thy beloved Son, Jesus Christ, our Lord, who liveth and reigneth with Thee and the Holy Ghost, one true God, world without end. Amen.

Introit.

(The same as for Pentecost Sunday).

The Collect.

O God, who didst give Thy Holy Spirit to Thine apostles: Grant unto Thy people the performance of their petitions, so that on us to whom Thou hast given faith Thou mayest also bestow peace; through our Lord Jesus Christ, Thy Son, who with Thee and the Holy Ghost liveth and reigneth, ever one God, world without end. Amen.

    I. *Lesson*, Acts x: 42—48.   *Gospel*, John iii: 16—21.
    II. *Epistle*, I Cor. xii: 12—20.   *Gospel*, John vi: 44—51.
    III. *Epistle*, I John iv: 9—15.   *Gospel*, John xii: 44—50.

TRINITY.

The Collect.

O Lord God, heavenly Father: We poor sinners confess that in our flesh dwelleth no good thing, and that, left to ourselves, we die and perish in sin, since that which is born of the flesh is flesh and cannot see the kingdom of God. But we beseech Thee: Grant us Thy grace and mercy, and for the sake of Thy Son, Jesus Christ, send Thy Holy Spirit into our hearts, that being regenerate, we may firmly believe the forgiveness of sins, according to Thy promise in baptism; and that we may daily increase in brotherly love, and in other good works, until we at last obtain eternal salvation, through the same, Thy beloved Son, Jesus Christ, our Lord, who liveth and reigneth with Thee and the Holy Ghost, one true God, world without end. Amen.

Introit.

Holy, Holy, Holy, is the Lord of Hosts: of Him, and through Him, and to Him, are all things.

Ps. O Lord, our Lord: How excellent is Thy name in all the earth.

Glory be to the Father, &c.

The Collect.

Almighty and everlasting God, who hast given unto us, Thy servants, grace, by the confession of a true faith, to acknowledge the glory of the eternal Trinity, and in the power of the divine majesty to worship the Unity: We beseech Thee, that Thou wouldst keep us steadfast in this faith, and evermore defend us from all adversities, who livest and reignest, one God, world without end. Amen.

    I. *Epistle*, Rom. xi: 33—36.   *Gospel*, John iii: 1—15.
    II. *Epistle*, I John iii: 1—10.   *Gospel*, John xv: 12—17.
    III. *Epistle*. Titus iii: 3—7.   *Gospel*, Matt. xxviii: 16—20.

Collects for the Church Year

FIRST SUNDAY AFTER TRINITY.

The Collect.

Lord God, heavenly Father, we beseech Thee so to rule and govern our hearts by Thy Holy Spirit, that we may not, like the rich man, hear Thy word in vain, and become so devoted to things temporal as to forget things eternal; but that we readily and according to our ability minister to such as are in need, and not defile ourselves with surfeiting and pride; in trial and misfortune keep us from despair, and grant us to put our trust wholly in Thy fatherly help and grace, so that in faith and Christian patience we may overcome all things, through Thy Son, Jesus Christ, our Lord, who liveth and reigneth with Thee and the Holy Ghost, one true God, world without end. Amen.

Introit.

O Lord, I have trusted in Thy mercy: my heart shall rejoice in Thy salvation.

I will sing unto the Lord: He hath dealt bountifully with me.

Ps. How long wilt Thou forget me, O Lord? How long wilt Thou hide Thy face from me?

Glory be to the Father, &c.

The Collect.

O God, the strength of all them that put their trust in Thee: Mercifully accept our prayers; and because through the weakness of our mortal nature we can do no good thing without Thee, grant us the help of Thy grace, that in keeping Thy commandments we may please Thee, both in will and deed; through Jesus Christ, our Lord, who liveth and reigneth with Thee and the Holy Ghost, ever one God, world without end. Amen.

I.	*Epistle*, I John iv: 16—21.	*Gospel*, Luke xvi: 19—31.
II.	*Epistle*, Rom. i: 1—17.	*Gospel*, Luke xii: 13—21.
III.	*Epistle*, I Tim. vi: 6—16.	*Gospel*, Matt. xvi: 24—27.

SECOND SUNDAY AFTER TRINITY.

The Collect.

Lord God, heavenly Father, we give thanks unto Thee, that through Thy holy word Thou hast called us to Thy great supper, and we beseech Thee: Quicken our hearts by Thy Holy Spirit, that we may not hear Thy word without fruit, but that we may prepare ourselves rightly for Thy kingdom, and not suffer ourselves to be hindered by any worldly care, through Thy beloved Son, Jesus Christ, our Lord, who liveth and reigneth with Thee and the Holy Ghost, one true God, world without end. Amen.

Introit.

The Lord was my stay; He brought me forth into a large place: He delivered me, because He delighted in me.

Ps. I will love Thee, O Lord, my Strength: The Lord is my Rock and my Fortress.

Glory be to the Father, &c.

The Collect.

O Lord, who never failest to help and govern those whom Thou dost bring up in Thy steadfast fear and love: Make us to have a perpetual fear and love of Thy holy name; through Jesus Christ, Thy Son, our Lord, who liveth and reigneth with Thee and the Holy Ghost, ever one God, world without end. Amen.

I. *Epistle*, I John iii : 13—18. *Gospel*, Luke xiv : 16—24.
II. *Epistle*, Rom. i : 18—25. *Gospel*, Luke xiv : 25—35.
III. *Epistle*, II Petr. i : 1—11. *Gospel*, Luke ix : 51—62.

THIRD SUNDAY AFTER TRINITY.

The Collect.

Lord God, heavenly Father, we all like sheep have gone astray, having suffered ourselves to be led away from the right path by Satan and our own sinful flesh: We beseech Thee graciously to forgive us all our sins for the sake of Thy Son, Jesus Christ; and quicken our hearts by Thy Holy Spirit, that we may abide in Thy word, and in true repentance and a steadfast faith continue in Thy Church unto the end, and obtain eternal salvation, through our Lord Jesus Christ, Thy Son, who liveth and reigneth with Thee and the Holy Ghost, one true God, world without end. Amen.

Introit.

Turn Thee unto me and have mercy upon me: for I am desolate and afflicted. Look upon mine affliction and my pain: and forgive all my sins.
Ps. Unto Thee, O Lord, do I lift up my soul: O my God, I trust in Thee, let me not be ashamed.
Glory be to the Father, &c.

The Collect.

O God, the protector of all that trust in Thee, without whom nothing is strong, nothing is holy: Increase and multiply upon us Thy mercy; that, Thou being our ruler and guide, we may so pass through things temporal that we finally lose not the things eternal; through Jesus Christ, our Lord, who liveth and reigneth with Thee and the Holy Ghost, ever one God, world without end. Amen.

I. *Epistle*, I Peter v : 6—11. *Gospel*, Luke xv : 1—10.
II. *Epistle*, Rom. ii : 1—16. *Gospel*, Luke xv : 11—24.
III. *Epistle*, Eph. ii : 1—9. *Gospel*, Matt. ix : 9—13.

FOURTH SUNDAY AFTER TRINITY.

The Collect.

Lord God, heavenly Father, who art merciful, and through Christ didst promise us, that Thou wilt neither judge nor condemn us, but graciously forgive us all our sins, and abundantly provide for all our wants of body and soul: We pray Thee, that by Thy Holy Spirit Thou wilt establish in our hearts a confident faith in Thy mercy, and teach us also to be merciful to our neighbor: that we may not judge or condemn others, but willingly forgive all men, and, judging only ourselves, lead blessed lives in Thy fear, through Thy dear Son, Jesus Christ our Lord, who liveth and reigneth with Thee and the Holy Ghost, one true God, world without end. Amen.

Collects for the Church Year

The Lord is my Light and my Salvation; whom shall I fear?: The Lord is the Strength of my life; of whom shall I be afraid?

When the wicked, even mine enemies and my foes came upon me: they stumbled and fell.

Ps. Though an host should encamp against me: my heart shall not fear.
Glory be to the Father, &c.

The Collect.

Grant, O Lord, we beseech Thee, that the course of this world may be so peaceably ordered by Thy governance that Thy Church may joyfully serve Thee in all godly quietness, through Jesus Christ, Thy Son, our Lord, who liveth and reigneth with Thee and the Holy Ghost, ever one God, world without end. Amen.

I. *Epistle*, Rom. viii: 18—23.　　*Gospel*, Luke vi: 36—42.
II. *Epistle*, Rom. ii: 17—29.　　*Gospel*, Matt. v: 38—42.
III. *Epistle*, Rom. xiv: 1—12.　　*Gospel*, Matt. vii: 1—6.

FIFTH SUNDAY AFTER TRINITY.

The Collect.

O Jesus Christ, Thou Son of the living God, who hast given us Thy holy word, and hast bountifully provided for all our temporal wants, we confess that we are unworthy of all these mercies, and that we have rather deserved punishment: But we beseech Thee, forgive us our sins, and prosper and bless us in our several callings, that by Thy strength we may be sustained and defended, now and forever, and so praise and glorify Thee eternally, Thou who livest and reignest with the Father and the Holy Ghost, one true God, world without end. Amen.

Introit.

Hear, O Lord, when I cry with my voice: Thou hast been my help.
Leave me not, neither forsake me: O God of my salvation.
Ps. The Lord is my Light and my Salvation: Whom shall I fear?
Glory be to the Father, &c.

The Collect.

O God, who hast prepared for them that love Thee such good things as pass man's understanding: Pour into our hearts such love toward Thee, that we, loving Thee above all things, may obtain Thy promises, which exceed all that we can desire; through Jesus Christ, Thy Son, our Lord, who liveth and reigneth with Thee and the Holy Ghost, ever one God, world without end. Amen.

I. *Epistle*, I Peter iii: 8—14.　　*Gospel*, Luke v: 1—11.
II. *Epistle*, Rom. iii: 1—20.　　*Gospel*, John i: 35—52.
III. *Lesson*, Acts xxvi: 1—18.　　*Gospel*, Matt. xvi: 13—19.

SIXTH SUNDAY AFTER TRINITY.

The Collect

Lord God, heavenly Father, we confess that we are poor, wretched sinners, and that there is no good in us, our hearts, flesh and blood being so corrupted by sin, that we never in this life can be without sinful lust and concupiscence;

therefore we beseech Thee, dear Father, forgive us these sins, and let Thy Holy Spirit so cleanse our hearts that we may desire and love Thy word, abide by it, and thus by Thy grace be forever saved; through our Lord Jesus Christ, Thy Son, who liveth and reigneth with Thee and the Holy Ghost, one true God, world without end. Amen.

Introit.

The Lord is the strength of His people: He is the saving strength of His anointed.

Save Thy people, and bless Thine inheritance: feed them also and lift them up forever.

Ps. Unto Thee will I cry, O Lord, my Rock; be not silent unto me: lest if Thou be silent to me, I become like them that go down into the pit.

Glory be to the Father, &c.

The Collect.

Lord of all power and might, who art the author and giver of all good things: Graft in our hearts the love of Thy name, increase in us true religion, nourish us with all goodness, and of Thy great mercy keep us in the same; through Jesus Christ, Thy Son, our Lord, who liveth and reigneth with Thee and the Holy Ghost, ever one God, world without end. Amen.

I.	*Epistle,* Rom. vi: 3—11.	*Gospel,* Matt. v: 20—26.
II.	*Epistle,* Rom. iii: 21—31.	*Gospel,* Matt. v: 17—19.
III.	*Epistle,* James ii: 8—17.	*Gospel,* Matt. v: 27—37.

SEVENTH SUNDAY AFTER TRINITY.

The Collect.

Lord God, heavenly Father, who in the wilderness didst by Thy Son abundantly feed four thousand men besides women and children with seven loaves and a few small fishes: We beseech Thee, graciously abide among us with Thy blessing, and keep us from covetousness and the cares of this life, that we may seek first Thy kingdom and Thy righteousness, and in all things needful for body and soul, experience Thine ever-present help; through Thy Son, our Lord Jesus Christ, who liveth and reigneth with Thee and the Holy Ghost, one true God, world without end. Amen.

Introit.

O clap your hands, all ye people: Shout unto God with the voice of triumph.

Ps. He shall subdue the people under us: and the nations under our feet.

Glory be to the Father, &c.

The Collect.

O God, whose never-failing providence ordereth all things both in heaven and earth: We humbly beseech Thee to put away from us all hurtful things, and to give us those things which be profitable for us; through Jesus Christ, Thy Son, our Lord, who liveth and reigneth with Thee and the Holy Ghost, ever one God, world without end. Amen.

I.	*Epistle,* Rom. vi: 19—23.	*Gospel,* Mark viii: 1—9.
II.	*Epistle,* Rom. iv: 1—8.	*Gospel,* Matt. xvi: 5—12.
III.	*Lesson,* Psalms xxiii: 1—6.	*Gospel,* Luke xiv: 12—15.

Collects for the Church Year

EIGHTH SUNDAY AFTER TRINITY.

The Collect.

Lord God, heavenly Father, we most heartily thank Thee that Thou hast caused us to come to the knowledge of Thy word. We pray Thee: graciously keep us steadfast in this knowledge unto death, that we may obtain eternal life; send us now and ever pious pastors, who faithfully preach Thy word, without offense or false doctrine, and grant them long life. Defend us from all false teachings, and frustrate Thou the counsels of all such as pervert Thy word, who come to us in sheep's clothing, but are inwardly ravening wolves, that Thy true Church may evermore be established among us, and be defended and preserved from such false teachers, through Jesus Christ, Thy Son, who liveth and reigneth with Thee and the Holy Ghost, one true God, world without end. Amen.

Introit.

We have thought of Thy loving-kindness, O God: in the midst of Thy temple.

According to Thy name, O God, so is Thy praise unto the ends of the earth: Thy right hand is full of righteousness.

Ps. Great is the Lord, and greatly to be praised: in the city of our God, in the mountain of His holiness.

Glory be to the Father, &c.

The Collect.

Grant to us, Lord, we beseech Thee, the spirit to think and do always such things as are right, that we, who cannot do anything that is good without Thee, may by Thee be enabled to live according to Thy will; through Jesus Christ, Thy Son, our Lord, who liveth and reigneth with Thee and the Holy Ghost, ever one God, world without end. Amen.

I.	*Epistle*, Rom. viii: 12—17.	*Gospel*, Matt. vii: 15—21.
II.	*Epistle*, Rom: iv: 9—25.	*Gospel*, Matt. vii: 12—14.
III.	*Epistle*, I John iv: 1—6.	*Gospel*, Mark vii: 5—16.

NINTH SUNDAY AFTER TRINITY.

The Collect.

Lord God, heavenly Father, who hast bountifully given us Thy blessing and our daily bread: We beseech Thee, preserve us from covetousness, and so quicken our hearts that we willingly share Thy blessed gifts with our needy brethren; that we may be found faithful stewards of Thy gifts, and abide in Thy grace when we shall be removed from our stewardship, and shall come before Thy judgment, through our Lord Jesus Christ, Thy Son, who liveth and reigneth with Thee and the Holy Ghost, one true God, world without end. Amen.

Introit.

Behold God is mine Helper: The Lord is with them that uphold my soul. He shall reward evil unto mine enemies: Cut them off in Thy truth, O Lord.

Ps. Save me, O God, by Thy name: and judge me by Thy strength.

Glory be to the Father, &c.

The Collect.

Let Thy merciful ears, O Lord, be open to the prayers **of Thy humble serv-**ants; and, that they may obtain their petitions, make them to ask such things

Collects for the Church Year

as shall please Thee; through Jesus Christ, Thy Son, our Lord, who liveth and reigneth with Thee and the Holy Ghost, ever one God, world without end. Amen.

   I. *Epistle*, I Cor. x: 6—13.   *Gospel*, Luke xvi: 1—9.
   II. *Epistle*, Rom. v: 1—11.   *Gospel*, Luke xii: 42—48.
   III. *Epistle*, II Thes. iii: 10—13.   *Gospel*, Luke xvi: 10—17.

TENTH SUNDAY AFTER TRINITY.

The Collect.

Almighty and everlasting God, who by Thy Holy Ghost hast revealed unto us the gospel of Thy Son, Jesus Christ: We beseech Thee so to quicken our hearts that we may sincerely receive Thy word, and not make light of it, or hear it without fruit, as did Thy people, the unbelieving Jews, but that we may fear Thee and daily grow in faith in Thy mercy, and finally obtain eternal salvation, through Thy Son, Jesus Christ our Lord, who liveth and reigneth with Thee and the Holy Ghost, one true God, world without end. Amen.

Introit.

As for me, I will call upon God; and He shall hear my voice: He hath delivered my soul in peace from the battle that was against me.

God shall hear and afflict them; even He that abideth of old: Cast thy burden upon the Lord, and He shall sustain thee.

Ps. Give ear to my prayer, O God: and hide not Thyself from my supplication.

Glory be to the Father, &c.

The Collect.

O God, who declarest Thine almighty power chiefly in showing mercy and pity: Mercifully grant unto us such a measure of Thy grace that we, running the way of Thy commandments, may obtain Thy gracious promises, and be made partakers of Thy heavenly treasure; through Jesus Christ, Thy Son, our Lord, who liveth and reigneth with Thee and the Holy Ghost, ever one God, world without end. Amen.

   I. *Epistle*, I Cor. xii: 2—11.   *Gospel*, Luke xix: 41—48.
   II. *Epistle*, Rom. v: 12—21.   *Gospel*, Matt. xi: 16—24.
   III. *Epistle*, Hebr. iii: 12—iv: 1.   *Gospel*, John vi: 66—71.

ELEVENTH SUNDAY AFTER TRINITY.

The Collect.

Lord God, heavenly Father, we beseech Thee so to guide and direct us by Thy Holy Spirit, that we may not forget our sins and be filled with pride, but continue in daily repentance and renewal, seeking our comfort only in the blessed knowledge that Thou wilt be merciful unto us, forgive us our sins, and grant us eternal life; through Thy beloved Son, Jesus Christ, our Lord, who liveth and reigneth with Thee and the Holy Ghost, one true God, world without end. Amen.

Introit.

God is in His holy habitation, He is God who setteth the solitary in families: The God of Israel is He that giveth strength and power unto His people.

Ps. Let God arise, let His enemies be scattered: let them also that hate Him flee before Him.

Glory be to the Father, &c.

Collects for the Church Year

The Collect.

Almighty and everlasting God, who art always more ready to hear than we to pray, and art wont to give more than either we desire or deserve: Pour down upon us the abundance of Thy mercy, forgiving us those things whereof our conscience is afraid, and giving us those good things which we are not worthy to ask, but through the merits and mediation of Jesus Christ, Thy Son, our Lord, who liveth and reigneth with Thee and the Holy Ghost, ever one God, world without end. Amen.

   I. *Epistle*, I Cor. xv: 1—in vs. 10.   *Gospel*, Luke xviii: 9—14.
  II. *Epistle*, Rom. vi: 1—23.   *Gospel*, Matt. xxi: 28—31.
 III. *Epistle*, I John i: 8—ii: 2.   *Gospel*, Matt. xxiii: 1—12.

TWELFTH SUNDAY AFTER TRINITY.

The Collect.

Almighty and everlasting God, who hast created all things: We thank Thee that Thou hast given us sound bodies, and hast graciously preserved our tongues and other members from the power of the adversary: We beseech Thee, grant us Thy grace, that we may rightly use our ears and tongues; help us to hear Thy word diligently and devoutly, and with our tongues so to praise and magnify Thy grace, that no one shall be offended by our words, but that all may be edified thereby, through Thy beloved Son, Jesus Christ, our Lord, who liveth and reigneth with Thee and the Holy Ghost, one true God, world without end. Amen.

Introit.

Make haste, O God, to deliver me: make haste to help me, O Lord.
Let them be ashamed and confounded: that seek after my soul.
Ps. Let them be turned backward, and put to confusion: that desire my hurt.
Glory be to the Father, &c.

The Collect.

Almighty and merciful God, of whose only gift it cometh that Thy faithful people do unto Thee true and laudable service: Grant, we beseech Thee, that we may so faithfully serve Thee in this life that we fail not finally to attain Thy heavenly promises; through Jesus Christ, Thy Son, our Lord, who liveth and reigneth with Thee and the Holy Ghost, one true God, world without end. Amen.

   I. *Epistle*, II Cor. iii: 4—9.   *Gospel*, Mark, vii: 31—37.
  II. *Epistle*, Rom. vii: 1—6.   *Gospel*, Matt. xii: 33—37.
 III. *Epistle*, I Cor. ii: 9—16.   *Gospel*, John ix: 24—38.

THIRTEENTH SUNDAY AFTER TRINITY.

The Collect.

Lord God, heavenly Father, we most heartily thank Thee that Thou **hast** granted us to live in this accepted time, when we may hear Thy holy gospel, know Thy fatherly will, and behold Thy Son, Jesus Christ! We pray Thee, most merciful Father: Let the light of Thy holy word remain with us, and so govern our hearts by Thy Holy Spirit, that we may never forsake Thy word, but remain steadfast in it, and finally obtain eternal salvation; through Thy beloved Son, Jesus Christ, our Lord, who liveth and reigneth with Thee and the Holy Ghost, one true God, world without end. Amen.

Introit.

Have respect, O Lord, unto Thy covenant: O let not the oppressed return ashamed.

Arise, O God, plead Thine own cause: and forget not the voice of Thine enemies.

Ps. O God, why hast Thou cast us off forever: Why doth Thine anger smoke against the sheep of Thy pasture?

Glory be to the Father, &c.

The Collect.

Almighty and everlasting God, give unto us the increase of faith, hope, and charity; and that we may obtain that which Thou dost promise, make us to love that which Thou dost command; through Jesus Christ, Thy Son, our Lord, who liveth and reigneth with Thee and the Holy Ghost, ever one God, world without end. Amen.

I.	*Epistle,* Gal. iii: 15—22.	*Gospel,* Luke x: 23—37.
II.	*Epistle,* Rom. vii: 7—25.	*Gospel,* Matt. v: 43—48.
III.	*Epistle,* I Cor. xiii: 1—13.	*Gospel,* John xiii: 34—35.

FOURTEENTH SUNDAY AFTER TRINITY.

The Collect.

Lord God, heavenly Father, who by Thy blessed word and Thy holy baptism hast mercifully cleansed all who believe from the fearful leprosy of sin, and daily dost grant us Thy gracious help in all our need: We beseech Thee so to enlighten our hearts by Thy Holy Spirit, that we may never forget these Thy blessings, but ever live in Thy fear, and, trusting fully in Thy grace, with thankful hearts continually praise and glorify Thee; through Thy Son, our Lord Jesus Christ, who liveth and reigneth with Thee and the Holy Ghost, one true God, world without end. Amen.

Introit.

Behold, O God, our shield, and look upon the face of Thine Anointed: For a day in Thy courts is better than a thousand.

Ps. How amiable are Thy tabernacles, O Lord of Hosts: My soul longeth, yea, even fainteth for the courts of the Lord.

Glory be to the Father, &c.

The Collect.

Keep, we beseech Thee, O Lord, Thy Church with Thy perpetual mercy; and, because the frailty of man without Thee cannot but fall, keep us ever by Thy help from all things hurtful, and lead us to all things profitable to our salvation; through Jesus Christ, Thy Son, our Lord, who liveth and reigneth with Thee and the Holy Ghost, ever one God, world without end. Amen.

I.	*Epistle,* Gal. v: 16—24.	*Gospel,* Luke xvii: 11—19.
II.	*Epistle,* Rom. viii: 1—17.	*Gospel,* John v: 1—14.
III.	*Lesson,* Revel. iii: 1—6.	*Gospel,* Luke iv: 23—30.

FIFTEENTH SUNDAY AFTER TRINITY.

The Collect.

Lord God, heavenly Father, we thank Thee for all Thy benefits: that Thou hast given us life and graciously sustained us unto this day: We beseech Thee, take not Thy blessing from us; preserve us from covetousness, that we may serve Thee only, love and abide in Thee, and not defile ourselves by idolatrous love of mammon, but hope and trust only in Thy grace, through Jesus Christ our Lord, who liveth and reigneth with Thee and the Holy Ghost, one true God, world without end. Amen.

Introit.

Bow down Thine ear, O Lord, hear me: O Thou, my God, save Thy servant that trusteth in Thee.

Be merciful to me, O Lord: for I cry unto Thee daily.

Ps. Rejoice the soul of Thy servant: for unto Thee, O Lord, do I lift up my soul.

Glory be to the Father, &c

The Collect.

O Lord, we beseech Thee, let Thy continual pity cleanse and defend Thy Church: And because it cannot continue in safety without Thy succor, preserve it evermore by Thy help and goodness; through Jesus Christ, Thy Son, our Lord, who liveth and reigneth with Thee and the Holy Ghost, ever one God, world without end. Amen.

I. *Epistle*, Gal. v: 25 —vi: 10.	*Gospel*, Matt. vi: 24—34.
II. *Epistle*, Rom. viii: 18—39.	*Gospel*, Luke x: 38—42.
III. *Epistle*, I Cor. vii: 29—31.	*Gospel*, Matt. vi: 19—23.

SIXTEENTH SUNDAY AFTER TRINITY.

The Collect.

Lord God, heavenly Father, who didst send Thy Son to be made flesh, that by His death He might atone for our sins and deliver us from eternal death: We pray Thee, confirm in our hearts the hope that our Lord Jesus Christ, who with but a word raised the widow's son, in like manner will raise us on the last day, and grant us eternal life: through Thy beloved Son, Jesus Christ, our Lord, who liveth and reigneth with Thee and the Holy Ghost, one true God, world without end. Amen.

Introit.

Be merciful unto me, O Lord: for I cry unto Thee daily.

For Thou, O Lord, art good, and ready to forgive: and plenteous in mercy unto all them that call upon Thee.

Ps. Bow down Thine ear, O Lord, hear me: for I am poor and needy.

Glory be to the Father, &c.

The Collect.

Lord, we pray Thee, that Thy grace may always go before and follow after us, and make us continually to be given to all good works; through Jesus Christ, Thy Son, our Lord, who liveth and reigneth with Thee and the Holy Ghost, ever one God, world without end. Amen.

I. *Epistle*, Eph. iii: 13—21.	*Gospel*, Luke, vii: 11—17.
II. *Epistle*, Rom. ix: 1—13.	*Gospel*, John xi: 19—29.
III. *Epistle*, Phil. i: 20—26.	*Gospel*, John xi: 32—45.

SEVENTEENTH SUNDAY AFTER TRINITY.

The Collect.

Lord God, heavenly Father: We beseech Thee so to guide and direct us by Thy Holy Spirit, that we may not exalt ourselves, but humbly fear Thee, with our whole hearts hear and keep Thy word, and hallow the Lord's day, that we also may be hallowed by Thy word; help us, first, to place our hope and confidence in Thy Son, Jesus Christ, who alone is our righteousness and Redeemer, and, then, so to amend and better our lives in accordance with Thy word, that we may avoid all offenses and finally obtain eternal salvation, through Thy grace in Christ, who liveth and reigneth with Thee and the Holy Ghost, one true God, world without end. Amen.

Introit.

Righteous art Thou, O Lord, and upright are Thy judgments:
Deal with Thy servant according to Thy mercy.
Ps. Blessed are the undefiled in the way: who walk in the law of the Lord.
Glory be to the Father, &c.

The Collect.

Lord, we beseech Thee, grant Thy people grace to withstand the temptations of the devil, and with pure hearts and minds to follow Thee, the only God; through Jesus Christ, Thy Son our Lord, who liveth and reigneth with Thee and the Holy Ghost, ever one God, world without end. Amen.

    I. *Epistle,* Eph. iv: 1—6.   *Gospel,* Luke xiv: 1—11.
   II. *Epistle,* Rom. ix: 14—33.   *Gospel,* Mark ii: 18—28.
  III. *Epistle,* Gal. v: 1—14.   *Gospel,* Matt. xviii: 1—7.

EIGHTEENTH SUNDAY AFTER TRINITY.

The Collect.

Lord God, heavenly Father: We are poor, miserable sinners; we know Thy will, but cannot fulfill it because of the weakness of our flesh and blood, and because our enemy, the devil, will not leave us in peace. Therefore we beseech Thee, shed Thy Holy Spirit in our hearts, that, in steadfast faith, we may cling to Thy Son Jesus Christ, find comfort in His passion and death, believe the forgiveness of sin through Him, and in willing obedience to Thy will lead holy lives on earth, until by Thy grace, through a blessed death, we depart from this world of sorrow, and obtain eternal life, through Thy Son, Jesus Christ, our Lord, who liveth and reigneth with Thee and the Holy Ghost, one true God, world without end. Amen.

Introit.

Reward them that wait for Thee, O Lord: and let Thy prophets be found faithful.
Hear the prayer of Thy servants: and of Thy people Israel.
Ps. I was glad when they said unto me: Let us go into the house of the Lord.
Glory be to the Father, &c.

The Collect.

O God, forasmuch as without Thee we are not able to please Thee: Mercifully grant, that Thy Holy Spirit may in all things direct and rule our hearts; through Jesus Christ, Thy Son our Lord, who liveth and reigneth with Thee and the Holy Ghost, ever one God, world without end. Amen.

    I. *Epistle,* I Cor. i: 4—8.   *Gospel,* Matt. xxii: 34—46.
   II. *Epistle,* Rom. x: 1—13.   *Gospel,* John x: 23—38.
  III. *Epistle,* I John ii: 7—17.   *Gospel,* Mark x: 17—2(

Collects for the Church Year

NINETEENTH SUNDAY AFTER TRINITY.

The Collect.

O mighty and everlasting God, who by Thy Son Jesus Christ didst mercifully help the palsied man both in body and soul: We beseech Thee, for the sake of Thy great mercy: Be gracious also unto us; forgive us all our sins, and so govern us by Thy Holy Spirit, that we may not ourselves be the cause of sickness and other afflictions; keep us in Thy fear, and strengthen us by Thy grace that we may escape temporal and eternal wrath and punishment, through Thy Son, Jesus Christ, our Lord, who liveth and reigneth with Thee and the Holy Ghost, one true God, world without end. Amen.

Introit.

Say unto my soul, I am thy salvation:

The righteous cry, and the Lord heareth; He delivereth them out of their troubles: He is their God for ever and ever.

Ps. Give ear, O my people, to my law: incline your ears to the words of my mouth.

Glory be to the Father, &c.

The Collect.

O Almighty and most merciful God, of Thy bountiful goodness keep us, we beseech Thee, from all things that may hurt us; that we, being ready, both in body and soul, may cheerfully accomplish those things that Thou wouldest have done; through Jesus Christ, Thy Son our Lord, who liveth and reigneth with Thee and the Holy Ghost, ever one God, world without end. Amen.

I. *Epistle*, Eph. iv: 22—28.	*Gospel*, Matt. ix: 1—8.
II. *Epistle*, Rom. x: 14—21.	*Gospel*, John. ix: 1—11.
III. *Epistle*, Colos. iii: 1—10.	*Gospel*, Luke xiii: 10—17.

TWENTIETH SUNDAY AFTER TRINITY.

The Collect.

Lord God, heavenly Father: We thank Thee, that of Thy great mercy Thou hast called us by Thy holy word to the blessed marriage-feast of Thy Son, and through Him dost forgive us all our sins; but, being daily beset by temptation, offense, and danger, and being weak in ourselves and given to sin, we beseech Thee graciously to protect us by Thy Holy Spirit, that we fall not; and if we fall and defile our wedding-garment, with which Thy Son hath clothed us, graciously help us again and lead us to repentance, that we fall not forever; preserve in us a constant faith in Thy grace, through our Lord Jesus Christ, who liveth and reigneth with Thee and the Holy Ghost, one true God, world without end. Amen.

Introit.

The Lord our God is righteous in all His works which He doeth: for we obeyed not His voice.

Give glory to Thy name, O Lord: and deal with us according to the multitude of Thy mercies.

Ps. Great is the Lord, and greatly to be praised: in the city of our God, in the mountain of His holiness.

Glory be to the Father, &c.

Collects for the Church Year

The Collect.

Grant, we beseech Thee, merciful Lord, to Thy faithful people pardon and peace, that they may be cleansed from all their sins, and serve Thee with a quiet mind; through Jesus Christ, Thy Son our Lord, who liveth and reigneth with Thee and the Holy Ghost, ever one God, world without end. Amen.

I.	*Epistle*, Eph. v: 15—21.	*Gospel*, Matt. xxii: 1—14.
II.	*Epistle*, Rom. xi: 1—12.	*Gospel*, Matt. xiii: 44—50.
III.	*Epistle*, Hebr. x: 19—31.	*Gospel*, Matt.xxi: 33—44.

TWENTY-FIRST SUNDAY AFTER TRINITY.

The Collect.

Almighty and everlasting God, who by Thy Son hast promised us the forgiveness of sins, righteousness, and everlasting life: We beseech Thee, do Thou by Thy Holy Spirit so quicken our hearts that we in daily prayer may seek our help in Christ against all temptations, and, constantly believing His promise, obtain that for which we pray, and at last be saved, through Thy Son Jesus Christ, who liveth and reigneth with Thee and the Holy Ghost, one true God, world without end. Amen.

Introit.

The whole world is in Thy power, O Lord, King Almighty: there is no man that can gainsay Thee.

For Thou hast made heaven and earth, and all the wondrous things under the heaven: Thou art Lord of all.

Ps. Blessed are the undefiled in the way: who walk in the law of the Lord.
Glory be to the Father, &c.

The Collect.

Lord, we beseech Thee to keep Thy household, the Church, in continual godliness; that through Thy protection it may be free from all adversities, and devoutly given to serve Thee in good works, to the glory of Thy name; through Jesus Christ, Thy Son our Lord, who liveth and reigneth with Thee and the Holy Ghost, ever one God, world without end. Amen.

I.	*Epistle*, Eph. vi: 10—17.	*Gospel*, John iv: in vs. 46—53.
II.	*Epistle*, Rom. xi: 13—24.	*Gospel*, Matt. xvi: 1—4.
III.	*Epistle*, Colos. i: 24—2, 3.	*Gospel*, Luke xviii: 1—8.

ALL SAINTS' DAY.

The Collect.

O almighty and everlasting God, who through Thine only-begotten and beloved Son, Jesus Christ, wilt sanctify all Thine elected and beloved: Give us grace to follow their faith, hope, and charity, that we together with them may obtain eternal life: through Thy Son, Jesus Christ, our Lord, who liveth and reigneth with Thee and the Holy Ghost, one true God, world without end. Amen.

Introit.

I know in whom I have believed: And am persuaded that He is able to keep that which I have committed to Him against that day.

There is laid up for me a crown of righteousness; which the Lord, the righteous Judge, shall give me.

Collects for the Church Year

Ps. O Lord, Thou hast searched me and known me: Thou knowest my downsitting and mine uprising.

Glory be to the Father, &c.

The Collect.

O Almighty God, who hast knit together Thine elect in one communion and fellowship in the mystical body of Thy Son, Christ our Lord: Grant us grace to follow Thy blessed saints in all virtuous and godly living, that we may come to those unspeakable joys which Thou hast prepared for those who unfeignedly love Thee; through Jesus Christ, our Lord, who liveth and reigneth with Thee and the Holy Ghost, ever one God, world without end. Amen.

I. *Lesson,* Revel. vii: 1—12.	*Gospel,* Matt. v: 1—12.	
II. *Lesson,* Revel. vii: 13—17.	*Gospel,* Matt. v: 13—16.	
III. *Lesson,* Revel. xxii: 1—7.	*Gospel,* Luke vi: 20—26.	

TWENTY-SECOND SUNDAY AFTER TRINITY.

The Collect.

O almighty, eternal God: We confess that we are poor sinners and cannot answer one of a thousand, when Thou contendest with us; but with all our hearts we thank Thee, that Thou hast taken all our guilt from us and laid it upon Thy dear Son Jesus Christ, and made Him to atone for it: We pray Thee graciously to sustain us in faith, and so to govern us by Thy Holy Spirit, that we may live according to Thy will, in neighborly love, service, and helpfulness, and not give way to wrath or revenge, that we may not incur Thy wrath, but always find in Thee a gracious Father, through Jesus Christ our Lord, who liveth and reigneth with Thee and the Holy Ghost, one true God, world without end. Amen.

Introit.

If Thou, Lord, shouldest mark iniquities: O Lord, who shall stand?

But there is forgiveness with Thee: that Thou mayest be feared, O God of Israel.

Ps. Out of the depths have I cried unto Thee, Lord: Lord, hear my voice.

Glory be to the Father, &c.

The Collect.

O God, our refuge and strength, who art the author of all godliness: Be ready, we beseech Thee, to hear the devout prayers of Thy Church; and grant that those things which we ask faithfully, we may obtain effectually; through Jesus Christ, Thy Son, our Lord, who liveth and reigneth with Thee and the Holy Ghost, ever one God, world without end. Amen.

I. *Epistle,* Phil. i: 6—11.	*Gospel,* Matt. xviii: 23—35.	
II. *Epistle.* Rom. xi: 25—36.	*Gospel,* Matt. xviii: 15—22.	
III. *Epistle,* II Tim. ii: 19—21.	*Gospel,* Mark. iv: 21—25.	

TWENTY-THIRD SUNDAY AFTER TRINITY.

The Collect.

Lord God, heavenly Father: we thank Thee that Thou hast hitherto granted us peace and graciously spared us from war and foreign dominion: We pray Thee, graciously let us continue to live in Thy fear according to Thy will, giving no cause for wars or other punishment; govern and direct our magistrates, that they may not hinder the obedience due to Thee, but maintain righteousness, that we may enjoy happiness and blessing under their government, through our Lord Jesus Christ, who liveth and reigneth with Thee and the Holy Ghost. one true God, world without end. Amen.

Introit.

I know the thoughts that I think toward you, saith the Lord: thoughts of peace, and not of evil.

Then shall ye call upon me, and pray unto me, and I will hearken unto you: and I will turn your captivity, and gather you from all nations and all places.

Ps. Lord, Thou hast been favorable unto Thy land: Thou hast brought back the captivity of Jacob.

Glory be to the Father. &c.

The Collect.

Absolve, we beseech Thee, O Lord, Thy people from their offenses; that from the bonds of our sins which, by reason of our frailty, we have brought upon us, we may be delivered by Thy bountiful goodness; through Jesus Christ, Thy Son, our Lord, who liveth and reigneth with Thee and the Holy Ghost, ever one God, world without end. Amen.

I.	*Epistle,* Phil. iii: 17—21.	*Gospel,* Matt. xxii: 15—22.
II.	*Epistle,* Tim ii: 1—6.	*Gospel,* Mark. xii: 41—44.
III.	*Epistle,* Rom. xiii: 1—7.	*Gospel,* Matt. xvii: 24—27.

TWENTY-FOURTH SUNDAY AFTER TRINITY.

The Collect.

O almighty and everlasting God, who by Thy Son hast promised us forgiveness of our sins and deliverance from eternal death: We pray that by Thy Holy Spirit Thou wilt daily increase our faith in Thy grace through Christ, and establish us in the certain hope that we shall not die, but peacefully sleep, and be raised again on the last day to eternal life and salvation; through our Lord, Jesus Christ, Thy Son, who liveth and reigneth with Thee and the Holy Ghost, one true God, world without end. Amen.

Introit.

O come, let us worship and bow down: let us kneel before the Lord, our Maker.

For He is our God: and we are the people of His pasture, and the sheep of His hand.

Ps. O come, let us sing unto the Lord: let us make a joyful noise to the Rock of our salvation.

Glory be to the Father, &c.

The Collect.

Stir up, we beseech Thee, O Lord, the wills of Thy faithful people; that they, plenteously bringing forth the fruit of good works, may of Thee be plenteously rewarded; through Jesus Christ, Thy Son, our Lord, who liveth and reigneth with Thee and the Holy Ghost, ever one God, world without end. Amen.

I.	*Epistle,* Colos. i: 9—14.	*Gospel,* Matt. ix: 18—26.
II.	*Epistle,* I Cor. xv: 50—56.	*Gospel,* John vi: 37—40.
III.	*Epistle,* II Cor. v: 1—10.	*Gospel,* Luke xx: 27—40.

Collects for the Church Year

TWENTY-FIFTH SUNDAY AFTER TRINITY.

The Collect.

Lord God, heavenly Father, we most heartily thank Thee that by Thy word Thou hast brought us out of the darkness of Papacy into the light of Thy grace: We beseech Thee, mercifully help us to walk in that light, guard us from all error and false doctrine, and grant that we may not, as the Jews, become ungrateful and despise and persecute Thy word, but receive it with all our heart, govern our lives according to it, and put all our trust in Thy grace through the merit of Thy dear Son, our Lord Jesus Christ, who liveth and reigneth with Thee and the Holy Ghost, one true God, world without end. Amen.

Introit.

Have mercy upon me, O Lord, for I am in trouble: deliver me from the hand of mine enemies, and from them that persecute me.

Let me not be ashamed, O Lord: for I have called upon Thee.

Ps. In Thee, O Lord, do I put my trust; let me never be ashamed.

Glory be to the Father, &c.

The Collect

Almighty God, we beseech Thee, show **Thy mercy** unto Thy humble servants, that we who put no trust in our own merits may not be dealt with after the severity of Thy judgment, but according to Thy mercy; through Jesus Christ, Thy Son, our Lord, who liveth and reigneth with Thee and the Holy Ghost, ever one God, world without end. Amen.

I.	*Epistle,* I Thes. iv: 13—18.	*Gospel,* Matt. xxiv: 15—28.
II.	*Epistle,* II Thes. ii: 1—12.	*Gospel,* Matt xxv: 1—13.
III.	*Epistle,* I Thes. v: 1—10.	*Gospel,* Matt. xxiv: 35—44.

TWENTY-SIXTH SUNDAY AFTER TRINITY.

The Collect.

O almighty, eternal and merciful God, who by Thy beloved Son, our Lord and Savior Jesus Christ, hast established the kingdom of grace for us, that we might believe the forgiveness of our sins, in Thy holy Church on earth, since Thou art a God who hath no pleasure in the death of the wicked, but that the wicked turn from his way and live: We beseech Thee, graciously forgive us all our sins, through the same, Thy Son Jesus Christ, who liveth and reigneth with Thee and the Holy Ghost, one true God, world without end. Amen.

Introit.

Save me, O God, by Thy name: and judge me by Thy strength.

Hear my prayer, O God: give ear to the words of my mouth.

Ps. He shall reward evil to mine enemies: cut them off in Thy truth.

Glory be to the Father, &c.

The Collect.

Almighty, everlasting, and merciful God, Thou who, through Thy dear Son, our Lord and Savior Jesus Christ, hast for our sakes established the kingdom of grace that here in Thy holy Church we should believe the forgiveness of our sins, inasmuch as Thou art a God who hath no pleasure in the death of the wicked, but that the wicked turn from his way and live: We pray Thee, graciously pardon all our sins, through the same, Thy Son, Jesus Christ, our Lord, who liveth and reigneth with Thee, in the unity of the Holy Spirit, ever one God, world without end. Amen.

II.	*Epistle*, I Thes. v: 12—23.	*Gospel*, Matt. xi: 25—30.
II.	*Epistle*, I Cor. xv: 22—28.	*Gospel*, Matt. xxv: 31—46.
III.	*Epistle*, Hebr. iv: 9—13.	*Gospel*, John v: 22—29.

TWENTY-SEVENTH SUNDAY AFTER TRINITY.

The Collect.

(The Collect for the Sixth Sunday after Epiphany shall be used on the last Sunday after Trinity in each year).

DAY OF HUMILIATION AND PRAYER.

The Collect.

O gracious God, merciful Father, who dost bountifully forgive and show mercy unto all who truly repent of their sins: We heartily beseech Thee, dear Father, forgive us all our sins, and grant us Thy grace, that all we who call upon Thy name, each day abstain from all unrighteousness and sin, and turn unto Thee with all our hearts, that by the power of Thy Spirit we may daily be found in sincere faith and obedience, bringing forth fruits of true repentance: grant us also that, seeking and calling upon Thee in faith and confidence, we may find Thee a merciful God and Father, and be assured of Thy gracious help and blessing in every need of body and soul, until at length, by Thy grace, we obtain eternal salvation; through Thy dear Son, our Lord and Savior, who liveth and reigneth with Thee and the Holy Ghost, one true God, world without end. Amen.

Introit.

Hear, O heavens, and give ear, for the Lord hath spoken: I have nourished and brought up children, and they have rebelled against me.

They have forsaken the Lord, they have provoked the Holy One of Israel unto anger: They are gone away backward.

Ps. If Thou, Lord, shouldst mark iniquities: O Lord, who shall stand?

Glory be to the Father. &c.

The Collect.

Almighty and most merciful God, our heavenly Father, of whose compassion there is no end, who art long-suffering, gracious, and plenteous in goodness and truth; forgiving iniquity, transgression and sin: We have sinned and done perversely, we have forsaken and grievously offended Thee; against Thee, Thee only, have we sinned and done evil in Thy sight; but we beseech Thee, O Lord, remember not against us former iniquities; let Thy tender mercies speedily forgive us, for we are brought very low; help us, O God of our salvation, and purge away our sins, for the glory of Thy holy name, for the sake of Thy dear Son, our Savior, Jesus Christ, who liveth and reigneth with Thee and the Holy Ghost, ever one God, world without end. Amen.

I.	*Lesson.* Is. lv 6—7.	*Gospel*, Matt. iii: 8—10.
II.	*Lesson*, Is. lv: 1—4.	*Gospel*, Luke xiii: 23—30.
III.	*Lesson*, Ps. xxxii; 1—11.	*Gospel*, Luke vi: 46—49.

Collects for the Church Year

THE FESTIVAL OF HARVEST.

Introit.

O Lord, Thou crownest the year with Thy goodness: and Thy paths drop fatness.

Thou visitest the earth and waterest it: Thou blessest the springing thereof.

Ps. Praise waiteth for Thee, O God, in Zion: and unto Thee shall the vow be performed.

Glory be to the Father, &c.

The Collect.

Almighty God, most merciful Father, who openest Thy hand, and satisfiest the desire of every living thing: We give Thee most humble and hearty thanks that Thou hast crowned the fields with Thy blessing, and hast permitted us once more to gather in the fruits of the earth; and we beseech Thee to bless and protect the living seed of Thy word sown in our hearts, that in the plenteous fruits of righteousness we may always present to Thee an acceptable thank-offering; through Jesus Christ, Thy Son, our Lord, who liveth and reigneth with Thee and the Holy Ghost, ever one God, world without end. Amen.

THE FESTIVAL OF THE REFORMATION.

Introit.

The Lord of Hosts is with us: the God of Jacob is our refuge.

Therefore will we not fear, though the earth be removed: and though the mountains be carried into the midst of the sea.

Ps. God is our refuge and strength: a very present help in trouble.

Glory be to the Father, &c.

The Collect.

O Lord God, heavenly Father: Pour out, we beseech Thee, Thy Holy Spirit upon Thy faithful people, keep them steadfast in Thy grace and truth, protect and comfort them in all temptation, defend them against all enemies of Thy word, and bestow upon Christ's Church militant Thy saving peace, through the same, Thy Son, our Lord, who liveth and reigneth with Thee and the Holy Ghost, ever one God, world without end. Amen.

A DAY OF GENERAL OR SPECIAL THANKSGIVING.

Introit.

Let every thing that hath breath praise the Lord: praise ye the Lord.

Praise Him for His mighty acts: praise Him according to His excellent greatness.

Ps. Praise ye the Lord; praise God in His sanctuary; praise Him in the firmament of His power.

Glory be to the Father, &c.

The Collect.

Almighty God, our heavenly Father, whose mercies are new unto us every morning, and who, though we have in no wise deserved Thy goodness, dost abundantly provide for all our wants of body and soul; Give us we pray Thee, Thy Holy Spirit, that we may heartily acknowledge Thy merciful goodness toward us, give thanks for all Thy benefits, and serve Thee in willing obedience; through Jesus Christ, Thy Son, our Lord, who liveth and reigneth with Thee and the Holy Ghost, ever one God, world without end. Amen.

A Selection of Psalms

PSALM 1.

Blessed is the man that walketh not in the counsel of the ungodly: Nor standeth in the way of sinners, nor sitteth in the seat of the scornful.

But his delight is in the law of the Lord: And in His law doth he meditate day and night.

And he shall be like a tree planted by the rivers of water: That bringeth forth his fruit in his season.

His leaf also shall not wither: And whatsoever he doeth shall prosper.

The ungodly are not so: But are like the chaff which the wind driveth away.

Therefore the ungodly shall not stand in the judgment: Nor sinners in the congregation of the righteous. For theLord knoweth the way of the righteous: But the way of the ungodly shall perish.

Glory be to the Father, and to the Son, and to the Holy Ghost; As it was in the beginning, is now, and ever shall be, world without end. Amen.

PSALM 2.

Why do the heathen rage: And the people imagine a vain thing?

The kings of the earth set themselves, and the rulers take counsel together: Against the Lord and against His anointed, saying,

Let us break their bands asunder: And cast away their cords from us.

He that sitteth in the heavens shall laugh: The Lord shall have them in derision.

Then shall He speak unto them in His wrath: And vex them in His sore displeasure.

Yet have I set my king: Upon my holy hill of Zion.

I will declare the decree: The Lord hath said unto me, Thou art my Son; this day have I begotten thee.

Ask of me, and I shall give thee the heathen for thine inheritance: And the uttermost parts of the earth for thy possession.

Thou shalt break them with a rod of iron: Thou shalt dash them in pieces like a potter's vessel.

Be wise now therefore, O ye kings: Be instructed, ye judges of the earth.

Serve the Lord with fear: And rejoice with trembling.

Kiss the Son, lest He be angry, and ye perish from the way, when His wrath is kindled but a little: Blessed are all they that put their trust in Him.

PSALM 8.

O Lord, our Lord, how excellent is Thy name in all the earth: Who hast set Thy glory above the heavens.

Out of the mouth of babes and sucklings hast Thou ordained strength because of Thine enemies: That Thou mightest still the enemy and the avenger.

When I consider Thy heavens, the work of Thy fingers: The moon and the stars, which Thou hast ordained;

What is man, that Thou art mindful of him: And the son of man, that Thou visitest him?

For Thou hast made him a little lower than the angels: And hast crowned him with glory and honor.

Thou madest him to have dominion over the works of Thy hands: Thou hast put all things under his feet:

All sheep and oxen: Yea, and the beasts of the field;

The fowl of the air, and the fish of the sea: And whatsoever passeth through the paths of the seas.

O Lord, our Lord: How excellent is Thy name in all the earth!

PSALM 19.

The heavens declare the glory of God: And the firmament showeth His handiwork.

Day unto day uttereth speech: And night unto night showeth knowledge.

There is no speech nor language: Where their voice is not heard.

Their line is gone out through all the earth: And their words to the end of the world.

In them hath He set a tabernacle for the sun: Which is as a bridegroom coming out of his chamber, and rejoiceth as a strong man to run a race.

His going forth is from the end of the heaven, and his circuit unto the ends of it: And there is nothing hid from the heat thereof.

The law of the Lord is perfect, converting the soul: The testimony of the Lord is sure, making wise the simple.

The statutes of the Lord are right, rejoicing the heart: The commandment of the Lord is pure, enlightening the eyes.

The fear of the Lord is clean, enduring forever: The judgments of the Lord are true and righteous altogether.

More to be desired are they than gold, yea, than much fine gold: Sweeter also than honey and the honeycomb.

Moreover by them is Thy servant warned: And in keeping of them there is great reward.

Who can understand his errors? Cleanse Thou me from secret faults.

Keep back Thy servant also from presumptuous sins; let them not have dominion over me: Then shall I be upright and I shall be innocent from the great transgression.

Let the words of my mouth, and the meditation of my heart, be acceptable in thy sight: O Lord, my strength, and my redeemer.

PSALM 23.

The Lord is my shepherd: I shall not want.

He maketh me to lie down in green pastures: He leadeth me beside the still waters.

He restoreth my soul: He leadeth me in the paths of righteousness for His name's sake.

Yea, though I walk through the valley of the shadow of death, I will fear no evil: For Thou art with me; Thy rod and Thy staff they comfort me.

Thou preparest a table before me in the presence of mine enemies: Thou anointest my head with oil; my cup runneth over.

Surely goodness and mercy shall follow me all the days of my life: And I will dwell in the house of the Lord forever.

PSALM 24.

The earth is the Lord's and the fullness thereof: The world, and they that dwell therein.

For He hath founded it upon the seas: And established it upon the floods.

Who shall ascend into the hill of the Lord?: Or who shall stand in His holy place?

He that hath clean hands, and a pure heart: Who hath not lifted up his soul unto vanity, nor sworn deceitfully.

He shall receive the blessing from the Lord: And righteousness from the God of his salvation.

This is the generation of them that seek him: That seek thy face, O Jacob.

Lift up your heads, O ye gates; and be ye lifted up, ye everlasting doors: And the King of glory shall come in.

Who is this King of glory?: The Lord strong and mighty, the Lord mighty in battle.

Lift up your heads, O ye gates; even lift them up, ye everlasting doors: And the King of glory shall come in.

Who is this King of glory?: The Lord of hosts, He is the King of glory.

PSALM 25.

Unto Thee, O Lord: Do I lift my soul.

O my God, I trust in Thee: Let me not be ashamed, let not mine enemies triumph over me:

Yea, let none that wait on Thee be ashamed: Let them be ashamed which transgress without cause.

Show me Thy ways, O Lord: Teach me Thy paths.

Lead me in Thy truth, and teach me: For Thou art the God of my salvation; on Thee do I wait all the day.

Remember, O Lord, Thy tender mercies, and Thy loving-kindnesses: For they have been ever of old.

Remember not the sins of my youth, nor my transgressions: According to Thy mercy remember Thou me for Thy goodness' sake, O Lord.

Good and upright is the Lord: Therefore will He teach sinners in the way.

The meek will He guide in judgment: And the meek will He teach His way.

All the paths of our Lord are mercy and truth: Unto such as keep His covenant and His testimonies.

For Thy name's sake, O Lord, pardon mine iniquity: For it is great.

What man is he that feareth the Lord?: Him shall He teach in the way that He shall choose.

His soul shall dwell at ease: And his seed shall inherit the earth.

The secret of the Lord is with them that fear Him: And He will show them His covenant.

Mine eyes are ever toward the Lord: For He shall pluck my feet out of the net.

Turn Thee unto me, and have mercy upon me: For I am desolate and afflicted.

The troubles of my heart are enlarged: O bring Thou me out of my distresses.

Look upon mine affliction and my pain: And forgive me all my sins.

Consider mine enemies, for they are many: And they hate me with cruel hatred.

O keep my soul and deliver me: Let me not be ashamed; for I put my trust in Thee.

Let integrity and uprightness preserve me: For I wait on Thee.

Redeem Israel, O God: Out of all his troubles.

Psalms

PSALM 27.

The Lord is my light and my salvation; whom shall I fear?: The Lord is the strength of my life; of whom shall I be afraid?

When the wicked, even mine enemies and my foes, came upon me to eat up my flesh: They stumbled and fell.

Though a host should encamp against me, my heart shall not fear: Though war should rise against me, in this will I be confident.

One thing have I desired of the Lord, that will I seek after: That I may dwell in the house of the Lord all the days of my life, to behold the beauty of the Lord, and to inquire in His temple.

For in the time of trouble He shall hide me in His pavilion: In the secret of His tabernacle shall He hide me; He shall set me upon a rock.

And now shall mine head be lifted up: Above mine enemies round about me.

Therefore will I offer in His tabernacle sacrifices of joy: I will sing, yea, I will sing praises unto the Lord.

Hear, O Lord, when I cry with my voice: Have mercy also upon me, and answer me.

When Thou saidst, seek ye my face: My heart said unto Thee, Thy face, Lord will I seek.

Hide not Thy face far from me: Put not Thy servant away in anger.

Thou hast been my help: Leave me not, neither forsake me, O God of my salvation.

When my father and my mother forsake me: Then the Lord will take me up.

Teach me Thy way, O Lord: And lead me in a plain path, because of mine enemies.

Deliver me not over unto the will of mine enemies: For false witnesses are risen up against me, and such as breathe out cruelty.

I had fainted: Unless I had believed to see the goodness of the Lord in the land of the living.

Wait on the Lord: Be of good courage, and He shall strengthen thine heart; wait, I say, on the Lord.

PSALM 30.

I will extol Thee, O Lord; for Thou hast lifted me up: And hast not made my foes to rejoice over me.

O Lord my God, I cried unto Thee: And Thou hast healed me.

O Lord, Thou hast brought up my soul from the grave: Thou hast kept me alive, that I should not go down to the pit.

Sing unto the Lord, O ye saints of His: And give thanks at the remembrance of His holiness.

For His anger endureth but a moment; in His favor is life: Weeping may endure for a night, but joy cometh in the morning.

And in my prosperity I said: I shall never be moved.

Lord, by Thy favor Thou hast made my mountain to stand strong: Thou didst hide Thy face, and I was troubled.

I cried to Thee, O Lord: And unto the Lord I made supplication.

What profit is there in my blood, when I go down to the pit?: Shall the dust praise Thee? shall it declare Thy truth?

Hear, O Lord, and have mercy upon me: Lord, be Thou my helper.

Thou hast turned for me my mourning into dancing: Thou hast put off my sackcloth, and girded me with gladness;

To the end that my glory may sing praise to Thee, and not be silent: O Lord, my God, I will give thanks unto Thee forever.

PSALM 32.

Blessed is he whose transgression is forgiven: Whose sin is covered.

Blessed is the man unto whom the Lord imputeth not iniquity: And in whose spirit there is no guile.

When I kept silence: My bones waxed old through my roaring all the day long.

For day and night Thy hand was heavy upon me: My moisture is turned into the drought of summer.

I acknowledged my sin unto Thee: And mine iniquity have I not hid.

I said, I will confess my transgressions unto the Lord: And Thou forgavest the iniquity of my sin.

For this shall every one that is godly pray unto Thee in a time when Thou mayest be found: Surely in the floods of great waters they shall not come nigh unto him.

Thou art my hiding place; Thou shalt preserve me from trouble: Thou shalt compass me about with songs of deliverance.

I will instruct thee and teach thee in the way which thou shalt go: I will guide thee with mine eye.

Be ye not as the horse, or as the mule, which have no understanding: Whose mouth must be held in with bit and bridle, lest they come near unto thee.

Many sorrows shall be to the wicked: But he that trusteth in the Lord, mercy shall compass him about.

Be glad in the Lord, and rejoice, ye righteous: And shout for joy, all ye that are upright in heart.

PSALM 42.

As the hart panteth after the water-brooks: So panteth my soul after Thee, O God.

My soul thirsteth for God; for the living God: When shall I come and appear before God?

My tears have been my meat day and night: While they continually say unto me, Where is thy God?

When I remember these things, I pour out my soul in me: For I had gone with the multitude.

I went with them to the house of God, with the voice of joy and praise: With a multitude that kept holy day.

Why art thou cast down, O my soul? and why art thou disquieted within me? Hope thou in God: For I shall yet praise Him for the help of His countenance.

O my God, my soul is cast down within me: Therefore will I remember Thee from the land of Jordan, and of the Hermonites, from the hill Mizar.

Deep calleth unto deep at the noise of Thy waterspouts: All Thy waves and Thy billows are gone over me.

Yet the Lord will command His loving-kindness in the daytime: And in the night His song shall be with me, and my prayer unto the God of my life.

I will say unto God my Rock, Why hast Thou forgotten me?: Why go I moaning because of the oppression of the enemy?

As with a sword in my bones, mine enemies reproach me: While they say daily unto me, Where is thy God?

Why art thou cast down, O my soul: And why art thou disquieted within me?

Hope thou in God: For I shall yet praise Him who is the health of my countenance, and my God.

PSALM 43.

Judge me, O God, and plead my cause against an ungodly nation: O deliver me from the deceitful and unjust man.

For Thou art the God of my strength, why dost Thou cast me off?: Why go I mourning because of the oppression of the enemy?

O send out Thy light and Thy truth, let them lead me: Let them bring me unto Thy holy hill, and to Thy tabernacles.

Then will I go nigh unto the altar of God, unto God my exceeding joy: Yea, upon the harp will I praise Thee, O God, my God.

Why art thou cast down, O my soul? and why art thou disquieted within me?

Hope in God: For I shall yet praise Him, who is the health of my countenance, and my God.

PSALM 46.

God is our refuge and strength: A very present help in trouble.

Therefore will not we fear, though the earth be removed: And though the mountains be carried into the midst of the sea;

Though the waters thereof roar and be troubled: Though the mountains shake with the swelling thereof.

There is a river, the streams whereof shall make glad the city of God: The holy place of the tabernacles of the Most High.

God is in the midst of her; she shall not be moved: God shall help her, and that right early.

The heathen raged, the kingdoms were moved: He uttered His voice, the earth melted.

The Lord of hosts is with us: The God of Jacob. is our refuge.

Come, behold the works of the Lord: What desolations He hath made in the earth.

He maketh wars to cease unto the ends of the earth: He breaketh the bow, and cutteth the spear in sunder; He burneth the chariot in the fire.

Be still, and know that I am God: I will be exalted among the heathen, I will be exalted in the earth.

The Lord of hosts is with us: The God of Jacob is our refuge.

PSALM 48.

Great is the Lord, and greatly to be praised: In the city of our God, in the mountain of His holiness.

Beautiful for situation, the joy of the whole earth, is mount Zion: On the sides of the north, the city of the great King.

God is known in her palaces: For a refuge.

For, lo, the kings were assembled: They passed by together.

They saw it, and so they marvelled: They were troubled, and hasted away.

Fear took hold upon them there, and pain: As of a woman in travail.

Thou breakest the ships of Tarshish: With an east wind.

As we have heard, so have we seen in the city of the Lord of hosts, in the city of our God: God will establish it forever.

We have thought of Thy loving-kindness, O God: In the midst of Thy temple.

According to Thy name, O God, so is Thy praise unto the ends of the earth: Thy right hand is full of righteousness.

Let mount Zion rejoice, let the daughters of Judah be glad: Because of Thy judgments.

Walk about Zion, and go round about her: Tell the towers thereof.

Mark ye well her bulwarks, consider her palaces: That ye may tell it to the generation following.

For this God is our God forever and ever: He will be our guide even unto death.

PSALM 51.

Have mercy upon me, O God, according to Thy loving-kindness: According unto the multitude of Thy tender mercies, blot out my transgressions.

Wash me thoroughly from mine iniquity: And cleanse me from my sin.

For I acknowledge my transgressions: And my sin is ever before me.

Against Thee, Thee only, have I sinned, and done this evil in Thy sight: That Thou mightest be justified when Thou speakest, and be clear when Thou judgest.

Behold, I was shapen in iniquity: And in sin did my mother conceive me.

Behold, Thou desirest truth in the inward parts: And in the hidden part Thou shalt make me to know wisdom.

Purge me with hyssop, and I shall be clean: Wash me, and I shall be whiter than snow.

Make me to hear joy and gladness: That the bones which Thou hast broken may rejoice.

Hide Thy face from my sins: And blot out all mine iniquities.

Create in me a clean heart, O God: And renew a right spirit within me.

Cast me not away from Thy presence: And take not Thy Holy Spirit from me.

Restore unto me the joy of Thy salvation: And uphold me with Thy free Spirit.

Then will I teach transgressors Thy ways: And sinners shall be converted unto Thee.

Deliver me from blood-guiltiness, O God, Thou God of my salvation: And my tongue shall sing aloud of Thy righteousness.

O Lord, open Thou my lips: And my mouth shall show forth Thy praise.

For Thou desirest not sacrifice, else would I give it: Thou delightest not in burnt-offering.

The sacrifices of God are a broken spirit: A broken and a contrite heart, O God, Thou wilt not despise.

Do good in Thy good pleasure unto Zion: Build Thou the walls of Jerusalem.

Then shalt Thou be pleased with the sacrifices of righteousness, with burnt-offering, and whole burnt-offering. Then shall they offer bullocks upon Thine altar.

PSALM 67.

God be merciful unto us, and bless us: And cause His face to shine upon us;

That Thy way may be known upon earth: Thy saving health among all nations.

Let the people praise Thee, O God: Let all the people praise Thee.

O let the nations be glad and sing for joy: For Thou shalt judge the people righteously, and govern the nations upon earth.

Let the people praise Thee, O God: Let all the people praise Thee.

Then shall the earth yield her increase: And God, even our own God, shall bless us.

God shall bless us: And all the ends of the earth shall fear Him.

PSALM 84.

How amiable are Thy tabernacles: O Lord of hosts!

My soul longeth, yea, even fainteth for the courts of the Lord: My heart and my flesh crieth out for the living God.

Yea, the sparrow hath found an house, and the swallow a nest for herself, where she may lay her young: Even Thine altar, O Lord of hosts, my King and my God.

Blessed are they that dwell in Thy house: They will be still praising Thee.

Blessed is the man whose strength is in Thee: In whose heart are the ways of them.

Who passing through the valley of Baca make it a well: The rain also filleth the pools..

They go from strength to strength: Every one of them in Zion appeareth before God.

O Lord of hosts, hear my prayer: Give ear, O God of Jacob.

Behold, O God our shield: And look upon the face of Thine Anointed.

For a day in Thy courts is better than a thousand: I had rather be a doorkeeper in the house of my God, than to dwell in the tents of wickedness.

For the Lord God is a sun and a shield: The Lord will give grace and glory.

No good thing will He withhold from Them that walk uprightly: O Lord of hosts, blessed is the man that trusteth in Thee.

PSALM 86.

Bow down Thine ear, O Lord, hear me: For I am poor and needy.

Preserve my soul; for I am holy: O Thou my God, save Thy servant that trusteth in Thee.

Be merciful unto me, O Lord: For I cry unto Thee daily.

Rejoice the soul of Thy servant: For unto Thee, O Lord, do I lift up my soul.

For Thou, Lord, art good, and ready to forgive: And plenteous in mercy unto all them that call upon Thee.

Psalms

Give ear, O Lord, unto my prayer: And attend to the voice of my supplications.

In the day of my trouble will I call upon Thee: For Thou wilt answer me.

Among the gods there is none like unto Thee, O Lord: Neither are there any works like unto Thy works.

All nations whom Thou hast made shall come and worship before Thee, O Lord: And shall glorify Thy name.

For Thou art great, and doest wondrous things: Thou art God alone.

Teach me Thy way, O Lord: I will walk in Thy truth: Unite my heart to fear Thy name.

I will praise Thee, O Lord my God, with all my heart: And I will glorify Thy name for evermore.

For great is Thy mercy toward me: And Thou hast delivered my soul from the lowest hell.

O God, the proud are risen against me: And the assemblies of the violent men have sought after my soul: and have not set Thee before them.

But Thou, O Lord, art a God full of compassion, and gracious: Long suffering and plenteous in mercy and truth.

O turn to me, and have mercy upon me: Give Thy strength unto Thy servant, and save the son of Thine hand-maid.

Show me a token for good, that they which hate me may see it, and be ashamed: Because Thou, O Lord, hast helped me, and comforted me.

PSALM 90.

Lord, Thou hast been our dwelling place: In all generations.

Before the mountains were brought forth, or ever Thou hadst formed the earth and the world: Even from everlasting to everlasting, Thou art God.

Thou turnest man to destruction: And sayest, Return, ye children of men

For a thousand years in Thy sight are but as yesterday when it is past: And as a watch in the night.

Thou carriest them away as with a flood; they **are as a** sleep: In the morning they are as the grass which groweth up.

In the morning it flourisheth and groweth up: In the evening it is cut down, and withereth.

For we are consumed by Thine anger: And by Thy wrath are we troubled.

Thou hast set our iniquities before Thee: Our secret sins in the light of Thy countenance.

For all our days are passed away in Thy wrath: We spend our years as a tale that is told.

The days of our years are threescore years and ten; and if by reason of strength they be fourscore years: Yet is their strength labor and sorrow; for it is soon cut off, and we fly away.

Who knoweth the power of Thine anger: Even according to Thy fear, so is Thy wrath.

So teach us to number our days: That we may apply our hearts unto wisdom.

Return, O Lord, how long?: And let it repent Thee concerning Thy servants

O satisfy us early with Thy mercy: That we may rejoice and be glad ... our days.

Make us glad according to the days wherein Thou hast afflicted us: And the years wherein we have seen evil.

Psalms

Let Thy work appear unto Thy servants: And Thy glory unto their children.

And let the beauty of the Lord God be upon us: And establish Thou the work of our hands upon us; yea, the work of our hands establish Thou it.

PSALM 97.

The Lord reigneth, let the earth rejoice: Let the multitude of isles be glad thereof.

Clouds and darkness are round about Him: Righteousness and judgment are the habitation of His throne.

A fire goeth before Him: And burneth up His enemies round about.

His lightnings enlightened the world: The earth saw, and trembled.

The hills melted like wax at the presence of the Lord: At the presence of the Lord of the whole earth.

The heavens declare His righteousness: And all the people see His glory.

Confounded be all they that serve graven images, that boast themselves of idols: Worship Him, all ye gods.

Zion heard, and was glad: And the daughters of Judah rejoiced because of Thy judgments, O Lord.

For Thou, Lord, art high above all the earth: Thou art exalted far above all gods.

Ye that love the Lord, hate evil: He preserveth the souls of His saints; He delivereth them out of the hand of the wicked.

Light is sown for the righteous: And gladness for the upright in heart.

Rejoice in the Lord, ye righteous: And give thanks to the remembrance of His holiness.

PSALM 98.

O sing unto the Lord a new song: For He hath done marvellous things.

His right hand, and His holy arm: Hath gotten Him the victory.

The Lord hath made known His salvation: His righteousness hath He openly showed in the sight of the heathen.

He hath remembered His mercy and His truth toward the house of Israel: All the ends of the earth have seen the salvation of our God.

Make a joyful noise unto the Lord of all the earth: Make a loud noise, and rejoice and sing praise.

Sing unto the Lord with the harp: With the harp, and the voice of a psalm.

With trumpets and sound of cornet: Make a joyful noise before the Lord, the King.

Let the sea roar and the fullness thereof: The world, and they that dwell therein.

Let the floods clap their hands, let the hills be joyful together before the Lord: For He cometh to judge the earth.

With righteousness shall He judge the world: And the people with equity.

PSALM 100.

Make a joyful noise unto the Lord, all ye lands: Serve the Lord with gladness, come before His presence with singing.

Know ye that the Lord He is God: It is He that hath made us, and not we ourselves; we are His people, and the sheep of His pasture.

Psalms

Enter into His gates with thanksgiving, and into His courts with praise. Be thankful unto Him, and bless His name.

For the Lord is good; His mercy is everlasting: And His truth endureth to all generations.

PSALM 103.

Bless the Lord, O my soul: And all that is within me, bless His holy name
Bless the Lord, O my soul: And forget not all His benefits;

Who forgiveth all thine iniquities: Who healeth all thy diseases;

Who redeemeth thy life from destruction: Who crowneth thee with loving-kindness and tender mercies;

Who satisfieth thy mouth with good things: So that thy youth is renewed like the eagle's.

The Lord executeth righteousness and judgment: For all that are oppressed.

He made known His ways unto Moses: His acts unto the children of Israel.

The Lord is merciful and gracious: Slow to anger and plenteous in mercy.

He will not always chide: Neither will He keep His anger forever.

He hath not dealt with us after our sins: Nor rewarded us according to our iniquities.

For as the heaven is high above the earth: So great is His mercy toward them that fear Him.

As far as the east is from the west: So far hath He removed our transgressions from us.

Like as a father pitieth his children. So the Lord pitieth them that fear Him.

For He knoweth our frame: He remembereth that we are dust.

As for man, his days are as grass: As a flower of the field, so he flourisheth.

For the wind passeth over it, and it is gone: And the place thereof shall know it no more.

But the mercy of the Lord is from everlasting to everlasting upon them that fear Him: And His righteousness unto children's children;

To such as keep His covenant: And to those that remember His commandments to do them.

The Lord hath prepared His throne in the Heavens: And His kingdom ruleth over all.

Bless the Lord, ye His angels, that excel in strength: That do His commandments, hearkening unto the voice of His word.

Bless ye the Lord, all ye His hosts: Ye ministers of His, that do His pleasure.

Bless the Lord, all His works in all places of His dominion: Bless the Lord, O my soul.

PSALM 111.

Praise ye the Lord. I will praise the Lord with my whole heart: In the assembly of the upright, and in the congregation.

The works of the Lord are great: Sought out of all them that have pleasure therein.

His work is honorable and glorious: And His righteousness endureth forever.

He hath made His wonderful works to be remembered: The Lord is gracious and full of compassion

He hath given meat unto them that fear Him: He will ever be mindful of His covenant.

He hath shown His people the power of His works: That He may give them the heritage of the heathen.

The works of His hands are verity and judgment: All His commandments are sure.

They stand fast for ever and ever: And are done in truth and uprightness.

He sent redemption unto His people: He hath commanded His covenant for ever; holy and reverend is His name.

The fear of the Lord is the beginning of wisdom: A good understanding have all they that do His commandments; His praise endureth for ever.

PSALM 115.

Not unto us, O Lord, not unto us, but unto Thy name give glory: For Thy mercy, and for Thy truth's sake.

Wherefore should the heathen say: Where is now their God?

But our God is in the heavens: He hath done whatsoever He hath pleased.

Their idols are silver and gold: The work of men's hands.

They have mouths, but they speak not: Eyes have they, but they see not;

They have ears, but they hear not: Noses have they, but they smell not;

They have hands, but they handle not; feet have they, but they walk not: Neither speak they, through their throat.

They that make them are like unto them: So is every one that trusteth in them.

O Israel, trust thou in the Lord: He is their help and their shield.

O house of Aaron, trust in the Lord: He is their help and their shield.

Ye that fear the Lord, trust in the Lord: He is their help and their shield.

The Lord hath been mindful of us; He will bless us: He will bless the house of Israel; He will bless the house of Aaron.

He will bless them that fear the Lord: Both small and great.

The Lord shall increase you more and more: You and your children.

Ye are blessed of the Lord: Which made heaven and earth.

The heaven, even the heavens, are the Lord's: But the earth hath He given unto the children of men.

The dead praise not the Lord: Neither any that go down into silence.

But we will bless the Lord: From this time forth and for evermore. Praise the Lord.

PSALM 118.

O give thanks unto the Lord, for He is good: Because His mercy endureth for ever.

Let Israel now say: That His mercy endureth for ever.

Let the house of Aaron now say: That His mercy endureth for ever.

Let them now that fear the Lord say: That His mercy endureth for ever.

I called upon the Lord in distress: The Lord answered me, and set me in a large place.

The Lord is on my side; I will not fear: What can man do unto me?

The Lord taketh my part with them that help me: Therefore shall I see my desire upon them that hate me.

It is better to trust in the Lord: Than to put confidence in man.

It is better to trust in the Lord: Than to put confidence in princes.

All nations compassed me about: But in the name of the Lord I will destroy them.

They compassed me about; yea, they compassed me about: But in the name of the Lord I will destroy them.

They compassed me about like bees; they are quenched as the fire of thorns: For in the name of the Lord I will destroy them.

Thou hast thrust sore at me that I might fall: But the Lord helped me.

The Lord is my strength and song: And is become my salvation.

The voice of rejoicing and salvation is in the tabernacles of the righteous: The right hand of the Lord doeth valiantly.

The right hand of the Lord is exalted: The right hand of the Lord doeth valiantly.

I shall not die, but live: And declare the works of the Lord.

The Lord hath chastened me sore: But He hath not given me over unto death.

Open to me the gates of righteousness: I will go into them, and I will praise the Lord:

This gate of the Lord: Into which the righteous shall enter.

I will praise Thee: for Thou hast heard me: And art become my salvation.

The stone which the builders refused: Is become the head stone of the corner.

This is the Lord's doing: It is marvellous in our eyes.

This is the day which the Lord hath made: We will rejoice and be glad in it.

Save now, I beseech Thee, O Lord: O Lord, I beseech Thee, send now prosperity.

Blessed be he that cometh in the name of the Lord: We have blessed you out of the house of the Lord.

God is the Lord, which hath showed us light: Bind the sacrifice with cords, even unto the horns of the altar.

Thou art my God, and I will praise Thee: Thou art my God, I will exalt Thee.

O give thanks unto the Lord; for He is good: For His mercy endureth for ever.

PSALM 121.

I will lift up mine eyes unto the hills: From whence cometh my help.

My help cometh from the Lord: Which made heaven and earth.

He will not suffer thy foot to be moved: He that keepeth thee will not slumber.

Behold, He that keepeth Israel: Shall neither slumber nor sleep.

The Lord is thy keeper: The Lord is thy shade upon thy right hand.

The sun shall not smite thee by day: Nor the moon by night.

The Lord shall preserve thee from all evil: He shall preserve thy soul.

The Lord shall preserve thy going out and thy coming in: From this time forth, and even for evermore.

PSALM 122.

I was glad when they said unto me: Let us go into the house of the Lord, Our feet shall stand within thy gates, O Jerusalem.

Jerusalem is builded: As a city that is compact together.

Whither the tribes go up; the tribes of the Lord: Unto the testimony of Israel, to give thanks unto the name of the Lord.

For there are set thrones of judgment: The thrones of the house of David.

Pray for the peace of Jerusalem: They shall prosper that love thee.

Peace be within thy walls: And prosperity within thy palaces.

For my brethren and companions' sakes: I will now say, Peace be within thee.

Because of the house of the Lord our God: I will seek thy good.

PSALM 125.

They that trust in the Lord shall be as mount Zion: Which cannot be removed, but abideth for ever.

As the mountains are round about Jerusalem: So the Lord is round about His people from henceforth even for ever.

For the rod of the wicked shall not rest upon the lot of the righteous: Lest the righteous put forth their hands unto iniquity.

Do good, O Lord, unto those that be good: And to them that are upright in their hearts.

As for such as turn aside unto their crooked ways: The Lord shall lead them forth with the workers of iniquity; but peace shall be upon Israel.

PSALM 130.

Out of the depths: Have I cried unto Thee, O Lord.

Lord, hear my voice: Let Thine ears be attentive to the voice of my supplications.

If Thou, Lord, shouldst mark iniquities: O Lord, who shall stand?

But there is forgiveness with Thee: That Thou mayest be feared.

I wait for the Lord, my soul doth wait: And in His word do I hope.

My soul waiteth for the Lord, more than they that watch for the morning: I say, more than they that watch for the morning.

Let Israel hope in the Lord, for with the Lord there is mercy: And with Him is plenteous redemption.

And He shall redeem Israel: From all his iniquities.

PSALM 143.

Hear my prayer, O Lord, give ear to my supplications: In Thy faithfulness answer me, and in Thy righteousness.

And enter not into judgment with Thy servant: For in Thy sight shall no man living be justified.

For the enemy hath persecuted my soul; he hath smitten my life down to the ground: He hath made me to dwell in darkness, as those that have been long dead.

Therefore is my spirit overwhelmed within me: My heart within me is desolate.

I remember the days of old; I meditate on all Thy works: I muse on the work of Thy hands.

I stretch forth my hands unto Thee: My soul thirsteth after Thee, as a thirsty land.

Hear me speedily, O Lord; my spirit faileth: Hide not Thy face from me, lest I be like unto them that go down into the pit.

Cause me to hear Thy loving-kindness in the morning; for in Thee do I trust: Cause me to know the way wherein I should walk; for I lift up my soul unto Thee.

Deliver me, O Lord, from my enemies: I flee unto Thee to hide me.

Teach me to do Thy will; for Thou art my God: Thy Spirit is good; lead me into the land of uprightness.

Quicken me, O Lord, for Thy name's sake: For Thy righteousness' sake bring my soul out of trouble.

And of Thy mercy cut off mine enemies: And destroy all them that afflict my soul; for I am Thy servant.

PSALM 145.

I will extol Thee, my God, O King: And I will praise Thy name for ever and ever.

Every day will I bless Thee: And I will praise Thy name for ever and ever.

Great is the Lord, and greatly to be praised: And His greatness in unsearchable.

One generation shall praise Thy works to another: And shall declare Thy mighty acts.

I will speak of the glorious honor of Thy majesty: And of Thy wondrous works.

And men shall speak of the might of Thy terrible acts: And I will declare Thy greatness.

They shall abundantly utter the memory of Thy great goodness: And shall sing of Thy righteousness.

The Lord is gracious and full of compassion: Slow to anger, and of great mercy.

The Lord is good to all: And His tender mercies are over all His works.

All Thy works shall praise Thee, O Lord: And Thy saints shall bless Thee.

They shall speak of the glory of Thy kingdom: And talk of Thy power;

To make known to the sons of men His mighty acts: And the glorious majesty of His kingdom.

Thy kingdom is an everlasting kingdom: And Thy dominion endureth throughout all generations.

The Lord upholdeth all that fall: And raise up all those that be bowed down.

The eyes of all wait upon Thee: And Thou givest them their meat in due season.

Thou openest Thine hand: And satisfiest the desire of every living thing.

The Lord is righteous in all His ways: And holy in all His works.

The Lord is nigh unto all them that call upon Him: To all that call upon Him in truth.

He will fulfill the desire of them that fear Him: He also will hear their cry and will save them.

The Lord preserveth all them that love Him: But all the wicked will He destroy.

My mouth shall speak the praise of the Lord: And let all flesh bless His holy name for ever and ever.

Psalms

PSALM 146.

Praise ye the Lord: Praise the Lord, O my soul.

While I live will I praise the Lord: I will sing praises unto my God while I have any being.

Put not your trust in princes: Nor the son of man, in whom there is no help.

His breath goeth forth, he returneth to his earth: In that very day his thoughts perish.

Happy is he that hath the God of Jacob for his help: Whose hope is in the Lord his God;

Which made heaven and earth, the sea, and all that therein is: Which keepeth truth for ever;

Which executeth judgment for the oppressed: Which giveth food to the hungry.

The Lord looseth the prisoners: The Lord openeth the eyes of the blind.

The Lord raiseth them that are bowed down: The Lord loveth the righteous.

The Lord preserveth the strangers; He relieveth the fatherless and widows: But the way of the wicked He turneth upside down.

The Lord shall reign forever, even thy God, O Zion, unto all generations: Praise ye the Lord.

PSALM 147.

Praise ye the Lord; for it is good to sing praises unto our God: For it is pleasant; and praise is comely.

The Lord doth build up Jerusalem: He gathereth together the outcasts of Israel.

He healeth the broken in heart: And bindeth up their wounds.

He telleth the number of the stars: He calleth them all by their names.

Great is our Lord and of great power: His understanding is infinite.

The Lord lifteth up the meek: He casteth the wicked down to the ground.

Sing unto the Lord with thanksgiving: Sing praise upon the harp unto our God.

Who covereth the heaven with clouds, who prepareth rain for the earth: Who maketh grass to grow upon the mountains.

He giveth to the beast his food: And to the young ravens which cry.

He delighteth not in the strength of the horse: He taketh not pleasure in the legs of a man.

The Lord taketh pleasure in them that fear Him: In those that hope in His mercy.

Praise the Lord, O Jerusalem: Praise thy God, O Zion.

For He hath strengthened the bars of thy gates: He hath blessed thy children within thee.

He maketh peace in thy borders: And filleth thee with the finest of the wheat.

He sendeth forth His commandment upon earth: His word runneth very swiftly.

He giveth snow like wool: He scattereth the hoarfrost like ashes.

He casteth forth His ice like morsels: Who can stand before His cold?

He sendeth His word and melteth them: He causeth the wind to blow, and the waters to flow.

He showeth His word unto Jacob: His statutes and His judgments unto Israel.

He hath not dealt so with any nation: And as for His judgments, they have not known them. Praise ye the Lord.

PSALM 150.

Praise ye the Lord. Praise God in His sanctuary: Praise Him in the firmament of His power.

Praise Him for His mighty acts: Praise Him according to His excellent greatness.

Praise Him with the sound of the trumpet: Praise Him with psaltery and harp.

Praise Him with the timbrel and dance: Praise Him with stringed instruments and organs.

Praise Him upon the loud cymbals: Praise Him upon the high sounding cymbals.

Let everything that hath breath praise the Lord: Praise ye the Lord.

Worship in General

1 L. M.

L. Bourgeois, 1551

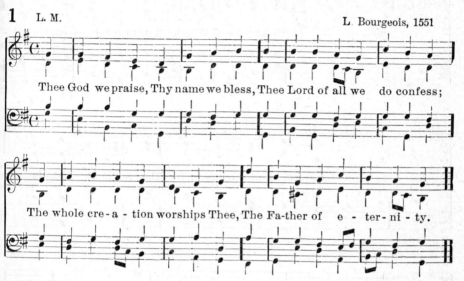

Thee God we praise, Thy name we bless, Thee Lord of all we do confess;

The whole cre-a-tion worships Thee, The Fa-ther of e-ter-ni-ty.

2 To Thee aloud all angels cry,
The heavens and all the powers on high,
The cherubs and the seraphs join,
And thus they hymn Thy praise divine:

3 O holy, holy, holy Lord,
Thou God of hosts, by all adored;
Earth and the heavens are full of Thee,
Thy light, Thy power, Thy majesty.

4 The apostles join the glorious throng,
The prophets swell the immortal song,
The white-robed hosts of martyrs bright
All serve and praise Thee day and night.

5 The holy Church in every place
Throughout the world exalts Thy praise
And ever doth acknowledge Thee,
Father of boundless majesty.

6 O God eternal, mighty King,
We unto Thee our praises bring;
And to Thy true and only Son,
And Holy Spirit, Three in One.

7 O King of glory, Christ the Lord,
God's everlasting Son—the Word,
To rescue mankind from its doom,
Thou didst our very flesh assume.

8 Thou overcamest death's sharp sting,
Believers unto heaven to bring;
At God's right hand, exalted there,
Thou dost the Father's glory share.

9 And we believe Thou wilt descend
To be our judge, when comes the end;
Thy servants help, whom Thou, O God,
Hast ransomed with Thy precious
blood.

10 Among Thy saints let us be found
With glory everlasting crowned;
Thy people save from age to age,
And bless Thy chosen heritage.

11 O guide them, lift them up for aye;
We magnify Thee day by day,
Thy name we worship and adore,
World without end, for evermore.

12 Vouchsafe, O Lord, we humbly pray,
To keep us safe from sin this day:
O Lord, have mercy on us all,
Have mercy on us, when we call.

13 Thy mercy, Lord, to us extend,
As on Thy mercy we depend:
Lord, I have put my trust in Thee,
Confounded let me never be.

Niceta of Remesiana? ca. 392

2 8, 7, 8, 7, 8, 8, 8.

14th cent. N. Decius, d. 1541

All glo-ry be to God on high, Who hath our race be-friend-ed! To us no harm shall now come nigh, The strife at last is end - - - ed; God show-eth His good will toward men, And peace shall dwell on earth a-gain; O thank Him for His good-ness!

2 We praise, we worship Thee, we trust,
   And give Thee thanks for ever,
O Father, that Thy rule is just
   And wise, and changes never;
Thy boundless power o'er all things reigns,
Done is whate'er Thy will ordains;
   Well for us that Thou rulest!

Prayer and Praise

3 O Jesus Christ, God's only Son,
  Who with Thy Father reignest,
Thou, who didst save a world undone,
  Our hope and stay remainest;
O Lamb of God, to Thee on high
From out our depths we sinners cry,
  Have mercy on us, Jesus!

4 O Holy Ghost, Thou precious gift,
  Thou Comforter unfailing,
O'er Satan's snares our souls uplift,
  And let Thy power availing
Avert our woes and calm our dread,
For us the Savior's blood was shed,
  We trust in Thee to save us!

Nicolaus Decius, 1525

Older form. 8, 7, 8, 7, 8, 8, 7.   14th cent. N. Decius, d. 1541

{All glo - ry be to God on high, Who hath our race be-
{To us no harm shall now come nigh, The strife at last is

friend - - - ed!}
end - - - ed;} God show - eth His good will toward men, And

peace shall dwell on earth a - gain; O thank Him for His good - ness!

Worship in General

Sing praise to God who reigns a-bove, The God of all cre-a - tion; The God of power, the God of love, The God of our sal-va - tion. With heal - ing balm my soul He fills, And ev - ery pain and sor - row stills: To God all praise and glo - ry!

2 The angel host, O King of kings,
    Thy praise forever telling,
In earth and sky all living things
    Beneath Thy shadow dwelling,
Adore the wisdom which could span,
And power which formed, creation's
        plan:
    To God all praise and glory!

3 What God's almighty power hath
        made,
    His gracious mercy keepeth;
By morning glow or evening shade,
    His watchful eye ne'er sleepeth;
Within the kingdom of His might,
Lo! all is just, and all is right:
    To God all praise and glory!

4

Prayer and Praise

4 I cried to God in my distress,
  His mercy heard me calling;
My Savior saw my helplessness
  And kept my feet from falling;
For this, Lord, praise and thanks to
    Thee!
Praise God most high, praise God
    with me!
  To God all praise and glory!

5 The Lord is never far away,
  Forsakes his people never;
He is their refuge and their stay,
  Their peace and trust forever;
And with a mother's watchful love
He guides them wheresoe'er they
    rove:
  To God all praise and glory!

6 When every earthly hope has flown
  From sorrow's sons and daughters,
Our Father from His heavenly throne

Beholds the troubled waters;
  And at His word the storm is stayed
Which made His children's heart a-
    fraid:
  To God all praise and glory.

7 Thus all my pilgrimage along
  I'll sing aloud Thy praises,
That men may hear the grateful song
  My voice unwearied raises:
Be joyful in the Lord, my heart!
Both soul and body, bear your part!
  To God all praise and glory!

8 O ye who bear Christ's holy name,
  Give God all praise and glory!
All ye who own His power, proclaim
  Aloud the wondrous story;
Cast each false idol from His throne,
The Lord is God, and He alone:
  To God all praise and glory!

J. J. Schutz, 1675

4 L. M.   Thomas Tallis, 1515—85

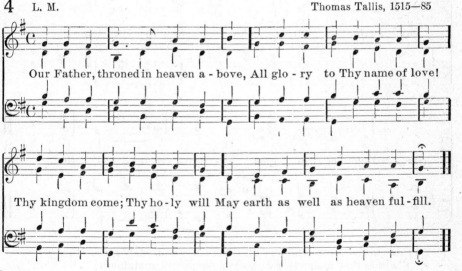

Our Father, throned in heaven a - bove, All glo - ry to Thy name of love!

Thy kingdom come; Thy ho - ly will May earth as well as heaven ful - fill.

2 Give us this day our daily food,
  With all we need of promised good;
  And freely all our sins remit,
  As we our debtors freely quit.

3 Defend us from the tempter's ways,
  Uphold when tried, when fallen raise:
  For power is Thine, and boundless reign,
  In glory evermore, Amen.

5   J. Guthrie, 1869

5 14, 14, 4, 7, 8.

German, 1668

Praise to the Lord, the Al-might-y, the King of cre - a - - - -
tion! O my soul, praise Him, for He is thy health and sal-
va - - tion! All ye who hear, Now to His tem-ple draw
near, Join me in glad a - do - ra - - - - - tion.

2 Praise to the Lord, who o'er all things so wondrously reigneth,
Shelters thee under His wings yea, so gently sustaineth;
Hast thou not seen
How thy desires e'er have been
Granted in what He ordaineth?

3 Praise to the Lord, who doth prosper thy work and defend thee;
Surely His goodness and mercy here daily attend thee;
Ponder anew
What the Almighty can do
If with His love He befriend thee!

'Prayer and Praise

4 Praise thou the Lord, who with marvelous wisdom hath made thee!
  Decked thee with health, and with loving hand guided and stayed thee;
      How oft in grief
      Hath not He brought thee relief,
          Spreading His wings for to shade thee!

5 Praise to the Lord! O let all that is in me adore Him!
  All that hath life and breath, come now with praises before Him!
      Let the Amen
      Sound from His people again;
          Gladly for aye we adore Him.

J. Neander, 1680

6 C. M.

O. Holden, 1793

All hail the power of Je-sus' name! Let an-gels prostrate fall;
Bring forth the roy-al di-a-dem, And crown Him Lord of all!
Bring forth the roy-al di-a-dem, And crown Him Lord....... of all!

2 Ye seed of Israel's chosen race,
    Ye ransomed from the fall,
  Hail Him who saves you by His grace,
    And crown Him Lord of all!

3 Hail Him, ye heirs of David's line,
    Whom David Lord did call;
  The God incarnate, Man divine:
    And crown Him Lord of all!

4 Ye Gentile sinners, ne'er forget
    The wormwood and the gall;
  Go spread your trophies at His feet,
    And crown Him Lord of all!

5 Let every kindred, every tribe,
    On this terrestrial ball,
  To Him all majesty ascribe,
    And crown Him Lord of all!

6 O that with yonder sacred throng
    We at His feet may fall;
  We'll join the everlasting song,
    And crown Him Lord of all!

E. Perronet, 1779

7 7, 8, 7, 8, 7, 6, 7, 6, 7, 6, 7, 6.

Ludv. M. Lindeman, 1812—87

My soul, now bless thy Mak - er! Let all with - in me bless His name, Who maketh thee par - tak - er Of mercies more than thou dar'st claim. For-get Him not, whose meekness For-giv-eth all thy sin; Who heal-eth all thy weakness, Re-news thy life with-in; Whose grace and care are end-less, Who saved thee through the past;

Prayer and Praise

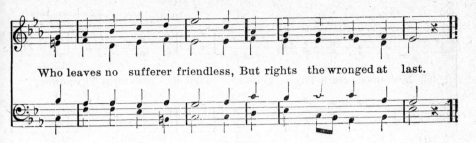

Who leaves no sufferer friendless, But rights the wronged at last.

2 He shows to man His treasure
   Of judgment, truth, and righteousness,
His love beyond all measure,
   His yearning pity o'er distress;
Nor treats us as we merit,
   But lays His anger by;
The humble, contrite spirit
   Finds His compassion nigh;
And high as heaven above us,
   As break from close of day,
So far, since He doth love us,
   He puts our sins away.

3 For, as a tender father
   Hath pity on his children here,
He in His arms doth gather
   All who are His in childlike fear;
He knows how frail our powers,
   Who but from dust are made:
We flourish as the flowers,
   And even so we fade;
A storm but o'er them passes,
   And all their bloom is o'er,—
We wither like the grasses,
   Our place knows us no more.

4 God's grace alone endureth,
   And children's children yet shall prove
How He with strength assureth
   The hearts of all that seek His love.
In heaven is fixed His dwelling,
   His rule is over all;
Angels, in might excelling,
   Bright hosts, before Him fall.
Praise Him who ever reigneth,
   All ye who hear His word,
Nor our poor hymns disdaineth,—
   My soul, O praise the Lord!

9   J. Graumann, 1540

8 7, 6. 6L.

M. Teschner, 1613

The heavens de-clare Thy glo - ry, The fir - ma - ment Thy power;

Day un - to day the sto - ry Re-peats from hour to hour;

Night un - to night re - ply - ing, Pro - claims in ev - ery land,

O Lord, with voice un - dy - ing, The won-ders of Thy hand.

2 The sun with royal splendor
  Goes forth to chant Thy praise;
And moonbeams soft and tender
  Their gentler anthem raise:
O'er every tribe and nation
  That music strange is poured;
The song of all creation
  To Thee, creation's Lord.

3 How perfect, just, and holy
  The precepts Thou hast given;
Still making wise the lowly,
  They lift the thoughts to heaven;
How pure, how soul-restoring
  Thy gospel's heavenly ray,
A brighter radiance pouring
  Than noon of brightest day!

Prayer and Praise

4 Thy statutes, Lord, with gladness
  Rejoice the humble heart;
And guilty fear and sadness
  From contrite souls depart:
Thy word hath richer treasure
  Than dwells within the mine,
And sweetness beyond measure
  Attends Thy voice divine.

5 O who can make confession
  Of every secret sin;
Or keep from all transgression
  His spirit pure within?

But let me never boldly
  From Thy commands depart,
Or render to Thee coldly
  The service of my heart.

6 All heaven on high rejoices
  To do its Maker's will;
The stars with solemn voices
  Resound Thy praises still:
So let my whole behavior,
  Thoughts, words, and actions be,
O Lord, my strength, my Savior,
  One ceaseless song to Thee.

T. R. Birks. 1874

9

8, 7, 6L.   Ludv. M. Lindeman, 1812—87

Praise, my soul, the King of heav-en, To His feet thy trib-ute bring;

Ransomed, healed, restored, for-giv-en, Ev-er-more His prais-es sing!

Hal-le-lu-jah! Hal-le-lu-jah! Praise the ev-er-last-ing King.

2 Praise Him for His grace and favor
  To our fathers in distress;
Praise Him, still the same as ever,
  Slow to chide, and swift to bless;
    Hallelujah! Hallelujah!
  Glorious in his faithfulness.

3 Father-like, He tends and spares us;
  Well our feeble frame He knows;
In His hands He gently bears us,

Rescues us from all our foes;
    Hallelujah! Hallelujah!
  Widely as His mercy goes.

4 Angels in the height, adore Him;
  Ye behold Him face to face;
Saints triumphant, bow before Him;
  Gathered in from every race.
    Hallelujah! Hallelujah!
  Praise with us the God of grace.

H. F. Lyte. 1834

Worship in General

9, 8, 9, 8, 8, 8.

Johann B. König, 1738

I praise Thee, O my God and Fa - ther, For
all I am and all I have, The bless-ings that we dai - ly
gath - er, E'en from our cra - dle to our grave; For Thy rich
grace hath scattered here What-e'er we need to help and cheer.

2 I praise Thee, Savior, whose compassion
    Hath brought Thee down to succor me;
Thy pitying heart sought my salvation,
    Though keenest woes were heaped on Thee,
Wrought me from bondage full release,
Made me Thine own and gave me peace.

3 Thee, too, I praise, O Holy Spirit,
    By whose deep teachings I am made
A heavenly kingdom to inherit,
    Who art my comforter, my aid;
Whate'er of good by me is done
Is of Thy grace and light alone.

Prayer and Praise

4 And as my life is onward gliding,
  With each fresh scene anew I mark
How Thou art holding me and guiding,
  Where all seems troubled, strange, and dark:
When cares oppress and hopes depart,
Thy light hath never failed my heart.

5 Shall I not then be filled with gladness,
  Shall I not praise Thee evermore?
And triumph o'er all fears and sadness,
  E'en when my cup of woes runs o'er?
Though heaven and earth may pass away,
I know Thy word stands fast for aye. .

J. Mentzer, 1704

11 11, 5, 11, 9.

Erik Hoff, b. 1832

Ye lands, to the Lord make a ju - bi - lant noise;
Glo-ry be to God! O serve Him with joy, in His presence now rejoice; Sing praise un - to God out of Zi - on!........

2 Not we, but the Lord is our Maker, our God;
    Glory be to God!
  His people we are, and the sheep led by His rod;
    Sing praise unto God out of Zion!

3 O enter His gates with thanksgiving and praise;
    Glory be to God!
  To bless Him and thank Him, our voices we will raise;
    Sing praise unto God out of Zion!

4 For good is the Lord, and His mercy is sure;
    Glory be to God!
  To all generations His truth shall still endure;
    Sing praise unto God out of Zion!

13

V. Koren, 1874

12 8, 7, 8 L.

F. J. Haydn, 1797

Praise the Lord, ye heavens, a-dore Him, Praise Him, an-gels, in the height;

Sun and moon, re-joice be-fore Him; Praise Him, all ye stars of light.

Praise the Lord, for He hath spok-en; Worlds His mighty voice o-beyed;

Laws which nev-er shall be brok-en, For their guidance He hath made.

2 Praise the Lord, for He is glorious;
  Never shall His promise fail;
God hath made His saints victorious;
  Sin and death shall not prevail.
Praise the God of our salvation;
  Hosts on high, His power proclaim;
Heaven and earth, and all creation,
  Laud and magnify His name.

Foundling Chapel Coll., 1796

Prayer and Praise

13 8, 7, 8, 7, 8, 8, 7.

German, 1523

With joy-ful heart your prais-es bring To God, the fount of bless-ing; His ev-er-last-ing goodness sing, His ho-ly name con-fess - ing; Our God let all cre - a - tion bless; He is our aid in all dis-tress: O bless His name for - ev - er.

2 Praise God, who to the cross and grave
Hath sent His Son from heaven;
His death that did the guilty save,
Eternal life hath given.
He hath redeemed our souls from hell;
Now peace from God with men doth dwell;
O bless His name forever!

3 Praise God, who by His Spirit's light
To faith our souls awaketh:
Our souls with gifts of grace and might,
He strong and steadfast maketh.
His word doth light our heavenward way;
His grace inclines us to obey;
O bless His name forever!

4 Ye mighty seraphim, your praise
Still to the Lord be bringing,
Let all in heaven their voices raise;
Let earth break forth in singing.
Whate'er hath breath shall Him a-dore,
Him first, Him last, Him evermore:
O bless His name forever!

C. Gunther. 1714

14 L. M.

L. Bourgeois, 1551

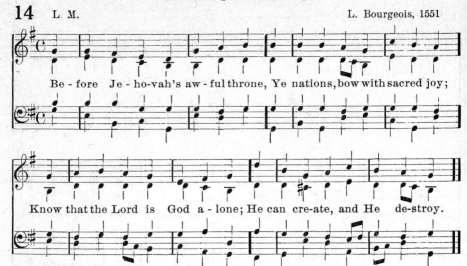

Be - fore Je - ho-vah's aw - ful throne, Ye nations, bow with sacred joy;

Know that the Lord is God a - lone; He can cre-ate, and He de-stroy.

2 His sovereign power, without our aid,
Made us of clay, and formed us men;
And when like wandering sheep we
strayed,
He brought us to His fold again.

3 We are His people, we His care,
Our souls and all our mortal frame;
What lasting honors shall we rear,
Almighty Maker, to Thy name?

4 We'll crowd Thy gates with thankful
songs,

High as the heavens our voices raise;
And earth, with her ten thousand
tongues,
Shall fill Thy courts with sounding
praise.

5 Wide as the world is Thy command,
Vast as eternity Thy love;
Firm as a rock Thy truth must stand,
When rolling years shall cease to
move.

I. Watts, 1719

15 8, 7, 8ʟ

J. A. Freylinghausen's Gesangbuch, 1704

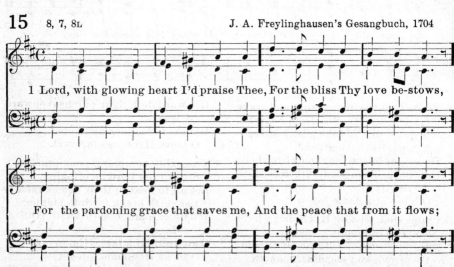

1 Lord, with glowing heart I'd praise Thee, For the bliss Thy love be-stows,

For the pardoning grace that saves me, And the peace that from it flows;

Prayer and Praise

Help, O God, my weak en-deav-or; This dull soul to rap-ture raise:

Thou must light the flame, or nev-er Can my love be warmed to praise.

2 Praise, my soul, the God that sought
  thee,
  Wretched wanderer, far astray;
Found thee lost, and kindly brought
  thee
From the paths of death away:
Praise, with love's devoutest feeling,
  Him who saw thy guilt-born fear,
And, the light of hope revealing,
  Bade the blood-stained cross appear.

3 Lord, this bosom's ardent feeling
  Vainly would my lips express;
Low before Thy footstool kneeling,
  Deign Thy suppliant's prayer to
    bless:
Let Thy grace, my soul's chief treas-
  ure,
  Love's pure flame within me raise;
And, since words can never measure,
  Let my life show forth Thy praise.

F. S. Key, 1826

16 7s. 4L.   J. H. Knecht, 1793

Come my soul, thy suit pre-pare, Je - sus loves to answer prayer;

He Him - self has bid thee pray, Therefore will not say thee nay.

2 Thou art coming to a king,
  Large petitions with thee bring;
For His grace and power are such,
None can ever ask too much.

3 With my burden I begin:
Lord, remove this load of sin!
Let Thy blood, for sinners spilt,
Set my conscience free from guilt.

4 God, my Lord, my king, Thou art,
Take possession of my heart,

There Thy blood-bought right main-
And without a rival reign.   [tain,

5 While I am a pilgrim here,
Let Thy love my spirit cheer;
Be my guide, my guard, my friend;
Lead me to my journey's end.

6 Show me what I have to do;
Every hour my strength renew;
Let me live a life of faith;
Let me die Thy people's death.

17   J. Newton. 1779

17 8, 7, 8, 7, 6, 6, 6, 6, 6, 7.

Martin Luther, 1529

Re - joice to - day with one ac-cord, Sing out with ex - ul-ta - tion! Re - joice and praise our might - y Lord, Whose arm hath brought sal - va - tion. The great-ness of His name His works of love pro - claim: His good - ness He hath shown, And He is God a - lone; Let all His saints a - dore Him.

Prayer and Praise

2 When in distress to Him we cried,
  He heard our sad complaining;
O trust in Him whate'er betide,
  His grace is all-sustaining;
    Our hearts to Him shall raise
    Triumphant songs of praise;
    And let all voices say,
"O praise the Lord alway,"
Let all His saints adore Him.

Sir H. W, Baker, 1861

18   8, 7, 8, 7, 8, 8, 7.   Joseph Klug, Wittenberg, 1535

O Ho-ly Spir-it, grant us grace That we our Lord and Sav-ior In faith and fer-vent love embrace, And tru-ly serve Him ev-er, So that when death is draw-ing nigh, We to His o-pen wounds may fly, And find in them sal-va-tion.

2 Help us that we Thy saving word
  In faithful hearts may treasure;
Let e'er that bread of life afford
  New grace in richest measure;
Yea, let us die to every sin,
For heaven create us new within,
  That fruits of faith may flourish.

3 And when our earthly race is run,
  Death's bitter hour impending,
Then may Thy work, in us begun,
  Continue till life's ending;
Until we gladly may commend
Our souls into our Savior's hand,
  To rest in peace eternal.

B. Ringwaldt, 1581
S. Jonassön, 1693

Worship in General

12s. 4L.

Ludv. M. Lindeman, 1812-87

Sing loud Hal-le-lu - jah in ju-bi-lant cho - rus, Ye
na - tions, O sing to the Lord who reigns o'er us! His
mer - ci - ful kind - ness and grace He re - veal - eth,
He par - dons our sins, and our sor - rows He heal - eth.

2 O lift up your voices in strains of thanksgiving!
Let praises ascend to our God ever living!
Now life and salvation from Him we inherit,
In Jesus, His Son, through His death and His merit.

3 Of mercy and grace God alone is the giver,
And all who believe, He will surely deliver;
His truth standeth fast, and it faileth us never:
His mercy endureth for ever and ever.

4 All glory and praise to the Father be given,
The Son, and the Spirit, from earth and from heaven;
As was, and is now, be supreme adoration,
And ever shall be, to the God of salvation.

J. Agricola, 1524

Prayer and Praise

20 C. M.   Este's Psalter, 1592

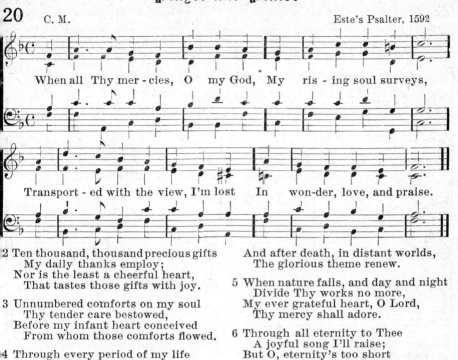

When all Thy mer - cies, O my God, My ris - ing soul surveys,

Transport - ed with the view, I'm lost In won-der, love, and praise.

2 Ten thousand, thousand precious gifts
  My daily thanks employ;
  Nor is the least a cheerful heart,
  That tastes those gifts with joy.

3 Unnumbered comforts on my soul
  Thy tender care bestowed,
  Before my infant heart conceived
  From whom those comforts flowed.

4 Through every period of my life
  Thy goodness I'll pursue;

And after death, in distant worlds,
  The glorious theme renew.

5 When nature fails, and day and night
  Divide Thy works no more,
  My ever grateful heart, O Lord,
  Thy mercy shall adore.

6 Through all eternity to Thee
  A joyful song I'll raise;
  But O, eternity's too short
  To utter all Thy praise!

J. Addison, 1712

21 L. M.   L. Bourgeois, 1551

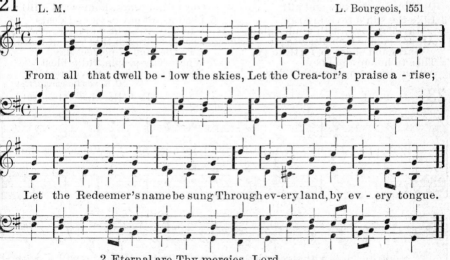

From all that dwell be - low the skies, Let the Crea-tor's praise a - rise;

Let the Redeemer's name be sung Through ev-ery land, by ev - ery tongue.

2 Eternal are Thy mercies, Lord,
  Eternal truth attends Thy word;
  Thy praise shall sound from shore to shore
  Till suns shall rise and set no more.

I. Watts, 1719

22 7s. 6L.

Ludv. M. Lindeman, 1812—87

Je - sus, Sun of right-eous-ness, Bright-est beam of love di-vine,

With the ear - ly morn-ing rays Do Thou on our darkness shine,

And dis - pel with pur - est light All our long and gloom-y night.

2 As on drooping herb and flower
  Falls the soft refreshing dew,
Let Thy Spirit's grace and power
  All our weary souls renew;
Showers of blessing softly fall
On Thy people, one and all!

3 Like the sun's reviving ray,
  May Thy love, with tender glow,
All our coldness melt away,
  Warm and cheer us forth to go,
Thee to honor and obey
All our life's short earthly day.

4 Thou our only hope and guide,
  Never leave us nor forsake:
In Thy light may we abide
  Till the endless morning break,
Moving to Thy holy hill
Onward, upward, homeward still!

5 Lead us all our days and years
  In Thy straight and narrow way;
Lead us through this vale of tears
  To the land of perfect day,
Where Thy people, fully blest,
Near Thy throne forever rest.

C. K. von Rosenroth, 1684

23 11, 10, 11, 10.

E. J. Hopkins, 1818—1901

Praise ye Je - ho - vah, praise the Lord most ho - ly, Who cheers the

contrite, girds with strength the weak; Praise Him who will with

Prayer and Praise

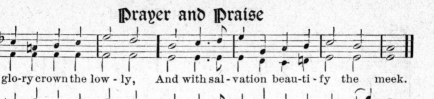

glo-ry crown the low-ly, And with sal-vation beau-ti-fy the meek.

2 Praise ye the Lord for all His loving kindness,
   And all the tender mercies He hath shown;
   Praise Him who pardons all our sin and blindness,
   And calls us sons, and takes us for His own.

3 Praise ye Jehovah, source of every blessing;
   Before His gifts earth's richest boons are dim;
   Resting in Him, His peace and joy possessing,
   All things are ours, for we have all in Him.

4 Praise ye the Father, God the Lord who gave us,
   With full and perfect love, His only Son;
   Praise ye the Son who died Himself to save us;
   Praise ye the Spirit, praise the Three in One!

M. Cockburn-Campbell, 1838

24 L. M.   Arr. fr. R. Schumann, 1839

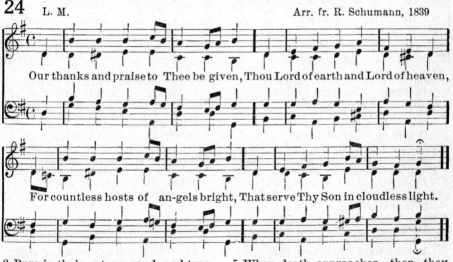

Our thanks and praise to Thee be given, Thou Lord of earth and Lord of heaven,

For countless hosts of an-gels bright, That serve Thy Son in cloudless light.

2 Pure in their nature, good, and true,
  'Tis their delight Thy will to do;
  From heaven they come the souls to
      guard
  That trust in Thy most holy word.

3 They joy when but one sinner turns;
  Their zeal for Jesus ever burns;
  They serve His people night and day,
  And turn full many an ill away.

4 All little ones, awake, asleep,
  And every child of Thine, they keep;
  O'er all Thy kingdom, far and near,
  They give their kind and loving care.

5 When death approaches, then they
      come,
  To soften pain, and guide us home;
  And when the spirit leaves the clay,
  To waft us to the realms of day.

6 Give us, O Lord, the grace and power
  To serve Thee well each day and hour;
  Grant us the zeal and fervent love
  To serve as angels serve above.

7 Let these good spirits with us be,
  When in Thy house we worship Thee;
  And bid them all our path defend
  Till this our life on earth shall end.

Latin, by Philip Melanchton, 1543
P. Eber, 1554

25 8, 7, 8, 7, 4, 7.

E. J. Hopkins, 1818—1901

Je-sus, Lord of life and glo-ry, Bend from heaven Thy gra-cious ear:

While our wait-ing souls a-dore Thee, Friend of help-less sin-ners, hear:

By Thy mer-cy, O de-liv-er us, good Lord!

2 Taught by Thine unerring Spirit,
  Boldly we draw nigh to God;
Only in Thy spotless merit,
  Only through Thy precious blood:
    By Thy mercy,
    O deliver us, good Lord!

3 From the depth of nature's blindness,
  From the hardening power of sin,
From all malice and unkindness,
  From the pride that lurks within,
    By Thy mercy,
    O deliver us, good Lord!

4 When temptation sorely presses,
  In the day of Satan's power,
In our times of deep distresses,
  In each dark and trying hour,
    By Thy mercy,
    O deliver us, good Lord!

5 When the world around is smiling,
  In the time of wealth and ease,
Earthly joys our hearts beguiling,
  In the day of health and peace,
    By Thy mercy,
    O deliver us, good Lord!

6 In the weary hours of sickness,
  In the times of grief and pain,
When we feel our mortal weakness,
  When all human help is vain:
    By Thy mercy,
    O deliver us, good Lord!

7 In the solemn hour of dying,
  In the awful judgment day,
May our souls, on Thee relying,
  Find Thee still our rock and stay:
    By Thy mercy,
    O deliver us, good Lord!

John James Cummins, 1839

26 6, 5, 6, 5, 11, 6, 6, 5.

Zinck's Koralbog, 1801

Give praise to God our King, O earth and heav-en!

Prayer and Praise

Of grace and mer-cy sing, So free-ly giv-en.

O Sav-ior, who hast died Our ex-pi-a-tion, Thy name be glo-ri-fied, Thy name be glo-ri-fied By all cre-a-tion.

2 O Holy Ghost, our guide
    To heavenly glory,
In all our hearts abide,
    Lord, we implore Thee;
In us, blest Spirit, reign,
    Thine aid bestowing;
[:Our souls with peace sustain,:‖
    Peace still o'erflowing.

3 Lift we our hearts on high
    In adoration;
Our Lord is ever nigh
    With consolation.
Let every grief be still;
    Light He will send us;
[:In life, in death, He will:‖
    Always defend us.

A. T. Russell, 1854

27 7s. 6L.　　　　　　　　　　　　　　　　　R. Redhead, 1853

Rock of A - ges, cleft for me, Let me hide my-self in Thee;

Let the wa - ter and the blood, From Thy riv - en side which flowed,

Be of sin the dou - ble cure, Cleanse me from its guilt and power.

2 Not the labors of my hands
Can fulfill Thy law's demands;
Could my zeal no respite know,
Could my tears forever flow,
All for sin would not atone;
Thou must save, and Thou alone.

3 Nothing in my hand I bring;
Simply to Thy cross I cling;
Naked, come to Thee for dress:

Helpless, look to Thee for grace;
Foul, I to the fountain fly:
Wash me, Savior, or I die!

4 While I draw this fleeting breath,
When mine eyelids close in death,
When I soar to worlds unknown,
See Thee on Thy judgment throne:
Rock of Ages, cleft for me,
Let me hide myself in Thee!

　　　　　　　　　　　　A. M. Toplady, 1776

Second Tune. 7. 6L.　　　　　　Thomas Hastings, 1784—1872

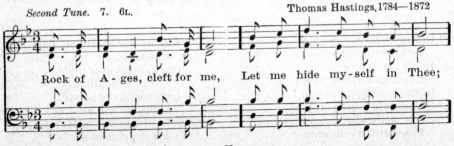

Rock of A - ges, cleft for me, Let me hide my-self in Thee;

Let the wa - ter and the blood, From Thy riv - en side which flowed,

Be of sin the dou - ble cure, Cleanse me from its guilt and power.

28 L. M.

J. Hatton, d. 1793

1 Give to our God im - mor - tal praise! Mercy and truth are all His ways;

Wonders of grace to God be - long: Repeat His mer - cies in your song.

2 Give to the Lord of lords renown,
The King of kings with glory crown:
His mercies ever shall endure,
When lords and kings are known no
more.

3 He built the earth, He spread the sky,
And fixed the starry lights on high:
Wonders of grace to God belong;
Repeat His mercies in your song.

4 He fills the sun with morning light;
He bids the moon direct the night:
His mercies ever shall endure.

When sun and moon shall shine no
more.

5 He sent His Son with power to save
From guilt and darkness, and the
grave:
Wonders of grace to God belong;
Repeat His mercies in your song.

6 Through this vain world He guides
our feet,
And leads us to His heavenly seat:
His mercies ever shall endure,
When this vain world shall be no more.

Watts, 1719

29   8, 7, 8, 7, 8, 7, 8, 7, 7.

German, 1523

May God be-stow on us His grace, With blessings rich pro - vide us,

And may the brightness of His face To life e - ter - nal guide us;

That we His gracious work may know, And what is His good pleas - ure,

And al - so to the hea - then show Christ's rich - es with - out

meas - ure, And un - to God con - vert them.

Prayer and Praise

2 To Thee let all the heathen bring
  Their joyful gratulations,
And all the world rejoice and sing
  With psalms and acclamations;
For Thou, O God, wilt judge the earth;
  Nor suffer sin to flourish:
The land no more shall mourn her
    dearth,
  Thy word shall keep and nourish
In righteous paths all people.

3 O let the people praise Thy worth,
  In all good works increasing;
The land shall plenteous fruit bring
  Thy word is rich in blessing. [forth.
Let God the Father, God the Son,
  And Holy Spirit, bless us:
To whom by all be honor done!
  Let solemn awe possess us,
Yea, fear Him, all ye people.

M. Luther, 1524

30 5, 5, 8, 8, 5, 5. A. Drese, 1620—1701

Who is there like Thee, Je-sus, un-to me? None are like Thee, none a-bove Thee, Thou art al-to-geth-er love-ly; None on earth have we, None in heaven like Thee.

2 Love that warmly glowed,
  Blood that freely flowed;
Life that stooped to death to save me,
And a deathless being gave me;
  Bore my guilty load,
  Brought me back to God!

3 Plant Thyself in me,
  I will learn of Thee,
To be holy, meek, and tender,

Wrath and pride and self surrender:
  Nothing shouldst Thou see
  But Thyself in me.

4 When on death's cold strand
  I one day shall stand,
Let Thy presence go beside me,
Through the gloomy waters guide me:
  Grant me then to stand,
  Lord, at Thy right hand.

J. A. Freylinghausen. 1704

31 6, 7, 6, 7, 6, 6, 6, 6.   Johann Crüger, 1647

Now thank we all our God, With heart and hands and voi - ces,

Who wondrous things hath done, In whom His world re - joi - ces;

Who from our mother's arms Hath blessed us on our way

With countless gifts of love, And still is ours to - day.

2 O may this bounteous God,
    Through all our life be near us,
With ever joyful hearts,
    And blessed peace to cheer us;
And keep us in His grace,
    And guide us when perplexed,
And free us from all ills,
    In this world and the next.

3 All praise and thanks to God
    The Father now be given,
The Son and Him who reigns
    With them in highest heaven;
The one eternal God,
    Whom earth and heaven adore;
For thus it was, is now,
    And shall be evermore!

M. Rinkart, 1648

Prayer and Praise

7s. 8L.

J. Richardson, 1853

Pleas-ant are Thy courts a-bove, In the land of light and love;

Pleas-ant are Thy courts be-low, In this land of sin and woe.

O, my spir-it longs and faints For the con-verse of Thy saints,

For the brightness of Thy face, For Thy full-ness, God of grace!

2 Happy souls! their praises flow
Even in this vale of woe;
Waters in the desert rise,
Manna feeds them from the skies;
On they go from strength to strength,
Till they reach Thy throne at length;
At Thy feet adoring fall,
Who hast led them safe through all.

3 Lord, be mine this prize to win;
Guide me through a world of sin,
Keep me by Thy saving grace,
Give me at Thy side a place.
Sun and shield alike Thou art;
Guide and guard my erring heart;
Grace and glory flow from Thee:
Shower, O shower them, Lord, on me!

H. F. Lyte, 1834

33 7, 8, 7, 8, 7 7. Lüneburgisches Gesangbuch, 1686

Light of light, en-light-en me, Now a-new the day is dawn - -ing; Sun of grace, the shad-ows flee, Brighten Thou my Sab-bath morn - ing; With Thy joy-ous sun-shine blest, Hap - py is my day of rest!

2 Fount of all our joy and peace,
   To Thy living waters lead me;
     Thou from earth my soul release,
   And with grace and mercy feed me;
     Bless Thy word, that it may prove
     Rich in fruits that Thou dost love.

3 Kindle Thou the sacrifice
   That upon my lips is lying;
     Clear the shadows from mine eyes,
   That, from every error flying,
     No strange fire may in me glow
     That Thine altar doth not know.

Beginning of Service

4   Let me with my heart today
    Holy, holy, holy singing,
      Rapt a while from earth away,
    All my soul to Thee upspringing,
      Have a foretaste, inly given,
      How they worship Thee in heaven.

5   Rest in me and I in Thee,
    Build a paradise within me;
      O reveal Thyself to me,

    Blessed Love, who died'st to win me:
      Fed from Thine exhaustless urn,
      Pure and bright my lamp shall burn.

6   Hence all care, all vanity,
    For the day to God is holy:
      Come, Thou glorious Majesty,
    Deign to fill this temple lowly;
      Naught to-day my soul shall move,
      Simply resting in Thy love.

B. Schmolck, 1714

34   7, 8, 7, 8, 8, 8.   Johann Rudolph Ahle, 1664

Bless-ed Je - sus, at Thy word We are gath-ered all to hear Thee;

Let our hearts and souls be stirred Now to seek and love and fear Thee;

By Thy teachings sweet and ho - ly Drawn from earth to love Thee sole-ly.

2 All our knowledge, sense, and sight
    Lie in deepest darkness shrouded,
Till Thy Spirit breaks our night
    With the beams of truth unclouded.
Thou alone to God canst win us,
Thou must work all good within us.

3 Glorious Lord, Thyself impart!
    Light of light, from God proceeding,
Open Thou our ears and heart,
    Help us by Thy Spirit's pleading;
Hear the cry Thy people raises,   [es.
Hear, and bless our prayers and prais-

T. Clausnitzer, 1663

35 8, 7, 8, 7, 7, 7.

A. P. Berggreen, 1849

O-pen now thy gates of beau-ty, Zi - on, let me en-ter there, Where my soul, in joy-ful du - ty, Waits for Him who an - swers prayer; O how bless-ed is this place, Filled with sol - ace, light, and grace.

2 Lord, my God, I come before Thee,
Do not hide Thy face from me;
Where we find Thee and adore Thee
There a heaven on earth must be;
To my heart, O enter Thou,
Let it be Thy temple now.

3 Here Thy praise is gladly chanted,
Here Thy seed is duly sown:
Let my soul, where it is planted,
Bring forth precious sheaves alone,
So that all I hear may be
Fruitful unto life in me.

Beginning of Service

4 Thou my faith increase and quicken,
　　Let me keep Thy gift divine;
Howsoe'er temptations thicken,
　　May Thy word forever shine
As my guiding star through life,
As my comfort in the strife.

5 Speak, O God, and I will hear Thee;
　　Let Thy will be done indeed;
May I undisturbed draw near Thee
　　While Thou dost Thy people feed;
Here the living waters flow,
Here is balm for all our woe.

B. Schmolck, 1732

36　L. M.

Cantionale Sacrum, Gotha, 1651

Lord Je-sus Christ, be pres-ent now, And let Thy Ho-ly

Spir - it bow All hearts in love and fear to - day,

To hear the truth and keep Thy way.

2 Unseal our lips to sing Thy praise,
　Our hearts in true devotion raise;
　Our faith increase, our minds enlight,
　That we may know Thy name aright:

3 Until we join the host that cry,
　"Holy art Thou, O Lord most high!"

And 'mid the light of that blest place
Shall gaze upon Thee face to face.

4 Glory to God, the Father, Son,
　And Holy Spirit, Three in One!
　To Thee, O blessed Trinity,
　Be praise throughout eternity!

Wilhelm II. Duke of Sachse-Weimar, 1648

35

37 8, 7, 8, 7, 7, 7, 8, 8.

Johann Schop, 1642

Dear-est Je-sus, draw Thou near me, Let Thy Spir-it

dwell with mine; O-pen now my ear to hear Thee,

Take my heart and seal it Thine; Keep me, lead me

on my way Thee to fol-low and o-bey, E'er to do Thy

will and fear Thee, And re-joice to know and hear Thee.

Beginning of Service

2 Underneath Thy wings abiding,
   In Thy Church, O Savior dear,
 Let me dwell, in Thee confiding,
   Hold me in Thy faith and fear;
 Take away from me each thought
   That with wickedness is fraught,
 Tempting me to disobey Thee,
   Root it out, O Lord, I pray Thee.

3 Thou, earth's greatest joy and glad-
   And salvation, full and free, [ness,
 Let Thy presence cheer my sadness,
   And prepare my soul for Thee!
 In the hour when I depart,
   Touch my spirit, lips and heart,
 With Thy word assure, uphold me
   Till the heavenly gates enfold me.

T. Kingo, 1699

38   7s. 6L.

John Dahle, 1911

Safe-ly through an-oth-er week God has brought us on our way;

Let us now a bless-ing seek, Wait-ing in His courts to-day:

Day of all the week the best, Emblem of e-ter-nal rest!

2 Mercies multiplied each hour
   Through the week our praise de-
 Guarded by almighty power, [mand;
   Fed and guided by His hand,
 Though ungrateful we have been,
   Only made returns of sin.

3 While we pray for pardoning grace,
   Through the dear Redeemer's name;
 Show Thy reconciléd face,

Take away our sin and shame:
From our worldly cares set free,
May we rest this day in Thee.

4 May Thy gospel's joyful sound
   Conquer sinners, comfort saints;
 Make the fruits of grace abound,
   Bring relief for all complaints:
 Thus may all our sabbaths prove
 Till we join the Church above.

J. Newton, 1774

39   8, 9, 6, 6, 6, 6, 5.   13th Century, Johann Walther, 1524

O Ho-ly Ghost, to Thee we pray For true faith to guide us in our way; Grant its faith-ful keep-ing Till our life's brief sto-ry, When in death we're sleep-ing, Ends at home in glo-ry. O have mer-cy, Lord!

2 Shine in our hearts, Thou blessèd Light,
    Teach us Jesus Christ to know aright,
    That we all may surely,
      In His grace confiding,
    Be with Him securely
      Evermore abiding.
    O have mercy, Lord!

3 Thou Fount of love, our hearts inspire
    With the holy flame of Thy pure fire;
    That in Christ united,
      One in all endeavor,

Loyal friendship plighted,
    We may walk together.
O have mercy, Lord!

4 Thou Comforter in every need,
    'Gainst the wicked foe and death we plead
    That Thy help may enter;
      When our courage faileth,
    And the evil tempter
      All our life assaileth.
O have mercy, Lord!

M. Luther, 1524
M. B. Landstad, 1861

Beginning of Service

Fa-ther, who the light this day Out of dark-ness didst cre-ate, Shine up-on us now, we pray, While with-in Thy courts we wait; Wean us from the works of night, Make us chil-dren of the light.

2 Savior, who this day didst break
  From the bondage of the tomb,
Bid our slumbering souls awake,
  And dispel their doubt and gloom;
Let us, from our bonds set free,
Rise from sin and live to Thee.

3 Blessed Spirit, Comforter,
  Sent this day from Christ on high,
Lord, on us Thy gifts confer,
  Cleanse, illumine, sanctify;
All Thine influence shed abroad;
Lead us to the truth of God.

Julia Anne Elliot, 1835

41 6, 7, 6, 7, 6, 6, 6, 6,

Meiningisches Gesangbuch, 1693

We love the place, O God, Wherein Thine hon-or dwell-eth;

The joy of Thine a-bode All earth-ly joy ex-cell-eth;

It is the house of prayer, Where-in Thy serv-ants meet;

And Thou, O Lord, art there Thy chos-en flock to greet.

2 We love Thine altar, Lord;
  O what on earth is dearer?
For there, in faith adored,
  We draw Thy presence nearer;
We love the word of life,
  The word that tells of peace,
Of comfort in the strife,
  And joys that never cease.

3 We love to sing below
  For mercies freely given;
But most we long to know
  The triumph-song of heaven.
Lord Jesus, give us grace
  On earth to love Thee more,
In heaven to see Thy face,
  And with Thy saints adore.

W Bullock, 1854
Sir H. W. Baker, 1860

Beginning of Service

Johann Crüger, 1649

42 8, 7, 8, 7, 8, 8, 7, 7.

Lord, we hum-bly bow be-fore Thee, In Thy courts on this Thy day;

Help us right-ly to a-dore Thee, Wor-thi-ly to praise and pray:

World-ly cares and thoughts dis-pell-ing, In our hearts Thy Spir-it dwelling;

Teach us meek-ly to o-bey, Learn Thy will, and keep Thy way.

2 Hear, O Lord, our full confession,
　　When to Thee we lift our cry;
　Pardon speak for each transgression;
　　To our suppliant souls draw nigh:
　Thy pure word our hearts directing,
　Thy good grace our steps protecting;
　　Look on us with pitying eye,
　　All we need, O Lord, supply.

Henry Thompson, 1836

43 10, 8, 8, 10, 7.

H. Thomissön's Psalmebog, 1569

Lord God, our Fa - ther, Thou our chief-est stay, Thou art our souls' de - light for aye! O heark - en to our hum - ble prayer: For - give our sins and us in mer - cy spare! Have mer - cy on us, O Lord! Lord! ......

2 Lord Jesus Christ, God's Son, true light and way,
Shepherd of souls, to Thee we pray:
Thou wast for our salvation slain,
Let not Thy death and sufferings be in vain!
Have mercy on us, O Lord!

3 Lord God, the Holy Ghost, Thee we implore
Be with us now and evermore!
Lead us to God, His grace to win,
And leave us not to perish in our sin.
Have mercy on us, O Lord!

Latin. M. B. Landstad, 1861

Beginning of Service

6, 7, 6, 7, 6, 6, 6, 6.

Johann Crüger, 1647

To Thee, O God, we raise Our voice, in cho-ral sing-ing;

We come, with prayer and praise, Our hearts' ob-la-tions bring-ing;

Thou art our fa-thers' God, And e-ver shalt be ours:

Our lips and lives shall laud Thy name, with all our powers.

2 Thy goodness, like the dew
 On Hermon's hill descending,
Is every morning new,
 And tells of love unending.
We bless Thy tender care
 That led our wayward feet,
Past every fatal snare,
 To streams and pastures sweet.

3 We bless Thy Son, who bore
 The cross, for sinners dying;
Thy Spirit we adore,
 The precious blood applying.
Let work and worship send
 Their incense unto Thee,
Till song and service blend,
 Beside the crystal sea.

A. T. Pierson, 1874

Worship in General

45 7, 8, 7, 8, 7, 7.   German, 1656

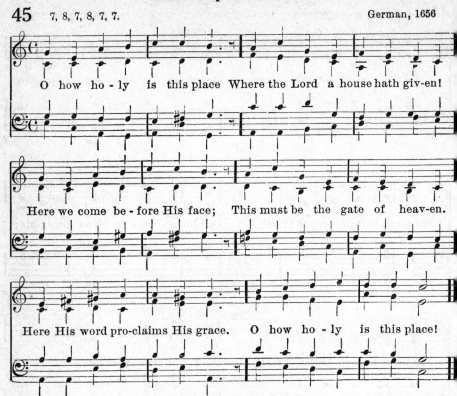

O how ho-ly is this place Where the Lord a house hath giv-en!

Here we come be-fore His face; This must be the gate of heav-en.

Here His word pro-claims His grace. O how ho-ly is this place!

2 Thousand thanks, great God, arise
　Unto Thee, in grace excelling.
Who, though filling all the skies,
　Yet dost make this house Thy dwelling,
　And to us dost here dispense
　Thy pure word and sacraments.

3 Hitherto upon this house
　Hath salvation surely rested.
Here our God hath been with us,
　And Himself hath manifested.
　Here His Spirit He hath given
　To reveal the way to heaven.

4 O how lovely, meet and right
　In His temple to adore Him!
Let us now in Him delight,
　And with gladness come before Him.
　Treasures lasting, precious, pure,
　From above we here secure.

5 Dearest Guest, with us abide,
　With Thy holy word still feed us;
Hitherto by Thee supplied,
　Still by living waters lead us!
　Keep Thy Church on earth secure
　While the earth itself endure.

B. Schmolck, 1712

Close of Service

8, 8, 7, 8, 8, 7. 7. H. Thomissön's Psalmebog 1569

How blest are they who hear God's word, And keep and heed what they have heard: They wis - dom dai - ly gath - er; Their light shines brighter day by day, And while they tread life's wea-ry way, They have the oil of glad - ness To soothe their pain and sad-ness.

2 God's word a treasure is to me,
   Through sorrow's night my sun shall
      The shield of faith in battle;   [be,
   The Father's hand hath written there
   My title as His child and heir,
      "The kingdom's thine forever;"
      That promise faileth never.

3 Today I was my Savior's guest,
   My soul was here so richly blest,
      The bread of life receiving.
   O may thereby my faith prevail,
   So that its fruit shall never fail
      Till my account is given
      Before the throne in heaven.

J. N. Brun, 1786

47   8, 7, 8, 7, 8, 7, 7, 8, 7, 7.

C. E. F. Weyse, 1838

Peace be to thy ev-ery dwel-ling, Ci - ty by Je - ho - vah blest;

Who, His grace to thee re-veal-ing Thee pre-serves in peace and rest.

May His pres-ence still at-tend thee; May'st thou sit by day and night

In His shadow with de-light; His all-power-ful arm de-fend thee;

Prize, O prize, thy lot of grace; Live un - to thy Sav-ior's praise.

Close of Service

2 Lord, we fervently implore Thee,
That, while pilgrims here below,
We may walk in truth before Thee,
And in all Thy knowledge grow;
Showing forth Thy matchless praises;
Thou who, out of sin's dark night,
Hast to Thine own marvelous light
Called Thy people, O Lord Jesus:
Keep and seal us ever Thine,
Leave with us Thy peace divine.

C. A. Pohlman, 1826

48 8, 7, 8, 7, 4, 4, 7.

Henry Smart, 1867

Lord, dis-miss us with Thy bless-ing, Fill our hearts with joy and peace!

Let us each, Thy love pos-sess-ing, Tri-umph in re - deem-ing grace.

O re-fresh us, O refresh us, Traveling through this wil-der-ness.

2 Thanks we give and adoration
For Thy gospel's joyful sound.
May the fruits of Thy salvation
In our hearts and lives abound.
‖:May Thy presence:‖
With us evermore be found.

3 So, whene'er the signal's given
Us from earth to call away,
Borne on angels' wings to heaven,
Glad the summons to obey,
‖:May we ready,:‖
Rise and reign in endless day.

J. Fawcett, 1773

49 7s. 6L.

J P. E. Hartmann, 1852

Peace, to soothe our bit-ter woes, God in Christ on

us be-stows; Je - sus bought our peace with God

With His ho - ly, pre - cious blood; Peace in Him for

sin - ners found, Is the gos - pel's joy - ful sound.

2 Peace to us the Church doth tell,
'Tis her welcome and farewell:
Peace was our baptismal dower,
Peace shall bless our dying hour;
Peace be with you, full and free,
Now and through eternity.

N. F. S. Grundtvig. 1845

Close of Service

50 8, 6, 8, 6, 8, 8, 8, 6.

Ludv. M. Lindeman, 1812—87

How bless-ed is the lit-tle flock, Whom Je-sus calls His own!

He is their Sav-ior and their rock, They trust in Him a-lone; They

walk by faith and hope and love, But they shall dwell with Him a-bove,

When hope and faith shall pass a-way, And love shall last for aye.

2 My Jesus, am I in that band,
　And wilt Thou call me Thine?
Do I among the chosen stand
　Whose lamps so brightly shine?
O let me not lie down to rest
Till this I know, my Savior blest,
Till I can say, by grace restored:
　"Thou know'st I love Thee, Lord!"

3 And even if with tears it be,
　That this to Thee I say,
Yet Thou in grace wilt look on me
　And wipe my tears away;
Yea, when but Thou who all dost know
In me canst find Thy love below
And own me Thine, then well is me,—
　My all I have in Thee.

N. J. Holm. 1829

51 11, 9, 11, 9, 5, 5, 9.

Ludv. M. Lindeman, 1812—87

And now we must bid one an-oth-er fare-well;

The peace of our God keep you ev-er!

God's peace in our bos-om, and all will be well,

Or wheth-er we meet or we sev-er.

May Christ, our dear Lord, Be our sure re-ward

Close of Service

When we from this world pass for - ev - er!

2 O help us, dear Father, and Christ, Thou the Son,
   That gladly our course we may finish!
   And Thou, Holy Spirit, Thou comforting One,
   Thy love in our hearts so replenish,
     That we by Thy might
      May fight the good fight,
   Till won is the crown everlasting.

Martha Clausen, ca. 1830

52   C. M.

Nicolaus Hermann, 1560

O hap - py day when we shall stand A - mid the heavenly
throng, And sing with hosts from eve - ry land The
new ce - les - tial song, The new ce - les - tial song.

2 O blessed day! From far and near
   The servants of the Lord
   Shall meet the ransomed millions there
   ‖: Who heard God's saving word.:‖

3 O what a mighty, rushing flood
   Of love without surcease,

Shall roll about the throne of God
‖:In joy and endless peace!:‖

4 God, may Thy bounteous grace inspire
  Our hearts so that we may
  All join the heavenly, white-robed
  ‖:Upon that glorious day.:‖ [choir

51

W. A. Wexels, 1846

Worship in General

53 8, 7, 8, 7, 7, 7, 8, 8. Louis Bourgeois, 1551

Praise to Thee and ad - o - ra - tion, Bless - ed Je - sus, Son of God, Who, to serve Thine own cre - a - tion, Didst par - take of flesh and blood; Teach me that I nev - er may From Thy fold or pastures stray, But with zeal and joy ex - ceed - ing Fol - low where Thy steps are lead - ing.

Close of Service

2 Let me never, Lord, forsake Thee,
    E'en though bitter pain and strife
On my way shall overtake me;
    But may I through all my life
Walk in fervent love to Thee,
In all woes for comfort flee
To Thy birth, Thy death and passion;
Till I see Thy full salvation.

T. Kingo, 1689

54 10s, 4 L.

E. J. Hopkins, 1867

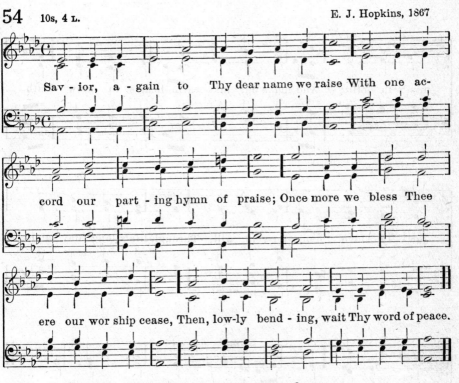

Sav - ior, a - gain to Thy dear name we raise With one accord our part - ing hymn of praise; Once more we bless Thee
ere our wor ship cease, Then, low-ly bend - ing, wait Thy word of peace.

2 Grant us Thy peace upon our homeward way;
  With Thee began, with Thee shall end the day;
  Guard Thou the lips from sin, the hearts from shame,
  That in this house have called upon Thy name.

3 Grant us Thy peace, Lord, through the coming night,
  Turn Thou for us its darkness into light;
  From harm and danger keep Thy children free,
  For dark and light are both alike to Thee.

4 Grant us Thy peace throughout our earthly life,
  Our balm in sorrow and our stay in strife;
  Then, when Thy voice shall bid our conflict cease,
  Call us, O Lord, to Thine eternal peace.

J. Ellerton, 1866

55 L. M. 6L.

W. H. Monk, 1861

Sweet Sav-ior, bless us ere we go; Thy word in-to our minds in-still; And make our luke-warm hearts to glow With low-ly love and fer-vent will. Through life's long day and death's dark night, O gen-tle Je-sus, be our light.

2 The day is gone, its hours have run,
And Thou hast taken count of all,
The scanty triumphs grace hath won,
The broken vow, the frequent fall.
Through life's long day and death's dark night,
O gentle Jesus, be our light.

Close of Service

3 Grant us, dear Lord, from evil ways
  True absolution and release,
And bless us, more than in past days,
  With purity and inward peace,
Through life's long day and death's dark night,
  O gentle Jesus, be our light.

4 For all we love, the poor, the sad,
  The sinful, unto Thee we call;
O let Thy mercy make us glad;
  Thou art our Savior, and our all.
Through life's long day and death's dark night,
  O gentle Jesus, be our light.

5 Sweet Savior, bless us; night is come;
  Through night and darkness near us be;
Good angels watch about our home,
  And we are one day nearer Thee.
Through life's long day and death's dark night.
  O gentle Jesus, be our light.

F. W. Faber, 1849

56 L. M.

Louis Bourgeois, 1547

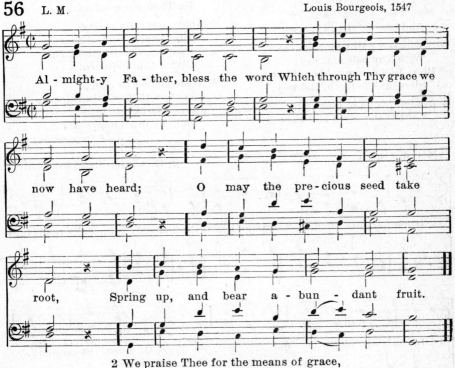

Al - might-y Fa - ther, bless the word Which through Thy grace we now have heard; O may the pre - cious seed take root, Spring up, and bear a - bun - dant fruit.

2 We praise Thee for the means of grace,
  As in Thy courts we seek Thy face.
Grant, Lord, that we who worship here
  May all, at last, in heaven appear.

Anon

Worship in General

57 7, 6, 7, 6.

Melchior Vulpius, 1609

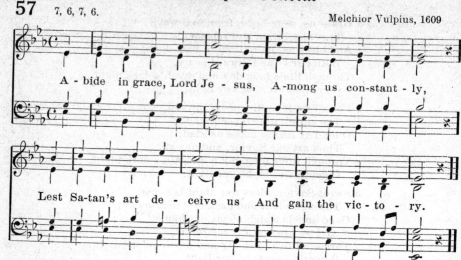

A - bide in grace, Lord Je - sus, A - mong us con-stant - ly,

Lest Sa-tan's art de - ceive us And gain the vic - to - ry.

2 Abide, Lord, with the story
Of Thy redeeming love;
May we the gospel's glory
And saving virtue prove.

3 Abide, our pathway brighten
With Thy celestial ray;
Blest Light, our souls enlighten,
Show us the truth, the way.

4 Abide with us in blessing,
Lord of the earth and sky;

Rich grace and strength possessing,
Do Thou our need supply!

5 Abide, our only safety,
Thy people's sure defence;
No power can withstand Thee
Divine Omnipotence!

6 Abide among us ever,
Lord, with Thy faithfulness;
Jesus, forsake us never,
Help us in all distress!

J. Stegmann, 1627

58 8, 7, 8, 7.

J. H. Schein's Cantional, 1627.

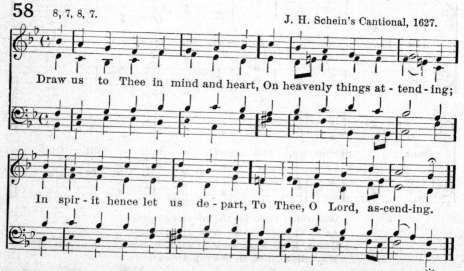

Draw us to Thee in mind and heart, On heavenly things at - tend-ing;

In spir - it hence let us de - part, To Thee, O Lord, as-cend-ing.

Close of Service

2 Draw us to Thee, O Christ, and guide
  Our erring feet to heaven;
  If Thou, O Lord, with us abide,
    Light to our path is given.

3 Draw us to Thee, O Thou whose love
  The angels praise adoring;

Receive our souls to Thee above,
  Thy name in death imploring.

4 Draw us to Thee, grant us to rise
  To yon abodes of glory;
  On Thee to rest our joyful eyes,
  And fall in praise before Thee.

F. Funcke, 1686

59   8, 7, 8, 7, 7, 7.

J. Chr. Bach, 1693

Sav - ior, now the day is end-ing, And the shades of eve-ning fall,

Let Thy heaven-ly Dove, de-scend-ing, Bring Thy mer-cy to us all;

Set Thy seal on ev-ery heart, Je - sus, bless us ere we part!

2 Bless the gospel message, spoken
  In Thine own appointed way;
  Give each fainting soul a token
  Of Thy tender love today;
  Set Thy seal on every heart,
  Jesus, bless us ere we part!

3 Comfort those in pain or sorrow,
  Watch each sleeping child of Thine;
  Let us all arise tomorrow

Strengthened by Thy grace divine;
Set Thy seal on every heart,
Jesus, bless us ere we part!

4 Pardon Thou each deed unholy;
  Lord, forgive each sinful thought;
  Make us contrite, pure, and lowly,
  By Thy great example taught:
  Set Thy seal on every heart,
  Jesus, bless us ere we part.

Sarah Doudney, 1871

60 10, 10, 11, 11.

W. Croft, 1678—1727

O wor-ship the King all-glorious a-bove; O grate-ful-ly sing His power and His love; Our shield and de-fend-er, the An-cient of Days, Pa-vil-ioned in splendor, and gird-ed with praise.

2 O tell of His might, O sing of His grace!
Whose robe is the light, whose canopy, space.
His chariots of wrath the deep thunderclouds form,
And dark is His path on the wings of the storm.

3 The earth, with its store of wonders untold,
Almighty, Thy power hath founded of old,
Hath 'stablished it fast by a changeless decree,
And round it hath cast, like a mantle, the sea.

4 Thy bountiful care, what tongue can recite?
It breathes in the air, it shines in the light,
It streams from the hills, it descends to the plain,
And sweetly distills in the dew and the rain.

5 Frail children of dust, and feeble as frail,
In Thee do we trust, nor find Thee to fail.
Thy mercies how tender! how firm to the end!
Our Maker, Defender, Redeemer, and Friend!

6 O measureless Might! ineffable Love!
While angels delight to hymn Thee above,
The humbler creation, though feeble their lays,
With true adoration shall sing to Thy praise.

Sir R. Grant. 1833

His Majesty and Glory

61   7, 6.   8L.

Samuel S. Wesley, 1864

O God, the Rock of A - ges, Who ev - er - more hast been,

What time the tem-pest ra - ges, Our dwell-ing-place se - rene;

Be - fore Thy first cre - a - tions, O Lord, the same as now,

To end - less gen - er - a - tions The Ev - er - last - ing, Thou!

2 Our years are like the shadows
    On sunny hills that lie,
Or grasses in the meadows
    That blossom but to die:
A sleep, a dream, a story
    By strangers quickly told,
An unremaining glory
    Of things that soon are old.

3 O Thou, who canst not slumber,
    Whose light grows never pale,
Teach us aright to number
    Our years before they fail;

On us Thy mercy lighten,
    On us Thy goodness rest,
And let Thy Spirit brighten
    The hearts Thyself hast blessed.

4 Lord, crown our faith's endeavor
    With beauty and with grace,
Till, clothed in light for ever,
    We see Thee face to face;
A joy no language measures,
    A fountain brimming o'er,
An endless flow of pleasures,
    An ocean without shore.

62 8, 7. 8L.

H. Smart, 1812—79

Lord, Thy glo - ry fills the heav-en; Earth is with its ful-ness stored;

Un - to Thee be glo - ry giv - en, Ho - ly, ho - ly, ho-ly Lord.

Heaven is still with an-thems ringing; Earth takes up the an-gels' cry,

Ho - ly, ho - ly, ho - ly, sing-ing, Lord of hosts, Thou Lord most high.

His Majesty and Glory

2 Ever thus in God's high praises,
  Brethren, let our tongues unite,
While our thoughts His greatness
    raises,
  And our love His gifts excite:
With His seraph train before Him,
  With His holy Church below,
Thus unite we to adore Him,
  Bid we thus our anthem flow.

3 Lord, Thy glory fills the heaven;
  Earth is with its fulness stored;
Unto Thee be glory given,
  Holy, holy, holy Lord.
Thus Thy glorious name confessing,
  We adopt the angels' cry,
Holy, holy, holy blessing
  Thee, the Lord our God most high.

R. Mant, 1837

53   7, 7, 7, 7.   J. A. Freylinghausen, 1704

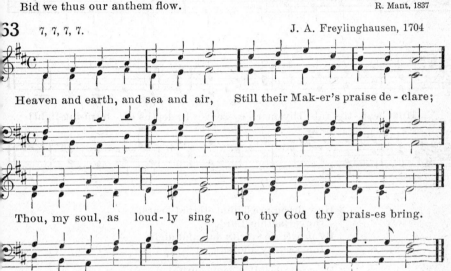

Heaven and earth, and sea and air,   Still their Mak-er's praise de-clare;

Thou, my soul, as loud-ly sing,   To thy God thy prais-es bring.

2 See, the sun his power awakes,
  As through clouds his glory breaks;
  See the moon and stars of light,
  Praising God in stillest night.

3 See how God this rolling globe
  Swathes with beauty as a robe;
  Forests, fields, and living things,
  Each its Master's glory sings.

4 Through the air Thy praises meet,
  Birds are singing clear and sweet;
  Fire, and storm, and wind, Thy will
  As Thy ministers fulfill.

5 The ocean waves Thy glory tell,
  At Thy touch they sing and swell;
  From the well-spring to the sea,
  Rivers murmur, Lord, of Thee.

6 O my God, what wonders lie
  Hid in Thine infinity!
  Stamp upon my inmost heart
  What I am, and what Thou art.

J. Neander, 1680

God

64 C. M.

Scotch Psalter, 1615

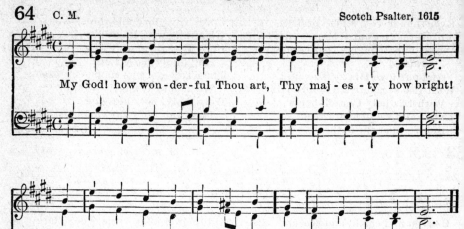

My God! how won-der-ful Thou art, Thy maj-es-ty how bright!

How beau-ti-ful Thy mer-cy-seat In depths of burn-ing light!

2 How dread are Thine eternal years,
    O everlasting Lord,
 By prostrate spirits day and night
    Incessantly adored!

3 How wonderful, how beautiful,
    The sight of Thee must be,
 Thine endless wisdom, boundless power,
    And awful purity!

4 O how I fear Thee, living God!
    With deepest, tenderest fears,
 And worship Thee with trembling hope,
    And penitential tears!

5 Yet, I may love Thee too, O Lord!
    Almighty as Thou art,
 For Thou hast stooped to ask of me
    The love of my poor heart.

6 No earthly father loves like Thee,
    No mother e'er so mild,
 Bears and forbears, as Thou hast done
    With me, Thy sinful child.

7 My God, how wonderful Thou art,
    Thou everlasting Friend!
 On Thee I stay my trusting heart,
    Till faith in vision end.

F. W. Faber, 1849

His Goodness and Love

65 S. M.

Arr. fr. R. Schumann, 1810—1856

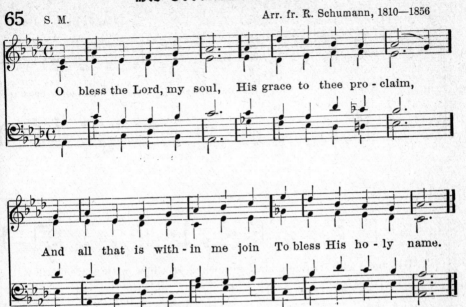

O bless the Lord, my soul, His grace to thee pro - claim,

And all that is with - in me join To bless His ho - ly name.

2 O bless the Lord, my soul;
   His mercies bear in mind;
 Forget not all His benefits:
   The Lord to thee is kind.

3 He will not always chide;
   He will with patience wait;
 His wrath is ever slow to rise,
   And ready to abate.

4 He pardons all thy sins;
   Prolongs thy feeble breath;
 He heals all thine infirmities,
   And ransoms thee from death.

5 He clothes thee with His love;
   Upholds thee with His truth;
 And like the eagle He renews
   The vigor of thy youth.

6 Then bless His holy name,
   Whose grace hath made thee whole,
 Whose lovingkindness crowns thy days:
   O bless the Lord, my soul!

J. Montgomery, 1819

66 C. M. 8L.

F. A. J. Hervey, 1867

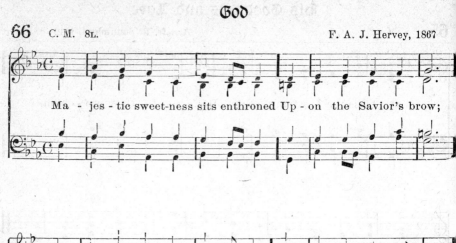

Ma - jes - tic sweet-ness sits enthroned Up - on the Savior's brow;

His head with ra-diant glories crowned, His lips with grace o'erflow.

No mortal can with Him com-pare, A-mong the sons of men;

Fair - er is He than all the fair That fill the heaven-ly train.

His Goodness and Love

2 He saw me plunged in deep distress,
   He flew to my relief;
For me He bore the shameful cross,
   And carried all my grief.
To Him I owe my life and breath,
   And all the joys I have;
He makes me triumph over death,
   He saves me from the grave.

3 To heaven, the place of His abode
   He brings my weary feet;
Shows me the glories of my God,
   And makes my joy complete.
Since from His bounty I receive
   Such proofs of love divine,
Had I a thousand hearts to give,
   Lord, they should all be Thine.

S. Stennett, 1787

67 L. M.

S. Webbe, 1782

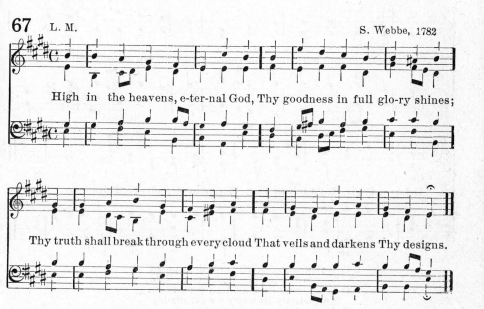

High in the heavens, e-ter-nal God, Thy goodness in full glo-ry shines;

Thy truth shall break through every cloud That veils and darkens Thy designs.

2 Forever firm Thy justice stands,
   As mountains their foundations keep;
Wise are the wonders of Thy hands;
   Thy judgments are a mighty deep.

3 My God, how excellent Thy grace,
   Whence all our hope and comfort spring!
The sons of Adam in distress
   Fly to the shadow of Thy wing.

4 Life, like a fountain rich and free,
   Springs from the presence of my Lord;
And in Thy light our souls shall see
   The glorious promise in Thy word.

I. Watts, 1719

68 8s. 6L.

J. H. Schein, 1586—1630

O Love, who formedst me to wear The im-age of Thy God-head here;

Who soughtest me with ten - der care Through all my wanderings wild and drear;

O Love, I give my-self to Thee, Thine ev-er, on - ly Thine to be.

2 O Love, who ere life's earliest morn
   On me Thy choice hast gently laid,
O Love, who here as man wast born,
   And wholly like to us wast made;
O Love, I give myself to Thee,
Thine ever, only Thine to be.

3 O Love, who once in time wast slain
   Pierced through and through with bitter woe
O Love, who wrestling thus didst gain
   That we eternal joy might know;
O Love, I give myself to Thee,
Thine ever, only Thine to be.

4 O Love, who lovedst me for aye,
   Who for my soul dost ever plead,
O Love, who didst that ransom pay
   Whose power sufficeth in my stead;
O Love, I give myself to Thee,
Thine ever, only Thine to be.

5 O Love, who once shalt bid me rise
   From out this dying life of ours;
O Love, who once o'er yonder skies
   Shalt set me in the fadeless bowers;
O Love, I give myself to Thee,
Thine ever, only Thine to be.

J. Scheffler, 1657

His Goodness and Love

69 S. M.

Arr. fr. R. Schumann, 1810—1856

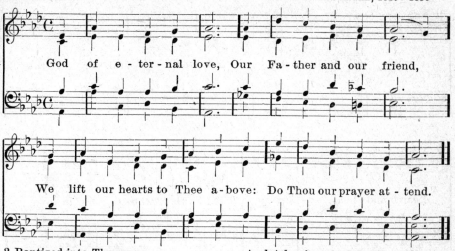

God of e-ter-nal love, Our Fa-ther and our friend,

We lift our hearts to Thee a-bove: Do Thou our prayer at-tend.

2 Baptized into Thy name,
  We all have Christ put on:
  O may Thy love our hearts inflame,
  The course of truth to run.

3 May earthly feelings die,
  And fruits of faith increase;

And Adam's nature prostrate lie
  Before the Prince of Peace.

4 Endue us, Lord, with strength,
  To triumph over sin:
  That we may with Thy saints at length
  Eternal glory win.

Seaton's Church H. B., 1855

70 C. M.

Albert L. Peace, 1885

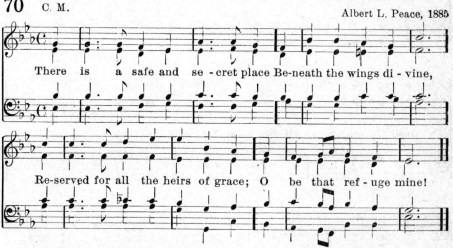

There is a safe and se-cret place Be-neath the wings di-vine,

Re-served for all the heirs of grace; O be that ref-uge mine!

2 The least and feeblest there may bide
  Uninjured and unawed;
  While thousands fall on every side,
  He rests secure in God.

3 He feeds in pastures large and fair
  Of love and truth divine;

O child of God, O glory's heir,
  How rich a lot is thine!

4 A hand almighty to defend,
  An ear for every call,
  An honored life, a peaceful end,
  And heaven to crown it all!

37

H. F. Lyte, 1834

71   8s. 10L.   (1417) Johann Walter, 1524

We all be-lieve in one true God, Mak - er of the
earth and heav - - en; The Fa-ther, who to us in love
Hath the right of chil-dren giv - en; He both soul and bod - y
feed - eth, All we want He doth pro - vide us;
He through snares and per - ils lead - eth, Watching that no

His Trinity

harm be - tide us; He cares for us by

day and night, All things are gov-erned by His might.

2 And we believe in Jesus Christ,
　His own Son, our Lord, possessing
An equal Godhead, throne, and might,
　Through whom comes the Father's blessing;
Of the Holy Ghost conceivéd,
　Born of Mary, virgin-mother,
That lost man might life inherit,
　Made true man, our Elder Brother,
Was crucified for sinful men,
And raised by God to life again.

3 Also the Holy Ghost we own,
　Who sweet grace and comfort giveth,
And with the Father and the Son
　In eternal glory liveth;
Who the Christian Church doth even
　Keep in unity of spirit;
Sins are truly here forgiven
　Through the blest Redeemer's merit:
All flesh shall rise again, and we
Shall live with God eternally.

M. Luther, 1524

God

72 11, 12, 12, 10.

John B. Dykes, 1860

Ho - ly, ho - ly, ho - ly, Lord God Al - might - y!

Ear - ly in the morn - ing our song shall rise to Thee;

Ho - ly, ho - ly, ho - ly! mer - ci - ful and might - y!

God in three per - sons, bless - ed Trin - i - ty!

2 Holy, holy, holy, all the saints adore Thee,
   Casting down their golden crowns around the glassy sea;
Cherubim and seraphim falling down before Thee,
   Which wert, and art, and evermore shalt be.

3 Holy, holy, holy! though the darkness hide Thee,
   Though the eye of sinful man Thy glory may not see:
Only Thou art holy; there is none beside Thee,
   Perfect in power, in love and purity.

His Trinity

4 Holy, holy, holy, Lord God Almighty!
  All Thy works shall praise Thy name, in earth and sky and sea;
  Holy, holy, holy, merciful and mighty!
  God in three persons, blessed Trinity!

R. Heber, 1827

73 6, 6, 4, 6, 6, 6, 4.

Felice de Giardini, 1769

Come, Thou al-might-y King, Help us Thy name to sing
Help us to praise! Fa-ther all glo-ri-ous, O'er all vic-
to-ri-ous, Come and reign o-ver us, An-cient of Days!

2 Jesus, our Lord, descend;
  From all our foes defend,
     Nor let us fall;
  Let Thine almighty aid
  Our sure defense be made:
  Our souls on Thee be stayed;
     Lord, hear our call!

3 Come, Thou incarnate Word,
  Gird on Thy mighty sword,
     Our prayer attend.
  Come and Thy people bless,
  And give Thy word success;
  Spirit of holiness,
     On us descend.

4 Come, holy Comforter,
  Thy sacred witness bear
     In this glad hour;
  Thou who almighty art,
  Now rule in every heart,
  And ne'er from us depart,
     Spirit of power!

5 To the great One in Three
  Eternal praises be,
     Hence evermore;
  His sovereign majesty
  May we in glory see,
  And to eternity
     Love and adore.

Anon. ca. 1757

74 11, 10. 4L.
E. J. Hopkins, 1818—1901.

An - cient of Days, who sittest throned in glo - ry; To Thee all
knees are bent, all voi-ces pray; Thy love hath blest the
wide world's wondrous sto - ry With light and life since E-den's dawning day.

2 O Holy Father, who hast led Thy children
  In all the ages, with the Fire and Cloud,
  Through seas, dry-shod, through weary wastes bewildering;
  To Thee, in reverent love, our hearts are bowed.

3 O Holy Jesus, Prince of Peace, and Savior,
  To Thee we owe the peace that still prevails,
  Stilling the rude wills of men's wild behavior,
  And calming passion's wild and stormy gales.

4 O Holy Ghost, the Lord and the Life-Giver,
  Thine is the quickening power that gives increase:
  From Thee have flowed, as from a pleasant river,
  Our plenty, wealth, prosperity, and peace.

5 O Triune God, with heart and voice adoring,
  Praise we the goodness that doth crown our days;
  Pray we, that Thou wilt hear us, still imploring
  Thy love and favor, kept to us always.

W. C. Doane, 1886

75 11, 11, 11, 5,

1584, Johann Crüger, 1640

Fa - ther most ho - ly,   mer - ci - ful and ten - der;   Je - sus our

Sav - ior, with the Fa - ther reign - ing; Spir - it of

mer - cy, Ad - vo - cate, de - fend - er, Light nev - er wan - ing;

2 Trinity sacred, Unity unshaken:
    Deity perfect, giving and forgiving,
  Light of the angels, Life of the forsaken,
    Hope of all living;

3 Maker of all things, all Thy creatures praise Thee;
    Lo, all things serve Thee through Thy whole creation:
  Hear us, Almighty, hear us as we raise Thee
    Heart's adoration.

4 To the almighty triune God be glory:
    Highest and greatest, help Thou our endeavor;
  We, too, would praise Thee, giving honor worthy,
    Now and for ever.

Latin, Anon., 10th Century

76 8, 7, 7, 7, 7, 7.

Darmstadt-Gesangbuch, 1699

We all be-lieve in one true God, Father, Son, and Ho-ly Ghost,

Pres - ent help-er in all need, Praised by all the heav'nly host.

By whose mighty power a - lone   All is made, and wisely done.

2 And we believe in Jesus Christ,
    Son of God and Mary's Son,
Who descended from His throne,
    And for us salvation won;
By whose death and agony
We are saved from misery.

3 And we confess the Holy Ghost,
    Who from Father, Son proceeds;
Who upholds and comforts us
    In the midst of fears and needs;
Blest and holy Trinity,
Praise forever be to Thee!

T. Clausnitzer, 1668

The Church

8, 7. 8L.

H. Smart, 1867

Praise the Rock of our sal - va-tion, Laud His name from zone to zone;

On that rock the Church is build-ed, Christ him-self the cor - ner-stone;

Vain a-gainst our rock-built Zi - on Winds and wa-ters, fire and hail;

Christ is in her midst; a-gainst her Sin and hell shall not pre - vail.

2 Built of living stones, cemented
  By the Spirit's unity,
Based on prophets and apostles,
  Firm in faith and stayed on Thee,
May Thy Church, O Lord Incarnate,
  Grow in grace, in peace, in love;
Emblem of the heavenly Zion,
  The Jerusalem above.

3 Where Thou reignest, King of Glory,
  Throned in everlasting light,
Midst Thy saints, no more is needed
  Sun by day, nor moon by night:
Soon may we those portals enter
  When this earthly strife is o'er;
There to dwell with saints and angels,
  In Thy presence evermore.

B. Webb, 1872

The Church

7, 6, 8L.

Samuel S. Wesley, 1864

The Church's one foun-da-tion Is Je-sus Christ her Lord;

She is His new cre-a-tion By wa-ter and the word;

From heaven He came and sought her To be His ho-ly bride;

With His own blood He bought her, And for her life He died.

2 Elect from every nation,
   Yet one o'er all the earth,
Her charter of salvation
   One Lord, one faith, one birth;
One holy name she blesses,
   Partakes one holy food,
And to one hope she presses,
   With every grace endued.

3 Though with a scornful wonder
   Men see her sore oppressed,
By schisms rent asunder,
   By heresies distressed;
Yet saints their watch are keeping,
   Their cry goes up, "How long?"
And soon the night of weeping
   Shall be the morn of song.

Foundation and Nature

4 'Mid toil and tribulation,
   And tumult of her war,
 She waits the consummation
   Of peace for evermore;
 Till with the vision glorious
   Her longing eyes are blest,
 And the great Church victorious
   Shall be the Church at rest.

5 Yet she on earth hath union
   With God the Three in One,
 And mystic sweet communion
   With those whose rest is won;
 O happy ones and holy!
   Lord, give us grace, that we,
 Like them, the meek and lowly,
   On high may dwell with Thee!

S. J. Stone, 1868

79 8, 7, 8, 7, 8, 8, 8   14th cent. N. Decius, d. 1541

Thou ho-ly Church, God's cit-y, shine, High on His moun-tain found-ed!

Sing praise to Christ, thy king di-vine, Who thee with walls sur-

round-ed; Thy chil-dren He doth bless and sends His

peace to thee, thy strife He ends: Now praise thy God, O Zi-on!

2 He sendeth out His holy word
   To every land and nation,
 It swiftly runs, 'tis from the Lord
   His message of salvation;
 The hearts that were like ice and snow,
 It melts so that in streams they flow
   With tears of true repentance.

3 Who now but will himself deny,
   And yield to God submission,
 His word receive, on Christ rely,
   Obtains a full remission;
 He is converted and made wise,
 And goes from hence to Paradise:
   Grant us this grace, O Savior!

M. B. Landstad, 1861

The Church

8, 9, 8, 8, 9, 8, 6, 6, 4, 4, 4, 8.

P. Nicolai, 1599

By the ho - ly hills sur - round - ed, On her firm base se - cure-ly found - ed, Stands fast the cit - y of the Lord; None shall rend her walls a - sun - der; On her men look with fear and won - der; And mark who here keeps watch and ward. He slum-bers not, nor sleeps,

Foundation and Nature

Who His loved Is-rael keeps. Hal - le - lu - jah! Hap-

py the race Who through God's grace Shall have in her their dwelling place!

2 Zion's gates Jehovah loveth,
    And with especial grace approveth;
        He maketh fast her bolts and bars;
    Those who dwell in her He blesses,
    And comforts them in their distresses
        Who cast on Him their griefs and cares.
    How wonderful the grace
    With which He doth embrace
        All His people!
    City of God,
    How sweet the abode
    On which such blessings are bestowed!

3 Taught in thee is a salvation
    Unknown to every other nation;
        There great and holy things are heard;
    In the midst of thee abiding,
    Enlightening, comforting, and guiding,
        Thou hast the Spirit and the word;
    There breathing peace around
    Is heard the joyful sound,
        Grace and mercy!
    How sweet that is
    Which here speaks peace,
    There crowns with everlasting bliss.

4 Mother thou of every nation
    Which here hath sought and found salvation,
        O Zion, yet on earth shalt be:
    Hark, what shouts the air are rending!
    What cries to heaven's gates ascending!
        All our fresh springs shall be in thee.
    From thee the waters burst,
    To slake our burning thirst,
        Hallelujah!
    From sin and death
    God's own word saith
    That He alone delivereth.

C. J. P. Spitta, 1843

79

The Church

8, 7. 8L.

J. A. Freylinghausen's Gesangbuch, 1704

Christ a - lone is our sal - va - tion, Christ the rock on which we stand;

Oth - er than this sure foun-da - tion Will be found but sink-ing sand.

Christ, His cross and re - sur - rec - tion, Is a - lone the sin-ner's plea;

At the throne of God's per - fec - tion Noth-ing else can set him free.

2 We have all things, Christ possessing;
    Life eternal, second birth;
Present pardon, peace, and blessing,
    While we tarry here on earth;
And by faith's anticipation,
    Foretaste of the joy above,
Freely given us with salvation,
    By the Father in His love.

3 When we perfect joy shall enter,
    'Tis in Him our bliss will rise;
He's the essence, soul, and center
    Of the glory in the skies:
In redemption's wondrous story
    Planned before our parents' fall,
From the cross unto the glory,
    Jesus Christ is all in all.

                       Anon.

82   C. M.   Este's Psalter, 1592

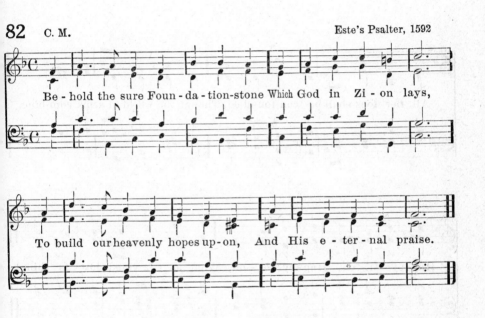

Be - hold the sure Foun - da - tion-stone Which God in Zi - on lays,
To build our heavenly hopes up - on, And His e - ter - nal praise.

2 Chosen of God, to sinners dear,
    Let saints adore the Name;
They trust their whole salvation here
    Nor shall they suffer shame.

3 The foolish builders, scribe and priest,
    Reject it with disdain;
Yet on this Rock the Church shall rest,
    And envy rage in vain.

4 What though the gates of hell withstood
    Yet must this building rise:
'Tis Thine own work, almighty God,
    And wondrous in our eyes.

                    I. Watts, 1719

The Church

83 8, 7, 8, 7, 4, 4, 7.

Henry Smart, 1867

Zi - on stands with hills sur-round-ed; Zi - on kept by power di-vine

All her foes shall be con-found-ed, Though the world in arms com-bine.

Hap-py Zi - on, Hap-py Zi - on, What a fa-vored lot is thine!

2 Every human tie may perish;
  Friend to friend unfaithful prove;
Mothers cease their own to cherish;
  Heaven and earth at last remove:
    ‖:But no changes:‖
  Can attend Jehovah's love.

3 In the furnace God may prove thee,
  Thence to bring thee forth more bright,
But can never cease to love thee;
  Thou art precious in His sight:
    ‖:God is with thee:‖
  God, thine everlasting light.

T. Kelly, 1806

Its Strength and Permanence

84 11, 11, 11, 5.

1584, Johann Crüger, 1640

Lord of our life, and God of our sal-va-tion, Star of our night, and hope of ev-ery na-tion, Hear and re-ceive Thy Church's sup-pli-ca-tion, Lord God Al-mighty.

2 See round Thine Ark the hungry billows curling,
See how Thy foes their banners are unfurling;
Lord, while their darts envenomed they are hurling,
Thou canst preserve us.

3 Lord, Thou canst help when earthly armor faileth;
Lord, Thou canst save when deadly sin assaileth;
Lord, o'er Thy Church nor death nor hell prevaileth:
Grant us Thy peace, Lord.

4 Peace in our hearts, our evil thoughts assuaging,
Peace in Thy Church where brothers are engaging,
Peace, when the world its busy war is waging,
Send us, O Savior.

5 Grant us Thy help till foes are backward driven;
Grant them Thy truth, that they may be forgiven;
Grant peace on earth, and, after we have striven,
Peace in Thy heaven.

Philip Pusey, 1840; based on. M. A. von Löwenstern, 1644

The Church

85 8, 8, 7. 6L.

German, 1530

Be not dis-mayed, thou lit - tle flock, Al - though the foe's fierce bat - tle-shock Loud on all sides as - sail thee; Though o'er thy fall they laugh se - cure, Their tri - umph can - not long en - dure: Let not thy cour - age fail thee.

2 Thy cause is God's; go at His call,
And to His hand commit thy all;
Fear thou no ill impending:
His Gideon shall arise for thee,
God's word and people manfully
In God's own time defending.

Its Strength and Permanence

3 Our hope is sure in Jesus' might;
    Against themselves the godless fight,
        Themselves, not us, distressing;
    Shame and contempt their lot shall be:
    God is with us, with Him are we,
        To us belongs His blessing.

                        J. M. Altenburg, 1632

Older Form.   8, 8, 7.   6L.   German, 1530

Be not dis-mayed, thou lit-tle flock, Although the foe's fierce bat-tle-shock Loud on all sides........ as-sail thee; Though o'er thy fall they laugh se-cure, Their tri-umph can-not long en-dure: Let not thy cour - - age fail thee.

The Church

8, 7. 8L.

H. Smart, 1812—79

Through the night of doubt and sor-row On-ward goes the pil-grim band,

Sing-ing songs of ex-pec-ta-tion, March-ing to the Promised Land.

Clear be-fore us, through the dark-ness, Gleams and burns the guiding light.

Brother clasps the hand of brother, Stepping fear-less through the night.

2 One the light of God's own presence,
  O'er His ransomed people shed,
Chasing far the gloom and terror,
  Brightening all the path we tread:
One the object of our journey,
  One the faith which never tires,
One the earnest looking forward,
  One the hope our God inspires.

Its Strength and Permanence

3 One the strain the lips of thousands
    Lift as from the heart of one;
One the conflict, one the peril,
    One the march in God begun:
One the gladness of rejoicing
    On the far eternal shore,
Where the One Almighty Father
    Reigns in love for evermore.

4 Onward therefore, pilgrim brothers!
    Onward, with the cross our aid!
Bear its shame and fight its battle,
    Till we rest beneath its shade!
Soon shall come the great awaking
    Soon the rending of the tomb,
Then the scattering of all shadows,
    And the end of toil and gloom.

B. S. Ingemann, 1843

87   8, 7, 8, 7, 7, 7.   Heinrich Albert, 1643

Rise, ye children of sal-va-tion, All who cleave to Christ the Head!

Wake, a-rise, O mighty na-tion, Ere the foe on Zi-on tread:

He draws nigh, and would de-fy All the hosts of God most high.

2 Saints and heroes, long before us,
    Firmly on this ground have stood;
See their banner waving o'er us,
    Conquerors through the Savior's
        blood!
Ground we hold, whereon of old,
Fought the faithful and the bold.

3 Fighting, we shall be victorious
    By the blood of Christ our Lord;
On our foreheads, bright and glorious,

Shines the witness of His word;
Spear and shield, on battlefield,
His great name: We cannot yield.

4 When His servants stand before Him,
    Each receiving his reward,
When His saints in light adore Him,
    Giving glory to the Lord,
"Victory!" our cry shall be,
Like the thunder of the sea.

J. Falckner. 1697

The Church

8, 7. 8L.

F. J. Haydn, 1797

Glorious things of thee are spok-en, Zi - on, cit - y of our God;

He, whose word can-not be brok-en, Formed thee for His own a - bode,

On the Rock of A - ges found-ed, What can shake thy sure re-pose!

With sal-va - tion's walls sur-rounded, Thou may'st smile at all thy foes.

2 See the streams of living waters
    Springing from eternal love,
Well supply thy sons and daughters,
    And all fear of want remove.
Who can faint while such a river
    Ever flows their thirst to assuage?
Grace, which like the Lord, the giver,
    Never fails from age to age.

Its Strength and Permanence

3 Round each habitation hovering,
  See the cloud and fire appear,
For a glory and a covering
  Showing that the Lord is near.
Thus they march, the pillar leading,
  Light by night and shade by day;
Daily on the manna feeding
  Which He gives them when they pray.

4 Savior, if of Zion's city
  I, through grace, a member am,
Let the world deride or pity,
  I will glory in Thy name.
Fading is the worldling's pleasure,
  All his boasted pomp and show;
Solid joys and lasting treasure
  None but Zion's children know.

J. Newton, 1779

89   S. M.   R. P. Stewart, 1825—1894

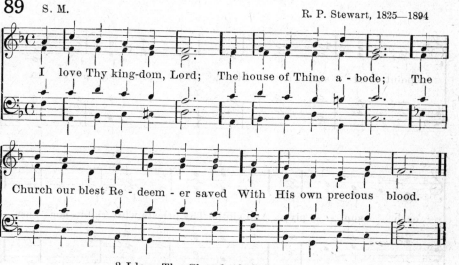

I love Thy king-dom, Lord; The house of Thine a - bode; The
Church our blest Re - deem - er saved With His own precious blood.

2 I love Thy Church, O God!
  Her walls before Thee stand,
Dear as the apple of Thine eye,
  And graven on Thy hand.

3 For her my tears shall fall,
  For her my prayers ascend;
To her my cares and toils be given,
  Till toils and cares shall end.

4 Beyond my highest joy
  I prize her heavenly ways,
Her sweet communion, solemn vows,
  Her hymns of love and praise.

5 Jesus, Thou Friend divine,
  Our Savior and our King,
Thy hand from every snare and foe
  Shall great deliverance bring.

6 Sure as Thy truth shall last,
  To Zion shall be given
The brightest glories earth can yield,
  And brighter bliss of heaven.

T. Dwight, 1800

The Church

L. M.

H. K. Oliver, 1832

Lord, pour Thy Spir - it from on high, And Thine appoint - ed serv - ants bless; Thy prom-ised power to
each sup - - ply, And clothe Thy priests with right - eous-ness.

2 Within Thy temple when they stand,
To teach the truth as taught by Thee,
Savior, like stars in Thy right hand,
Let all Thy Church's pastors be.

3 Wisdom and zeal and faith impart,
Firmness and meekness from above;
To bear Thy people on their heart,
And love the souls whom Thou dost love;

4 To watch, and pray, and never faint;
By day and night their watch to keep;
To warn the sinner, cheer the saint,
Protect Thy lambs, and feed Thy sheep.

5 And, when their work is finished here,
Let them in hope their charge resign;
Before the throne with joy appear,
And there with endless glory shine.

J. Montgomery, 1833.

The Ministry

9, 8, 9, 8.

Ludv. M. Lindeman, 1812—87

O Rock of A - ges, one foun - da - tion, On
which the liv - ing Church doth rest,— The Church, whose walls are
strong sal - va - tion, Whose gates are praise,— Thy name be blest!

2 Son of the living God, O call us
   Once and again to follow Thee;
And give us strength, whate'er befall us,
   Thy true disciples still to be.

3 When fears appall, and faith is failing,
   Make Thy voice heard o'er wind and wave,
"Why doubt?"—and in Thy love prevailing
   Put forth Thine hand to help and save.

4 And if our coward hearts deny Thee,
   In inmost thought, in deed, or word,
Let not our hardness still defy Thee,
   But with a look subdue us, Lord.

5 O strengthen Thou our weak endeavor
   Thee in Thy sheep to serve and tend,
To give ourselves to Thee for ever,
   And find Thee with us to the end.

H. A. Martin, 1871

The Church

7s. 8L.

J. B. Dykes, 1861

Fa-ther, be Thy blessing shed On Thy chos-en serv-ant's head;

Sav-ior, need-ed grace im-part To sus-tain and keep his heart;

Ho-ly Spir-it, with Thy fire Touch his lips, his soul in-spire,

That Thy truth through him be told Fear-less-ly to young and old.

2 Seal this day the vows that hold
Flock and shepherd in one fold.
May he Jesus' mandates keep,
"Feed My lambs," and "Feed My sheep!"
By Thee to Thy people sent
With Thy word and sacrament,
May he so proclaim the word
That who hear him, hear Thee, Lord.

The Ministry

3 In Thy vineyard called to toil,
  Wisely may he search the soil;
  Sinners may he love and win,
  While he hates and brands the sin.
  Give him boldness for the right,
  Give him meekness in the fight,
  Teach him zeal and care to blend,
  Give him patience to the end.

4 Grant him in his charge to find
  Listening ear and fervent mind,
  Helpful counsels, deepening peace,
  Earnest life, and glad increase;
  May they, by each other led,
  Grow to one in Christ, their head,
  And at last, together be
  Ripe for heaven and meet for Thee.

Samuel Gilman, 1863

93   S. M.

C. Lockhart, c. 1769

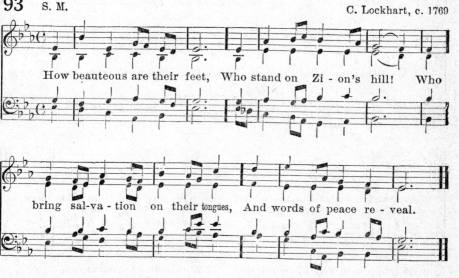

How beauteous are their feet, Who stand on Zi - on's hill! Who bring sal-va - tion on their tongues, And words of peace re - veal.

2 How charming is their voice!
  How sweet the tidings are!
"Zion, behold thy Savior-King,
  He reigns and triumphs here."

3 How happy are our ears,
  That hear this joyful sound,
Which kings and prophets waited for,
  And sought, but never found!

4 How blessed are our eyes,
  That see this heavenly light!

Prophets and kings desired it long,
  But died without the sight.

5 The watchmen join their voice,
  And tuneful notes employ;
Jerusalem breaks forth in songs,
  And deserts learn the joy.

6 The Lord makes bare His arm
  Through all the earth abroad;
Let all the nations now behold
  Their Savior and their God.

I. Watts, 1707

The Church

7, 6. 8L.

Jacques Arcadelt, 1572

Lord of the liv-ing har-vest, That whit-ens o'er the plain,

Where an-gels soon shall gath-er Their sheaves of gold-en grain,

Ac-cept these hands to la-bor, These hearts to trust and love,

And deign with them to hast-en Thy king-dom from a-bove.

2 As laborers in Thy vineyard,
  Send us, O Christ, to be
Content to bear the burden
  Of weary days for Thee;
We ask no other wages,
  When Thou shalt call us home,
But to have shared Thy travail
  And see Thy kingdom come.

3 Come down, Thou Holy Spirit,
  And fill our souls with light;
Clothe us in spotless raiment,
  In linen clean and white;

Within Thy sacred temple
  Be with us, where we stand,
And sanctify Thy people
  Throughout this happy land.

4 Be with us, God the Father,
  Be with us, God the Son,
Be with us, God the Spirit,
  O blessed Three in One!
Make us a royal priesthood,
  Thee rightly to adore,
And fill us with Thy fullness,
  Now, and for evermore.

J. S. B Monsell. 1866

95   8, 3, 6, 8, 8, 6.   A. H. Brown, b. 1830

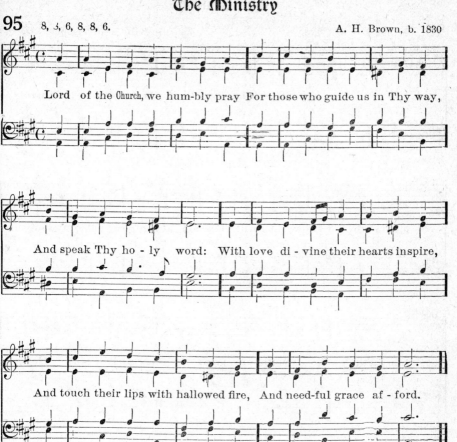

Lord of the Church, we hum-bly pray For those who guide us in Thy way,

And speak Thy ho - ly word: With love di - vine their hearts inspire,

And touch their lips with hallowed fire, And need-ful grace af - ford.

2 Help them to preach the truth of God,
  Redemption through the Savior's blood:
    Nor let the Spirit cease
  On all the Church His gifts to shower;
  To them a messenger of power,
    To us, of life and peace.

3 So may they live to Thee alone:
  Then hear the welcome word, "Well done!"
    And take their crown above:
  Enter into their Master's joy,
  And all eternity employ
    In praise, and bliss, and love.

E. Osler, 1836

The Church

8, 7, 8, 7, 8, 8, 8, 4, 8.   Valentin Babst's Gesangbuch, 1545

In Thee a-lone, O Christ, my Lord, My hope on earth re-main-eth; I know Thou wilt Thine aid af-ford, Naught else my soul sus-tain-eth. No strength of man, no earth-ly stay Can help us in the e-vil day: Thou, on-ly Thou, canst aid sup-ply, To Thee I cry, On Thee I bid my heart re-ly.

96

Confession

2 My sins a heavy burden rise;
  I mourn them with contrition,
Grant through Thy death and sacri-
  To me a full remission!   [fice,
Lord, show before the Father's throne
That Thou didst for my sins atone
So shall I from my load be freed,
  Thy word I plead.
Keep me, O Lord, each hour of need.

3 O Lord, in mercy stay my heart
  On faith's most sure foundation,
And to my inmost soul impart
  Thy perfect consolation.
My life be love supreme to Thee,—
To all men with sincerity:
And at the last, when comes my end,
  Thy succor send,
From Satan's wiles my soul defend.

J. Schneesing, ca., 1540

97 8s. 6L.

Schumann's Gesangbuch, 1539

Be - fore Thee, God, who know-est all With grief and shame I pros-trate fall; I see my sins a - gainst Thee, Lord, The sins of thought, of deed, and word, They press me sore, I cry to Thee: O God, be mer - ci - ful to me!

2 O Lord, my God, to Thee I pray:
O cast me not in wrath away,
Let Thy good Spirit ne'er depart,
But let Him draw to Thee my heart,
That truly penitent I be:
O God, be merciful to me!

3 O Jesus, let Thy precious blood
Be to my soul a cleansing flood;
Turn not, O Lord, Thy guest away,
But grant that justified I may
Go to my house with peace from Thee:
O God, be merciful to me!

M. B. Landstad, 1861

98 8, 6, 8, 6, 8, 8, 7.

Rev. G. W. Torrance, 1835—1907

Lord Jesus Christ, Thou high-est good! To whom Thy ran-somed flee, Be-hold in pen-i-ten-tial mood A sup-pliant bows to Thee. Through Thee I seek the Fa-ther's throne, For-give-ness ask through Thee a-lone, And strength for ho-ly liv-ing.

2 Beneath a load of guilt I sigh;
  Relieve my fainting heart—
Thou who in mortal agony
  Didst bear my sin and smart.
Of Thee alone I crave relief;
Leave me not now in fear and grief
  And dark despair to perish.

3 O where for comfort shall I turn,
  When I the past survey?
How oft I've dared Thy grace to spurn,
  And cast my bliss away:
Yet Thine availing merit, Lord,
Deliverance and peace afford;
  Thy word is all my solace.

4 This word, for ever precious, saith
  The humble, contrite mind
That looks to Thee in simple faith
  Shall full salvation find;
And then, from sin's dominion free,
Display true thankfulness to Thee,
  Devoted to Thy glory.

5 To Thee I come at Thy behest,
  Atoner of my sin!
Forgiveness and the promised rest
  Through Thy desert to win.
Be merciful, my God, to me,
And let no more remembered be
  The days of sin and folly.

Confession

6 Teach me, O Lord, before Thy face
 This wayward heart to still;
With joyfulness to run my race,
 And do Thy blessed will.
In a plain path do Thou me guide,
That faithful I may still abide,
 And quit me to Thine honor.

7 And pour Thine oil of joy on me
 When, the last moment nigh,
The parting spirit would be free
 To join Thy saints on high.
Then may Thy death, Lord, cheer my
  heart;
And in Thy faith may I depart
 To dwell with Thee for ever.

B. Ringwaldt, 1588

99 L. M.   Arr. from a Gregorian Chant by L. Mason, 1834

O Thou that hear'st when sin-ners cry, Though all my crimes be--fore Thee lie, Be-hold them not with an-gry look, But blot their memo-ry from Thy book.

2 Create my nature pure within,
 And form my soul averse to sin;
Let Thy good Spirit ne'er depart,
Nor hide Thy presence from my heart.

3 I cannot live without Thy light,
 Cast out and banished from Thy sight;
Thy holy joys, my God, restore,
And guard me that I fall no more.

4 A broken heart, my God, my King,
 Is all the sacrifice I bring:
The God of grace will ne'er despise
A broken heart for sacrifice.

5 O may Thy love inspire my tongue;
 Salvation shall be all my song,
And all my powers shall join to bless
The Lord, my strength and righteous-
  ness.

I. Watts, 1719

The Church

We stand in deep re - pent - ance Be - fore Thy throne of love;

O God of grace, for - give us, The stain of guilt re - move;

Be - hold us while with weep - ing We lift our eyes to Thee,

And, all our sins sub - du - ing, Our Fa - ther, set us free.

2 O shouldst Thou from us sinners
   Withhold Thy grace to guide,
 Forever we should wander
   From Thee, and peace, aside;
 But Thou to spirits contrite
   Dost light and life impart,
 That man may learn to serve Thee
 With thankful, joyous heart.

3 Our souls—on Thee we cast them,
   Our only refuge Thou!
 Thy cheering words revive us,
   When pressed with grief we bow:
 Thou bear'st the trusting spirit
   Upon Thy loving breast,
 And givest all Thy ransomed
 A sweet, unending rest.

Ray Palmer, 1834

Confession

L. M.

L. Bourgeois, 1547

I come to Thee, O bless-ed Lord, In-vit-ed by Thy gra-cious word To this Thy feast, to sup with Thee, Grant that a wor-thy guest I be.

2 I come to Thee with sin and grief,
For Thou alone canst give relief,
Thy death for me, dear Lord, I plead:
O Jesus, help me in my need!

3 Shouldst Thou a strict account demand,
Who could, O Lord, before Thee stand?
Purge all my secret sins away:
Be Thou, O Christ, the sinner's stay!

4 O Jesus, Lamb of God, alone,
Who didst for all our sins atone,
Though I have sinned and gone astray,
Turn not, O Lord, Thy guest away!

5 O Jesus, Lamb of God alone,
Who didst for all our sins atone,
Be merciful, I Thee implore,
Have mercy, Lord, for evermore!

M. B. Landstad, 1861

The Church

8, 7, 8, 7, 8, 8, 7.

Johann Walther, 1524

Oppressed by sin, O Lord, to Thee I come in my af-flic-tion:
O, full of pit-y, look on me, Im-part Thy ben-e-dic-tion. My sins are great, where shall I flee? The blood of Je-s speaks for me; For all our sins He car-ried.

2 Repentant at Thy feet I fall,
To Thy cross humbly clinging,
O Jesus, hear me when I call,
My wants before Thee bringing.
My trust is in Thy grace and power;
For all was finished in that hour,
When Thou didst make atonement.

3 When I approach Thine altar, Lord,
   May I this comfort cherish,
That on the cross Thy blood was poured
   For me, lest I should perish.
Thou didst for me God's law fulfill,
That holy joy my heart might thrill
   When on Thy love I'm feasting.

4 Be Thou my shield 'gainst Satan's power,
   Whene'er he would assail me;
The victor's crown, when comes death's hour,
   O let it never fail me!
Lord Jesus, Thou who savedst me,
My life I would devote to Thee,
   To praise Thy name forever.

C. F. Gellert, 1757.

103 S. M.

W. H. Monk, 1875

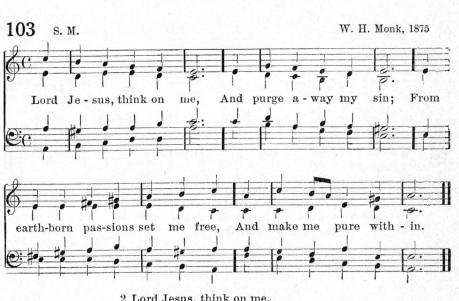

Lord Je - sus, think on me, And purge a - way my sin; From
earth-born pas-sions set me free, And make me pure with - in.

2 Lord Jesus, think on me,
   With many a care oppressed,
Let me Thy loving servant be,
   And taste Thy promised rest.

3 Lord Jesus, think on me,
   Nor let me go astray;
Through darkness and perplexity
   Point Thou the heavenly way.

4 Lord Jesus, think on me,
   That, when the flood is passed,
I may the eternal brightness see,
   And share Thy joy at last.

Synesius, ca. 400

The Church

11, 11, 11, 5.

1584, Johann Crüger, 1640

Turn, Lord, Thy wrath a - way, in mer-cy spare us! Lay down Thy
rod and let Thy love up - bear us! Hear us poor
sin - ners, lo, sin hath un - done us, Have mer-cy on us!

2 For if Thou shouldst, O Lord, in anger smite us,
And for our sins with righteous meed requite us,
Then we would perish, in our lost condition
Doomed to perdition.

3 O Lord, we pray Thee, grant to us remission!
Pardon our sins, we mourn them with contrition,
Thou who desirest not the sinner's dying,
Grace art supplying.

4 Our frame remember, Thou who life bestowest,
We are but dust, this Thou, O Father, knowest,
Subject to death we are from life's beginning,
For we are sinning.

5 Look to Thy Son's most bitter death and passion,
Who on the cross did purchase our salvation,
When from His wounds His blood was freely streaming,
The world redeeming.

6 Therefore, O Father, through Thy dear Son's merit,
Spare us and let us grace through Him inherit,
That we in heaven, with Thee, of life the giver,
May live forever.

G. Thymus, 1541

Confirmation

105 8, 7. 6L.

M. Vulpius, 1560—1616

Fa - ther, Son, and Ho - ly Spir - it, I'm bap-tized in Thy dear name;

In the seed Thou dost in - her - it, With the peo - ple Thou dost claim,

I am reck-oned, I am reckoned, And for me the Savior came.

2 Thou receivest me, O Father,
  As a child and heir of Thine:
Jesus, Thou who diedst, yea, rather
  Ever livest, Thou art mine.
    ‖: Thou, O Spirit :‖
  Art my guide, my light divine.

3 I have pledged, and would not falter,
  Truth, obedience, love to Thee;
I have vowed upon Thine altar
  Ever Thine alone to be,
    ‖: And forever :‖
  Sin and all its lusts to flee.

4 Gracious God, all Thou hast spoken
  In this covenant shall take place;
But if I, alas, have broken

These my vows, hide not Thy face;
  ‖: And from falling :‖
O restore me by Thy grace!

5 Lord, to Thee I now surrender
  All I have, and all I am;
Make my heart more true and tender,
  Glorify in me Thy name.
    ‖: Let obedience :‖
  To Thy will be all my aim.

6 Help me in this high endeavor,
  Father, Son, and Holy Ghost!
Bind my heart to Thee forever,
  Till I join the heavenly host;
    ‖: Living, dying :‖
  Let me make in Thee my boast.

J. J. Rambach, 1734

The Church

8, 7, 8, 7, 6, 6, 6, 6, 6, 7.

Martin Luther, 1529

Our Lord and God, O bless this day, And hear us, we implore Thee: None of our dear ones turn a - way Who
now are here be - fore Thee. We come be - fore Thy face
And pray: Let Thy rich grace De - scend from heaven a - bove
In all Thy might-y love, And keep us by Thy Spir - - it!

Confirmation

2 O bless Thy word to all the young,
   Let each, Thy truth possessing,
Bear witness true with heart and tongue,
   Their faith and ours confessing;
      From mother's arms Thy grace
      With love did them embrace;
      Baptized into Thy name
      As Thine Thou didst them claim,
   O Lord, as Thine now own them!

3 When they their vows today renew,
   Accept them with Thy favor;
And when they speak the great "I do,"
   May they forget it never!
      But they are weak and frail,
      When Satan's hosts assail;
      O arm them with Thy might,
      And grant that in the fight
   They unto death be faithful.

4 And when they leave their childhood home,
   And Satan would undo them,
May their baptismal grace become
   A shield and buckler to them!
      Blest he who then can say;
      God's covenant stands for aye:
      He ne'er shall be undone
      Who trusts in God alone—
   God is his mighty Father!

J. N. Brun, 1786

107   7s. 4L.

J. H. Knecht, 1799

Thine for ev-er! God of love, Hear us from Thy throne a-bove;

Thine for ev-er may we be Here and in e-ter-ni-ty.

2 Thine for ever! O how blest
They who find in Thee their rest!
Savior, Guardian, heavenly Friend,
O defend us to the end.

3 Thine for ever! Lord of life,
Shield us through our earthly strife;
Thou the life, the truth, the way,
Guide us to the realms of day.

4 Thine for ever! Shepherd, keep
These thy frail and trembling sheep;
Safe alone beneath Thy care,
Let us all Thy goodness share.

5 Thine for ever! Thou our guide,
All our wants by Thee supplied,
All our sins by Thee forgiven,
Lead us, Lord, from earth to heaven.

Mary F. Maude, 1847

The Church

7, 6, 7, 6, 3, 3, 6, 6.

Johann Rosenmüller, 1655

Fa - ther, Son, and Ho - ly Ghost, Bless the young before Thee; Thou their wants and dangers know'st Watch them, we implore Thee. Here they stand, Hope-ful band, Faith in Thee confess - ing, Wait - ing for Thy bless - ing.

2 Gentle Savior, they are Thine,
  Thou wilt never lose them;
May Thy life and love divine
  Melt their tender bosom.
    Lord, we pray
    That they may
  All like Thee, be holy,
  Loving, meek, and lowly.

3 Giver Thou of gifts to all,
  No good thing deny them:
Hear, O hear our earnest call,
  Life and light supply them.
    Strength renew,
    Keep them true;
  All that stand before Thee,
  Bless them, we implore Thee.

C. A. Döring, 1821

Confirmation

8, 7. 8L.   From a Gregorian Chant by L. Mason, 1839

Bles-sed Sav-ior, who hast taught me   I should live to Thee a - lone;

All these years Thy hand hath brought me, Since I   first was made Thine own.

At the font my vows were spok-en   By my par-ents in the Lord,

That my vows shall be un - broken,   At the   al-tar   I   re - cord.

2 I would trust in Thy protecting,
    Wholly rest upon Thine arm;
  Follow wholly Thy directing,
    O my only guard from harm!
  Meet me now with Thy salvation,
    In the Church's ordered way;
  Let me feel Thy confirmation
    In Thy truth and fear today:

3 So that, might and firmness gaining,
    Hope in danger, joy in grief,
  Now and evermore remaining
    Steadfast in the true belief;
  Resting in my Savior's merit,
  Strengthened, with the Spirit's strength
  With Thy Church I may inherit
    All my Father's joy at length.

                                          J. M. Neale, 1842

The Church

110 7s. 8L.

German, 1544

Fear, my child, thy God and Lord, And re-vere His name and
word, Ho-ly keep the Sab-bath day, Hon-or to thy
par-ents pay, Kill not, shun a-dul-ter-y, Steal not,
lies and slan-der flee, Keep from cov-et-ous-ness free.

2 In the Father I believe,
  Who to all did being give,
  And in Jesus Christ His Son,
  Who for man redemption won;
    And my faith I also place
    In the Holy Ghost, whose grace
    Sanctifies our souls and ways.

3 Father, throned in heaven above,
  Hallowed be Thy name in love;
  Let Thy kingdom come, we pray,
  And Thy will be done alway;
    Give us food, forgiveness send,
    In temptations aid extend,
    Save us, Thou, when comes our end

Confirmation

4 God the Father, God the Son,
   God the Spirit, Three in One.
   I, baptized into Thy name,
   As Thy child Thy blessing claim:
     Grant that in Thy covenant grace
     I my trust in Thee may place,
     Till in heaven I see Thy face.

5 Jesus, let my soul be fed
   With Thyself, the living bread,
   For Thy flesh is meat indeed,
   And Thy cleansing blood I need;
     Let it cleanse from sin and shame,
     That Thy death I may proclaim,
     And forever bless Thy name.

B. Pedersen, 1608

111   C. M.   W. H. Havergal, 1846

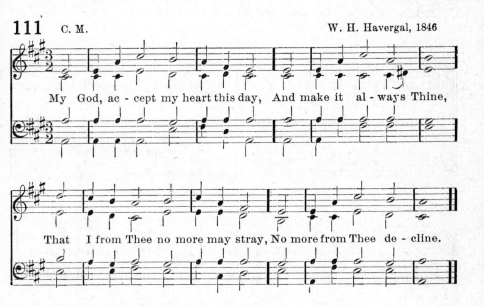

My God, ac-cept my heart this day, And make it al-ways Thine,

That I from Thee no more may stray, No more from Thee de-cline.

2 Before the cross of Him who died,
   Behold I prostrate fall;
  Let every sin be crucified,
   Let Christ be all in all!

3 Anoint me with Thy Spirit's grace,
   And seal me for Thine own;
  That I may see Thy glorious face,
   And worship at Thy throne!

4 May the dear blood, once shed for me,
   My blest atonement prove,
  That I from first to last may be
   The purchase of Thy love!

5 Let every thought, and work, and word,
   To Thee be ever given:
  Then life shall be Thy service, Lord,
   And death the gate of heaven!

M. Bridges, 1848

The Church

11, 10, 11, 10.

L. Mason, 1830

Hail to the brightness of Zi - on's glad morning, Joy to the lands that in dark-ness have lain! Hush'd be the ac-cents of sor-row and mourn-ing, Zi - on in tri-umph be - gins her mild reign.

2 Hail to the brightness of Zion's glad morning,
  Long by the prophets of Israel foretold;
  Hail to the millions from bondage returning!
  Gentiles and Jews the blest vision behold.

3 Lo, in the desert rich flowers are springing,
  Streams ever copious are gliding along;
  Loud from the mountain-tops echoes are ringing,
  Wastes rise in verdure and mingle in song.

4 See, from all lands, from the isles of the ocean,
  Praise to Jehovah ascending on high;
  Fallen are the engines of war and commotion,
  Shouts of salvation are rending the sky.

T. Hastings, 1832

Missions

113 7, 6. 8L.

G. J. Webb, 1837

The morn-ing light is break-ing; The dark-ness dis-ap-pears;

The sons of earth are wak-ing To pen-i-ten-tial tears;

Each breeze that sweeps the o-cean Brings ti-dings from a-far

Of na-tions in com-mo-tion, Pre-pared for Zi-on's war.

2 See heathen nations bending
　　Before the God we love,
And thousand hearts ascending
　　In gratitude above;
While sinners, now confessing,
　　The gospel call obey,
And seek the Savior's blessing,
　　A nation in a day.

3 Blest river of salvation,
　　Pursue thy onward way;
Flow thou to every nation,
　　Nor in thy richness stay;
Stay not till all the lowly
　　Triumphant reach their home;
Stay not till all the holy
　　Proclaim "The Lord is come!"

S. F Smith, 1832

114 8, 7. 8L.

G. F. Le Jeune, 1872

Sav - ior, sprinkle ma - ny na - tions, Fruit-ful let Thy sorrows be!

By Thy pains and con - so - la-tions Draw the gen-tiles un - to Thee!

Of Thy cross the wondrous sto - ry Be it to the nations told;

Let them see Thee in Thy glo - ry, And Thy mer - cy man-i-fold!

2 Far and wide, though all unknowing,
    Pants for Thee each mortal breast:
Human tears for Thee are flowing,
    Human hearts in Thee would rest.
Thirsting, as for dews of even,
    As the new-mown grass for rain,
Thee they seek, as God of heaven,
    Thee as man for sinners slain.

3 Savior, lo, the isles are waiting,
    Stretched the hand, and strained the sight,
For Thy Spirit new-creating,
    Love's pure flame, and wisdom's light.
Give the word, and of the preacher
    Speed the foot, and touch the tongue,
Till on earth, by every creature,
    Glory to the Lamb be sung.

A. C. Coxe, 1851

Missions

St. Alban's Tune-Book

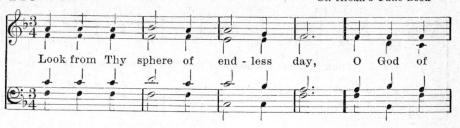

Look from Thy sphere of end - less day, O God of

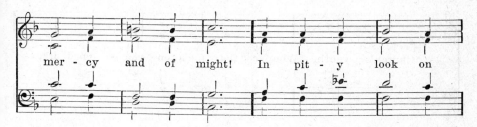

mer - cy and of might! In pit - y look on

those who stray, Be - night-ed in this land of light.

2 In peopled vale, in lonely glen,
   In crowded mart, by stream or sea;
How many of the sons of men
   Hear not the message sent from Thee!

3 Send forth Thy heralds, Lord, to call
   The thoughtless young, the hardened old,
A scattered, homeless flock, till all
   Be gathered to Thy peaceful fold.

4 Send them Thy mighty word, to speak
   Till faith shall dawn, and doubt depart.
To awe the bold, to stay the weak,
   And bind and heal the broken heart.

5 Then all these wastes, a dreary scene
   That make us sadden as we gaze,
Shall grow, with living waters, green,
   And lift to heaven the voice of praise.

W. C. Bryant, 1840

The Church

J. Barnby, 1872

116 8s. 6L.

A-wake, Thou Spir - it, who didst fire The watchmen of the Church's youth, Who faced the foe's en - ven - omed ire, Who wit - nessed day and night Thy truth, Whose voices loud are ring - - ing still, And bring-ing hosts to know Thy will.

2 Lord, let our earnest prayer be heard,
   The prayer Thy Son hath bid us pray,
   For lo, Thy children's hearts are stirred
   In every land in this our day,
   To cry with fervent soul to Thee,
   O help us, Lord! so let it be!

3 O haste to help, ere we are lost!
   Send preachers forth, in spirit strong,
   Armed with Thy word, a dauntless host,
   Bold to attack the rule of wrong;
   Let them the earth for Thee reclaim,
   Thy heritage, to know Thy name.

116

Missions

4 Would there were help within our walls!
O let Thy Spirit come again,
Before whom every barrier falls,
And now once more shine forth as then!
O rend the heavens and make us free!
Come, Lord, and bring us back to Thee!

5 And let Thy word have speedy course,
Through every land be glorified,
Till all the heathen know its force,
And fill Thy churches far and wide;
Wake Israel from his sleep, O Lord,
And spread the conquest of Thy word!

6 The Church's desert paths restore;
Let stumbling-blocks that in them lie
Hinder Thy word henceforth no more:
Error destroy, and heresy,
And let Thy Church, from hirelings free,
Bloom as a garden fair to Thee!

C. A. von Bogatzky, 1750

117 L. M.   J. Hatton, d. 1793

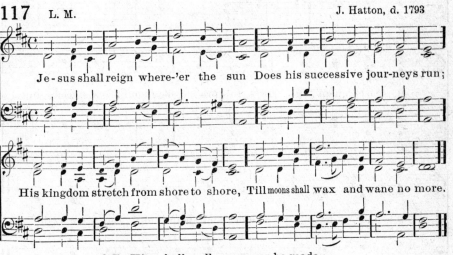

Je-sus shall reign where-'er the sun Does his successive jour-neys run;
His kingdom stretch from shore to shore, Till moons shall wax and wane no more.

2 To Him shall endless prayer be made,
And praises throng to crown His head;
His name like sweet perfume shall rise
With every morning sacrifice.

3 People and realms of every tongue
Dwell on His love with sweetest song;
And infant voices shall proclaim
Their early blessings on His name.

4 Blessings abound where'er He reigns;
The prisoner leaps to burst his chains,
The weary find eternal rest,
And all the sons of want are blest.

5 Let every creature rise and bring
Peculiar honors to our King:
Angels descend with songs again,
And earth repeat the loud Amen.

I. Watts, 1719

The Church

8s. 6L.

Schumann's Gesangbuch, 1539

Through midnight gloom from Ma - ce - don The cry of myri - ads as of one, The voice - ful si - lence of de - spair, Is el - o - quent in aw - ful prayer, The soul's ex - ceed - ing bit - ter cry, "Come o'er and help us, or we die".

2 How mournfully it echoes on!
   For half the earth is Macedon;
   These brethren to their brethren call,
   And by the Love which loved them all,
   And by the whole world's Life they cry,
   "O ye that live, behold we die!"

3 By other sounds the world is won
   Than that which wails from Macedon;
   The roar of gain is round it rolled,
   Or men unto themselves are sold,
   And cannot list the alien cry,
   "O hear and help us, lest we die."

Missions

4 Yet with that cry from Macedon,
   The very car of Christ rolls on:
   "I come; who would abide My day
   In yonder wilds prepare My way;
   My voice is crying in their cry:
   Help ye the dying, lest ye die."

5 Jesus, for men of Man the Son,
   Yea, Thine the cry from Macedon;
   O by the kingdom and the power
   And glory of Thine advent hour,
   Wake heart and will to hear their cry;
   Help us to help them, lest we die.

S. J. Stone, 1871

119 7s. 4L.   J. H. Knecht, 1799

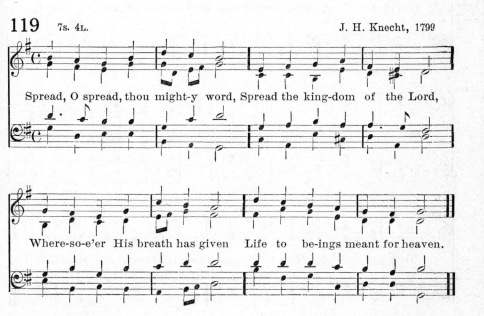

Spread, O spread, thou might-y word, Spread the king-dom of the Lord,

Where-so-e'er His breath has given Life to be-ings meant for heaven.

2 Tell them how the Father's will
   Made the world, and keeps it still,
   How He sent His Son to save
   All who help and comfort crave.

3 Tell of our Redeemer's love,
   Who for ever doth remove
   By His holy sacrifice
   All the guilt that on us lies.

4 Tell them of the Spirit given
   Now to guide us up to heaven,
   Strong and holy, just and true,
   Working both to will and do.

5 Word of life, most pure and strong,
   Lo, for thee the nations long;
   Spread, till from its dreary night
   All the world awakes to light.

6 Up! the ripening fields ye see,
   Mighty shall the harvest be;
   But the reapers still are few,
   Great the work they have to do.

7 Lord of harvest, let there be
   Joy and strength to work for Thee,
   Till the nations, far and near,
   See Thy light, and learn Thy fear.

J. F. Bahnmaier, 1827

The Church

7, 6. 8L.

L. Mason, 1823

From Greenland's i - cy moun-tains, From India's co - ral strand,

Where Af-ric's sun - ny foun-tains Roll down their gold-en sand;

From many an an-cient riv - er, From many a palm - y plain,

They call us to de - liv - er Their land from er-ror's chain.

2 What though the spicy breezes
  Blow soft o'er Ceylon's isle;
Though every prospect pleases,
  And only man is vile;
In vain with lavish kindness
  The gifts of God are strown;
The heathen in his blindness
  Bows down to wood and stone.

3 Shall we, whose souls are lighted
  With wisdom from on high,
Shall we to men benighted
  The lamp of life deny?

Salvation! O salvation!
  The joyful sound proclaim,
Till earth's remotest nation
  Has learned Messiah's name.

4 Waft, waft, ye winds, His story,
  And you, ye waters, roll,
Till, like a sea of glory,
  It spreads from pole to pole;
Till o'er our ransomed nature
  The Lamb for sinners slain,
Redeemer, King, Creator,
  In bliss returns to reign!

R. Heber, 1819

Missions

121 8, 7. 8L.

James Langran, 1835

Hark! the voice of Je-sus cry-ing, "Who will go and work to-day?

Fields are white, and harvests waiting, Who will bear the sheaves away?"

Loud and long the Mas-ter call-eth, Rich re-ward He of-fers thee:

Who will an-swer, glad-ly say-ing, "Here am I; send me, send me"?

2 If you cannot cross the ocean,
  And the heathen lands explore,
You can find the heathen nearer,
  You can help them at your door.
If you cannot give your thousands,
  You can give the widow's mite;
And the least you do for Jesus
  Will be precious in His sight.

3 If you cannot be a watchman,
  Standing high on Zion's wall,
Pointing out the path to heaven,
  Offering life and peace to all;

With your prayers and with your
    bounties
  You can do what heaven demands;
You can be like faithful Aaron,
  Holding up the prophet's hands.

4 Let none hear you idly saying,
  "There is nothing I can do,"
While the souls of men are dying,
  And the Master calls for you.
Take the task He gives you gladly,
  Let His work your pleasure be;
Answer quickly when He calleth—
  "Here am I; send me, send me."

D. March, 1868.

The Church

122   8s. 8L.

John Goss, 1864

O God of God! O Light of light! Thou Prince of Peace, Thou King of kings,

To Thee, where an-gels know no night The song of praise for - ev - er rings:

To Him who sits up - on the throne, The Lamb once slain for sin - ful men,

Be honor, might; all by Him won; Glo - ry and praise! A-men, A-men.

2 Deep in the prophets' sacred page,
    Grand in the poet's wingèd word,
Slowly in type, from age to age,
    Nations beheld their coming Lord;
Till through the deep Judean night
    Rang out the song, "Good-will to men!"
Hymned by the first-born sons of light,
    Re-echoed now, "Good-will!" Amen.

3 That life of truth, those deeds of love,
    That death of pain, 'mid hate and scorn;
These all are past, and now above,
    He reigns our King, once crowned with thorn
Lift up your heads, ye heavenly gates;
    So sang His hosts, unheard by men;
Lift up your heads, for you He waits.
    We lift them up! Amen, Amen!

4 Nations afar, in ignorance deep;
   Isles of the sea, where darkness lay;
These hear His voice, they wake from sleep,
   And throng with joy the upward way.
They cry with us, "Send forth Thy light,"
   O Lamb, once slain for sinful men;
Burst Satan's bonds, O God of might;
   Set all men free! Amen, Amen!

5 Sing to the Lord a glorious song,
   Sing to His name, His love forth tell;
Sing on, heaven's host, His praise prolong;
   Sing, ye who now on earth do dwell:
Worthy the Lamb for sinners slain;
   From angels, praise; and thanks from men;
Worthy the Lamb, enthroned to reign,
   Glory and power! Amen, Amen!

J. Julian, 1883

123 6, 6, 4, 6, 6, 6, 4.   Felice de Giardini, 1769

Thou, whose al - might - y word Cha - os and dark - ness heard,

And took their flight; Hear us, we hum - bly pray, And where the

gos - pel day Sheds not its glo - rious ray, Let there be light!

2 Thou who didst come to bring
  On Thy redeeming wing
    Healing and sight,
Health to the sick in mind,
Sight to the inly blind,
O now, to all mankind,
    Let there be light!

3 Spirit of truth and love,
  Life-giving, holy Dove,
    Speed forth Thy flight;
Move on the waters' face

Spreading the beams of grace,
And, in earth's darkest place,
    Let there be light!

4 Holy and blessed Three,
  Glorious Trinity,
    Wisdom, Love, Might;
Boundless as ocean's tide
Rolling in fullest pride,
Through the world, far and wide,
    Let there be light!

J. Marriot, 1813

The Church

124   6, 6, 6, 6, 8, 8.

John Goss, 1800—80

A - rise, O God, and shine, In all Thy sav-ing might, And pros-per each de - sign To spread Thy glo - rious light: Let healing streams of mer-cy flow, That all the earth Thy truth may know.

2 Bring distant nations near,
   To sing Thy glorious praise;
Let every people hear
   And learn Thy holy ways!
Reign, mighty God, assert Thy cause,
And govern by Thy righteous laws!

3 Put forth Thy glorious power,
   That Gentiles all may see,
And earth present her store
   In converts born to Thee:
God, our own God, His Church will bless,
And fill the world with righteousness.

4 To God the only wise,
   The one immortal King,
Let Hallelujahs rise
   From every living thing:
Let all that breathe, on every coast,
Praise Father, Son, and Holy Ghost.

                        W. Hurn, 1813

Missions

125 L. M.

German, 1677

O Spir-it of the liv — ing God! In all the full — ness of Thy grace, Where'er the foot of man hath trod, De - scend on our a - pos - tate race!

2 Give tongues of fire and hearts of love,
To preach the reconciling word;
Give power and unction from above,
Where'er the joyful sound is heard.

3 Be darkness, at Thy coming, light!
Confusion, order in Thy path!
Souls without strength inspire with might;
Bid mercy triumph over wrath.

4 O Spirit of the Lord! prepare
All the round earth her God to meet;
Breathe Thou abroad, like morning air,
Till hearts of stone begin to beat.

5 Baptize the nations; far and nigh
The triumphs of the cross record;
The name of Jesus glorify,
Till every kindred call Him Lord.

6 God from eternity hath willed
All flesh shall His salvation see
So be the Father's love fulfilled,
The Savior's sufferings crowned through Thee.

J. Montgomery, 1823

The Church

10. 4L.   W. H. Monk, 1861

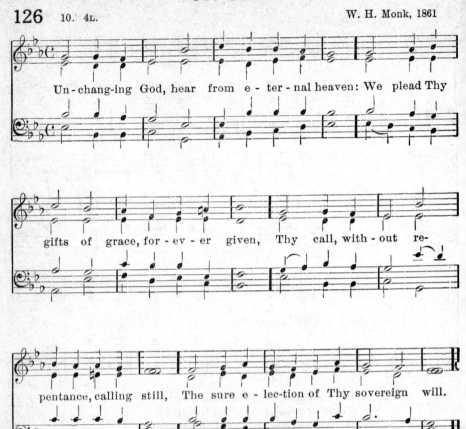

Un-chang-ing God, hear from e-ter-nal heaven: We plead Thy gifts of grace, for-ev-er given, Thy call, with-out re-pentance, calling still, The sure e-lec-tion of Thy sovereign will.

2 Out of our faith in Thee, who canst not lie,
Out of our heart's desire, goes up the cry,
From hope's sweet vision of the thing to be,
From love to those who still are loved by Thee.

3 Bring Thy beloved back, Thine Israel,
Thine own elect who from Thy favor fell,
But not from Thine election!—O forgive,
Speak but the word, and, lo! the dead shall live.

4 Father of mercies! these the long astray,
These in soul-blindness now the far-away,
These are not aliens, but Thy sons of yore,
O, by Thy Fatherhood, restore, restore!

Mission to the Jews

5 Breathe on Thy Church, that it may greet the day;
  Stir up her will to toil, and teach, and pray,
  Till Zionward again salvation come,
  And all her outcast children are at home.

6 Triune Jehovah, Thine the grace and power,
  Thine all the work, its past, its future hour;
  O Thou, who failest not, Thy gifts fulfill,
  And crown the calling of Thy changeless will.

S. J. Stone, 1885

127 7s. 4L.

J. A. Freylinghausen, 1704

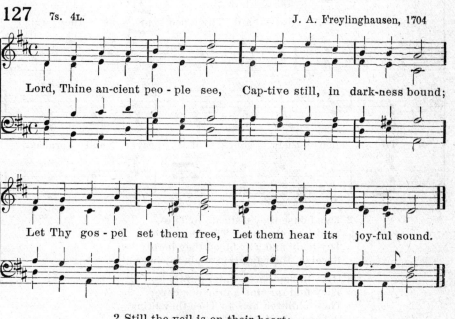

Lord, Thine an-cient peo-ple see, Cap-tive still, in dark-ness bound;

Let Thy gos-pel set them free, Let them hear its joy-ful sound.

2 Still the veil is on their heart:
    Rend it, Lord, at length in twain;
  Bid their unbelief depart,
    Bring them to Thy fold again.

3 Let Thy love their blindness heal;
    God of Israel, hear our prayer;
  Let Thy grace their pardon seal,
    Still Thy covenant let them share.

4 Harp of Judah, long unstrung,
    Sound at length the Savior's praise;
  Jew and Gentile, old and young,
    Loud the glad Hosanna raise.

E. Harland, 185

128   L. M.   Cantionale Sacrum, Gotha, 1651

E - ter - nal Son of God, O Thou, Be - fore whom earth and
heav - en bow, Re - gard Thy peo - ple as they raise
To Thee their songs of prayer and praise.

2 This house they dedicate to Thee,
   That here they may Thy glory see;
   Thy body and Thy blood they here
   Receive, their fainting souls to cheer.

3 Here in baptismal water pure
   They find for sins a gracious cure;
   Their children here to Thee they bring,
   O Thou, our death-subduing King.

4 Here sin's diseases healing find,
   The weak grow strong, light cheers the blind;
   The troubled heart with peace is blest,
   And weariness finds heavenly rest.

5 When tempests shake the world around,
   The rock-built Church secure is found;
   The gates of hell may here assail
   Whom Christ defends, but not prevail.

6 Praise to the Father, and the Son,
   And Holy Spirit, Three in One,
   Blest Trinity whom we adore,
   Teach us to praise Thee evermore.

Latin, 11th Century
A. J. Rambach, 1817

Church Buildings

8, 7. 6L.

John Goss, 1869

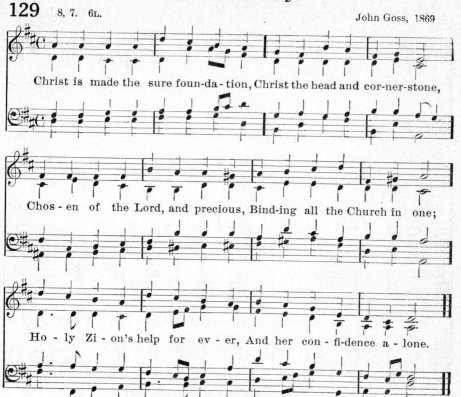

Christ is made the sure foun-da-tion, Christ the head and cor-ner-stone,

Chos-en of the Lord, and precious, Bind-ing all the Church in one;

Ho-ly Zi-on's help for ev-er, And her con-fi-dence a-lone.

2 All that dedicated city,
  Dearly loved of God on high,
In exultant jubilation
  Pours perpetual melody:
God the one in Three adoring
In glad hymns eternally.

3 To this temple, where we call Thee,
  Come, O Lord of host, today:
With Thy wonted loving-kindness
  Hear Thy people as they pray;
And Thy fullest benediction
Shed within its walls alway.

4 Here vouchsafe to all Thy servants
  What they ask of Thee to gain,
What they gain from Thee for ever
  With the blessed to retain,
And herafter in Thy glory
Evermore with Thee to reign.

5 Laud and honor to the Father,
  Laud and honor to the Son,
Laud and honor to the Spirit,
  Ever Three and ever One;
One in might, and One in glory,
While unending ages run.

Latin, 6th or 7th Century

The Church

6, 6, 6, 6, 8, 8.

J. Darwall, 1770

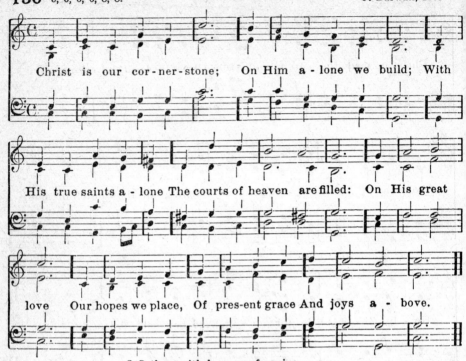

Christ is our cor-ner-stone; On Him a-lone we build; With

His true saints a-lone The courts of heaven are filled: On His great

love Our hopes we place, Of pres-ent grace And joys a-bove.

2 O then with hymns of praise
    These hallowed courts shall ring!
Our voices we will raise,
    The Three in One to sing;
      And thus proclaim
        In joyful song,
        Both loud and long,
      That glorious name.

3 Here, gracious God, do Thou
    For evermore draw nigh:
Accept each faithful vow,
    And mark each suppliant sigh;
      In copious shower
        On all who pray,
        Each holy day,
      Thy blessing pour.

4 Here may we gain from heaven
    The grace which we implore,
And may that grace, once given,
    Be with us evermore,
      Until that day
        When all the blest
        To endless rest
      Are called away

Latin, 6th or 7th Century

Church Buildings

131 8, 7. 6L.

C. Ett. Cantica Sacra, 1840

Come Thou now, and be a-mong us, Lord and Maker, while we pray:

Let Thy presence fill the tem-ple Which we ded-i-cate to-day;

And, Thyself its con-se-cra-tor, Dwell with-in its walls al-way.

2 Grant that all Thy faithful people
  May Thy truer temple be;
Neither flesh, nor soul, nor spirit,
  Know another Lord than Thee;
But, to Thee once dedicated,
  Serve Thee everlastingly.

3 Bright be here Jehovah's altar
  With the presents that we bring,
Held in holy veneration,
  Rich with many an offering;
Ever hallowed, ever quiet,
  Ever dear to God, its king.

4 Here our souls, as Thy true altars,
  Deign to hallow and to bless,
O Thou future Judge of all men,
  With Thy grace and holiness:
That Thy gifts sent down from heaven,
  We may evermore possess.

Latin, 6th or 7th Century

The Church

132 8s. 7L. Ludv. M. Lindeman, 1812—87

Built on the Rock the Church doth stand, E-ven when steeples are fall-ing; Crumbled have spires in ev-ery land, Bells still are chim-ing and call - ing; Call-ing the young and old to rest, But a-bove all the soul dis-trest, Longing for rest ev - er - last - ing.

2 Surely in temples made with hands,
   God, the Most High, is not dwelling,
High above earth His temple stands,
   All earthly temples excelling;
Yet He whom heavens cannot contain
Chose to abide on earth with men—
   Built in our bodies His temple.

3 We are God's house of living stones,
   Builded for His habitation;
He through baptismal grace us owns
   Heirs of His wondrous salvation;
Were we but two His name to tell,
Yet He would deign with us to dwell,
   With all His grace and His favor.

4 Now we may gather with our King;
   E'en in the lowliest dwelling;
Praises to Him we there may bring,
   His wondrous mercy forth telling;
Jesus His grace to us accords,
Spirit and life are all His words,
   His truth doth hallow the temple.

5 Still we our earthly temples rear,
   That we may herald His praises;
They are the homes where He draws near
   And little children embraces; [near
Beautiful things in them are said,
God there with us His cov'nant made,
   Making us heirs of His kingdom.

Church Buildings

6 Here stands the font before our eyes
  Telling how God did receive us;
Th' altar recalls Christ's sacrifice
  And what His table doth give us;
Here sounds the word that doth proclaim
Christ yesterday, today the same,
  Yea, and for aye our Redeemer.

7 Grant then, O God, where'er men roam,
  That when the church bells are ringing,
Many in Jesus' faith may come
  Where He His message is bringing:
I know mine own, mine own know me,
Ye, not the world, my face shall see:
My peace I leave with you, Amen.

N. F. S. Grundtvig, 1837

133   L. M.

German, 1539

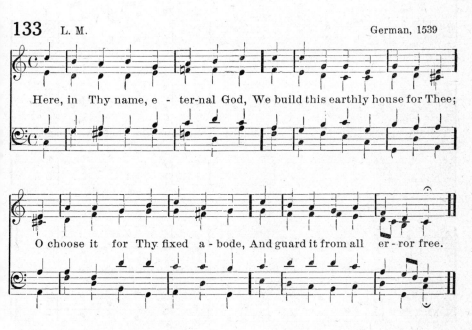

Here, in Thy name, e - ter-nal God, We build this earthly house for Thee;

O choose it for Thy fixed a - bode, And guard it from all er - ror free.

2 Here, when Thy people seek Thy face,
  And dying sinners pray to live,
Hear Thou in heaven, Thy dwelling-
      place, [give.
And when Thou hearest, Lord, for-

3 Here, when Thy messengers proclaim
  The blessed gospel of Thy Son,
Still, by the power of Thy great name,
Be mighty signs and wonders done.

4 When children's voices raise the song,
  Hosanna to the heavenly King,
Let heaven, with earth, the strain
      prolong,
Hosanna let the angels sing.

5 Thy glory never hence depart;
  Yet choose not, Lord, this house alone,
Thy kingdom come to every heart;
In every bosom fix Thy throne.

J. Montgomery, 1822

The Means of Grace

The Word of God

7, 6. 8L.

Meiningisches Gesangbuch, 1693

O Word of God in-car-nate, O Wis-dom from on high,
O Truth unchanged, un-chang-ing, O Light of our dark sky;
We praise Thee for the ra-diance That from the hal-lowed page,
A lamp un-to our foot-steps, Shines on from age to age.

2 The Church from her dear Master
　Received the gift divine,
And still that light she lifteth
　O'er all the earth to shine.
It is the golden casket
　Where gems of truth are stored;
It is the heaven-drawn picture
　Of Christ, the living Word.

3 It floateth like a banner
　Before God's host unfurled;
It shineth like a beacon
　Above the darkling world;
It is the chart and compass
　That o'er life's surging sea,
Amid the rocks and quicksands
　Still guides, O Christ, to Thee.

The Word of God

4 O make Thy Church, dear Savior,
  A lamp of burnished gold,
  To bear before the nations
  Thy true light as of old;
  O teach Thy wandering pilgrims
  By this their path to trace,
  Till, clouds and darkness ended,
  They see Thee face to face
  W. W. How, 1867

135 C. M.

W. H. Havergal, 1846

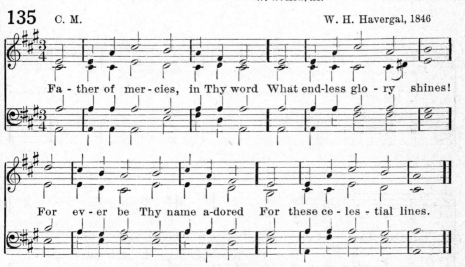

Fa - ther of mer - cies, in Thy word What end-less glo - ry shines!

For ev - er be Thy name a-dored For these ce - les - tial lines.

2 Here may the blind and hungry come,
    And light and food receive;
  Here shall the lowliest guest have room,
    And taste and see and live.

3 Here springs of consolation rise
    To cheer the fainting mind,
  And thirsting souls receive supplies,
    And sweet refreshment find.

4 Here the Redeemer's welcome voice
    Spreads heavenly peace around;
  And life and everlasting joys
    Attend the blissful sound.

5 O may these heavenly pages be
    My ever dear delight;
  And still new beauties may I see,
    And still increasing light.

6 Divine Instructor, gracious Lord!
    Be Thou for ever near;
  Teach me to love Thy sacred word,
    And view my Savior there!

Anne Steele, 1760

The Means of Grace

136 8, 6. 8L.

Thy word, O Lord, like gen-tle dews, Falls soft on hearts that pine; Lord, to Thy gar-den ne'er re-fuse This heavenly balm of Thine. Wa-tered by Thee, let ev-ery tree Forth blossom to Thy praise, By grace of Thine bear fruit di-vine, Through all the com-ing days.

2 Thy word is like a flaming sword,
   A wedge that cleaveth stone;
Keen as a fire, so burns Thy word,
   And pierceth flesh and bone.
Let it go forth o'er all the earth,
   To cleanse our hearts within,
To show Thy power in Satan's hour
   And break the might of sin.

3 Thy word, a wondrous guiding star,
   On pilgrim hearts doth rise,
Leads those to God who dwell afar,
   And makes the simple wise.
Let not its light e'er sink in night;
   In every spirit shine,
That none may miss heaven's final [bliss.
   Led by Thy light divine.

C. B. Garve, 1825

The Word of God

8, 7, 8, 7, 6, 6, 6, 6, 7.

Martin Luther, 1529

God's word is our great her-it-age, And shall be ours for ev - er; To spread its light from age to age Shall be our chief en-deav - or; Through life it guides our way, In death it is our stay; Lord grant, while worlds en - dure, We keep its teachings pure, Throughout all gen - er - a - - tions.

N. F. S. Grundtvig, 1817

The Means of Grace

138 L. M.

German, 1543

Lord, keep us stead-fast in Thy word: Curb those who fain by craft or sword Would wrest the king-dom from Thy Son, And set at naught all He hath done.

2 Lord Jesus Christ, Thy power make
   known;
For Thou art Lord of lords alone:
Defend Thy Christendom, that we
May evermore sing praise to Thee.

3 O Comforter, of priceless worth,
Send peace and unity on earth;
Support us in our final strife,
And lead us out of death to life.

M. Luther, 1541

139 C. M.

J. B. Dykes, 1866

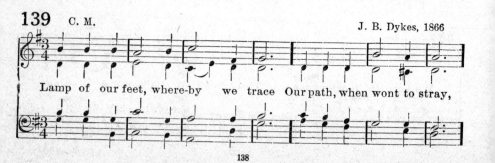

Lamp of our feet, where-by we trace Our path, when wont to stray,

The Word of God

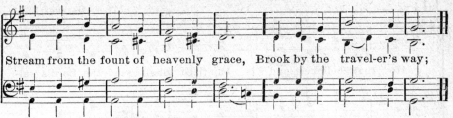

Stream from the fount of heavenly grace, Brook by the travel-er's way;

2 Bread of our souls, whereon we feed,
   True manna from on high;
   Our guide and chart, wherein we read
   Of realms beyond the sky;

3 Pillar of fire through watches dark,
   Or radiant cloud by day;
   When waves would 'whelm our tossing bark,
   Our anchor and our stay:

4 Word of the ever-living God,
   Will of His glorious Son;
   Without Thee how could earth be trod,
   Or heaven itself be won?

5 Lord, grant us all aright to learn
   The wisdom it imparts;
   And to its heavenly teaching turn,
   With simple, childlike hearts.

B. Barton, 1826

140   6s. 4L.   18th Century

Lord, Thy word a - bid - eth, And our footsteps guid - eth;

Who its truth be - liev - eth Light and joy re - ceiv - eth.

2 When our foes are near us,
   Then Thy word doth cheer us,
   Word of consolation,
   Message of salvation.

3 When the storms are o'er us.
   And dark clouds before us,
   Then its light directeth,
   And our way protecteth.

4 Who can tell the pleasure,
   Who recount the treasure,

By Thy word imparted
To the simple-hearted?

5 Word of mercy, giving
   Succor to the living;
   Word of life, supplying
   Comfort to the dying!

6 O that we, discerning
   Its most holy learning,
   Lord, may love and fear Thee,
   Evermore be near Thee!

139   Sir H. W. Baker, 186.

The Means of Grace

8, 7, 8, 7, 8, 8, 7.

German, 1523

He that believes and is bap-tized Shall see the Lord's sal-va - tion; Baptized in - to the death of Christ, He is a new cre-a - - tion; Through Christ's re - demp-tion he shall stand A-mong the glo-rious heavenly band Of ev - ery tribe and na - tion.

2 With one accord, O God, we pray:
    Grant us Thy Holy Spirit;
Look Thou on our infirmity
    Through Jesus' blood and merit!
Grant us to grow in grace each day
By holy baptism that we may
    Eternal life inherit!

T. Kingo, 1689

Baptism

Ludv. M. Lindeman, 1812—87

A - bide a - mong us, we im - plore Thee,

Lord Je - sus Christ, Thy Spir - it breathe! And let the babes we

bring be - fore Thee Now be baptized in - to Thy death.

2 Lord, after Thee we Christians call them,
   O let them in Thy name arise!
And keep them Thine whate'er befall them,
   That they may reach Thy Paradise.

3 If Thou their earthly race shouldst lengthen,
   Thy faithful servants let them prove;
If few their days, their weakness strengthen,
   That they may share Thy dying love.

4 O write Thy blessed name, dear Savior,
   Upon their hearts, we Thee implore;
And on Thy palms engrave this favor,
   That they are Thine for evermore.

N. F. S. Grundtvig, 1837

The Means of Grace

143   10, 6, 10, 6, 8, 8, 4.   John Dahle, 1911

O Fa-ther, Thou who hast cre-at-ed all In wis-est
love, we pray, Look on this babe, who at Thy gra-cious call
Is enter-ing on life's way; Bend o'er him in his noth-ing-ness,
Thine im-age on his soul im-press; O Fa-ther, hear!

2 O Son of God, who diedst for us, behold,
    We bring our child to Thee;
Thou tender Shepherd, take him to Thy fold,
    Thine own for aye to be;
Defend him through this earthly strife,
And lead him in Thy way of life,
      O Son of God!

Baptism

3 O Holy Ghost, who broodedst o'er the **wave**,
   Descend upon this child;
 Give him undying life, his spirit lave
   With waters undefiled;
 Grant him from earliest years to be
 Thy learner apt, a home for Thee,
       O Holy Ghost!

4 O Triune God, what Thou command'st is done;
   We speak, but Thine the might;
 This child has scarce yet seen our earthly sun,
   O pour on him Thy light,
 In faith and hope, in joy and love,
 Thou Sun of all below, above,
       O Triune God!

A. Knapp, 1841

144   C. M.
German

O Lord, our lit-tle ones to Thee In faith and hope we give;
We know that through this mys-ter-y Their new-born souls shall live.

2 We pour the water on their brow,
    The sacred words we say;
  Baptize them with the Spirit now,
    And keep them Thine alway.

3 Help them to go from strength to strength,
    Until, full-grown in Thee,
  They come before Thy face at length,
    And all Thy glory see.

4 And then, with all the heavenly host,
    In everlasting songs,
  Praise Father, Son, and Holy Ghost,
    To whom all praise belongs.

W. Whiting, 1872

The Means of Grace

145   7, 8, 7, 8, 8, 8.   Johann Rudolph Ahle, 1664

Bless - ed Je - sus! here we stand, Met to do as Thou hast spok-en;

And this child, at Thy com-mand, Now we bring to Thee, in tok - en

That to Christ it here is giv-en; For of such shall be His heav - en.

2 Yes, Thy warning voice is plain,
   And we fain would keep it duly:
He who is not born again,
   Heart and life renewing truly,
Born of water and the Spirit,
Shall God's kingdom ne'er inherit.

3 Therefore hasten we to Thee;
   Take the pledge we bring, O take it!
Let us here Thy glory see,
   And in tender pity make it
Now Thy child, and leave it never,
Thine on earth and Thine forever.

4 Make it, Head, Thy member now;
   Shepherd, take Thy lamb and feed it;
Prince of Peace, its peace be Thou;
   Way of life, to heaven, O lead it:
Vine, this branch may nothing sever,
Grafted firm in Thee for ever.

5 Now upon Thy heart it lies,
   What our hearts so dearly treasure;
Heavenward lead our burdened sighs,
   Pour Thy blessing without measure;
Write the name we now have given,
Write it in the book of heaven.

B. Schmolk, 1709

Baptism

Sav - ior, who Thy flock art feed - ing

With the shep - herd's kind - est care, And the fee - ble

gent - ly lead - ing, While the lambs Thy bos - om share:

2 Now, these little ones receiving,
    Fold them in Thy gracious arm!
  There, we know, Thy word believing,
    Only there secure from harm!

3 Never, from Thy presence roving,
    Let them be the lion's prey;
  Let Thy tenderness so loving
    Keep them through life's dangerous way.

4 Then, within Thy fold eternal,
    Let them find a resting-place,
  Feed in pastures ever vernal,
    Drink the rivers of Thy grace.

W. A. Muhlenberg, 1826

The Means of Grace

O Lamb of God most ho - ly! Who on the cross didst suf - fer,

And patient still and low - ly, Thy - self to scorn didst of - fer;

Our sins by Thee were tak - en, Or hope had us for - sak - en:

Have mer - cy on us, O Je - sus!

2 O Lamb of God most holy
  Who on the cross didst suffer,
And patient still and lowly,
  Thyself to scorn didst offer;
Our sins by Thee were taken,
Or hope had us forsaken:
  Have mercy on us, O Jesus!

3 O Lamb of God most holy!
  Who on the cross didst suffer,
And patient still and lowly,
  Thyself to scorn didst offer;
Our sins by Thee were taken,
Or hope had us forsaken:
  Thy peace be with us, O Jesus!

N. Decius, 1531

The Lord's Supper

148 7, 6. 8L. Zinck's Koralbog, 1801

O liv-ing Bread from heav-en, How hast Thou fed Thy guest!

The gifts Thou now hast giv-en Have filled my heart with rest. O

wondrous food of bless-ing, O cup that heals our woes!

My heart this gift pos-sess-ing, In thank-ful song o'er-flows.

2 My Lord, Thou here hast led me
  Within Thy holiest place,
And there Thyself hast fed me
  With treasures of Thy grace:
And Thou hast freely given,
  What earth could never buy,—
The bread of life from heaven,
  That now I shall not die.

3 Thou gav'st the food I wanted,
  Its power can death destroy;
And Thou hast freely granted
  The cup of endless joy.

Ah, Lord, I do not merit
  The favor Thou hast shown,
And all my soul and spirit
  Bow down before Thy throne.

4 Lord, grant me that, thus strengthened
  With heavenly food, while here
My course on earth is lengthened,
  I serve with holy fear:
And when Thou call'st my spirit
  To leave this world below,
I enter, through Thy merit,
  Where joys unmingled flow.

J. Rist, 1651

The Means of Grace

8s. 8l.

Johann Crüger, 1649

Deck thy-self, my soul, with glad-ness, Leave the gloomy haunts of

sad - ness, Come in - to the day-light's splen - dor,

There with joy thy prais-es ren - der Un - to him whose grace un-

bound-ed, Hath this won-drous ban-quet found-ed, High o'er

The Lord's Supper

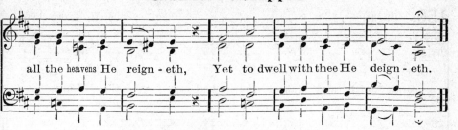

all the heavens He reign - eth, Yet to dwell with thee He deign - eth.

2 Hasten as a bride to meet Him,
And with loving reverence greet Him,
For with words of life immortal
Now He knocketh at thy portal;
Haste to ope the gates before Him,
Saying, while thou dost adore Him,
"Suffer, Lord, that I receive Thee,
And I never more will leave Thee."

3 Ah, how hungers all my spirit
For the love I do not merit!
Oft have I, with sighs fast thronging,
Thought upon this food with longing,
In the battle well-nigh worsted,
For this cup of life have thirsted,
For the Friend, who here invites us,
And to God Himself unites us.

4 Now I sink before Thee lowly,
Filled with joy most deep and holy,
As with trembling awe and wonder
On Thy mighty work I ponder,
How by mystery surrounded,
Depths no man hath ever sounded,
None may dare to pierce unbidden,
Secrets that with Thee are hidden.

5 Sun, who all my life dost brighten,
Light, who dost my soul enlighten,
Joy, the sweetest man e'er knoweth,
Fount, whence all my being floweth.
At Thy feet I cry, my Maker,
Let me be a fit partaker
Of this blessed food from heaven,
For our good, Thy glory, given.

6 Jesus, Bread of life, I pray Thee,
Let me gladly here obey Thee.
Never to my hurt invited,
Be Thy love with love requited;
From this banquet let me measure,
Lord, how vast and deep its treasure;
Through the gifts Thou here dost give me
As Thy guest in heaven receive me.

J. Franck, 1649

The Means of Grace

150   10s. 2L.   A. H. Brown, 1889

Draw nigh and take the bod-y of the Lord,

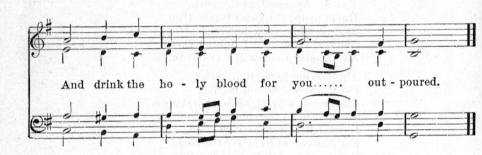

And drink the ho-ly blood for you...... out-poured.

2 By that pure body and that holy blood
   Saved and refreshed, we render thanks to God.

3 Salvation's giver, Christ, the only Son,
   By His dear cross and blood the world hath won.

4 Offered was He for greatest and for least,
   Himself the victim and Himself the priest.

5 Victims were offered by the law of old,
   Which in a type this heavenly mystery hold.

6 He, Lord of light, and Savior of our race,
   Hath given to His saints a wondrous grace.

7 Approach ye, then, with faithful hearts sincere,
   And take the earnest of salvation here.

8 He who His saints in this world rules and shields,
   To all believers life eternal yields.

9 He feeds the hungry with the bread of heaven,
   And living streams to those who thirst are given.

10 Alpha and Omega, to whom shall bow,
   All nations at the doom, is with us now.

Latin, Anon., 691

The Lord's Supper

151 C. M.

Scotch Psalter, 1615

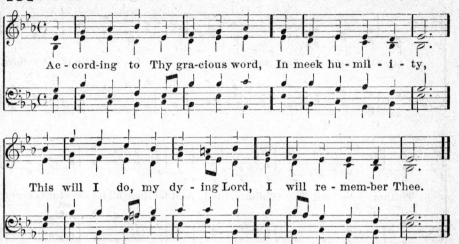

Ac-cord-ing to Thy gra-cious word, In meek hu-mil-i-ty,

This will I do, my dy-ing Lord, I will re-mem-ber Thee.

2 Thy body, broken for my sake,
 My bread from heaven shall be;
Thy testamental cup I take,
 And thus remember Thee.

3 Gethsemane can I forget,
 Or there Thy conflict see,
Thine agony and bloody sweat,
 And not remember Thee?

4 When to the cross I turn mine eyes,
 And rest on Calvary,

O Lamb of God, my sacrifice,
 I must remember Thee.

5 Remember Thee, and all Thy pains,
 And all Thy love to me;
Yes, while a breath, a pulse remains,
 Will I remember Thee.

6 And when these failing lips grow
 And mind and memory flee, [dumb,
When Thou shalt in Thy kingdom
 Jesus, remember me. [come
J. Montgomery, 1825

152

1 O God, unseen, yet ever near,
 Thy presence may we feel;
And thus, inspired with holy fear,
 Before Thine altar kneel.

2 Here may Thy faithful people know
 The blessings of Thy love;
The streams that through the desert flow,
 The manna from above.

3 We come, obedient to Thy word,
 To feast on heavenly food:
Our meat, the body of the Lord;
 Our drink, His precious blood.

4 Thus would we all Thy words obey,
 For we, O God, are Thine;
And go rejoicing on our way,
 Renewed with strength divine.

E. Osler, 1836

The Means of Grace

153 L. M.

German, 1605

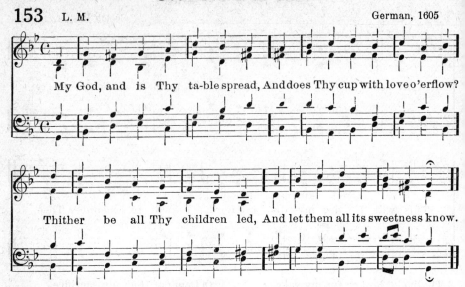

My God, and is Thy ta-ble spread, And does Thy cup with love o'erflow?

Thither be all Thy children led, And let them all its sweetness know.

2 Hail, sacred feast, which Jesus makes,
Rich banquet of His flesh and blood!
Thrice happy he who here partakes
That sacred stream, that heavenly
flood!

3 O let Thy table honored be,
And furnished well with worthy
guests;
And may each soul salvation see
That here its sacred pledges tastes!

P. Doddridge, 1755

154

1 Jesus, the very thought is sweet;
In that dear name all heart-joys meet;
But O, than honey sweeter far,
The glimpses of His presence are.

2 No word is sung more sweet than this;
No name is heard more full of bliss;
No thought brings sweeter comfort nigh
Than Jesus, Son of God most high.

3 Jesus, the hope of souls forlorn,
How good to them for sin that mourn!
To them that seek Thee, O how kind!
But what art Thou to them that find?

4 Jesus, Thou sweetness, pure and blest,
Truth's fountain, light of souls distressed,
Surpassing all the heart requires,
Exceeding all the soul desires!

5 No tongue of mortal can express,
No pen can write its blessedness:
He only who hath proved it knows
What bliss from love of Jesus flows.

The Lord's Supper

6 O Jesus, King of wondrous might!
   O Victor, glorious from the fight!
   Sweetness that may not be expressed,
   And altogether loveliest!

7 Remain with us, O Lord, today!
   In every heart Thy grace display:
   That now the shades of night are fled,
   On Thee our spirits may be fed.

8 I seek for Jesus in repose,
   When round my heart its chambers close;
   Abroad, and when I shut the door,
   I long for Jesus evermore.

9 With Mary in the morning gloom
   I seek for Jesus at the tomb;
   For Him, with love's most earnest cry,
   I seek with heart and not with eye.

10 Jesus, to God the Father gone,
   Is seated on the heavenly throne:
   My heart hath also passed from me,
   That where He is there it may be.

11 We follow Jesus now, and raise
   The voice of prayer, the hymn of praise,
   That He at last may make us meet
   With Him to gain the heavenly seat.

Bernard of Clairvaux, ca. 1150

155   L. M.   L. Bourgeois, 1551

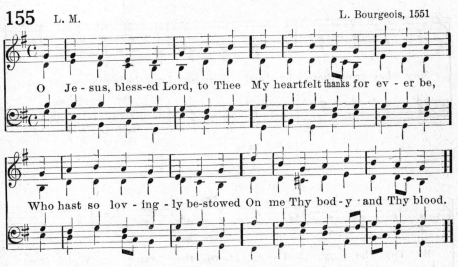

O Jesus, blessed Lord, to Thee My heartfelt thanks for ever be,
Who hast so lovingly bestowed On me Thy body and Thy blood.

2 Break forth, my soul, for joy, and say:
   hat wealth is come to me this day!
   fy Savior dwells within me now:
   How blest am I! how good art Thou!

T. Kingo, 1689

156

Johann Walther, 1524

May God be praised henceforth and blest for-ev - er! Who, Him-self both

gift and giv - er, With His own flesh and blood our souls doth nourish;

May they grow there - by and flour-ish! Lord, have mer-cy on us.

By Thy ho - ly bod - y, Lord, the same Which from

The Lord's Supper

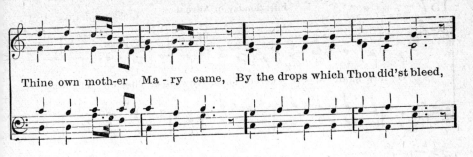

Thine own moth-er Ma - ry came, By the drops which Thou did'st bleed,

Help us in the hour of need. Lord, have mer - cy on us.

2 Thou hast to death Thy holy body given,
  Life to win for us in heaven
By stronger love, dear Lord, Thou could'st not bind us,
  Whereof this should well remind us.
    Lord, have mercy on us.
Lord, Thy love constrained Thee for our good
Mighty things to do by Thy dear blood,
  Thou hast paid the debt we owed,
  Thou hast made our peace with God.
    Lord, have mercy on us.

3 May God bestow on us His grace and blessing,
  That, His holy footsteps tracing,
We walk as brethren dear in love and union,
  Nor repent this sweet communion.
    Lord, have mercy on us.
Let not us the Holy Ghost forsake,
May He grant that we the right way take;
  That poor Christendom may see
  Days of peace and unity.
    Lord, have mercy on us.

M. Luther, 1524

The Church Year

First Sunday in Advent.

Zinck's Koralbog, 1801

O how shall I re-ceive Thee, How meet Thee on Thy way;

Blest hope of ev-ery na-tion, My soul's de-light and stay? O

Je-sus, Je-sus, give me, By Thine il-lum-ing light,

To know what-e'er is pleas-ing And wel-come in Thy sight.

2 Thy Zion palms is strewing
  With branches fresh and fair;
And every soul awaking,
  Her anthem shall prepare;
Perpetual thanks and praises
  Forth from our hearts shall spring;
And to Thy name the service
  Of all our powers we bring.

3 O ye who sorrow, sinking
  Beneath your grief and pain,
Rejoice in His appearing,
  Who shall your souls sustain:
He comes, He comes with gladness!
  How great is His good-will!
He comes, all grief and anguish
  Shall at His word be still.

4 Ye who with guilty terror
  Are trembling, fear no more;
With love and grace the Savior
  Shall you to hope restore:
He comes, who contrite sinners
  Will with the children place,
The children of His Father,
  The heirs of life and grace.

5 He comes, the Lord, to judgment;
  Woe, woe to them who hate!
To those who love and seek Him
  He opes the heavenly gate.
Come quickly, gracious Savior,
  And gather us to Thee,
That in the light eternal
  Our joyous home may be.

P. Gerhardt, 1653

First Sunday in Advent

158 8, 8, 8, 8, 8, 8, 6, 6.

J. Stobæus, 1634

Lift up your heads, ye mighty gates, Be - hold the King of glo - ry waits;

The King of kings is draw-ing near, The Sav-ior of the world is here.

Life and sal - va-tion doth He bring, Wherefore re - joice and gladly sing:

We praise Thee, Fa - ther, now, Cre - a - tor, wise art Thou.

2 The Lord is just, a helper tried,
Mercy is ever at His side;
His kingly crown is holiness,
His sceptre, pity in distress.
The end of all our woes He brings;
Wherefore the earth is glad and sings,
We praise Thee, Savior, now;
Mighty indeed art Thou.

3 O blest the land, the city blest
Where Christ the ruler is confessed:
O happy hearts and happy homes,
To whom this King in triumph comes!
The cloudless sun of joy He is,
Who bringeth pure delight and bliss;
O Comforter divine!
What boundless grace is Thine!

4 Fling wide the portals of your heart,
Make it a temple set apart
From earthly use for heaven's employ
Adorned with prayer and love and joy;
So shall your Sovereign enter in,
And new and nobler life begin,
To Thee, O God, be praise,
For word, and deed, and grace!

5 Redeemer, come, I open wide
My heart to Thee; here, Lord, abide.
Let me Thine inner presence feel,
Thy grace and love in me reveal.
Thy Holy Spirit guide us on
Until our glorious goal is won!
Eternal praise and fame
We offer to Thy name!

G. Weissel, 1642

159 12, 5, 12, 5, 6, 6, 5, 8.

Ludv. M. Lindeman, 1812—87

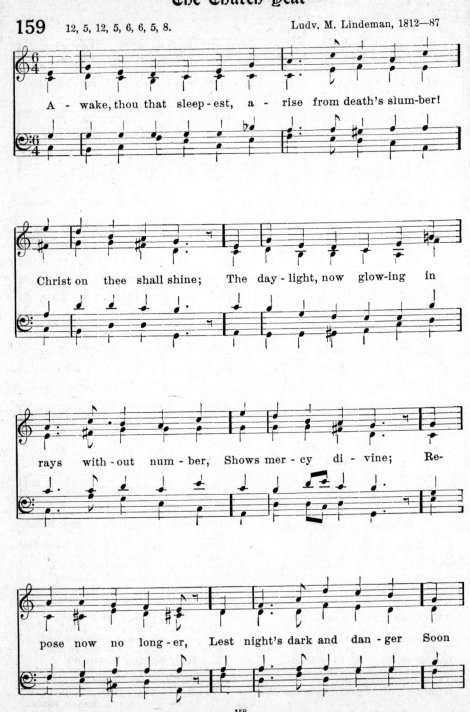

A - wake, thou that sleep-est, a - rise from death's slum-ber!
Christ on thee shall shine; The day-light, now glow-ing in
rays with-out num-ber, Shows mer-cy di-vine; Repose now no long-er, Lest night's dark and dan-ger Soon

First Sunday in Advent

come o'er thy soul.   A - wake now, a - rise, and be whole!

2 In earth's vale of sorrows the cold mists enshroud thee,
    And tears often flow;
  And suffering and grief seem the portion allowed thee
    In this life below;
    Yet, hear the glad message,
    That rescue doth presage,
  And pardon and peace
  Through Him who doth bring thee release.

3 In earth's dreary deserts the sharp thorns will wound thee,
    And rough is the way;
  And often thou longest from ills that surround thee
    To hasten away;
    Yet, cease now thy sadness,
    God's springtime of gladness
  Through Christ thou shalt see:
  Awake, for He calleth to thee!

4 O lift up thine eyes now with hope unto heaven,
    The daybreak is here:
  Thy Lord let all blessing and honor be given,
    Go meet Him with cheer;
    When hearts are convicted
    Of sin, and afflicted
  His welcome will rise
  In anthems of praise to the skies.

5 To God be all glory, who graciously sendeth
    From heaven His light;
  The way and the truth and the life my soul findeth,
    And peace is my right.
    O Christ, shine upon us!
    From death Thou hast won us
  To follow, O Lord,
  Thy steps in the light of Thy word.

M. B. Landstad, 186.

159

The Church Year

8, 8, 7, 7, 8, 8, 8.

Ludv. M. Lindeman, 1812—87

Wake! the wel - come day ap - pear - eth,

How with joy our hearts it cheer-eth! Wake, the Lord's great

year be - hold! That which ho - ly men of old,

Those who throng the sa - cred pag - es, Wait - ed for through

First Sunday in Advent

count - less a - ges; Hal - le - lu - jah! Hal - le - lu - jah!

2 Patriarchs and priests aspiring,
  Kings and prophets long desiring,
      Saw not this before they died:
      Lo, the light to them denied!
  See its beams to earth directed!
  Welcome, O Thou long-expected!
      Hallelujah! Hallelujah!

3 He, the Savior sent by heaven,
  Once through faith to Abram given,
      Israel's Son and glorious King,
      Hope to which the heathen cling,
  Now on earth with men abiding,
  Comes to Zion meekly riding;
      Hallelujah! Hallelujah!

4 Lo! He comes, a victim willing,
  All His Father's will fulfilling;
      He will, through His precious blood,
      All things once again make good,
  Pain and shame of death sustaining,
  What was lost with joy regaining;
      Hallelujah! Hallelujah!

5 In our stead Himself He offers,
  On th' accursed tree He suffers,
      That His death's sweet savor may
      Take our curse for aye away,
  Cross and curse for us enduring,
  Hope and heaven to us securing;
      Hallelujah! Hallelujah!

6 Moses' law no longer rules us,
  Christ's free Spirit gently schools us;
      Ended now our captive thrall;
      He who God obeys in all,
  Through his Savior's death and merit,
  Now enjoys adoption's spirit;
      Hallelujah! Hallelujah!

7 Rent the temple curtain's center,
  Fearless each may strive to enter,
      Through the veil, the holy place,
      There to stand before His face;
  He who once came down from heaven,
  Fear from all our breasts hath driven;
      Hallelujah! Hallelujah!

8 Hence thy King, O Zion, praising,
  Heart and voice to Him upraising,
      Shout with joy, for once thou art
      In His reign to bear thy part;
  Come, thyself as offering bringing,
  Come, thou Bride, for ever singing
      Hallelujah! Hallelujah!

                    J. A. Freylinghausen, 1714

The Church Year

161 6, 6, 7, 7, 7, 7.

German, 15?4

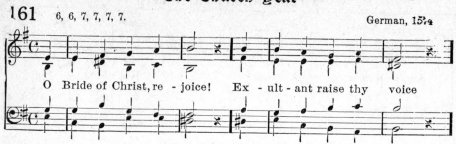

O Bride of Christ, re - joice! Ex - ult - ant raise thy voice

To hail the day of glo - ry, Fore-told in sa - cred sto - ry:

Ho-san - na, praise, and glo - ry, Our King, we bow be - fore Thee

2 Let shouts of gladness rise
Triumphant to the skies.
Here comes the King most glorious
To reign o'er all victorious:
Hosanna, etc.

3 He wears no kingly crown,
Yet as a king He's known;
Though not arrayed in splendor:
He still makes death surrender:
Hosanna, etc.

4 The weak and timid find
Him gentle, good and kind;
To them He gives a treasure
Of bliss beyond all measure:
Hosanna, etc.

5 Thy heart now open wide,
Bid Christ with thee abide;
He graciously will hear thee,
And be forever near thee:
Hosanna, etc.

6 Then go thy Lord to meet;
Strew palm-leaves at His feet:
Thy garments spread before Him,
And honor and adore Him:
Hosanna, etc.

7 E'en babes with one accord
With thee shall praise the Lord,
And every Gentile nation
Respond with exultation:
Hosanna, etc.

Anon., Danish, ca. 1600

Second Sunday in Advent

7, 6, 7, 6, 6, 7, 7, 6.

German, 1598

Rise, children of the king - dom! The King is drawing nigh:
A - rise, and hail with glad - ness The Rul - er from on high.
Ye Christians, hast - en forth! Your praise and hom - age bring Him,
And glad Ho - san - nas sing Him; Naught else your love is worth.

2 Arise, ye drooping mourners!
　The King is very near;
Away with grief and sorrow.
　For lo! your help is here.
Behold, in many a place—
　O blessed consolation!—
We find Him, our salvation,
In His pure means of grace.

3 Arise, ye much afflicted!
　The King is not afar;
Rejoice, ye long dejected!
　Behold the Morning Star.
The Lord will give you joy!
　Though troubles now distress you,
　With comfort He will bless you,
E'en death He will destroy.

4 Arise, ye poor and needy!
　The King provides for you;
He comes with succor speedy,
　With mercy ever new.
Receive your gracious King,
　The giver of all blessing;
　Hail Him, His name confessing,
And glad Hossannas sing.

5 O rich the gifts Thou bring'st us,
　Thyself made poor and weak;
O love beyond expression,
　That thus can sinners seek!
For this, O Lord, will we
　Our joyous tribute bring Thee,
　And glad Hossannas sing Thee,
And ever grateful be.

J. Rist, 1651

163   8, 7, 8, 7, 8, 8, 7.   M. Prætorius, 1610

I place my-self in Je-sus' hands, And there a-bide for ev - er;

No griefs, no joys, shall loose the bands, Nor our sweet un - ion sev - er;

In those dread days When earth de-cays, Who stays on Him, and

whom He stays, Shall be pre - served for ev - er.

2 A rock and castle is the Lord,
    And they shall see and wonder
Who build on His almighty word,
    And thereon deeply ponder;
And what He saith,
In life and death,
My heart shall trust with steadfast faith,
    Though earth be rent asunder.

3 Let Him do with me what He will,
   He cannot fail to please me,
I cleave to Him with strong faith still,
   And hope that He will bless me;
He must be blest
Who loves Him best,
And on His word doth firmly rest;
   Lord, with this truth impress me.

4 When things are at their worst, I will
   Still joy in His protection,
Who loves to bring out good from ill,
   And grieves in my affliction:
His trials sent
Are all well meant,
His blows a Father's chastisement,
   And tokens of affection.

5 My confidence unshaken stands
   Upon His blessed promise,
That none shall pluck us from His hands,
   Nor any foe o'ercome us.
He will not break
The word He spake.
He will not leave us, nor forsake,
   Nor take His Spirit from us.

C. J. P. Spitta, 1833

164 8, 7. 4L.

John B. Dykes, 1823—76

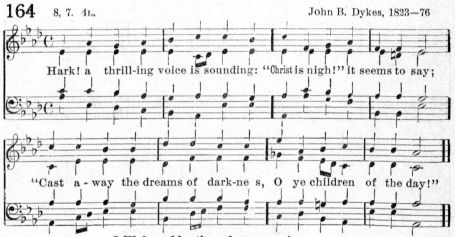

Hark! a thrill-ing voice is sounding: "Christ is nigh!" it seems to say;

"Cast a - way the dreams of dark-ness, O ye children of the day!"

2 Wakened by the solemn warning,
   Let the earth-bound soul arise;
All the powers of darkness vanish:
   Christ, our Day-star, mounts the skies.

3 Lo, the Lamb, so long expected,
   Comes with pardon down from heaven,
Let us haste, with tears of sorrow,
   One and all, to be forgiven.

4 So, when next He shines with glory,
   Wrapping all the earth in fear,
Not for chastening, but salvation
   Unto us He shall appear.

5 Honor, glory, might, dominion,
   To the Father and the Son,
With the everlasting Spirit,
   While eternal ages run.

Anon., Latin, 5th Century.

165 8, 9, 8, 8, 9, 8, 6, 6, 4, 4, 4, 8.

P. Nicolai, 1599

Christians, prayer may well em-ploy you, The powers of dark-

ness would de-stroy you: Yea, Sa-tan's self has planned your

fall. Wield God's word, a weap-on glo-rious,

A-gainst each foe; and soon vic-to-rious Our

God will make you o'er them all. Is Sa-tan strong and fell?

Second Sunday in Advent

Here is Im-man-u-el. Sing Ho-san-na! The strong ones yield, With Christ our shield, And we as conquerors hold the field.

2 Cast afar this world's vain pleasures,
  Aye, boldly fight for heavenly treasures,
    And steadfast be in Jesus' might,
He will help, whate'er betide you:
And naught will harm with Christ beside you:
    By faith you'll conquer in the fight.
      Then shame, O weary soul!
      Look forth toward the goal:
        There joy waits you.
      The race then run,
      The combat done,
    Your crown of glory will be won.

3 Wisely fight, for time is fleeting,
  The hours of grace are swift retreating!
    And life is shortest to the wise.
When the trump the dead is waking,
And sinners all with fear are quaking,
    Then will the saints with joy arise.
      Bless God: our triumph's sure,
      Though long we did endure
        Scorn and trial.
      Thou, Son of God,
      To Thy abode
    Wilt lead the way Thyself hast trod.

4 Jesus, all Thy children cherish,
  And keep them that they never perish,
    Whom Thou hast purchased with Thy blood
Give new life, that our desiring
Be ever heavenward aspiring,
    For what is holy, true and good.
      Thy Spirit on us pour,
      That we may love Thee more—
        Hearts o'erflowing:
      And then will we
      Be true to Thee
    In death and life eternally.

W. E. Arends, 1714

The Church Year

8, 7, 8, 7, 4, 7.

J. G. C. Störl, 1734

Lo, He comes with clouds de-scend-ing, Once for our sal-va-tion slain; Thousand an-gel-hosts at-tend-ing Swell the triumph of His train: Hal-le-lu-jah! Christ, the Lord, re-turns to reign.

2 Every eye shall now behold Him,
   Robed in dreadful majesty;
Those who set at naught and sold Him
   Pierced and nailed Him to the tree,
     Deeply wailing,
   Shall the true Messiah see.

3 Now redemption, long expected,
   See in solemn pomp appear;
All His saints, by men rejected,
   Now shall meet Him in the air:
     Hallelujah!
   See the day of God appear.

4 Yea, Amen, let all adore Thee,
   High on Thine eternal throne;
Savior, take the power and glory;
   Claim the kingdoms for Thine own:
     Hallelujah!
   Thou shalt reign, and Thou alone.

C. Wesley, 1758, et al.

167   7, 6, 7, 6, 7, 7, 6.   German, 1524

The on-ly Son from heav-en, Fore-told by an-cient
seers, By God, the Fa-ther, giv-en, In hu-man shape appears; No sphere His light con-fin-ing, No
star so bright-ly shin-ing As He, our Morning Star.

2 O time of God appointed,
   O bright and holy morn!
He comes, the King anointed,
   The Christ, the virgin-born;
His home on earth He maketh,
And man of heaven partaketh,
   Of life again an heir.

3 O Lord, our hearts awaken,
   To know and love Thee more,
In faith to stand unshaken,
   In Spirit to adore,
That we still heavenward hasting,
Yet here Thy joy foretasting,
   May reap its fulness there.

Elisabeth Cruciger, 1524

168 6, 6. 6L.   M. Teschner, 1613

Hail to the Lord's A-noint-ed, Great Da-vid's great-er Son!

Hail, in the time ap-point-ed, His reign on earth be-gun!

He comes to break op-pres-sion, To set the cap-tive free,

To take a-way trans-gres-sion And rule in eq-ui-ty.

2 He comes with succor speedy
  To those who suffer wrong;
To help the poor and needy,
  And bid the weak be strong;
To give them songs for sighing;
  Their darkness turn to light,
Whose souls, condemned and dying,
  Were precious in His sight.

3 He shall come down like showers
  Upon the fruitful earth;
And love and joy, like flowers,
  Spring in His path to birth.
Before Him, on the mountains,
  Shall peace, the herald, go:
And righteousness, in fountains,
  From hill to valley flow.

Third Sunday in Advent

4 Kings shall fall down before Him,
   And gold and incense bring;
All nations shall adore Him,
   His praise all people sing;
For He shall have dominion
   O'er river, sea and shore,
Far as the eagle's pinion
   Or dove's light wing can soar.

5 For Him shall prayer unceasing
   And daily vows ascend;
His kingdom still increasing,
   A kingdom without end.

The mountain-dews shall nourish
   A seed in weakness sown,
Whose fruit shall spread and flourish
   And shake like Lebanon.

6 O'er every foe victorious,
   He on His throne shall rest,
From age to age more glorious,
   All-blessing and all-blest.
The tide of time shall never
   His covenant remove;
His name shall stand for ever;
   That name to us is love!

J. Montgomery, 1821

169   7s. 4L.   Ludv. M. Lindeman, 1812—87

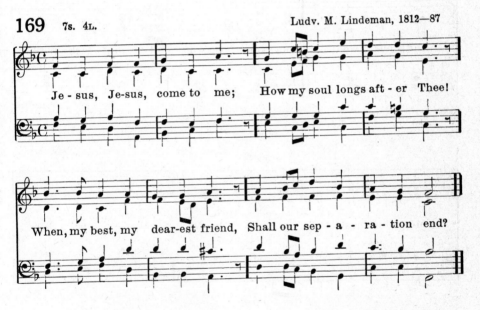

Je - sus, Je - sus, come to me; How my soul longs aft - er Thee!

When, my best, my dear-est friend, Shall our sep - a - ra - tion end?

2 Lord, my longings never cease;
   Without Thee I find no peace;
'Tis my constant cry to Thee,—
Jesus, Jesus, come to me!

3 Mean the joys of earth appear,
   All below is dark and drear;
Naught but Thy beloved voice
Can my wretched heart rejoice.

4 Thou alone, my gracious Lord,
   Art my shield and great reward;

All my hope, my Savior Thou,—
To Thy sovereign will I bow.

5 Come, and dwell within my heart;
   Purge its sin, and heal its smart;
See, I ever cry to Thee,—
Jesus, Jesus, come to me!

6 Patiently I wait Thy day;
   For this gift alone I pray,
That, when death shall visit me,
Thou my light and life wilt be.

J. Scheffler, 1657

170 8, 7, 8, 7, 7, 7, 8, 8.

Louis Bourgeois, 1551

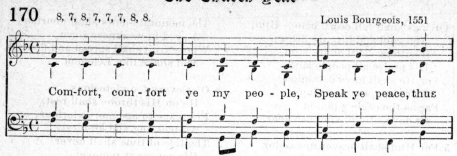

Com-fort, com-fort ye my peo-ple, Speak ye peace, thus

saith our God; Com-fort those who sit in dark-ness,

Mourning 'neath their sor-rows' load. Speak ye to Je-

ru-sa-lem Of the peace that waits for them; Tell her that her

Third Sunday in Advent

sins I cov-er, And her war-fare now is o - - ver.

2 Yea, her sins our God will pardon,
　Blotting out each dark misdeed;
That which well deserved His anger
　He will no more see or heed.
She hath suffered many a day,
Now her griefs have passed away,
God will change her pining sadness
Into ever springing gladness.

3 For the herald's voice is crying
　In the desert far and near,
Bidding all men to repentance,
　Since the kingdom now is here.
O that warning cry obey!
Now prepare for God a way;
Let the valleys rise to meet Him,
And the hills bow down to greet Him.

4 Make ye straight what long was crooked,
　Make the rougher places plain,
Let your hearts be true and humble,
　As befits His holy reign.
For the glory of the Lord
Now o'er earth is shed abroad,
And all flesh shall see the token
That His word is never broken.

J. Olearius. 1671

The Church Year

171 9, 8, 9, 8, 9, 9.   Ludv. M. Lindeman, 1812—87

Sav - ior of sin-ners, now re - vive us   With Thy free mer - cy

from a - bove;   Friend of the sin - ful and the wea - ry,

Turn un - to us Thy heart of love!   O come, Thy sweet com-

pas - sion show - ing,   On our poor souls Thy grace be-stow - ing.

2 O Thou, our only hope and helper;
   The Wonderful is still Thy name,
Who comes to Thee in every sorrow
   Shall ever find Thy love the same,
Thy grace and mercy never failing,
O'er every foe Thy might prevailing.

3 Thou knowest how poor mortals wan-
      der
In error's shade, deceived and blind;
Come, Lord, and graciously enlighten
   The darkness of our heart and mind.

Thy glory every truth revealing,
Which sin and Satan are concealing.

4 Father, our misery Thou knowest,
Our joy, our peace, our glory gone.
The message of Thy mercy send us,
   The precious gospel of Thy Son.
Then life shall change to peace and
      blessing,
In Christ our Lord our good possess-
      ing.

L. A. Gotter, 1714

Third Sunday in Advent

172 L. M. 6L.   D. S. Bortniansky, 1752—1828

O come, O come, Im-man-u-el, And ran-som cap-tive Is-ra-el, That mourns in lone-ly ex-ile here Un-til the Son of God ap-pear. Re-joice! re-joice! Im-man-u-el Shall come to thee, O Is-ra-el!

2 O come, Thou Rod of Jesse, free
Thine own from Satan's tyranny;
From depths of hell Thy people save
And give them victory o'er the grave.
Rejoice! rejoice! Immanuel
Shall come to thee, O Israel!

3 O come, Thou Day-spring, come and cheer
Our spirits by Thine advent here:
And drive away the shades of night,
And pierce the clouds and bring us [light!
Rejoice! rejoice! Immanuel
Shall come to thee, O Israel!

4 O come, Thou Key of David, come,
And open wide our heavenly home:
Make safe the way that leads on high,
And close the path to misery.
Rejoice! rejoice! Immanuel
Shall come to thee, O Israel!

5 O come, O come, Thou Lord of might,
Who to Thy tribes, on Sinai's height
In ancient times didst give the law
In cloud, and majesty, and awe.
Rejoice! rejoice! Immanuel
Shall come to thee, O Israel!

Anon., Latin, ca. 12th Century

173 9, 8, 9, 8, 8, 8.   Fourth Sunday in Advent   J. D. Meier, 1692

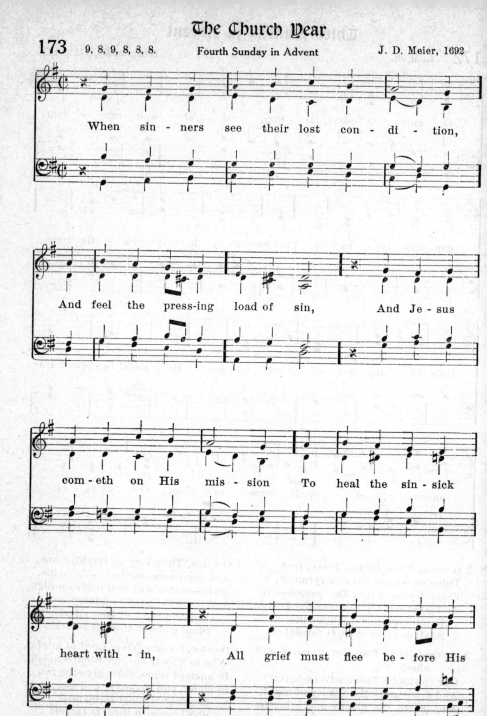

When sin-ners see their lost con-di-tion,

And feel the press-ing load of sin, And Je-sus

com-eth on His mis-sion To heal the sin-sick

heart with-in, All grief must flee be-fore His

Fourth Sunday in Advent

grace, And joy di-vine will take its place.

2 When Jesus enters meek and lowly,
    To fill the home with sweetest peace;
When hearts have felt His blessing holy,
    And found from sin complete release,
Then light and calm within shall reign,
And hearts divided love again.

3 When Jesus enters land and nation,
    And moves the people with His love,
When yielding to His kind persuasion,
    Our hearts His truth and blessings prove,
Then shall our life on earth be blest
The peace of God on us shall rest.

4 When Jesus comes, O blessed story!
    He works a change in heart and life;
God's kingdom comes with power and glory
    To young and old, to man and wife;
Through sacrament and living word,
Faith, love and hope are now conferred.

5 Then stilled are cries and lamentation,
    Then loosed is every Satan's band,
In death is hope and consolation,
    The soul is safe in Jesus' hand:
When we shall walk through death's dark vale
His rod and staff shall never fail.

6 O may He soon to every nation
    Find entrance where He is unknown,
With life and light and full salvation
    That heathendom may be o'erthrown,
And healing to the hearts may come
In heathen land and Christian home!

7 Behold, He at the door is knocking!
    Hark, how He pleads our souls to win!
Who hears His voice— the door unlocking—
    To sup with Him He enters in!
How blest the day, my soul, how blest!
When Jesus comes to be thy guest!

8 Behold, He at the door is calling,
    O heed, my soul, what He doth say;
Deny Him not— O thought appalling—
    And turn Him not from thee away.
My soul gives answer deep within:
Thou blessed of the Lord, come in.

9 Come Thou who spreadest joy and gladness,
    Forever bide with me and mine,
And bring to those who sit in sadness
    And gloom of death Thy light divine:
A voice comes from my soul within;
Thou blessed of the Lord, come in!

M. B. Landstad, 1863

The Church Year

174 L. M.

L. Bourgeois, 1551

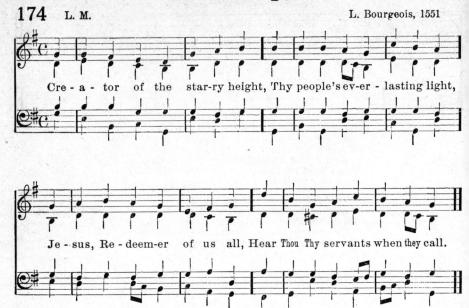

Cre - a - tor of the star-ry height, Thy people's ev-er-lasting light, Je - sus, Re - deem-er of us all, Hear Thou Thy servants when they call.

2 Thou, sorrowing at the helpless cry
Of all creation doomed to die,
Didst save our lost and guilty race,
By healing gifts of heavenly grace.

3 Love drew Thee down, the world to win
From common stain of common sin;
Proceeding from a virgin shrine
The spotless victim all divine.

4 At Thy great name, exalted now,
All knees in lowly homage bow;

All things in heaven and earth adore,
And own Thee King for evermore.

5 To Thee, O holy One, we pray,
Our Judge in that tremendous day,
Ward off, while yet we dwell below,
The weapons of our crafty foe.

6 To God the Father, God the Son,
And God the Spirit, Three in One,
Praise, honor, might, and glory be
From age to age eternally.

Anon, Latin, 10th Century

175 C. M.

J. Clarke, 1670—1707

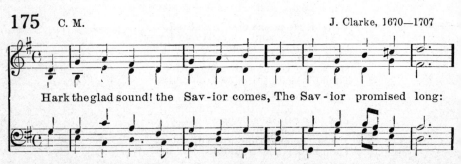

Hark the glad sound! the Sav - ior comes, The Sav - ior promised long:

Fourth Sunday in Advent

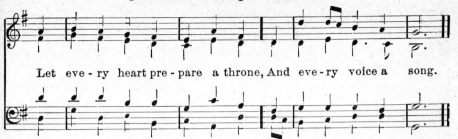

Let eve-ry heart pre-pare a throne, And eve-ry voice a song.

2 He comes, the prisoners to release,
   In Satan's bondage held;
   The gates of brass before Him burst,
   The iron fetters yield.

3 He comes, the broken heart to bind,
   The bleeding soul to cure,
   And with the treasures of His grace
   To bless the humble poor.

4 Our glad Hosannas, Prince of Peace,
   Thy welcome shall proclaim,
   And heaven's eternal arches ring
   With Thy beloved name.

P. Doddridge, 1735

176 L. M.

Christopher Edwin Willing, 1830—1894

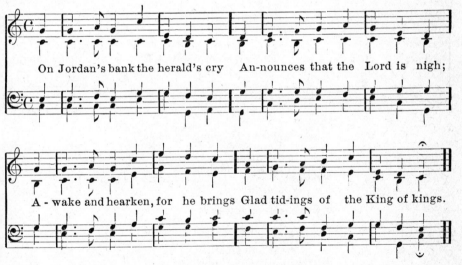

On Jordan's bank the herald's cry An-nounces that the Lord is nigh;

A-wake and hearken, for he brings Glad tid-ings of the King of kings.

2 Then cleansed be every Christian breast
   And furnished for so great a guest;
   Yea, let us each our hearts prepare
   For Christ to come and enter there.

3 For Thou art our salvation, Lord,
   Our refuge and our great reward;
   Without Thy grace we waste away,
   Like flowers that wither and decay.

4 To heal the sick stretch out Thine hand,
   And bid the fallen sinner stand;
   Once more upon Thy people shine,
   And fill the world with love divine.

5 All praise, eternal Son, to Thee,
   Whose advent set Thy people free:
   Whom with the Father we adore,
   And Holy Ghost, for evermore.

C. Coffin, 1736

The Church Year

8, 3, 3, 6, 8, 3, 3, 6.

Christmas Eve

J. G. Ebeling, 1666

All my heart this night re-joi - ces, As I hear, Far and near sweetest an - gel voic - es; "Christ is born," their choirs are sing-ing, Till the air Ev-erywhere Now with joy is ring - ing.

2 Hark, a voice f om yonder manger,
    Soft and sweet,
    Doth entreat,
"Flee from woe and danger;
Brethren, come; from all that grieves you
    You are freed;
    All you need
I will surely give you."

3 Come then, let us hasten yonder,
    Here let all,
    Great and small,
Kneel in awe and wonder;
Love Him who with love is yearning;
    Hail the Star
    That from far
Bright with hope is burning.

4 Ye who pine in weary sadness,
    Weep no more,
    For the door
Now is found of gladness:
Cling to Him, for He will guide you
    Where no cross,
    Pain or loss
Can again betide you.

Christmas Eve

5 Hither come, ye heavy-hearted
  Who for sin,
  Deep within,
Long and sore have smarted:
For the poisoned wounds you're feeling
  Help is near,
  One is here,
Mighty for their healing.

6 Thee, dear Lord, with heed I'll cherish,
  Live to Thee,
  And with Thee
Dying shall not perish;
But shall dwell with Thee forever,
  Far on high,
  In the joy
That can alter never.

P. Gerhardt, 1656

178   6, 6, 8, 8, 6, 6.   Franz Gruber, 1818

Ho - ly night! peaceful night! Through the dark-ness beams a light,

Yon-der, where they sweet vig-ils keep   O'er the Babe who, in si - lent sleep,

Rests in heav-en-ly peace,   Rests in heav - en-ly peace.

2 Silent night! holiest night!
  Darkness flies, and all is light!
  Shepherds hear the angels sing:
  "Hallelujah! hail the King!
    ‖:Jesus the Savior is here!":‖

3 Silent night! holiest night!
  Guiding Star, O lend thy light!
  See the eastern wise men bring

Gifts and homage to our King!
  ‖:Jesus the Savior is here!:‖

4 Silent night! holiest night!
  Wondrous Star, O lend thy light!
  With the angels let us sing
  Hallelujah to our King!
    ‖:Jesus our Savior is here!:‖

J. Mohr, 1818.

The Church Year

179 L. M.

J. A. P. Schulz, 1747—1800

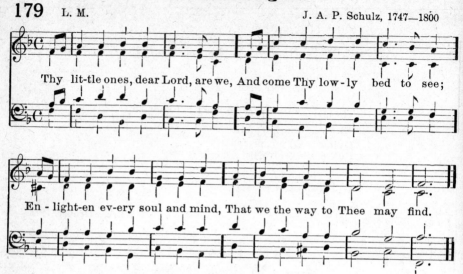

Thy lit-tle ones, dear Lord, are we, And come Thy low-ly bed to see;

En - light-en ev-ery soul and mind, That we the way to Thee may find.

2 With songs we hasten Thee to greet,
   And kiss the dust before Thy feet,
   O blessed hour, O sweetest night,
   That gave Thee birth, our soul's delight.

3 Now welcome! From Thy heavenly home
   Thou to our vale of tears art come;
   Man hath no offering for Thee, save
   The stable, manger, cross, and grave.

4 Jesus, alas! how can it be
   So few bestow a thought on Thee,
   Or on the love, so wondrous great,
   That drew Thee down to our estate?

5 O draw us wholly to Thee, Lord,
   Do Thou to us Thy grace accord,
   True faith and love to us impart,
   That we may hold Thee in our heart.

6 Keep us, howe'er the world may lure,
   In our baptismal covenant pure;
   That every yearning thought may be
   Directed only unto Thee:

7 Until at last we, too, proclaim,
   With all Thy saints, Thy glorious name;
   In Paradise our songs renew,
   And praise Thee as the angels do.

8 We gather round Thee, Jesus dear,
   So happy in Thy presence here;
   Grant us, our Savior, every one,
   To stand in heaven before Thy throne.

H. A. Brorson, 1732

Christmas

L. M.

William Gardiner's Sacred Melodies, 1815

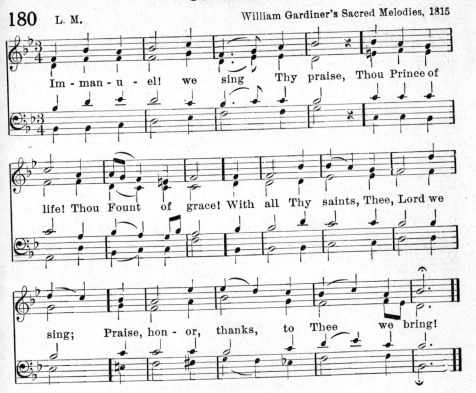

Im - man - u - el! we sing Thy praise, Thou Prince of
life! Thou Fount of grace! With all Thy saints, Thee, Lord we
sing; Praise, hon - or, thanks, to Thee we bring!

2 E'er since the world began to be,
How many a heart hath longed for Thee!
And Thou, O long-expected Guest,
Hast come at last to make us blest!

3 Now art Thou here; we know Thee now;
In lowly manger liest Thou:
A child, yet makest all things great;
Poor, yet is earth Thy robe of state.

4 Now fearless I can look on Thee:
From sin and grief Thou set'st me free:
Thou bearest wrath, Thou conquerest death,
Fear turns to joy Thy glance beneath.

5 Thou art my Head, my Lord divine;
I am Thy member, wholly Thine;
And in Thy Spirit's strength would still
Serve Thee according to Thy will.

6 Thus will I sing Thy praises here,
With joyful spirit year by year:
And when we reckon years no more,
May I in heaven Thy name adore.

P. Gerhardt, 1653

The Church Year

L. M.

German, 1539

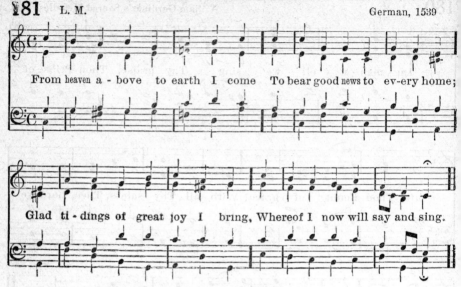

From heaven a-bove to earth I come To bear good news to ev-ery home;

Glad ti-dings of great joy I bring, Whereof I now will say and sing.

2 To you this night is born a child
Of Mary, chosen mother mild;
This little child, of lowly birth,
Shall be the joy of all the earth.

3 'Tis Christ, our God, who far on high
Hath heard your sad and bitter cry;
Himself will your salvation be,
Himself from sin will make you free.

4 He brings those blessings, long ago
Prepared by God for all below;
Henceforth His kingdom open stands
To you, as to the angel bands.

5 These are the tokens ye shall mark,
The swaddling clothes and manger dark;
There shall ye find the young child laid,
By whom the heavens and earth were made.

6 Now let us all with gladsome cheer
Follow the shepherds, and draw near
To see this wondrous gift of God,
Who hath His only Son bestowed.

7 Give heed, my heart, lift up thine eyes!
Who is it in yon manger lies?
Who is this child so young and fair?
The blessed Christ-child lieth there.

8 Welcome to earth, Thou noble Guest,
Through whom the sinful world is blest!
Thou com'st to share our misery,
What can we render, Lord, to Thee!

9 Ah, Lord, who hast created all,
How hast Thou made Thee weak and small.
That Thou must choose Thine infant bed
Where ass and ox but lately fed!

Christmas

10 Were earth a thousand times as fair,
   Beset with gold and jewels rare,
   She yet were far too poor to be
   A narrow cradle, Lord, for Thee.

11 For velvets soft and silken stuff
   Thou hast but hay and straw so rough,
   Whereon Thou, King, so rich and great,
   As 'twere Thy heaven, art throned in state.

12 Thus hath it pleased Thee to make plain
   The truth to sinners poor and vain,
   That this world's honor, wealth and might
   Are naught and worthless in Thy sight.

13 Ah, dearest Jesus, Holy Child,
   Make Thee a bed, soft undefiled,
   Within my heart, that it may be
   A quiet chamber kept for Thee.

14 My heart for very joy doth leap,
   My lips no more can silence keep;
   I, too, must raise with joyous tongue
   That sweetest ancient cradle song:

15 Glory to God in highest heaven,
   Who unto man His Son hath given!—
   While angels sing with pious mirth
   A glad New Year to all the earth.

M. Luther, 1535

182 7, 6. 4L.

Melchior Vulpius, 1609

A great and might-y won-der Our Christmas fes-tal brings:
On earth, a low-ly in-fant, Be-hold the King of kings!

2 The Word is made incarnate,
   Descending from on high;
   And cherubim sing anthems
   To shepherds, from the sky.

3 And we with them triumphant,
   Repeat the hymn again:
   "To God on high be glory,
   And peace on earth to men!"

4 Since all He comes to ransom,
   By all be He adored,
   The Infant born in Bethlehem,
   The Savior and the Lord!

5 All idol forms shall perish,
   And error shall decay,
   And Christ shall wield His scepter,
   Our Lord and God for aye.

St. Germannus, 631—7?

183   8, 8, 7. 8, 8, 7, 4, 4, 4, 4, 8.

P. Nicolai, 1599

Re-joice, re-joice this hap-py morn, A Sav-ior un-to us is born, The Christ, the Lord of glo - ry; His low-ly birth in Beth-le - hem The an-gels from on high pro-claim, And sing redemption's sto - ry; My soul, ex - tol God's great fav-or, Bless him ev - er for sal-va - tion, Give Him praise and a - dor - a - tion!

Birgitte C. Boye. 1778

Christmas

8, 8, 8, 8, 4.

Johann Walther, 1424

O Je - sus Christ, all praise to Thee, Thou who art pleased a

man to be; To dwell with men Thou dost not scorn, And ang-els shout to

see Thee born, Hal - le - lu - jah.   -le - lu - jah............

2 The eternal Father's only Son
   Now takes a manger for His throne:
   The everlasting fount of good,
   Assumes our mortal flesh and blood.
      Hallelujah.

3 He whom the world can not enclose
   In Mary's bosom doth repose;
   To be a little child He deigns
   Who all things by Himself sustains.
      Hallelujah.

4 The eternal Light to us descends,
   Its brightness to the earth it lends,
   And purely shines upon our night,
   To make us children of the light.
      Hallelujah.

5 The only Son, true God confessed,
   To His own world now comes a Guest;
   And through this vale of tears our
         Guide,
   Doth in His heaven our home provide.
      Hallelujah.

6 In poorest guise to us He came,
   Himself He bears our sin and shame,
   That, as His heirs in heaven above,
   We may with angels share His love.
      Hallelujah.

7 His love to show, surpassing thought!
   God's Son this wondrous work hath
         wrought;
   Then let us all unite to raise
   Our song of glad, unceasing praise.
      Hallelujah.

M Luther, 1524

The Church Year

185 8, 7, 8, 7, 8, 8, 7, 8, 8, 7.

German, 14th Century

In this our hap-py Christmas-tide The joy-ful bells are ring - ing;

To praise be all our powers ap-plied, God's grace and mer-cy sing - ing;

In Him by whom the world was made, Now in the low - ly man-ger laid,

Re-joice we in the spir - it; Thy praise, O Sav-ior, we will sound

Un - to the earth's re - mot-est bound, That all the world shall hear it.

Christmas

2 A little Son, the virgin-born,
　　True God from everlasting
　To rescue us who were forlorn,
　　His lot with us is casting:
　It moved His tender heart to see
　This world of sin and misery
　　In condemnation lying;
　Therefore He came from realms above
　Down to our earth, drawn by His love,
　　To soothe our grief and sighing.

3 Our thanks we offer Him today,
　　Although a poor oblation,
　Hallelujah! our joyful lay
　　Shall sound through every nation;
　Now in our camp the Ark we see,
　Therefore we shout the victory
　　With joyful hearts unfearing;
　We sing of peace, the peace profound,
　That hell shall tremble at the sound,
　　Our Christmas anthem hearing.

4 That God has laid His anger by,
　　He by His gift hath shown us;
　He gives His Son for us to die,
　　In Him He now doth own us;
　These joyful tidings tell abroad,
　That Jesus Christ, the Son of God,
　　From sin doth us deliver;
　Who then should not be glad today
　When Christ is born, the sinners' stay,
　　Who is of grace the giver?

5 As darkest night must fade and die
　　Before the sun's appearing,
　So fades my grief away, when I
　　Think on these tidings cheering,
　That God from all eternity
　Hath loved the world, and hath on me
　　Bestowed His grace and favor;
　I'll ne'er forget the angels' strain:
　Peace—peace on earth, good will to
　　To you is born a Savior!　　[men,

6 Although my joyful Christmas lay
　　Is mingled with my sighing,
　The cross shall never take away
　　My joy and praise undying;
　For when the heart is most opprest,
　The harp of joy is tuned the best,
　　The better strains are ringing,
　The cross itself, at Jesus' will,
　Must aid my soul, that I may still
　　In grief His praise be singing.

7 Hallelujah! our strife is o'er,
　　Who, then, should pine in sadness?
　Who now should grieve in anguish
　　In these our days of gladness? [sore
　Thou Church of God, O sing this morn:
　To us is Christ the Savior born,
　　O joy that none can sever!
　Hallelujah! sing thou my heart,
　Now Christ is mine, I can depart
　　To be with Him for ever.

H. A. Brorson, 1732

186　7s. 4L.　　　German medieval, adapted by Luther or Walther　1524

Come, Thou Savior of our race, Choicest gift of heavenly grace!

O Thou bless-ed vir-gin's Son, Be Thy race on earth be-gun.

2 Not of mortal blood or birth,
　He descends from heaven to earth:
　By the Holy Ghost conceived,
　Truly man to be believed.

3 Wondrous birth! O wondrous Child!
　Of the virgin undefiled!
　Though by all the world disowned,
　Still to be in heaven enthroned.

4 From the Father forth He came,
　And returneth to the same,

Captive leading death and hell:
High the song of triumph swell!

5 Equal to the Father now,
　Though to dust Thou once didst bow;
　Boundless shall Thy kingdom be:
　When shall we its glories see?

6 Brightly doth Thy manger shine,
　Glorious is its light divine:
　Let not sin o'ercloud this light,
　Ever be our faith thus bright.

Ambrose, d. 397
M. Luther, 1524

187 14, 14, 4, 7, 8.

German, 1668

Triumph, ye heav-ens! re - joice ye with high a - dor - a -
tion! Sing to the Lord, to the Sav - ior, in glad ex - ul -
ta - tion! An - gels give ear! God un - to men draw - eth
near, Bring - ing to lost ones sal - va - tion.

2 Triumph, ye heavens! rejoice, O ye nations and wonder!
God and the sinner no power of the devil may sunder.
  "Peace and good-will!"
  Hark! it is echoing still,
  Silencing Sinai's thunder!

3 God in man's nature! O mystery past comprehending!
Now is the temple thrown wide and the incense ascending!
  Christ is the way!
  We who were once far away,
  Now at His footstool are bending.

Christmas

4 Hast Thou, O Holy One, deigned of my need to be thinking?
Chosen me, callèd me, the waters of life to be drinking?
    Shall not my mind
    Fullness of blessing here find,
Deep in humility sinking?

5 King of all glory! what grace in Thy humiliation!
Thou wert a child who of old wert the Lord of creation!
    Thee will I own,
    Thee would I follow alone,
Heir of Thy wondrous salvation.

6 Faithful Immanuel! let me Thy glories be telling;
Ever, my Savior, be Thou in mine inmost heart dwelling.
    With me abide;
    Teach me to stay at Thy side,
Where the love-fountain is welling.

7 Friend of the sinner! Lord Jesus! my spirit is soaring
Where Thou art throned, on Thy head the sweet spikenard still pouring.
    Take me above,
    There will I sing of Thy love,
Ever Thy person adoring.

                    G. Tersteegen, 1735

188 C. M.   Este's Psalter, 1592

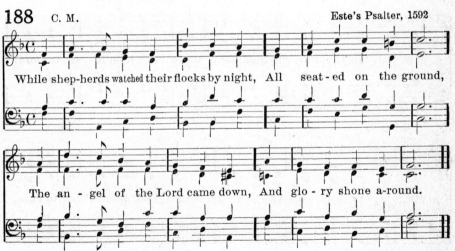

While shep-herds watched their flocks by night, All seat-ed on the ground,
The an - gel of the Lord came down, And glo - ry shone a-round.

2 "Fear not," said he—for mighty dread
Had seized their troubled mind—
"Glad tidings of great joy I bring,
To you and all mankind.

3 "To you in David's town this day,
Is born of David's line
The Savior, who is Christ the Lord,
And this shall be the sign—

4 The heavenly Babe you there shall
To human view displayed,   [find,

All meanly wrapped in swathing bands
And in a manger laid."

5 Thus spake the seraph— and forth-
Appeared a shining throng [with
Of angels, praising God, who thus
Addressed their joyful song:—

6 "All glory be to God on high,
And to the earth be peace;
Good-will henceforth from heaven to
Begin and never cease." [men

                    Nahum Tate, 1702

189 8, 7, 8, 7, 8, 8, 7, 8, 8, 7. German, 14th Century

To us is born a bless-ed child, To us a Son is giv - en,

Born of a vir - gin un - de - filed, He is our hope of heav - en;

Had not this Child to us been born, We all had been in sin for-lorn,

He is our sole sal - va - tion; All thanks, Lord Jesus Christ, to Thee,

That Thou wert pleased a man to be: Save us from con-dem-na - tion!

192 German, Anon., Before 1422

Christmas

8, 7. 8L.

R. Redhead, 1820—88

Hark! what mean those ho - ly voi-ces, Sweet-ly sound-ing through the skies?

Lo! th'an-gel - ic host re - joic - es, Heav'n-ly Hal-le - lu-jahs rise.

List - en to the wondrous stor - y Which they chant in hymns of joy:

"Glo - ry in the high-est, glo - ry! Glo - ry be to God most high!"

2 "Peace on earth, good-will from
  heaven,
  Reaching far as man is found,
Souls redeemed, and sins forgiven,
  Loud our golden harps shall sound.
Christ is born, the great Anointed:
  Heaven and earth His praises sing;
O receive whom God appointed
  For your prophet, priest, and king.

3 "Hasten, mortals, to adore Him;
  Learn His name, and taste His joy;
Till in heaven ye sing before Him,
  'Glory be to God most High!'"
Let us learn the wondrous story
  Of our great Redeemer's birth;
Spread the brightness of His glory
  Till it cover all the earth.

J. Cawood, 1819

The Church Year

191   8, 7, 8, 7, 7, 7, 8, 8.   Ludv. M. Lindeman, 1812—87

Thou, whose com-ing seers and sa-ges Long fore-told to Is - ra - el,

Hast appeared in these last a - ges, Je - sus Christ Im-man - u - el.

O thou precious day of grace, Fraught with bless-ings to our race! None need now de-

spair of par - don, Bowed beneath a hope - less bur - den.

2 Simeon longed for Thy salvation;
    David, wrapt with holy fire,
  Poured forth strains of inspiration,
    As he swept his royal lyre;
  Righteous men and gifted seers
  Longed for Thee in bygone years,
  Some in silence, some loud crying,
  Mingling prayers with tears and sighing.

3 God be blessèd, who hath granted
    In His grace to you and me,
  That for which so many panted,—
    Vainly hoped to hear and see.
  Now God's counsel is revealed,
  And the vision is unsealed;
  God hath heard your supplication,
  And is come to bring salvation.

Christmas

4 Joyfully we sing Hosanna!
   Blessed Savior, enter in;
Feed us with the living manna,
   Cleanse our hearts from every sin.
See, we open wide the door!
Enter, to depart no more;
Come, and let us now enthrone Thee
In the hearts that long to own Thee.

5 Sin, alas! hath long compelled us
   Her dread bidding to obey,
And, both soul and body, held us
   Captive with resistless sway;
All our efforts have been vain

To cast off her iron chain;
Thou, and Thou alone, Lord Jesus,
Canst from all our sins release us.

6 Take Thy kingdom, wait no longer,
   Since to Thee it doth belong;
And He only who is stronger
   Can release us from the strong.
Make us happy, God's dear Son,
Reap the fruit Thy love has won;
Till earth's farthest realms adore
   Thee,
And her kings fall down before Thee.

C. J. P. Spitta, 1843

192   8, 7, 8, 7, 4, 7.

E. J. Hopkins, 1818—1901

An-gels, from the realms of glo-ry, Wing your flight o'er all the earth;

Ye, who sang cre-a-tion's sto-ry, Now pro-claim Mes-si-ah's birth:

Come and wor-ship— Wor-ship Christ the new-born King!

2 Shepherds, in the fields abiding,
   Watching o'er your flocks by night,
God with man is now residing,
   Yonder shines the heavenly light:
   Come and worship—
Worship Christ, the new-born King!

3 Sages, leave your contemplations;
   Brighter visions beam afar:
Seek the great Desire of nations,

Ye have seen His natal star:
   Come and worship—
Worship Christ, the new-born King!

4 Saints, before the altar bending,
   Watching long in hope and fear,
Suddenly the Lord, descending,
   In His temple shall appear:
   Come and worship—
Worship Christ, the new-born King!

J. Montgomery, 1816

193 L. M.

C. Balle, 1850

The hap-py Christ-mas comes once more, The heaven-ly Guest at the door, The bless-ed words the shep-herds thrill, The joy-ous ti-dings: Peace, good-will.

2 To David's city let us fly,
Where angels sing beneath the sky;
Through plain and village pressing near,
And news from God with shepherds hear.

3 O let us go with quiet mind,
The gentle Babe with shepherds find,
To gaze on Him who gladdens them,
The loveliest flower on Jesse's stem.

4 The lowly Savior meekly lies,
Laid off the splendor of the skies;
No crown bedecks His forehead fair,
No pearl, nor gem, nor silk is there.

5 No human glory, might, and gold,
The lovely Infant's form enfold;
The manger and the swaddlings poor
Are His, whom angels' songs adore.

6 O wake our hearts, in gladness sing,
And keep our Christmas with our King,
Till living song, from loving souls,
Like sound of mighty water rolls!

7 O holy Child, Thy manger gleams
Till earth and heaven glow with its beams,
Till midnight hath noon's brightness won,
And Jacob's Star outshines the sun.

Christmas

8 Thou patriarchs' joy, Thou prophets' song,
Thou heavenly Day-spring looked for long,
Thou Son of Man, incarnate Word,
Great David's Son, great David's Lord!

9 Come, Jesus, glorious heavenly Guest,
Keep Thine own Christmas in our breast;
Then David's harp-string, hushed so long,
Shall swell our jubilee of song.

N. F. S. Grundtvig, 1817

194   8, 4, 8, 8.   Ludv. M. Lindeman, 1312—8?

A Babe is born in Beth-le-hem, In Beth-le-hem; Therefore re-joice, Je-ru-sa-lem. Hal-le-lu-jah, Hal-le-lu-jah.

2 He doth within a manger lie,
    A manger lie;
  Whose throne is set above the sky.
    Hallelujah, Hallelujah.

3 Stillness was all the manger round,
    The manger round;
  The creature its Creator found.
    Hallelujah, Hallelujah.

4 The wise men came, led by the star,
    Led by the star;
  Gold, myrrh and incense, brought
      from far.
    Hallelujah, Hallelujah.

5 His mother is the virgin mild,
    The virgin mild;
  And He the Father's only Child.
    Hallelujah, Hallelujah.

6 Like us, in flesh of human frame,
    Of human frame;
  Unlike in sin alone He came.
    Hallelujah, Hallelujah.

7 To fallen man Himself He bowed,
    Himself He bowed;
  That He might lift us up to God.
    Hallelujah, Hallelujah.

8 On this most blessed Jubilee,
    Blest Jubilee,
  All glory be, O God, to Thee.
    Hallelujah, Hallelujah.

9 The Holy Trinity be praised,
    Hallelujah;
  To God our ceaseless thanks be raised
    Hallelujah, Hallelujah.

Anon., Latin, 14th Century

195 11s. 5L.

J. F. Wade's Cantus Diversi, 1751

Come hith - er, ye faith - ful, tri - umph - ant - ly sing! Come, see in the man - ger the an - gels' great King! To Beth - le - hem hast - en with joy - ful ac - cord; O come ye, come

Christmas

hith - er to wor - - ship the Lord!....... O

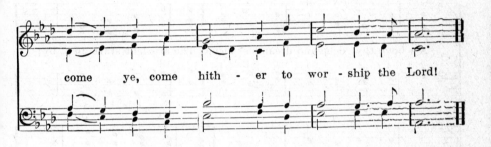

come ye, come hith - er to wor - ship the Lord!

2 True Son of the Father, He comes from the skies;
  To be born of a virgin He does not despise:
  To Bethlehem hasten with joyful accord;
  O come ye, come hither to worship the Lord!
  O come ye, come hither to worship the Lord!

3 Hark! hark to the angels! all singing in heaven,
  "To God in the highest all glory be given!"
  To Betlehem hasten with joyful accord;
  O come ye, come hither to worship the Lord!
  O come ye, come hither to worship the Lord!

4 To Thee, then, O Jesus, this day of Thy birth,
  Be glory and honor through heaven and earth;
  True Godhead incarnate! omnipotent Word!
  O come, let us hasten to worship the Lord!
  O come, let us hasten to worship the Lord!

Anon., Latin, 17th or 18th Century

196 8, 6, 8, 6, 7, 6, 8, 6. J. Barnby, 1838—96

O lit-tle town of Beth-le-hem, How still we see thee lie!......

A-bove thy deep and dreamless sleep The si-lent stars go by;

Yet in thy dark streets shin-eth The ev-er-last-ing light;

The hopes and fears of all the years Are met in thee to-night.

2 For Christ is born of Mary,
   And, gathered all above,
 While mortals sleep, the angels keep
   Their watch of wondering love.
 O morning stars, together
   Proclaim the holy birth!
 And praises sing to God the King
   And peace to men on earth.

3 How silently, how silently,
   The wondrous gift is given!
 So God imparts to human hearts
   The blessings of His heaven.

No ear may hear His coming,
   But in this world of sin,
 Where meek souls will receive Him
     still,
   The dear Christ enters in.

4 O holy Child of Bethlehem!
   Descend to us, we pray;
 Cast out our sin, and enter in;
   Be born in us today.
 We hear the Christmas angels
   The great glad tidings tell;
 O come to us, abide with us,
   Our Lord Immanuel!

P. Brooks, 1868.

Christmas

7, 6. 8L.

Zinck's Koralbog, 1801

Re-joice, re - joice, ye Chris-tians, With all your hearts, this morn!

O hear the bless-ed ti - dings, "The Lord, the Christ, is born," Now

brought us by the an - gels That stand a - bout God's throne;

O love-ly are the voic - es That make such ti-dings known!

2 O hearken to their singing!
　This Child shall be your friend;
　The Father so hath willed it,
　That thus your woes should end.
　The Son is freely given,
　That in Him ye may have
　The Father's grace and blessing,
　And know He loves to save.

3 Nor deem the form too lowly
　That clothes Him at this hour;
　For know ye what it hideth?
　'Tis God's almighty power.

Though now within the manger
　So poor and weak He lies,
　He is the Lord of all things,
　He reigns above the skies.

4 Sin, death, and hell, and Satan
　Have lost the victory;
　This Child shall overthrow them,
　As ye shall surely see.
　Their wrath shall naught avail them;
　Fear not, their reign is o'er;
　This Child shall overthrow them,—
　O hear, and doubt no more!

German. Anon.. 1540

198 7s. 8L.

Arr. fr. Mendelssohn, 1855

Hark! the her - ald an - gels sing Glo - ry to the

new - born King; Peace on earth, and mer - cy mild,

God and sin - ners rec - on-ciled! Joy-ful, all ye na-tions, rise,

Join the tri - umph of the skies; U - ni - ver - sal

na - ture say, Christ the Lord is born to - day. Hark! The her - ald

Organ Pedal

Christmas

an - gels sing   Glo - ry   to   the new - born King.

2 Christ, by highest heaven adored:
   Christ, the everlasting Lord;
   Late in time behold Him come,
   Offspring of a virgin's womb:
   Veiled in flesh the Godhead see;
   Hail the incarnate Deity,
   Pleased as man with men to dwell,
   Jesus, our Immanuel!
      Hark! The herald angels sing
      Glory to the new-born King.

3 Hail the heavenly Prince of Peace,
   Hail the Sun of Righteousness;
   Life and light to all He brings,
   Risen with healing in His wings.
   Mild, He lays His glory by
   Born that man no more may die,
   Born to raise the sons of earth,
   Born to give them second birth.
      Hark! The herald angels sing
      Glory to the new-born King.

4 Come, Desire of nations, come,
   Fix in us Thy humble home;
   Rise, the woman's conquering seed,
   Bruise in us the serpent's head.
   Adam's likeness, Lord, efface;
   Stamp Thy likeness in its place;
   O to all Thyself impart,
   Formed in each believing heart.
      Hark! The herald angels sing
      Glory to the new-born King.

C. Wesley, 1739

199 6, 6, 7, 6, 7, 6, 5, 5.

14th Century, J. Klug, 1535

Now sing we, now re - joice, Now raise to heaven our voice; Lo! He from whom joy streameth, Poor in the man - ger lies; Yet not so bright-ly beam-eth The sun in yon - der skies! Thou my Sav - ior art! Thou my Sav - ior art!

2 Given from on high to me,
I cannot rise to Thee:
O cheer my wearied spirit:
O pure and holy Child,
Through all Thy grace and merit,
Blest Jesus! Lord most mild,
‖: Draw me after Thee! :‖

3 Now through His Son doth shine
The Father's grace divine:
Death over us hath reignéd
Through sin and vanity:

The Son for us obtainéd
Eternal joy on high.
‖: May we praise Him there! :‖

4 O wnere shall joy be found?
Where but on heavenly ground?
Where now the angels singing
With all His saints unite,
Their sweetest praises bringing
In heavenly joy and light:
‖: May we praise Him there! :‖

Latin and German, 15th Century

Christmas

200 11, 11, 12, 11.

J. Goss, 1800—80

Shout the glad tidings, ex-ult-ing-ly sing; Je-ru-sa-lem triumphs, Mes-si-ah is King. 1. Zi-on, the mar-vel-ous sto-ry be tell-ing, The Son of the Highest, how low-ly His birth; The brightest arch-an-gel in glo-ry ex-cel-ling, He stoops to re-deem thee, He reigns up-on earth.

2 Tell how He cometh; from nation to nation
The heart-cheering news let the earth echo round:
How free to the faithful He offers salvation,
How His people with joy everlasting are crowned.
Shout the glad tidings, etc.

3 Mortals, your homage be gratefully bringing,
And sweet let the gladsome Hosanna arise:
Ye angels, the full Hallelujah be singing:
One chorus resound through the earth and the skies.
Shout the glad tidings, etc.

W. A. Muhlenberg, 1826

The Church Year

201   C. M.   Arr. fr. G F. Händel, by L. Mason, 1830

Joy to the world! the Lord is come: Let earth receive her King; Let ev-ery heart pre-pare Him room,

And heaven and na-ture sing, And heaven and na-ture
And heaven and na-ture sing,................
And heaven and na-ture sing, And

sing, And heaven, and heaven and na-ture sing.
heaven and na-ture sing,

2 Joy to the world! the Savior reigns:
    Let men their songs employ,
   While fields and floods, rocks, hills,
       and plains,
     ‖:Repeat the sounding joy.:‖

3 No more let sins and sorrows grow,
    No thorns infest the ground;

He comes to make His blessings flow
   ‖:Far as the curse is found.:‖

4 He rules the world with truth and
     grace,
   And makes the nations prove
  The glories of His righteousness,
   ‖:And wonders of His love.:‖

                              I. Watts. 1719

202 8, 7. 8L.

J. A. Freylinghausen's Gesangbuch, 1704

Come, Thou long-ex-pect-ed Je-sus, Born to set Thy peo-ple free;

From our fears and sins re-lease us, Let us find our rest in Thee.

Israel's strength and con-so-la-tion, Hope of all the earth Thou art;

Dear de-sire of ev-ery na-tion, Joy of ev-ery longing heart.

2 Born Thy people to deliver;
Born a child, and yet a king;
Born to reign in us for ever,
Now Thy gracious kingdom bring,
By Thine own eternal Spirit,
Rule Thou in our hearts alone;
By Thine all-sufficient merit,
Raise us to Thy glorious throne.

C. Wesley. 1744

203　7, 6. 8L.

J. Stainer, 1875

Light of the Gen-tile na-tions, Thy peo-ple's joy and love!

Drawn by Thy Spir-it hith-er, We glad-ly come to prove

Thy pres-ence in Thy tem-ple, And wait with ear-nest mind,

As Simeon once had wait-ed His Sav-ior God to find.

2 Yes, Lord, Thy servants meet Thee,
　E'en now, in every place
Where Thy true word hath promised,
　That they should see Thy face.
Thou yet wilt gently grant us,
　Who gather round Thee here,
In faith's strong arms to bear Thee,
　As once that aged seer.

3 Be Thou our joy, our brightness,
　That shines 'mid pain and loss,
Our sun in times of terror,
　The glory round our cross:
A glow in sinking spirits,
　A sunbeam in distress,
Physician, friend in sickness,
　In death our happiness.

4 Let us, O Lord, be faithful
　With Simeon to the end,
That so his dying song may
　From all our hearts ascend:
"O Lord, let now Thy servant
　Depart in peace for aye,
Since I have seen my Savior,
　Have here beheld His day."

5 My Savior, I behold Thee
　Now with the eye of faith:
No foe of Thee can rob me,
　Though bitter words he saith.
Within my heart abiding
　As Thou dost dwell in me,
No pain, no death hath terrors
　To part my soul from Thee!

J. Franck 1674

Sunday after Christmas

204 7, 6. 8L.

A. H. Mann, 1897

O Sav-ior, pre-cious Sav-ior, Whom yet un-seen we love,

O Name of might and fa - vor, All oth-er names a - bove!

We wor-ship Thee, we bless Thee, To Thee, O Christ, we sing;

We praise Thee and con - fess Thee Our ho - ly Lord and King.

2 O Bringer of salvation,
　Who wondrously hast wrought,
Thyself the revelation
　Of love beyond our thought:
We worship Thee, we bless Thee,
　To Thee, O Christ, we sing;
We praise Thee, and confess Thee
　Our gracious Lord and King.

3 In Thee all fullness dwelleth,
　All grace and power divine;
The glory that excelleth,
　O Son of God, is Thine;
We worship Thee, we bless Thee,
　To Thee, O Christ, we sing;
We praise Thee, and confess Thee
　Our glorious Lord and King.

4 O grant the consummation
　Of this our song above,
In endless adoration,
　And everlasting love;
Then shall we praise and bless Thee
　Where perfect praises ring,
And evermore confess Thee
　Our Savior and our King.

Frances R. Havergal, 1870

205 8, 7, 8, 7, 8, 8, 7.

German, 1523

To us sal - va - tion now is come, Through free-est grace and fa - vor, Our works could not a - vert our doom, They keep and save us nev - er; Faith looks to Je - sus Christ a - lone, Who did for all the world a - tone; He is our one Re - deem - er.

Sunday after Christmas

2 What God doth in His law demand,
   No man to Him doth render;
Before His bar all guilty stand;
   His law speaks curse in thunder,
The law demands a perfect heart;
We were defiled in every part,
   And lost was our condition,

3 False dreams deluded minds did fill,
   That God His law did tender,
As if to Him we could, at will,
   The due obedience render:
The law is but a mirror bright
To bring the inbred sin to sight,
   That lurks within our nature.

4 To cleanse ourselves from sinful stain,
   According to our pleasure,
Was labor lost— works were in vain—
   Sin grew beyond all measure;
For when with power the precept came,
It did reveal sin's guilt and shame
   And awful condemnation.

5 Still all the law fulfilled must be,
   Else we were lost forever,
Then God His Son sent down that He
   Might us from doom deliver;
He all the law for us fulfilled
And thus His Father's anger stilled
   Which over us impended.

6 As Christ hath full atonement made
   And brought to us salvation,
So may each Christian now be glad
   And build on this foundation:
Thy grace alone, dear Lord, I plead,
Thy death now is my life indeed,
   For Thou hast paid my ransom.

7 Not doubting this, I trust in Thee,
   Thy word cannot be broken,
Thou all dost call, "Come unto Me!"
   No falsehood hast Thou spoken:
"He who believes and is baptized,
He shall be saved," say'st Thou, O Christ,
   And he shall never perish.

8 The just is he— and he alone—
   Who by this faith is living,
The faith that by good works is shown,
   To God the glory giving;

Faith gives thee peace with God above,
But thou thy neighbor, too, must love,
   If thou art new created.

9 The law reveals the guilt of sin,
   And makes man conscience-stric-
The gospel then doth enter in, [ken
   The sin-sick soul to quicken:
Come to the cross, look up and live!
The law no peace to thee doth give,
   Nor can its deeds afford it.

10 Faith to the cross of Christ doth
   And rests in Him securely; [cling
And forth from it good works must
   As fruits and tokens surely; [spring
Still faith doth justify alone,
Works serve thy neighbor and make known
   The faith that lives within thee.

11 Hope waits for the accepted hour—
   Till God give joy for mourning,
When He displays His healing pow-
   Thy sighs to songs are turning; [er,
Thy needs are known unto thy Lord,
And He is faithful to His word,
   This is our hope's foundation.

12 Though it may seem, He hears thee
   Count not thyself forsaken; [not,
Thy wants are ne'er by Him forgot,
   Let this thy hope awaken;
His word is sure, here is thy stay,
Although thy heart to this saith nay,
   Let not thy faith be shaken.

13 All blessing, honor, thanks and praise,
   To Father, Son and Spirit,
The God who saved us by His grace,
   All glory to His merit:
O Father in the heavens above,
The work begun performs Thy love,
   Thy worthy name be hallowed.

14 Thy kingdom come, Thy will be done
   In earth, as 'tis in heaven:
Keep us in life, by grace led on,
   Forgiving and forgiven;
Save Thou us in temptation's hour,
And from all ills; Thine is the power,
   And all the glory, Amen!

P. Speratus, 1523

The Church Year

8, 7, 8, 7, 8, 8, 7.　　　　New Year's Eve　　　　J. Wolff, 1569

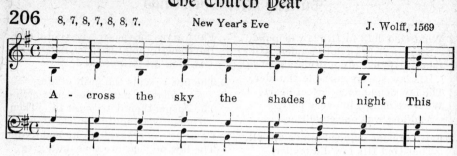

A - cross the sky the shades of night This

win - ter's eve are fleet - ing: We deck Thine al - tar,

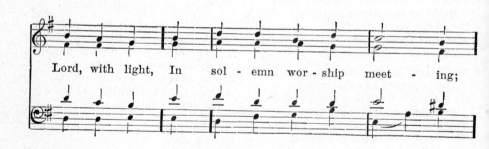

Lord, with light, In sol - emn wor - ship meet - ing;

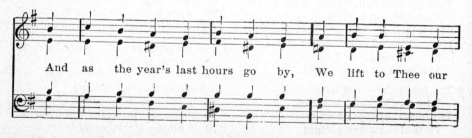

And as the year's last hours go by, We lift to Thee our

New Year's Eve

ear - nest cry, Once more Thy love en - treat - ing.

2 Before the cross subdued we bow,
    To Thee our prayers addressing;
Recounting all Thy mercies now,
    And all our sins confessing;
Beseeching Thee, this coming year,
To hold us in Thy faith and fear,
    And crown us with Thy blessing.

3 And while we pray we lift our eyes
    To dear ones gone before us,
Safe housed with Thee in Paradise,
    Whose peace descendeth o'er us:
And beg of Thee, when life is past,
To re-unite us all at last,
    And to our lost restore us.

4 We gather up, in this brief hour,
    The memory of Thy mercies:
Thy wondrous goodness, love and power.
    Our grateful song rehearses:
For Thou hast been our strength and stay
In many a dark and dreary day
    Of sorrow and reverses.

5 In many an hour, when fear and dread,
    Like evil spells have bound us,
And clouds were gathering overhead,
    Thy providence hath found us:
In many a night when waves ran high,
Thy gracious presence, drawing nigh,
    Hath made all calm around us.

6 Then, O great God, in years to come,
    Whatever fate betide us,
Right onward through our journey home
    Be Thou at hand to guide us:
Nor leave us till, at close of life,
Safe from all perils, toil, and strife,
    Heaven shall unfold and hide us.

Jas. Hamilton. 1882.

The Church Year

New Year

Louis Bourgeois, 1547

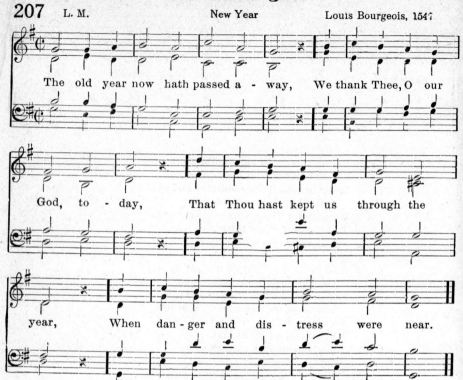

The old year now hath passed a - way, We thank Thee, O our God, to - day, That Thou hast kept us through the year, When dan - ger and dis - tress were near.

2 We pray Thee, O eternal Son,
   Who with the Father **reign'st** as one,
   To guard and rule Thy Christendom
   Through all the ages yet to come.

3 Take not Thy saving word away,
   Our souls' true comfort, staff, and stay;
   Abide with us and keep us free
   From errors, following only Thee.

4 O help us to forsake all sin,
   A new and holier course begin;
   Mark not what once was done amiss,
   A happier, better year be this:

5 Wherein as Christians we may live,
   Or die in peace that Thou canst give,
   To rise again when Thou shalt come,
   And enter our eternal home,

6 There shall we thank Thee, and adore,
   With all the angels evermore;
   Lord Jesus Christ, increase our faith
   To praise Thy name through life and death.

Jacob Tapp? 1588

208 8s. 7s. 6L.

Arr. fr. J. M. Haydn (?)

To the Name of our sal-va-tion Laud and hon-or let us pay,

Which for many a gen-er-a-tion Hid in God's foreknowledge lay,

But with ho-ly ex-ul-ta-tion We may sing a-loud to-day.

2 Jesus is the name we treasure,
　Name beyond what words can tell;
Name of gladness, name of pleasure,
　Ear and heart delighting well;
Name of sweetness passing measure,
　Saving us from sin and hell.

3 'Tis the name for adoration,
　Name for songs of victory,
Name for holy meditation
　In this vale of misery,
Name for joyful veneration
　By the citizens on high.

4 'Tis the name that whoso preacheth
　Speaks like music to the ear;
Who in prayer this name beseecheth

Sweetest comfort findeth near;
Whc its perfect wisdom reacheth
Heavenly joy possesseth here.

5 Jesus is the name exalted
　Over every other name,
In this name, whene'er assaulted,
　We can put our foes to shame;
Strength to them who else had halted,
　Eyes to blind, and feet to lame.

6 Therefore we in love adoring
　This most blesséd name revere,
Holy Jesus, Thee imploring
　So to write it in us here,
That hereafter heavenward soaring
　We may sing with angels there.

Anon., Latin, 1496

The Church Year

To God the an-them rais - ing, Sing, Christians, great and small,

Sing out, His goodness prais - ing, O thank Him one and all!

Be - hold, how God this year, Which now is safe-ly end - ed,

Hath in His love be - friend - ed His children far and near.

2 Let us consider rightly
   His mercies manifold,
And let us not think lightly
   Of all His gifts untold!
Let thankfulness recall
How God this year hath led us,
How He hath clothed and fed us,
   The great ones and the small.

3 To Church and State He granted
   His peace in every place,
His vineyard He hath planted
   Among us by His grace;
His ever-bounteous hand
Prosperity hath given,
And want and famine driven
   From this our Christian land.

4 Our God us well defended,
   He kept us through His grace;
But if He had contended
   With us, our sins to trace,
   And given us our meed,
We all had then been lying
In sin and sorrow, dying
   Each one for his misdeed.

5 His Father-heart is yearning
   To take us for His own,
When our transgressions mourning,
   We trust in Christ alone;
   When in His name we pray,
And humbly make confession,
He pardons our transgression,
   And is our faithful stay.

New Year

6 O Father dear in heaven,
 For all Thy gifts of love,
Which Thou to us hast given,
 We lift our thanks above.
‖:In Jesus' name we here,

To Thee our prayers addressing,
Still ask Thee for Thy blessing:‖
(1) Grant us a joyful year!
(2) Grant us a peaceful year!
(3) With mercies crown this year!
(Second half of verse sung three times,
each time with a different ending.)
P. Eber, ca., 1569

210 8, 7, 8, 7, 7, 7.

J Chr. Bach, 1693

Help, Lord Je - sus, let Thy blessing Rest up - on this opening year;

May we now, new strength possess-ing, Walk in love and ho - ly fear;

Dear-est Sav - ior, speed our way; Strength be - stow from day to day.

2 In our hearts one purpose keeping,
 May we live alone to Thee;
In our waking and our sleeping,
 Jesus, Thou our portion be;
Going out, be Thou our guide;
In our home with us abide.

3 May we, in unfeigned repentance,
 Seek forgiveness in Thy name,
Nor the law's condemning sentence
 Fill our hearts with fear and shame;
Thou alone canst pardon give,
Dearest Lord, our sins forgive.

4 Lord, Thy blessing now receiving,
 Grant Thou us a hallowed year;
Firmly on Thy word believing,

May our service be sincere;
That on earth we may become
Fitted for our heavenly home.

5 Jesus, Thou our footsteps guiding,
 May we never stray from Thee;
Jesus, near us still abiding,
 Thou our constant guardian be:
Jesus, Thou our thoughts inspire,
Jesus be our hearts' desire.

6 Savior, when this year is closing,
 Marked by mercies large and free,
May we, in Thy love reposing,
 Leave the future all with Thee;
Gladly in Thy courts appear,
Gladly wait Thy summons here.

J. Rist, 1642

211 7s. 4L.   J. H. Knecht, 1793

Je - sus, name of wondrous love, Name all oth - er names a - bove!

Un - to which must ev - ery knee Bow in deep hu - mil - i - ty.

2 Jesus, name decreed of old,
To the maiden mother told,
Kneeling in her lowly cell,
By the angel Gabriel.

3 Jesus, name of priceless worth
To the fallen sons of earth,
For the promise that it gave,
"Jesus shall His people save."

4 Jesus, name of mercy mild,
Given to the holy Child,

When the cup of human woe
First He tasted here below.

5 Jesus, only name that's given
Under all the mighty heaven,
Whereby man, to sin enslaved,
Bursts his fetters, and is saved.

6 Jesus, name of wondrous love,
Human name of God above:
Pleading only this we flee,
Helpless, O our God, to Thee.
            W. W. How, 1854

212 C. M.   W. Croft, 1708

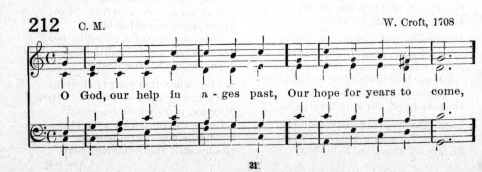

O God, our help in a - ges past, Our hope for years to come,

New Year

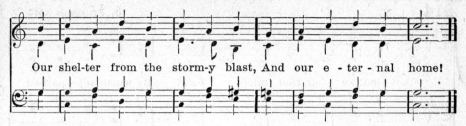

Our shel-ter from the storm-y blast, And our e - ter - nal home!

2 Under the shadow of Thy throne
   Thy saints have dwelt secure;
Sufficient is Thine arm alone,
   And our defense is sure.

3 Before the hills in order stood,
   Or earth received her frame,
From everlasting Thou art God,
   To endless years the same.

4 A thousand ages in Thy sight
   Are like an evening gone;

Short as the watch that ends the night,
   Before the rising sun.

5 Time, like an ever rolling stream,
   Bears all its sons away;
They fly, forgotten, as a dream
   Dies at the opening day.

6 O God, our help in ages past,
   Our hope for years to come!
Be Thou our guard while life shall
   And our eternal home.   [last,

I. Watts, 1719

213 7s. 4L.   J. A. Freylinghausen, 1705

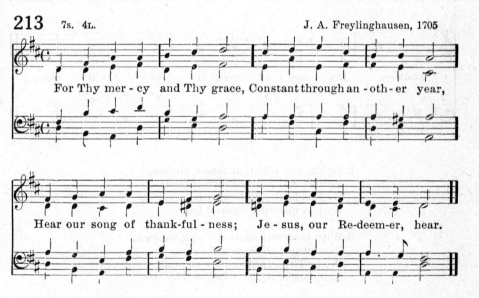

For Thy mer - cy and Thy grace, Constant through an-oth-er year,

Hear our song of thank-ful - ness; Je - sus, our Re-deem-er, hear.

2 Lo, our sins on Thee we cast,
   Thee, our perfect sacrifice;
And, forgetting all the past,
   Press toward our glorious prize.

3 Dark the future; let Thy light
   Guide us, bright and morning Star:
Fierce our foes, and hard the fight;
   Arm us, Savior, for the war.

4 In our weakness and distress,
   Rock of strength, be Thou our stay;

In the pathless wilderness
   Be our true and living way.

5 Who of us death's awful road
   In the coming year shall tread?
With Thy rod and staff, O God,
   Comfort Thou his dying bed.

6 Keep us faithful, keep us pure,
   Keep us evermore Thine own;
Help, O help us to endure;
   Fit us for the promised crown.

                 H. Downton. 1841

The Church Year

214 L. M.

L. Bourgeois, 1547

Great God! we sing that might-y hand By which sup-port-ed still we stand; The open-ing year Thy mer-cy shows— Let mer-cy crown it to its close.

2 By day, by night, at home, abroad,
  Still we are guarded by our God;
  By His incessant bounty fed,
  By His unerring counsel led.

3 With grateful hearts the past we own;
  The future, all to us unknown,
  We to Thy guardian care commit,
  And, peaceful, leave before Thy feet.

4 In scenes exalted or depressed,
  Be Thou our joy, and Thou our rest;
  Thy goodness all our hopes shall raise,
  Adored through all our changing days.

5 When death shall interrupt our songs,
  And seal in silence mortal tongues,
  Our helper, God, in whom we trust,
  Shall keep our souls and guard our dust.

P. Doddridge, publ. 1755

Sunday after New Year

F. Filitz, 1804—76

215 8, 7, 8, 7, 4, 7.

Lead us, heavenly Fa-ther, lead us O'er the world's tempestuous sea:

Guard us, guide us, keep us, feed us, For we have no help but Thee;

Yet pos-sess-ing ev-ery bless-ing, If our God our Father be.

2 Savior, breathe forgiveness o'er us,
    All our weakness Thou dost know;
Thou didst tread this earth before us,
    Thou didst feel its keenest woe;
        Lone and dreary, faint and weary,
Through the desert Thou didst go.

3 Spirit of our God, descending,
    Fill our hearts with heavenly joy,
Love all other love transcending,
    Pleasure that can never cloy:
        Thus provided, pardoned, guided,
Nothing can our peace destroy.

J. Edmeston, 1821

The Church Year

8, 8, 8, 8, 8, 8, 7.

John Dahle, 1911

As God doth lead me I will go; I do not ask to choose my way; Content with what He doth be-stow, As-sured He will not let me stray. So as He leads, my path I make, And step by step I glad-ly take, A child in Him con-fid-ing.

2 As God doth lead I am content;
I rest me calmly in His hands;
That which He has decreed and sent—
That which His will for me commands,
I would that He should all fulfill:
That I should do His gracious will
In living or in dying.

3 As God doth lead I all resign;
I trust me to my Father's will;
When reason's rays deceptive shine,
His counsel would I yet fulfill—
That which His love ordained as right,
Before He brought me to the light,—
My all to Him resigning.

4 As God doth lead me I abide,
In faith, in hope, in suffering true,
His strength is ever by my side—
Can aught my hold on Him undo?
So patiently I wait and know
That God, who doth my life bestow,
In kindness all is sending.

5 As God doth lead I onward go,
Though oft 'mid thorns and briers keen;
God does not yet His guidance show—
But in the end it shall be seen
How, by a loving Father's will,
Faithful and true, He leads me still,—
Thus anchored, faith is resting.

L. Gedicke, 1711

Sunday after New Year

217　　6, 7, 6, 7, 6, 6, 6, 6.　　　　　　　　　　German, 1648

Why do the heathen rage? What are the na-tions dream - ing?

In vain a-gainst the Lord And His An - oint - ed schem - ing,

Kings of the earth a - rise, And leaguéd rul - ers say:

"Come, let us break Their bands, And cast their cords a - way."

2 He who is throned in heaven
　Derides their preparation;
The Lord upon them pours
　His scornful indignation:
Soon shall His voice of wrath
　Their souls with terror thrill:
"Yet I have set my King
　On Zion's holy hill."—

3 Now will I cry aloud
　And tell the Lord's great token:
"Thou art My Son," He saith:
　To me the word was spoken:
"Yea, Thee have I this day
　Begotten: ask of Me,
And Thine the heathen, Thine
　Earth's utmost parts shall be:

4 Beneath Thine iron rod
　Thy foemen shall be shattered,
As by the potter's hand
　The broken shreds lie scattered."
Be wise, then, O ye kings,
　Ye earthly judges, hear;
Serve ye the Lord with awe,
　Rejoice with trembling fear.

5 Bow down and kiss the Son,
　Lest, if His wrath awaken,
Ye fail and fade away,
　For evermore forsaken.
Soon may His anger burn,
　A lightly kindled flame;
Then blessed are all they
　That trust His holy name.
　　　　　　B. H. Kennedy, 1860

218   7, 6. 8L.   Composed or adapted by L. Bourgeois, c. 1545

O Lord, hear Thou my call - ing, Out of the deep I cry:

O make my prayer a - vail - ing; With aid to me draw nigh:

O mark my lam - en - ta - tion, My rest - less sigh - ing hear,

And to my sup - pli - ca - tion In - cline Thy gra - cious ear.

2 If Thou shouldst mark abuses
  And strict account demand,
O Lord, with what excuses
  Could we before Thee stand?
But if with true contrition
  Our sins we mourn and blame,
Thou savest from perdition
  That we may fear Thy name.

3 In God my hope abideth,
  My trust is in the Lord,
My soul in Him confideth
  And builds upon His word:

My soul for Him is yearning,
  More longing for His grace
Than daylight's sweet returning
  The watchman longs to trace.

4 Be God thy strong foundation,
  Thou chosen Israel;
Thy God with whom salvation
  And mercy ever dwell;
His river ever streameth,
  With pardon full and free,
He Israel redeemeth
  From all iniquity.

Clement Marot, 1557

Epiphany

219   7s. 6L.   Arr. from C. Köcher, 1786—1872

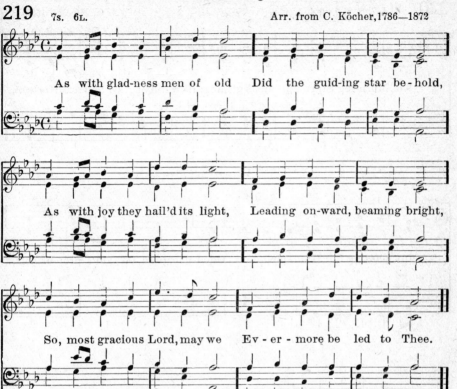

As with glad-ness men of old   Did the guid-ing star be-hold,

As with joy they hail'd its light,   Leading on-ward, beaming bright,

So, most gracious Lord, may we   Ev - er - more be led to Thee.

2 As with joyful steps they sped
  To that lowly manger-bed,
  There to bend the knee before
  Him whom heaven and earth adore,
  So may we with willing feet
  Ever seek Thy mercy-seat.

3 As they offered gifts most rare
  At that manger rude and bare,
  So may we with holy joy,
  Pure and free from sin's alloy,
  All our costliest treasures bring,
  Christ, to Thee, our heavenly King.

4 Holy Jesus! every day
  Keep us in the narrow way;
  And, when earthly things are past,
  Bring our ransomed souls at last
  Where they need no star to guide,
  Where no clouds Thy glory hide.

5 In the heavenly country bright,
  Need they no created light;
  Thou its light, its joy, its crown,
  Thou its sun which goes not down;
  There for ever may we sing
  Hallelujahs to our King.

W. C. Dix, 1861

220 8, 8, 7, 8, 8, 7, 4, 4, 4, 4, 8.

Ph. Nicolai, 1599

The Morn-ing Star up - on us gleams; How full of grace and truth His beams,

How passing fair His splen-dor! Good Shepherd, Da - vid's prop-er heir,

My King in heaven, Thou dost me bear Up - on Thy bos-om ten - der.

Near - est, Dear - est, High-est, brightest, Thou de-light-est

Still to love me, Thou, so high enthroned a - bove me.

2 Strike deep into this heart of mine
  Thy rays of love, Thou Star divine,
    And fire its dying embers:
  And grant that naught have power to part
  Me from Thy body, Lord, who art
    The life of all Thy members.
        I stand,
        Thy hand
      Ever taking,
      Ne'er forsaking:
      Naught shall ail me;
  Bread of life, Thou wilt not fail me.

3 O holy Jesus, when the light
  Of Thy dear face shines on me bright,
    Then heavenly joy doth thrill me.
  O Lord, my sure and steadfast good,
  Thy word, Thy Spirit, body, blood,—
    With life, new life, they fill me.
        This day,
        I pray:
      Mercy showing,
      Grace bestowing,
      Look on me, Lord,
  Thy own word is all my plea, Lord.

4 Thou, mighty Father, in Thy Son
  Didst love me, ere Thou hadst begun
    This ancient world's foundation.
  Thy Son hath made a friend of me,
  And when in spirit Him I see
    I've done with tribulation.
        What bliss
        Is this!
      Where He liveth
      Me He giveth
      Life for ever;
  Nothing me from Him can sever.

5 Lift up the voice and strike the string,
  Let all glad sounds of music ring
    In God's high praises blended.
  Christ will be with me all the way,
  Today, tomorrow, every day,
    Till traveling days be ended.
        Sing out,
        Ring out
      Triumph glorious,
      O victorious,
      Chosen nation;
  Praise the God of your salvation.
                    Philipp Nicolai, 1599.

The Church Year

221   L. M.   J. Clauder's "Psalmodia Nova," 1630

O Christ, our true and on - ly light, Il - lu - mine those who sit in night; Let those a - far now hear Thy voice, And in Thy fold with us re - joice.

2 Fill with the radiance of Thy grace
　The souls now lost in error's maze,
　And all whom in their secret minds
　Some dark delusion haunts and blinds.

3 And all who else have strayed from Thee,
　O gently seek! Thy healing be
　To every wounded conscience given,
　And let them also share Thy heaven.

4 O make the deaf to hear Thy word,
　And teach the dumb to speak, dear Lord,
　Who dare not yet the faith avow,
　Though secretly they hold it now.

5 Shine on the darkened and the cold,
　Recall the wanderers from Thy fold,
　Unite all those who walk apart,
　Confirm the weak and doubting heart.

6 So they with us may evermore
　Such grace with wondering thanks adore
　And endless praise to Thee be given
　By all Thy Church in earth and heaven.

J. Heermann, 1630

222 6, 7, 6, 7, 6, 6, 6, 6.

Meiningisches Gesangbuch, 1693

O bless-ed Babe di - vine, What offerings shall we give Thee?
The gold of faith be Thine: For we will still be - lieve Thee.
O fill our ea - ger hearts With Thy re - fresh-ing grace,
And make them fit to be Thy chos-en dwell-ing - place.

2 Let frankincense aspire,
  Pure sighs of sweetest savor,
Which pine with fond desire
  To find Thy gracious favor.
O make them purer yet,
  And send Thy Spirit down,
The altar of our hearts
  With holy fire to crown.

3 And myrrh, too, we prepare,
  Our bitter tribulation,
Such grief as Thou didst bear
  For us and our salvation.

Be strength and courage ours
  In toil and tears and pain,
With Thee to wear the yoke,
  The cross with Thee sustain.

4 Lo, all of ours is Thine,
  Each hope and thought and feeling;
Come, blessed Babe divine,
  Thyself in us revealing.
To Thee, and God in Thee,
  Our dearest wishes tend:
O make us Thine and His
  Through ages without end.

F. J. Burmeister, 1662

The Church Year

Rise, O Sa-lem, rise and shine! Lo, the Gen-tiles hail Thy wak-ing;
Her-ald of a morn di-vine, See the Day-spring o'er us breaking,
Tell-ing God has called to mind Those who long in darkness pined.

2 O how blindly did we stray,
    Ere this sun our earth had brightened:
Heaven we sought not, for no ray
    Had our 'wildered eyes enlightened;
All our looks were earthward bent,
All our strength on earth was spent.

3 But the Day-spring from on high
    Hath aris'n with beams unclouded,
And we see before it fly
    All the heavy gloom that shrouded
This sad earth, where sin and woe
Seemed to reign o'er all below.

4 Thy appearing, Lord, shall fill
    All my thoughts in sorrow's hour;
Thy appearing, Lord, shall still
    All my dread of death's dark power;
Whether joys or tears be mine,
Through them still Thy light shall shine.

5 Let me, when my course is run,
    Calmly leave a world of sadness
For the place that needs no sun,
    For Thou art its light and gladness,
For the mansions fair and bright,
Where Thy saints are crowned with light.

                                        J. Rist, 1655

Epiphany

11, 10. 4L.   Sir Herbert S. Oakeley, 1830—1903

Brightest and best of the sons of the morn-ing, Dawn on our

dark-ness and lend us thine aid; Star of the east, the ho - ri - zon a-

dorn - ing, Guide where our in - fant Re - deem-er is laid.

2 Cold on His cradle the dew-drops are shining,
　　Low lies His head with the beasts of the stall;
　Angels adore Him in slumber reclining,
　　Maker and Monarch and Savior of all.

3 Shall we not yield Him, in costly devotion,
　　Odors of Edom, and offerings divine,
　Gems of the mountain, and pearls of the ocean,
　　Myrrh from the forest, and gold from the mine?

4 Vainly we offer each ample oblation,
　　Vainly with gifts would His favor secure;
　Richer by far is the heart's adoration,
　　Dearer to God are the prayers of the poor.

5 Brightest and best of the sons of the morning,
　　Dawn on our darkness and lend us thine aid;
　Star of the east, the horizon adorning,
　　Guide where our infant Redeemer is laid.

R. Heber, 1811

231

The Church Year

225   8s. 6L.   First Sunday after Epiphany   German

O who like Thee, so calm, so bright, Lord Je-sus Christ, Thou Light of light,

O who like Thee did ev-er go So patient through a world of woe;

So meek, so low-ly, yet so high, So glo-rious in hu-mil-i-ty?

2 O wondrous Lord, our souls would be
  Still more and more conformed to Thee;
  Would lose the pride, the taint of sin,
  That burns these fevered veins within;
  And learn of Thee, the lowly one,
  And like Thee all our journey run.

3 O grant us ever on the road
  To trace the footsteps of our God;
  That when Thou shalt appear, arrayed
  In light to judge the quick and dead,
  We may to life immortal soar,
  Through Thee, who livest evermore.

A. C. Coxe, ca. 1840

226 11, 10. 4L.

F. R. Havergal, 1871.

We are the Lord's: His all-suf-fi-cient mer-it, Sealed on the cross to us this grace ac-cords; We are the Lord's, and all things shall in-her-it; Wheth-er we live or die, we are the Lord's.

2 We are the Lord's; then let us gladly tender
　Our souls to Him, in deeds, not empty words;
Let heart and tongue and life combine to render
　No doubtful witness that we are the Lord's.

3 We are the Lord's: no darkness brooding o'er us
　Can make us tremble, whilst this star affords
A steady light along the path before us—
　Faith's full assurance that we are the Lord's.

4 We are the Lord's: no evil can befall us
　In the dread hour of life's fast loosening cords;
No pangs of death shall even then appall us;
　Death we shall vanquish, for we are the Lord's.

C. J. P. Spitta. 1843

227 8, 7, 8, 7, 12, 12, 11, 11.

J. A. Freylinghausen, 1704

One thing need-ful! This one treasure Teach me, Sav-ior, to es-teem;

Oth-er things may prom-ise pleasure, But are nev-er what they seem;

They prove to be bur-dens that vex us and chafe us, And true lasting

hap-pi-ness nev-er vouchsafe us; This one pre-cious treas-ure, that

all else ex-ceeds, Gives joy a-bove measure and fills all my needs.

First Sunday after Epiphany

2 Seekest thou the one thing needful,
  Leave all cares that hindering prove;
Be of earthly joys unheedful,
  Fix thy heart on things above;
For where God and man both in one
    are united,
With God's perfect fullness the heart
    is delighted;
There, there is the worthiest lot and
    the best,
My one and my all, and my joy, and
    my rest.

3 Then with Mary's full surrender,
  I would offer Thee my heart,
At Thy feet my tribute render,
  As my chosen better part.
For Mary's heart burning with fer-
    vent emotion,
Was quickened to serve Thee with
    perfect devotion;
And there filled with love for her Sav-
    ior and Lord,
Was, with the One needful, in blessed
    accord.

4 Thus, O Jesus, my endeavor
  Is to be forever Thine.
Let no mortal love whatever
  Hindering now my heart entwine.
Though great be the host that refuses
    to heed Thee,
I'll faithfully follow where'er Thou
    wilt lead me;
For Thy word is Spirit and life to my
    soul,
And through it, O Jesus, my conduct
    control.

5 Wisdom's fountain everflowing
  Has its highest source in Thee.
By Thy grace confine my going
  In Thy footsteps, trod for me;
In which I with lowly and perfect
    submission
May bend to Thy wisdom my will and
    ambition;
And when, O my Savior, I know Thee
    aright
I then shall have risen to wisdom's
    great height.

6 I have naught, my God, to offer,
  Save the blood of Thy dear Son;
Graciously accept the proffer:
  Make His righteousness mine own.
His holy life gave He, was crucified
    for me;

His righteousness perfect He now
    pleads before Thee;
His own robe of righteousness, my
    highest good,
Shall clothe me in glory, through
    faith in His blood.

7 In Thine image then awaking,
  May my soul be all Thine own;
Of Thy holy life partaking,
  Sanctified to Thee alone.
For all that I need here, to serve and
    obey Thee,
In Thee I receive— and my Savior, I
    pray Thee:
From things transitory, absorbing my
    love,
Withdraw mine affections, and fix
    them above.

8 Jesus, in Thy cross are centered
  All the marvels of Thy grace;
Thou, my Savior, once hast entered
  Through Thy blood the holy place:
Thy sacrifice holy there wrought my
    redemption,
From Satan's dominion I now have
    exemption;
The way is now free to the Father's
    high throne,
Where I may approach Him, in Thy
    name alone.

9 Joys unnumbered, peace and blessing,
  Are the comforts full and free,
Richly now I am possessing,
  For my Savior shepherds me.
How sweet the communion, beyond
    all expression,
To have Thee, O Jesus, as my heart's
    possession.
O nothing in me can such ardor unfold
As when I Thee, Savior, in faith shall
    behold.

10 Henceforth Thou alone, my Savior,
  Shalt be all in all to me.
Search my heart and my behavior,
  Cast out all hypocrisy.
Restrain me from wandering in path-
    ways unholy,
And throughout life's pilgrimage keep
    my heart lowly;
I'll value but lightly earth's treasure
    and store:
Thou art the One needful, and mine
    evermore!

J. H. Schröder, 1697

The Church Year

228 S. M.

German, 1720

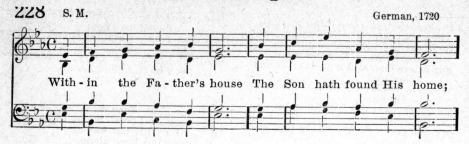

With-in the Fa-ther's house The Son hath found His home;

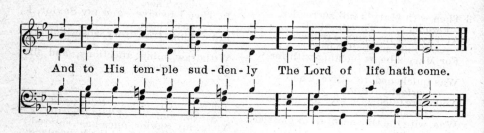

And to His tem-ple sud-den-ly The Lord of life hath come.

2 The doctors of the law
　　Gaze on the wondrous child,
And marvel at His gracious words
　　Of wisdom undefiled.

3 Yet not to them is given
　　The mighty truth to know,
To lift the earthly veil which hides
　　Incarnate God below.

4 The secret of the Lord
　　Escapes each human eye,
And faithful pondering hearts await
　　The full Epiphany.

5 Lord, visit Thou our souls
　　And teach us by Thy grace,
Each dim revealing of Thyself
　　With loving awe to trace;

6 Till from our darkened sight
　　The cloud shall pass away,
And on the cleanséd soul shall burst
　　The everlasting day;

7 Till we behold Thy face,
　　And know, as we are known,
Thee, Father, Son, and Holy Ghost,
　　Co-equal Three in One.

J. R. Woodford. 1863

229 8, 8, 7. 6L.   German, 1530

In house and home where man and wife To-geth-er lead a
god-ly life, By deeds their faith con-fess-ing, There
many a hap-py day is spent, There Je-sus glad-ly
will con-sent To tar-ry with His bless-ing.

2 If thou hast given Him thine heart,
The place of honor set apart
   For Him each night and morrow;
Then He the storms of life will calm,
Will bring for every wound a balm,
   And change to joy thy sorrow.

3 And if thy home be dark and drear,
The cruse be empty, hunger near,
   All hope within thee dying;
Despair not in thy sore distress,

Lo, Christ is there the bread to bless
   The fragments multiplying.

4 O Lord, we come before Thy face;
In every home bestow Thy grace
   On children, father, mother;
Relieve their wants, their burdens
   ease,
Let them together dwell in peace
   And love to one another!

M. B. Landstad, 1861

230 9, 8, 9, 8, 8, 8.

Georg Neumark, 1622—81

If thou but suf-fer God to guide thee, And hope in Him through all thy ways,

He'll give thee strength, whate'er be-tide thee, And bear thee through the e-vil days;

Who trusts in God's unchanging love Builds on the rock that naught can move.

2 What can these anxious cares avail thee,
    These never-ceasing moans and sighs?
What can it help if thou bewail thee
    O'er each dark moment as it flies?
Our cross and trials do but press
The heavier for our bitterness.

3 Only be still, and wait His leisure
    In cheerful hope, with heart content
To take whate'er thy Father's pleasure
    And all-discerning love have sent;
Nor doubt our inmost wants are known
To Him who chose us for His own.

4 He knows the time for joy, and truly
    Will send it when He sees it meet:
When He has tried and purged thee duly,
    And finds thee free from all deceit,
He comes to thee all unaware
And makes thee own His loving care.

Second Sunday after Epiphany

5 Nor think amid the heat of trial
   That God hath cast thee off unheard,
That he whose hopes meet no denial
   Must surely be of God preferred;
Time passes and much change doth bring,
And sets a bound to everything.

6 All are alike before the Highest;
   'Tis easy for our God, we know,
To raise thee up though low thou liest,
   To make the rich man poor and low;
True wonders still by Him are wrought
Who setteth up and brings to naught.

7 Sing, pray, and keep His ways unswerving;
   So do thine own part   faithfully,
And trust His word,—though undeserving;
   Thou yet shalt find it true for thee:
God never yet forsook at need
The soul that trusted Him indeed.

G. Neumark, 1657

Older Form. 9, 8, 9, 8, 8, 8.   Georg Neumark, 1622—81

If thou but suf-fer God to guide thee, And hope in Him through all thy ways,

He'll give thee strength, whate'er betide thee, And bear thee through the e - vil days;

Who trusts in God's unchanging love Builds on the rock that naught can move.

231 7, 6. 8L.

H. L. Hassler, 1601.

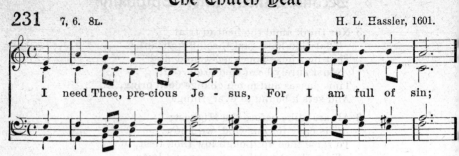

I need Thee, pre-cious Je - sus, For I am full of sin;

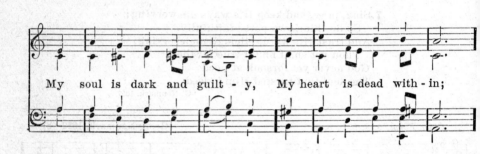

My soul is dark and guilt - y, My heart is dead with-in;

I need the cleans-ing foun-tain Where I can al-ways flee,

The blood of Christ most pre - cious, The sin-ner's per-fect plea.

Second Sunday after Epiphany

2 I need Thee, blessed Jesus,
   For I am very poor;
A stranger and a pilgrim,
   I have no earthly store.
I need the love of Jesus
   To cheer me on my way,
To guide my doubting footsteps,
   To be my strength and stay.

3 I need Thee, blessed Jesus;
   I need a friend like Thee,
A friend to soothe and pity,
   A friend to care for me.

I need the heart of Jesus
   To feel each anxious care,
To tell my every trial,
   And all my sorrows share.

4 I need Thee, blessed Jesus,
   And hope to see Thee soon,
Encircled with the rainbow
   And seated on Thy throne:
There, with Thy blood-bought chil-
   My joy shall ever be   [dren,
To sing Thy praise, Lord Jesus,
   To gaze, my Lord, on Thee.

F. Whitfield, 1855

232   S. M.

J. Stephenson

All praise to Thee, O Lord, Who by Thy might-y power

Didst man-i-fest Thy glo-ry forth In Ca-na's marriage hour.

2 Thou speakest, it is done:
   Obedient to Thy word,
The water reddening into wine
   Proclaims the present Lord.

3 Blest were the eyes which saw
   That wondrous mystery,
The great beginning of Thy works,
   That kindled faith in Thee.

4 And blessed they who know
   Thine unseen presence true,
When in the kingdom of Thy grace
   Thou makest all things new.

5 For by Thy loving hand
   Thy people still are fed;
Thou art the cup of blessing, Lord,
   And Thou the heavenly bread.

6 O may that grace be ours,
   In Thee for aye to live,
And drink of those refreshing streams
   Which Thou alone canst give.

7 So, led from strength to strength
   Grant us, O Lord, to see
The marriage supper of the Lamb,
   Thy great Epiphany.

H. W. Beadon, 1863

233 6s. 8L.

Charles J. Dale, 1904

My Je - sus, as Thou wilt! O may Thy will be mine!

In - to thy hand of love I would my all re - sign.

Through sor - row, or through joy, Con-duct me as Thine own,

And help me still to say, My Lord, Thy will be done!

Second Sunday after Epiphany

2 My Jesus, as Thou wilt!
   If needy here and poor,
Give me Thy people's bread,
   Their portion rich and sure.
The manna of Thy word
   Let my soul feed upon;
And if all else should fail,
   My Lord, Thy will done!

3 My Jesus, as Thou wilt!
   Though seen through many a tear,
Let not my star of hope
   Grow dim or disappear:
Since Thou on earth hast wept
   And sorrowed oft alone,
If I must weep with Thee,
   My Lord, Thy will be done!

4 My Jesus, as Thou wilt!
   When death itself draws nigh,
To Thy dear wounded side
   I would for refuge fly:
Leaning on Thee, to go
   Where Thou before hast gone;
The rest as Thou shalt please:
   My Lord, Thy will be done!

5 My Jesus, as Thou wilt!
   All shall be well for me:
Each changing future scene
   I gladly trust with Thee.
Thus to my home above
   I travel calmly on,
And sing, in life or death,
   My Lord, Thy will be done!

B. Schmolck, 1709

234   L. M.

Henry K. Oliver, 1839

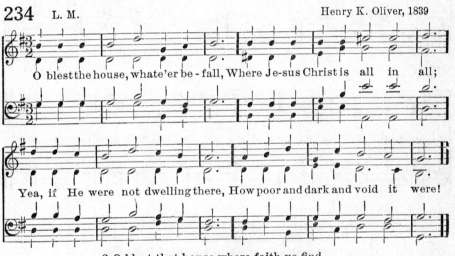

O blest the house, whate'er be-fall, Where Jesus Christ is all in all; Yea, if He were not dwelling there, How poor and dark and void it were!

2 O blest that house where faith ye find,
And all within have set their mind
To trust their God and serve Him still,
And do, in all, His holy will.

3 O blest the parents who give heed
Unto their children's foremost need,
And weary not of care or cost:
To them and heaven shall none be lost.

4 Blest such a house, it prospers well,
In peace and joy the parents dwell,
And in their children's lot is shown
How richly God can bless His own.

5 Then here will I and mine to-day
A solemn covenant make and say:
Though all the world forsake Thy word,
I and my house will serve the Lord.

C. C. L. von Pfeil, 1782

235 10s. 4L. Third Sunday after Epiphany T. Hewlett, 1845—74

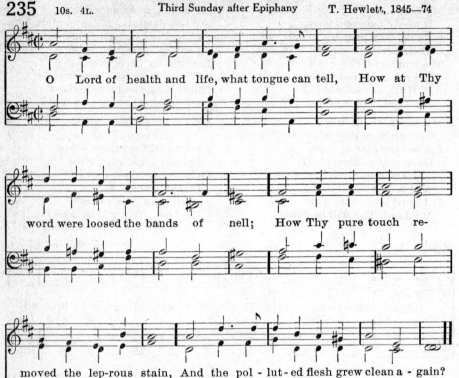

O Lord of health and life, what tongue can tell, How at Thy word were loosed the bands of nell; How Thy pure touch re-moved the lep-rous stain, And the pol - lut- ed flesh grew clean a - gain?

2 O wash our hearts, restore the contrite soul,
   Stretch forth Thy healing hand, and make us whole;
   O bend our stubborn knees to kneel to Thee,
   Speak but the word and we once more are free.

3 Yea, Lord, we claim the promise of Thy love,
   Thy love, which can all guilt, all pain remove;
   Nigh to our souls Thy great salvation bring,
   Then sickness hath no pang, and death no sting.

4 We hail this pledge in all Thy deeds of grace,
   As once disease and sorrow fled Thy face,
   So when that face again unveiled we see,
   Sickness, and tears, and death no more shall be.

5 Then grant us strength to pray, "Thy kingdom come,"
   When we shall know Thee in Thy Father's home,
   And at Thy great Epiphany adore
   The co-eternal Godhead evermore.

G. Phillmore, 1863

236 8s. 6L.

J. W. Elliott, b. 1833-

My hope is built on noth-ing less Than Je-sus' blood and righteousness;

I dare not trust the sweet-est frame, But wholly lean on Je-sus' name.

Unison.

On Christ, the sol-id rock, I stand: All oth-er ground is sinking sand.

2 When clouds and darkness veil His face,
　I rest on His unchanging grace,
　In every high and stormy gale
　My anchor holds within the veil;
　On Christ, the solid rock, I stand:
　All other ground is sinking sand.

3 His oath, His covenant, and blood
　Support me in the whelming flood;
　When all around my soul gives way,
　He then is all my hope and stay.
　On Christ, the solid rock, I stand:
　All other ground is sinking sand.

4 When He shall come, with trumpet sound,
　O may I then in Him be found!
　Clothed in His righteousness alone,
　Faultless to stand before the throne.
　On Christ, the solid rock, I stand:
　All other ground is sinking sand.

Ed. Mote, 1834

237   7, 8, 7, 8, 7, 7.   German, 1656

Why art thou cast down, my soul? O what mean thy sighs and sad-ness?

Trust in Him who makes thee whole, And thy griefs can turn to glad-ness,—

Oft - en in the dark-est hour He re - veals His love and power.

2 On this ground thy anchor cast;
    Safe thou art, in Christ confiding;
All the griefs which here thou hast
    Are but shadows unabiding.
Soon thy cross shall pass away,
Joy shall come that lasts for aye.

3 Christ's own way is always good,
    Christians find this consolation:
He who bought thee with His blood,
    Now stands pledged for thy salvation.
Rest upon His sacred word—
That assurance doth afford!

4 Jesus gives us joy and tears,
    Blesséd be His name forever!
When thy way most dark appears,
    Trust in Him, despond thou never;
Weary soul, when sore distressed,
Call on Him and be at rest.

5 Surely, narrow is the way
    To the land of gladness yonder;
While on this sad earth we stay,
    We must here as pilgrims wander.
Through the desert we must roam,
Till we Canaan reach, our home.

6 Upward, then, my weary soul,
    Where the crown of life is given!
Pressing onward to the goal,
    I shall win the bliss of heaven;
For, O Jesus, I am Thine,
Blest am I, for Thou art mine!

B. Schmolck, 1704
H. A. Brorson, 1734

238 8, 8, 8, 4.   J. Hullah, 1867

My God and Fa-ther, while I stray Far from my home, on life's rough way,

O teach me from my heart to say, "Thy will be done!"
"Thy will be done!"

2 Though dark my path, and sad my lot,
    Let me be still and murmur not,
Or breathe the prayer divinely taught,
    "Thy will be done!"

3 What though in lonely grief I sigh
    For friends beloved, no longer nigh,
Submissive still would I reply,
    "Thy will be done!"

4 If Thou hast called me to resign
    What most I prize, it ne'er was mine;
I only yield Thee what is Thine:
    "Thy will be done!"

5 Let but my fainting heart be blest
    With Thy sweet Spirit for its guest,
My God, to Thee I leave the rest,—
    "Thy will be done!"

6 Renew my will from day to day,
    Blend it with Thine, and take away
All that now makes it hard to say,
    "Thy will be done!"

7 Then, when on earth I breathe no more
    The prayer oft mixed with tears before,
I'll sing upon a happier shore,
    "Thy will be done!"

Charlotte Elliott, 1834

The Church Year

239   11, 9, 11, 9, 9.

Swedish, 1695

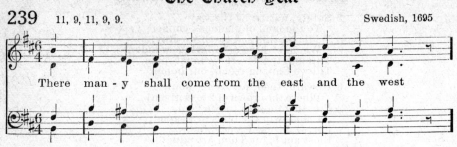

There man-y shall come from the east and the west

And sit at the feast of sal - va - tion

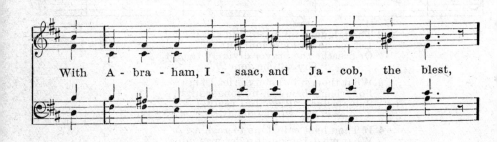

With A - bra - ham, I - saac, and Ja - cob, the blest,

O - bey - ing the Lord's in - vi - ta - tion.

Third Sunday after Epiphany

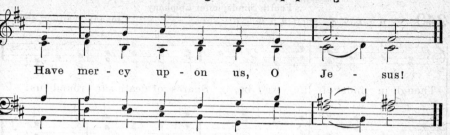

Have mer-cy up-on us, O Je-sus!

2 But they who have always resisted His grace
   And on their own virtue depended,
Shall then be condemned and cast out from His face,
   Eternally lost and unfriended.
      Have mercy upon us, O Jesus!

3 O may we all hear when our Shepherd doth call,
   In accents persuasive and tender,
That while there is time we make haste one and all
   And find Him, our mighty defender.
      Have mercy upon us, O Jesus!

4 O that we the throng of the ransomed may swell,
   To whom He hath granted remission.
God graciously make us in heaven to dwell,
   And save us from endless perdition.
      Have mercy upon us, O Jesus!

5 God grant that I may of His infinite love
   Remain in His merciful keeping;
And sit with the King at His table above,
   When here in the grave I am sleeping.
      Have mercy upon us, O Jesus!

6 All trials are then like a dream that is past,
   Forgotten all trouble and sorrow;
All questions and doubts have been answered at last;
   Then dawneth eternity's morrow.
      Have mercy upon us, O Jesus!

7 The heavens shall ring with an anthem more grand
   Than ever on earth was recorded;
The blest of the Lord shall receive at His hand
   The crown to the victors awarded.
      Have mercy upon us, O Jesus!

M. B. Landstad, 1861

The Church Year

Fourth Sunday after Epiphany

240 7, 6, 7, 6, 7, 8, 7, 6, 6, 9, 5, 6, 7, 5.

Johann Walther, 1524

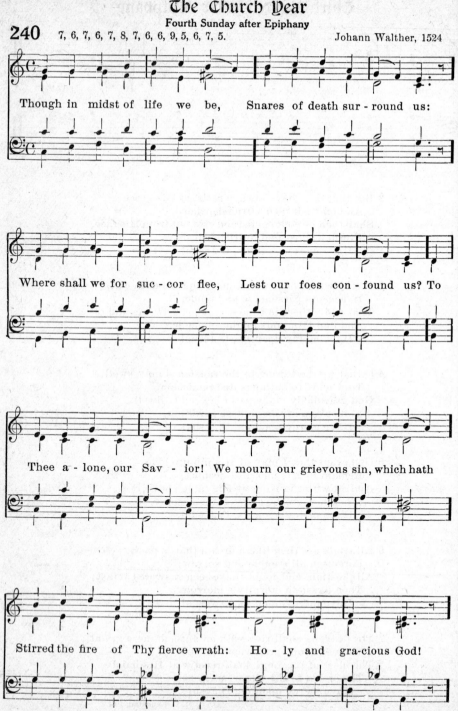

Though in midst of life we be, Snares of death sur-round us:

Where shall we for suc-cor flee, Lest our foes con-found us? To

Thee a-lone, our Sav - ior! We mourn our grievous sin, which hath

Stirred the fire of Thy fierce wrath: Ho - ly and gra-cious God!

250

Fourth Sunday after Epiphany

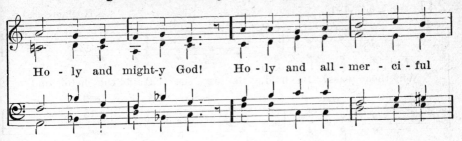

Ho - ly and might-y God! Ho - ly and all - mer - ci - ful

Sav - ior! Thou e - ter - nal God! Save us, Lord, from

sink - ing In the deep and bit - ter flood: Have mer-cy, O Lord!

2 While in midst of death we be,
  Hell's grim powers o'ertake us:
Who from such distress will free,
  Who secure will make us?
Thou only, Lord, canst do it!
It moves Thy tender heart to see
Our great sin and misery:
  Holy and gracious God!
  Holy and mighty God!
Holy and all-merciful Savior!
  Thou eternal God!
  Let not hell dismay us
With its deep and burning flood:
  Have mercy, O Lord!

3 Into hell's fierce agony
  Sin doth headlong drive us:
Where shall we for succor flee,
  Who, O who will hide us?
Thou only, blesséd Savior;
Thy precious blood was shed to win
Peace and pardon for our sin:
  Holy and gracious God!
  Holy and mighty God!
Holy and all-merciful Savior!
  Let us not, we pray,
  From the true faith's comfort
Fall in our last need away.
  Have mercy, O Lord!

M. Luther, 1524

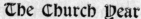

241 8, 7, 8, 7, 4, 7. A. H. Mann, 1885

Why those fears? Be-hold, 'tis Je-sus Holds the helm and guides the ship: Spread the sails, and catch the breez-es Sent to waft us through the deep; To the regions Where the mourn-ers cease to weep

2 Though the shore we hope to land on
Only by report is known,
Yet we freely all abandon,
Led by that report alone;
And with Jesus
Through the trackless deep move on.

3 Led by that, we brave the ocean;
Led by that, the storms defy;
Calm amidst tumultuous motion,
Knowing that our Lord is nigh:
Waves obey Him,
And the storms before Him fly.

4 O what pleasures there await us:
There the tempests cease to roar;
There it is that those who hate us
Can molest our peace no more;
Trouble ceases
On that tranquil happy shore.

T. Kelly, 1809

242 8, 8, 8, 3. J. B. Dykes, 1823—76

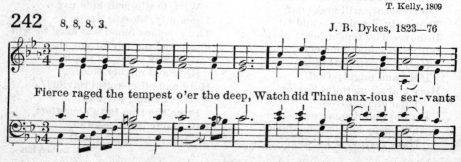

Fierce raged the tempest o'er the deep, Watch did Thine anx-ious ser-vants

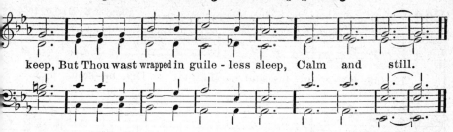

keep, But Thou wast wrapped in guile - less sleep, Calm and still.

"Save, Lord, we perish," was their
"O save us in our agony!" [cry,
Thy word above the storm rose high,
"Peace, be still."

The wild winds hushed; the angry deep
Sank, like a little child, to sleep;

The sullen billows ceased to leap,
At Thy will.

4 So, when our life is clouded o'er,
And storm-winds drift us from the shore,
Say, lest we sink to rise no more,
"Peace, be still."

G. Thring. 1861

243 C. M.   R. Redhead, 1820—1901

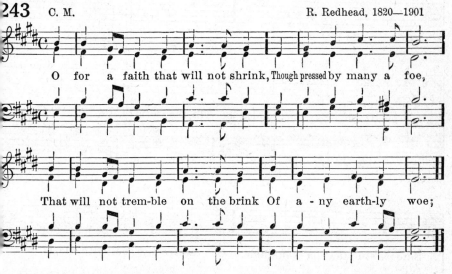

O for a faith that will not shrink, Though pressed by many a foe,

That will not trem-ble on the brink Of a - ny earth-ly woe;

That will not murmur nor complain
Beneath the chastening rod,
But, in the hour of grief or pain,
Will lean upon its God;

A faith that shines more bright and clear
When tempests rage without;[clear
That when in danger knows no fear,
In darkness feels no doubt;

That bears unmoved the world's dread frown,
Nor heeds its scornful smile;

That seas of trouble cannot drown,
Nor Satan's arts beguile;

5 A faith that keeps the narrow way
Till life's last hour is fled,
And with a pure and heavenly ray
Lights up a dying bed!

6 Lord, give us such a faith as this,
And then, whate'er may come,
We'll taste e'en here, the hallowed bliss
Of an eternal home.

W. H. Bathurst. 1831

The Church Year

244 7. 8L.

Simeon B Marsh, 1834

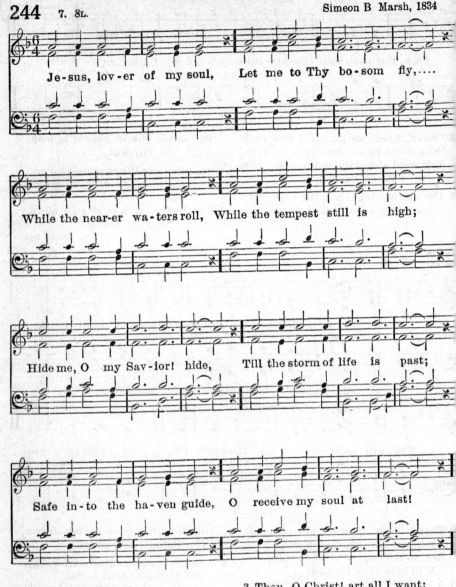

Je-sus, lov-er of my soul, Let me to Thy bo-som fly,....

While the near-er wa-ters roll, While the tempest still is high;

Hide me, O my Sav-ior! hide, Till the storm of life is past;

Safe in-to the ha-ven guide, O receive my soul at last!

2 Other refuge have I none;
 Hangs my helpless soul on Thee;
Leave, ah, leave me not alone,
 Still support and comfort me!
All my trust on Thee is stayed;
 All my help from Thee I bring;
Cover my defenseless head
 With the shadow of Thy wing.

3 Thou, O Christ! art all I want;
 More than all in Thee I find;
Raise the fallen, cheer the faint,
 Heal the sick, and lead the blind!
Just and holy is Thy name,
 I am all unrighteousness;
Vile and full of sin I am,
 Thou art full of truth and grace.

Fourth Sunday after Epiphany

4 Plenteous grace with Thee is found,
   Grace to pardon all my sin;
Let the healing streams abound,
   Make and keep me pure within;
Thou of life the fountain art,
   Freely let me take of Thee;
Spring Thou up within my heart!
   Rise to all eternity!

C. Wesley. 1740

7s. 8L.   *Second Tune.*   J. B. Dykes, 1861

Je-sus, lov-er of my soul, Let me to Thy bo-som fly,

While the near-er wa-ters roll, While the tem-pest still is high;

Hide me, O my Sav-ior! hide, Till the storm of life is past;

Safe in-to the ha-ven guide, O re-ceive my soul at last!

The Church Year

245 8, 6, 8, 6, 6, 6, 8, 6.   Ludv. M. Lindeman, 1812—87

O Fa-ther, may Thy word pre-vail A-gainst the gates of hell!

Be - hold the vine-yard Thou hast tilled With thorns and this - tles filled.

'Tis true, Thy plants are there; But, ah, how weak and rare!

How slight the power and ev - i-dence Of word and sac - ra-ments!

2 Come, Jesus, come and contemplate
Thy vineyard's sad estate:
Baptized are millions in Thy name,
But where is faith's pure flame?
Of what avail that we
Know of Thine agony
So long as we do not o'erthrow
In faith the wicked foe?

3 O Holy Ghost, to Thee, our light,
We cry by day, by night:
Come, grant us of the light and power
Our fathers had of yore;
When Thy dear Church did stand
A tree, deep-rooted, grand;
Full-crowned with blossoms white as
With purple fruits aglow!   [snow,

H. A. Brorson, ca. 1760

256

Fifth Sunday after Epiphany

246   L. M.

J. Clauder's "Psalmodia Nova," 1630

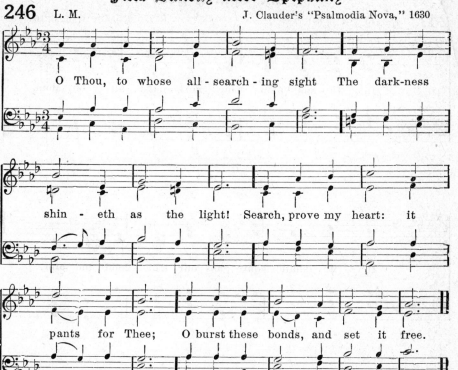

O Thou, to whose all-search-ing sight The dark-ness shin-eth as the light! Search, prove my heart: it pants for Thee; O burst these bonds, and set it free.

2 Wash out its stains, refine its dross,
Nail my affections to the cross!
Hallow each thought; let all within
Be clean, as Thou, my Lord, art clean.

3 If in this darksome wild I stray,
Be Thou my light, be Thou my way;
No foes, no violence I fear,
No harm, while Thou, my God, art near.

4 When rising floods my soul o'erflow,
When sinks my heart in waves of woe,
Jesus, Thy timely aid impart,
And raise my head, and cheer my heart.

5 Savior, where'er Thy steps I see,
Dauntless, untired, I'd follow Thee;
O let Thy hand support me still,
And lead me to Thy holy hill!

6 If rough and thorny be the way,
My strength proportion to my day;
Till toil and grief and pain shall cease,
Where all is calm, and joy and peace.

N. L. von Zinzendorf, 1721

The Church Year

4, 6, 10, 7, 4, 6, 6, 6, 7, 7, 7.   Kingo's Gradual, 1699

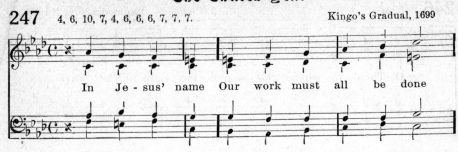

In Je-sus' name Our work must all be done

If it shall com-pass our true good and aim,

And not end in shame a - lone; For ev - ery

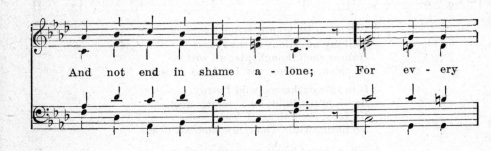

deed Which in it doth pro - ceed, Suc-

Fifth Sunday after Epiphany

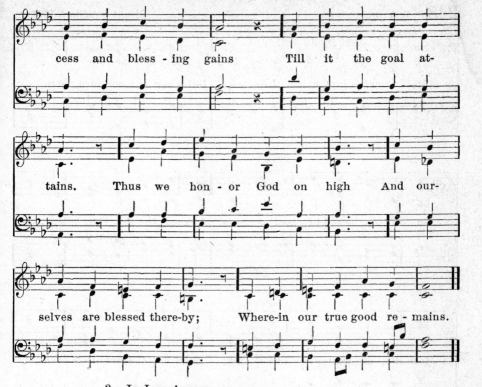

cess and bless - ing gains Till it the goal at-
tains. Thus we hon - or God on high And our-
selves are blessed there-by; Where-in our true good re - mains.

2 In Jesus' name
    We praise our God on high,
    He blesses them who spread abroad His fame,
      And we do His will thereby.
        E'er hath the Lord
        Done great things by His word,
        And still doth bare His arm
        His wonders to perform;
    Hence we should in every clime
    Magnify His name sublime,
    Who doth shield us from all harm.

3 In Jesus' name
    We live and we will die;
    If then we live, His love we will proclaim;
      If we die, we gain thereby.
        In Jesus' name,
        Who from heaven to us came,
        We shall again arise
        To meet Him in the skies,
    When at last, saved by His grace,
    We shall see Him face to face,
    Live with Him in Paradise.

J. Frederiksen, 1639

The Church Year

248   7, 6. 8L.   Claude Goudimel, 1565

In heaven is joy and glad-ness, But while I so-journ here,

So oft-en, bowed in sad - ness, I shed the bit - ter tear.

Here ills, al - way pre - vail - ing, Dis-tress the Saviors's bride;

Here mirth is lost in wail - ing; In heaven but joys a - bide.

2 I do not strive for pleasures
  That fools pursue on earth,
I sow in tears for treasures
  That have more lasting worth.
If, when my journey endeth,
  The sheaves I gather in,
The bliss the fool pretendeth
  I do not yearn to win.

3 For I shall see my Jesus,
  He is my hope and stay;
The cross that me oppresses
  Anon He takes away.
Then nothing more shall grieve me,
  And no adversity
Shall of my joy bereave me;
  Soon I shall Jesus see.

J. N. Brun, 1786

Sixth Sunday after Epiphany

249   8, 7, 8, 7, 8, 8, 7.   Joseph Klug, Wittenberg, 1535

With trembling awe the chos-en three The ho - ly mount as-cend - ed, Where, wrapped in bliss-ful ec - sta-cy, They saw the vi - sion splen - did— Their Lord ar - rayed in liv - ing light, And on His left hand and His right, By glo-rious saints at - tend - ed.

2 O vision bright, too bright to tell,
The joys of heaven unveiling!
How precious on those hearts it fell,
When earthly hopes were failing;
When, saints no more on either side,
Between the thieves the Savior died,
'Mid hate, and scorn, and railing!

3 Grant us, dear Lord, some vision
Of future triumph telling, [brief
Gilding with hope our night of grief,
Our clouds of fear dispelling.
If the dim foretaste was so bright,
O what shall be the dazzling light
Of Thine eternal dwelling!

W. W. How, 1867

The Church Year

250 8, 7, 9, 7, 8, 7.

Henry Smart, 1867

Light's a-bode, ce-les-tial Sa-lem, Vi-sion whence true peace doth spring,

Bright-er than the heart can fan-cy, Man-sion of the High-est King;

O how glorious are the praises Which of Thee the prophets sing!

2 There for ever and for ever
   Hallelujah is outpoured;
For unending, for unbroken
   Is the feast-day of the Lord;
All is pure and all is holy
   That within thy walls is stored.

3 There no cloud nor passing vapor
   Dims the brightness of the air;
Endless noon-day, glorious noon-day,
   From the Sun of suns is there;
There no night brings rest from labor,
   For unknown are toil and care.

4 O how glorious and resplendent,
   Fragile body, shalt thou be,
When endued with so much beauty,
   Full of health, and strong, and free,
Full of vigor, full of pleasure
   That shall last eternally!

5 Now with gladness, now with courage,
   Bear the burden on Thee laid,
That hereafter these Thy labors
   May with endless gifts be paid,
And in everlasting glory
   Thou with brightness be arrayed.

Thomas a Kempis d. 1471

251 8, 7, 8, 7, 8, 8.

Johann Crüger, 1649

Deep and glo-rious, word vic-to-rious, Word di-vine that ev-er lives! Call thou sin-ners to be win-ners Of the life that Je-sus gives; Tell a-broad what God hath giv-en; Je-sus is our way to heav-en.

2 Savior tender, thanks we render
  For the grace Thou dost afford;
Time is flying, time is dying,
  Yet eternal stands Thy word;
With Thy word Thy grace endureth,
And a refuge us secureth.

3 By Thy Spirit, through Thy merit,
  Draw all weary souls to Thee!
End their sighing, end their dying,
  Let them Thy salvation see!
Lead us in life's pathway tending.
To the life and bliss unending.

T. V. Oldenburg. 1840

252 8, 8, 7, 8, 8, 7, 4, 4, 4, 4, 8. P. Nicolai, 1599

Be-hold, how glo-rious is yon sky! Lo, there the righteous never die,

But dwell in peace for ev - er: Then who would wear this earthly clay,

When bid to cast life's chains away, And win Thy gracious fa - vor?

Ho - ly, Ho - ly, O for-give us; And re - ceive us,

heaven-ly Fa - ther, When a-round Thy throne we gath - er.

Sixth Sunday after Epiphany

2 Confiding in Thy sacred word,
  Our Savior is our hope, O Lord,
    The guiding star before us;
  Our Shepherd, leading us the way,
  If from Thy paths our footsteps stray,
    To Thee He will restore us:
      Holy, Holy, ever hear us,
    And receive us, while we gather
    Round Thy throne, Almighty Father.

K. W. Ramler, 1756

253 L. M.

German, 1543

O won-drous type, O vi-sion fair Of glo-ry that the Church shall share, Which Christ up-on the moun-tain shows, Where bright-er than the sun He glows!

2 From age to age the tale declare,
  How with the three disciples there,
  Where Moses and Elias meet,
  The Lord holds converse high and
    sweet.

3 The law and prophets there have place,
  The chosen witnesses of grace;
  The Father's voice from out the cloud
  Proclaims His only Son aloud.

4 With shining face and bright array,
  Christ deigns to manifest today
  What glory shall to faith be given
  When we enjoy our God in heaven.

5 And Christian hearts are raised on
    high
  By that great vision's mystery,
  For which in thankful strains we raise
  On this glad day the voice of praise.

6 O Father, with th' eternal Son
  And Holy Spirit, ever One,
  Vouchsafe to bring us by Thy grace
  To see Thy glory face to face.

Anon.. Latin, 15th Century

254 8, 6. 8L.

Septuagesima

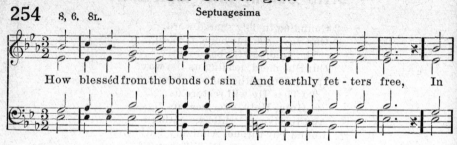

How blessèd from the bonds of sin And earthly fet-ters free, In

sin-gle-ness of heart and aim Thy servant, Lord, to be! The

hard-est toil to un-der-take With joy at Thy com-mand,

The meanest of-fice to receive With meekness at Thy hand!

Septuagesima

2 With willing heart and longing eyes
   To watch before Thy gate,
Ready to run the weary race,
   To bear the heavy weight;
No voice of thunder to expect,
   But follow calm and still,
For love can easily divine
   The One Beloved's will.

3 Thus may I serve Thee, gracious
   Thus ever Thine alone,   [Lord!
My soul and body given to Thee,
   The purchase Thou hast won:

Through evil or through good report
   Still keeping by Thy side,
And by my life or by my death,
   Let Christ be magnified!

4 How happily the working days
   In this dear service fly!
How rapidly the closing hour,
   The time of rest, draws nigh!
When all the faithful gather home,
   A joyful company,
And ever where the Master is,
   Shall His blest servants be.

C. J. P. Spitta, 1833

255   8, 7. 4L.   German, 1735

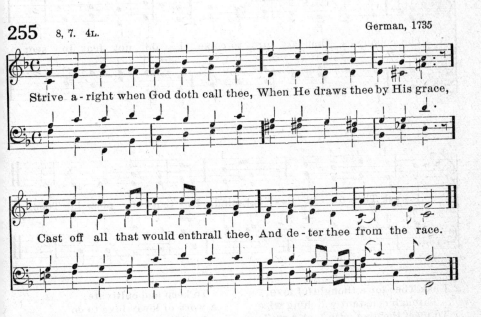

Strive a-right when God doth call thee, When He draws thee by His grace,

Cast off all that would enthrall thee, And de-ter thee from the race.

2 Wrestle, till thy zeal is burning,
   And thy love is glowing warm,
All that earth can give thee spurning —
   Half love will not bide the storm.

3 Combat, though thy life thou givest,
   Storm the kingdom, but prevail;
Let not him with whom thou strivest
   Ever make thee faint or quail.

4 Perfect truth will never waver,
   Wars with evil day and night,
Changes not for fear or favor,
   Only cares to win the fight.

5 Perfect truth will love to follow
   Watchfully our Master's ways;
Seeks not comfort poor and hollow,
   Looks not for reward or praise.

6 Perfect truth from worldly pleasure,
   Worldly turmoil, stands apart;
For in heaven is hid our treasure,
   There must also be the heart.

7 Soldiers of the cross, take courage!
   Watch and war 'mid fear and pain;
Daily conquering sin and sorrow,
   Till our King o'er earth shall reign.

J. J. Winckler, 1714

The Church Year

256   8, 6.   6L.   Dr. C. Steggall, 1826—1905

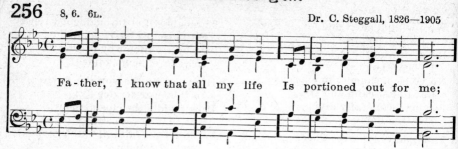

Fa-ther, I know that all my life   Is portioned out for me;

The chang-es that are sure to come, I do not fear to see:

I ask Thee for a pres-ent mind, In-tent on   pleas-ing Thee.

2 I ask Thee for a thoughtful love,
  Through constant watching wise,
To meet the glad with joyful smiles,
  To wipe the weeping eyes;
A heart at leisure from itself
  To soothe and sympathize.

3 I would not have the restless will
  That hurries to and fro,
Seeking for some great thing to do,
  Or secret thing to know;
I would be treated as a child
  And guided where I go.

4 Wherever in the world I am,
  In whatsoe'er estate,
I have a fellowship with hearts

To keep and cultivate;
A work of lowly love to do
  For Him on whom I wait.

5 I ask Thee for the daily strength,
  To none that ask denied,
A mind to blend with outward life,
  While keeping at Thy side,
Content to fill a little space,
  If Thou be glorified.

6 In service which Thy will appoints
  There are no bonds for me;
My secret heart is taught the truth
  That makes Thy children free;
A life of self-renouncing love
  Is one of liberty.

Anna L. Waring, 1850

Septuagesima

257 7s. 6L. W. D. Maclagan, 1885

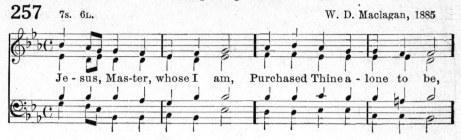

Je - sus, Mas-ter, whose I am, Purchased Thine a - lone to be,

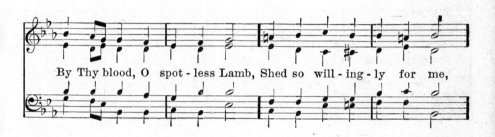

By Thy blood, O spot - less Lamb, Shed so will - ing - ly for me,

Let my heart be all Thine own, Let me live to Thee a - lone.

2 Other lords have long held sway,
  Now Thy name alone to bear,
Thy dear voice alone obey,
  Is my daily, hourly prayer;
Whom have I in heaven but Thee?
Nothing else my joy can be.

3 Jesus, Master, I am Thine;
  Keep me faithful, keep me near;
Let Thy presence in me shine
  All my homeward way to cheer.
Jesus, at Thy feet I fall,
O be Thou my all in all.

4 Jesus, Master, whom I serve,
  Though so feebly and so ill,
Strengthen hand and heart and nerve

All Thy bidding to fulfill;
Open Thou mine eyes to see
All the work Thou hast for me.

5 Lord, Thou needest not, I know,
  Service such as I can bring;
Yet I long to prove and show
  Full allegiance to my King.
Thou an honor art to me;
Let me be a praise to Thee.

6 Jesus, Master, wilt Thou use
  One who owes Thee more than all?
As Thou wilt! I would not choose;
  Only let me hear Thy call.
Jesus, let me always be,
In Thy service, glad and free.

Frances R. Havergal, 1874

The Church Year

Herbert Oakeley, 1874

Fight the good fight with all thy might, Christ is thy
strength, and Christ thy right; Lay hold on life, and
it shall be Thy joy and crown e - ter - nal - ly.

2 Run the straight race through God's good grace
Lift up thine eyes, and seek His face;
Life with its way before us lies,
Christ is the path, and Christ the prize.

3 Cast care aside, lean on thy guide,
His boundless mercy will provide;
Trust, and the trusting soul shall prove
Christ is its life, and Christ its love.

4 Faint not nor fear, for He is near,
He changeth not, and thou art dear;
Only believe, and thou shalt see
That Christ is all in all to thee.

J. S Monsell. 1863

Sexagesima

O One with God the Father, In maj-es-ty and might,

The brightness of His glo-ry, E-ter-nal Light of light,

O'er this our home of dark-ness Thy rays are streaming now;

The shadows flee be-fore Thee; The world's true light art Thou.

2 Yet, Lord, we see but darkly:
  O heavenly Light, arise,
Dispel these mists that shroud us,
  And hide Thee from our eyes.
We long to track the footprints
  That Thou Thyself hast trod;
We long to see the pathway
  That leads to Thee, our God.

3 O Jesus, shine around us
  With radiance of Thy grace;
O Jesus, turn upon us
  The brightness of Thy face.
We need no star to guide us,
  As on our way we press,
If Thou Thy light vouchsafest,
  O Sun of righteousness.

W. W. How. 1871

The Church Year

8, 7, 8, 7, 7, 7, 8, 8.

Johann Schop, 1642

Speak, O Lord, Thy serv-ant hear-eth, To Thy word I
now give heed; Life and spir-it Thy word bear-eth,
All Thy word is truth in-deed; Death's dread power in
me is rife; Je-sus, may Thy word of life Fill my soul with
love's strong fer-vor, That I cling to Thee for ev-er.

Seragesima

2 O what blessing to be near Thee,
  And to hearken to Thy voice;
May I ever love and fear Thee,
  That Thy word may be my choice
Oft were hardened sinners, Lord,
Struck with terror by Thy word;
But to him for sin who grieveth
Comfort sweet and hope it giveth.

3 Lord, Thy words are waters living,
  Where I quench my thirsty need;
Lord, Thy words are bread life-giving;
  On Thy words my soul doth feed;
Lord, Thy words shall be my light
Through death's vale and dreary
    night;
Yea, they are my sword prevailing,
And my cup of joy unfailing.

4 Precious Jesus, I beseech Thee:
  May Thy words take root in me;
May this gift from heaven enrich me,
  So that I bear fruit for Thee;
Take them never from my heart
Till I see Thee as Thou art,
When in heavenly bliss and glory
I shall see Thee and adore Thee.

5 All the world is full of sorrow;
  Dearest Jesus, hear Thou me:
Come what may today, tomorrow,
  May I firmly stand with Thee
On Thy word's unfaltering ground;
And when death's dread call shall
    sound,
I shall sing in its dark mazes
To Thy name my grateful praises.

Anna Sophia of Hesse-Darmstadt, 1658
M. B. Landstad, 1861

261 C. M. W. Croft, 1708

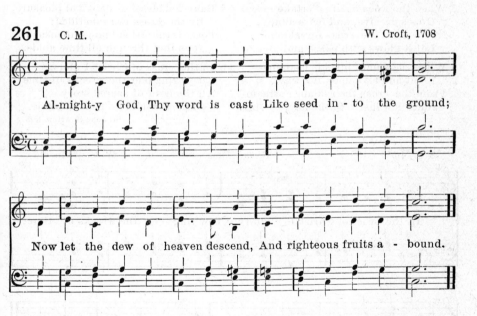

Al-might-y God, Thy word is cast Like seed in-to the ground;

Now let the dew of heaven descend, And righteous fruits a - bound.

2 Let not the foe of Christ and man
    This holy seed remove;
  But give it root in every heart,
    To bring forth fruits of love.

3 Let not the world's deceitful cares
    The rising plant destroy;

But let it yield a hundred-fold
    The fruits of peace and joy.

4 Oft as the precious seed is sown,
    Thy quickening grace bestow,
  That all whose souls the truth receive,
    Its saving power may know.

J. Cawood, 1816

The Church Year

262 8, 7. 4L. I. Conkey, 1851

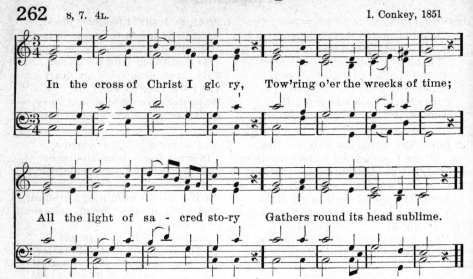

In the cross of Christ I glory, Tow'ring o'er the wrecks of time;

All the light of sa - cred sto-ry Gathers round its head sublime.

2 When the woes of life o'ertake me,
 Hopes deceive, and fears annoy,
 Never shall the cross forsake me;
 Lo! it glows with peace and joy.

3 When the sun of bliss is beaming
 Light and love upon my way,
 From the cross the radiance stream-
 Adds new lustre to the day.   [ing

4 Bane and blessing, pain and pleasure,
 By the cross are sanctified;
 Peace is there that knows no measure,
 Joys that through all time abide.

5 In the cross of Christ I glory,
 Tow'ring o'er the wrecks of time;
 All the light of sacred story
 Gathers round its head sublime.

Sir John Bowring, 1825

8, 7. 4L.   *Second Tune.*   W. G. Whinfield

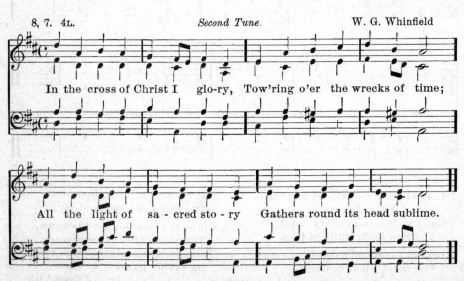

In the cross of Christ I glo-ry, Tow'ring o'er the wrecks of time;

All the light of sa - cred sto - ry Gathers round its head sublime.

Sexagesima

263   8, 6, 8, 6, 8, 8, 6.

Ludv. M. Lindeman, 1812—87.

In heaven a-bove, in heaven a-bove, Where God, our Fa-ther, dwells: How boundless there the bless-ed-ness! No tongue its greatness tells: There face to face, and full and free, Ev-er and ev-er-more we see— We see the Lord of hosts!

2 In heaven above, in heaven above,
   What glory deep and bright!
The splendor of the noonday sun
   Grows pale before its light:
The mighty sun that ne'er goes down,
Around whose gleam clouds never
   Is God, the Lord of hosts. [frown,

3 In heaven above, in heaven above,
   Behold a countless throng!
Angels in mystic radiance garbed
   Lead the triumphal song:
Angels and saints are one, and I
Join glad the gladdest company,
   And hail the Lord of hosts.

4 In heaven above, in heaven above,
   No tears of pain are shed:
Nothing can there or fade or die;
   Life's fulness round is spread,

And like an ocean, joy o'erflows,
And with immortal mercy glows
   Our God the Lord of hosts.

5 In heaven above, in heaven above,
   God hath a joy prepared,
Which mortal ear had never heard,
   Nor mortal vision shared,
Which never pierced to mortal breast,
By mortal lips was ne'er expressed,
   O God the Lord of hosts!

6 O Father, Son, and Holy Ghost,
   Accept my thankful praise:
Give me, as to the happy ones,
   Treasure of endless days.
If firm in faith and hope I stand,
I gain the crown, the better land,
   O God the Lord of hosts.

J. Aström, 1819

264 8s, 7s. 8L. Quinquagesima W. H. Monk 1823—89

Je - sus, ref - uge of the wea-ry, Ob-ject of the spir-it's love,

Fountain in life's des-ert drear-y, Sav-ior, from the world a - bove:

O how oft Thine eyes, of - fend-ed, Gaze up-on the sin-ner's fall!

Yet up - on the cross ex - tend-ed, Thou didst bear the pain of all.

2 Do we pass that cross unheeding,
   Breathing no repentant vow,
Though we see Thee wounded, bleed-
   See Thy thorn-encircled brow? [ing,
Yet Thy sinless death hath brought us
   Life eternal, peace and rest;
Only what Thy grace hath taught us
   Calms the sinner's troubled breast.

3 Jesus, may our hearts be burning,
   With more fervent love for Thee;
May our eyes be ever turning
   To Thy cross of agony;
Till in glory, parted never
   From the blessed Savior's side,
Graven in our hearts for ever,
   Dwell the cross, the Crucified.

                                       G. Savonarola, d. 1498

Quinquagesima

265   6, 6, 6, 4, 8, 8, 4.   J. B. Dykes, 1823—76

Be - hold the Lamb of God! O Thou for sin-ners slain,
Let it not be in vain That Thou hast died:
Thee for my Sav - ior let me take, My on - ly
ref - uge let me make Thy pierc - éd side.

2 Behold the Lamb of God!
Into the sacred flood
Of Thy most precious blood
  My soul I cast;
Wash me and make me clean within,
And keep me pure from every sin,
  Till life be past.

3 Behold the Lamb of God!
All hail, incarnate Word,
Thou everlasting Lord,
  Savior most blest;

Fill us with love that never faints,
Grant us, with all Thy blessed saints,
  Eternal rest.

4 Behold the Lamb of God!
Worthy is He alone
That sitteth on the throne
  Of God above;
One with the Ancient of all days,
One with the Comforter in praise,
  All light and love.

M. Bridges, 1848

266 7, 6, 7, 6, 6, 7, 7, 6.

German, 1571

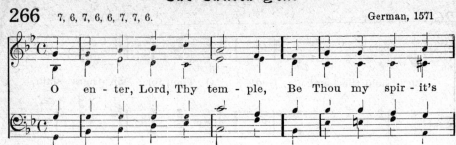

O en-ter, Lord, Thy tem-ple, Be Thou my spir-it's

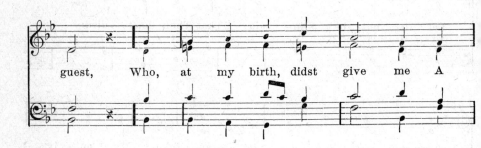

guest, Who, at my birth, didst give me A

sec - ond birth more blest; Thou in the God - head,

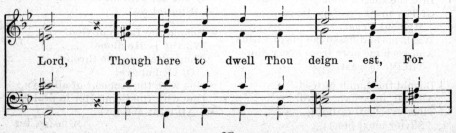

Lord, Though here to dwell Thou deign - est, For

Quinquagesima

ev - er e - qual reign - est, Art e - qual - ly a - dored.

2 O enter, let me know Thee,
   And feel Thy power within,
The power that breaks our fetters,
   And rescues us from sin.
O wash and cleanse Thou me,
That I may serve Thee truly,
To render honor duly
   With perfect heart to Thee.

3 'Tis Thou, O Spirit, teachest
   The soul to pray aright;
Thy songs have sweetest music,
   Thy prayers have wondrous might;
Unheard they cannot fall,
They pierce the highest heaven,
Till He His help hath given
   Who surely helpeth all.

4 Joy is Thy gift, O Spirit!
   Thou wouldst not have us pine;
In darkest hours Thy comfort
   Doth aye most brightly shine;
Ah, then how oft Thy voice
Hath shed its sweetness o'er me,
And opened heaven before me,
   And bid my heart rejoice.

5 All love is Thine, O Spirit!
   Thou hatest enmity;
Thou lovest peace and friendship,
   All strife wouldst have us flee;

Where wrath and discord reign
Thy whisper inly pleadeth,
And to the heart that heedeth
Brings love and light again.

6 The whole wide world, O Spirit,
   Doth on Thy presence rest:
Our wayward hearts Thou turnest
   As it may seem Thee best.
Once more Thy power make known,
As Thou hast done so often,
Convert the wicked, soften
   And break the heart of stone.

7 With holy zeal then fill us,
   To keep the faith still pure;
And bless our lands and houses
   With wealth that may endure;
And make that foe to flee
Who in us with Thee striveth,
From out our heart he driveth
   Whate'er delighteth Thee.

8 Order our path in all things
   According to Thy mind,
And when this life is over,
   And all must be resigned,
O grant us then to die
With calm and fearless spirit,
And after death inherit
   Eternal life on high.

P. Gerhardt, 1653

267 7, 6, 7, 6, 7, 6, 7, 7, 6.

J. B. Dykes, 1874

The way is long and drear - y, The path is bleak and bare,

Our feet are worn and wea - ry, But we will not de - spair.

More heav - y was Thy bur - den, More des - o - late Thy

way: O Lamb of God, who tak - est

The sin of the world a - way, Have mer - cy up - on us!

Quinquagesima

2 The snows lie thick around us
  In the dark and gloomy night,
The tempest roars above us,
  The stars have hid their light;
But blacker was the darkness
  Round Calvary's cross that day:
O Lamb of God, who takest
  The sin of the world away,
    Have mercy upon us!

3 Our hearts are faint with sorrow,
  Heavy and sad to bear;
We dread the bitter morrow,
  But we will not despair.
Thou knowest all our anguish,
  And Thou wilt bid it cease:
O Lamb of God, who takest
  The sin of the world away,
    O give to us Thy peace!

Adelaide A. Procter, 1858

268   8, 7, 8, 7, 3.   J B. Dykes, 1823—76

Lord, I hear of showers of bless-ing Thou art scattering full and free! Showers the thirst-y land re-fresh-ing; Let some drops de-scend on me— Ev-en me.

2 Pass me not, O gracious Father!
  Sinful though my heart may be:
Thou might'st leave me, but the rather
  Let Thy mercy light on me—
    Even me.

3 Pass me not, O tender Savior!
  Let me love and cling to Thee;
I am longing for Thy favor;
  When Thou comest, call for me—
    Even me.

4 Pass me not, O mighty Spirit!
  Thou canst make the blind to see;
Witnesser of Jesus' merit,
  Speak the word of power to me—
    Even me.

5 Have I long in sin been sleeping?
  Long been slighting, grieving Thee?
Has the world my heart been keeping?
  O forgive and rescue me—
    Even me.

6 Love of God, so pure and changeless;
  Blood of God, so rich and free;
Grace of God, so strong, and bound-
  Magnify it all in me—   [less,
    Even me.

7 Pass me not, but pardon bringing,
  Bind my heart, O Lord, to Thee!
Whilst the streams of life are spring-
  Blessing others, O bless me— [ing,
    Even me.

Elizabeth Codner, 1860

269 8, 7, 8, 7, 6, 6, 8, 8.   **First Sunday in Lent** Freylinghausen's Gesangbuch, 1704

I walk in dan-ger all the way; The thought shall nev-er leave me, That Sa-tan, who has marked his prey, Is plot-ting to de-ceive me. This foe with hid-den snares May seize me un-a-wares If e'er I fail to watch and pray:

First Sunday in Lent

I walk in dan - ger all the way.

2 I pass through trials all the way,
　　With sin and ills contending;
　In patience I must bear each day
　　The cross of God's own sending;
　Oft in adversity
　I know not where to flee;
　When storms of woe my soul dismay,
　I pass through trials all the way.

3 Death doth pursue me all the way,
　　Nowhere I rest securely,
　He comes by night, he comes by day,
　　And takes his prey most surely;
　A failing breath— and I
　In death's strong grasp may lie
　To face eternity foraye:
　Death doth pursue me all the way.

4 I walk 'mongst angels all the way
　　They shield me and befriend me;
　All Satan's power is held at bay
　　When heavenly hosts attend me;
　They are my sure defense,
　All fear and sorrow hence!
　Unharmed by foes, do what they may,
　I walk 'mongst angels all the way.

5 I walk with Jesus all the way,
　　His guidance never fails me,
　Within His wounds I find a stay,
　　When Satan's power assails me;
　And by His footsteps led,
　My path I safely tread,
　In spite of ills that threaten may,
　I walk with Jesus all the way.

6 My walk is heavenward all the way,
　　Await, my soul, the morrow,
　When thou shalt find release for aye
　　From all thy sin and sorrow;
　All worldly pomp, begone,
　To heaven I now press on;
　For all the world I would not stay,
　My walk is heavenward all the way.

H. A. Brorson, 1734

270 8, 7, 8, 7, 6, 6, 6, 6, 7.

Martin Luther, 1529

A might-y for-tress is our God, A trusty shield and weap-on;
Our help is He in all our need, Our stay, whate'er doth hap - pen;
For still our an-cient foe Doth seek to work us woe: Strong mail of craft and
power He wear-eth in this hour; On earth is not his e - qual.

2 Stood we alone in our own might,
  Our striving would be losing;
For us the one true Man doth fight,
  The Man of God's own choosing.
  Who is this chosen One?
  'Tis Jesus Christ, the Son,
  The Lord of hosts, 'tis He
  Who wins the victory
  In every field of battle.

3 And were the world with devils filled,
  All watching to devour us,
Our souls to fear we need not yield,
  They cannot overpower us;
  Their dreaded prince no more
  Can harm us as of yore;
  His rage we can endure;
  For lo! his doom is sure,
  A word shall overthrow him.

First Sunday in Lent

4 Still must they leave God's word its
    might,
  For which no thanks they merit;
  Still is He with us in the fight,
  With His good gifts and Spirit.
  And should they, in the strife,
  Take kindred, goods, and life,
  We freely let them go,
  They profit not the foe;
  With us remains the kingdom.

M. Luther, 1529

271   8, 8, 7, 8, 8, 7.

Zinck's Koralbog, 1801

Sav-ior, when we call, O hear us; In the try-ing hour be near us,

Lest the foe should prove too strong: To Thy mer-cy we be-take us;

Nev-er leave us, nor for-sake us; Power and grace to Thee be-long.

2 Other help than Thine we have not;
  Other help than Thine we crave not;
    'Tis enough if we have this:
  This from every ill secures us;
  Every blessing this ensures us;
    More than life Thy favor is.

3 Keep us on Thy strength relying,
  In Thy name the foe defying;
    Till Thy coming bring us peace.
  O how sweet the thought, and cheer-
  In the day of Thine appearing   [ing,
    Trouble shall for ever cease.

T. Kelly, ca. 1845

272   7, 6.   8L.   Zinck's Koralbog, 1801

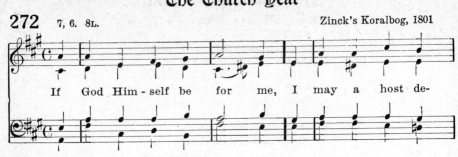

If God Him-self be for me, I may a host de-

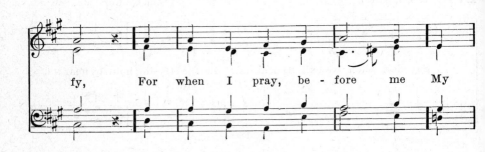

fy, For when I pray, be-fore me My

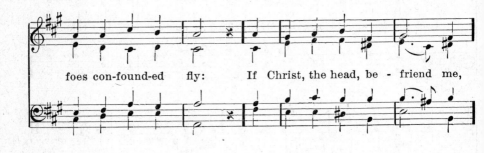

foes con-found-ed fly: If Christ, the head, be-friend me,

If God be my sup-port, The mis-chief they in-

First Sunday in Lent

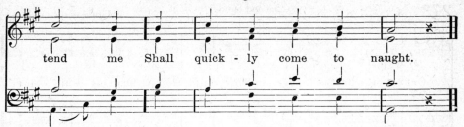

tend   me   Shall   quick - ly   come   to   naught.

2 This I believe— yea, rather,
   In this I make my boast,
That God is my dear Father,
   The friend who loves me most;
And that, whate'er betide me,
   My Savior is at hand,
Through stormy seas to guide me,
   And bring me safe to land.

3 I build on this foundation,—
   That Jesus and His blood
Alone are my salvation,
   The true eternal good:
Without Him, all that pleases
   Is valueless on earth;
The gifts I owe to Jesus
   Alone my love are worth.

4 His Holy Spirit dwelleth
   Within my willing heart,
Tames it when it rebelleth,
   And soothes the keenest smart:
He crowns His work with blessing,
   And helpeth me to cry
"My Father!" without ceasing,
   To Him who dwells on high.

5 And when my soul is lying
   Weak, trembling, and oppressed,
He pleads with groans and sighing
   That cannot be expressed;
But God's quick eye discerns them
   Although they give no sound,
And into language turns them,
   E'en in the heart's deep ground.

6 To mine His Spirit speaketh
   Sweet words of soothing power,
How God to him that seeketh
   For rest, hath rest in store:
There God Himself prepareth
   My heritage and lot,
And though my body weareth,
   My heaven shall fail me not.

7 Who clings with resolution
   To Him whom Satan hates,
Must look for persecution
   Which never here abates;
Reproaches, griefs and losses
   Rain fast upon his head,
A thousand plagues and crosses
   Become his daily bread.

8 All this I am prepared for,
   Yet am I not afraid;
By Thee shall all be cared for,
   To whom my vows were paid:
Though life and limb it cost me,
   And all the earthly store
Which once so much engrossed me,—
   I love Thee all the more.

9 Not fire, nor sword, nor thunder,
   Shall sever me from Thee;
Though earth be rent asunder
   Thou'rt mine eternally:
Not hunger, thirst, nor danger,
   Not pain, nor pinching want,
Nor mighty princes' anger,
   My fearless soul shall daunt.

10 No angel, and no gladness,
   No throne, no pomp, nor show,
No love, no hate, no sadness,
   No pain, no depth of woe,
No scheme of man's contrivance,
   Though it be great or small,
Shall draw me from Thy guidance,
   Not one of these, nor all!

11 My merry heart is springing,
   And knows not how to pine;
'Tis full of joy and singing,
   And radiancy divine;
The sun whose smiles so cheer me
   Is Jesus Christ alone:
To have Him always near me
   Is heaven itself begun.

P. Gerhardt, 1656

273   8, 7, 8, 7, 8, 8, 7.

Second Sunday in Lent

Johann Walther, 1524

Out of the depths I cry to Thee, Lord, God, O hear my wail-ing!

Thy gra-cious ear in-cline to me, And make my prayer a-

vail-ing. On my mis-deeds in mer-cy look, O

deign to blot them from Thy book, Or who can stand be-fore Thee?

2 Thy sovereign grace and boundless
     love,
   Make Thee, O Lord, forgiving;
My purest thoughts and deeds but
     prove
   Sin in my heart is living:
None guiltless in Thy sight appear;
All who approach Thy throne must
     fear,
   And humbly trust Thy mercy.

3 Thou canst be merciful while just,—
   This is my hope's foundation;
On Thy redeeming grace I trust,
   Grant me, then, Thy salvation.
Shielded by Thee, I stand secure;
Thy word is firm, Thy promise sure,
   And I rely upon Thee.

Second Sunday in Lent

4 Like those who watch the midnight's
    hour
  To hail the dawning morrow,
I wait for Thee, I trust Thy power,
  Unmoved by doubt or sorrow.
So let Thy Israel hope in Thee,
And he shall find Thy mercy free,
  And Thy redemption plenteous.

5 Where'er the greatest sins abound,
  By grace they are exceeded;
Thy helping hand is always found
  With aid where aid is needed;
Thy hand, the only hand to save,
Will rescue Israel from the grave,
  And pardon his transgression.

M. Luther, 1523

274   8, 7, 8, 7, 7, 7.   Ludv. M. Lindeman, 1812—87.

Thou to whom the sick and dy-ing Ev-er came, nor came in vain,

Still with heal-ing word re-ply-ing To the wea-ried cry of pain;

Hear us, Je-sus, as we meet, Suppliants at Thy mer-cy-seat.

2 Still the weary, sick, and dying
  Need a brother's, sister's care,
On Thy higher help relying,
  May we now their burden share,
Bringing all our offerings meet,
Suppliant to Thy mercy-seat.

3 May each child of Thine be willing,
  Willing both in hand and heart,
All the law of love fulfilling,

  Comfort ever to impart,
Ever bringing offerings meet,
Suppliant at Thy mercy-seat.

4 Then shall sickness, sin, and sadness,
  To Thy healing power yield,
Till the sick and sad, in gladness,
  Rescued, ransomed, cleansed, and healed,
One in Thee together meet, [healed,
Pardoned at Thy judgment-seat.

G. Thring, 1866

275   8, 7, 8, 7, 8, 7, 4, 6, 8.

J. Klug, Wittenberg, 1535

Lord, hear the voice of my com-plaint, To Thee I now com-mend me, Let not my heart and hope grow faint, But deign Thy grace to send me; True faith from Thee, my God, I seek, The faith that loves Thee sole-ly Keeps me low-ly, And prompt to aid the weak, And mark each word that Thou dost speak.

Second Sunday in Lent

2 Yet more from Thee I dare to claim,
   Whose goodness is unbounded;
O let me ne'er be put to shame,
   My hope be ne'er confounded;
But e'en in death still find Thee true,
   And in that hour, else lonely,
     Trust Thee only,
Not aught that I can do,
For such false trust I sore should rue.

3 O grant that from my very heart
   My foes be all forgiven,
Forgive my sins and heal their smart,
   And grant new life from heaven;
Thy word, that blessed food, bestow,
   Which best the soul can nourish;
     Make it flourish
Through all the storms of woe
That else my faith might overthrow.

4 Then be the world my foe or friend,
   Keep me to her a stranger,
Thy steadfast soldier to the end,
   Through pleasure and through dan-
     ger;
From Thee alone comes such high
   No works of ours obtain it, [grace,
     Or can gain it;
Our pride hath here no place,
'Tis Thy free promise we embrace.

5 Help me, for I am weak; I fight,
   Yet scarce can battle longer;
I cling but to Thy grace and might,
   'Tis Thou must make me stronger;
When sore temptations are my lot,
   And tempests round me lower,
     Break their power;
So through deliverance wrought,
I know that Thou forsak'st me not!

J. Agricola, 1529

276   8, 7.   6L.

Darmstadt-Gesangbuch, 1698

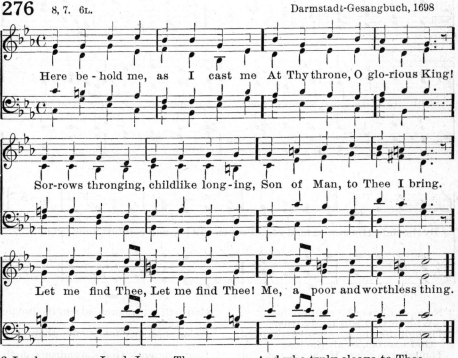

Here be-hold me, as I cast me At Thy throne, O glo-rious King!

Sor-rows thronging, childlike long-ing, Son of Man, to Thee I bring.

Let me find Thee, Let me find Thee! Me, a poor and worthless thing.

2 Look upon me, Lord, I pray Thee,
   Let Thy Spirit dwell in mine;
Thou hast sought me, Thou hast bought
   Only Thee to know I pine. [me,
   ‖:Let me find Thee!:‖
Take my heart, and own me Thine!

3 Naught I ask for, naught I strive for,
   But Thy grace so rich and free;
That Thou givest whom Thou lovest,

And who truly cleave to Thee.
   ‖:Let me find Thee!:‖
He hath all things who hath Thee.

4 Earthly treasure, mirth and pleasure,
   Glorious name, or golden hoard,
Are but weary, void and dreary,
   To the heart that longs for God.
   ‖:Let me find Thee!:‖
I am Thine, O mighty Lord!

J. Neander, 1677

The Church Year

8, 7, 8, 7, 7, 7, 8, 8.

Louis Bourgeois, 1551

When af-flic-tions sore op-press you, Low with grief and an-guish bowed,

Then to ear-nest prayer ad-dress you; Prayer will help you, through the cloud

Still to see your Sav-ior near, Un-der ev-ery cross you bear;

By the light His word doth lend you, Prayer will joy and comfort send you.

2 None shall ever be confounded,
  Who in God will freely trust;
Though they be by woes surrounded,
  God's a rock to all the just:
Though you deem He hears you not,
Still your wants are ne'er forgot:
Cry to Him when storms assail you,
Let your courage never fail you.

3 Call on God, knock, seek, implore Him,
  'Tis the Christian's noblest skill;
He who comes with faith before Him,
  Meets with help and favor still:
Who on God most firmly rest,
Are the wisest and the best;

God will with such strength imbue
  them,
Ne'er shall any foe subdue them.

4 Learn to mark God's wondrous deal-
  ing
  With the people that He loves;
When His chastening hand they're
  feeling,
  Then their faith the strongest proves:
God is nigh, and notes their tears,
Though He answers not, He hears;
Pray with faith, for though He try
  you,
No good thing can God deny you.

Second Sunday in Lent

5 Ponder all God's truth can teach you,
Let His word your footsteps guide;
Satan's wiles shall never reach you,
Though he draw the world aside:
Lo! God's truth is thy defense,
Light, and hope, and confidence:
Trust in God, He'll not deceive you,
Pray, and all your foes will leave you.

J. Olearius, 1671

278   4, 4, 7, 4, 4, 4, 7.   Ludv. M. Lindeman, 1812—87

Lord Je-sus Christ, My Sav-ior blest, My hope and my sal-
va - - tion! I trust in Thee, De-liv-er me
From mis-er - y; Thy word's my con-so-la-tion.

2 As Thou dost will,
Lead Thou me still,
That I may truly serve Thee.
My God, I pray,
Teach me Thy way,
To my last day
In Thy true faith preserve me.

3 Most heartily
I trust in Thee,
Thy mercy fails me never;
Dear Lord, abide
My helper tried,
Thou Crucified,
From evil keep me ever.

4 Now henceforth must
I put my trust
In Thee, O dearest Savior;
Thy comfort choice,
Thy word and voice
My heart rejoice,
Despite my ill behavior.

5 When sorrows rise,
My refuge lies
In Thy compassion tender;
Within Thine arm
Can naught alarm;
Keep me from harm,
Be Thou my strong defender.

6 I have Thy word,
Christ Jesus, Lord,
Thou never wilt forsake me;
This will I plead
In time of need;
O help with speed,
When troubles overtake me!

7 Grant, Lord, we pray,
Thy grace each day,
That we, Thy law revering,
May live with Thee,
And happy be
Eternally,
Before Thy throne appearing.

H C. Sthen, ca. 1578

The Church Year

Third Sunday in Lent

279   8, 9, 8, 8, 9, 8, 6, 6, 4, 4, 4, 8.   Ph. Nicolai, 1599

Ho - ly Je - sus! Fountain stream - ing Of ho - li - ness

and grace re - deem - ing,   As   clear as crys-tal, pure and

free;   Cher - u - bim   in robes of   white - ness

And ser - a - phim in all their bright - ness   Are

Third Sunday in Lent

dark-ness when com-pared with Thee; Be Thou my pat-tern bright,

My glo-ry and de-light, Ho-ly Sav-ior! O

teach Thou me, that I may be All pure and ho-ly, like to Thee.

2 Gentle Jesus! self-denying,
　And with Thy Father's will complying,
　　Yea, even unto death resigned;
　Let me e'er, Thy way pursuing,
　And pride and haughtiness subduing,
　　Be guided by Thy gentle mind;
　　　Like Thee may I be mild
　　　And gentle as a child,
　　　　Gentle Savior!
　O teach Thou me, that I may be
　Meek and obedient, like to Thee.

3 Loving Jesus! Thou my treasure,
　Whose love to man no thought can measure,
　　Conform me to Thine image bright;
　Send Thy Spirit, grace bestowing,
　That I, in every virtue growing,
　　May ripen for the realms of light;
　　　O draw me after Thee,
　　　Forever Thine to be,
　　　　Loving Savior!
　Thou givest rest to souls distressed,
　And all who learn of Thee are blest.

J. van Lodenstein, 1676
B. Crasselius, 1700

280 7, 6, 7, 6, 6, 7, 7, 6.

German, Hamburg, 1598

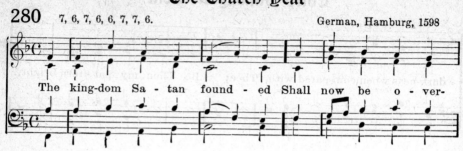

The king-dom Sa-tan found-ed Shall now be o-ver-

thrown, For Christ its fall hath sound-ed,

And through His power a-lone Shall Sa-tan meet his

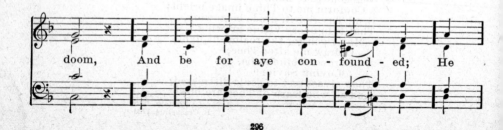

doom, And be for aye con-found-ed; He

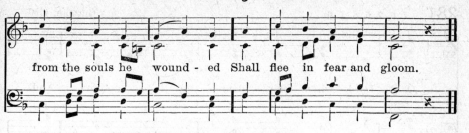

from the souls he wound - ed Shall flee in fear and gloom.

2 Though he would bind forever
   Our lips with bands of hell,
   Yet Christ, sent to deliver,
   Can loose those bands full well,
   That e'en the dumb may raise
His voice with joy and pleasure
And sing in sweetest measure
   To God his thanks and praise.

3 O Jesus! my distresses
   To Thee are known full well,
   Thou seest how Satan presses
   My soul's weak citadel;
   His aim is to control
My members and my senses,
With sin and with offenses
   He steals into my soul.

4 Anon my tongue he bindeth,
   That God it shall not praise;
   Anon my eyes he blindeth,
   To hide the light of grace;
   Now he my ears doth close,
To hinder me from hearing
The gospel's sound so cheering
   And soothing in my woes.

5 To God I raise my crying,
   Before the mercy-seat,
   And on His word relying,
   I grace of Him entreat,
   That He for Jesus' sake
Would cleanse my soul and spirit
'Through Jesus' blood and merit,
   And Satan's power break.

6 God, let not love of sinning
   Thy fear drive from my breast,
   Lest Satan, triumph winning,
   Be of my heart possessed;
   O let Thy chastening rod
Each day give me direction,
To seek Thy sure protection
   And tell Thy grace abroad.

7 My heart must Thou have solely,
   My Savior and my God!
   Come, Jesus, take it wholly,
   And make it Thine abode!
   Mould it to Thy control,
That I, Thy word receiving,
May find, in Thee believing,
   Salvation for my soul.

T. Kingo, 1689

281 7. 6, 7, 6, 8, 7, 6. German, 1790

O Lord, when con - dem - na - tion And

guilt op - press my soul, Then let Thy bit - ter

pas - sion The ris - ing storm con - trol: Re-

mind me that Thy blood was spilt For me, O most un-

Third Sunday in Lent

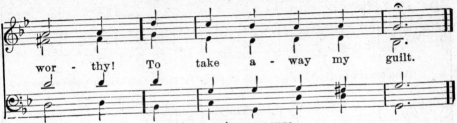

wor - thy!   To   take   a - way   my   guilt.

2 O wonder passing measure
   To faith's enlightened eye!
   For slaves it was the pleasure
   Of their own Lord to die!
   The mighty God stoops from on high
   For me, lost, ruined creature,
   And deigns as man to die.

3 My sins rise up to heaven,—
   And countless is their host;
   But Christ Himself hath given,
   And paid the mighty cost:
   Since then on Him my sins were laid,
   Of hell and all its torments,
   I am no more afraid.

4 Henceforth my heart shall bless
   Thee
   Whilst here its pulses move;
   Its songs of praise address Thee
   For all Thy dying love:
   Thy wrongs and last deep agony
   Shall be my meditation
   Till I am called to Thee.

5 Lord, let Thy bitter passion
   My soul with strength inspire
   To flee with indignation
   All sinful, low desire:
   Ah! never would I, Lord, forget
   The greatness of that ransom
   Which paid my endless debt.

6 Should earthly griefs assail me,
   If need be, shame and scorn,
   Let patience never fail me
   To bear as Thou hast borne:
   Grant that the world I may forsake,
   And Thee for my example,
   Oh! may I daily take.

7 Still let me do to others
   As Thou hast done to me,
   And look on all as brothers,
   Their willing servant be:
   O may I never seek my own,
   But help as Thou hast helped,
   With purest love alone.

8 At length when I am bidden
   With all things here to part,
   The wounds in which I'm hidden
   Speak peace into my heart:
   Relying then upon Thy blood,
   O give me full assurance
   That I shall see my God.

J. Gesenius, 1646

282 8, 7. 8L.

Breitendich's Koralbog, 1764

Who trusts in God, a strong a-bode In heaven and earth pos-sess-es;

Who looks in love to Christ a-bove, No fear his heart op-press-es.

In Thee a-lone, dear Lord, we own Sweet hope and con-so-la-tion;

Our shield from foes, our balm for woes, Our great and sure sal-va-tion.

2 Though Satan's wrath beset our path,
And worldly scorn assail us,
While Thou art near we will not fear,
Thy strength shall never fail us:
Thy rod and staff shall keep us safe,
And guide our steps forever;
Nor shades of death, nor hell beneath,
Our souls from Thee shall sever.

3 In all the strife of mortal life
Our feet shall stand securely;
Temptation's hour shall lose its power,
For Thou shalt guard us surely.
O God, renew, with heavenly dew,
Our body, soul, and spirit,
Until we stand at Thy right hand,
Through Jesus' saving merit.

J. Magdeburg, 1572, et al.

Third Sunday in Lent

283 7, 6. 8L.

Samuel S. Wesley, 1864

O Thou be-fore whose pres-ence Naught e-vil may come in,

Yet who dost look in mer-cy Down on this world of sin;

O give us no-ble pur-pose To set the sin-bound free,

And Christ-like ten-der pit-y To seek the lost for Thee.

2 Fierce is our subtle foeman:
  The forces at his hand
With woes that none can number
  Despoil the pleasant land;
All they who war against them,
  In strife so keen and long,
Must in their Savior's armor
  Be stronger than the strong.

3 So hast Thou wrought among us
  The great things that we see:
For things that are we thank Thee,
  And for the things to be.

For bright hope is uplifting
  Faint hands and feeble knees,
To strive beneath Thy blessing
  For greater things than these.

4 Lead on, O Love and Mercy,
  O Purity and Power,
Lead on till peace eternal
  Shall close this battle-hour:
Till all who prayed and struggled
  To set their brethren free,
In triumph meet to praise Thee,
  Most Holy Trinity

S. J. Stone, 1889

284 7, 6. 8L.   Fourth Sunday in Lent   H. L. Hassler, 1601.

Thy way and all thy sor - rows, Give thou in - to His hand,

His gra-cious care un - fail - ing, Who doth the heavens command;

Their course and path He giv - eth To clouds and air and wind:

A way thy feet may fol - low He, too, for thee will find.

2 On Him be thy reliance,
   If thou would'st prosper well:
To make thy work enduring
   Thy mind on Him must dwell,
God yieldeth naught to sorrow
   And self-tormenting care:
Naught, naught with Him availeth,
   No power save that of prayer.

3 Thy truth and grace, O Father,
   Behold and surely know,
Both what is good and evil,
   For mortal man below:
And whatsoe'er Thou choosest
   Thou dost, great God, fulfill,
And into being bringest
   Whate'er is in Thy will.

4 Thy way is ever open;
   Thou dost on naught depend;
Thine act is only blessing,
   Thy path light without end.
Thy work can no man hinder;
   Thy purpose none can stay,
Since Thou to bless Thy children
   Through all dost make a way.

5 In vain the powers of darkness
   Thy will, O God, oppose:
High over all undoubting,
   Thy pleasure onward goes:
Whate'er Thy will resolveth,
   Whate'er Thou dost intend,
Its destined work performeth
   True to its aim and end.

6 Then hope, my feeble spirit,
   And be thou undismayed:
God helps in every trial,
   And makes thee unafraid.
Await God's time with pleasure,
   Then shall thine eyes behold
The sun of joy and gladness
   His brightest beams unfold.

7 Arise, arise! thy sadness,
   Thy cares send far away;
Away each thought afflicting
   That on the heart doth prey.

Not in thy hands the guidance
   Of all events doth dwell;
God on His throne o'erruleth,
   He guideth all things well.

8 Leave all to His direction:
   In wisdom He doth reign:
Thy wonder far exceeding,
   He will His course maintain:
So He as Him beseemeth
   His wonder-working skill,
Shall put away the sorrows,
   That now thy spirit fill.

9 Awhile His consolation
   He will to thee deny,
And seem as though in spirit
   He far from thee would fly;
Awhile distress and anguish
   Shall compass thee around,
Nor to thy supplication
   An answering voice be found,

10 But if thou ne'er forsake Him,
   Thou shalt deliverance find;
Behold all unexpected,
   He will thy soul unbind.
He from thy heavy burden
   Will soon thy heart set free:
Yea, from that weight no evil
   Hath yet befallen thee.

11 Thou child of truth, how blessèd!
   A conqueror soon shalt be,
With songs of glad thanksgiving
   A crown awaiteth thee.
To thee the palm triumphal
   By God's own hand is giv'n,
Thine, to His name who saved thee,
   To sing the songs of heaven.

12 Give, Lord, this consummation
   To all our heart's distress,
Our hands, our feet, O strengthen,
   In death our spirits bless.
Thy truth and Thy protection
   Forevermore we pray:
With these in heavenly glory
   Shall end our certain way.

P. Gerhardt. 1656

285   8, 7, 8, 7, 4, 7.

J. Filitz, 1804—1876

Guide me, O Thou great Je-ho-vah, Pil-grim through this bar-ren land; I am weak, but Thou art might-y; Hold me with Thy power-ful hand: Bread of heav-en, Bread of heav-en, Feed me now and ev-er-more.

2 Open now the crystal fountain,
   Whence the healing streams do flow;
Let the fiery, cloudy pillar
Lead me all my journey through:
   ‖:Strong Deliverer,:‖
Be Thou still my strength and shield.

3 When I tread the verge of Jordan,
   Bid my anxious fears subside;
Death of death and hell's destruction,
Land me safe on Canaan's side:
   ‖:Songs of praises:‖
I will ever give to Thee.

W. Williams, 1745, et al.

Fourth Sunday in Lent

286 C. M.

Scotch Psalter, 1615

O God of Beth-el, by whose hand Thy
peo-ple still are fed; Who through this wea-ry
pil-grim-age Hast all our fa-thers led:

2 Our vows, our prayers, we now present
    Before Thy throne of grace:
God of our fathers, be the God
    Of their succeeding race.

3 Through each perplexing path of life
    Our wandering footsteps guide.
Give us each day our daily bread,
    And raiment fit provide.

4 O spread Thy sheltering wings around,
    Till all our wanderings cease.
And at our Father's loved abode,
    Our souls arrive in peace!

5 Such blessings from Thy gracious hand
    Our humble prayers implore;
And Thou shalt be our chosen God,
    And portion evermore.

P. Doddridge, 1737, et al.

287 7, 7, 6, 7, 7, 8.

Heinrich Isaac, 1490

O Bread of life from heav - en, To wea - ry pil-grims giv - en,
O Man-na from a - bove: The souls that hun - ger feed Thou, The
hearts that seek Thee feed Thou, With Thy most sweet and ten - der love.

2 O Fount of grace redeeming,
   O River ever streaming
     From Jesus' holy side:
   Come Thou, Thyself bestowing
   On thirsting souls, and flowing
     Till all their wants are satisfied.

3 Jesus, this feast receiving,
   Thy word of truth believing,
     We Thee unseen adore:
   Grant, when our race is ended,
   That we, to heaven ascended,
     May see Thy glory ever more.

Anon., Latin, 1661

Fifth Sunday in Lent

288 8s. 6L.

W. H. Monk, 1861

O Sav-ior, who in love didst take A hu-man bod-y, for our sake; To share with us the griefs of life, Its watch-ings, wea-ri-ness, and strife: All that be-long to man but sin, Thou didst this day Thy-self be-gin

2 Savior of infants, Thou didst rest,
Helpless, upon Thy mother's breast;
Savior of children, Thou didst play,
And grow beside her, day by day.
All human life to soothe and save,
Up from the cradle to the grave.

3 Savior, as low as Thou didst bend
From heaven to be the sinner's friend,
So high our nature lift with Thine,
Till human things become divine.
And Thy eternal love once more
God's image to the soul restore.

4 And when we cling too close to earth,
Forgetful of our heavenly birth,
And for the love of its poor dross,
Despise Thy crown or shun Thy cross.
O let this festal day reprove
Such wrong to Thine incarnate love.

J. S. B. Monsell, 1857

307

The Church Year

289 S. M.

R. S. Ambrose, 1876

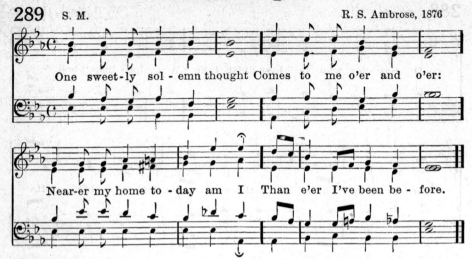

One sweet-ly sol - emn thought Comes to me o'er and o'er:

Near-er my home to - day am I Than e'er I've been be - fore.

2 Nearer my Father's house,
　Where many mansions be;
　Nearer today the great white throne,
　Nearer the crystal sea.

3 Nearer the bound of life
　Where burdens are laid down;
　Nearer to leave the heavy cross;
　Nearer to gain the crown.

4 But, lying dark between,
　Winding down through the night,

There rolls the silent, unknown stream
That leads at last to light.

5 Ev'n now, perchance, my feet
　Are slipping on the brink,
And I, to-day, am nearer home,—
　Nearer than now I think.

6 Jesus, perfect my trust;
　Strengthen my spirit's faith;
Nor let me stand, at last, alone
　Upon the shore of death.

Phoebe Cary, 1852

290　8, 7, 8, 7, 8, 4, 7.

J. C. Gebauer

On Ma - ry, vir - gin un - de - filed, Did God be - stow His

fa - vor; She bore a son, the spot-less child, To him be praise for-

Fifth Sunday in Lent

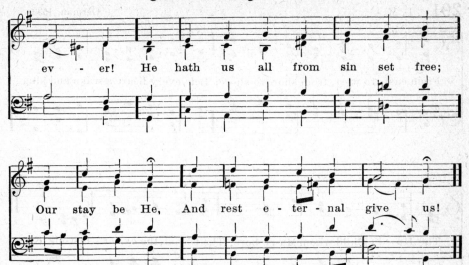

ev - er! He hath us all from sin set free;

Our stay be He, And rest e - ter - nal give us!

2 Were all the sages here below
  All human wisdom showing,
The mystery of Christ to know
  Were far beyond their knowing;
For full of grace and truth is He;
  O may He be
Our comfort in our dying!

3 Inspired of God the prophets spake,
  And faithful proved their saying,
That Christ the bonds of sin doth break,
  Deliverance conveying
To all by Satan's wiles enslaved;
  All shall be saved
Who trust in Him, believing.

4 O Root of Jesse, David's Son,
  And Jacob's Star of heaven!
Thou art the Christ, the blessed One;
  Thy name all praise be given:
By grace Thou hast redeemed us all
  From Adam's fall,
And Thou wilt guide and tend us.

5 O could I speak in every tongue,
  The Scripture's deep expounding,
Were in my mouth the angels' song
  That through high heaven is sounding,
I on my knees would humbly fall,
  On Jesus call,
And worship Him forever!

6 My sins are countless as the sands,
  My crimes, O God, are crying,
Deliver me from sin's dread bands
  And save me, Lord, when dying;
O let me not, for evil past,
  Be lost at last,
Grant me Thy grace, I pray Thee!

Anon., H. Thomissön, 1569

291   L. M.   German, 1539

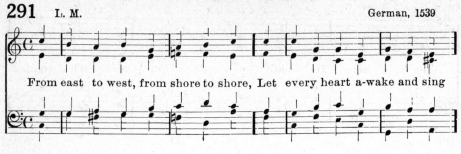

From east to west, from shore to shore, Let every heart a-wake and sing

The Ho - ly Child whom Ma-ry bore, The Christ, the ev - er - last-ing King.

2 Behold! the world's Creator wears
  The form and fashion of our frame;
  Our very flesh our Maker shares,
  To save a fallen world He came.

3 For this how wondrously He wrought!
  A maiden, in her lowly place,
  Became, in ways beyond all thought,
  The chosen vessel of His grace.

4 She bowed her to the angel's word,
  Declaring what the Father willed,
  And suddenly the promised Lord
  That pure and hallowed temple filled.

5 He shrank not from the oxen's stall,
  He lay within the manger bed,
  And He whose bounty feedeth all
  At Mary's breast Himself was fed.

6 And while the angels in the sky
  Sang praise above the silent field,
  To shepherds poor the Lord most high,
  The one great Shepherd, was revealed.

7 All glory for this blessed morn
  To God the Father ever be;
  All praise to Thee, O Virgin-born,
  All praise, O Holy Ghost, to Thee.

C. Sedulius, 5th Century

Sixth Sunday in Lent

Palm Sunday

J. B. Dykes, 1866

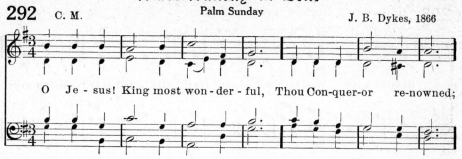

O Je - sus! King most won - der - ful, Thou Con-quer-or re-nowned;

Thou Sweetness most in - ef - fa - ble, In whom all joys are found!

2 When once Thou visitest the heart,
  Then truth begins to shine:
  Then earthly vanities depart,
  Then kindles love divine.

3 O Jesus, light of all below!
  Thou Fount of life and fire!
  Surpassing all the joys we know,
  All that we can desire,—

4 May every heart confess Thy name,
  And ever Thee adore;
  And, seeking Thee, itself inflame
  To seek Thee more and more.

5 Thee may our tongues forever bless;
  Thee may we love alone:
  And ever in our lives express
  The image of Thine own.

Bernard of Clairvaux, d. 1153

293 L. M.

J. B. Dykes, 1862

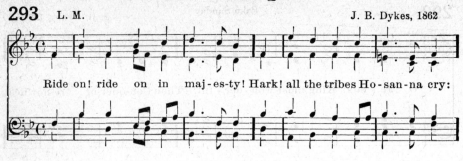

Ride on! ride on in maj-es-ty! Hark! all the tribes Ho-san-na cry:

O Sav-ior meek, pur-sue Thy road With palms and scattered garments strowed.

2 Ride on, ride on in majesty!
In lowly pomp ride on to die!
O Christ, Thy triumphs now begin
O'er captive death and conquered sin.

3 Ride on, ride on in majesty!
The angel armies of the sky
Look down with sad and wondering
   eyes,
To see the approaching Sacrifice.

4 Ride on, ride on in majesty!
Thy last and fiercest strife is nigh:
The Father on His sapphire throne
Expects His own anointed Son.

5 Ride on, ride on in majesty!
In lowly pomp ride on to die;
Bow Thy meek head to mortal pain,
Then take, O God, Thy power and
   reign.

H. H. Milman, 1827

294 11, 10. 4L.

J. B. Dykes, 1876

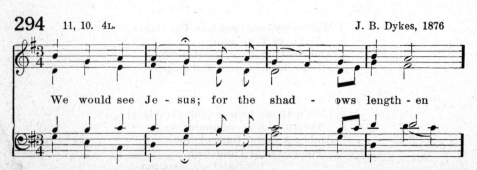

We would see Je - sus; for the shad - ows length-en

Sixth Sunday in Lent

A - cross this lit - tle land-scape of our life;

We would see Je - sus, our weak faith to strength-en,

For the last wea - ri - ness, the fi - nal strife.

2 We would see Jesus, the great rock foundation
　　Whereon our feet were set by sovereign grace:
　Nor life nor death, with all their agitation,
　　Can thence remove us, if we see His face.

3 We would see Jesus: other lights are paling,
　　Which for long years we have rejoiced to see;
　The blessings of our pilgrimage are failing;
　　We would not mourn them, for we go to Thee.

4 We would see Jesus; yet the spirit lingers
　　Round the dear objects it has loved so long,
　And earth from earth can scarce unclasp its fingers;
　　Our love to Thee makes not this love less strong.

5 We would see Jesus: sense is all too binding,
　　And heaven appears too dim, too far away;
　We would see Thee, Thyself our hearts reminding
　　What Thou hast suffered, our great debt to pay.

6 We would see Jesus: this is all we're needing;
　　Strength, joy, and willingness come with the sight;
　We would see Jesus, dying, risen, pleading;
　　Then welcome day, and farewell mortal night!

Anna Warner, 1852

The Church Year

8, 7. 8L.

S. Webbe, 1740—1816

Love di - vine, all love ex - cel-ling, Joy of heaven, to earth come down!

Fix in us Thy hum - ble dwell-ing, All Thy faith-ful mercies crown.

Je - sus, Thou art all com-pas-sion, Pure, un - bound-ed love Thou art,

Vis - it us with Thy sal - va - tion, En - ter ev - ery trembling heart!

2 Breathe, O breathe Thy loving Spirit
  Into every troubled breast!
Let us all in Thee inherit,
  Let us find Thy promised rest.
Take away the love of sinning,
  Alpha and Omega be;
End of faith, as its beginning,
  Set our hearts at liberty.

3 Come, almighty to deliver,
  Let us all Thy life receive;
Graciously return, and never,
  Never more Thy temples leave!

Thee we would be always blessing,
  Serve Thee as Thy hosts above,
Pray, and praise Thee without ceasing,
  Glory in Thy perfect love.

4 Finish, then, Thy new creation,
  Pure and spotless let us be;
Let us see Thy great salvation,
  Perfectly restored in Thee,
Changed from glory into glory,
  Till in heaven we take our place,
Till we cast our crowns before Thee,
  Lost in wonder, love, and praise.

C. Wesley, 1747

Lent and Passion Week

296   8, 7. 8L.   German, 1525

His tri-al o'er, and now, be-neath His own cross faintly bend-ing,

Je-sus the fa-tal hill of death Is wea-ri-ly as-cend-ing.

And now, His hands and feet pierced through, Up-on the cross they raise Him,

Where e-ven now, in dis-tant view, The eye of faith sur-veys Him.

2 O wondrous love, which God most high
　　Towards man was pleased to cher-
His sinless Son He gave to die,　[ish!
　　That sinners might not perish.
Our sins's pollution to remove,
　　His blood was asked and given;
So mighty was the Saviors's love,
　　So vast the wrath of heaven.

3 Yes! 'tis the cross that breaks the rod
　　And chain of condemnation,
And makes a league 'twixt man and
　　For our entire salvation.　[God,
O praise the Father, praise the Son,
　　The Lamb for sinners given,
And Holy Ghost, through whom alone
　　Our hearts are raised to heaven.

C. Coffin, 1736

297   8, 7, 8, 7, 7, 7, 8, 8.

Louis Bourgeois, 1551

O what pre-cious balm and heal-ing, Je-sus, in Thy
wounds I find! Ev-ery hour that I am feel-ing
Pains of bod-y and of mind: Should some e-vil
thought rush in, And pro-voke my soul to sin, Thoughts of Thy deep
wounds, from sinning Keep me in its first be-gin-ning.

2 Should some lust or sharp temptation
  Prove too strong for flesh and blood,
Lo! I think upon Thy passion,
  And the breach is soon made good:
Or should Satan press me hard,
Thinking I am off my guard,
Christ, I say, for me was wounded,
And the tempter flees confounded.

3 If the world my heart entices
  On the broad and easy road,
And doth by its gay devices
  Silence every thought of God,
When the heavy load I see
Which, dear Lord, was laid on Thee,
I can still each wild emotion,
Calm and blest in my devotion.

4 Yes, whate'er may pain or grieve me,
  Thy dear wounds can make me whole;
When my heart sinks, they revive me,
  Life pours in upon my soul:
May Thy comfort render sweet
Every bitter cup I meet;
Thou who by Thy death and passion
Hast procured my soul's salvation.

5 Lord, on Thee alone I stay me,
  Safely hide beneath Thy wing;
Death can neither hurt nor slay me,
  Thy death took away his sting:
That I may in Thee have part,
Comfort, strengthen, heal my heart;
Light, and life, and love bestowing,
All from Thy free mercy flowing.

6 Well of life, if Thou art nigh me,
  Springing deep within my heart,
When the last dread hour shall try me,
  I can feel no inward smart:
If I hide myself in Thee,
Not a foe can injure me;
He shall overcome who hideth
In Thy wounds, and there abideth.

J. Heerman, after Bernard of Clairvaux, 1644

298
Same Tune.

1 On my heart imprint Thine image,
  Blessed Jesus, King of grace,
That life's riches, cares, and pleasures,
  Have no power Thee to efface;
This the superscription be:
Jesus, crucified for me,
Is my life, my hope's foundation,
And my glory and salvation.

T. Kingo, 1689

299 8, 7, 8, 7, 8, 8.

Johann Crüger, 1649

Je - sus, who for my trans-gres - sion Didst the shameful cross en-dure, And didst there the blest pos - ses - sion Of Thy joys to me in - sure: May my praise be ev - er tell - ing Of Thy love, all love ex - cel - ling.

2 Wondrous woes that brought salva-
    tion!
  Wondrous grace to sinners shown!
  Heaven is wrapt in contemplation
  Of His love, whom men disown!
  O my soul! wilt thou disown Him?
  Wilt not thou, my heart, enthrone
    Him?

3 Who but He can bless thy weeping?
  Who but He can soothe thy grief?

Only safe beneath His keeping,
  Thou in Him hast sure relief:
To the cross He came to bless thee;
Let His love, my soul, possess thee!

4 Lord! each thought and inclination,
  All my heart and will inspire,
  That my soul, Thy new creation,
    Thee may serve with pure desire;
  Daily Thy great love reviewing,
  Daily thus my sins subduing!

A. T. Russell, 1851

Lent and Passion Week

300   11, 11, 11, 5.   Johann Crüger, 1640

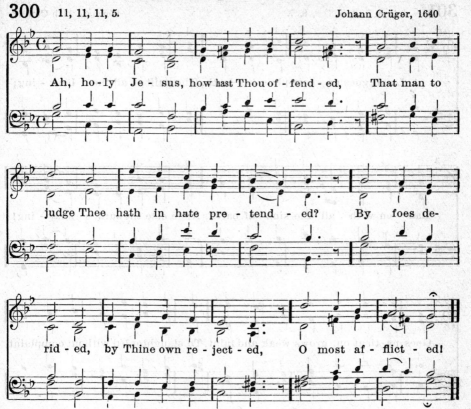

Ah, ho-ly Je - sus, how hast Thou of - fend - ed, That man to judge Thee hath in hate pre - tend - ed? By foes de-rid - ed, by Thine own re - ject - ed, O most af - flict - ed!

2 Who was the guilty? Who brought this upon Thee?
Alas, my treason, Jesus, hath undone Thee!
'Twas I, Lord Jesus, I it was denied Thee:
     I crucified Thee.

3 Lo, the good Shepherd for the sheep is offered;
The slave hath sinnéd, and the Son hath suffered;
For man's atonement, while he nothing heedeth,
     God intercedeth.

4 For me, kind Jesus, was Thy incarnation,
Thy mortal sorrow, and Thy life's oblation;
Thy death of anguish and Thy bitter passion,
     For my salvation.

5 Therefore, kind Jesus, since I cannot pay Thee,
I do adore Thee, and will ever pray Thee:
Think on Thy pity and Thy love unswerving,
     Not my deserving.

                                        J. Heermann, 1630

301 8, 7, 8, 7, 8, 8, 7, 8, 8, 7. German, 14th Century

A Lamb goes un - com-plain-ing forth, The guilt of all men bear - ing;

Lad - en with all the sins of earth, None else the burden shar - ing!

Goes pa-tient on, grows weak and faint, To slaughter led without complaint,

That spot-less life to of - fer; Bears shame, and stripes, and wounds and death,

An-guish and mock-er - y, and saith, "Will-ing all this I suf - fer."

2 That Lamb is Lord of death and life,
   God over all forever;
  The Father's Son, whom to that strife
   Love doth for us deliver!
  O mighty Love! what hast Thou done!
  The Father offers up His Son —
   The Son content descendeth!
  O Love, O Love! how strong art Thou!
  In shroud and grave Thou lay'st Him low
   Whose word the mountains rendeth!

3 Him on the cross, O Love, Thou lay'st,
   Fast to that torture nailing,
  Him as a spotless Lamb Thou slay'st;
   His heart and flesh are failing —
  The body with that crimson flood,
  That precious tide of noble blood,
   The heart with anguish breaking!
  O Lamb! what shall I render Thee
  For all Thy tender love to me,
   Or what return be making?

4 My lifelong days would I still Thee
   Be steadfastly beholding;
  Thee ever, as Thou ever me,
   With loving arms enfolding.
  And when my heart grows faint and chill,
  My heart's undying light, O still
   Abide unchanged before me!
  Myself Thy heritage I sign,
  Ransomed to be forever Thine,
   My only hope and glory.

5 I of Thy majesty and grace
   Would night and day be singing;
  A sacrifice of joy and praise
   Myself to Thee still bringing.
  My stream of life shall flow to Thee

Its steadfast current ceaselessly
   In praise to Thee outpouring;
  And all the good Thou dost to me
  I'll treasure in my memory,
   Deep in my heart's depths storing

6 Shrine of my heart, give larger space
   For wealth that passeth measure!
  Thou must become a royal place
   For all-excelling treasure.
  Away, world, with thy golden hoard,
  And all the glories in thee stored,
   My treasure is in heaven:
  For I have found true riches now;
  My treasure, Christ, my Lord art Thou,
   Thy blood so freely given!

7 This treasure ever I employ,
   This ever aid shall yield me:
  In sorrow it shall be my joy,
   In conflict it shall shield me.
  In joy, the music of my feast;
  And when all else has lost its zest.
   This manna still shall feed me;
  In thirst my drink, in want my food
  My company in solitude,
   To comfort and to lead me!

8 And when I enter on Thy joys,
   With Thee Thy kingdom sharing,
  Thyself my robe of triumph, Lord,
   Thy blood my right declaring,
  Shall place upon my head the crown,
  Shall lead me to the Father's throne,
   And raiment fit provide me;
  Till I, by Him to Thee betrothed,
  By Thee in bridal costume clothed,
   Stand as a bride beside Thee!

P. Gerhardt, 1648

302 8, 7, 8, 7, 7, 7, 8, 8.

Ludv. M. Lindeman, 1812—87

O-ver Ke-dron Je-sus tread-eth To His pas-sion for us all; Ev-ery hu-man eye be weep-ing, Tears of bit-ter grief let fall! Round His spir-it flock the foes, Place their shafts and bend their bows, Aim-ing at the Sav-ior sole-ly,

Lent and Passion Week

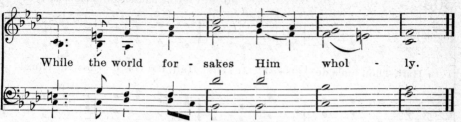

While the world for-sakes Him whol-ly.

2 David once, with heart afflicted,
    Crossed the Kedron's narrow strand,
  Clouds of gloom and grief about him
    When an exile from his land.
  But, O Jesus, blacker now
  Bends the cloud above Thy brow,
  Hasting to death's dreary portals
  For the shame and sin of mortals.

3 See how, anguish-struck, He falleth
    Prostrate, and with struggling breath,
  Three times on His God He calleth,
    Praying that the bitter death
  And the cup of doom may go,
  Still He cries, in all His woe:
  "Not My will, but Thine, O Father!"
  And the angels round Him gather.

4 See how, in that hour of darkness,
    Battling with the evil power,
  Agonies untold assail Him,
    On His soul the arrows shower;
  All the garden flowers are wet
  With the drops of bloody sweat,
  From His anguished frame distilling—
  World's redemption thus fulfilling!

5 But, O flowers, so sadly watered
    By this pure and precious dew,
  In some blessed hour your blossoms
    'Neath the olive-shadows grew!
  Eden's garden did not bear
  Aught that can with you compare,
  For the blood, thus freely given,
  Makes my soul the heir of heaven.

6 When as flowers themselves I wither,
    When I droop and fade like grass,
  When the life-streams through my pulses
    Dull and ever duller pass,
  When at last they cease to roll,
  Then, to cheer my sinking soul,
  Grace of Jesus, be Thou given—
  Source of triumph! pledge of heaven!
                    Thomas Kingo, 1689

303   8, 7. 8L.

J. A. Freylinghausen's Gesangbuch, 1704

Hail, Thou once de-spis-ed Je-sus! Hail, Thou Ga-li-le-an King!

Thou didst suf-fer to re-lease us; Thou didst free sal-va-tion bring.

Hail, Thou ag-o-niz-ing Sav-ior, Bear-er of our sin and shame!

By Thy mer-its We find fa-vor; Life is giv-en through Thy name.

2 Paschal Lamb, by God appointed,
  All our sins on Thee were laid;
By almighty love anointed,
  Thou hast full atonement made.
All Thy people are forgiven,
  Through the virtue of Thy blood:
Opened is the gate of heaven;
  Peace is made 'twixt man and God.

3 Jesus, hail, enthroned in glory,
  There for ever to abide!
All the heavenly hosts adore Thee,
  Seated at Thy Father's side:

There for sinners Thou art pleading,
  There Thou dost our place prepare,
Ever for us interceding,
  Till in glory we appear.

4 Worship, honor, power, and blessing,
  Thou art worthy to receive;
Loudest praises, without ceasing,
  Meet it is for us to give.
Help, ye bright angelic spirits,
  Bring your sweetest, noblest lays,
Help to sing our Savior's merits,
  Help to chant Immanuel's praise.

J. Bakewell, 1757

Lent and Passion Week

304 7s. 6L.   R. Redhead, 1853

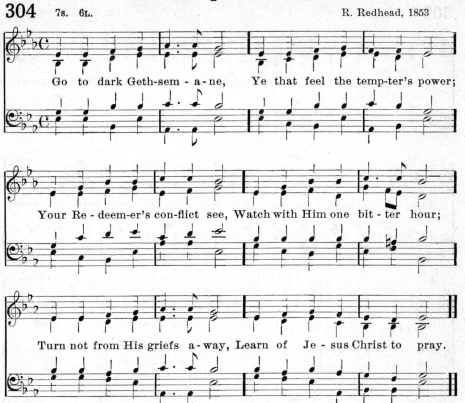

Go to dark Geth-sem - a - ne, Ye that feel the temp-ter's power;
Your Re - deem-er's con-flict see, Watch with Him one bit - ter hour;
Turn not from His griefs a - way, Learn of Je - sus Christ to pray.

2 Follow to the judgment-hall,
    View the Lord of life arraigned;
O the wormwood and the gall!
    O the pangs His soul sustained!
Shun not suffering, shame or loss,
Learn of Him to bear the cross.

3 Calvary's mournful mountain climb,
    There, adoring at His feet,
Mark that miracle of time,
    God's own sacrifice complete;
"It is finished," hear the cry,
Learn of Jesus Christ to die.

4 Early hasten to the tomb
    Where they laid His breathless clay;
All is solitude and gloom,
    Who hath taken Him away?
Christ is risen! He meets our eyes.
Savior, teach us so to rise.

J. Montgomery, 1825

The Church Year

305 7s. 8L.

J. Stainer, 1840—1901

Sav-ior, when in dust to Thee Low we bend the a-dor-ing knee;

When, re-pent-ant, to the skies Scarce we lift our weep-ing eyes;

O by all Thy pains and woe Suf-fered once for man be-low

Bend-ing from Thy throne on high, Hear our sol-emn lit-a-ny!

2 By Thy helpless infant years,
By Thy life of want and tears,
By Thy days of sore distress
In the savage wilderness;
By the dread mysterious hour
Of the insulting tempter's power;
Turn, O turn a favoring eye,
Hear our solemn litany!

3 By Thine hour of dire despair,
By Thine agony of prayer;
By the cross, the nail, the thorn,
Piercing spear, and torturing scorn;

By the gloom that veiled the skies
O'er the dreadful sacrifice;
Listen to our humble cry,
Hear our solemn litany!

4 By Thy deep expiring groan
By the sad sepulchral stone;
By the vault whose dark abode
Held in vain the rising God;
O from earth to heaven restored,
Mighty, re-ascended Lord,
Listen, listen to the cry,
Hear our solemn litany!

Sir Robert Grant, 1815

306 L. M.

E. Miller, 1735—1807

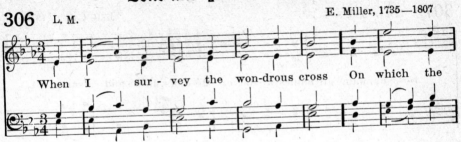

When I sur-vey the won-drous cross On which the

Prince of glo - - ry died, My rich-est gain I

count but loss, And pour con-tempt on all my pride.

2 Forbid it, Lord, that I should boast
 Save in the death of Christ, my God:
 All the vain things that charm me most,
 I sacrifice them to His blood.

3 See from His head, His hands, His feet,
 Sorrow and love flow mingled down!
 Did e'er such love and sorrow meet,
 Or thorns compose so rich a crown?

4 Were the whole realm of nature mine,
 That were a tribute far too small;
 Love so amazing, so divine,
 Demands my soul, my life, my all.
                         I. Watts, 1707

The Church Year

307 7, 6, 7, 6, 8, 8, 7, 7.

J. B. Calkin, 1872

Je - sus, name all names a - bove, Je - sus, best and dear - est,

Je - sus, fount of per - fect love, Ho - liest, ten - derest, near - est;

Je - sus, source of grace com-plet - est, Je - sus, pur - est, Je-sus sweetest,

Je - sus, well of power di - vine, Make me, keep me, seal me Thine!

2 Jesus, open me the gate,
   That the robber entered,
Who in that most lost estate
   Wholly on Thee ventured.
Thou whose wounds are ever pleading,
And Thy passion interceding,
   From my misery let me rise
   To a home in Paradise!

3 Jesus, crowned with thorns for me,
   Scourged for my transgression!
Witnessing, through agony,
   That Thy good confession;

Jesus, clad in purple raiment,
For my evil making payment:
   Let not all Thy woe and pain,
   Let not Calvary, be in vain!

4 When I cross death's bitter sea,
   And its waves roll higher,
Help the more forsaking me,
   As the storm draws nigher:
Jesus, leave me not to languish,
Helpless, hopeless, full of anguish!
   Tell me, "Verily, I say,
   Thou shalt be with Me today."

Theoctistus of the Studium, ca. 890

328

Lent and Passion Week

308 L. M.

German, 1543

We bless Thee, Je - sus Christ our Lord; For

ev - er be Thy name a - dored: For Thou, the sin - less

One, hast died, That sin - ners might be jus - ti - fied.

2 O very Man, and very God,
Who hast redeemed us with Thy blood;
From death eternal set us free,
And make us one with God in Thee.

3 From sin and shame defend us still,
And work in us Thy steadfast will,
The cross with patience to sustain,
And bravely bear its utmost pain.

4 In Thee we trust, in Thee alone;
For Thou forsakest not Thine own;
To all the meek Thy strength is given,
Who by Thy cross ascend to heaven.

C. Vischer, 1597

The Church Year

309 8, 7, 8, 7, 8, 8, 7.

Johann Walther, 1424

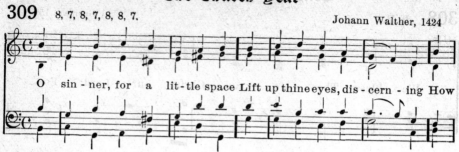

O sin-ner, for a lit-tle space Lift up thine eyes, dis-cern-ing How

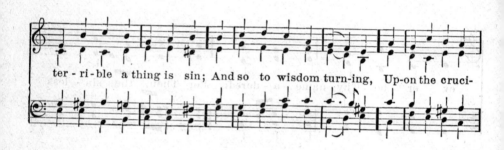

ter-ri-ble a thing is sin; And so to wisdom turn-ing, Up-on the cruci-

fied One look, And thou shalt read, as in a book, What well is worth thy learning.

2 Look on His head, that bleeding head,
  With crown of thorns surrounded;
Look on His sacred hands and feet,
  Which piercing nails have wounded;
See every limb with scourges rent;
On Him, the just, the innocent,
  What malice hath abounded!

3 'Tis not alone those tender limbs
  With so much pain are aching;
For the ingratitude of man
  His heart within is breaking.
O fearful was the chastisement
The Son of Mary underwent,
  The place of sinners taking.

4 No man has any sorrow borne
  Like unto that affliction,
When Jesus for our sake endured
  His people's contradiction;

Beyond imagination were
The sufferings He willed to bear
  In that dread crucifixion.

5 Now mark, O man, and ponder well
  Sin's awful condemnation.
For whom were all those wounds en-
  To purchase thy salvation. [dured?
Had Jesus never bled and died,
Then what could thee and all betide
  But fiery reprobation?

6 Flee, therefore, sinner, flee from sin
  And Satan's wiles ensnaring;
Flee from those everlasting flames
  For evil ones preparing.
O thank thy Savior, and entreat
To rest hereafter at His feet,
  The life eternal sharing.

Anon., Latin, 1678

330

310 10s. 4L.

W. H. Monk, 1861

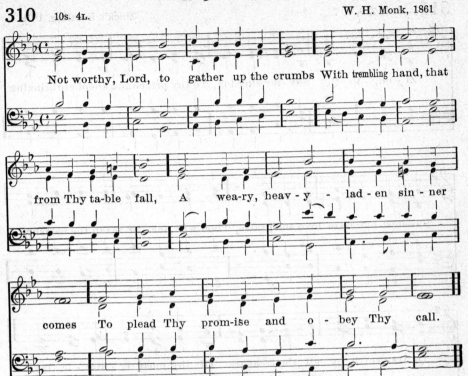

Not worthy, Lord, to gather up the crumbs With trembling hand, that from Thy ta-ble fall, A wea-ry, heav-y - lad-en sin - ner comes To plead Thy prom-ise and o - bey Thy call.

2 I am not worthy to be thought Thy child,
  Nor sit the last and lowest at Thy board;
Too long a wanderer, and too oft beguiled,
  I only ask one reconciling word.

3 One word from Thee, my Lord, one smile, one look,
  And I could face the cold, rough world again;
And with that treasure in my heart could brook
  The wrath of devils and the scorn of men.

4 And is not mercy Thy prerogative—
  Free mercy, boundless, fathomless, divine?
Me, Lord, the chief of sinners, me forgive,
  And Thine the greater glory, only Thine.

5 I hear Thy voice; Thou bidst me come and rest:
  I come, I kneel, I clasp Thy piercéd feet:
Thou bid'st me take my place, a welcome guest
  Among Thy saints, and of Thy banquet eat.

6 My praise can only breathe itself in prayer,
  My prayer can only lose itself in Thee;
Dwell Thou for ever in my heart, and there,
  Lord, let me sup with Thee; sup Thou with me.

E. H. Bickersteth, 1872

311 8, 8, 7, 8, 8, 7.

Zinck's Koralbog, 1801

Zi - on, to thy Sav-ior sing-ing, To thy prince and shepherd bringing Sweetest hymns of love and praise, Thou wilt nev - er reach the measure Of His worth, by all the treasure Of thy most ec - stat - ic lays.

2 Of all wonders that can thrill thee,
And with adoration fill thee,
   What than this can greater be,
That Himself to thee He giveth?
He that eateth ever liveth,
   For the Bread of life is He.

3 Fill thy lips to overflowing
With sweet praise, His mercy showing
   Who this heavenly table spread:
On this day so glad and holy,
To each longing spirit lowly
   Giveth He the living bread.

4 Here the King hath spread His table
Whereon eyes of faith are able
   Christ our Passover to trace:
Shadows of the law are going,
Light and life and truth inflowing,
   Night to day is giving place

Holy Thursday

5 Lo, this blessed food descending
  Heavenly love is hither sending,
    Hungry lips on earth to feed:
So the paschal lamb was given,
So the manna came from heaven,
    Isaac was His type indeed.

6 O good Shepherd, bread life-giving,
  Us, Thy grace and life receiving,
    Feed and shelter evermore;
Thou on earth our weakness guiding
We in heaven with Thee abiding
    With all saints will Thee adore.

Thomas Aquinas, ca. 1260

312   L. M.

German, 1605

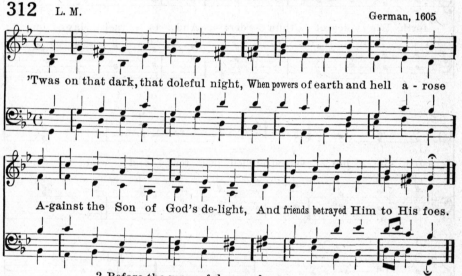

'Twas on that dark, that doleful night, When powers of earth and hell a - rose
A-gainst the Son of God's de-light, And friends betrayed Him to His foes.

2 Before the mournful scene began,
  He took the bread, and blessed, and brake;
What love through all His actions ran!
  What wondrous words of grace He spake!

3 "This is my body, broke for sin;
  Receive and eat the living food:"
Then took the cup and blessed the wine;
  "'Tis the new covenant in my blood."

4 "Do this," He said, "till time shall end,
  In memory of your dying Friend
Meet at my table and record
  The love of your departed Lord."

5 Jesus, Thy feast we celebrate;
  We show Thy death, we sing Thy name,
Till Thou return, and we shall eat
  The marriage supper of the Lamb.

I. Watts, 1709

The Church Year

Good Friday

8, 7, 8, 7, 8, 8, 7.

J. Wolff, 1569

The Lord of might, from Si-nai's brow, Gave forth His voice of thun-der; And Is-rael lay on earth be-low, Out-stretched in fear and won-der; Be-neath His feet was pitch-y night, And at His left hand and His right The rocks were rent a-sun-der.

Good Friday

2 The Lord of love, on Calvary,
  A meek and suffering stranger,
Upraised to heaven His languid eye
  In nature's hour of danger;
For us He bore the weight of woe,
For us He gave His blood to flow,
  And met His Father's anger.

3 The Lord of love, the Lord of might,
  The King of all created,
Shall back return to claim His right,
  On clouds of glory seated;
With trumpet-sound and angel-song,
And Hallelujahs loud and long,
  O'er death and hell defeated!

H. Heber, publ. 1827

314 C. M.

Arr. from C. Tye, 1553

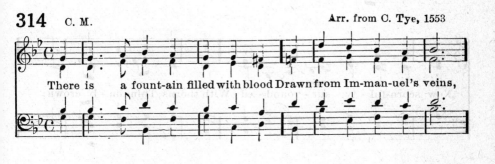

There is a fount-ain filled with blood Drawn from Im-man-uel's veins,

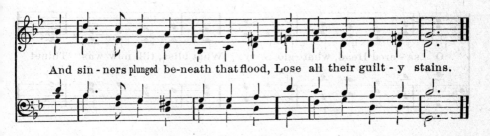

And sin-ners plunged be-neath that flood, Lose all their guilt-y stains.

2 The dying thief rejoiced to see
  That fountain in his day;
And there have I, as vile as he,
  Washed all my sins away.

3 Dear dying Lamb, Thy precious blood
  Shall never lose its power,
Till all the ransomed Church of God
  Be saved, to sin no more.

4 E'er since, by faith, I saw the stream
  Thy flowing wounds supply,
Redeeming love has been my theme,
  And shall be till I die.

5 Then in a nobler, sweeter song,
  I'll sing Thy power to save,
When this poor, lisping, stammering tongue
  Lies silent in the grave.

W. Cowper, 1771

315   7, 6. 8L.   H. L. Hassler, 1601

O sa-cred Head, now wound-ed, With grief and shame weighed down,

Now scorn-ful-ly sur-round-ed With thorns, Thine on-ly crown;

O sa-cred Head, what glo-ry, What bliss, till now was Thine!

Yet, though de-spised and go-ry, I joy to call Thee mine.

2 I see Thy strength and vigor
    All fading in the strife,
And death with cruel rigor
    Bereaving Thee of life;
O agony of dying!
    O love to sinners free!
Jesus, all grace supplying,
    O turn Thy face on me.

3 What Thou, my Lord, hast suffered
    Was all for sinners' gain:
Mine, mine was the transgression,
    But Thine the deadly pain:
Lo, here I fall, my Savior!
    'Tis I deserve Thy place;
Look on me with Thy favor,
    Vouchsafe to me Thy grace.

Good Friday

4 In this Thy bitter passion,
  Good Shepherd, think of me
With Thy most sweet compassion,
  Unworthy though I be:
Beneath Thy cross abiding
  Forever would I rest,
In Thy dear love confiding,
  And with Thy presence blest.

5 The joy can ne'er be spoken,
  Above all joys beside,
When in Thy body broken
  I thus with safety hide:
My Lord of Life, desiring
  Thy glory now to see,
Beside the cross expiring,
  I'd breathe my soul to Thee.

6 What language shall I borrow
  To thank Thee, dearest Friend,
For this Thy dying sorrow,
  Thy pity without end?

O make me Thine forever;
  And should I fainting be,
Lord, let me never, never,
  Outlive my love to Thee.

7 And when I am departing,
  O part not Thou from me;
When mortal pangs are darting,
  Come, Lord, and set me free:
And when my heart must languish
  Amidst the final throe,
Release me from mine anguish,
  By Thine own pain and woe.

8 Be near me when I'm dying,
  O show Thy cross to me;
And to my succor flying,
  Come, Lord, and set me free:
These eyes, new faith receiving,
  From Jesus shall not move;
For he who dies believing,
  Dies safely, through Thy love.

Ascribed to Bernard of Clairvaux (1091-1153)
P. Gerhardt, 1656

316 8, 7. 4L.   Ludv. M. Lindeman, 1812—87

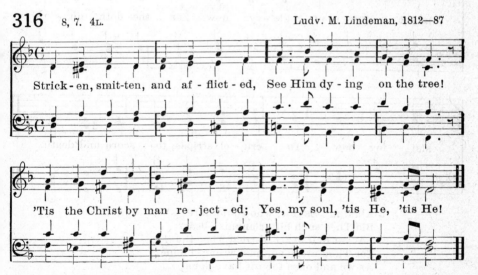

Strick-en, smit-ten, and af-flict-ed, See Him dy-ing on the tree!

'Tis the Christ by man re-ject-ed; Yes, my soul, 'tis He, 'tis He!

2 Mark the sacrifice appointed!
  See who bears the awful load;
'Tis the Word, the Lord's Anointed,
  Son of Man, and Son of God!

3 Here we have a firm foundation;
  Here the refuge of the lost:

Christ the Rock of our salvation:
  His the name of which we boast.

4 Lamb of God for sinners wounded!
  Sacrifice to cancel guilt!
None shall ever be confounded
  Who on Thee their hope have built.

T. Kelly, 1804

317   8s. 6L.   Schumann's Gesangbuch, 1539

O world, be-hold! up - on the tree Thy Life is hang-ing now for thee: Thy Sav - ior yields His dy - ing breath. The might - y Prince of glo - ry now For thee doth un - re- sist - ing bow To cru - el stripes, to scorn and death.

2 Alas! my Savior, who could dare
    Bid Thee such bitter anguish bear?
      What evil heart ill-treat Thee thus?
    For Thou art good, hast wrongéd none,
    As we and ours too oft have done;
      Thou hast not sinned, dear Lord, like us.

3 My grievous sins, that number more
    Than yonder sands upon the shore,
      Have brought to pass this agony:
    'Tis I have caused the floods of woe,
    That now Thy soul in death o'erflow,
      And those sad hearts that watch by Thee.

Good Friday

4 'Tis I to whom these pains belong;
  'Tis I should suffer for my wrong,
    Bound hand and foot in heavy chains:
  Thy scourge, Thy fetters, whatsoe'er
  Thou bearest, 'tis my soul should bear,
    For I have well deserved such pains.

5 Lord, from Thy sorrows I will learn
  How fiercely wrath divine doth burn,
    How terribly its thunders roll;
  How sorely this our loving God
  Can smite with His avenging rod;
    How deep His floods o'erwhelm the soul.

6 And I will nail me to Thy cross,
  And learn to count all things but dross,
    Wherein the flesh doth pleasure take;
  Whate'er is hateful in Thine eyes,
  With all the strength that in me lies,
    Will I cast from me and forsake.

7 Thy heavy groans, Thy bitter sighs,
  The tears that from Thy dying eyes
    Were shed when Thou wast sore oppressed,
  Shall be with me, when at the last
  Myself on Thee I wholly cast,
    And enter with Thee into rest.

P. Gerhardt, 1648

318 C. M.   Archdeacon Pry's Llyfr y Psalmau, 1621

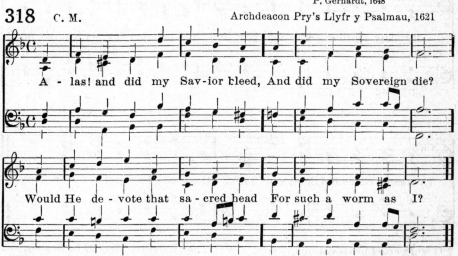

A - las! and did my Sav-ior bleed, And did my Sovereign die?

Would He de - vote that sa - cred head For such a worm as I?

2 Was it for crimes that I had done
    He groaned upon the tree?
  Amazing pity! grace unknown!
    And love beyond degree!

3 Well might the sun in darkness hide,
    And shut his glories in,
  When God, the mighty Maker, died
    For man, the creature's sin!

4 Thus might I hide my blushing face,
    While His dear cross appears;
  Dissolve, my heart, in thankfulness!
    And melt, my eyes, to tears.

5 But drops of grief can ne'er repay
    The debt of love I owe.
  Here, Lord, I give myself away:
    'Tis all that I can do.

I. Watts, 1707

319 8, 7, 8, 7, 8, 8, 7, 7.

Johann Crüger, 1649

Of my life the life, O Je-sus! Of my death the death al-so;

Who hast given Thy-self to ease us From our load of guilt and woe:

By Thy death our ran-som buy-ing, And pre-serv-ing us from dy-ing,

Thousand, thousand thanks to Thee, Bless-ed Je-sus! ev-er be.

2 O what cruel provocations,
　Scourges of the tongue and rod,
Spitting, shame, and accusations,
　Hast Thou borne, Thou Son of God!
To redeem my soul from evil,
And the bondage of the devil,
　Thousand, thousand thanks to Thee!
　Blessed Jesus! ever be.

3 Thou didst let Thyself be beaten,
　To deliver me from pain;
Falsely charged, and sorely smitten,
　That Thy loss might be my gain.
Thou hast suffered crucifixion
For my comfort in affliction:
　Thousand, thousand thanks to Thee,
　Blessed Jesus! ever be.

Good Friday

4 For my proud and haughty spirit,
   Thy humiliation paid;
For my death Thy death and merit
   Have a full atonement made:
Thy reproaches and dishonor
All have tended to my honor:
   Thousand, thousand thanks to Thee,
   Blessed Jesus! ever be.

5 From the heart, I thank Thee, Jesus,
   For the vast, stupendous load,
Which Thou bearest to release us
   From the dreadful wrath of God:
For Thy cruel death and passion,
Agony and sore temptation,
   For Thy sharp and bitter pain,
   Thanks forever, Lord, Amen.

E. C. Homburg, 1659

320   8, 8, 7, 8, 8, 7.   Zinck's Koralbog, 1801

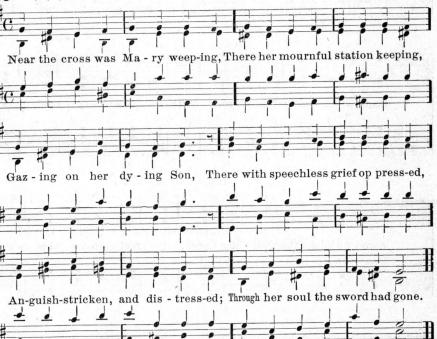

Near the cross was Ma-ry weep-ing, There her mournful station keeping, Gaz-ing on her dy-ing Son, There with speechless grief op press-ed, An-guish-stricken, and dis-tress-ed; Through her soul the sword had gone.

2 Who upon that Sufferer gazing,
  Bowed in sorrow so amazing,
    Would not with His mother mourn?
  'Twas our sins brought Him from heaven;
  These the cruel nails had driven;
    All His griefs for us were borne.

3 When no eye its pity gave us,
  When there was no arm to save us,
    He His love and power displayed;
  By His stripes He wrought our healing;
  By His death, our life revealing,
    He for us the ransom paid.

4 Jesus, may Thy love constrain us
  That from sin we may refrain us,
    In Thy griefs may deeply grieve.
  Thee our best affections giving,
  To Thy glory ever living,
    May we in Thy glory live.

After Stabat mater. H. Mills, 1845.

The Church Year

321   7, 6, 8, 6, 8, 6, 8, 6.   F. C Maker, 1881

Be-neath the cross of Je - sus I fain would take my stand, The
shad-ow of a might-y rock With-in a wea-ry land; A
home with-in the wil - der - ness, A rest up-on the way,
From the burning of the noon-tide heat, And the bur-den of the day.

2 Upon the cross of Jesus,
  Mine eye at times can see
The very dying form of One
  Who suffered there for me.
And from my smitten heart with tears,
  These wonders I confess,—
The wonder of His glorious love,
  And my own worthlessness.

3 I take, O cross, thy shadow
  For my abiding-place;
I ask no other sunshine than
  The sunshine of His face;
Content to let the world go by,
  To know no gain or loss,
My sinful self my only shame,
  My glory all the cross.

Elizabeth C. Clephane, 1872

Good Friday

4, 4, 7, 7, 6.

German, 1628

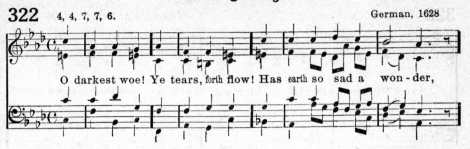

O darkest woe! Ye tears, forth flow! Has earth so sad a won-der,

That the Father's on-ly Son Now lies bur-ied yon-der!

2   O sinful man,
It was the ban
Of death on thee that brought Him
Down to suffer for thy sins,
And such woe hath wrought Him.

3   Behold thy Lord,
The Lamb of God,
Blood-sprinkled lies before thee,
Pouring out His life that He
May to life restore thee.

4   O Ground of faith,
Laid low in death!
Sweet lips now silent sleeping!
Surely all that live must mourn
Here with bitter weeping.

5   Yea, blest is he
Whose heart shall be
Fixed here, and apprehendeth
Why the Lord of glory thus
To the grave descendeth.

6   O Jesus blest!
My help and rest!
With tears I pray—Lord, near me;
Make me love Thee to the last,
In the grave be near me!

J. Rist, 1641

The Church Year

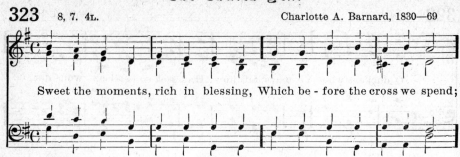

Sweet the moments, rich in blessing, Which be - fore the cross we spend;

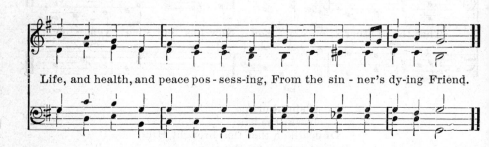

Life, and health, and peace pos - sess-ing, From the sin - ner's dy-ing Friend.

2 Truly blessed is this station,
  Low before His cross to lie,
  While we see divine compassion
  Beaming in His gracious eye.

3 For Thy sorrows we adore Thee,
  For the pains that wrought our peace;
  Gracious Savior! we implore Thee,
  In our souls Thy love increase!

4 Here we feel our sins forgiven,
  While upon the Lamb we gaze;
  And our thoughts are all of heaven,
  And our lips o'erflow with praise.

5 Lord, in loving contemplation,
  Fix our hearts and eyes on Thee,
  Till we taste Thy full salvation,
  And Thine unveiled glory see.

W. Shirley, 1770

Easter

From Palestrina

The strife is o'er, the bat - tle done! The vic-to-ry of life is

won! The song of tri-umph hath be - gun. Hal - le - lu - jah!

Coda, after the last verse only.

Hal - le - lu - jah! Hal - le - lu - jah! Hal - le - lu - jah!

2 The powers of death have done their worst,
  But Christ their legion hath dispersed:
  Let shouts of holy joy outburst.
    Hallelujah!

3 The three sad days have quickly sped;
  He rises glorious from the dead:
  All glory to our risen Head!
    Hallelujah!

4 He closed the yawning gates of hell;
  The bars from heaven's high portals fell;
  Let hymns of praise His triumphs tell.
    Hallelujah!

5 Lord, by the stripes which wounded Thee,
  From death's dread sting Thy servants free,
  That we may live and sing to Thee,
    Hallelujah!

Anon., Latin, 1753

325   8, 7, 8, 7, 7, 7, 8, 8.

Johann Schop, 1642

Like the gold-en sun as-cend-ing, Break-ing through the
gloom of night, On the earth his glo-ry spend-ing
So that dark-ness takes to flight; Thus my Je-sus
from the grave And death's dismal, dreadful cave, Rose tri-um-phant
Eas-ter morn-ing, At the ear-ly pur-ple dawn-ing

2 Thanks to Thee, O Christ victorious!
 Thanks to Thee, O Lord of life!
Death hath now no power o'er us,
 Thou hast conquered in the strife;
Thanks because Thou didst arise,
And hast opened Paradise!
None can fully sing the glory
Of the resurrection story.

3 For my heart finds consolation,
 And my fainting soul grows brave,
When I stand in contemplation
 At Thy dark and dismal grave;
When I see where Thou didst sleep
In death's dungeon dark and deep,
Yet didst break all bands asunder,
Must I not rejoice and wonder?

4 Though I be by sin o'ertaken,
 Though I lie in helplessness,
Though I be by friends forsaken,
 And must suffer sore distress,
Though I be despised, contemned,
And by all the world condemned,
Though the dark grave yawn before
 me,
Yet the light of hope shines o'er me.

5 Thou hast died for my transgression,
 All my sins on Thee were laid;
Thou hast won for me salvation,
 On the cross my debt was paid;
From the grave I shall arise,
And shall meet Thee in the skies;
Death itself is transitory,
I shall lift my head in glory.

6 Satan's arrows all lie broken,
 Death and hell have met their doom;
Christ, Thy rising is the token:
 Thou hast triumphed o'er the tomb;

Thou hast buried all my woe,
And my cup doth overflow;
By Thy resurrection glorious
I shall wave my palms victorious.

7 As the Son of God I know Thee,
 For I see Thy sovereign power;
Sin and death shall not o'erthrow me
 Even in my dying hour;
For Thy resurrection is
Surety for my heavenly bliss,
And my baptism a reflection
Of Thy death and resurrection.

8 Unto life Thou shalt arouse me
 By Thy resurrection's power;
Though the hideous grave shall house
 me,
 And my flesh the worms devour;
Fire and water may destroy
My frail body, yet with joy
I shall rise as Thou hast risen
From the deep sepulchral prison.

9 Grant me grace, O blessed Savior,
 And Thy Holy Spirit send,
That my walk and my behavior
 May be pleasing to the end;
That I may not fall again
Into death's grim pit and pain
Whence by grace Thou hast retrieved
 me,
And from which Thou hast relieved
 me.

10 For the joy Thy birth doth give me,
 For Thy holy, precious word;
For Thy baptism which doth save me,
 For Thy gracious festal board;
For Thy death, the bitter scorn,
For Thy resurrection morn,
Lord, I thank Thee and extol Thee,
And in heaven I shall behold Thee.
       T. Kingo, 1689

The Church Year

326   7s. 6L.

Ludv. M. Lindeman, 1812—87

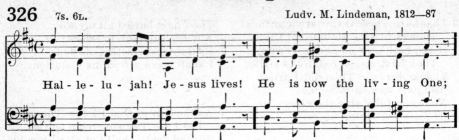

Hal - le - lu - jah! Je - sus lives! He is now the liv - ing One;

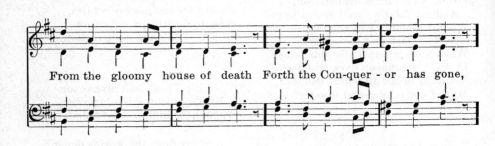

From the gloomy house of death Forth the Con-quer - or has gone,

Bright fore - run - ner to the skies Of His peo - ple, yet to rise.

2 Jesus lives! let all rejoice!
   Praise Him, ransomed ones of earth!
Praise Him in a nobler song,
   Cherubim of heavenly birth!
Praise the Victor-King, whose sway
Sin, and death, and hell obey.

3 Jesus lives! why weepest thou?
   Why that sad and frequent sigh?
He who died our Brother here,
   Lives our Brother still on high,—
Lives for ever, to bestow
Blessings on His Church below.

4 Jesus lives! and thus, my soul,
   Life eternal waits for thee;
Joined to Him, thy living Head,

Where He is, thou too shalt be;
With Himself, at His right hand,
Victor over death shalt stand.

5 Jesus lives! To Him my heart
   Draws with ever new delight:
Earthly vanities, depart!
   Hinder not my heavenward flight!
Let this spirit ever rise
To its magnet in the skies.

6 Hallelujah, angels, sing!
   Join us in our hymn of praise,
Let your chorus swell the strain
   Which our feebler voices raise:
Glory to our God above,
And on earth His peace and love!

C. B. Garve, 1825

348

327 7, 6. 8L.

Berthold Tours, 1875

The day of res - ur - rec - tion, Earth, tell it out a - broad, The Pass-o - ver of glad-ness, The Pass - o - ver of God. From death to life e - ter - nal, From earth un - to the sky, Our Christ hath brought us o - ver, With hymns of vic - to - ry.

2 Our hearts be pure from evil
  That we may see aright
The Lord in rays eternal
  Of resurrection light;
And, listening to His accents,
  May hear so calm and plain
His own "All hail!" and hearing,
  May raise the victor strain.

3 Now let the heavens be joyful,
  Let earth her song begin,
Let all the world keep triumph,
  And all that is therein:
In grateful exultation,
  Their notes let all things blend,
For Christ the Lord hath risen,
  Our joy that hath no end.

John of Damascus (8th Century)

328 7, 6. 8L.   Ludv. M. Lindeman, 1812—87

Come, ye faith-ful, raise the strain Of tri-umph-ant glad-'ness,

God hath brought His Is-ra-el In-to joy from sad-ness;

Loosed from Pharaoh's bit-ter yoke Ja-cob's sons and daughters,

Led them with un-moist-ened foot Through the Red Sea wa-ters.

2 'Tis the spring of souls to-day,
  Christ hath burst His prison,
And from three days' sleep in death
  As a sun hath risen;
All the winter of our sins,
  Long and dark, is flying
From His light, to whom we give
  Laud and praise undying.

3 Now the queen of seasons, bright
  With the day of splendor,
With the royal feast of feasts,
  Comes its joy to render;

Comes to glad Jerusalem,
  Who with true affection
Welcomes, in unwearied strains,
  Jesus' resurrection.

4 Neither might the gates of death,
  Nor the tomb's dark portal,
Nor the watchers, nor the seal,
  Hold Thee as a mortal;
But today amidst Thine own
  Thou didst stand, bestowing
That Thy peace, which evermore
  Passeth human knowing.

John of Damascus, (8th Century)

329 8, 8, 7, 8, 8, 7, 4, 4, 4, 4, 8.   Ph. Nicolai, 1599

He is a-ris-en! Glorious word! Now rec-on-ciled is God, my Lord;

The gates of heaven are o - pen. My Je - sus died tri - umph-ant - ly,

And Sa-tan's ar-rows brok-en lie, Destroyed hell's dir-est weap - on.

O hear What cheer! Christ vic - to-rious Ris - eth glorious,

Life He giv - eth— He was dead, but see, He liv - eth!

Birgitte C. Boye, 1778

330   8, 7, 8, 7, 7, 8, 7, 4.   Enchiridion, Erfurt, 1524

Christ Je-sus lay in death's strong bands, For our of-fens-es giv - en;

But now at God's right hand He stands, And brings us life from heav - en:

Wherefore let us joy-ful be And sing to God right thankful - ly

Loud songs of Hal - le - lu - jah! Hal - le - lu - jah!

2 It was a strange and dreadful strife,
    When life and death contended;
  The victory remained with life,
    The reign of death was ended:
  Stripped of power, no more he reigns;
  An empty form alone remains;
  His sting is lost for ever!
        Hallelujah!

3 So let us keep the festival
    Whereto the Lord invites us;
  Christ is Himself the joy of all,
    The sun that warms and lights us:

By His grace He doth impart
Eternal sunshine to the heart;
  The night of sin is ended!
        Hallelujah!

4 Then let us feast this Easter day
    On the true bread of heaven;
  The word of grace hath purged away
    The old and wicked leaven;
  Christ alone our souls will feed;
  He is our meat and drink indeed;
  Faith lives upon no other!
        Hallelujah!

M. Luther, 1524

331 7, 8, 7, 8, 7, 7.

German, 1656

Je - sus lives! thy ter - rors now Can no lon-ger, Death, ap - pall me;

Je - sus lives! by this I know, From the grave He will re - call me.

Brighter scenes will then commence: This shall be my con - fi - dence.

2 Jesus lives! to Him the throne
   High o'er heaven and earth is given:
I shall go where He is gone,
   Live and reign with Him in heaven.
God through Christ forgives offense;
This shall be my confidence.

3 Jesus lives! for me He died:
   Hence will I, to Jesus living,
Pure in heart and act abide,
   Praise to Him and glory giving.
Freely God doth aid dispense;
This shall be my confidence.

4 Jesus lives! I know full well,
   Naught from me His love shall
      sever;
Life, nor death, nor powers of hell,
   Part me now from Christ forever.
God will be a sure defense:
This shall be my confidence.

5 Jesus lives! henceforth is death
   But the gate of life immortal;
This shall calm my trembling breath,
   When I pass the gloomy portal.
Faith shall cry, as fails each sense,
"Lord, Thou art my confidence."

C. F. Gellert, 1757

332 8, 6, 8, 6, 8, 8, 7.

G. W. Torrance, 1835—1907

I know that my Re-deem-er lives, In this my faith is fast; And what-so-e'er against Him strives Will sure-ly fall at last. He lives, the might-y One, I know, Whose arm overcomes the stron-gest foe, Who death and hell hath van-quished.

2 He lives, He lives; though dust shall
Upon my mouldering head, [lie
Yet He will call me, by and by,
To quit an earthy bed;
And I shall waken at His voice,
Rise re-embodied, and rejoice
To look on my Redeemer.

3 His promise, who hath ne'er deceived,
In life and death I trust;
The Lord in whom I have believed
Will raise my sleeping dust:
In this my very flesh that dies
I shall revive, and with these eyes
Shall see the God who made me.

4 Myself shall see Him in my flesh,
With all His glory bright;
His presence shall my heart refresh,
And fill my soul with light.
Myself shall ever on Him gaze,
Myself shall ever sound His praise,
Myself, and not another.

5 Rise then, my soul, e'en now, and live
In hope's divine abode!
Let earth and Satan vainly strive
To tear thee from thy God.
The bier, the coffin, let them show
The grave; the gloom, the worm—
"I know
That my Redeemer liveth."

P. Gerhardt, 1667

Easter

333 9, 8, 9, 8, 8, 8.

Georg Neumark, 1622—81

Abide with us, the day is waning, Thus prayed the two while on the way;

We read that Thou, O Lord, remaining, Didst all their doubts and fears allay.

Incline Thine ear, Thou King of grace, When, praying thus, we seek Thy face.

2 At eventide, Thy Spirit sending,
    Help us, O Lord, our watch to keep,
In prayer devout, before Thee bending,
    Ere we our eyelids close in sleep,
Confessing sin in deed and word,
With hope of mercy from the Lord.

3 Abide with us; with heavenly gladness
    Illumine, Lord, our darkest day;
And when we weep in pain and sadness
    Be Thou our solace, strength and stay;
Tell of Thy woe, Thy victory won,
When Thou didst pray: God's will be done.

4 Abide with us, O Savior tender,
    That bitter day when life shall end,
When to the grave we must surrender,
    And fear and pain our hearts shall rend;
The shield of faith do Thou bestow,
When trembling we must meet the foe.

5 When earthly help no more availeth,
    To sup with us Thou wilt be nigh;
Thou givest strength that never faileth,
    In Thee we grave and death defy:
While earth is fading from our sight,
Our eyes behold the realms of light.

C. J. Boye, 1834

The Church Year

334 7s. With Hallelujah.

Lyra Davidica, 1708

Christ the Lord is risen a-gain; Hal - le-lu - jah!

Christ hath brok-en ev-ery chain; Hal - le-lu - jah!

Hark, ang-el-ic voic-es cry, Hal - le-lu - jah!

Sing-ing ev-er-more on high, Hal - le-lu - jah!

2 He who gave for us His life,
Who for us endured the strife,
Is our Paschal Lamb to-day;
We too, sing for joy and say,
    Hallelujah!

3 He who bore all pain and loss
Comfortless upon the cross,
Lives in glory now on high,
Pleads for us and hears our cry;
    Hallelujah!

4 He whose path no records tell,
Who descended into hell,
Who the strong man armed hath bound,
Now in highest heaven is crowned.
    Hallelujah!

5 He who slumbered in the grave,
Is exalted now to save;
Now through Christendom it rings
That the Lamb is King of kings.
    Hallelujah!

6 Now He bids us tell abroad,
How the lost may be restored,
How the penitent forgiven,
How we, too, may enter heaven.
    Hallelujah!

7 Thou our Paschal Lamb indeed,
Christ, Thy ransomed people feed;
Take our guilt and sins away,
That we all may sing for aye
    Hallelujah!

M. Weisse, 1531

335 8, 8, 8, 8, 4.

Johann Walther, 1524

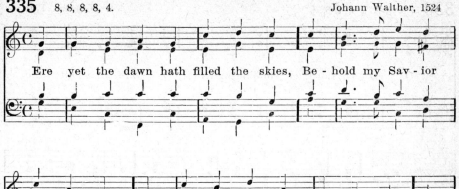

Ere yet the dawn hath filled the skies, Be - hold my Sav - ior

Christ a - rise, He chas - eth from us sin and night, And

6th v. only.

brings us joy and life and light. Hal - le - lu - jah! - le - lu - jah!..........

2 O stronger Thou than death and hell,
Where is the foe Thou canst not quell?
What heavy stone Thou canst not roll
From off the prisoned, suff'ring soul!
  Hallelujah!

3 If Jesus lives, can I be sad?
I know He loves me, and am glad:
Though all the world were dead to me,
Enough, O Christ, if I have Thee!
  Hallelujah!

4 He feeds me, comforts, and defends,
And when I die His angel sends
To bear me whither He is gone,

For of His own He loseth none.
  Hallelujah!

5 No more to fear or grief I bow,
God and the angels love me now;
The joys prepared for me today
Drive fear and mourning far away.
  Hallelujah!

6 Strong Champion! For this comfort, see,
The whole world bringeth thanks to Thee!
And once we, too, shall raise above
More sweet and loud the song we love:
  Hallelujah!

J. Heermann, 1630

336 8, 7, 8, 7, 4, 4, 8, 8.

German, 1704

O ris - en Lord! O conquering King! O Life of all the
liv - ing! To - day that peace of Eas - ter bring Which comes but of Thy
giv - ing! Once death, our foe, Had laid Thee low; Now hast Thou rent his
bonds in twain, Now art Thou risen who once wast slain!

2 O that to know Thy victory
To us were inly granted,
And these cold hearts might catch from Thee
The glow of faith undaunted;
Thy quenchless light,
Thy glorious might
Still comfortless and lonely leave
The soul that cannot yet believe.

3 Then break through our hard hearts Thy way,
O Jesus, Lord of glory!
Kindle the lamp of faith today,
Teach us to sing before Thee
For joy at length,
That in Thy strength
We, too, may rise whom sin had slain,
And Thine eternal rest attain.

First Sunday after Easter

4 And when our tears for sin o'erflow,
Do Thou in love draw near us,
Thy precious gift of peace bestow,
Let Thy bright presence cheer us,
That so may we,
O Christ, from Thee
Drink in the life that cannot die,
And keep true Easter feasts on high.

J. H. Böhmer, 1704

337 L. M.

J. Clauder's "Psalmodia Nova," 1630

Faith is a liv - ing power from heaven That grasps the prom - ise God hath given, A trust that can - not be o'er-thrown, Fixed heart - i - ly on Christ a - lone.

2 Faith finds in Christ whate'er we need
To save or strengthen us indeed.
Receives the grace He sends us down,
And makes us share His cross and crown.

3 Faith in the conscience worketh peace,
And bids the mourner's weeping cease;
By faith the children's place we claim,
And give all honor to one Name.

4 Faith feels the Spirit's kindling breath
In love and hope that conquer death;
Faith worketh hourly joy in God,
And trusts and blesses e'en the rod.

5 We thank Thee, then, O God of heaven,
That Thou to us this faith hast given
In Jesus Christ, Thy Son, who is
Our only fount and source of bliss.

6 And from His fullness grant each soul
The rightful faith's true end and goal,
The blessedness no foes destroy,
Eternal love, and light, and joy.

P. Herbert, 1566

The Church Year

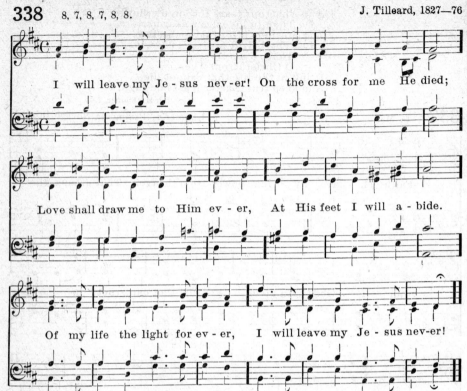

338 8, 7, 8, 7, 8, 8. J. Tilleard, 1827—76

I will leave my Je-sus nev-er! On the cross for me He died;

Love shall draw me to Him ev-er, At His feet I will a-bide.

Of my life the light for ev-er, I will leave my Je-sus nev-er!

2 In His name I stand acquitted
  While upon the earth I stay:
What I have to Him committed
He will keep until that day.
Be His service my endeavor;
I will leave my Jesus never!

3 Dwelling in His presence holy,
  I at length shall reach the place
Where with all His saints in glory
  I shall see His lovely face;
Nothing then but bliss for ever:
I will leave my Jesus never!

4 Not the earth with all its treasure
  Could content this soul of mine;
Not alone for heavenly pleasure
  Doth my thirsty spirit pine;
For its Savior yearning ever:
I will leave my Jesus never!

5 From that living fountain drinking,
  Walking always at His side,
Christ shall lead me without sinking
  Through the river's rushing tide,
With the blest to sing for ever:
I will leave my Jesus never!

Chr. Keimann, 1658

8, 7, 8, 7, 8, 8. *Second Tune.* H Pape, 1648

I will leave my Je-sus nev-er! On the cross for me He died;

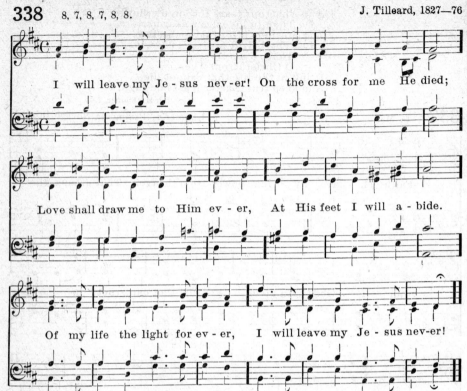

330

Love shall draw me to Him ev-er, At His feet I will a-bide.

Of my life the light for ev-er, I will leave my Je-sus nev-er!

339 C. M. German

Thou art the Way: to Thee a-lone From sin and death we flee:

And he who would the Fa-ther seek, Must seek Him, Lord, by Thee.

2 Thou art the Truth: Thy word alone
  Sound wisdom can impart:
Thou only canst inform the mind,
  And purify the heart.

3 Thou art the Life: the rending tomb
  Proclaims Thy conquering arm·

And those who put their trust in Thee
Nor death nor hell shall harm.

4 Thou art the Way, the Truth, the Life:
  Grant us that Way to know,
That Truth to keep, that Life to win.
  Whose joys eternal flow.

G. W. Doane, 1824

340 11s. 5L.

J. F. Wade's Cantus Diversi, 1751

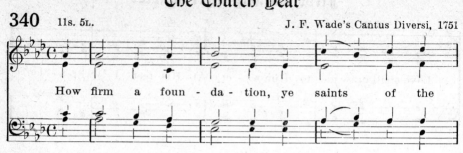

How firm a foun - da - tion, ye saints of the

Lord, Is laid for your faith in His

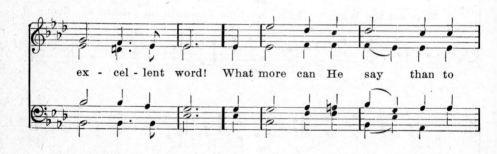

ex - cel - lent word! What more can He say than to

you He hath said, Who un - to the

First Sunday after Easter

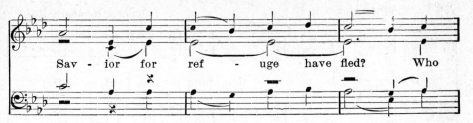

Sav - ior for ref - uge have fled? Who

un - to the Sav - ior for ref - uge have fled?

2 "Fear not, I am with thee, O be not dismayed,
For I am thy God, and will still give thee aid;
I'll strengthen thee, help thee, and cause thee to stand,
‖:Upheld by My righteous, omnipotent hand.:‖

3 "When through the deep waters I call thee to go,
The rivers of sorrow shall not overflow;
For I will be with thee, thy troubles to bless,
‖:And sanctify to thee thy deepest distress.:‖

4 "When through fiery trials thy pathway shall lie,
My grace, all-sufficient, shall be thy supply;
The flame shall not hurt thee; I only design
‖:Thy dross to consume, and thy gold to refine.:‖

5 "E'en down to old age all my people shall prove
My sovereign, eternal, unchangeable love;
And when hoary hairs shall their temples adorn,
‖:Like lambs they shall still in my bosom be borne.:‖

6 "The soul that on Jesus hath leaned for repose,
I will not, I will not desert to his foes;
That soul, though all hell should endeavor to shake,
‖:I'll never, no never, no never forsake!":‖

Keen. 1787

341 7, 6, 7, 6, 6, 7, 7, 6.

German, Hamburg, 1598

O sing with ex-ul-ta-tion, Sing to the Lord, re-joice!
And in His con-gre-ga-tion Shout with tri-umph-ant voice!
For, lo, at God's right hand Is Christ in glo-ry seat-ed;
With death and hell de-feat-ed As vic-tor He doth stand.

2 Since Christ, our Lord, is living
  We never more shall die;
To God the glory giving
  We rise to Him on high;
    Though chastened we may be,
And to our graves be taken,
We unto life shall waken
    And live eternally.

3 Christ is the sure foundation
    The builders did reject,
But He for our salvation
    Is precious and elect,

And made the cornerstone,
On which the Church is founded,
This marvel now is sounded
  The work of God alone.

4 To Thee, O Christ, be glory,
    Who camest in His name!
Thy people sing the story
    Thy praises to proclaim;
We thank Thee and adore,
O Christ, Our Lord and Savior,
Thy grace and boundless favor
    Stand fast forevermore

A. C. Arrebo. 1623

First Sunday after Easter

342   8, 3, 3, 6, 8, 8, 3, 3, 6.

J. G. Ebeling, 1666

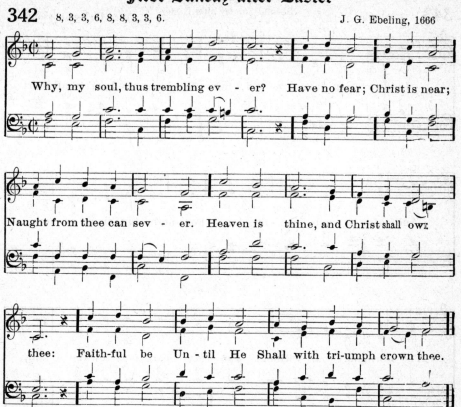

Why, my soul, thus trembling ev - er? Have no fear; Christ is near;
Naught from thee can sev - er. Heaven is thine, and Christ shall owe
thee: Faith-ful be Un - til He Shall with tri-umph crown thee.

2 Painful cross if He should send me,
   Shall I faint
   With complaint,
  Lest the grief should end me?
He hath borne the cross before me:
   Soon no pain
   Shall remain,
  Only peace be o'er me.

3 Hopeful, cheerful, and undaunted,
   Everywhere
   They appear
  Who in Christ are planted:
Death itself cannot appall them:
   They rejoice
   When the voice
  Of their Lord doth call them.

4 Death cannot destroy forever:
   From our fears,
   Cares and tears,
  Soon shall it deliver.

Doors of grief and gloom it closes,
   While the soul,
   Free and whole,
  With the saints reposes.

5 Lord, my Shepherd, take me to Thee:
   I am Thine,
   Thou art mine,
  Even ere I knew Thee.
I am Thine, for Thou hast bought me,
   Lost I stood,
   But Thy blood
  Free salvation brought me.

6 Thou art mine, and, for my guiding,
   Be Thy bright
   Shining light
  In my heart abiding!
Savior dear! let me, attaining
   To Thy side,
   There abide,
  With Thee ever reigning!

P. Gerhardt, 1653

The Church Year

7, 6. 8L.

Second Sunday after Easter

F. Mendelssohn

In heaven-ly love a-bid-ing, No change my heart shall fear;

And safe is such con-fid-ing, For noth-ing chang-es here.

The storm may roar with-out me, My heart may low be laid,

But God is round a-bout me, And can I be dis-mayed?

2 Wherever He may guide me,
   No want shall turn me back;
My Shepherd is beside me,
   And nothing can I lack.
His wisdom ever waketh,
   His sight is never dim,
He knows the way He taketh,
   And I will walk with Him.

3 Green pastures are before me,
   Which yet I have not seen;
Bright skies will soon be o'er me,
   Where darkest clouds have been.
My hope I cannot measure,
   My path to life is free,
My Savior has my treasure,
   And He will walk with me.

Anna L. Waring, 1850

344   8, 7, 8, 7, 6, 6, 8, 8.

Freylinghausen's Gesangbuch, 1704

Whene'er we con-tem-plate the grace, The love and con-de-scen-sion Of Christ to our a-pos-tate race, Which pass all com-pre-hen-sion, Low at His feet we bend; Own Him the sinner's friend; De-termined naught to know be-side Christ Je-sus, and Him cru-ci-fied.

2 How pleasant is our lot, how good
    And blest beyond expression;
For, having cleansed us by His blood,
    He bears us with compassion,
    Applies His healing power
    To us, each day and hour;
Yea, we in Him redemption have,
In death itself and in the grave.

3 And this our joyful theme shall be
    When, called to see our Savior,
We join the glorious company
    Around His throne forever;
    Then we in highest strain
    Shall praise the Lamb once slain,
Who hath redeemed us by His blood,
And made us kings and priests to God.

                            Chr. Gregor, 1778

The Church Year

345   8, 7, 8, 7, 8, 8, 7.   Joseph Klug, Wittenberg, 1535

The Lord my faith-ful shep-herd is, And me He safe-ly guid-eth, I shall not want, for I am His Who all things good pro-vid-eth: I fol-low Him, I hear His voice, In Him my Lord I do re-joice: Blest am I in His keep-ing!

2 A tender shepherd leads his sheep,
   Where pastures green are growing,
And there His flock doth guard and keep,
   Beside still waters flowing, [keep,
Thus Christ, my shepherd, leadeth me,
My soul and body feedeth He, [me,
   And for their wants provideth.

3 And if I ever go astray,
   My wayward soul He turneth,
To save the lost, to guide the way,
   For this He ever yearneth;

He leadeth me, my soul to bless,
In His own path of righteousness
   For His name's sake and glory.

4 Why should I ever fear, O Lord,
   Whilst Thee I have beside me?
Thou by Thy Spirit and Thy word
   Dost comfort and dost guide me;
In death's dark vale I'll fear no ill,
For Thou, O Lord, art with me still,
   Thy rod and staff shall stay me.

5 Thou art my host; for me, Thy guest,
  A table Thou providest.
Though foes be near, I am at rest;
  Thou still with me abidest.
With oil anointest Thou my head;
On me Thy blessing rich is shed,
  My cup with bliss o'erfloweth.

6 Thy goodness and Thy mercy, Lord,
  Shall follow me, attending
The days Thou dost to me afford,
  Until they reach their ending:
Thereafter shall I in Thy love
Dwell in Thy house in heaven above
  Forever and forever.

A. C. Arrebo, 1623

346 S. M.

Arr. from G. F. Händel, 1685—1759

The Lord my shep - herd is; I shall be well sup - plied: Since He is mine and I am His, What can I want be - side?

2 He leads me to the place
   Where heavenly pasture grows;
Where living waters gently pass,
   And full salvation flows.

3 If e'er I go astray,
   He doth my soul reclaim;
And guides me in His own right way,
   For His most holy name.

4 While He affords His aid,
   I cannot yield to fear;

Though I should walk through death's
     dark shade
   My Shepherd's with me there.

5 In spite of all my foes,
   Thou dost my table spread;
My cup with blessings overflows,
   And joy exalts my head.

6 The bounties of Thy love
   Shall crown my following days;
Nor from Thy house will I remove,
   Nor cease to speak Thy praise.

I. Watts, 1719

347   8s. 6L.   S. S. Wesley, 1810—76

Je - sus, Thy boundless love to me No thought can reach, no tongue de - clare: O knit my thank - ful heart to Thee And reign with-out a ri - val there. Thine whol - ly, Thine a - lone, I am, Be Thou a - lone my con - stant flame.

2 O grant that nothing in my soul
   May dwell, but Thy pure love alone;
O may Thy love possess me whole,
   My joy, my treasure, and my crown:
Strange fires far from my soul re-
   move;
My every act, word, thought, be love.

3 O love, how cheering is thy ray!
   All pain before thy presence flies:
Care, anguish, sorrow, melt away
   Where'er thy healing beams arise.
O Jesus, nothing may I see,
Nothing desire or seek, but Thee.

4 Unwearied may I this pursue,
   Dauntless to the high prize aspire;
Hourly within my soul renew

This holy flame, this heavenly fire;
And day and night be all my care
To guard the sacred treasure there.

5 Still let Thy love point out my way;
   What wondrous things Thy love
     hath wrought!
Still lead me, lest I go astray:
   Direct my word, inspire my thought;
And if I fall, soon may I hear
Thy voice, and know that love is near.

6 In suffering, be Thy love my peace;
   In weakness, be Thy love my power;
And when the storms of life shall
    cease,
Jesus, in that important hour
In death, as life, be Thou my guide,
And save me, who for me hast died.

P. Gerhardt, 1653

348 6, 6, 6, 6, 8, 8. J. Darwall, 1770

Re - joice, the Lord is King! Your Lord and King a - dore; Mor-

tals, give thanks and sing, And tri - umph ev - er - more; Lift up your

heart, lift up your voice, Re-joice, a - gain I say, re - joice.

2 Jesus, the Savior, reigns,
   The God of truth and love;
When He had purged our stains
   He took His seat above.
Lift up your heart, etc.

3 His kingdom cannot fail,
   He rules o'er earth and heaven:
The keys of death and hell
   Are to our Jesus given.
Lift up your heart, etc.

4 He sits at God's right hand,
   Till all His foes submit,
And bow to His command,

   And fall beneath His feet.
Lift up your heart, etc.

5 He all His foes shall quell,
   Shall all our sins destroy;
And every bosom swell
   With pure seraphic joy:
Lift up your heart, etc.

6 Rejoice in glorious hope;
   Jesus, the Judge, shall come,
And take His servants up
   To their eternal home:
We soon shall hear the archangel's
   voice.
The trump of God shall sound, rejoice!
C. Wesley, 1744

349 7, 6, 7, 6, 6, 7, 7, 6.

German, 1571

From God shall naught di-vide me, For He is true for aye, And on my path will guide me, Who else should oft-en stray; His ev-er bounteous hand By night and day is heed-ful, And

Third Sunday after Easter

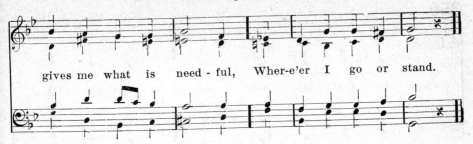

gives me what is need-ful, Wher-e'er I go or stand.

2 If sorrow comes, He sent it,
   In Him I put my trust;
I never shall repent it,
   For He is true and just,
   And loves to bless us still;
My life and soul, I owe them
To Him who doth bestow them,
   Let Him do as He will.

3 Whate'er shall be His pleasure
   Is surely best for me;
He gave His dearest treasure,
   That our weak hearts might see
   How good His will toward us;
And in His Son He gave us
Whate'er could bless and save us:
   Praise Him who loveth thus!

4 O praise Him, for He never
   Forgets our daily need;
O blest the hour whenever
   To Him our thoughts can speed;
   Yea, all the time we spend
Without Him is but wasted,
Till we His joy have tasted,
   The joy that hath no end.

5 For when the world is passing
   With all its pomp and pride,
All we were here amassing
   No longer may abide;
   But in our earthly bed,
Where softly we are sleeping,
God hath us in His keeping,
   To wake us from the dead.

6 Then, though on earth I suffer
   Much trial, well I know
I merit ways still rougher,
   And 'tis to heaven I go;
   For Christ I know and love,
To Him I now am hasting,
And gladness everlasting
   With Him this heart shall prove.

7 For such His will who made us;
   The Father seeks our good;
The Son hath grace to aid us,
   And save us by His blood;
   His Spirit rules our ways,
By faith in us abiding,
To heaven our footsteps guiding;
   To Him be thanks and praise.

L. Helmbold, 1563

350 5, 6. 10L.

Zinck's Koralbog, 1801

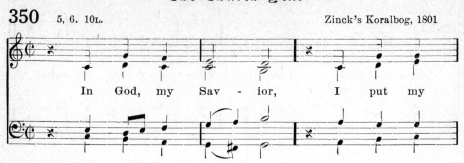

In God, my Sav - ior, I put my

trust a - lone; His word and fa - vor My help in

need I own; My life I ten - der,

And all I have as well, In full sur-

Third Sunday after Easter

ren - der   To Thee, whose grace I tell,   My soul's be-

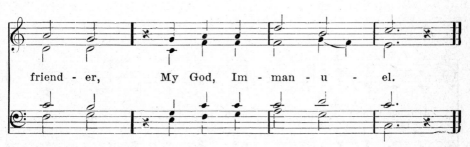

friend - er,   My God, Im - man - u - el.

2 The loss sin wrought me,
  Through Satan's wiles, O Lord,
Thou, who hast bought me,
  Hast all by grace restored:
My thanks I render,
  Myself to Thee I yield,
My Savior tender,
  My rock, my sun and shield,
My soul's defender,
  On Thee my hopes I build.

3 Keep me Thy servant,
  Let me obey Thee, Lord,
In spirit fervent,
  According to Thy word;
When doth forsake me
  The frowning world for aye,
And sufferings shake me,
  Grant patience, be my stay,
Until Thou take me
  From this ill world away.

4 My consolation
  Thou art in every need,
For my salvation
  Thou on the cross didst bleed;
In heaven dwelling,

I shall, when past all pain,
  Thy praise be telling,
O Lamb for sinners slain!
When, anthems swelling,
  I sing the angels' strain.

5 O faithful Savior,
  My sweetest rest and stay!
O let me never
  From Thee in darkness stray!
My soul deliver,
  And guide Thy weary dove,
By grace and favor,
  Home to the place I love—
My home forever—
  Jerusalem above.

6 There, past life's sadness,
  'Tis good to be at rest,
In joy and gladness,
  With saints forever blest;
Lord, let me ever
  Walk in Thy faith and fear,
That, past death's river,
  I may Thy welcome hear:
"Come blest forever,
  Come in, my servant dear!"

Anon.. (Danish) ca 1600

351   6, 6, 5, 6, 6, 5, 7, 8, 6.

Ludv. M. Lindeman, 1812—87

Je-sus, price-less treas - ure, Source of pur-est pleas-ure,

tru-est friend to me: Ah, how long I've pant - ed

And my heart hath faint - ed, Thirst - ing, Lord, for Thee.

Thine I am, O spot-less Lamb! I will suf - fer

Third Sunday after Easter

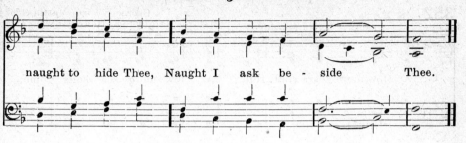

naught to   hide Thee,   Naught I   ask   be - side   Thee.

2 In Thine arms I rest me,
   Foes who would molest me
      Cannot reach me here;
   Though the earth be shaking,
   Every heart be quaking,
      Jesus calms my fear;
   Fires may flash and thunder crash,
   Yea, and sin and hell assail me,
      Jesus will not fail me.

3 Hence with earthly treasure!
   Thou art all my pleasure,
      Jesus, all my choice;
   Hence, thou empty glory!
   Naught to me thy story,
      Told with tempting voice;
   Pain or loss, or shame, or cross,
   Shall not from my Savior move me,
      Since He deigns to love me.

4 Fare thee well that errest,
   Thou that earth preferrest,
      Thou wilt tempt in vain;
   Fare thee well, trangression,
   Hence, abhorred possession,
      Come not forth again.
   Past your hour, O pride and power,
   Worldly life, thy bonds I sever,
      Fare thee well forever!

5 Hence, all fear and sadness!
   For the Lord of gladness,
      Jesus, enters in;
   Those who love the Father,
   Though the storms may gather,
      Still have peace within;
   Yea, whate'er I here must bear,
   Thou art still my purest pleasure,
      Jesus, priceless treasure.

J. Franck, 1655

The Church Year

352 S M. 8L.

George William Martin, 1862
Har. by Sir Arthur Sullivan, 1874

A few more years shall roll, A few more sea - sons come, And we shall be with those that rest, A - sleep with-in the tomb.

A few more suns shall set O'er these dark hills of time, And we shall be where suns are not, A far se - ren - er clime.

2 A few more storms shall beat
  On this wild, rocky shore,
And we shall be where tempests cease,
  And surges swell no more.
A few more struggles here,
  A few more partings o'er,
A few more toils, a few more tears,
  And we shall weep no more.

3 'Tis but a little while,
  And He shall come again,
Who died that we might live, who lives
  That we with Him may reign;
Then, O my Lord, prepare
  My soul for that glad day;
O wash me in Thy precious blood,
  And take my sins away!

H. Bonar, 1844

378

353 8, 7, 8, 7, 7, 7.

Ludv. M. Lindeman, 1812—87

Je-sus, Je-sus, on - ly Je - sus, Can my heart-felt longing still;

See, I pledge my-self to Je - sus, What He wills, a - lone to will.

For my heart, which He hath filled, Ev - er cries: Lord, as Thou wilt.

2 One there is for whom I'm living,
   Whom I love most tenderly;
Jesus, unto whom I'm giving,
   What in love He gave to me,
Jesus' blood hides all my guilt;
Lead me, Lord, then, as Thou wilt.

3 Seems a thing to me a treasure,
   Which displeasing is to Thee,
Then remove such dangerous pleasure;
   Give instead what profits me.
Let my heart by Thee be stilled,
Make me Thine, Lord, as Thou wilt.

4 Grant that I may e'er endeavor
   Thy good pleasure to fulfill,
In me, through me, with me ever,
   Lord, accomplish Thou Thy will.
Let me die, Lord, on Thee built,
When, and where, and as Thou wilt.

5 Lord, my praise shall be unceasing,
   For Thou gav'st Thyself to me,
And besides so many a blessing
   That I now sing joyfully:
Be it unto me, my shield,
As Thou wilt, Lord, as Thou wilt.

Ludämilie Elisabeth of Schwartzburg-Rudolstadt, 1687

354 8, 8, 6, 8, 8, 6.

S. Reay, 1876

Spir - it of wis - dom, turn our eyes From earth and earth - ly van - i - ties To heaven - ly truth and love; Spir - it of un - der - stand - - ing true, Our souls with heaven-ly light en - due To seek the things a - bove.

2 Spirit of counsel, be our guide;
  Teach us, by earthly struggles tried,
    Our heavenly crown to win:
  Spirit of fortitude, Thy power
  Be with us in temptation's hour,
    To keep us pure from sin.

3 Spirit of knowledge, lead our feet
  In Thine own paths, so safe and sweet,
    By angel footsteps trod;
  Where Thou our guardian true shalt be,
  Spirit of gentle piety,   [be,
    To keep us close to God.

Fourth Sunday after Easter

4 Through all our life be ever near,
  Spirit of God's most holy fear,
   In our heart's inmost shrine:
  Our souls with awful reverence fill,
  To worship His most holy will,
   All-righteous and divine.

5 So lead, us, Lord, through peace or
  Onward to everlasting life,   [strife,
   To win our high reward:
  So may we fight our lifelong fight,
  Strong in Thine own unearthly might,
   And reign with Christ, our Lord.

Anon., ca. 1860

355   L. M.

German, 1524

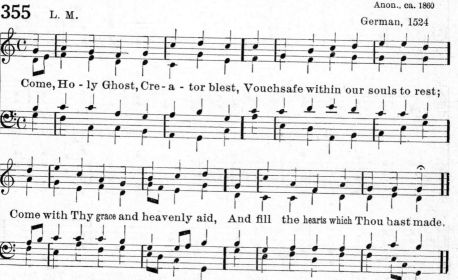

Come, Ho - ly Ghost, Cre - a - tor blest, Vouchsafe within our souls to rest; Come with Thy grace and heavenly aid, And fill the hearts which Thou hast made.

2 To Thee, the Comforter, we cry
  To Thee, the gift of God most high,
  The fount of life, the fire of love,
  The souls' anointing from above.

3 The sevenfold gifts of grace are Thine,
  O finger of the hand divine;
  True promise of the Father Thou,
  Who dost the tongue with speech endow.

4 Thy light to every thought impart,
  And shed Thy love in every heart;
  The weakness of our mortal state
  With deathless might invigorate.

5 Drive far away our wily foe,
  And Thine abiding peace bestow;
  If Thou be our preventing guide,
  No evil can our steps betide.

6 Make Thou to us the Father known;
  Teach us th' eternal Son to own,
  And Thee, whose name we ever bless,
  Of both the Spirit, to confess.

7 Praise we the Father and the Son,
  And Holy Spirit, Three in One:
  And may the Son on us bestow
  The gifts that from the Spirit flow.

A Rabanus Maurus. d. 856

The Church Year

7, 7, 6, 7, 7, 8.

Heinrich Isaac, 1490

O Thou, who dost ac - cord us The high-est prize and guer - don,

Thou hope of all our race, Je - sus, do Thou af - ford us The

gift we ask of par - don For all who hum-bly seek Thy face.

2 With whispered accusation
   Our conscience tells of sinning
   In thought, and word, and deed;
Thine is our restoration,
   The work of grace beginning
   For souls from every burden freed.

3 For who, if Thou reject us,
   Shall raise the fainting spirit?
   'Tis Thine alone to spare:
If Thou to life elect us,
   With cleansèd hearts to near it,
   Shall be our task, our lowly prayer.

4 O Trinity most glorious,
   Thy pardon free bestowing,
   Defend us evermore;
That in Thy courts victorious,
   Thy love more truly knowing,
   We may with all Thy saints adore.

Anon. (Latin, 11th Century)

Fifth Sunday after Easter

357   6, 6, 6, 6, 8, 8.   J. Goss, 1800—80

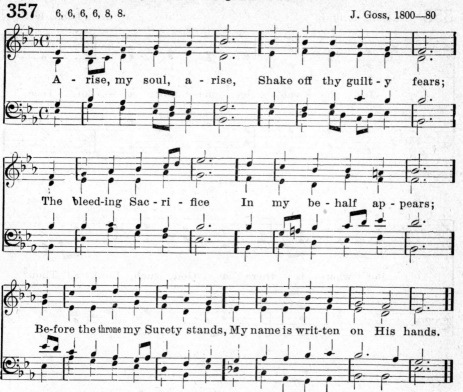

A - rise, my soul, a - rise, Shake off thy guilt-y fears;

The bleed-ing Sac - ri - fice In my be-half ap - pears;

Be-fore the throne my Surety stands, My name is writ-ten on His hands.

2 He ever lives above,
   For me to intercede;
His all-redeeming love,
   His precious blood to plead;
His blood atoned for all our race,
And sprinkles now the throne of grace.

3 Five bleeding wounds He bears,
   Received on Calvary;
They pour effectual prayers,
   They strongly speak for me;
Forgive him, O forgive, the cry,
Nor let that ransomed sinner die!

4 The Father hears Him pray,
   His dear anoninted One;
He cannot turn away
   The presence of His Son;
His Spirit answers to the blood,
And tells me I am born of God.

5 My God is reconciled,
   His pardoning voice I hear:
He owns me for His child,
   I can no longer fear;
With confidence I now draw nigh,
And "Father, Abba, Father!" cry.

C. Wesley, 1742

358   9, 10, 9, 10, 10, 10.

John Dahle, 1911

Je - ho - vah, let me now a - dore Thee,

For where is there a God, such, Lord, as Thou?

With songs I fain would come be - fore Thee; O let Thy

Spir - it deign to teach me now To praise Thee in His name, through

Fifth Sunday after Easter

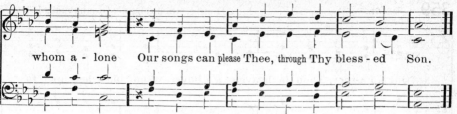

whom a - lone   Our songs can please Thee, through Thy bless - ed   Son.

2 Yes, draw me to the Son, O Father,
   That so the Son may draw me up to Thee.
Let every power within me gather,
   To own Thy sway, O Spirit—rule in me,
That so the peace of God may in me dwell,
And I may sing for joy and praise Thee well.

3 Grant me Thy Spirit; then my praises
   Will sound aright, no jarring tone or word;
Sweet are the songs the heart then raises,
   Then I can pray in truth and spirit, Lord;
Thy Spirit bears mine up on eagles' wing,
To join the psalms the heavenly choirs now sing.

4 For He can plead for me with sighings
   That are unutterable to lips like mine;
He bids me pray with earnest cryings,
   Bears witness with my soul that I am Thine,
Co-heir with Christ, and thus may dare to say,
O Abba, Father, hear me when I pray.

5 When thus Thy Spirit in me burneth,
   And makes this cry to break from out my heart,
Thy heart, O Father, toward me yearneth,
   And longs all precious blessings to impart;
Thy ready love rejoiceth to fulfill
The prayer breathed out according to Thy will

6 And what Thy Spirit thus hath taught me
   To seek from Thee, must needs be such a prayer
As Thou wilt grant, through Him who bought me,
   And raised me up to be Thy child and heir;
In Jesus' name I fearless seek Thy face,
And take from Thee, my Father, grace for grace.

7 O joy, our hope and trust are founded
   On His sure word and witness in the heart;
I know Thy mercies are unbounded,
   And all good gifts Thou freely wilt impart,
Nay, more is lavished by Thy bounteous hand
Than we can ask or seek or understand.

8 O joy! In His name we draw near Thee,
   Who ever pleadeth for the sons of men;
I ask in faith and Thou wilt hear me,
   In Him Thy promises are all Amen.
O joy for me! and praise be ever Thine,
Whose wondrous love has made such blessings mine!

       B. Crasselius, 1697

359 8s. 6L.

Schumann's Gesangbuch, 1539

Our Fa-ther, Thou in heaven a-bove, Who bid-dest us to

dwell in love, As breth-ren of one fam-i-ly, And

cry for all we need to Thee; Teach us to mean the

words we say, And from the in-most heart to pray.

2 All hallowed be Thy name, O Lord!
O let us firmly keep Thy word,
And lead, according to Thy name,
A holy life, untouched by blame;
Let no false teachings do us hurt—
All poor deluded souls convert.

3 Thy kingdom come! Thine let it be
In time and through eternity!
O let Thy Holy Spirit dwell
With us, to rule and guide us well;
From Satan's mighty power and rage
Preserve Thy Church from age to age.

4 Thy will be done on earth, O Lord,
As where in heaven Thou art adored!
Patience in time of grief bestow,
Obedience true in weal and woe;
Our sinful flesh and blood control
That thwart Thy will within the soul.

5 Give us this day our daily bread,
Let us be duly clothed and fed;
And keep Thou from our homes afar
Famine and pestilence and war,
That we may live in godly peace,
Unvexed by cares and avarice.

Fifth Sunday after Easter

6 Forgive our sins, that they no more
  May grieve and haunt us as before,
  As we forgive their trespasses
  Who unto us have done amiss;
  Thus let us dwell in charity,
  And serve each other willingly.

7 Into temptation lead us not,
  And when the foe doth war and plot
  Against our souls on every hand,
  Then armed with faith, O may we
      stand
  Against him as a valiant host
  Through comfort of the Holy Ghost.

8 Deliverance from all evil give,
  For yet in evil days we live;
  Redeem us from eternal death,
  And when we yield our dying breath,
  Console us, grant us calm release,
  And take our souls to Thee in peace.

  Amen! that is, So let it be!
  Strengthen our faith and trust in Thee,
  That we may doubt not, but believe,
  That what we ask we shall receive;
  Thus in Thy name and at Thy word
  We say Amen; now hear us, Lord!

  M. Luther, 1539

360 C. M.

W H. Havergal, 1846

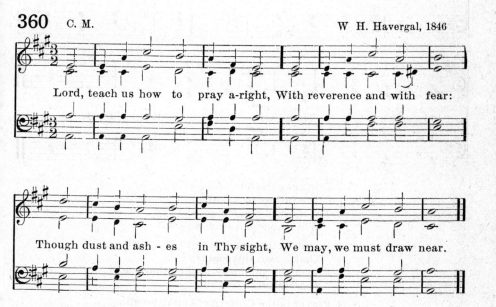

Lord, teach us how to pray a-right, With reverence and with fear:

Though dust and ash - es in Thy sight, We may, we must draw near.

2 Burdened with guilt, convinced of sin,
    In weakness, want, and woe,
  Fightings without and fears within,
    Lord, whither shall we go?

3 God of all grace, we come to Thee
    With broken, contrite hearts;
  Give what Thine eye delights to see,
    Truth in the inward parts.

4 Give deep humility; the sense
    Of godly sorrow give;

A strong desire, with confidence,
    To hear Thy voice and live;

5 Faith in the only sacrifice
    That can for sin atone,
  To cast our hopes, to fix our eyes,
    On Christ, on Christ alone.

6 Give these, and then Thy will be done;
    Thus strengthened with all might,
  We, through Thy Spirit and Thy Son,
    Shall pray, and pray aright.

  J. Montgomery, 1818

361 C. M.   John Dahle, 1911

Prayer is the soul's sin - - cere de - - sire,

Un - ut - tered or ex - pressed; The mo - tion of a

hid - den fire That trem - bles in the breast.

2 Prayer is the burden of a sigh,
   The falling of a tear,
   The upward glancing of the eye,
   When none but God is near.

3 Prayer is the simplest form of speech
   That infant lips can try;
   Prayer the sublimest strains that reach
   The Majesty on high.

4 Prayer is the Christian's vital breath,
   The Christian's native air;
   His watchword at the gates of death:
   He enters heaven with prayer.

5 Prayer is the contrite sinner's voice
   Returning from his ways
   While angels in their songs rejoice,
   And cry, "Behold, he prays!"

6 O Thou, by whom we come to God,
   The life, the truth, the way!
   The path of prayer Thyself hast trod;
   Lord, teach us how to pray.

                    J. Montgomery, 1818

362 8, 7, 8, 7, 8, 8, 7.

14th Cent., N. Decius, d. 1541

The Lord as-- cend - eth up on high, Loud anthems round Him swell - ing;

The Lord hath tri-umphed glo - rious - ly, In power and might ex-

cel - - - ling: Hell and the grave are cap - tive led; Lo,

He re-turns, our glo-rious head, To His e - ter - nal dwell - ing!

2 The heavens with joy receive their Lord;
  O day of exultation!
By saints, by angel-hosts, adored
For His so great salvation!
O earth, adore thy glorious King:
His rising, His ascension sing
  With grateful adoration!

3 By saints in earth and saints in heaven,
  With songs for ever blended,
All praise to Christ, our King, be given,
Who hath to heaven ascended;
To Father, Son, and Holy Ghost,
The God of heaven's resplendent host
  In bright array extended!

A. T. Russell, 1851

363 8, 7, 8, 7, 8, 8, 7, 7.

Ludv. M. Lindeman, 1812—87

Conquering Prince and King of glo-ry, Maj-es-ty sub-lime-ly bright! Heaven and all the heavens a-dore Thee, Throned a-bove their far-thest height. Shall I not, en-rap-tured gaz-ing, At Thy feet fall pros-trate, prais-ing,

Ascension

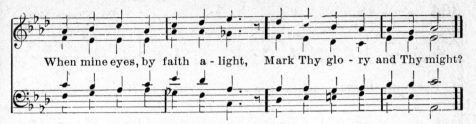

When mine eyes, by faith a-light, Mark Thy glo-ry and Thy might?

2 Far on high art Thou ascended,
    Sitting at Thy Father's right,
Pure, seraphic voices blended,
    Crying, Glory! at the sight.
Shall I not fall down before Thee,
And with joyful heart adore Thee,
    When the heavens exultant ring
    With the triumph of my King?

3 Far and wide Thy brightness spreading
    Lights the land whose sun Thou art,
Nobler bliss and glory shedding
    On each heavenly spirit's heart.
There in highest glory seated,
By rejoicing angels greeted;
    Here, though child of earth, I cry
    Hallelujah! Lord most high!

4 Of Thy cup shall I be fearful
    When Thy glory whelms my sight?
Shall my courage not be cheerful
    When I recognize Thy might?
Lord, I trust Thee, though Thou slay me;
Now, not earth and hell dismay me.
    Thou my King, my Savior Thou,
    At Thy name alone I bow.

5 Might and spirit now o'erflowing,
    With Thy power perform Thy word.
All Thine enemies o'erthrowing,
    Make Thy foes Thy footstool, Lord.
O'er the earth, O Judah's Lion,
Send the scepter out of Zion,
    Spread Thy sway from sea to sea,
    Till the earth acknowledge Thee.

6 Throned on high, and all things filling,
    Thou art with us evermore.
Now my soul, with rapture thrilling,
    Opens wide for Thee its door.
Come, O come, Thou King of glory;
'Stablish Thy dominion o'er me;
    Live in me and reign alone,
    As upon Thy heavenly throne.

7 Thou ascended, gifts art giving;
    God and heaven are inly near.
By Thee in the Spirit living,
    I shall stand before Thee there.
Alien here to time and senses,
Hid in Thee from their offenses;
    Set in heavenly place with Thee,
    Jesus, Thou art joy to me.

G. Tersteegen, 1735

364 8, 9, 8, 8, 9, 8, 6, 6, 4, 4, 4, 8.

Ph. Nicolai, 1599

Praise the Lord through ev - e. y na - - tion, His ho - ly arm hath wrought sal - va - tion; Ex - alt Him on His Fa - ther's throne; Praise your King, ye Chris - tian le - - gions, Who now pre - pares in heaven - ly re - gions Un - fail - ing man-sions for His own: With voice and min-strel - sy,

Ascension

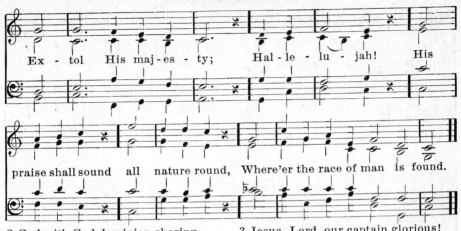

Ex - tol His maj - es - ty; Hal - le - lu - jah! His

praise shall sound all nature round, Where'er the race of man is found.

2 God with God dominion sharing,
  And man with man our image bearing,
    Gentiles and Jews to Him are given;
  Praise your Savior, ransomed sinners,
  Of life, through Him, immortal win-
      ners,
    No longer heirs of earth, but heaven;
    O beatific sight,
    To view His face in light!
  Hallelujah!
  And while we see, transformed to be
  From bliss to bliss eternally!

3 Jesus, Lord, our captain glorious!
  O'er sin and death and hell victorious;
    Wisdom and might to Thee belong;
  We confess, proclaim, adore Thee;
  We bow the knee, we fall before Thee;
    Thy love henceforth shall be our
        song;
    The cross meanwhile we bear;
    The crown e'er long to wear;
  Hallelujah!
  Thy reign extend, world without end
  Let praise from all to Thee ascend.

R. Feith, 1806

365 C. M.

J. Clarke, 1670—1707

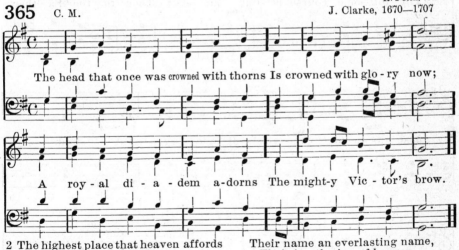

The head that once was crowned with thorns Is crowned with glo - ry now;

A roy - al di - a - dem a-dorns The might-y Vic - tor's brow.

2 The highest place that heaven affords
    Is His by sovereign right:
  The King of kings, and Lord of lords,
    And heaven's eternal Light.

3 The joy of all who dwell above,
    The joy of all below,
  To whom He manifests His love,
    And grants His name to know.

4 To them the cross, with all its shame,
    With all its grace, is given;

  Their name an everlasting name,
    Their joy the joy of heaven.

5 They suffer with their Lord below,
    They reign with Him above;
  Their profit and their joy to know
    The mystery of His love.

6 His cross to us is life and health,
    Though shame and death to Him:
  His people's hope, His people's wealth
    Their everlasting theme.

T. Kelly, 1820

393

366   8, 8, 7, 8, 8, 7, 4, 4, 4, 4, 8.   Ph. Nicolai, 1599

O won-drous Con-quer-or and great, Scorned by the world Thou

didst cre-ate, Thy work is all com-plet-ed!

Thy toil-some course is at an end; Thou to the Fa-ther

dost as-cend, In roy-al glo-ry seat--ed.

Low-ly, ho-ly, now vic-to-rious, High and glo-rious:

Ascension

Earth and heav - en To Thy rule, O Christ, are giv - en.

2 Thou, Lord, art now our head, and we
Thy members are, and draw from Thee
  Our life and full salvation.
For comfort, peace, joy, light and power,
For balm to heal in sorrow's hour,
  We yield Thee adoration.
Kneeling, feeling, Thou art nearest,
Lord, and dearest: we're receiving
Grace surpassing our conceiving.

3 Lord Jesus, keep our eyes on Thee;
Help us Thy servants true to be,
  Fulfilling Thy good pleasure,
Set Thou our minds on things above,
Let this vain world ne'er win our love,
  Be Thou our only treasure.
Wholly, lowly, we would own Thee,
And enthrone Thee: wisdom learning,
All Thy perfect ways discerning.

4 Thou, Jesus, art our shield and guide,
O let Thy words in us abide,
  Directing all our going.
Teach us to love Thy blessed will,
To suffer meekly and be still,
  Nor fear grief's tide o'erflowing.
Weeping, keeping low before Thee,
We adore Thee. 'Midst our sorrow,
Lord, we hail the coming morrow.

5 Lord Jesus, hasten Thy return;
Our longing hearts expectant yearn
  To prove the joys of heaven.
Thy precious blood has set us free,
We owe our present all to Thee,
  For us Thy life was given.
Singing, bringing praise abounding
Now we're sounding never-ending
Triumph, Lord, in Thy ascending.

E. C. Homburg, 1659

367 7, 6, 7, 6, 6, 7, 7, 6.

German, Hamburg, 1598

Lo, God to heaven as - cend - eth! Throughout its re - gions vast, With shouts tri - umph - ant
blend - - eth The trump - et's thrill - ing blast:
Sing praise to Christ, the Lord, Sing
praise with ex - ul - ta - - tion! King of each hea - then

Ascension

na - - - tion! The God of hosts a - dored.

2 With joy is heaven resounding,
   Christ's glad return to see;
Behold the saints surrounding
   The Lord who set them free:
Bright myriads thronging come;
   The cherub-band rejoices,
   And loud seraphic voices
Welcome Messiah home.

3 No more the way is hidden,
   Since Christ, our head, arose:
No more to man forbidden,
   The road to heaven that goes;
Our Lord is gone before,
   Yet here He will not leave us,
   But soon in heaven receive us:
He opens wide the door.

4 Christ is our place preparing.
   To heaven we, too, shall rise,
And, joys angelic sharing,
   Be where our treasure lies:
There may each heart be found,
   Where Jesus Christ has entered!
   There let our hopes be centered,
Our course still heavenward bound!

5 May we, His servants, thither
   In heart and mind ascend,
And let us sing together,—
   We seek Thee, Christ, our friend,
Thee, God's anointed Son,
   Our life, and way to heaven,
   To whom all power is given,
Our joy, and hope, and crown.

G. W. Sacer. 1665

The Church Year

368   S. M. 8L.

H. S. Gauntlett, 1805—76

Thou art gone up on high To man-sions in the skies;

And round Thy throne un-ceas-ing-ly The songs of praise a-rise;

But we are lin-gering here, With sin and care op-pressed:

Lord, send Thy prom-ised Com-fort-er, And lead us to Thy rest.

2 Thou art gone up on high;
  But Thou didst first come down,
Through earth's most bitter agony
  To pass unto Thy crown;
And girt with griefs and fears
  Our onward course must be;
But only let that path of tears
  Lead us at last to Thee.

3 Thou art gone up on high;
  But Thou shalt come again,
With all the bright ones of the sky
  Attendant in Thy train.
O by Thy saving power,
  So make us live and die,
That we may stand in that dread hour
  At Thy right hand on high.

Emma L. Toke. 1851

369 L. M.

H. K. Oliver, 1832

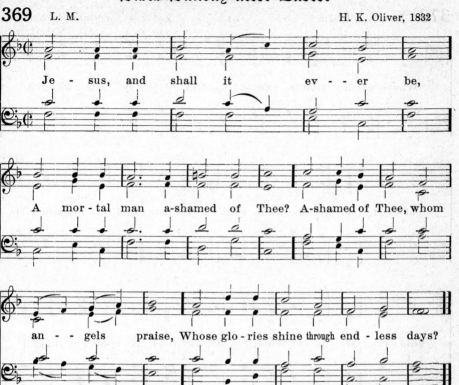

Je - sus, and shall it ev - - er be,

A mor - tal man a-shamed of Thee? A-shamed of Thee, whom

an - - gels praise, Whose glo - ries shine through end - less days?

2 Ashamed of Jesus! sooner far
Let evening blush to own a star:
He sheds the beams of light divine
O'er this benighted soul of mine.

3 Ashamed of Jesus! just as soon
Let midnight be ashamed of noon;
'Tis midnight with my soul, till He,
Bright morning star, bid darkness flee.

4 Ashamed of Jesus, that dear Friend
On whom my hopes of heaven depend!
No, when I blush, be this my shame,
That I no more revere His name.

5 Ashamed of Jesus! yes, I may,
When I've no guilt to wash away,
No tear to wipe, no good to crave,
No fear to quell, no soul to save.

6 Till then, nor is my boasting vain,
Till then I boast a Savior slain;
And O may this my glory be,
That Christ is not ashamed of me.

J. Grigg, 1765

370 8, 7, 8, 7, 4, 4, 8.   Ludv. M. Lindeman, 1812—87

What-e'er my God or-dains is right: Ho-ly His will a-
bid-eth; I will be still whate'er He doth, And fol-low where He
guid-eth. He is my God; Though dark my road, He holds me that I
shall not fall, Where-fore to Him I leave it all.

2 Whate'er my God ordains is right
He never will deceive me;
He leads me by the proper path;
I know He will not leave me,
And take, content,
What He hath sent;
His hand can turn my griefs away,
And patiently I wait His day.

3 Whate'er my God ordains is right:
Though now this cup in drinking
May bitter seem to my faint heart,
I take it, all unshrinking.
Tears pass away
With dawn of day;
Sweet comfort yet shall fill my heart,
And pain and sorrow shall depart.

4 Whate'er my God ordains is right:
Here shall my stand be taken;
Though sorrow, need, or death be mine,
Yet I am not forsaken;
My Father's care
Is round me there;
He holds me that I shall not fall,
And so to Him I leave it all.

400   S. Rodigast. 1675

371 6, 5. 8L.   G. J. Elvey, 1816—93

In the hour of tri - al, Je - sus, plead for me,

Lest by base de - ni - al I de - part from Thee;

When Thou seest me wav - er, With a look re - call,

Nor for fear or fa - vor Suf - fer me to fall.

2 With forbidden pleasures
   Would this vain world charm;
 Or its sordid treasures
   Spread to work me harm;
 Bring to my remembrance
   Sad Gethsemane,
 Or, in darker semblance,
   Cross-crowned Calvary.

3 Should Thy mercy send me
   Sorrow, toil, and woe;
 Or should pain attend me
   On my path below;

Grant that I may never
   Fail Thy hand to see;
 Grant that I may ever
   Cast my care on Thee.

4 When my last hour cometh,
   Fraught with strife and pain,
 When my dust returneth
   To the dust again;
 On Thy truth relying,
   Through that mortal strife,
 Jesus, take me, dying,
   To eternal life.

                                    J. Montgomery, 1834

The Church Year

O Je-sus, I have prom-ised To serve Thee to the end;

Be Thou for ev - er near me, My Mas-ter and my Friend!

I shall not fear the bat - tle If Thou art by my side,

Nor wan-der from the path-way If Thou wilt be my guide.

2 O let me feel Thee near me—
    The world is ever near;
  I see the sights that dazzle,
    The tempting sounds I hear.
  My foes are ever near me,
    Around me and within;
  But, Jesus, draw Thou nearer,
    And shield my soul from sin.

3 O let me hear Thee speaking
    In accents clear and still,
  Above the storms of passion,
    The murmurs of self-will.
  O speak to reassure me,
    To hasten or control:
  O speak, and make me listen,
    Thou Guardian of my soul!

4 O Jesus, Thou hast promised
    To all who follow Thee
  That where Thou art in glory
    There shall Thy servant be;
  And, Jesus, I have promised
    To serve Thee to the end;
  O give me grace to follow,
    My Master and my Friend!

5 O let me see Thy footmarks,
    And in them plant mine own;
  My hope to follow duly
    Is in Thy strength alone.
  O guide me, call me, draw me,
    Uphold me to the end;
  And then in heaven receive me,
    My Savior and my Friend!

J. E. Bode, 1869

373 C. M.

Nicolaus Hermann, 1560

O Christ, our hope, our hearts' de - sire, Re-demp-tion's on - ly spring! Cre - a - tor of the world art Thou, Its Sav - ior and its King, Its Sav - ior and its King.

2 How vast the mercy and the love,
　Which laid our sins on Thee,
　And led Thee to a cruel death,
　‖:To set Thy people free!:‖

3 But now the bands of death are burst,
　The ransom has been paid;
　And Thou art on Thy Father's throne,
　‖:In glorious robes arrayed.:‖

4 O may Thy mighty love prevail
　Our sinful souls to spare!
　O may we come before Thy throne,
　‖:And find acceptance there!:‖

5 O Christ, be Thou our present joy,
　Our future great reward;
　Our only glory may it be
　‖:To glory in the Lord!:‖

Anon.. Latin. 7th or 8th Century

The Church Year

Pentecost

Ph. Nicolai, 1599

O Ho - ly Spir - it, en - ter in, And in our hearts Thy

work be - gin, Thy tem - ple deign to make us;

Sun of the soul, Thou Light di - vine, A - round and in us

bright-ly shine, To joy and glad - ness wake us.

That we to Thee tru - ly liv - ing, To Thee giv - ing

Pentecost

prayer un - ceas - ing, Still may be in love in - creas - ing.

2 Give to Thy word impressive power,
   That in our hearts, from this good
      hour,
      As fire it may be glowing;
   That we confess the Father, Son,
   And Thee, the Spirit, Three in One,
      Thy glory ever showing.
   O stay and sway our souls ever,
   That they never may forsake Thee,
   But by faith their refuge make Thee.

3 Thou Fountain whence all wisdom
      flows,
   Which God on pious hearts bestows,
      Grant us Thy consolation,
   That in our pure faith's unity
   We faithful witnesses may be
      Of grace that brings salvation.
   Hear us, cheer us by Thy teaching;
   Let our preaching and our labor
   Praise Thee, Lord, and bless our
      neighbor.

4 Left to ourselves we shall but stray;
   O lead us in the narrow way,
      With wisest counsel guide us,
   And give us steadfastness, that we
   May ever faithful prove to Thee,
      Whatever woes betide us.
   Lord, now heal Thou all hearts broken,
   And betoken Thou art near us,
   Whom we trust to light and cheer us.

5 Thy heavenly strength sustain our
      heart,
   That we may act the valiant part
      With Thee as our reliance;
   Be Thou our refuge and our shield,

That we may never quit the field,
   Bidding all foes defiance;
Descend, defend from all errors
And earth's terrors: Thy salvation
Be our constant consolation.

6 O mighty Rock, O Source of life,
   Let Thy dear word, 'mid doubt and
      strife,
      Be so within us burning,
   That we be faithful unto death,
   In Thy pure love and holy faith,
      From Thee true wisdom learning!
   Thy grace and peace on us shower;
   By Thy power Christ confessing,
   Let us win our Savior's blessing.

7 O gentle Dew, from heaven now fall
   With power upon the hearts of all,
      Thy tender love instilling:
   That heart, to heart more closely
      bound,
   Fruitful in kindly deeds be found,
      The law of love fulfilling;
   Then, Lord, discord shall not grieve
      Thee;
   We receive Thee; where Thou livest,
   Peace, and love, and joy Thou givest.

8 Grant that our days, while life shall
      last,
   In purest holiness be passed,
      Be Thou our strength forever;
   Grant that our hearts henceforth be
      free
   From sinful lust and vanity,
      Which us from Thee must sever.
   Keep Thou pure now from offenses
   Heart and senses. Blessed Spirit!
   Let us heavenly life inherit.
                        M. Schirmer. 1640

The Church Year

375 8s. 9L.

Johann Walther, 1524

Come, Ho-ly Spir-it, God and Lord! Be all Thy gra-ces now out poured On each be-liev-er's soul and heart; Thy fer-vent love to them im-part. Lord, by the brightness of Thy light, Thou in the faith dost men u-nite Of ev-ery land and ev-ery tongue; This to Thy praise, O

Pentecost

Lord, be sung: Hal-le-lu-jah! Hal-le-lu-jah!

2 Thou holy Light, and Guide divine!
  O cause the word of life to shine;
  Teach us to know our God aright,
  And call Him Father with delight!
  From error, Lord, our souls defend,
  That they on Christ alone attend;
  In Him with living faith confide,
  And in unfaltering trust abide.
      Hallelujah! Hallelujah!

3 Sweet Source of comfort, holy Love,
  Send us Thy succor from above,
  That in Thy service we may stay,
  And trouble drive us not away.
  Lord, with Thy grace our souls refresh,
  Confirm our frail and feeble flesh,
  That we may battle manfully,
  And press through life and death to
      Hallelujah! Hallelujah! [Thee.

M. Luther, 1524
German medieval
Adapted by Luther or J. Walther, 1524

376 7s. 4L.

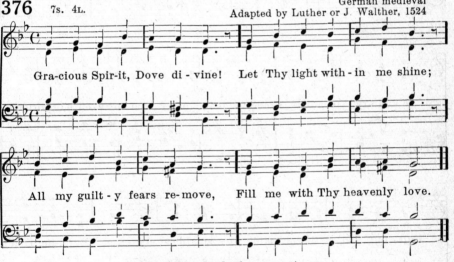

Gra-cious Spir-it, Dove di-vine! Let Thy light with-in me shine;

All my guilt-y fears re-move, Fill me with Thy heavenly love.

2 Speak Thy pardoning grace to me,
  Set the burdened sinner free;
  Lead me to the Lamb of God;
  Wash me in His precious blood.

3 Life and peace to me impart,
  Seal salvation on my heart;
  Breathe Thyself into my breast,
  Earnest of eternal rest.

4 Let me never from Thee stray,
  Keep me in the narrow way;
  Fill my soul with joy divine,
  Keep me, Lord, for ever Thine.

John Stocker, 1777

The Church Year

Heav-en-ly Spir-it, all oth-ers tran-scend-ing, Thou who with

Fa-ther and Son dost a-bide! Come Thou, our spir-its in

u-ni-ty blend-ing, Come and make read-y the heav-en-ly bride!

Call-ing and gathering, and Je-sus de-clar-ing, Build-ing God's

Church, shedding light from a-bove, Come, O Thou Spir-it of

God, nev-er tir - ing, Come and in-terpret God's won-der-ful love!

2 Merciful Jesus, with love never failing,
  Sending Thy Spirit, the pledge ever new,
That Thy atonement for all is availing,
  Faith ever sees that Thy promise is true.
Crowned are Thy servants with heavenly fire,
  Speaking with hearts and with tongues all aflame;
Heavenly Spirit, our voices inspire,
  That we may sing of His glorious name!

3 Heavenly Consoler, with unction celestial,
  Heal Thou the wounds of each sin-burdened heart!
Strengthen our faith, and with zeal Pentecostal
  Fill our faint souls, and Thy blessings impart!
Create within us new hearts and new spirits;
  Lead us in truth, and sustain us in woe;
Teach us true faith in the dear Savior's merits,
  So that at death we Thy power may know!

J. N. Brun, 1786

378 7, 7, 7.

W. H. Monk, 1823—89

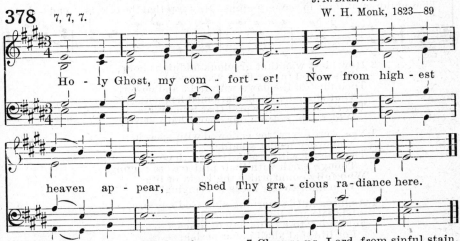

Ho - ly Ghost, my com - fort-er! Now from high-est
heaven ap - pear, Shed Thy gra - cious ra-diance here.

2 Come to them who suffer dearth,
  With Thy gifts of priceless worth,
  Lighten all who dwell on earth.

3 Thou the heart's most precious guest,
  Thou, of comforters the best,
  Give to us, the o'er-laden, rest.

4 Come! in Thee our toil is sweet,
  Shelter from the noonday heat,
  From whom sorrow flieth fleet.

5 Blessed Sun of grace! o'er all
  Faithful hearts who on Thee call
  Let Thy light and solace fall.

6 What without Thy aid is wrought,
  Skillful deed or wisest thought,
  God will count but vain and naught.

7 Cleanse us, Lord, from sinful stain,
  O'er the parchéd heart, O rain!
  Heal the wounded of its pain.

8 Bend the stubborn will to Thine,
  Melt the cold with fire divine,
  Erring hearts to right incline.

9 Grant us, Lord, who cry to Thee,
  Steadfast in the faith to be,
  Give Thy gift of charity.

10 May we live in holiness,
  And in death find happiness,
  And abide with Thee in bliss!

Anon., Latin. 13th Century.
M. Moller, 1584

The Church Year

O day full of grace, which we be-hold, Now gent-ly to view as - cend-ing;

Thou o - ver the earth thy reign unfold, Good cheer to all mor - tals lend - ing:

That children of light in ev-ery clime May prove that the night is end - ing.

2 How blest was that gracious midnight hour,
    When God in our flesh was given;
Then flushéd the dawn with light and power,
    That spread o'er the darkened heaven;
Then rose o'er the world that Sun divine
    Which gloom from our hearts hath driven.

3 Yea, were every tree endowed with speech,
    And every leaflet singing,
They never with praise His worth could reach,
    Though earth with their praise were ringing.
Who fully could praise the Light of life
    Who light to our souls is bringing?

4 As birds in the morning sing God's praise,
    His fatherly love we cherish,
For giving to us this day of grace,
    For life that shall never perish.
His Church He hath kept these thousand years,
    And hungering souls did nourish.

5 Pass on to thy close, O Whit-Sunday,
    With sunlight about thee beaming,
And scatter thy blessings on thy way,
    As brooks through the meadows streaming
E'er leave in their wake the woods and fields
    In beauty and fruitfulness dreaming.

6 With joy we depart for our fatherland,
    Where God our Father is dwelling,
Where ready for us His mansions stand,
    Where heaven with praise is swelling;
And there we shall walk in endless light,
    With blest ones His praise forth telling.

Anon.,(Danish, 14th Century).
N. F. S. Grundtvig, 1826

Pentecost

380   8, 7, 8, 7, 8, 8, 7,   German, 1524

O Ho-ly Ghost, Thou gift di-vine, And giv-er of all bless-ing, Thou, with the Father and the Son, True Godhead art pos-sess-ing, And from them both art shed a-broad, E-ter-nal Spir-it Lord and God, In Thee all Chris-tians glo-ry.

2 O Spirit blest, we Thee entreat:
  O grant us that we ever,
With heart and soul, as it is meet,
  May serve our Lord and Savior
And Him confess till our last breath,
As Lord of life and Lord of death
  And give Him praise and honor.

3 Our hearts let new-created be,
  Our walk make pure and holy.
Help us offense and sin to flee,
  And ever serve God solely,
So that our faith in Christ, our Lord,
May prove itself in deed and word
  Before the world about us.

4 Thy gracious heavenly dew let fall,
  The fainting Church to quicken;
Thy soothing ointment pour on all
  Whose souls are sad and stricken;
Sustain us, Lord in evil days,
And let our lives in all our ways,
  Abound in love and mercy.

5 Give strength and courage to contend
  Against the hosts of evil,
That we may vanqish, in the end,
  The world, the flesh, the devil;
And when death's billow o'er us rolls,
Bear Thou to heaven our ransomed
  souls,
  While dust to dust returneth.

B. Ringwaldt, 1681
S. Jonassøn, 1693

411

381   8, 7, 8, 7, 7, 7, 8, 8.   Johann Schop, 1642

Ho - ly Ghost, dis - pel our sadness, Pierce the clouds of sin-ful night;

Come, Thou source of sweet-est gladness, Breathe Thy life, and spread Thy light!

Lov - ing Spir - it, God of peace! Great dis-trib - u - ter of grace!

Rest up - on this con - gre - ga-tion, Hear, O hear our sup-pli - ca-tion!

2 From that height which knows no
    measure
As a gracious shower descend,
Bringing down the richest treasure
Men can wish, or God can send!
O Thou Glory, shining down
From the Father and the Son,
    Grant us Thy illumination!
    Rest upon this congregation!

3 Known to Thee are all recesses
Of the earth and spreading skies;
Every sand the shore possesses
Thy omniscient mind descries.
Holy Fountain! wash us clean
Both from error and from sin!
    Make us fly what Thou refusest,
    And delight in what Thou choos-
    est!

Pentecost

4 Manifest Thy love for ever;
  Fence us in on every side;
In distress be our reliever,
  Guard and teach, support and guide!
Let Thy kind effectual grace
Turn our feet from evil ways;
  Show Thyself our new creator,
  And conform us to Thy nature!

5 Be our friend on each occasion,
  God, omnipotent to save!
When we die, be our salvation,
  When we're buried, be our grave!
And, when from the grave we rise,
Take us up above the skies.
  Seat us with Thy saints in glory,
  There for ever to adore Thee!

P. Gerhardt, 1648

382   6, 6, 4, 6, 6, 6, 4.

J. R. Fairlamb

Come, Ho - ly Ghost, in love Shed on us from above

Thine own bright ray! Di - vine - ly good Thou art; Thy sa - cred

gifts im - part To glad - den each sad heart: O come to - day!

2 Come, tenderest Friend, and best,
  Our most delightful guest,
    With soothing power:
  Rest, which the weary know,
  Shade, 'mid the noontide glow,
  Peace, when deep griefs o'erflow,
    Cheer us this hour!

3 Come, Light serene, and still,
  Our inmost bosoms fill;
    Dwell in each breast;
  We know no dawn but Thine:
  Send forth Thy beams divine,
  On our dark souls to shine,
    And make us blest!

4 Exalt our low desires;
  Extinguish passion's fires;
    Heal every wound:
  Our stubborn spirits bend;
  Our icy coldness end;
  Our devious steps attend,
    While heavenward bound.

5 Come, all the faithful bless;
  Let all who Christ confess,
    His praise employ:
  Give virtue's rich reward;
  Victorious death accord,
  And, with our glorious Lord,
    Eternal joy!

Anon. (Latin, 13th Century)

The Church Year

383   8, 7, 8, 7, 8, 8, 7, 8, 8, 7.

German, 14th Century

O Light of God's most wondrous love, Who dost our darkness bright - en,

Shed on Thy Church from heaven a - bove, Our eye of faith en - light - en!

As in Thy light we gath - er here, Show us that Christ's own promise clear

Is Yea and A - men ev - - er. O ris - en and as - cen-ded Lord,

We wait ful - fill-ment of Thy word: O bless us with Thy fa - vor!

Birgitte C. Boye, 1778

Trinity Sunday

384 8, 6. 8L.

I sing to Thee with voice and heart, Of all my joys the well; I

sing, that, what I know Thou art My lips o all may tell: That

Thou a foun-tain art of grace, With blessings rich-ly stored

For all, in ev-ery time and place, This well I know, O Lord.

2 Cheer up, faint heart, rejoice and sing,
   All anxious fear resign;
For God, the sovereign Lord and King,
   Is thy God, even thine:
He is thy portion, He thy joy,
   Thy life, and light, and Lord;
Thy counsellor when doubts annoy,
   Thy shield and great reward.

3 In restless thoughts or dark despair
   Why spend the day and night?
On Him who loves thee cast thy care;
   He makes our burdens light:

Did not His love, and truth, and power
   Watch o'er thy childhood's day?
Hath He not oft, in threatening hour
   Turned dreaded ills away!

4 His wisdom never plans in vain,
   Ne'er falters, or mistakes;
All that His counsels wise ordain
   A happy ending makes:
Upon thy mouth, then, lay thy hand,
   And trust His guiding eye;
Thus, firm as rock, thy feet shall
   Now and eternally.   [stand,

P. Gerhardt 1653

The Church Year

385   7, 8, 7, 8, 7, 6, 7, 6, 7, 6, 7, 6.

Hans Kugelmann, 1540

To Thee all praise as-cend - eth, Al-might-y ev - er - bless-ed God;

The an-them nev - er end - eth Around Thy throne, O ho - ly Lord!

E'en here, in trib-u-la - tion, When we are sore-ly tried,

Thou art our con-so-la - tion, The ref-uge where we hide.

Day un-to day Thy glo - ry, Thy good-ness doth con - fess,

Trinity Sunday

And we take up the sto - ry Of all Thy faith - ful - ness.

2 Our hearts o'erflow with gladness,
   For we have learned Thy power and
      grace
   We may not sink in sadness,
   We stand, in Christ, before Thy face.
      Thy name be ever praiséd,
         Thou doest wonders great;
      Our voice may well be raiséd,
         Thy mercies to relate.
      Oh! be it all our pleasure
         Whilst pilgrim-days endure,
      To find in Thee our treasure,
         To rest in Thee secure.

3 Thy name, O Lord, abideth,
   Thou shalt be honored on the earth,
   Thy hand our all provideth,
   Thou caredst for us ere our birth.
      O Lord! what shall we render
         For all the debt we owe,
      For all Thy care so tender,
         Thy love too vast to know?
      The theme of Thy salvation
         Shall be our one employ,
      We bless Thee for creation,
         And for eternal joy!

J. Rist, 1651

386   C. M.   Carl G. Gläser, 1828

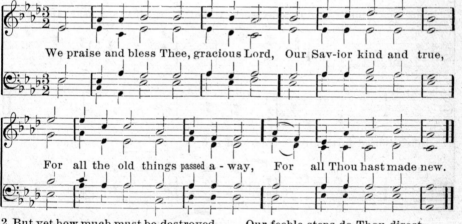

We praise and bless Thee, gracious Lord, Our Sav-ior kind and true,

For all the old things passed a - way, For all Thou hast made new.

2 But yet how much must be destroyed,
   How much renewed must be,
   Ere we can fully stand complete
   In likeness, Lord, to Thee!

3 Thou, only Thou must carry on
   The work Thou hast begun;
   Of Thine own strength Thou must
      impart,
   In Thine own ways to run.

4 O leave us not! from day to day
   Revive, restore again!

Our feeble steps do Thou direct,
   Our enemies restrain.

5 When flesh shall fail, then strengthen
      Thou
   The spirit from above;
   Make us to feel Thy service sweet,
   And light Thy yoke of love.

6 So shall we faultless stand at last
   Before Thy Father's throne;
   The blessedness for ever ours,
   The glory all Thine own.

417

C. J. P. Spitta, 1843

387 14, 14, 4, 7, 8.

German, 1668

Praise to the Fa-ther, the glo-ri-ous King of cre-a-tion! Swell the loud cho-rus, ye chos-en of ev-er-y na - - tion! O my soul, wake! Harp, lute and psal-ter-y take, Sound forth thy true ad-o-ra - - - tion.

2 Praise to the Son: for the cross that once shamefully bore Him,
Now, on the throne of His power let all creatures adore Him!
　　Man reigns on high!
　　Lo! all the hosts of the sky
Bow down and worship before Him!

3 Praise to the Spirit, whose strong, rushing wind, ever blowing,
Still through the world, wheresoever it listeth, is going:
　　Darkness and death
　　Drink, from Thy quickening breath,
Life, light and joy overflowing.

Trinity Sunday

4 Lord God Almighty, Creator, Redeemer and Giver,
   Thy praise resounds by the shore of the bright crystal river:
   We, too, would fain,
   Echoing humbly the strain,
   Praise Thee for ever and ever.

J. Hopkins, 1866

388 L. M.

J. B. Dykes, 1866

Fa - ther of all, whose love pro - found A ran - som for our

souls hath found, Be - fore Thy throne we sin - - ners

bend; To us Thy par - doning love ex - tend.

2 Almighty Son, incarnate Word,
   Our Prophet, Priest, Redeemer, Lord,
   Before Thy throne we sinners bend;
   To us Thy saving grace extend.

3 Eternal Spirit, by whose breath
   The soul is raised from sin and death,
   Before Thy throne we sinners bend;
   To us Thy quickening power extend.

4 Jehovah, Father, Spirit, Son,
   Mysterious Godhead, Three in One,
   Before Thy throne we sinners bend;
   Grace, pardon, life, to us extend!

Ed. Cooper, 1805

The Church Year

L. M.

Ralph Harrison, 1748—1810

O hap-py day, that stays my choice On Thee, my Sav-ior and my God! Well may this glow-ing heart re-joice, And tell its rap-tures all a-broad.

2 O happy bond, that seals my vows
   To Him who merits all my love!
   I'll praise Him in His sacred house,
   And gladly to His altar move.

3 'Tis done, the great transaction's done;
   I am my Lord's, and He is mine:
   He drew me, and I followed on,
   Glad to obey the voice divine.

4 High heaven, that heard the solemn vow,
   That vow renewed shall daily hear;
   Till in life's latest hour I bow,
   And bless in death a bond so dear.

P. Doddridge, publ. 1755

Trinity Sunday

390 8, 8, 6, 8, 8, 6.

A. H. Brown, b. 1830

Au-thor of faith, to Thee I cry, To Thee, who wouldst not have me die, But know the truth and live: O-pen mine eyes to see Thy face, Work in my heart the sav-ing grace, The life e-ter-nal give.

2 I know the work is only Thine,
The gift of faith is all divine;
   But if on Thee we call,
Thou wilt the benefit bestow,
And give us hearts to feel and know
   That Thou hast died for all.

3 Thou bid'st us knock and enter in,
Come unto Thee and rest from sin,
   The blessing seek and find;
Thou bid'st us ask Thy grace, and have;
Thou can'st, Thou would'st, this moment save
   Both me and all mankind.

4 Be it according to Thy word!
Now let me find my pardoning Lord,
   Let what I ask be given;
The bar of unbelief remove,
Open the door of faith and love,
   And take me into heaven.

C. Wesley, 1745

The Church Year
First Sunday after Trinity

391 8, 8, 7, 8, 8, 7, 8, 7. Ludv. M. Lindeman, 1812—87

A - mid the world's de - ceit-ful cares Thou dost not heed how un - awares
Thy day of life is end - ing! Se - cure thou liv-est, strong and wise,
The world pur-su-ing, 'tis the prize For which thou art con - tend - ing:—
O man, O man! the end draws near! Thy life thou art ex - pend - ing!

2 While here thou toilest at thy best,
Death comes, an uninvited guest—
His summons is appalling—
The most secure awakes with fears,
And for the wise no way appears,
The strongest then is falling:—
O man, O man! Death thee and all
Away from earth is calling!

3 When sounds the voice: "The soul
of thee,
This very night required shall be!"
Thou to the grave art tending—
Vain is resistance—vain thy nay—

For tread thou must that downward
Which none is reascending: [way
O man, O man! from danger flee,
Thy soul to God commending!

4 For if thou shouldst the whole world
gain
And lose thy soul, all were in vain,
No gain is thee afforded!
Thy works are counted at God's
throne,
And thou shalt reap what thou hast
When judgment is awarded! [sown,
O man, O man! thy peril know!
'Tis in God's word recorded!

422

First Sunday after Trinity

5 Wide is the gate, and broad the way,
　That to destruction leads astray,
　　The many yet pursue it;
　The narrow gate and narrow way
　Leads unto life and bliss for aye,
　　And few be they that find it:
　O man, O man! O care betimes
　　For thine immortal spirit!

6 Awake! awake! repent and pray!
　By faith prepare thyself each day
　　To die in peace unfearing!
　The Christ embrace, thy sins deplore,

The naked clothe, and feed the poor,
　By works thy faith declaring!
O man, O man! before thy God
　Thou soon shalt have a hearing!

7 In alms, in works put not thy trust,
　But do thou pray: My God most just,
　　Thy mercy I am needing!
　Out of the deep I cry to Thee;
　O judge me not by just decree!
　　Thy mercy I am pleading!
　O Savior Christ! O Savior Christ!
　　For me be interceding!

L. P. Gothus. 1572
J. O. Wallin, 1816

392　C. M.

R. Redhead 1820—1901

Lord, as to Thy dear cross we flee, And plead to be for-given,

So let Thy life our pat-tern be, And form our souls for heaven.

2 Help us through good report and ill
　Our daily cross to bear,
Like Thee to do our Father's will,
　Our brethren's grief to share.

3 Let grace our selfishness expel,
　Our earthliness refine
And kindness in our bosoms dwell
　As free and true as Thine.

4 If joy shall at Thy bidding fly,
　And grief's dark day come on,

We in our turn would meekly cry,
　"Father, Thy will be done."

5 Should friends misjudge, or foes de-
　　fame,
　Our brethren faithless prove,
Then, like Thine own, be all our aim
　To conquer them by love.

6 Kept peaceful in the midst of strife,
　Forgiving and forgiven,
O may we lead the pilgrim's life,
　And follow Thee to heaven.

J. H. Gurney, 1838

393   8, 8, 7, 8, 8, 7, 8, 8, 8, 8, 8, 4, 8, 8.

German, 1577

With all my heart I love Thee, Lord; For-sake me not, but
still af-ford Thy read-y help and fa-vor:
The world,—its joys de-light me not, Nor earth nor heaven could
be my lot, Wert Thou not mine for-ev-er.
And should my heart with sor-row break, Thy-self my por-tion

First Sunday after Trinity

I will make, My trust, my heart's de - light, my all, Whose blood re-deemed me from the fall: Lord Je - sus Christ! My God and Lord! Thy gracious name Preserve me from e - ter-nal shame.

2 My body, soul, and all I have
Are Thine, O Lord, to keep and save,
   In this our life of sadness:
I pray Thee, grant me daily grace,
To use each gift to Thy sole praise,
   For others' good and gladness:
From doctrine false, from error wild,
From Satan's lies, protect Thy child!
My soul with Thy whole strength prepare,
My cross in meekest love to bear:
     Lord Jesus Christ!
My God and Lord! Thy gracious name
Preserve me from eternal shame.

3 My soul let Thine own angels dear.
To Abram's bosom bear and cheer,
   When she her flight is taking:
My body, in its chamber still,
Securely keep from wrong and ill,
   Till earth's last great awaking:
Then raise me, Lord, to be with Thee,
That these mine eyes with joy may see,
O Son of God, Thy glorious face,
My Savior, and my fount of grace!
     Lord Jesus Christ,
Thy servant hear! hear, I implore,
That I may praise Thee evermore!

M. Schalling, 1567

394 L. M.

J. Clauder's "Psalmodia Nova," 1630

Take up thy cross, the Sav-ior said, If thou wouldst my dis-ci-ple be; De-ny thy-self, the world for-sake, And hum-bly fol--low af-ter me.

2 Take up thy cross; let not its weight
   Fill thy weak soul with vain alarm:
   My strength shall bear thy spirit up,
   And brace thine heart and nerve thine arm.

3 Take up thy cross, nor heed the shame,
   Nor let thy foolish pride rebel;
   Thy Lord for thee the cross endured,
   To save thy soul from death and hell.

4 Take up thy cross, then, in His strength,
   And calmly every danger brave;
   'Twill guide thee to a better home,
   And lead to victory o'er the grave.

5 Take up thy cross and follow Him,
   Nor think till death to lay it down;
   For only he who bears the cross
   May hope to wear the glorious crown.

C. W. Everest, 1833.

395   8, 6. 8L.

A. H. Mann, 1885

I heard the voice of Je - sus say, "Come un - to Me and rest;

Lay down, thou wea-ry one, lay down Thy head up - on My breast."

I came to Je - sus as I was, Wea-ry, and worn and sad;

I found in Him a rest-ing-place, And He has made me glad.

2 I heard the voice of Jesus say,
    "Behold, I freely give
The living water; thirsty one,
    Stoop down and drink, and live."
I came to Jesus, and I drank
    Of that life-giving stream;
My thirst was quenched, my soul re-
        vived,
    And now I live in Him.

3 I heard the voice of Jesus say,
    "I am this dark world's light;
Look unto Me, thy morn shall rise,
    And all thy day be bright."
I looked to Jesus, and I found
    In Him my star, my sun;
And in that light of life I'll walk
    Till travelling days are done.

H. Bonar. 1846

The Church Year

396   10s. 6L.   E. W. Bullinger, b. 1837

Long did I toil, and knew no earth-ly rest, Far did I rove, and

found no cer - tain home; At last I sought them in His sheltering breast,

Who opes His arms, and bids the wea-ry come: With Him I found a

home, a rest di - vine, And I since then am His, and He is mine.

2 The good I have is from His stores supplied,
   The ill is only what He deems the best;
   He for my friend, I'm rich with naught beside,
     And poor without Him, though of all possessed:
   Changes may come, I take, or I resign,
   Content, while I am His, while He is mine.

428

Second Sunday after Trinity

3 Whate'er may change, in Him no change is seen,
 A glorious sun that wanes not nor declines,
 Above the clouds and storms He walks serene,
 And on His people's inward darkness shines:
 All may depart, I fret not, nor repine,
 While I my Savior's am, while He is mine.

4 While here, alas! I know but half His love,
 But half discern Him, and but half adore;
 But when I meet Him in the realms above
 I hope to love Him better, praise Him more,
 And feel, and tell, amid the choir divine,
 How fully I am His, and He is mine.

H. F. Lyte, 1833

397 7s. 4L.   J. H. Knecht, 1799

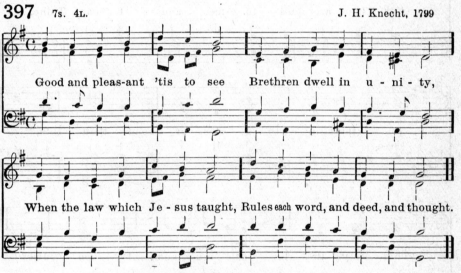

Good and pleas-ant 'tis to see Brethren dwell in u - ni - ty,

When the law which Je - sus taught, Rules each word, and deed, and thought.

2 God has promised there, we know,
 Blessings richly to bestow,
 Life on earth, with all s store,
 Life in heaven for evern re.

3 Sun of righteousness, arise!
 Shine on our benighted eyes;
 To Thy Church Thy light unfold,
 That the nations may behold.

4 Jesus! Head of Christians all!
 Grant that we, both great and small,
 Through Thy gospel's light divine,
 May be one and wholly Thine.

5 Bring back all that go astray,
 Heavenly Shepherd! to Thy way;
 'Neath Thy favor and Thy light,
 All Thy pasture-sheep unite.

M. Muller, 1700

398 10s. 4L. G. Lomas, 1834—1884

I lift my heart to Thee, Sav - ior di - vine,
For Thou art all to me, and I am Thine.
Is there on earth a clos - er bond than this,
That "My Be - lov - ed's mine, and I am His?"

2 To Thee, Thou bleeding Lamb, I all things owe;
All that I have and am, and all I know.
All that I have is now no longer mine,
And I am not mine own;—Lord, I am Thine.

3 How can I, Lord, withhold life's brightest hour
From Thee; or gathered gold, or any power?
Why should I keep one precious thing from Thee,
When Thou hast given Thine own dear self for me?

4 I pray Thee, Savior, keep me in Thy love,
Until death's holy sleep shall me remove
To that fair realm, where, sin and sorrow o'er,
Thou and Thine own are one for evermore.

C. E. Mudie, 1872

399 8, 7, 8, 7, 7, 7.

Ludv. M. Lindeman, 1812—87

Come to Calvary's ho - ly mountain, Sinners, ruined by the fall;

Here a pure and heal-ing fountain Flows to you, to me, to all;

In a full per - pet - ual tide, O-pened when our Savior died.

2 Come in poverty and meanness,
    Come defiled, without, within;
From infection and uncleanness,
    From the leprosy of sin,
Wash your robes and make them white;
Ye shall walk with God in light.

3 Come in sorrow and contrition,
    Wounded, impotent, and blind;
Here the guilty free remission,
    Here the troubled peace my find:
Health this fountain will restore;
He that drinks shall thirst no more.

4 He that drinks shall live for ever;
    'Tis a soul-renewing flood:
God is faithful; God will never
    Break His covenant of blood,
Signed when our Redeemer died,
Sealed when He was glorified.

J. Montgomery, 1819

400   8s. 6L.   Third Sunday after Trinity   J. H. Schein, 1586—1630

The abyss of many a for-mer sin En-clos-es me, and bars me in;

Like bil-lows my transgressions roll— Be Thou the pi-lot of my soul;

And to salvation's har-bor bring, Thou Savior and Thou glo-rious King!

2 My Father's heritage abused,
Wasted by lust, by sin misused;
To shame and want and misery brought,
The slave to many a fruitless thought;—
I cry to Thee, who lovest men,
O pity and receive again!

3 In hunger now, no more possessed
Of that my portion bright and blest,
The exile and the alien see,
Who yet would fain return to Thee!
Accept me, Lord, I seek Thy grace;
And let me see a Father's face!

4 With that blest thief my prayer I make,
Remember for Thy mercy's sake!
With that poor publican I cry,
Be merciful, O God, most high!
With that lost prodigal I fain,
Back to my home would turn again!

5 Mourn, mourn, my soul, with earnest care,
And raise to Christ the contrite prayer;—
O Thou who freely wast made poor,
My sorrows and my sins to cure,
Me, poor of all good works, embrace,
Enriching with Thy boundless grace!

    Joseph of the Studium, ca. 860

Third Sunday after Trinity

Schumann's Gesangbuch, 1539

Yea, as I live, Je-ho-vah saith, I would not have the sin-ner's death. Far rath-er 'tis My ho-ly will, That in his course he should stand still. Re-pent-ant sin-ners I for-give, Then let them hear, be-lieve, and live.

2 Think of this word, O guilty soul!
Despair not: Christ can make thee
　whole,
In Him there's pardon, peace, and
　grace;
A sure and blessed hiding-place.
The covenant, confirmed by blood,
Doth stand upon the oath of God.

3 O trifle not the time away!
Say not, "I'll come another day."
Say not, "I'll have my soul's desire,
And turn when of the world I tire."
Say not, "I'll then converted be,
God will be merciful to me."

4 'Tis true that God is rich in grace,—
Beholding His Anointed's face.

The blood of Christ atoned for sin,
He died eternal life to win;
Yet God doth not vouchsafe to say
That thou shalt live "another day."

5 O hasten, sinner, to be wise!
Nor dare God's message to despise.
He who this hour supplies thy breath,
The next, may give thee o'er to death.
And if thy sins are not forgiven,
Thou'lt never, never enter heaven.

6 Then cry: "Lord Jesus, help Thou
This very day I come to Thee! [me,
O give me peace, and from this hour
Deliver me from Satan's power;
That henceforth and eternally,
Thyself my all in all may be!"

433　　　　　　　　　J. Heermann, 1630

402   8, 7, 8, 7, 8, 8.   Johann Crüger, 1649

Though we long, in sin-wrought blindness, From Thy gracious paths have strayed,

Cold to Thee and all Thy kind-ness, Wil - ful, reckless, or a - fraid;

Through dim clouds that gather round us Thou hast sought, and Thou hast found us.

2 Oft from Thee we veil our faces,
   Children-like, to cheat Thine eyes,
Sin, and hope to hide the traces!
   From ourselves ourselves disguise;
'Neath the webs enwoven round us,
Thy soul-piercing glance has found us.

3 Sudden, 'midst our idle chorus,
   O'er our sin Thy thunders roll,
Death his signal waves before us,
   Night and terror take the soul;
Till through double darkness round us,
Looks a star,—and Thou hast found us.

4 O most Merciful, most Holy,
   Light Thy wanderers on their way;
Keep us ever Thine, Thine wholly,
   Suffer us no more to stray!
Cloud and storm oft gather round us;
We were lost, but Thou hast found us.

F. T. Palgrave, 1868

Third Sunday after Trinity

403 7, 8, 7, 8, 7, 7.

German, 1656

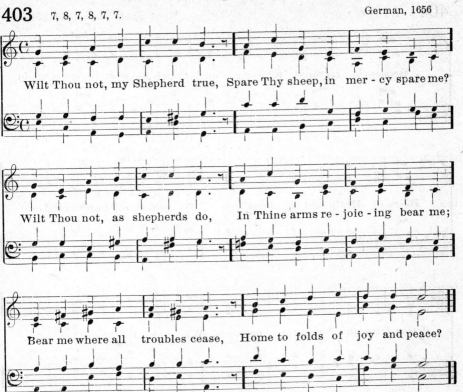

Wilt Thou not, my Shepherd true, Spare Thy sheep, in mer - cy spare me?

Wilt Thou not, as shepherds do, In Thine arms re - joic - ing bear me;

Bear me where all troubles cease, Home to folds of joy and peace?

2 With Thy flock I long to be,
    With the flock to whom 'tis given
Safe to feed, and, praising Thee,
    Roam the happy plains of heaven:
Free from fear of sinful stain,
They can never stray again.

3 Lord! I here am sore beset,
    Fears at every step confound me;
Lo! my foes have spread their net,
    And with craft and might surround me:
Such their snares on every side,
Safe Thy sheep can ne'er abide.

4 See, on earth's wide desert way
    How my truant steps mislead me;
Bring me back, no more to stray,
    In Thine own green pastures feed me.
Gather me within the fold,
Where Thy lambs Thy light behold.

J. Scheffler, 1657

404 7, 6. 8L.   Meiningisches Gesangbuch, 1693

Redeemed, restored, for-giv-en Through Jesus' precious blood,

Heirs of His home in heav-en, O praise our pardoning God!

Praise Him in tune-ful meas-ures, Who gave His Son to die;

Praise Him whose sevenfold treasures, En-rich and sanc-ti-fy!

2 Once on the dreary mountain
   We wandered far and wide,
Far from the cleansing fountain,
   Far from the piercéd side;
But Jesus sought and found us,
   And washed our guilt away;
With cords of love He bound us
   To be His own for aye.

3 Dear Master, Thine the glory
   Of each recovered soul;
Ah! who can tell the story
   Of love that made us whole?

Not ours, not ours the merit;
   Be Thine alone the praise,
And ours a thankful spirit
   To serve Thee all our days.

4 Now keep us, Holy Savior,
   In Thy true love and fear;
And grant us of Thy favor
   The grace to persevere;
Till, in Thy new creation,
   Earth's time-long travail o'er,
We find our full salvation,
   And praise Thee evermore.

Sir H. W. Baker, 1876

Fourth Sunday after Trinity

405   6, 6, 6, 6, 8, 8.

John Adcock, 1882

Be - hold, how good a thing It is to dwell in peace;

How pleas-ing to our King This fruit of right-eous-ness;

When brethren in the faith a-gree—How joy-ful is such u - ni - ty!

2 Where unity is found,
  The sweet anointing grace
Extends to all around,
  And consecrates the place;
To every waiting soul it comes,
And fills it with divine perfumes.

3 Grace, every morning new,
  And every night we feel
The soft, refreshing dew
  That falls on Hermon's hill!
On Zion it doth sweetly fall:
The grace of one descends on all.

4 E'en now our Lord doth pour
  The blessing from above,
A kindly, gracious shower

Of heart-reviving love,
The former and the latter rain,
The love of God and love of man.

5 In Him when brethren join,
  And follow after peace,
The fellowship divine
  He promises to bless:
His choicest graces to bestow,
Where two or three are met below.

6 The riches of His grace
  In fellowship are given
To Zion's chosen race,
  The citizens of heaven;
He fills them with His choicest store,
He gives them life for evermore.

C. Wesley, 1742

The Church Year

8s. 6L.

Schumann's Gesangbuch, 1539

How fair the Church of Christ shall stand, A bea-con-light in all the land, When love and faith all hearts in-spire, And all u-nite in one de-sire To be as broth-ers, and a-gree To live in peace and u-ni-ty.

2 'Tis all in vain that you profess
The doctrines of the Church, unless
You live according to your creed,
And show your faith by word and deed.
Observe the rule: To others do
As you would have them do to you.

3 Resentment, hate, and cruel jest,
Must not be harbored in the breast
Where love and charity should dwell;
Then, think and speak of others well,
Refrain from all that causes strife
And mars a truly Christian life.

4 So let your tongue, your heart, and mind,
Agree to banish every kind
Of malice, falsehood, and disguise,
And here on earth a paradise
Of peace and harmony maintain,
Where concord and good-will shall reign.

5 For God observes our thoughts and deeds,
The secrets of our heart He reads;
The wicked can not be concealed,
Their evil ways shall be revealed,
He every true believer knows,
And love and grace on him bestows.

6 My soul, be therefore of good cheer,
  Though sinners threaten, scoff and
    sneer,
  Serenely on your way proceed,
  Nor worldly strife and clamor heed,
  For Jesus' sake the cross you bear,
  And soon with Him the crown shall
    wear.

7 O gracious God, wilt Thou my heart
  So fashion in each secret part,
  That Thou be sanctified in me,
  Till Thee in heaven above I see,
  Where holy, holy, holy, Lord,
  We sing to Thee with sweet accord.

T. Kingo, 1699

407 8, 7, 8, 7, 7, 7.

J. Chr. Bach, 1693

Brethren, called by one vo - ca - tion, Members of one fam - i - ly,

Heirs through Christ of one sal - va - tion, Let us live in har - mo - ny;

Nor by strife em - bit - ter life, Journeying to e - ter - ni - ty.

2 In a land where all are strangers,
    And our sojourning so short,
  In the midst of common dangers,
    Concord is our best support;
  Heart with heart divides the smart,
    Lightens grief of every sort.

3 Let us shun all vain contention
    Touching words and outward things,
  Whence, alas! so much dissension
    And such bitter rancor springs;
  Troubles cease, where Christ brings
      peace
    And sweet healing on His wings.

4 Judge not hastily of others,
    But thine own salvation mind;
  Nor be captious to thy brother's,
    To thine own offenses blind;
  God alone discerns thine own,
    And the hearts of all mankind.

5 Let it be our chief endeavor,
    That we may the Lord obey,
  Then shall envy cease forever,
    And all hate be done away;
  Free from strife shall be his life
    Who serves God both night and day!

C. J. P. Spitta, 1833

439

408 8, 7. 8L.

J. Rosenmüller, 1649

Je - sus, I my cross have tak - en, All to leave, and fol - low Thee; Des - ti - tute, de - spised, for - sak - en, Thou, from hence, my all shalt be. Per - ish ev - ery fond am - bi - tion, All I've sought, and hoped, and known, Yet how

Fourth Sunday after Trinity

rich is my con - di - tion! God and heaven are still my own.

2 Let the world despise and leave me;
    They have left my Savior, too;
Human hearts and looks deceive me;
    Thou art not, like them, untrue;
And while Thou shalt smile upon me,
    God of wisdom, love and might,
Foes may hate, and friends may shun me;
    Show Thy face and all is bright.

3 Go, then, earthly fame and treasure!
    Come disaster, scorn and pain!
In Thy service, pain is pleasure;
    With Thy favor, loss is gain.
I have called Thee Abba, Father;
    I have stayed my heart on Thee;
Storms may howl, and clouds may gather,
    All must work for good to me.

4 Man may trouble and distress me,
    'Twill but drive me to Thy breast;
Life with trials hard may press me,
    Heaven will bring me sweeter rest.
O 'tis not in grief to harm me,
    While Thy love is left to me,
O 'twere not in joy to charm me,
    Were that joy unmixed with Thee.

5 Take, my soul, thy full salvation;
    Rise o'er sin, and fear, and care;
Joy to find, in every station,
    Something still to do or bear.
Think what Spirit dwells within thee,
    What a Father's smile is thine,
What a Savior died to win thee;
    Child of heaven, shouldst thou repine?

6 Haste, then, on from grace to glory,
    Armed by faith, and winged by prayer;
Heaven's eternal day's before thee,
    God's own hand shall guide thee there.
Soon shall close thy earthly mission,
    Swift shall pass thy pilgrim days,
Hope soon change to glad fruition,
    Faith to sight, and prayer to praise.

H. F. Lyte. 1824

The Church Year

409 7, 6, 7, 6, 7, 7, 7, 6.

J. H. Cornell, 1872

Rise, my soul, and stretch thy wings, Thy bet-ter por-tion trace;

Rise from trans-i-to-ry things Toward heaven, thy na-tive place.

Sun, and moon, and stars de-cay; Time shall soon this earth re-move;

Rise, my soul, and haste a-way To seats pre-pared a-bove.

2 Rivers to the ocean run,
  Nor stay in all their course;
Fire ascending seeks the sun;
  Both speed them to their source;
So a soul that's born of God
Pants to view His glorious face;
Upward tends to His abode,
  To rest in His embrace.

3 Cease, my soul, O cease to mourn!
  Press onward to the prize;
Soon thy Savior will return,
  To take thee to the skies ;
There is everlasting peace,
Rest, enduring rest in heaven,
There will sorrow ever cease,
  And crowns of joy be given.

R. Seagrave, 1742

Fifth Sunday after Trinity

410 7, 6. 8L.

H. L. Hassler, 1601

Let me be Thine for - ev - er, My gra-cious God and Lord,

May I for-sake Thee nev - er, Nor wan - der from Thy word:

Pre-serve me from the maz - es Of er - ror and dis - trust,

And I shall sing Thy prais - es For - ev - er with the just.

2 Lord Jesus! bounteous giver
  Of light and life divine,
Thou didst my soul deliver,
  To Thee I all resign:
Thou hast in mercy bought me
  With blood and bitter pain;
Let me, since Thou hast sought me,
  Eternal life obtain.

3 O Holy Ghost, who pourest
  Sweet peace into my heart,
And all my soul restorest,
  Let not Thy grace depart.
And while His name confessing
  Whom I by faith have known,
Grant me Thy constant blessing;
  Make me for aye Thine own.

N. Selnecker, 1572, et al.

The Church Year

7, 8, 7, 8, 7, 7.

German, 1656

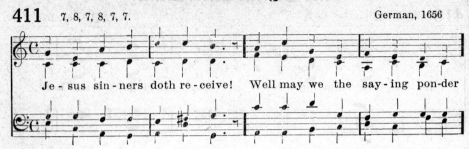

Je - sus sin - ners doth re - ceive! Well may we the say - ing pon - der

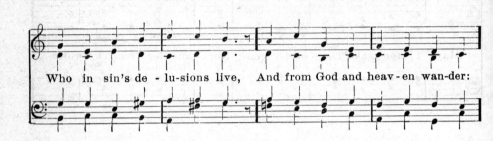

Who in sin's de - lu - sions live, And from God and heav - en wan - der:

This a - lone can hope re - vive— Je - sus sin - ners doth re - ceive!

2 We deserve but grief and shame,—
   Yet His words, rich grace revealing,
Pardon, peace, and life proclaim;
   Here their ills have perfect healing
Who with humble hearts believe,
Jesus sinners doth receive!

3 As the shepherd seeks to find
   His lost sheep that from him stray-
      eth,
So hath Christ each soul in mind,
   And for its salvation prayeth;
Fain He'd have each wanderer live:
Jesus sinners doth receive.

4 Come, then, all by guilt oppressed,
   Jesus calls, and He would make you
God's own children, pure and blest,
   And to glory He would take you;
Think on this, and well believe
Jesus sinners doth receive.

5 Savior, now I come to Thee:
   Great my sins, a weary burden!
Wilt Thou mercy show to me?
   Can I hope to find a pardon?
I will trust: my soul relieve!
Me, a sinner, Lord, receive!

Fifth Sunday after Trinity

6 Rich Thy mercy—strangely good!
    O how oft have I offended!
  But, through Thy redeeming blood
    All my fear of wrath is ended:
  Yes, I now can witness give:
  Jesus sinners doth receive!

7 Now my conscience is at peace;
    From the Law I stand acquitted;
  Christ hath purchased my release,

And my every sin remitted.
Naught remains my soul to grieve:
Jesus sinners doth receive.

8 Jesus sinners doth receive!
    Happy in His ceaseless favor,
  Here for heaven I will live,
    There shall live with Him forever,
  Joy in death these tidings give;
  "Jesus sinners doth receive!"

412 L. M.

T. E. Aylward, b. 1844

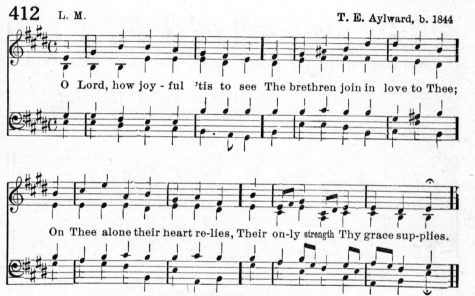

O Lord, how joy-ful 'tis to see The brethren join in love to Thee;
On Thee alone their heart re-lies, Their on-ly strength Thy grace sup-plies.

2 How sweet within Thy holy place
   With one accord to sing Thy grace,
   Besieging Thine attentive ear
   With all the force of fervent prayer!

3 O may we love the house of God,
   Of peace and joy the blest abode;
   O may no angry strife destroy
   That sacred peace, that holy joy.

4 The world without may rage, but we
   Will only cling more close to Thee,
   With hearts to Thee more wholly given,
   More weaned from earth, more fixed on heaven

5 Lord, shower upon us from above
   The sacred gift of mutual love;
   Each other's wants may we supply,
   And reign together in the sky.

C. Coffin, 1736

The Church Year

7, 8, 7, 8, 7, 7.   Swedish

Je-sus, Master! at Thy word   I   will work what-e'er be-tide me,

And I know Thou wilt, O Lord,   By Thy word and Spir-it guide me;

At Thy word my faith shall see   All things work for good to me.

2 Though my toil may seem unblest,
   And my lot appointed dreary,
When at eve I go to rest,
   From my labor faint and weary;
At Thy word I will each morn
To my work with joy return.

3 Though I be of joys bereft,
   And by sorrows overtaken,
Yet I know a solace left:
   I am not by Thee forsaken;
Jesus, Thou canst aid afford,
Fraught with comfort is Thy word.

4 At Thy word in faith I press
   Onward through this vale of sadness;
By Thy grace I shall possess
   Victor-palms in heavenly gladness;
To my latest hour, O Lord,
I will trust Thee at Thy word.

M. F. Liebenberg, 1823

414 S. M. D.

J. Goss, 1854

Not what these hands have done Can save this guilt-y soul;
Not what this toil-ing flesh has borne Can make my spir-it whole.
Not what I feel or do Can give me peace with God;
Not all my prayers, and sighs, and tears, Can bear my aw-ful load.

2 Thy grace alone, O God,
    To me can pardon speak;
Thy power alone, O Son of God,
    Can this sore bondage break.
No other work save Thine,
    No meaner blood will do;
No strength, save that which is divine,
    Can bear me safely through.

3 I bless the Christ of God;
    I rest on love divine;
And with unfaltering lip and heart
    I call this Savior mine.
'Tis He that saveth me,
    And freely pardon gives;
I love, because He loveth me;
    I live, because He lives.

H. Bonar, 1862

415 L. M.   German, 1605

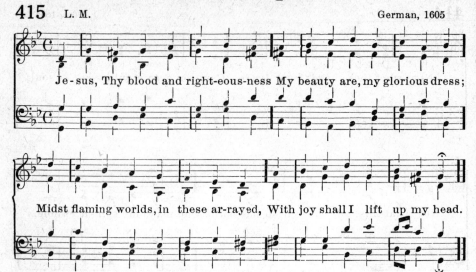

Je-sus, Thy blood and right-eous-ness My beauty are, my glorious dress;

Midst flaming worlds, in these ar-rayed, With joy shall I lift up my head.

2 Bold shall I stand in Thy great day;
 For who aught to my charge shall
  lay?
 Fully absolved through these I am,
 From sin and fear, from guilt and
  shame.

3 The holy, meek, unspotted Lamb,
 Who from the Father's bosom came,
 Who died for me, sin to atone,
 Now as my Lord and God I own.

4 Lord, I believe Thy precious blood,
 Which at the mercy-seat of God

For ever doth for sinners plead,
For me, e'en for my soul was shed.

5 Lord, I believe, were sinners more
 Than sands upon the ocean shore,
 Thou hast for all a ransom paid,
 For all a full atonement made.

6 When from the dust of death I rise
 To claim my mansion in the skies,
 Even then this shall be all my plea,—
 Jesus hath lived, hath died for me!

N. L. von Zinzendorf, 1739

416 L. M.   German, 1543

The Law of God is good. and wise, And

sets His will be-fore our eyes; Shows us the way of

Sixth Sunday after Trinity

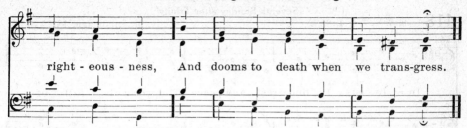

right - eous - ness, And dooms to death when we trans-gress.

2 Its light of holiness imparts
  The knowledge of our sinful hearts,
  That we may see our lost estate,
  And seek deliverance ere too late.

3 To those who help in Christ have
      found,
  And would in works of love abound,
  It shows what deeds are His delight,
  And should be done as good and right.

4 When men the offered help disdain,
  And dead in sin and woe remain,

Its terror in their ear resounds,
And keeps their wickedness in bounds.

5 The law is good, but since the fall
  Its holiness condemns us all:
  It dooms us for our sin to die,
  And has no power to justify.

6 To Jesus we for refuge flee,
  Who from the curse has set us free,
  And humbly worship at His throne,
  Saved by His grace through faith
      alone.

M. Loy, 1880

417 C. M.   A. R. Reinagle, 1830

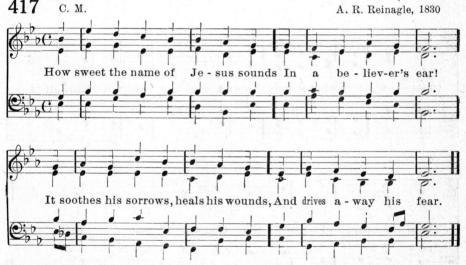

How sweet the name of Je - sus sounds In a be - liev-er's ear!

It soothes his sorrows, heals his wounds, And drives a - way his fear.

2 It makes the wounded spirit whole,
    And calms the troubled breast!
  'Tis manna to the hungry soul,
    And to the weary, rest.

3 Dear Name! the rock on which I build,
    My shield and hiding-place,
  My never-failing treasury, filled
    With boundless stores of grace;

4 Jesus, my Shepherd, Guardian,
      Friend,
    My Prophet, Priest, and King;

My Lord, my Life, my Way, my End,
  Accept the praise I bring.

5 Weak is the effort of my heart,
    And cold my warmest thought;
  But when I see Thee as Thou art,
    I'll praise Thee as I ought.

6 Till then I would Thy love proclaim
    With every fleeting breath:
  And may the music of Thy name
    Refresh my soul in death.

J. Newton, 1779

The Church Year

Seventh Sunday after Trinity

418   8, 7, 8, 7, 4, 4, 8, 7.   Ludv. M. Lindeman, 1812—87

In Je-sus I find rest and peace—The world is full of sor-row; His wounds are my a-bid-ing-place; Let the unknown to-mor-row Bring what it may, There I can stay, My faith finds all I need to-day, I will not trou-ble bor-row.

2 Until I found that crystal spring,
  My way was dull and dreary;
I looked for peace in many a thing;
  But still my soul grew weary.
Unsatisfied,
All things I tried,
And yet my soul had not espied
  The fount of life so near me.

3 My soul was carnal, blind, and bound
  By sin, and never sought Thee,
Lord Jesus, though I ever found
  All else no comfort brought me,
No peace, no rest
Within my breast;
My troubled soul remained unblest,
  Of Thee I ne'er bethought me.

Seventh Sunday after Trinity

4 In pity, then, Thou cam'st to me,
  Thine arms to me extending;
I heard Thy voice: Come unto me
  And rest in peace unending.
Immanuel
Loves thee full well,
He saves thy soul from death and
  hell,
  In perils thee defending.

5 O Jesus, I must now confess
  The world hath but vexation
And anguish, sorrow, dire distress,
  As is Thy declaration.
In Thee is peace
And sweet surcease;
Thy bosom is my resting-place
  Where I find consolation.

6 To me the preaching of the cross
  Is wisdom everlasting;
Thy death alone redeems my loss;
  On Thee my burden casting,
I, in Thy name,
A refuge claim
From sin and death and from all
  shame—
  Blest be Thy name, O Jesus!

7 O Jesus, may I constant be,
  Forever with Thee staying!
O may I feel love's mastery,
  My every fear allaying!
The dove at last
Hath found sweet rest
From all her weary, futile quest,
  Although she long went straying.

Anon., Danish, 1740

419 L. M.

German, 1605

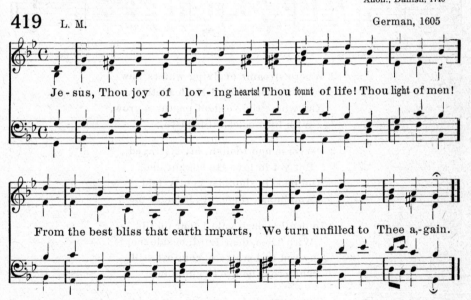

Je-sus, Thou joy of lov-ing hearts! Thou fount of life! Thou light of men!

From the best bliss that earth imparts, We turn unfilled to Thee a-gain.

2 Thy truth unchanged hath ever stood;
  Thou savest those that on Thee call;
To them that seek Thee, Thou art
  good,
To them that find Thee, all in all.

3 We taste Thee, O Thou living bread,
  And long to feast upon Thee still;
We drink of Thee, the fountain head,
  And thirst our souls from Thee to fill.

4 Our restless spirits yearn for Thee,
  Where'er our changeful lot is cast;
Glad, that Thy gracious smile we see,
  Blest, that our faith can hold Thee fast.

5 O Jesus, ever with us stay!
  Make all our moments calm and
    bright;
Chase the dark night of sin away,
  Shed o'er the world Thy holy light.

Bernard of Clairvaux, ca. 1150

420 8, 7. 4L. J. B. Dykes, 1868

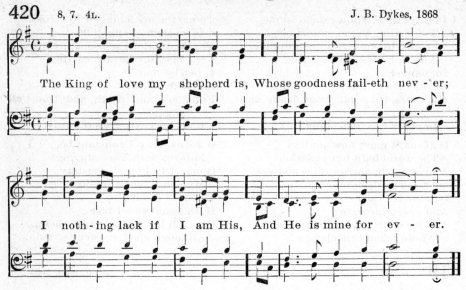

The King of love my shepherd is, Whose goodness fail-eth nev-er;
I noth-ing lack if I am His, And He is mine for ev-er.

2 Where streams of living waters flow
  My ransomed soul He leadeth,
  And where the verdant pastures grow,
  With food celestial feedeth.

3 Perverse and foolish, oft I strayed,
  But yet in love He sought me,
  And on His shoulder gently laid,
  And home, rejoicing, brought me.

4 In death's dark vale I fear no ill
  With Thee, dear Lord, beside me,
  Thy rod and staff my comfort still
  Thy cross before to guide me.

5 Thou spread'st a table in my sight,
  Thy unction grace bestoweth;
  And, O the transport of delight
  With which my cup o'erfloweth!

6 And so through all the length of days
  Thy goodness faileth never;
  Good Shepherd! may I sing Thy praise
  Within Thy house for ever.

  Sir H. W. Baker, 1868

Seventh Sunday after Trinity

421 C. M.   W. Croft, 1708

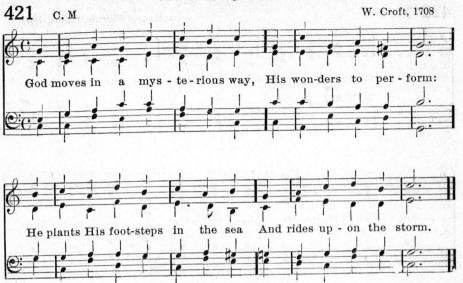

God moves in a mys-te-rious way, His won-ders to per-form:

He plants His foot-steps in the sea And rides up-on the storm.

2 Deep in unfathomable mines
    Of never-failing skill,
  He treasures up His bright designs,
    And works His sovereign will.

3 Ye fearful saints, fresh courage take:
    The clouds ye so much dread
  Are big with mercy, and shall break
    In blessings on your head.

4 Judge not the Lord by feeble sense,
    But trust Him for His grace;
  Behind a frowning providence
    He hides a smiling face.

5 His purposes will ripen fast,
    Unfolding every hour.
  The bud may have a bitter taste,
    But sweet will be the flower.

6 Blind unbelief is sure to err,
    And scan His works in vain;
  God is His own interpreter,
    And He will make it plain.

                                      W. Cowper. 1774

The Church Year

422 L. M.

Cantionale Sacrum, Gotha, 1654

O gra-cious Hand that free-ly gives The fruit of earth, our toil to bless! O Love, by which the sin-ner lives, O let our tongue that love con-fess!

2 Our God for all our need provides;
His sun alike o'er all doth shine;
From none his glorious beams he hides;
So rich, so free, His love divine.

3 Again this love our garners fills;
This love again let all adore;
The cry of want this bounty stills,
Who biddeth all His name implore.

4 O may our lives through grace abound,
In holy fruits and Thee proclaim!
Let all Thy courts with praises sound
Thy gracious hand, Thy wondrous name.

5 Lord, when Thou shalt descend from heaven,
Thy ransomed harvest here to reap,
O in that day Thy joy be given
To those who now go forth and weep.

A. T. Russell, 1851

Eighth Sunday after Trinity

423 C. M.

Nicolaus Hermann, 1560

Straight is the gate to heaven a - bove, And nar - row is the
way; Yet there is room in God's great love For
thee, for thee al - way, For thee, for thee al - way.

2 In Paradise there still is room,
   There still is room for thee;
   For thee the Savior hath a home,
   ‖:Where heavenly mansions be.:‖

3 Though thousand times ten thousands stand
   White-robed in glory there,
   There is a place at God's right hand
   ‖:For thee in heaven so fair.:‖

4 In Jesus' heart there still is room,
   In heaven is room also,
   The gospel message bids thee come,
   ‖:Praise God who loves thee, too.:‖

5 Now God be praised, who even me
   A glorious diadem
   Will grant when I His glory see
   ‖:In His Jerusalem.:‖

Lina Sandell. ca. 1860

424 8, 7, 8, 7, 8, 8, 7. Erfurter Enchiridion, 1524

Look down, O Lord, from heaven be-hold, And let Thy pit-y
wak - en! How few the flock with-in Thy fold, Neg-lect-ed and forsak - - en! Men suf-fer not Thy word to stand, And
faith seems quenched on eve-ry hand, Dark times have us o'er-tak - en.

2 With frauds which they themselves invent
   The truth they have confounded:
Their hearts are not with one consent
   On Thy pure doctrine grounded;
And, whilst they gleam with outward
They lead Thy people to and fro,[show,
   In error's maze astounded.

3 God surely will uproot all those
   Who with deceits now store us;
With haughty tongue they God op-
   pose,
   And say, "Who stands before us?
By right or might we shall prevail;
What we determine cannot fail,
   For who can lord it o'er us?"

Eighth Sunday after Trinity

4 Then saith our God: I will arise,
These wolves My flock are rending;
I've heard My people's bitter sighs
To heaven, My throne, ascending:
My saving word for them shall fight
And fearlessly and sharply smite,
The poor with might defending.

5 As silver tried by fire is pure
From all adulteration;
So, through God's word, shall men
endure
Each trial and temptation:

Its worth gleams brighter through
the cross,
And, purified from human dross,
It shines through every nation.

6 Defend, O God, Thy truth, and stay
This evil generation;
And from the error of their way
Keep Thine own congregation.
The wicked everywhere abound,
And would Thy little flock confound,
Which, Lord, forbid them. Amen

M. Luther, 1524

425 C. M.

W. H. Havergal, 1846

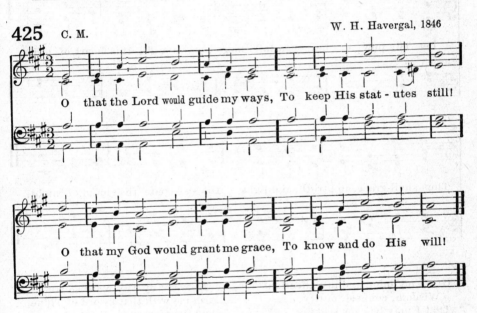

O that the Lord would guide my ways, To keep His stat-utes still!

O that my God would grant me grace, To know and do His will!

2 Order my footsteps by Thy word,
And make my heart sincere;
Let sin have no dominion, Lord,
But keep my conscience clear.

3 Assist my soul, too apt to stray,
A stricter watch to keep;
And should I e'er forget Thy way,
Restore Thy wandering sheep.

4 Make me to walk in Thy commands;
'Tis a delightful road:
Nor let my head, or heart, or hands,
Offend against my God.

I. Watts, 1719

426 8, 7, 8, 7, 7, 7.

J. Chr. Bach, 1693

Come, O come, Thou quickening Spir-it, Thou for-ev-er art di-vine;

Let Thy pow-er nev-er fail me, Al-ways fill this heart of mine;

Thus shall grace, and truth, and light, Dis-si-pate the gloom of night.

2 Grant my mind and my affections
  Wisdom, counsel, purity,
That I may be ever seeking
  Naught but that which pleases Thee,
Let Thy knowledge spread and grow,
And all error overthrow.

3 Lead me to green pastures, lead me
  By the true and living way;
Shield me from each strong tempta-
    tion,
  That might lead my heart astray;
And if e'er my feet should turn,
For each error let me mourn.

4 Holy Spirit, strong and mighty,
  Thou who makest all things new,
Make Thy work within me perfect,

  Help me by Thy word so true,
Arm me with that sword of Thine,
And the victory shall be mine.

5 In the faith, O make me steadfast;
  Let not Satan, death, or shame,
Of my confidence deprive me;
  Lord, my refuge is Thy name
When the flesh inclines to ill,
Let Thy word prove stronger still.

6 And when my last hour is nearing,
  O assure me ever more,
As the chosen heir of heaven,
  Of that bliss for me in store,
Greater far than tongue can tell,
There, redeemed by Christ, to dwell.

H. Held, ca. 1664

427 L. M.

German, 1543

Lord Je-sus Christ, with us a-bide, For round us falls the e-ven-tide; Nor let Thy word, that heaven-ly light, For us be ev-er veiled in night.

2 While sin and death around we see,
   O grant that we may constant be;
   And pure retain, till life is spent,
   Thy precious word and sacrament.

3 Dear Savior, help, Thy Church up-
   hold;
   For we are sluggish, thoughtless,
   cold;
   Indue Thy word with power and grace,
   And spread its truth in every place.

4 Yes, leave us but Thy word, we pray;
   The fatal wiles of Satan stay;
   O smile upon Thy Church; give grace,
   And courage, patience, love, and peace.

5 O God! how sin's dread works abound,
   Throughout the earth no rest is found;
   And wide has falsehood's spirit spread,
   And error boldly rears its head.

6 And ever is there something new
   Devised to change Thy doctrines true;
   Lord Jesus! as Thou still dost reign,
   Those vain, presumptuous minds re-
   strain;

7 And as the cause and glory, Lord,
   Are Thine, not ours, do Thou afford
   Us help and strength and constancy,
   And keep us ever true to Thee.

8 Thy word shall fortify us hence,
   It is Thy Church's sure defense;
   O let us in its power confide,
   That we may seek no other guide.

9 Here on Thy word in faith we lean,
   There Thou shalt be forever seen;
   And when our journey endeth here,
   Receive us, Lord, in glory there.

N. Selnecker, 1572

428   8, 7, 8, 7, 4, 4, 7, 4, 4, 7.

H. Thomissöns Salmebog, 1569

Withhold not, Lord, the help I crave, Forsake not, nor for-get me,

For from the cra-dle to the grave A thousand foes be-set me.

A-las! Thy child, Deceived, beguiled, To guide him-self un-a-ble,

In devious ways Of er-ror strays, Blind, fee-ble, and un-sta-ble.

2 To guard and keep me, never cease,
　From all that is defiling;
Preserve me also from false peace,
　When life is smooth and smiling.
　　Should dangers rise,
　　And me surprise,
And clouds around me gather,
　　Teach me to pray,
　　And childlike say,
"Help me, my God and Father!"

3 Let me throughout my life esteem
　Thy word as precious manna,
And make Thy name my constant
　My song and my Hosanna; [theme,
　　Thy Son alone
　　The gracious throne,
Where I may find compassion;
　　His precious blood
　　My strength and food,
And shield against temptation.

4 Then take not, Lord, Thy hand away,
  Withdraw not Thy protection,
But grant me to the grave, I pray,
  Thy guidance and direction.
    At my last end
    I will commend
To Thee my soul and spirit;
    Then shall I be,
    My God, with Thee,
And endless joy inherit.

C. J. P. Spitta, 1843

429 S. M.

German Chorale
Adapted by W. H. Havergal, 1793—1870

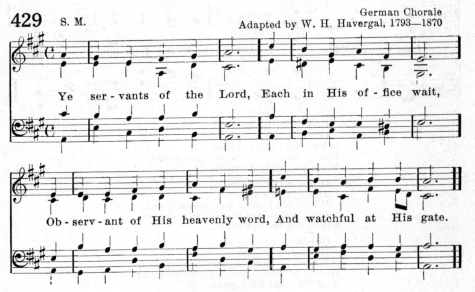

Ye ser-vants of the Lord, Each in His of-fice wait,

Ob-serv-ant of His heavenly word, And watchful at His gate.

2 Let all your lamps be bright,
  And trim the golden flame;
Gird up your loins, as in His sight,
  For awful is His name.

3 Watch! 'tis your Lord's command;
  And while we speak, He's near.
Mark the first signal of His hand,
  And ready all appear.

4 O happy servant he,
  In such a posture found!
He shall His Lord with rapture see,
  And be with honor crowned.

5 Christ shall the banquet spread
  With His own royal hand,
And raise the faithful servant's head
  Amid th' angelic band.

P. Doddridge. Publ. 1755

430 4, 4, 7, 7, 6.

German, 1628

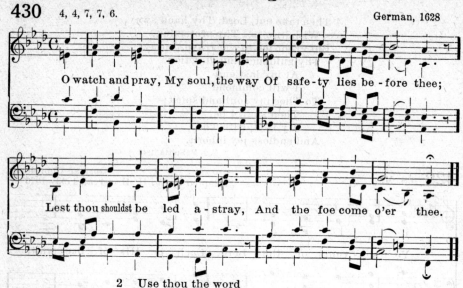

O watch and pray, My soul, the way Of safe-ty lies be-fore thee;

Lest thou shouldst be led a-stray, And the foe come o'er thee.

2 Use thou the word
Of God, thy Lord;
All else is unavailing;
Every thought and passion guard
With this shield unfailing.

3 O make thy choice
The Spirit's voice
When He comes to remind thee;
Then shall peace thine heart rejoice,
Satan get behind thee.

4 One secret thought
With evil fraught,
Which in the heart was cherished,
Havoc of God's grace hath wrought,
And the soul hath perished.

5 Our evil mind,
To sin inclined,
Is drawn by sin around us;
If a wicked thought we mind,
Satan soon hath bound us.

6 One word from hell
Cast its foul spell
On Adam with temptation;
So by one man all men fell
Under condemnation.

7 Each soul astray
From Christ, the way,
Should keep God's people humble;
Jesus warns, "O watch and pray,
Lest ye fall and stumble."

8 Be on your guard,
Keep watch and ward
Beware of Satan's cunning!
Watch and pray and trust your Lord
Till ye see Him coming!

H. A. Brorson, 1735

431   6. 6L.

J. Barnby, 1838—96

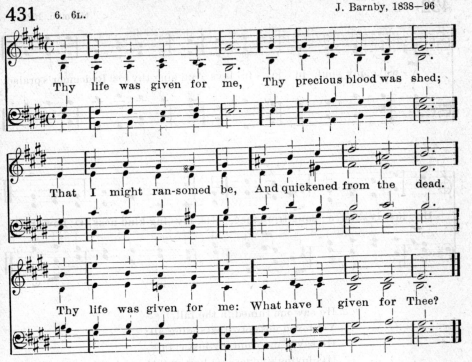

Thy life was given for me, Thy precious blood was shed;

That I might ran-somed be, And quickened from the dead.

Thy life was given for me: What have I given for Thee?

2 Long years were spent for me
  In weariness and woe,
That through eternity
  Thy glory I might know.
Long years were spent for me:
Have I spent one for Thee?

3 Thy Father's home of light,
  Thy rainbow-circled throne,
Were left for earthly night,
  For wanderings sad and lone.
Yea, all was left for me:
Have I left aught for Thee?

4 And Thou hast brought to me,
  Down from Thy home above,
Salvation full and free,
  Thy pardon and Thy love.
Great gifts Thou broughtest me:
What have I brought to Thee?

5 O let my life be given,
  My years for Thee be spent,
World-fetters all be riven,
  And joy and suffering blent!
Thou gavest Thyself for me;
I give myself for Thee.

Frances R. Havergal, 1858

432 L. M.

German, 1524

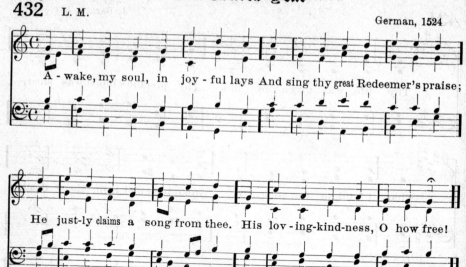

A-wake, my soul, in joy-ful lays And sing thy great Redeemer's praise;

He just-ly claims a song from thee. His lov-ing-kind-ness, O how free!

2 He saw me ruined in the fall,
Yet loved me notwithstanding all;
He saved me from my lost estate,
His lovingkindness, O how great!

3 Though numerous hosts of mighty foes;
Though earth and hell my way oppose,
He safely leads my soul along.
His lovingkindness, O how strong!

4 When trouble, like a gloomy cloud,
Has gathered thick and thundered loud,
He near my soul has always stood,
His lovingkindness, O how good!

5 Often I feel my sinful heart,
Prone from my Savior to depart;
But though I oft have Him forgot,
His lovingkindness changes not.

6 Soon shall I pass the gloomy vale,
Soon all my mortal powers must fail;
O may my last expiring breath
His lovingkindness praise in death.

M. Medley, 1782

Tenth Sunday after Trinity

433 L. M.

H. K. Oliver, 1832

God call-ing yet!— shall I not hear? Earth's pleasures

shall I still hold dear? Shall life's swift pass - ing

years all fly, And still my soul in slum-bers lie?

2 God calling yet!— shall I not rise?
Can I His loving voice despise,
And basely His kind care repay?
He calls me still: can I delay?

3 God calling yet! and shall He knock
And I my heart the closer lock?
He still is waiting to receive,
And shall I dare His Spirit grieve?

4 God calling yet!—and shall I give
No heed, but still in bondage live?
I wait, but He does not forsake;
He calls me still: My heart, awake!

5 Ah, yield Him all; in Him confide:
Where but with Him doth peace abide?
Break loose, let earthly bonds be riven,
And let the spirit rise to heaven!

6 God calling yet! — I cannot stay;
My heart I yield without delay:
Vain world, farewell! from thee I part;
The voice of God hath reached my heart!

G. Tersteegen, 1735

434 8, 7. 8L.

German, 1525

Thy love, O gra-cious Lord and God, All oth-er loves ex-

cel - - - ling, At-tunes my heart to sweet ac-cord,

And pass-es power of tell-ing; For when Thy wondrous love I see,

My heart yields glad sub-mis- -sion; I love Thee for Thy

Tenth Sunday after Trinity

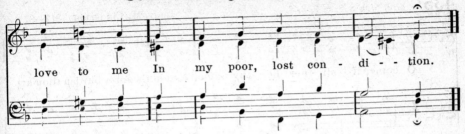

love   to   me   In   my   poor,   lost   con - di - - tion.

2 Yea, Thou hast loved our fallen race,
   And rather than condemn us,
   Cast out and banish from Thy face,
   Thine only Son didst send us;
   Who died upon the cross, that we
   Should all be saved forever;
   Hence Jesus also died for me,
   My soul, forget it never.

3 Thy love, O God, embraces all,
   And Jesus' merits cover
   The guilt of all, both great and small,
   The world of sinners over.
   Thy Spirit doth Thy light afford
   To all who will receive it,
   And from Thy knowledge bars Thy
      word
   No soul who will believe it.

4 But what hath moved Thee, gracious
      Lord?
   Why is Thine heart still yearning,
   Since the great world rejects Thy
      word,
   Thy love and mercy spurning?
   For men go on in sin each day
   In carnal-minded blindness,
   And O how few Thy call obey,
   And heed Thy lovingkindness!

5 In us no beauty Thou couldst see,
   And no intrinsic merit;
   We all were poor—but misery
   And sin we did inherit.
   We wandered each a different path,
   And in our lost condition,
   By nature children of His wrath,
   Whom sin doomed to perdition.

6 Our virtues and our own good deeds
   With God cannot avail us;
   With these the enemy misleads,
   Such righteousness shall fail us;
   Our will and strength and soul are
      dead
   In evil inclination;
   Christ Jesus has the ransom paid,
   And gained for us salvation.

7 O gracious God, Thy loving heart
   Was full of sweet compassion;
   And felt our woe and desperate smart,
   And planned our restoration;
   Thy grace and justice found a way
   To save us from death's horror;
   And everlasting judgment stay,
   And give us joy for sorrow.

8 On Christ, the rock, I'm anchored
      fast,
   By faith in Him remaining;
   I'll weather every stormy blast,
   My peace of soul retaining;
   On Father, Son, and Holy Ghost,
   My ever firm foundation,
   Until the harbor bar is crossed,
   And I see God's salvation.

9 O Jesus, at my dying breath
   Hold Thou my hand securely,
   And may I in a living faith
   Hold fast to Thee most surely;
   That my last prayer to Thee may rise,
   My soul to Thee commending,
   And I shall find in Paradise
   The joys of life unending.

T. Kingo, 1699

467

435 8, 9, 8, 9, 8, 8, 9, 9, 8, 8.

Ludv. M. Lindeman, 1812—87

O come, if sin-ner be thy name, And sin's sore burden thou art feel-ing, To Him who nev-er put to shame The suppliant at His foot-stool kneel-ing. Why wilt thou gloom for glo-ry choose, And His free gift of life re-fuse? Wilt thou vile bond-age love for ev-er, When

Tenth Sunday after Trinity

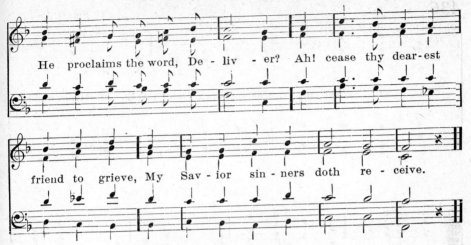

He proclaims the word, De - liv - er? Ah! cease thy dear-est

friend to grieve, My Sav - ior sin - ners doth re - ceive.

2 Come, heavy laden, bending low,
  Come as thou canst, to Him returning;
If 'neath the weight thou'rt weak and slow,
  Yet creep,—who found Him any spurning?
Fear not, His heart in love doth beat;
If thou art slow, He hastes to meet.
Long hath He called with warm entreaty;
His soul doth melt in deepest pity:
So come, poor worm, this may relieve,
My Savior sinners doth receive.

3 Say not: My sins are crimson dyed,
  I've scorned His mercy's richest treasure,
His call I've mocked, His threats defied,
  Now wrath is mine in fullest measure.
Go seek Him, if thy heart be bent,
And earnestly its sin repent,
His grace o'ersteps guilt's every mountain,
And opens free the cleansing fountain.
Hope on,—this word can all retrieve,
My Savior sinners doth receive.

4 Yet say not: I may still delay,
  Taste of sin's joy, and be forgiven,
God will not yet this very day
  Close the wide gate of grace and heaven.
His gift He offers; hasten thou
With both thy hands and seize it now;
He who dreams on, by sin deluded,
Will find himself at last excluded;
Burst now the net thy foe doth weave,
Now Jesus sinners doth receive.

5 Friend of the sinner, in Thy grace,
  Teach us to seek Thy succor speedy;
Reveal to anxious souls Thy face,
  To us, to all the poor and needy.
When conscience feels sin's bitter smart,
Show us Thy pierced and open heart;
When anguish on our soul is preying,
Let us not stand, in doubt delaying;
Let each one say: Lord, I believe;
'Tis done—me Jesus doth receive.

L. F. F. Lehr, ca. 1733

436   8, 7. 8L.   H. Smart, 1867

I will sing my Mak-er's prais-es, And in Him most

joy-ful be, For in all things I see tra-ces Of the good He

mean-eth me: Noth-ing else but love could move Him

With such sweet and ten-der care All who try to

Tenth Sunday after Trinity

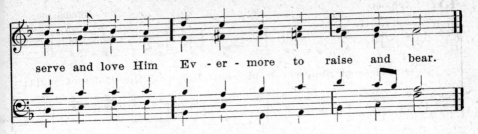

serve and love Him   Ev - er - more   to   raise   and   bear.

2 Yea, so dear doth He esteem me,
    That the Son He loves so well
He hath given to redeem me
    From the quenchless flames of hell;
Well of life that springeth ever!
    Sea of love that hath no ground!
Fruitless were my best endeavor
    Depth of love like Thine to sound.

3 All which for my soul is needful
    He will carefully provide
Nor of that is he unheedful
    Which my body needs beside:
When my strength cannot avail me—
    At the best a broken reed—
God appears; He will not fail me
    In the time of utmost need.

4 As a father ne'er removeth
    All his love for some lost child,
But the prodigal still loveth,
    Yearning to be reconciled;
So my sins and many errors
    Find a tender pardoning God,
Who doth not with penal terrors
    Chasten them, but with the rod.

5 All His blows and scourges truly
    For the moment grievous prove,
And yet, when I weigh them duly,
    Are but tokens of His love;
Proofs that He is watching o'er me,
    And would, by the cross and rod,
From this wicked world restore me
    To my Father and my God.

6 Since then neither change nor coldness
    In His precious love can be,
Lo! I lift my hands with boldness,
    As a child I come to Thee.
Grant me grace, O God, I pray Thee,
    That I may with all my might
Love, and trust Thee, and obey Thee,
    Till I reach the realms of light.
                                    P. Gerhardt. 1653

The Church Year

437   7, 6. 8L.   F. Mendelssohn

O bless-ed Sun, whose splen-dor Dis - pels the shades of night;

O Je - sus, my de - fend - er, My soul's su-preme de - light,—

Though fortune should be - reave me Of all I love the best,

(If) If Thou Thy love still leave me, I free - ly give the rest.

2 I know no life divided,
  O Lord of life, from Thee;
In Thee is life provided
  For all mankind and me;
I know no death, O Jesus,
  Because I live in Thee;
Thy death it is which frees us
  From death eternally.

3 I fear no tribulation,
  Since, whatsoe'er it be,
It makes no separation
  Between my Lord and me.

If Thou, my God, my teacher,
  Vouchsafe to be my own,
Though poor, I shall be richer
  Than monarch on his throne.

4 If, while on earth I wander,
  My heart is light and blest,
Ah, what shall I be yonder,
  In perfect peace and rest?
O blessed thought in dying,
  We go to meet the Lord,
Where there shall be no sighing,
  A kingdom our reward.

C. J. P. Spitta, 1833

Eleventh Sunday after Trinity

438 11, 10. 4L.

Samuel Webbe, 1792

Come, ye dis-con-so-late, wher-e'er ye lan-guish,
Come to the mer-cy-seat, fer-vent-ly kneel;
Here bring your wound-ed hearts, here tell your an-guish;
Earth has no sor-row that Heaven can-not heal.

2 Joy of the desolate, light of the straying,
   Hope of the penitent, fadeless and pure,
Here speaks the Comforter, tenderly saying,
   Earth has no sorrow that Heaven cannot cure.

3 Here see the bread of life, see waters flowing
   Forth from the throne of God, pure from above;
Come to the feast of love, come, ever knowing
   Earth has no sorrow but Heaven can remove.

T. Moore, 1816. v. 3. T. Hastings, 1832

439 7, 6. 8L.

J. Barnby, 1883

I lay my sins on Je - sus, The spot - less Lamb of God;

He bears them all, and frees us From the ac - curs - ed load.

I bring my guilt to Je - sus, To wash my crim - son stains

White in His blood most pre - cious, Till not a stain re - mains.

2 I lay my wants on Jesus;
　All fullness dwells in Him;
He heals all my diseases,
　He doth my soul redeem:
I lay my griefs on Jesus,
　My burdens and my cares;
He from them all releases,
　He all my sorrows shares.

474

Eleventh Sunday after Trinity

3 I rest my soul on Jesus,
    This weary soul of mine;
His right hand me embraces,
    I on His breast recline:
I love the name of Jesus,
    Immanuel, Christ, the Lord:
Like fragrance on the breezes
    His name abroad is poured.

4 I long to be like Jesus,
    Meek, loving, lowly, mild;
I long to be like Jesus,
    The Father's Holy Child:
I long to be with Jesus
    Amid the heavenly throng,
To sing with saints His praises,
    To learn the angels' song.

H. Bonar. 1843

440 C. M.

Scotch Psalter, 1615

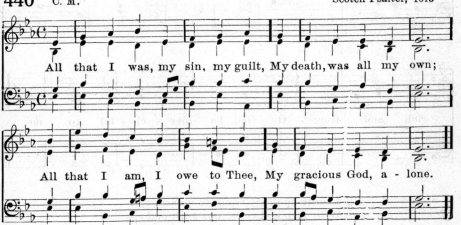

All that I was, my sin, my guilt, My death, was all my own;

All that I am, I owe to Thee, My gracious God, a - lone.

2 The evil of my former state
    Was mine, and only mine;
The good in which I now rejoice
    Is Thine, and only Thine.

3 The darkness of my former state,
    The bondage, all was mine;
The light of life in which I walk,
    The liberty, is Thine.

4 Thy grace first made me feel my sin,
    It taught me to believe;
Then in believing, peace I found,
    And now I live, I live.

5 All that I am, e'en here on earth,
    All that I hope to be
When Jesus comes and glory dawns,
    I owe it, Lord, to Thee.

475 H. Bonar. 1853

441 L. M.

J. B. Dykes, 1823—76

With brok-en heart and con - trite sigh, A trembling sin - ner, Lord, I cry: Thy pardoning grace is rich and free: O God, be mer - ci - ful to me.

2 I smite upon my troubled breast,
With deep and conscious guilt oppressed;
Christ and His cross my only plea:
O God, be merciful to me.

3 Far off I stand with tearful eyes,
Nor dare uplift them to the skies;
But Thou dost all my anguish see,
O God, be merciful to me.

4 Nor alms, nor deeds that I have done
Can for a single sin atone;
To Calvary alone I flee:
O God, be merciful to me.

5 And when, redeemed from sin and hell,
With all the ransomed throng I dwell,
My raptured song shall ever be,
God has been merciful to me.

Cornelius Elven, 1852

Eleventh Sunday after Trinity

142 C .M.

Arr. by L. Mason, 1836

Ap - proach, my soul, the mer - cy - seat,

Where Je - sus an - swers prayer; There hum - bly fall be-

fore His feet, For none can per - ish there.

2 Thy promise is my only plea,
   With this I venture nigh;
   Thou callest burdened souls to Thee,
   And such, O Lord, am I.

3 Bowed down beneath a load of sin,
   By Satan sorely pressed,
   By wars without and fears within,
   I come to Thee for rest.

4 Be Thou my shield and hiding-place,
   That, sheltered near Thy side,
   I may my fierce accuser face,
   And tell him, Thou hast died.

5 O wondrous love, to bleed and die,
   To bear the cross and shame,
   That guilty sinners, such as I,
   Might plead Thy gracious name!

J. Newton, 1779

477

443 9, 8, 9, 8, 8, 8.   Twelfth Sunday after Trinity   J. D. Meier, 1692
Arr. by Chr. Möck, d. 1818

O would, my God, that I could praise Thee With
thousand tongues, by day and night! How many a song my lips should
raise Thee, Who or-der'st all things here a - right! My thankful
heart would ev - er be Tell - ing what God hath done for me.

2 O all ye powers that He implanted,
   Arise, keep silence thus no more,
Put forth the strength that He hath granted,
   Your noblest work is to adore;
O soul and body, make ye meet
With heartfelt praise your Lord to greet.

3 Ye forest leaves so green and tender,
   That dance for joy in summer air;
Ye meadow-grasses bright and slender,
   Ye flowers so wondrous sweet and fair;
Ye live to show His praise alone.
Help me to make His glory known.

4 O all things that have breath and motion;
   That throng with life, earth, sea, and sky,
 Now join me in my heart's devotion,
   Help me to raise His praises high.
 My utmost powers can ne'er aright
 Declare the wonders of His might.

5 But I will tell, while I am living,
   His goodness forth with every breath,
 And greet each morning with thanksgiving,
   Until my heart is still in death.
 Nay, when at last my lips grow cold,
 His praise shall in my sighs be told.

6 O Father, deign Thou, I beseech Thee,
   To listen to my earthly lays;
 A nobler strain in heaven shall reach Thee,
   When I with angels hymn Thy praise,
 And learn amid their choirs to sing
 Loud Hallelujahs to my King.

J. Mentzer, 1704

444   L. M.

J Hatton, d. 1793

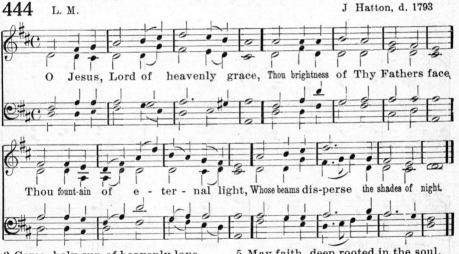

O Jesus, Lord of heavenly grace, Thou brightness of Thy Fathers face, Thou fount-ain of e-ter-nal light, Whose beams dis-perse the shades of night.

2 Come, holy sun of heavenly love,
  Send down Thy radiance from above;
  And to our inmost hearts convey
  The Holy Spirit's cloudless ray.

3 And we the Father's help will claim,
  And sing the Father's glorious name:
  His powerful succor we implore,
  That we may stand, to fall no more.

4 May He our actions deign to bless,
  And loose the bonds of wickedness;
  From sudden falls our feet defend,
  And guide us safely to the end.

5 May faith, deep rooted in the soul,
  The flesh subdue, the mind control:
  May guile depart, and discord cease,
  And all within be joy and peace.

6 O hallowed thus be every day!
  Let meekness be our morning ray,
  And faithful love our noonday light,
  And hope our sunset, calm and bright.

7 O Christ, with each returning morn,
  Thine image to our hearts is borne:
  O may we ever clearly see
  Our Savior and our God in Thee!

Ambrose of Milan, (340-397)

The Church Year

9, 8, 9, 8, 8, 8.

German, Hamburg, 1690

Begone! vain world, with all thy pleasures, And keep thy joys far from my sight; In thee and in thy tempting treas-ures My soul no long-er finds de-light. The world may seek and love its own: I love my Je-sus, Him a-lone.

2 He is my glory and my treasure,
My wisdom and my soul's delight,
In Him I find my sweetest pleasure
And all my comfort day and night.
The world may seek and love its own:
I love my Jesus, Him alone.

3 In weakness He my strength abideth,
He comforts me, when sad my lot;
In gloom of death He light provideth,
In death as life He fails me not.
The world may seek and love its own:
I love my Jesus, Him alone.

Twelfth Sunday after Trinity

4 He rules on high, His throne shall
   never
   Like earthly empires pass away,
   His kingdom stands and grows for-
   ever,
   Till all creation owns His sway.
   The world may seek and love its own:
   I love my Jesus, Him alone.

5 He is the fairest—all excelling—
   He whom the world refused to know,

His riches are beyond all telling,
   And these He doth on me bestow.
   The world may seek and love its own,
   I love my Jesus, Him alone.

6 Now let me be despised, forsaken,
   And in a humble state remain,
   Soon I to glory shall be taken,
   And with my Savior ever reign.
   The world may seek and love its own:
   I love my Jesus, Him alone.

J. Scheffler, 1657
H. A. Brorson, 1734

446 C. M.

T. Haweis, 1733—1820

O for a thou-sand tongues to sing My dear Re-
deem-er's praise, The glo--ries of my
God and King, The tri-umphs of His grace!

2 My gracious Master and my God,
   Assist me to proclaim,
   To spread, through all the earth
   The honors of Thy name. [abroad,

3 Jesus! the name that charms our fears,
   That bids our sorrows cease;
   'Tis music in the sinner's ears;
   'Tis life, and health, and peace.

4 He breaks the power of reigning sin,
   He sets the prisoner free;
   His blood can make the foulest clean;
   His blood availed for me.

5 He speaks, and, listening to His voice,
   New life the dead receive;
   The mournful, broken hearts rejoice;
   The humble poor believe.

C. Wesley, 1738

The Church Year

447 L. M.

W. B. Bradbury, 1849

Just as I am, with-out one plea, But that Thy blood was shed for me, And that Thou bid'st me come to Thee, O Lamb of God, I come, I come.

2 Just as I am and waiting not
   To rid my soul of one dark blot,
   To Thee, whose blood can cleanse each spot,
   O Lamb of God, I come, I come.

3 Just as I am, though tossed about
   With many a conflict, many a doubt,
   Fightings and fears within, without,
   O Lamb of God, I come, I come.

4 Just as I am, poor, wretched, blind;
   Sight, riches, healing of the mind,
   Yea, all I need, in Thee to find,
   O Lamb of God, I come, I come.

5 Just as I am, Thou wilt receive,
   Wilt welcome, pardon, cleanse, relieve;
   Because Thy promise I believe,
   O Lamb of God, I come, I come.

6 Just as I am; Thy love unknown
   Has broken every barrier down;
   Now to be Thine, yea, Thine alone,
   O Lamb of God, I come, I come.

Charlotte Elliott, 1836

Thirteenth Sunday after Trinity

448 8, 7, 8, 7, 8, 8, 7, 7.

Ludv. M. Lindeman, 1812—87

Love, the fount of light from heav-en, Is the root and source of life;

Therefore God's de-crees are giv - en With His lov - ing-kind-ness rife,

As our Sav - ior God de - clar - eth, And the Spir-it witness bear-eth,

As we in God's peace do prove, God is light and God is love.

2 Love doth crown the life eternal,
   Love the brightness is of light,
Therefore on His throne supernal
   Jesus sits in glory bright;
He, the light and life of heaven,
Who Himself for us hath given,
   Still abides and reigns above
   In His Father's boundless love.

3 Love, alone the law fulfilling,
   Is the bond of perfectness,
Love, who came a victim willing,
   Paid our debt and brought us peace;
Therefore love and peace in union
Ever grow in sweet communion,
   And through love we may abide
   One with Him who for us died.

N. F. S. Grundtvig, 1853

449 8, 7. 8L.

J. Rosenmüller, 1648

Lord of glo - ry, Thou hast bought us With Thy
life - blood as the price, Nev - er grudg - ing for the
lost ones That tre - men-dous sac - ri - fice, And with that hast
free - ly giv - en Bless-ings count-less as the sand, To th' un-
thank-ful and the e - vil With Thine own un - spar-ing hand.

Thirteenth Sunday after Trinity

2 Grant us hearts, dear Lord, to yield
   Gladly, freely of Thine own;[Thee,
With the sunshine of Thy goodness
   Melt our thankless hearts of stone;
Till our cold and selfish natures,
   Warmed by Thee, at length believe
That more happy and more blessed
   'Tis to give than to receive.

3 Wondrous honor hast Thou given
   To our humblest charity,
In Thine own mysterious sentence,
   "Ye have done it unto Me."

Can it be, O gracious Master,
   Thou dost deign for alms to sue,
Saying, by Thy poor and needy,
   "Give as I have given to you?"

4 Lord of glory, who hast bought us
   With Thy life-blood as the price,
Never grudging for the lost ones
   That tremendous sacrifice.
Give us faith, to trust Thee boldly
   Hope to stay our souls on Thee:
But, O best of all Thy graces,
   Give us Thine own charity.

Eliza S. Alderson, 1864

450   8, 8, 8, 6.   J. Barnby, 1883

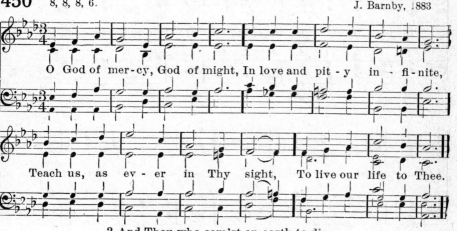

O God of mer-cy, God of might, In love and pit-y in - fi - nite,

Teach us, as ev - er in Thy sight, To live our life to Thee.

2 And Thou who cam'st on earth to die,
   That fallen man might live thereby,
   O hear us, for to Thee we cry;
     In hope, O Lord, to Thee.

3 Teach us the lesson Thou hast taught,
   To feel for those Thy blood hath bought,
   That every word, and deed, and thought,
     May work a work for Thee.

4 For all are brethren, far and wide,
   Since Thou, O Lord, for all hast died;
   Then teach us, whatsoe'er betide,
     To love them all in Thee.

5 In sickness, sorrow, want or care,
   Whate'er it be, 'tis ours to share;
   May we, where help is needed, there
     Give help as unto Thee.

6 And may Thy Holy Spirit move
   All those who live, to live in love,
   Till Thou shalt greet in heaven above
     All those who give to Thee.

451   8, 6, 8, 6, 6, 6, 7, 6.   Ludv. M. Lindeman, 1812—87

Come, brethren, let us hast-en on! The eve-ning clos-eth round;

'Tis per-il-ous to lin-ger here On this wild des-ert ground.

Come, toward e-ter-ni-ty, Press on from strength to strength,

Nor dread your journey's toil and length, For good its end shall be.

2 We shall not rue our final choice,
　　Though straight our path and steep;
　We know that He who called us here,
　　His word shall ever keep.
　　　Then follow, trusting, come,
　And let each set his face
　Toward yonder fair and blessed place,
　　Intent to reach our home.

3 Come, children, let us onward go!
　　We travel hand in hand;
　Each in his brother find his joy
　　In this wild stranger land.
　　　As children let us be,
　Nor by the way fall out,
　The angels guard us round about,
　　And help us brotherly.

4 Let all the strong be quick to raise
  The weaker when they fall;
Let love and peace and patience bloom
  In ready help for all.
  In love yet closer bound,
Each would be least, yet still
On love's fair path most pure from ill,
  Most loving would be found.

5 Come, brothers, wander on with joy,
  For shorter grows the way,
The hour that frees us from the flesh
  Draws nearer day by day.
  A little truth and love,
A little courage yet,
More free from earth, more apt to set
  Your hopes on things above.

6 It will not last for very long,
  A little farther roam;
It will not last much longer now
  Ere we shall reach our home;
  There shall we ever rest,
There with our Father dwell,
With all the saints who served Him
  There truly, deeply blest.   [well,

7 Friend of our dear and perfect choice,
  Thou joy of all that live,
Being that know'st not chance or
    change,
  What courage dost Thou give!
  All beauty, Lord, we see,
All bliss and life and love,
In Him in whom we live and move,
  And we are glad in Thee.

G. Tersteegen, 1738

452   8, 8, 8, 4.   F. A. G. Ouseley, 1825—89

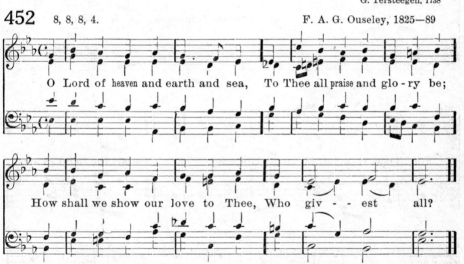

O Lord of heaven and earth and sea, To Thee all praise and glo-ry be;

How shall we show our love to Thee, Who giv--est all?

2 The golden sunshine, vernal air,
  Sweet flowers and fruit, Thy love de-
    clare:
When harvests ripen, Thou art there,
    Who givest all.

3 For peaceful homes, and healthful
    days,
For all the blessings earth displays,
We owe Thee thankfulness and
    Who givest all.   [praise,

4 Thou didst not spare Thine only Son,
But gav'st Him for a world undone,
And freely with that blessed One
    Thou givest all.

5 Thou giv'st the Spirit's holy dower,
Spirit of life, and love, and power,
And dost His sevenfold graces shower
    Upon us all.

6 For souls redeemed, for sins forgiven,
For means of grace and hopes of
    heaven,
What can to Thee, O Lord, be given,
    Who givest all?

7 We lose what on ourselves we spend.
We have, as treasure without end,
Whatever, Lord, to Thee we lend,
    Who givest all.

8 Whatever, Lord, we lend to Thee,
Repaid a thousand fold will be;
Then gladly will we give to Thee
    Who givest all,—

9 To Thee, from whom we all derive,
Our life, our gifts, our power to give:
O may we ever with Thee live,
    Who givest all!

C. Wordsworth, 1653

The Church Year

453 9, 8, 9, 8, 9, 9, 8.

Ludv. M. Lindeman, 1812—87

As aft - er the wa-ter-brooks pant - eth The hart, when it

sinks in the chase, So thirsteth my soul, as it faint - eth,

For Thee, O my God, and Thy grace; For Thou art the fount ev-er-

liv - - - ing, Who un - to the thirst-y art giv - - - ing

The wa - ter of life that I need.

Fourteenth Sunday after Trinity

2 By day and by night in her anguish
My soul is lamenting in woe:
O Lord, in my grief I must languish,
No counsel, no help do I know;
When shall I Thy mercy awaken?
When shall I, the poor and forsaken,
Before Thee appear, O my God?

3 Great fears now my bosom are rend-
ing,
For near the abyss I am brought,
My way on the brink I am wending,
My journey with peril is fraught;
I faint, I see terrors appalling,
And into the deep I am falling—
O hearken, O Lord, to my cries!

4 Thou, Thou art my rock of salva-
tion,
My house I have built upon Thee;
O if Thou shouldst fail as founda-
tion,
My ruin it surely would be;
Lord, deep unto deep now is calling,
Thy waves and Thy billows appalling
Arise to go over my soul.

5 When others sing anthems of glad-
ness,
And offer thanksgiving and praise,
I sit in the gloom of my sadness
And hear not the anthems they raise;
My song is the voice of my sighing,
The festal days pass in my crying—
I languish in grief and in woe.

6 Why art thou disquiet within me?
Why art thou cast down, O my soul?
Confide in thy God, let Him win thee!
Still hope in thy God, Him extol!
For surely once dawneth a morrow,
When, freed from thy care and thy
sorrow,
Thou praises shalt sing to thy God.

7 His light and His truth, they shall
lead me
In peace to His temple at last;
I rest on His word, He will speed me,
And conflict and sorrow are past;
Yea, joyful I anthems will raise Him.
With heart and with voice will I
praise Him—
My health and my life and my God.

N. F. S. Grundtvig, 1812

454 C. M.   S. Howard, 1750

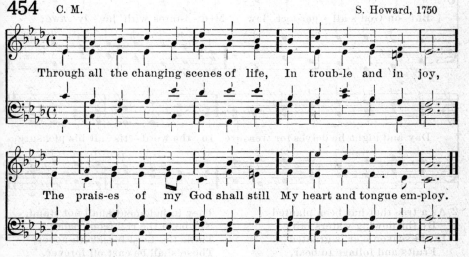

Through all the changing scenes of life, In trouble and in joy,

The praises of my God shall still My heart and tongue employ.

2 Of His deliverance I will boast,
Till all that are distressed,
From mine example comfort take,
And soothe their griefs to rest.

3 O magnify the Lord with me,
With me exalt His name;
When in distress to Him I called,
He to my rescue came.

4 The hosts of God encamp around
The dwellings of the just;

Deliverance He affords to all
Who on His succor trust.

5 O make but trial of His love,
Experience will decide
How blest are they, and only they,
Who in His truth confide.

6 Fear Him, ye saints, and you will
Have nothing else to fear;   [then
Make but His service your delight,
Your wants shall be His care.

Tate and Brady, 1696

The Church Ye

455   8, 7, 8, 7, 7, 7, 8, 8.

Johann Schop, 1642

Bless-ed is the man that nev - er Doth in god-less counsel meet;

Nor in sin-ners' way stands ev - er, Nor sits in the scorner's seat,

But on God's all - per-fect law Med - i-tates with ho - ly awe;

Day and night he delves for treasure In the word—'tis all his pleasure.

2 As a tree that has been planted
  By the flowing waters fair,
In its season e'er is granted
  Fruits and foliage to bear,
So is he, the righteous, seen
Ever fruitful, ever green,
And his leaf shall wither never,
All he does shall prosper ever.

3 To the wicked 'tis not given
  Such a happy lot to share;
As the chaff by wind is driven
  So shall the ungodly fare;

They in judgment shall not stand,
Nor be in the righteous band:
These the Lord forsaketh never,
Those shall be cast off forever.

4 For the Lord His people knoweth,
  His pure eyes behold their way,
And the blessing He bestoweth
  Is their heritage for aye:
But the wicked ever tend
To their doom and to their end:
God will all the righteous cherish,
But the wicked ones shall perish.

P. Gerhardt, 1553
M. B. Landstad, 1861

456 6, 6, 4, 6, 6, 6, 4.   L. Mason, 1832

My faith looks up to Thee, Thou Lamb of Cal-va-ry,
Sav-ior di-vine; Now hear me while I pray; Take all my
guilt a-way; O let me from this day Be whol-ly Thine.

2 May Thy rich grace impart
  Strength to my fainting heart,
    My zeal inspire;
  As Thou hast died for me,
  O may my love to Thee
  Pure, warm, and changeless be,
    A living fire.

3 While life's dark maze I tread,
  And griefs around me spread,
    Be Thou my guide;
  Bid darkness turn to day,
  Wipe sorrow's tears away,
  Nor let me ever stray
    From Thee aside.

4 When ends life's transient dream,
  When death's cold, sullen stream
    Shall o'er me roll;
  Blest Savior, then, in love,
  Fear and distrust remove;
  O bear me safe above—
    A ransomed soul!

491   R. Palmer. 1830

457 6, 7, 6, 7, 6, 6, 6, 6.

Meiningisches Gesangbuch, 1693

O God, Thou faith-ful God, Thou foun-tain ev - er flow - ing,

With - out whom noth-ing is, All per - fect gifts be - stow - ing;

A pure and health-y frame O give me, and with - in

A conscience free from blame, A soul un - hurt by sin.

2 And grant me, Lord, to do,
  With ready heart and willing,
Whate'er Thou shalt command,
  My calling here fulfilling;
And do it when I ought,
  With all my strength, and bless
The work I thus have wrought,
  For Thou must give success.

3 And let me promise naught
  But I can keep it truly,
Abstain from idle words,
  And guard my lips still duly;

And grant, when in my place
  I must and ought to speak,
My words due power and grace;
  Nor let me wound the weak.

4 If dangers gather round,
  Still keep me calm and fearless:
Help me to bear the cross
  When life is dark and cheerless;
To overcome my foe
  With words and actions kind;
When counsel I would know,
  Good counsel let me find.

Fifteenth Sunday after Trinity

5 And let me be with all
   In peace and friendship living,
As far as Christians may;
   And if Thou aught art giving
Of wealth and honors fair,
   O this refuse me not,
That naught be mingled there
   Of goods unjustly got.

6 And if a longer life
   Be here on earth decreed me,
And Thou through many a strife
   To age at last wilt lead me,
Thy patience in me shed,
   Avert all sin and shame,
And crown my hoary head
   With pure untarnished fame.

7 Let nothing that may chance,
   Me from my Savior sever:
And dying with Him, take
   My soul to Thee for ever;
And let my body have
   A little space to sleep
Beside my fathers' grave,
   And friends that o'er it weep.

8 And when the end is come,
   And all the dead are waking,
O reach me down Thy hand,
   Thyself my slumbers breaking;
Then let me hear Thy voice,
   And change this earthly frame,
And bid me aye rejoice
   With those who love Thy name.

J. Heermann, 1630

458   7s. 4L.   L Pleyel, 1790

Chil-dren of the heavenly King, As ye jour-ney, sweetly sing;

Sing your Sav-ior's wor-thy praise, Glo-rious in His works and ways.

2 We are traveling home to God,
   In the way the fathers trod;
They are happy now, and we
   Soon their happiness shall see.

3 Lift your eyes, ye sons of light,
   Zion's city is in sight;
There our endless home shall be,
   There our Lord we soon shall see.

4 Fear not, brethren; joyful stand
   On the borders of your land;
Jesus Christ, your Father's Son,
   Bids you undismayed go on.

5 Lord, obediently we go,
   Gladly leaving all below;
Only Thou our leader be,
   And we still will follow Thee.

J. Cennick, 1742

The Church Year

459   8, 8, 6, 8, 8, 6.   H. W. Hardy

O Love divine, how sweet Thou art! When shall I find my willing heart

All tak-en up by Thee? I thirst, I faint, I die to prove

The greatness of re-deem-ing love, The love of Christ to me.

2 Stronger His love than death or hell;
  Its riches are unsearchable;
    The first-born sons of light
  Desire in vain its depths to see,
  They cannot reach the mystery,
    The length, and breadth, and height.

3 God only knows the love of God:
  O that it now were shed abroad
    In this poor stony heart!
  For love I sigh, for love I pine:
  This only portion, Lord, be mine,
    Be mine this better part.

4 O that I could for ever sit
  Like Mary at the Master's feet!
    Be this my happy choice:
  My only care, delight, and bliss,
  My joy, my heaven on earth, be this,
    To hear the Bridegroom's voice!

C. Wesley, 1749

Fifteenth Sunday after Trinity

460 7, 6. 8L.

M. Teschner, 1613

In ho - ly con-tem - pla - tion We sweet-ly now pur-sue

The theme of God's sal - va - tion, And find it ev - er new.

Set free from pres-ent sor - row, We cheer-ful - ly can say,

Let the unknown to - mor - row Bring with it what it may.

2 It can bring with it nothing,
　　But He will bear us through;
　Who gives the lilies clothing
　　Will clothe His people too.
　Beneath the spreading heavens
　　No creature but is fed;
　And He who feeds the ravens
　　Will give His children bread.

3 Though vine or fig tree neither
　　Their wonted fruit should bear;
　Though all the field should wither,
　　Nor flocks nor herds be there;
　Yet God the same abiding,
　　His praise shall tune my voice;
　For while in Him confiding,
　　I cannot but rejoice.

W. Cowper, 1779

The Church Year

461 11, 10. 8L.

Schörring's Koralbog, 1781

Je-sus, I long for Thy bless-ed com-mun - ion, Yearning for

Thee fills my heart and my mind; Draw me from all that would

hin-der our un - ion, May I to Thee, my be - gin-ning, be joined;

Show me more clear-ly my hope-less con - di - tion; Show me the

depth of cor - rup-tion in me, So that my na - ture may

Fifteenth Sunday after Trinity

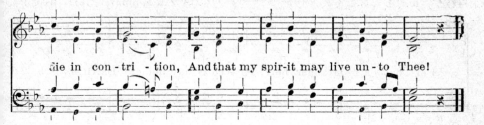

die in con-tri-tion, And that my spir-it may live un-to Thee!

2 Mightily strengthen my spirit within
    me,
    That I may learn what Thy Spirit
      can do;
O take Thou captive each passion and
    win me,
    Lead Thou and guide me my whole
      journey through!
All that I am and possess I surrender,
    If Thou alone in my spirit mayst
      dwell,
Everything yield Thee, O Savior
    most tender,
    Thou, only Thou, canst my sadness
      dispel.

3 O that I only might learn consecra-
    tion,
    Make full surrender of heart day by
      day!
O that my Jesus might be my sole
    portion,
    I am, alas! all too far, far away.
Jesus, whose voice full of love's
    gentle warning,
    Gladly I follow, O give me Thy
      hand,
That in pure holiness, faith's bright
    adorning,
    Like a true Christian I walk to the
      end.

4 Jesus, O hear Thou Thy dove's gentle
    cooing!
    Shepherd, go seek the lost, wander-
      ing lamb!
Thou, who hast won me by love's ten-
    der wooing,
    Cleanse Thou my heart from its sin
      and its shame.
May I not be like a sepulchre whited,
    Fair and all beautiful outside alone:
But may Thy law in my heart be in-
    dited,
    That in full truth I may call me
      Thine own.

5 Jesus, when shall I find rest in th'
    haven?
    Heavy the burden, remove it from
      me!
When shall I see Thee, my Savior
    in heaven?
    Rise, Lord, and quiet the wild troub-
      led sea!
O loving Jesus, show mercy right
    speedy;
    Hide not Thy countenance always
      from me;
Thou, purest wealth of the inwardly
    needy;
    Fill Thou my heart, precious Sav-
      ior, with Thee!

6 Jesus, my love let not go unrequited:
    See my poor soul growing weary,
      O Lord,
Let us, Immanuel, now be united,
    When Thou art with me, my soul is
      restored.
Once Thou didst say, "They will hun-
    ger and perish,
    If I permit them to go on their
      way;"
Love everlasting! Refuse not to
    nourish
    Souls that are hungering for frag-
      ments today.

7 Merciful Jesus, now hear how I bind
    Thee
    To the sure pledge of Thy covenant
      word:
"Ask, and receive: when ye seek, ye
    shall find me;"
    Thus have Thy lips, ever faithful,
      averred.
I with the woman of Canaan unrest-
    ing,
    Cry after Thee till my longing is
      stilled,
Till Thou shalt add, my petitions at-
    testing,
    "Amen, yea, amen: it be as thou
      wilt!"

German, Anon., 1712
P. J. Hygom, ca. 1740

The Church Year

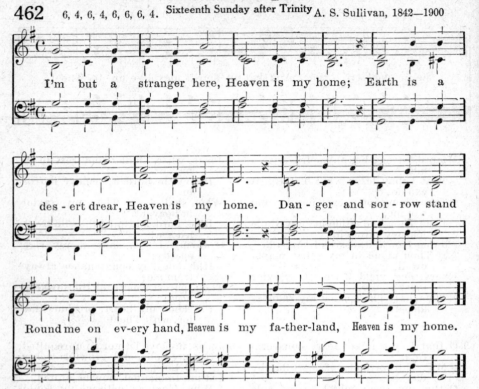

I'm but a stranger here, Heaven is my home; Earth is a
des - ert drear, Heaven is my home. Dan - ger and sor - row stand
Round me on ev-ery hand, Heaven is my fa-ther-land, Heaven is my home.

2 What though the tempests rage?
    Heaven is my home;
  Short is my pilgrimage,
    Heaven is my home;
  And time's wild wintry blast
  Soon shall be overpast,
  I shall reach home at last;
    Heaven is my home.

3 There, at my Savior's side,
    Heaven is my home;
  May I be glorified,
    Heaven is my home;
  There are the good and blest,
  Those I love most and best,
  Grant me with them to rest;
    Heaven is my home.

4 Therefore I murmur not,
    Heaven is my home;
  Whate'er my earthly lot,
    Heaven is my home.
  And I shall surely stand
  There at my Lord's right hand,
  Heaven is my fatherland:
    Heaven is my home!

Thomas R. Taylor, 1835

Sixteenth Sunday after Trinity

463 8, 7, 8, 7, 7, 7.

C. H. Dretzel, 1731

Je - sus wept! those tears are o - ver, But His heart is still the same;

Kinsman, friend, and el - der broth-er, Is His ev - er - last-ing name.

Sav-ior, who can love like Thee, Gracious One of Beth-a - ny?

2 When the pangs of trial seize me,
　　When the waves of sorrow roll,
　I will lay my head on Jesus,
　　Pillow of the troubled soul.
　Surely none can feel like Thee,
　Weeping One of Bethany.

3 Jesus wept! and still in glory
　　He can mark each mourner's tear:
　Living to retrace the story
　　Of the hearts He solaced here;
　Lord, when I am called to die,
　Let me think of Bethany.

4 Jesus wept! that tear of sorrow
　　Is a legacy of love;
　Yesterday, today, tomorrow,
　　He the same doth ever prove.
　Thou art all in all to me,
　Living One of Bethany.

John R. Macduff, 1853

The Church Year

7s. 4L.

German medieval
Adapted by Luther or J. Walther, 1524

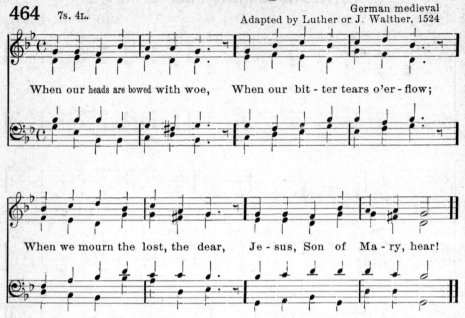

When our heads are bowed with woe, When our bit-ter tears o'er-flow;

When we mourn the lost, the dear, Je-sus, Son of Ma-ry, hear!

2 Thou our throbbing flesh hast worn,
Thou our mortal griefs hast borne,
Thou hast shed the human tear;
Jesus, Son of Mary, hear!

3 When the solemn death-bell tolls
For our own departing souls,
When our final doom is near,
Jesus, Son of Mary, hear!

4 Thou hast bowed the dying head,
Thou the blood of life hast shed,

Thou hast filled a mortal bier;
Jesus, Son of Mary, hear!

5 When the heart is sad within
With the thought of all its sin,
When the spirit shrinks with fear,
Jesus, Son of Mary, hear!

6 Thou the shame, the grief, hast known,
Though the sins were not Thine own;
Thou hast deigned their load to bear;
Jesus, Son of Mary, hear!

H. H. Milman, 1827

7s. 4L.   *Second Tune.*   R. Redhead, 185)

When our heads are bowed with woe, When our bit-ter tears o'erflow;

Sixteenth Sunday after Trinity

When we mourn the lost, the dear, Je - sus, Son of Ma - ry, hear!

465 7, 6, 7, 6. Melchior Vulpius, 1609

Long hast thou wept and sor-rowed, Poor mourner, dry thy tears;

Be - hold, with light and com - fort, Je - sus Him-self ap - pears.

2 All other hope must perish,
  All earthly props decay;
Then let the seed be buried,
  The husk be blown away.

3 Yet think not God has granted
  But to recall again,—
His gifts of love and goodness
  Shall ever thine remain.

4 The seed, before it flourish,
  Must low in darkness lie:
And love, to live for ever,
  Must for a season die.

5 But those like thee, bereavèd
  Within earth's darkened home,
Are rich in many a promise
  And pledge, of joys to come.

6 "Trust in my mercy ever,
  My people!" saith the Lord;
Hold fast in deepest sorrow
  That soul-sustaining word.

7 The harvest day is hasting—
  The rest from toil and pain,
When those who sleep in Jesus
  Shall come with Him again.

8 And, more than all the treasures
  That morning shall restore,
Himself, Himself shall meet thee,
  Thy portion evermore!

9 Then rest, sad heart, in patience,
  With this petition still,
"Lord, all these vacant places
  With Thine own fullness fill!"

Meta Heusser-Schweizer, 1837

The Church Year

466 6, 4, 6, 4, 6, 6, 4.

L. Mason, 1792-1872

Near - er, my God, to Thee, Near - er to Thee!

E'en though it be a cross That rais - eth me;

Still all my song shall be, Near - er, my God, to Thee,

Near - er, my God, to Thee, Near - er to Thee!

2 Though like the wanderer,
    The sun gone down,
Darkness be over me,
    My rest a stone;
Yet in my dreams I'd be
Nearer, my God, to Thee,
    Nearer to Thee!

3 There let the way appear
    Steps unto heaven;
All that Thou sendest me
    In mercy given;
Angels to beckon me
Nearer, my God, to Thee!
    Nearer to Thee!

4 Then, with my waking thoughts
    Bright with Thy praise,
Out of my stony griefs,
    Bethel I'll raise;
So by my woes to be
Nearer, my God, to Thee,
    Nearer to Thee!

5 Or if on joyful wing,
    Cleaving the sky,
Sun, moon, and stars forgot,
    Upward I fly,
Still all my song shall be,
Nearer, my God, to Thee,
    Nearer to Thee!

502

Sarah F. Adams, 1841

467   8s. 6L.   J. Goss, 1800—80

O Je-sus, source of calm re-pose, Thy like no man nor an-gel knows,

Fair-est a-mong ten thousand fair! E'en those whom death's sad fet-ters bound,

Whom thickest darkness compassed round, Find light and life, if Thou ap-pear.

2 Renew Thine image, Lord, in me,
  Lowly and gentle may I be;
    No charms but these to Thee are dear;
  No anger may'st Thou ever find,
  No pride, in my unruffled mind,
    But faith, and heaven-born peace, be there.

3 A patient, a victorious mind,
  That life and all things cast behind,
    Springs forth obedient to Thy call.
  A heart that no desire can move,
  But still to adore, believe, and love,
    Give me, my Lord, my life, my all!

              J. A. Freylinghausen, 1704

468 7, 8, 7, 8, 7, 6, 7, 6, 7, 6, 7, 6.

Hans Kugelmann, 1540

One is our God and Fa - ther! The flock and all its shepherds cry;

One Spir - it us doth gath - er, One is our Lord, who reigns on high;

One well of life doth lave us, One hope our souls in - spires,

One faith, our stay, doth save us, One love us ev - er fires,

One peace our spir - its bless - es, One fight for our re - ward,

Seventeenth Sunday after Trinity

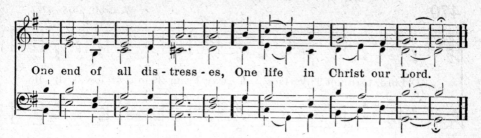

One end of all dis-tress-es, One life in Christ our Lord.

2 One in the Spirit's union,
　　We onward march, a pilgrim throng,
And sing in sweet communion
　　The ransomed Zion's victor-song;
Through night and tribulation,
　　Through death our way we wend,
With hope and expectation
　　To see our journey's end—
The cross, the grave, death's prison,
　　We leave behind, and rise
To meet our Savior risen,
　　And enter Paradise.

B. S. Ingemann, 1843

469 S. M.

Samuel S. Wesley, 1810—76

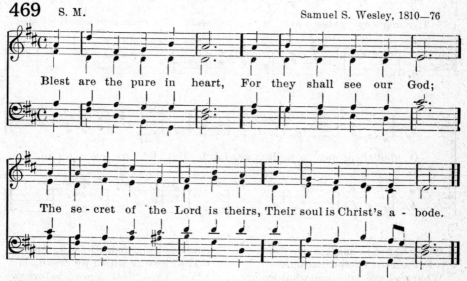

Blest are the pure in heart, For they shall see our God;

The se-cret of the Lord is theirs, Their soul is Christ's a - bode.

2 The Lord, who left the heavens,
　　Our life and peace to bring,
To dwell in lowliness with men,
　　Their pattern and their King,—

3 He to the lowly soul
　　Doth still Himself impart,

And for His dwelling and His throne,
　　Chooseth the pure in heart.

4 Lord, we Thy presence seek;
　　May ours this blessing be:
Give us a pure and lowly heart,
　　A temple meet for Thee.

J. Keble, 1819, et al.

470 3, 6. 8L.   W. Croft, 1678—1727

O Lord, turn not Thy face a - way From them that low - ly lie,

La-ment-ing sore their sin - ful life, With tears and bit - ter cry.

Thy mer - cy gates are o - pen wide To them that mourn their sin;

O shut them not a - gainst us, Lord, But let us en - ter in.

2 We need not to confess our fault,
　For surely Thou canst tell;
What we have done, and what we are,
　Thou knowest very well.
Wherefore, to beg and to entreat,
　With tears we come to Thee,
As children that have done amiss
　Fall at their father's knee.

3 And need we, then, O Lord, repeat
　The blessing which we crave,
When Thou dost know, before we
　　speak,
　The thing that we would have?
Mercy, O Lord, we mercy ask,
　This is the total sum;
For mercy, Lord, is all our prayer;
　O let Thy mercy come!

J. Marckant, 1661

Seventeenth Sunday after Trinity

471 7, 6. 8L.

Samuel S. Wesley, 1364

O day of rest and glad-ness, O day of joy and light,

O balm of care and sad-ness, Most beau-ti-ful, most bright,

On thee the high and low-ly, Through a-ges joined in tune,

Sing ho-ly, ho-ly, ho-ly! To the great God Tri-une.

2 On thee, at the creation,
　The light first had its birth;
On thee for our salvation,
　Christ rose from depths of earth;
On thee our Lord, victorious,
　The Spirit sent from heaven;
And thus on thee, most glorious,
　A triple light was given.

3 Thou art a port protected
　From storms that round us rise;
A garden intersected
　With streams of Paradise;
Thou art a cooling fountain,
　In life's dry, dreary sand;
From thee, like Pisgah's mountain,
　We view our promised land.

4 Today on weary nations
　The heavenly manna falls;
To holy convocations
　The silver trumpet calls,
Where gospel-light is glowing
　With pure and radiant beams,
And living water flowing
　With soul-refreshing streams.

5 New graces ever gaining
　From this our day of rest,
We reach the rest remaining
　To spirits of the blest.
To Holy Ghost be praises;
　To Father, and to Son;
The Church her voice upraises
　To Thee, blest Three in One.

C. Wordsworth, 186?

The Church Year

472 · 7, 6. 8L.

Eighteenth Sunday after Trinity

J. Stainer, 1840—1901

I could not do with-out Thee, O Sav-ior of the lost,

Whose won-drous love re-deemed me, At such tre-men-dous cost;

Thy righteousness, Thy par-don, Thy precious blood must be

My on-ly hope and com-fort, My glo-ry and my plea.

2 I could not do without Thee,
  I cannot stand alone,
I have no strength or goodness,
  No wisdom of my own;
But Thou, beloved Savior,
  Art all in all to me;
And weakness will be power
  If leaning hard on Thee.

3 I could not do without Thee,
  For O the way is long,
And I am often weary,
  And sigh replaces song:
How could I do without Thee?
  I do not know the way;
Thou knowest, and Thou leadest.
  And wilt not let me stray.

Eighteenth Sunday after Trinity

4 I could not do without Thee,
O Jesus, Savior dear;
E'en when my eyes are holden,
I know that Thou art near.
How dreary and how lonely
This changeful life would be,
Without the sweet communion,
The secret rest with Thee!

5 I could not do without Thee,
For years are fleeting fast,
And soon in solemn loneliness
The river must be passed;
But Thou wilt never leave me,
And though the waves roll high,
I know Thou wilt be near me,
And whisper, "It is I."

Frances R. Havergal, 1873

473 C. M.

Arr. by L. Mason, 1836

Fa - ther, what - e'er of earth - ly bliss
Thy sover - eign will de - nies,
Ac - cept-ed at Thy
throne of grace, Let this pe - ti - tion rise:

2 Give me a calm, a thankful heart,
From every murmur free;
The blessings of Thy grace impart,
And let me live to Thee.

3 Let the sweet hope that Thou art mine
My path of life attend;
Thy presence through my journey shine,
And bless its happy end.

Anne Steele, 1760

The Church Year

Henri F. Hemy, 1865
Altered by J. G. Walton, 1871

474　8s. 6L.

Thee will I love, my strength, my tower, Thee will I love, my
joy, my crown; Thee will I love with all my power,
In all my works, and Thee a - lone: Thee will I
love, till the pure fire Fill my whole soul with chaste de - sire.

2 I thank Thee, uncreated Sun,
　　That Thy bright beams on me have shined;
I thank Thee, who hast overthrown
　　My foes, and healed my wounded mind;
I thank Thee, whose enlivening voice
Bids my freed heart in Thee rejoice.

3 Uphold me in the doubtful race,
　　Nor suffer me again to stray;
Strengthen my feet, with steady pace
　　Still to press forward in Thy way;
That all my powers, with all their might,
In Thy sole glory may unite.

Eighteenth Sunday after Trinity

4 Thee will I love, my joy, my crown;
   Thee will I love, my Lord, my God!
  Thee will I love, beneath Thy frown
   Or smile, Thy scepter or Thy rod.
  What though my flesh and heart decay?
  Thee shall I love in endless day.

J. Scheffler, 1657

475   L. M.   W. Knapp, 1698—1768

O Je-sus, cru-ci-fied for man, O Lamb, all glo--rious on Thy throne, Teach Thou our wonder-ing souls to scan The mys-tery of Thy love un-known.

2 We pray Thee, grant us strength to take
   Our daily cross, whate'er it be,
  And gladly for Thine own dear sake
   In paths of pain to follow Thee.

3 As on our daily way we go,
   Through light or shade, in calm or strife,
  O may we bear Thy marks below
   In conquered sin and chastened life.

4 And week by week this day we ask
   That holy memories of Thy cross
  May sanctify each common task,
   And turn to gain each earthly loss.

5 Grant us, dear Lord, our cross to bear
   Till at Thy feet we lay it down,
  Win through Thy blood our pardon there,
   And through the cross attain the crown.

W. W. How 1871

The Church Year

476   8s. 6L.   J. Stainer, 1875

Thou hid-den love of God, whose height, Whose depth un-fath-omed no man knows,

I see from far Thy beauteous light, In-ly I sigh for Thy repose:

Voices in unison.   *Harmony.*

My heart is pained, nor can it be At rest, till it find rest in Thee.

2 Is there a thing beneath the sun
   That strives with Thee my heart to share?
   Ah! tear it thence, and reign alone,
   The Lord of every motion there.
   Then shall my heart from earth be free,
   When it hath found repose in Thee.

3 O hide this self from me, that I
   No more, but Christ in me, may live!
   My base affections crucify,
   Nor let one favorite sin survive;
   In all things nothing may I see,
   Nothing desire, or seek, but Thee.

4 Each moment draw from earth away
   My heart that lowly waits Thy call!
   Speak to my inmost soul, and say:
   I am thy love, thy God, thy all!
   To feel Thy power, to hear Thy voice,
   To taste Thy love, be all my choice!
                                    G. Tersteegen, 1729

Nineteenth Sunday after Trinity

477   7, 6. 8L.

H. L. Hassler, 1601

O Je-sus, our sal-va-tion, Low at Thy cross we lie:

Lord, in Thy great com-pas-sion, Hear, our be-wail-ing cry.

We come to Thee with mourn-ing, We come to Thee in woe;

With con-trite hearts re-turn-ing, And tears that o-ver-flow.

2 O gracious Intercessor!
   O Priest within the veil,
Plead for each lost transgressor
   The blood that cannot fail.
We spread our sins before Thee,
   We tell them one by one:
O, for Thy name's great glory,
   Forgive all we have done.

3 O, by Thy cross and passion,
   Thy tears and agony,
And crown of cruel fashion,
   And death on Calvary;

By all that untold suffering,
   Endured by Thee alone;
O Priest, O spotless Offering,
   Plead, for Thou didst atone!

4 And in these hearts now broken
   Re-enter Thou and reign,
And say, by that dear token,
   We are absolved again.
And build us up, and guide us,
   And guard us day by day;
And in Thy presence hide us,
   And take our sins away.

James Hamilton, 1867

The Church Year

478   8s. 6L.   Schumann's Gesangbuch, 1539

Now I have found the ground where-in Sure my soul's an-chor may re-main— The wounds of Je-sus, for my sin Be-fore the world's foun-da-tion slain; Whose mer-cy shall un-shak-en stay, When heaven and earth are fled a-way.

2 Father, Thine everlasting grace
  Our scanty thought surpasses far,
  Thy heart still melts with tender-
       ness,
  Thy arms of love still open are,
  Returning sinners to receive,
  That mercy they may taste and live.

3 O Love, Thou bottomless abyss,
  My sins are swallowed up in Thee!
  Covered is my unrighteousness,
  Nor spot of guilt remains on me,
  While Jesus' blood, through earth
       and skies
  Mercy, free, boundless mercy! cries.

Nineteenth Sunday after Trinity

4 With faith I plunge me in this sea,
  Here is my hope, my joy, my rest;
  Hither, when hell assails, I flee,
  I look into my Savior's breast:
  Away, sad doubt and anxious fear!
  Mercy is all that's written there.

5 Though waves and storms go o'er my
      head,
  Though strength, and health, and
      friends be gone,

Though joys be withered all and dead,
Though every comfort be withdrawn,
On this my steadfast soul relies,—
Father, Thy mercy never dies!

6 Fixed on this ground will I remain,
  Though my heart fail and flesh decay;
  This anchor shall my soul sustain,
  When earth's foundations melt away:
  Mercy's full power I then shall prove,
  Loved with an everlasting love.

J. A. Rothe, 1727

479   7, 6, 7, 6.

Kingo's Gradual, 1699

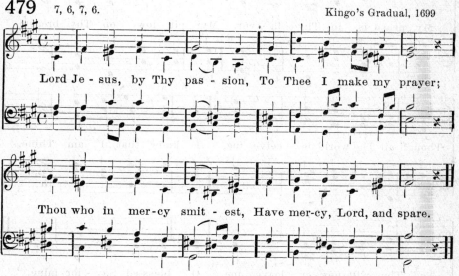

Lord Je-sus, by Thy pas-sion, To Thee I make my prayer;

Thou who in mer-cy smit-est, Have mer-cy, Lord, and spare.

2 O wash me in the fountain
   That floweth from Thy side!
 O clothe me in the raiment
   Thy blood hath purified!

3 O hold Thou up my goings,
   And lead from strength to strength,
 That unto Thee in Zion
   I may appear at length!

4 O hearken to my knocking,
   And open wide the door,
 That I may enter freely
   And never leave Thee more!

5 O bring me, loving Jesus,
   To that most blessed place,
 Where angels and archangels
   Look ever on Thy face;

6 Where gladsome Hallelujahs
   Unceasingly resound;
 Where martyrs, now triumphant,
   Walk robed in white and crowned'

7 O make my spirit worthy
   To join that ransomed throng!
 O teach my lips to utter
   That everlasting song!

8 O give that last, best blessing,
   That even saints can know,
 To follow in Thy footsteps
   Wherever Thou dost go!

9 Not wisdom, might, or glory,
   I ask to win above;
 I ask for Thee, Thee only,
   O Thou eternal Love!

Richard E. Littledale, 1864

480 7s, 6s. 8L.

A. Ewing, 1830—95

To Thee, O dear, dear Sav-ior! My spir-it turns for rest,

My peace is in Thy fa-vor, My pil-low on Thy breast;

Though all The world de-ceive me, I know that I am Thine.

And Thou wilt nev-er leave me, O bless-ed Sav-ior mine.

2 In Thee my trust abideth,
  On Thee my hope relies,
O Thou whose love provideth
  For all beneath the skies;
O Thou whose mercy found me
  From bondage set me free,
And then for ever bound me
  With threefold cords to Thee.

3 My grief is in the dullness
  With which this sluggish heart
Doth open to the fullness
  Of all Thou wouldst impart;
My joy is in Thy beauty
  Of holiness divine,
My comfort in the duty
  That binds my life in Thine.

4 Alas, that I should ever
  Have failed in love to Thee,
The only one who never
  Forgot or slighted me!
O for a heart to love Thee
  More truly as I ought,
And nothing place above Thee
  In deed, or word, or thought.

5 O for that choicest blessing
  Of living in Thy love,
And thus on earth possessing
  The peace of heaven above;
O for the bliss that by it
  The soul securely knows
The holy calm and quiet
  Of faith's serene repose!

John S. B. Monsell, 1863

Nineteenth Sunday after Trinity

481 8, 8, 8, 4, 8.

Ludv. M. Lindeman, 1812—87

My all I to my God commend, Who all doth to His
pur - pose bend; My life re - sign - ing to His will;
Mine to lie still, Or His de - signs a - lone ful - fill.

2 This earth is but a vale of tears,
Where grief on every side appears;
Sad hours of conflict, toil, and woe
    Here ebb and flow,
Till we are summoned hence to go.

3 Today with joy our hearts beat high;
Tomorrow in the grave we lie:
Though as the rose we bloom today,
    We soon decay,
And sorrow everywhere hath sway.

4 Lord, may we meditate aright
How soon we all must fade from
    sight,
How swiftly from the earth we fly,
    All born to die,
Rich, poor, wise, simple, low and high.

5 Few are our days and sad below,
Our daily bread is toil and woe:

But God in His good time will send
    A peaceful end:
Death from a foe is made a friend.

6 And though our sins against us rise
To heaven we lift our trusting eyes,
For God is merciful, and gave,
    Our souls to save,
His Son belovèd to the grave.

7 This thought in every pain and grief
Brings comfort, sweet and full relief,
That we shall rise when Christ ap-
    No more in tears,   [pears,
As now, in these our pilgrim years.

8 O Jesus Christ, the Son of God,
Who hast redeemed us with Thy
    blood,
Thy precious wounds our refuge be:
    For rest we flee,
O Lord, our only hope, to Thee.

J. Leon, 1581

The Church Pear

482   6, 5, 6, 5, 11, 6, 6, 5.   Zinck's Koralbog, 1801

O Je-sus, blest is he Who Thine a-bid-eth: Thy light his steps in peace Se-cure-ly guid-eth; On Thee our rock most high His hope en-dur - eth: Him of e-ter-nal rest, Him of e-ter-nal rest, Thy word as-sur - eth.

2 His care he casts on Thee,
  Nor evil feareth:
Him on his heavenward way
  Thy presence cheereth.
The world he leaves for Thee;
  Thou art his treasure;
‖:The joys laid up in Thee:‖
  No thought can measure.

3 What though on earth he mourn,
  His pain Thou healest;
When all is dark and drear,
  Hope Thou revealest;
Thou him in death wilt stay
  With consolation;
‖:Thou soon in bliss to be:‖
  His contemplation.

A. T. Russell. 1851

483 L. M.

S. Webbe, 1782

We sing the praise of Him who died, Of Him who died up-on the cross;

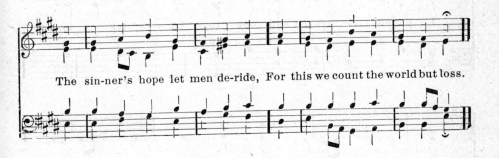

The sin-ner's hope let men de-ride, For this we count the world but loss.

2 Inscribed upon the cross we see
   In shining letters, God is love;
   He bears our sins upon the tree,
   He brings us mercy from above.

3 The cross, it takes our guilt away,
   It holds the fainting spirit up,
   It cheers with hope the gloomy day,
   And sweetens every bitter cup.

4 It makes the coward spirit brave,
   And nerves the feeble arm for fight,
   It takes the terror from the grave,   .
   And gilds the bed of death with light.

5 The balm of life, the cure of woe,
   The measure and the pledge of love,
   The sinner's refuge here below,
   The angels' theme in heaven above.

T. Kelly, 1815

484 10s. 4L.

Samuel Langford

Wea - ry of earth and la - den with my sin,
I look to heaven and long to en - ter in,
But there no e - vil thing may find a home;
And yet I hear a voice that bids me, "Come!"

2 So vile I am, how dare I hope to stand
In the pure glory of that holy land?
Before the whiteness of that throne appear?
Yet there are hands stretched out to draw me near.

3 The while I fain would tread the heavenly way,
Evil is ever with me day by day;
Yet on mine ears the gracious tidings fall,
"Repent, confess, thou shalt be loosed from all."

4 It is the voice of Jesus that I hear,
His are the hands stretched out to draw me near;
And His the blood that can for all atone,
And set me faultless there before the throne.

5 'Twas He who found me on the deathly wild,
And made me heir of heaven, the Father's child.
And day by day, whereby my soul may live,
Gives me His grace of pardon, and will give.

6 O great Absolver, grant my soul may wear
The lowliest garb of penitence and prayer,
That in the Father's courts my glorious dress
May be the garment of Thy righteousness.

7 Yea, Thou wilt answer for me, righteous Lord,
Thine all the merits, mine the great reward;
Thine the sharp thorns, and mine the golden crown,
Mine the life won, and Thine the life laid down.

8 Naught can I bring, dear Lord, for all I owe,
Yet let my full heart what it can bestow;
Myself my gift, let my devotion prove,
Forgiven greatly, how I greatly love.

S. J Stone, 1866

485 S. M.   Arr. fr. R. Schumann, 1810—56

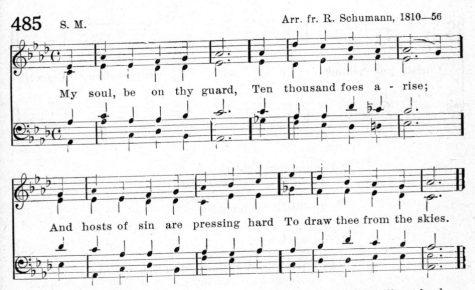

My soul, be on thy guard, Ten thousand foes a - rise;
And hosts of sin are pressing hard To draw thee from the skies.

2 O watch, and fight, and pray!
The battle ne'er give o'er;
Renew it boldly every day,
And help divine implore.

3 Ne'er think the victory won,
Nor lay thine armor down;

Thine arduous work will not be done,
Till thou obtain thy crown.

4 Fight on, my soul, till death
Shall bring thee to thy God!
He'll take thee at thy parting breath
Up to His blest abode.

George Heath, 1711

The Church Year

L. Mason, 1832

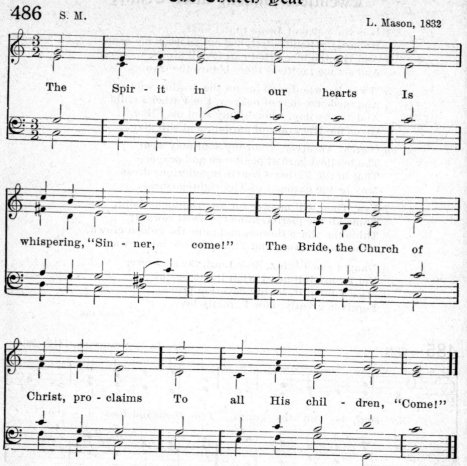

The Spir-it in our hearts Is whispering, "Sin-ner, come!" The Bride, the Church of Christ, pro-claims To all His chil-dren, "Come!"

2 Let him that heareth say
    To all about him, "Come!"
Let him that thirsts for righteousness,
    To Christ the fountain come.

3 Yes, whosoever will,
    O let him freely come,
And freely drink the stream of life,
    'Tis Jesus bids him come.

4 Lo, Jesus, who invites,
    Declares, "I quickly come:"
Lord, even so; we wait Thine hour;
    O blest Redeemer, come.

Henry U. Onderdonk, 1826

Twenty=first Sunday after Trinity

487   S. M. D.

J. Goss, 1854

Je-sus, my strength, my hope, On Thee I cast my care;
With hum-ble con-fi-dence look up, And know Thou hear'st my prayer.
Give me on Thee to wait, Till I can all things do;
On Thee, al-might-y to cre-ate, Al-might-y to re-new.

2 Give me a true regard,
   A single, steady aim,
Unmoved by threatening or reward,
   To Thee and Thy great name;
A jealous, just concern
   For Thine immortal praise;
A pure desire that all may learn
   And glorify Thy grace.

3 I rest upon Thy word;
   The promise is for me;
My succor and salvation, Lord
   Shall surely come from Thee
But let me still abide,
   Nor from my hope remove,
Till Thou my patient spirit guide
   Into Thy perfect love.

C. Wesley, 1742

The Church Year

488 8, 7. 8L.

H. Smart, 1867

What a . friend we have in Je-sus, All our sins and griefs to bear! What a priv-i-lege to car-ry Ev-ery-thing to God in prayer! O what peace we oft-en for-feit, O what need-less pain we bear— All be-cause we do not car-ry Ev-ery-thing to God in prayer!

Twenty=first Sunday after Trinity

2 Have we trials and temptations?
  Is there trouble anywhere?
We should never be discouraged;
  Take it to the Lord in prayer!
Can we find a friend so faithful,
  Who will all our sorrows share?
Jesus knows our every weakness—
  Take it to the Lord in prayer!

3 Are we weak and heavy-laden,
  Cumbered with a load of care?
Precious Savior, still our refuge!--
  Take it to the Lord in prayer!
Do thy friends despise, forsake thee?
  Take it to the Lord in prayer!
In His arms He'll take and shield
Thou wilt find a solace there. [thee.

Joseph Scriven, ca. 1855

489 S. M   James Nares, 1715—83

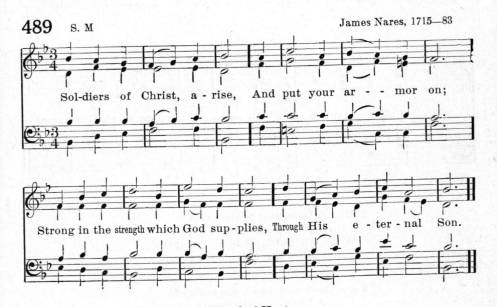

Sol-diers of Christ, a-rise, And put your ar- -mor on;

Strong in the strength which God sup-plies, Through His e-ter-nal Son.

2 Strong in the Lord of Hosts,
    And in His mighty power;
  Who in the strength of Jesus trusts
    Is more than conqueror.

3 Stand then in His great might,
    With all His strength endued;
  And take, to arm you for the fight,
    The panoply of God:

4 From strength to strength go on,
    Wrestle, and fight, and pray;
  Tread all the powers of darkness down,
    And win the well-fought day.

5 That having all things done
    And all your conflicts past,
  Ye may o'ercome, through Christ alone,
    And stand complete at last.

C. Wesley, 1749

490 C. M.

J. H. Casson, 1875

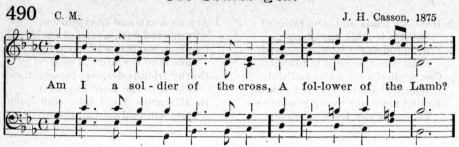

Am I a sol-dier of the cross, A fol-lower of the Lamb?

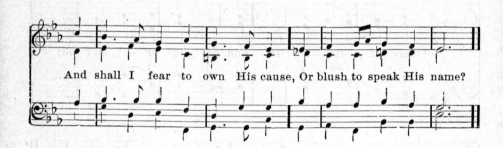

And shall I fear to own His cause, Or blush to speak His name?

2 Must I be carried to the skies
   On flowery beds of ease,
   While others fought to win the prize,
   And sailed through bloody seas?

3 Are there no foes for me to face?
   Must I not stem the flood?
   Is this vile world a friend to grace,
   To help me on to God?

4 Sure I must fight if I would reign:
   Increase my courage, Lord;
   I'll bear the cross, endure the pain,
   Supported by Thy word.

5 Thy saints, in all this glorious war,
   Shall conquer, though they die;
   They view the triumph from afar,
   And seize it with their eye.

6 When that illustrious day shall rise,
   And all Thy armies shine
   In robes of victory through the skies,
   The glory shall be Thine.

I. Watts, ca. 1723

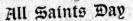

All Saints Day

H. S. Cutler, 1872

491 8, 6. 8L.

The Son of God goes forth to war, A king-ly crown to gain;

His blood-red ban-ner streams a-far, Who fol-lows in His train?

Who best can drink his cup of woe, Tri-um-phant o-ver pain,

Who pa-tient bears his cross be-low, He fol-lows in His train.

2 That martyr first, whose eagle eye
　　Could pierce beyond the grave;
Who saw his Master in the sky;
　　And called on Him to save;
Like Him, with pardon on His tongue;
　　In midst of mortal pain,
He prayed for them that did the
　　　　wrong:
　　Who follows in His train?

3 A noble band, the chosen few,
　　On whom the Spirit came,
Twelve valiant saints, their hope they
　　　　knew
　　And mocked the torch of flame;

They met the tyrant's brandished
　　The lion's gory mane,　　[steel,
They bowed their necks the stroke to
　　　　feel:
　　Who follows in their train?

4 A noble army, men and boys,
　　The matron and the maid,
Around the Savior's throne rejoice,
　　In robes of light arrayed.
They climbed the steep ascent of
　　　　heaven
　　Through peril, toil, and pain:
O God, to us may grace be given
　　To follow in their train.

R. Heber. publ. 1827

492   8, 8, 8, 6. 12L.

Ludv. M. Lindeman, 1812—87

Be-hold a host, ar-rayed in white, Like thousand snow-clad moun-tains bright,

With palms they stand—Who are this band Be - fore the throne of light?

Lo, these are they, of glo-rious fame, Who from the great af - flic-tion came

And in the flood of Je - sus' blood Are cleansed from guilt and blame;

Now gath-ered in the ho - ly place Their voic-es they in worship raise,

Their anthems swell where God doth dwell, 'Mid an - gels' songs of praise.

All Saints Day

2 Despised and scorned they sojourned
    here,
But now, how glorious they appear!
Those martyrs stand, a priestly band,
    God's throne forever near.
So oft, in troubled days gone by,
In anguish they would weep and sigh;
At home above the God of love
    For aye their tears shall dry.
They now enjoy their sabbath rest,
The paschal banquet of the blest;
The Lamb, their Lord, at festal board
    Himself is host and guest.

3 Then hail! ye mighty legions, yea,
    All hail! now safe and blest for aye;
And praise the Lord, who with His
    Sustained you on the way.   [word
Ye did the joys of earth disdain,
Ye toiled and sowed in tears and pain;
Farewell, now bring your sheaves,
    Salvation's glad refrain.   [and sing
Swing high your palms, lift up your
    song,
Yea, make it myriad voices strong:
Eternally shall praise to Thee,
    God, and the Lamb belong!

H. A. Brorson, ca. 1760

Second Tune.

Norwegian Folk-Tune

8, 8, 8, 6. 12L.

Be-hold a host, ar-rayed in white, Like thousand snow-clad mountains bright,
Lo, these are they, of glo-rious fame, Who from the great af-fliction came,

With palms they stand—Who are this band Be-fore the throne of light?
And in the flood of Je-sus' blood Are cleansed from guilt and blame;

Now gath-ered in the ho-ly place Their voic-es they in worship raise,

Their anthems swell where God doth dwell 'Mid an-gels' songs of praise.

529

493 8, 7, 8, 7, 7, 7.

A. P. Berggreen, 1849

Who are these like stars ap - pear - ing, These, before God's throne who stand? Each a gold - en crown is
wear - ing; Who are all this glo - rious band? Hal - le-
lu - jah! hark, they sing, Prais - ing loud their heavenly King.

2 Who are these of dazzling bright-
　　ness,
　These in God's own truth arrayed,
Clad in robes of purest whiteness,
　Robes whose luster ne'er shall fade,
Ne'er be touched by time's rude
　　hand?
　Whence comes all this glorious band?

3 These are they who have contended
　For their Savior's honor long,
Wrestling on till life was ended,
　Following not the sinful throng;
These, who well the fight sustained,
　Triumph by the Lamb have gained.

4 These are they whose hearts were
　　riven,
　Sore with woe and anguish tried,
Who in prayer full oft have striven
　With the God they glorified:
Now, their painful conflict o'er,
　God has bid them weep no more.

5 These, like priests, have watched and
　　waited,
　Offering up to Christ their will,
Soul and body consecrated,
　Day and night they serve Him still.
Now in God's most holy place,
　Blest they stand before His face.

H. T. Schenk, 1719

All Saints Day

494 7, 6. 8L. Samuel S. Wesley, 1864

From all Thy saints in war - fare, For all Thy saints at rest,

To Thee, O bless - ed Je - sus, All prais - es be ad - dressed

Thou, Lord, didst win the bat - tle, That they might conquerors be;

Their crowns of liv - ing glo - ry Are lit with rays from Thee.

2 Apostles, prophets, martyrs,
  And all the sacred throng,
Who wear the spotless raiment,
  Who raise the ceaseless song;
For these, passed on before us,
  Savior, we Thee adore,
And, walking in their footsteps,
  Would serve Thee more and more.

3 Then praise we God the Father,
  And praise we God the Son,
And God the Holy Spirit,
  Eternal Three in One;
Till all the ransomed number
  Fall down before the throne,
And honor, power, and glory
  Ascribe to God alone.

Earl Nelson, 1864

531

495   8, 6. 8L.

H. J. Gauntlett, 1805—76

Come, let us join our friends a - bove That have ob-tained the prize,

And on the ea - gle wings of love To joys ce - les - tial rise:

Let all the saints ter - res-trial sing, With those to glo - ry gone;

For all the servants of our King, In earth and heaven, are one.

2 One family we dwell in Him,
    One Church, above, beneath,
  Though now divided by the stream,
    The narrow stream of death:
  One army of the living God,
    To His command we bow;
  Part of His host have crossed the
    And part are crossing now. [flood,

3 Ten thousand to their endless home
    This solemn moment fly;
  And we are to the margin come,
    And we expect to die:
  His militant embodied host,
    With wistful looks we stand,
  And long to see that happy coast,
    And reach that heavenly land.

All Saints Day

4 Our old companions in distress
  We haste again to see,
And eager long for our release
  And full felicity:
E'en now by faith we join our hands
  With those that went before,
And greet the blood-besprinkled bands
  On the eternal shore.

5 Our spirits, too, shall quickly join,
  Like theirs with glory crowned,
And shout to see our Captain's sign,
  To hear His trumpet sound.
O that we now might grasp our Guide!
  O that the word were given!
Come, Lord of hosts, the waves di-
  And land us all in heaven.   [vide,

C. Wesley, 1759

R. P. Stewart, 1868

496   8, 7, 8, 7, 7, 7.

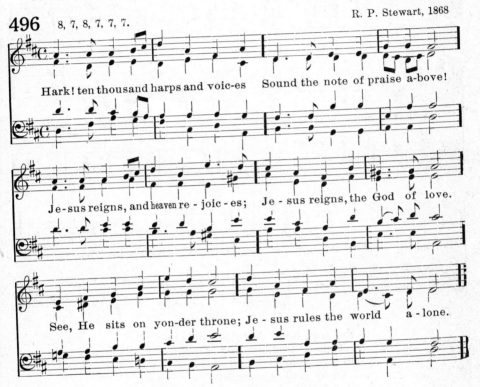

Hark! ten thousand harps and voic-es Sound the note of praise a-bove!

Je-sus reigns, and heaven re-joic-es; Je-sus reigns, the God of love.

See, He sits on yon-der throne; Je-sus rules the world a-lone.

2 Jesus, hail! Whose glory brightens
  All above, and makes it fair:
Lord of life, Thy smile enlightens,
  Cheers, and charms Thy people here.
When we think of love like Thine,
Lord, we own it love divine.

3 King of glory, reign for ever;
  Thine an everlasting crown:
Nothing from Thy love shall sever
  Those whom Thou hast made Thine own;
Happy objects of Thy grace,
Destined to behold Thy face.

4 Savior, hasten Thine appearing;
  Bring, O bring the glorious day,
When the awful summons hearing,
  Heaven and earth shall pass away.
Then, with golden harps, we'll sing,
"Glory, glory, to our King."

T. Kelly, 1806

497 8, 7, 8, 7, 8, 8. Twenty-second Sunday after Trinity   Johann Crüger, 1649

Lord, to Thee I make con-fes-sion, I have sinned and gone a-stray,

I have mul-ti-plied transgression, Chos-en for my-self my way:

Forced at last to see my er-rors, Lord, I tremble at Thy ter-rors.

2 But from Thee how can I hide me,
  Thou, O God, art everywhere;
Refuge from Thee is denied me,
  Or by land or sea or air;
Nor death's darkness can enfold me,
So that Thou shouldst not behold me.

3 Yet, though conscience' voice appall me,
  Father, I will seek Thy face;
Though Thy child I scarce dare call me,
  Yet restore me to Thy grace;
Do not for my sins forsake me,
Do not let Thy wrath o'ertake me;

4 For Thy Son hath suffered for me,
  And the blood He shed for sin,
That can heal me and restore me,
  Quench this burning fire within;
'Tis alone His cross can vanquish
These dark fears and soothe this anguish.

Twenty=second Sunday after Trinity

5 Then on Him I cast my burden,
 Sink it in the depths below!
Let me know Thy gracious pardon,
 Wash me, make me white as snow.
Let Thy Spirit leave me never,
 Make me only Thine forever!

J. Franck, 1649

498   7, 7, 7, 5. F. Filitz, 1804—1876

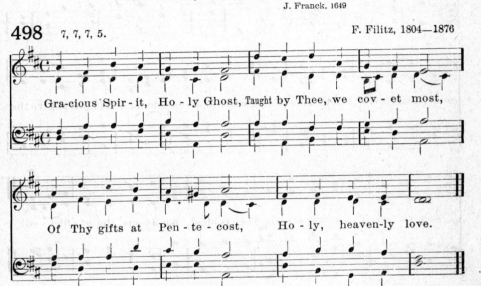

Gra-cious Spir-it, Ho-ly Ghost, Taught by Thee, we cov-et most,

Of Thy gifts at Pen-te-cost, Ho-ly, heaven-ly love.

2 Faith that mountains could remove,
 Tongues of earth or heaven above,
 Knowledge, all things, empty prove
 Without heavenly love.

3 Though I as a martyr bleed,
 Give my goods the poor to feed,
 All is vain if love I need;
 Therefore give me love.

4 Love is kind, and suffers long,
 Love is meek and thinks no wrong,
 Love than death itself more strong,
 Therefore give me love.

5 Prophecy will fade away,
 Melting in the light of day;
 Love will ever with us stay:
 Therefore give me love.

6 Faith and hope and love we see,
 Joining hand in hand, agree;
 But the greatest of the three,
 And the best, is love.

C. Wordsworth, 1862

The Church Year

8, 7, 8, 7, 8, 8, 7.

Johann Walther, 1524

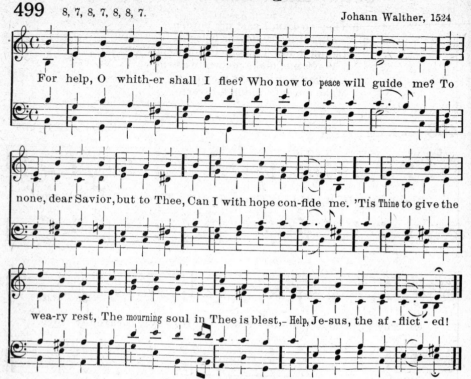

For help, O whith-er shall I flee? Who now to peace will guide me? To none, dear Savior, but to Thee, Can I with hope con-fide me. 'Tis Thine to give the wea-ry rest, The mourning soul in Thee is blest,— Help, Je-sus, the af-flict-ed!

2 My sin, O Lord, is now my grief,
   Against my will it rages:
Thy grace alone can bring relief,
   While sin its warfare wages,
All that I need is known to Thee,
And now a part myself can see,—
   Help, Jesus, the sin-burdened!

3 Good Shepherd, bearest Thou the weak?
   Sustain me in my weakness!
Thou great Physician of the sick,
   Heal Thou my moral sickness!
A prey to death I helpless fall,—
For health and strength to Thee I call,
   Save, Jesus, or I perish!

4 To those who trust Thee—"Nothing fear!
   I am the life!"—Thou criest;
Seeks not my soul, with strong desire,
   The life which Thou suppliest?
Through all my sorrows Thou canst lead,
In death provide for every need—
   Help, Jesus, the confiding.

5 I would do good, but still I fail,—
   Must I thus always waver?
What grief it gives Thou knowest well.
   Who shall my soul deliver,
And set the slave for ever free
From sin and death to live with Thee?—
   I thank Thee, God, through Jesus!

J. Neander, 1680

Twenty=third Sunday after Trinity

500   8, 8, 8, 7.

German, 15th Century

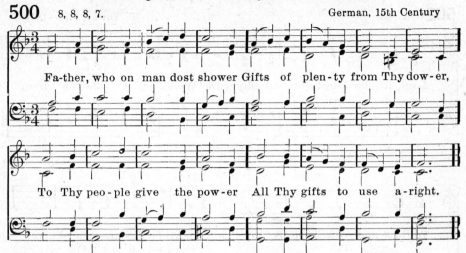

Fa-ther, who on man dost shower Gifts of plen-ty from Thy dow-er,

To Thy peo-ple give the pow-er All Thy gifts to use a-right.

2 Give pure happiness in leisure,
  Temperance in every pleasure,
  Holy use of earthly treasure,
    Bo ies clear and spirits bright.

3 Lift from this and every nation
  All that brings us degradation;
  Quell the forces of temptation;
    Put Thine enemies to flight.

4 Be with us, Thy strength supplying,
  That with energy undying,

Every foe of man defying,
  We may rally to the fight.

5 Thou who art our captain ever
  Lead us on to great endeavor;
  May Thy Church the world deliver,
    Give us wisdom, courage, might.

6 Father, who hast sought and found us,
  Son of God, whose love hath bound us,
  Holy Ghost, within us, round us,
    Hear us, Godhead infinite.

Percy Dearmer, 1906

501   C. M.

Scotch Psalter, 1615

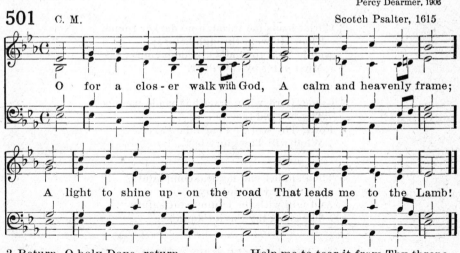

O for a clos-er walk with God, A calm and heavenly frame;

A light to shine up-on the road That leads me to the Lamb!

2 Return, O holy Dove, return,
    Sweet messenger of rest;
  I hate the sins that made Thee mourn,
    And drove Thee from my breast.

3 The dearest idol I have known,
    Whate'er that idol be,

Help me to tear it from Thy throne,
    And worship only Thee.

4 So shall my walk be close with God,
    Calm and serene my frame;
  So purer light shall mark the road
    That leads me to the Lamb!

W. Cowper, 1772

The Church Year

502 C. M.

T. Turton, 1780—1864

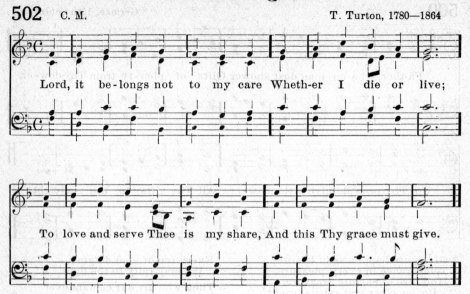

Lord, it be-longs not to my care Wheth-er I die or live;
To love and serve Thee is my share, And this Thy grace must give.

2 If life be long, I will be glad
   The longer to obey:
  If short, no laborer is sad,
   To end this toilsome day.

3 Christ leads me through no darker rooms
   Than He went through before;
  And he that to God's kingdom comes
   Must enter by this door.

4 Come, Lord, when grace has made me meet
   Thy blessed face to see;
  For if Thy work on earth be sweet,
   What will Thy glory be?

5 Then shall I end my sad complaints,
   And weary, sinful days,
  And join with the triumphant saints
   That sing my Savior's praise.

6 My knowledge of that life is small;
   The eye of faith is dim;
  But 'tis enough that Christ knows all,
   And I shall be with Him.

Richard Baxter, 1681

503 7s. 8L.

J. B. Dykes, 1861

When a-long life's thorn-y road, Faints the soul be-neath the load,

By its cares and sins op-prest, Finds on earth no peace or rest;

When the wil-y tempter's near, Fill-ing us with doubt and fear:

Je-sus, to Thy feet we flee, Je-sus, we will look to Thee

2 Thou, our Savior, from the throne
Listenest to Thy people's moan;
Thou, the living Head, dost share
Every pang Thy members bear;
Full of tenderness Thou art,
Thou wilt heal the broken heart;
Full of power, Thine arm shall quell
All the rage and might of hell.

3 Mighty to redeem and save,
Thou hast overcome the grave;
Thou the bars of death hast riven,
Opened wide the bars of heaven;
Soon in glory Thou shalt come,
Taking Thy poor pilgrims home;
Jesus, then we all shall be,
Ever, ever, Lord, with Thee.

James G. Deck. 1838

504 7, 6. 8L.

Welsh Hymn Melody

A pil-grim and a stran-ger, I jour-ney here be-low, Far dis-tant is my coun-try, The home to which I go. Here I must toil and trav-ail, Oft wea-ry and oppressed, But there my God shall lead me To ev-er-last-ing rest.

2 I've met with storms and danger,
　E'en from my early years,
With enemies and conflicts,
　With fightings and with fears.
There's nothing here that tempts me
　To wish a longer stay,
So I must hasten forward,
　No halting or delay.

3 It is a well-worn pathway—
　Many have gone before;
The holy saints and prophets,
　The patriarchs of yore.
They trod the toilsome journey
　In patience and in faith;
And them I fain would follow,
　Like them in life and death.

Twenty=fourth Sunday after Trinity

4 Who would share Abraham's bless- [ing,
Must Abraham's path pursue.
A stranger and a pilgrim,
Like him, must journey through.
The foes must be encountered,
The dangers must be passed;
Only a faithful soldier,
Receives the crown at last.

5 So I must hasten forwards,—
Thank God, the end will come!
This land of my sojourning
Is not my destined home.
That evermore abideth,
Jerusalem above,
The everlasting city,
The land of light and love.

6 There still my thoughts are dwelling
'Tis there I long to be;
Come, Lord, and call Thy servant
To blessedness with Thee!
Come, bid my toils be ended,
Let all my wanderings cease;
Call from the wayside lodging
To the sweet home of peace.

7 There I shall dwell for ever,
No more a stranger guest,
With all Thy blood-bought children,
In everlasting rest:
The pilgrim toils forgotten,
The pilgrim conflicts o'er,
All earthly griefs behind us,
Eternal joys before!

P. Gerhard, 1666

505   5, 5, 8, 8, 5, 5.   A. Drese, 1620—1701

Je - sus, still lead on, Till our rest be won! And al-though the way be cheer - less, We will fol - low, calm and fear-less; Guide us by Thy hand To our fa - ther - land!

2   If the way be drear,
     If the foe be near,
Let not faithless fears o'ertake us,
Let not faith and hope forsake us;
     For through many a foe
     To our home we go!

3   When we seek relief
     From a long-felt grief;
When temptations come alluring,

Make us patient and enduring:
     Show us that bright shore
     Where we weep no more!

4   Jesus, still lead on,
     Till our rest be won;
Heavenly Leader, still direct us,
Still support, console, protect us,
     Till we safely stand
     In our fatherland!

N. L. von Zinzendorf, 1721

506 9, 8. 6L. C. E. F. Weyse, 1826

I know of a sleep in Je-sus' name, A rest from all toil and sor-row;

Earth folds in her arms my wea-ry frame, And shelters it till the mor - row;

My soul is at home with God in heaven, Her sorrows are past and o - ver.

2 I know of a peaceful eventide;
  And when I am faint and weary,
At times with the journey sorely tried,
  Through hours that are long and
    dreary;
Then often I yearn to lay me down,
  And sink into blissful slumber.

3 I know of a morning bright and fair,
  When tidings of joy shall wake us,
When songs from on high shall fill
    the air,
  And God to His glory take us,
When Jesus shall bid us rise from
    sleep—
  How joyous that hour of awaking!

4 O that is a morning dear to me,
  And oft, o'er the mountains stream-
    ing,
In spirit its heavenly light I see,
  As golden the peaks are beaming;
Then sing I for joy like birds at dawn
  That carol in lofty lindens.

5 God's Son to our graves then wends
    His way,

His voice hear all tribes and na-
    tions;
The portals are rent that guard our
    clay,
  And moved are the sea's founda-
    tions.
He calls out aloud: "Ye dead, come
    forth!"
  In glory we rise to meet Him.

6 Now opens the Father's house above,
  The names of the blest are given:
Lord, gather us there; let none we
    love
  Be missed in the joys of heaven.
Vouchsafe Thou us all a place with
    Thee;
  We ask through our dear Redeem-
    er.

7 O Jesus, draw near my dying bed,
  And take me into Thy keeping,
And say when my spirit hence is fled:
  "This child is not dead, but sleep-
    ing."
And leave me not, Savior, till I rise,
  To praise Thee in life eternal.

M. B. Landstad, 1861

507 7, 8, 7, 8, 7, 7.

Lüneburgisches Gesangbuch, 1686

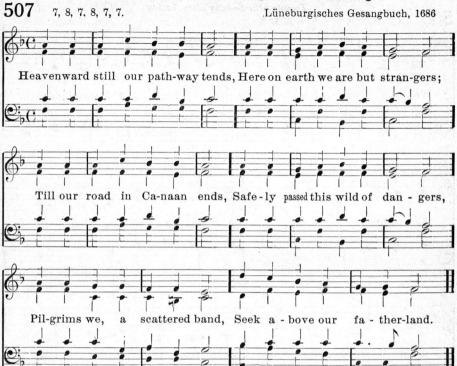

Heavenward still our path-way tends, Here on earth we are but stran-gers;

Till our road in Ca-naan ends, Safe-ly passed this wild of dan-gers,

Pil-grims we, a scattered band, Seek a-bove our fa-ther-land.

2 Heavenward still, my soul, ascend!
　Thou art one of heaven's creations;
Earth can ne'er give aim or end
　Fit to fill thy aspirations:
Turns a heaven-illumined mind
Evermore its source to find.

3 Heavenward still! God's volume blest,
　Thus, throughout its sacred pages,
Calls on me, and speaks its rest,
　Rest with Him through endless ages;
While my heart that call attends,
Still to heaven my path ascends.

4 Heavenward still my thoughts arise,
　When His festal board invites me;
Then my spirit upward flies,
　Foretaste then of heaven delights
　　me:
When on earth this food hath ceased,
Comes the Lamb's own marriage-
　　feast.

5 Heavenward still my spirit wends,
　That fair land by faith exploring;

Heavenward still my heart ascends,
　Sun and moon and stars out-soar-
　　ing;
Their faint rays in vain would try
Once with light of heaven to vie.

6 Heavenward still, when life shall
　　close,
　Death to my true home shall guide
　　me;
There, triumphant o'er my woes,
　Lasting bliss shall God provide me;
Christ Himself the way has led,
Joyful in His steps I tread.

7 Still then heavenward! heavenward
　　still!
　That shall be my watchword ever!
Joys of heaven my heart shall fill,
　Chasing joys that filled it never;
Heavenward still my joys shall run.
Till the gate of heaven is won.

B. Schmolck, 1731

508   8, 9, 8, 8, 9, 8, 6, 6, 4, 4, 4, 8.

Ph. Nicolai, 1599

Wake, a - wake, for night is fly - ing: The watchmen on

the heights are cry - ing, A - wake, Je - ru - sa - lem, a-

rise! Mid - night's sol - emn hour is toll - ing,

His char - iot wheels are near - er roll - ing; He

comes; pre-pare, ye vir - gins wise. Rise up; with will - ing feet

Twenty=fifth Sunday after Trinity

Go forth, the Bridegroom meet; Hal-le-lu-jah! Bear

through the night your well-trimmed light, Speed forth to join the marriage rite.

2 Zion hears the watchmen singing,
  Her heart with deep delight is springing,
    At once she wakes, she hastes away:
  Forth her Bridegroom hastens glorious,
  In grace arrayed, by truth victorious;
    Her grief is joy, her night is day:
  All hail, incarnate Lord,
  Our crown, and our reward!
        Hallelujah!
  We haste along, in pomp of song,
  And gladsome join the marriage throng.

3 Hear Thy praise, O Lord, ascending
  From tongues of men and angels, blending
    With harp and lute and psaltery.
  By Thy pearly gates in wonder
  We stand, and swell the voice of thunder,
    In bursts of choral melody:
  No vision ever brought,
  No ear hath ever caught,
        Such bliss and joy:
  We raise the song, we swell the throng,
  To praise Thee ages all along.

Philipp Nicolai, 1599

The Church Year

509 7, 8, 7, 8, 7, 7.   German, 1756

Je-sus Christ, my sure de-fense And my Sav-ior, ev-er liv-eth;

Know-ing this; my con-fi-dence Rests up-on the hope it giv-eth,

Though the night of death be fraught Still with many an anxious thought.

2 Jesus, my Redeemer, lives!
    I, too, unto life shall waken;
He will have me where He is:
    Should my courage then be shaken?
Should I fear? Or can the Head
Rise and leave its members dead?

3 Nay, too closely am I bound
    Unto Him by hope forever;
Faith's strong hand the rock hath found,
    Grasped it, and will leave it never:
Not the ban of death can part
From its Lord the trusting heart.

4 I shall see God with these eyes,
    Shall behold my blessed Savior;
I, the selfsame, shall arise,
    In my flesh see God forever;
Then shall wholly disappear
Frailties that oppress me here.

5 What now sickens, mourns, and sighs,
    Christ with Him to glory bringeth;
Earthly is the seed and dies,
    Heavenly from the grave it springeth;
Glorified we then shall rise
To our mansions in the skies.

6 Savior, draw away our heart
    Now from pleasures base and hollow,
Let us there with Thee have part,
    Here on earth Thy footsteps follow.
Fix our hearts beyond the skies,
Whither we ourselves would rise.

Anon., 1653

Twenty=fifth Sunday after Trinity

510   8, 7, 8, 7, 4, 7.   E. J. Hopkins, 1818—1901

O'er the dis-tant mountains breaking, Comes the reddening dawn of day;

Rise, my soul, from sleep a - wak-ing, Rise, and sing, and watch, and pray;

'Tis   thy   Sav - ior   On His bright re - turn - ing   way.

2 O Thou Long-expected, weary
　　Waits my anxious soul for Thee,
　Life is dark, and earth is dreary,
　　Where Thy light I do not see;
　　　O my Savior,
　　When wilt Thou return to me?

3 Nearer is my soul's salvation,
　　Spent the night, the day at hand;
　Keep me, in my lowly station,
　　Watching for Thee, till I stand,
　　　O my Savior,
　　In Thy bright, Thy promised land.

4 With my lamp well trimmed and burning,
　　Swift to hear and slow to roam,
　Watching for Thy glad returning
　　To restore me to my home.
　　　Come, my Savior,
　　Thou hast promised, quickly come.

J. S. B. Monsell, 1863

511   8, 6. 8L.

Soon will the heavenly Bridegroom come; Ye wedding-guests, draw near,
And slum-ber not in sin when He, The Son of God, is here.
With lamps a-light and oil in store, Let ev-ery guest ad-vance,
Nor shrink ashamed in trembling awe From His bright coun-te-nance.

2 Come, let us haste to meet our Lord,
  And hail Him with delight,
Who saved us by His precious blood
  And sorrows infinite:
Beside Him all the patriarchs old
  And holy prophets stand,
The glorious apostolic choir,
  The noble martyr-band.

3 As brethren dear they welcome us,
  And lead us to the throne,
Where angels bow their veiled heads
  Before the Three in One,

Where we, with all the saints of
  A white-robed multitude, [Christ,
Shall praise the ascended Lord, who
  To wear our flesh and blood [deigns

4 His gracious hand will ope for us
  The gates of paradise,
And spread the glories of His heaven
  Before our dazzled eyes:
Our lot will be for aye to share
  His reign of peace above,
And drink with unexhausted joy
  The river of His love.

J Walther, 1552

512 14s. 4L T. Tallis, 1515—85

Be - hold, the Bridegroom com-eth in the mid-dle of the night,

And blest is he whose loins are girt, whose lamp is burn-ing bright;

But woe to that dull ser-vant whom the Mas-ter shall sur-prise

With lamp un-trimmed, un - burning, and with slum-ber in his eyes.

2 Do thou, my soul, beware, beware lest thou in sleep sink down,
Lest thou be given o'er to death, and lose the golden crown;
But see that thou be sober, with a watchful eye, and thus
Cry, "Holy, holy, holy God, have mercy upon us!"

3 That day, the day of fear, shall come; my soul, slack not thy toil,
But light thy lamp, and feed it well, and make it bright with oil;
Thou knowest not how soon may sound the cry at eventide,
"Behold, the Bridegroom comes! Arise! He comes to meet the Bride!"

4 Beware, my soul! take thou good heed lest thou in slumber lie,
And, like the five, remain without, and knock, and vainly cry;
But watch, and bear thy lamp undimmed, and Christ shall gird thee on
His own bright wedding robe of light,—the glory of the Son.

(Greek) Anon.

The Church Year

513 8, 7, 8, 7, 8, 8, 7, 7.

Ludv. M. Lindeman, 1812—87

Death in all this world pre-vail-eth: Hu-man life, a sum-mer flower;
Blooms at morn, at e-ven fail-eth, But there comes a brighter hour.
When o'er death shall rise vic-to-rious, And ap-pear in forms more glorious,
To a bet-ter life re-stored, Who have loved and served their Lord.

2 Jesus yielded up His spirit,
  And His ransomed people gain
Life eternal by His merit;
  Death has armed his sting in vain.
For the unfettered soul ascendeth
To the world which never endeth,
  There without a veil to see
  God's true face eternally.

3 There is life that knows no sadness,
  There, a numberless array,
White-robed denizens of gladness,
  Unto God their homage pay:
Choir aloud to choir rejoices,
Seraphs with delighted voices
  Holy, holy, holy, sing
  To their Triune God and King.

4 There the patriarchs abiding,
  There the prophets all have rest,
There the noble twelve residing
  In their Master's love are blest;
There the saints in holy splendor
To the Lamb their praises render,
  Harping sweet in solemn strains
  "Hallelujah! Jesus reigns."

J. G. Albinus. 1652

514　7, 6. 8L.

J. Stainer, 1840—1901

"Come un-to Me, ye wea-ry, And I will give you rest."

O bless-ed voice of Je - sus, Which comes to hearts op-pressed;

It tells of ben - e - dic - tion, Of par-don, grace, and peace,

Of joy that hath no end - ing, Of love which can-not cease.

2 "Come unto Me, ye wanderers,
　　And I will give you light."
　O loving voice of Jesus,
　　Which comes to cheer the night;
　Our hearts were filled with sadness,
　　And we had lost our way;
　But morning brings us gladness,
　　And songs the break of day.

3 "Come unto Me, ye fainting,
　　And I will give you life."
　O cheering voice of Jesus,
　　Which comes to aid our strife;

The foe is stern and eager,
　The fight is fierce and long;
But Thou hast made us mighty,
　And stronger than the strong.

4 "And whosoever cometh,
　　I will not cast him out."
　O patient love of Jesus,
　　Which drives away our doubt
Which, though we be unworthy
　Of love so great and free,
Invites us very sinners
　To come, dear Lord, to Thee.

W. C. Dix, 1867

The Church Year

515 7s. 4l. Orlando Gibbons, 1623

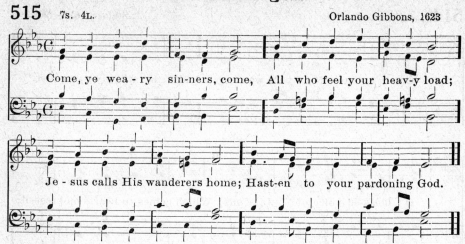

Come, ye wea-ry sin-ners, come, All who feel your heav-y load;

Je - sus calls His wanderers home; Hast-en to your pardoning God.

2 Come, ye guilty souls opprest,
Answer to the Savior's call:
"Come, and I will give you rest;
Come, and I will save you all."

3 Jesus, full of truth and love,
We Thy gracious call obey:
Faithful let Thy mercies prove,
Take our load of guilt away.

4 Fain we would on Thee rely,
Cast on Thee our sin and care:
To Thine arms of mercy fly,
Find our lasting quiet there.

5 Lo, we come to Thee for ease:
True and gracious as Thou art,
Now our weary souls release,
Write forgiveness on our heart.

C. Wesley, 1746

516 8, 7. 4l. "Psalmodia Sacra," Gotha, 1715

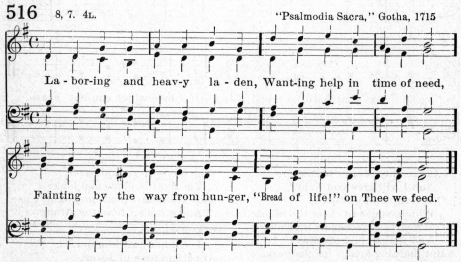

La - bor-ing and heav-y la - den, Want-ing help in time of need,

Fainting by the way from hun-ger, "Bread of life!" on Thee we feed.

2 Thirsting for the springs of waters
That, by love's eternal law,
From the stricken rock are flowing,
"Well of life!" from Thee we draw.

3 In the land of cloud and shadow,
Where no human eye can see,

Light to those who sit in darkness,
"Light of life!" we walk in Thee.

4 Thou the grace of life supplying,
Thou the crown of life wilt give;
Dead to sin and daily dying,
"Life of life!" in Thee we live.

J. S. B. Monsell. 1863

Twenty=sixth Sunday after Trinity

517 11, 10. 4L. F. R. Havergal, 1871

Come un - to Me, when shadows dark-ly gath - er, When the sad heart is wea-ry and dis-tressed; Seek - ing for com-fort from your heavenly Fa - ther, Come un - to Me, and I will give you rest.

2 Ye who have mourned when tender flowers were taken,
When the ripe fruit fell richly to the ground,
When the loved slept, in brighter homes to waken,
Where their pale brows with spirit-wreaths are crowned.

3 Large are the mansions in thy Father's dwelling,
Glad are the homes that sorrows never dim;
Sweet are the harps in holy music swelling,
Soft are the tones which raise the heavenly hymn.

4 There like an Eden blossoming in gladness,
Bloom the fair flowers the earth too rudely pressed:
Come unto Me, all ye who droop in sadness,
Come unto Me, and I will give you rest.

Catherine H. Esling, 1839

518 6, 6, 6, 6, 8, 8.   J. Goss, 1800—80

To Thee our God we fly For mer-cy and for grace;

O hear our low-ly cry, And hide not Thou Thy face.

O Lord, stretch forth Thy mighty hand, And guard and bless our fa-ther-land.

2 Arise, O Lord of hosts;
    Be jealous for Thy name,
And drive from out our coasts
    The sins that put to shame.
O Lord, stretch forth Thy mighty hand,
And guard and bless our fatherland.

3 Thy best gifts from on high
    In rich abundance pour,
That we may magnify
    And praise Thee more and more.
O Lord, stretch forth Thy mighty hand,
And guard and bless our fatherland.

4 The powers ordained by Thee,
    With heavenly wisdom bless;
May they Thy servants be,
    And rule in righteousness.
O Lord, stretch forth Thy mighty hand,
And guard and bless our fatherland.

National

5 The Church of Thy dear Son
  Inflame with love's pure fire,
Bind her once more in one,
  And life and truth inspire.
O Lord, stretch forth Thy mighty hand,
And guard and bless our fatherland.

6 Give peace, Lord, in our time:
  O let no foe draw nigh,
Nor lawless deed of crime
  Insult Thy Majesty.
O Lord, stretch forth Thy mighty hand,
And guard and bless our fatherland.

W. W. How, 1871

519 6, 6, 4, 6, 6, 6, 4.   H. Carey, 1743

God bless our na-tive land! Firm may she ev-er stand,
Through storm and night; When the wild tem-pests rave, Rul-er of
wind and wave, Do Thou our coun-try save By Thy great might.

2 For her our prayer shall rise
  To God above the skies;
    On Him we wait:
  Thou who art ever nigh,
  Guarding with watchful eye,
  To Thee aloud we cry,
    God save the state!

C. T. Brooks, ca. 1833
J. S. Dwight, 1844

555

520 6, 6, 6, 6, 8, 8.

J. Goss, 1800—80

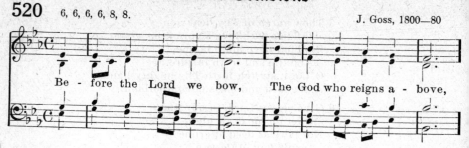

Be - fore the Lord we bow, The God who reigns a - bove,

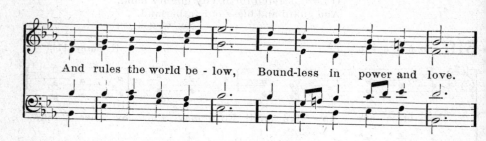

And rules the world be - low, Bound-less in power and love.

Our thanks we bring In joy and praise, Our hearts we raise To heaven's high King.

2 The nation Thou hast blest,
　May well Thy love declare,
From foes and fears at rest,
Protected by Thy care.
　For this fair land,
　　For this bright day,
　Our thanks we pay—
　　Gifts of Thy hand.

3 May every mountain height,
　Each vale and forest green,
Shine in Thy word's pure light,
And its rich fruits be seen!
　May every tongue
　　Be tuned to praise,
　And join to raise
　　A grateful song.

4 Earth! hear thy Maker's voice,
　Thy great Redeemer own;
Believe, obey, rejoice,
And worship Him alone;
　Cast down thy pride,
　　Thy sin deplore,
　And bow before
　　The Crucified.

5 And when in power He comes,
　O may our native land,
From all its rending tombs,
Send forth a glorious band,
　A countless throng,
　　Ever to sing
　To heaven's high King
　　Salvation's song.

F. S. Key, 1832

Day of Common Prayer

521   6, 7, 6, 7, 6, 6, 6, 6.

German, 1648

For-sake me not, my God, Thou God of my sal - va - tion!

Give me Thy light, to be My sure il - lu - mi - na - tion.

My soul to fol - ly turns, Seek - ing she knows not what:

O lead her to Thy - self; My God, for - sake me not!

2   Forsake me not, my God!
Take not Thy Spirit from me,
And suffer not the might
Of sin to overcome me.
A father pitieth
The children he begot:
My Father, pity me!
My God, forsake me not!

3   Forsake me not, my God,
Thou God of life and power!
Enliven, strengthen me,
In every evil hour:
And when the sinful fire
Within my heart is hot,
Be not Thou far from me:
My God, forsake me not!

4   Forsake me not, my God!
Uphold me in my going,
That evermore I may
Please Thee in all well-doing:
And that Thy will, O Lord,
May never be forgot
In all my works and ways:
My God, forsake me not!

5   Forsake me not, my God!
I would be Thine for ever:
Confirm me mightily
In every right endeavor:
And when my hour is come,
Cleansed from all stain and spot
Of sin, receive my soul:
My God, forsake me not!

S. Franck, 1714

522   7, 6, 7, 6, 3, 3, 6, 6.   Johann Rosenmüller, 1655

Not in an-ger, might-y God, Not in an-ger smite us. We must per-ish if Thy rod Just-ly should re-quite us. We are naught, Sin hath brought, Lord, Thy wrath up-on...... us, Yet have mer-cy on...... us!

2 Show me now a Father's love,
  And His tender patience,
Heal my wounded soul, remove
  These too sore temptations;
    I am weak,
    Father, speak
Thou of peace and gladness,
Comfort Thou my sadness.

3 Weary am I of my pain,
  Weary with my sorrow,
Sighing still for help in vain,
  Longing for the morrow;
    Why wilt Thou
    Tarry now?
Wilt Thou friendless leave me
And of hope bereave me?

4 Hence, ye foes! He comes in grace,
  God hath deigned to hear me;
I may come before His face,
  He is inly near me;
    He o'erthrows
    All my foes,
Death and hell are vanquished,
In whose bonds I languished.

5 Father, hymns to Thee we raise,
  Here and once in heaven;
And the Son and Spirit praise,
  Who our bonds have riven!
    Evermore
    We adore
Thee whose love hath stirred us,
And whose pity heard us.

J. G. Albinus, 1655

Day of Common Prayer

523   8, 7. 4L.

German, 16th Century

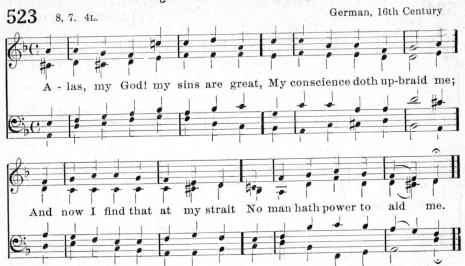

A - las, my God! my sins are great, My conscience doth up-braid me;

And now I find that at my strait No man hath power to aid me.

2 And fled I hence, in my despair,
   In some lone spot to hide me,
   My griefs would still be with me there,
   Thy hand still hold and guide me.

3 Nay, Thee I seek;—I merit naught,
   Yet pity and restore me;
   Be not Thy wrath, just God, my lot,
   Thy Son hath suffered for me.

4 If pain and woe must follow sin,
   Then be my path still rougher;

Here spare me not; if heaven I win,
On earth I gladly suffer.

5 But curb my heart, forgive my guilt,
   Make Thou my patience firmer,
   For they must miss the good Thou wilt,
   Who at Thy teachings murmur.

6 Then deal with me as seems Thee best,
   Thy grace will help me bear it,
   If but at last I see Thy rest,
   And with my Savior share it.

                                    J. Gross, 1613

8, 7. 4L.   *Older Form.*   German, 16th Century

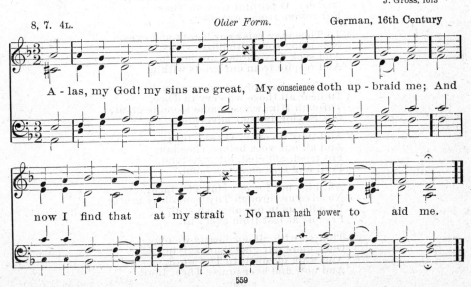

A - las, my God! my sins are great, My conscience doth up - braid me; And

now I find that at my strait No man hath power to aid me.

Various Occasions

524 L. M.

Louis Bourgeois, 1547

When in the hour of ut-most need We know not where to look for aid; When days and nights of anx-ious thought Nor help nor coun-sel yet have brought;

2 Then this our comfort is alone,
That we may meet before Thy throne,
And cry, O faithful God, to Thee
For rescue from our misery:

3 To Thee may raise our hearts and eyes,
Repenting sore with bitter sighs,
And seek Thy pardon for our sin,
And respite from our griefs within.

4 For Thou hast promised graciously
To hear all those who cry to Thee,
Through Him whose name alone is great,
Our Savior and our advocate.

5 And thus we come, O God, today,
And all our woes before Thee lay;
For tried, afflicted, lo! we stand,
Peril and foes on every hand.

6 Ah, hide not for our sins Thy face;
Absolve us through Thy boundless grace;
Be with us in our anguish still,
Free us at last from every ill.

7 That so with all our hearts we may
Once more our glad thanksgiving pay,
And walk obedient to Thy word,
And now and ever praise Thee, Lord.

P. Eber, 1566

Reformation Day

525   8, 7. 8L.   Arthur Sullivan, 1874

We hail Thee, Lord, Thy Church's rock, With joy-ful ac-cla-ma-tion!

Thou guardian Shepherd of Thy flock, Come, feed Thy con-gre-ga-tion.

We own the doc-trine of Thy cross To be our sole foun-da-tion:

Ac-cept from ev-ery one of us The deep-est a-dor-a-tion.

2 O Thou, who always dost abide
   Thy Church's head and Savior,
Be still Thy servants' constant guide,
   Direct our whole behavior.
Thy statutes to Thy Church declare,
   Still watch o'er its salvation:
Each member make Thy special care,
   And aid him in his station.

3 Jesus, the Church's head and Lord,
   Who as a shepherd leadest,
And with Thy sacrament and word
   Thy people richly feedest:
For mercies in such countless throng
   We bow our hearts before Thee,
And hope we shall in heaven ere long
   More worthily adore Thee.

N. L. von Zinzendorf. 1741

526   8, 7, 8, 7, 8, 8, 7.

German, 1523

Dear Christians, one and all, re-joice, With ex-ult-a-tion spring-ing,

And, with u-nit-ed heart and voice And ho-ly rap-ture

sing - - ing, Pro-claim the won-ders God hath done, How

His right arm the vic-tory won; Right dear-ly it hath cost Him.

Reformation Day

2 Fast bound in Satan's chains I lay,
  Death brooded darkly o'er me,
Sin was my torment night and day,
  In sin my mother bore me;
Deeper and deeper still I fell,
Life had become a living hell,
  So firmly sin possessed me.

3 My good works so imperfect were,
  They had no power to aid me;
My will God's judgments could not
  Yea, prone to evil made me; [bear,
Grief drove me to despair, and I
Had nothing left me but to die;
  To hell I fast was sinking.

4 Then God beheld my wretched state
  With deep commiseration;
He thought upon His mercy great,
  And willed my soul's salvation;
He turned to me a Father's heart;
Not small the cost! to heal my smart,
  He gave His best and dearest.

5 He spoke to His beloved Son:
  'Tis time to take compassion:
Then go, bright Jewel of my crown,
  And bring to man salvation;
From sin and sorrow set him free,
Slay bitter death for him, that he
  May live with Thee forever.

6 The Son obeyed Him cheerfully,
  And born of virgin mother,
Came down upon the earth to me,
  That He might be my brother:

His mighty power doth work unseen,
He came in fashion poor and mean,
  And took the Devil captive.

7 He sweetly said, Hold fast by me,
  I am thy rock and castle,
Thy ransom I myself will be,
  For thee I strive and wrestle:
For I am with thee, I am thine,
And evermore thou shalt be mine,
  The foe shall not divide us.

8 The foe shall shed My precious blood,
  Me of my life bereaving;
All this I suffer for thy good,
  Be steadfast and believing:
Life shall from death the victory win,
My innocence shall bear thy sin,
  So art thou blest forever.

9 Now to My Father I depart,
  From earth to heaven ascending,
Thence heavenly wisdom to impart,
  The Holy Spirit sending:
He shall in trouble comfort thee,
Teach thee to know and follow me,
  And to the truth conduct thee.

10 What I have done and taught, teach
    thou,
  My ways forsake thou never;
So shall my kingdom flourish now,
  And God be praised forever:
Take heed lest men with base alloy
The heavenly treasure should destroy:
  This counsel I bequeath thee.

M. Luther, 1523

Various Occasions

527 8, 7, 8, 7, 8, 8, 7. Joseph Klug, Wittenberg, 1535

Had God not come, may Is-rael say, Had God not come to aid us, Our en-e-mies on that sad day Would sure-ly have dis-mayed us; A rem-nant now, and hand-ful small, Held in con-tempt and scorn by all, Who cruel-ly would op-press us.

2 Their furious wrath, did God permit,
    Would quickly have consumed us,
And in the deep and yawning pit
    With life and limb entombed us;
Like men o'er whom dark waters roll,
The streams had gone e'en o'er our [soul,
    And mightily o'er whelmed us.

3 Thanks be to God, who from the pit
    Snatched us, when it was gaping:
Our souls, like birds that break the [net,
    To the blue sky escaping;
The snare is broken—we are free!
The Lord our helper praiséd be,
    The God of earth and heaven.

564

M. Luther, 1524

Thanksgiving Day

528 8, 7. 8L.   Arthur Sullivan, 1874

To Thee, O Lord, our hearts we raise In hymns of ad - o - ra - tion,

To Thee bring sac - ri - fice of praise With shouts of ex - ult - a - tion;

Bright robes of gold the fields a - dorn, The hills with joy are ring - ing,

The val-leys stand so thick with corn That e - ven they are sing - ing.

2 And now, on this our festal day,
   Thy bounteous hand confessing,
Upon Thine altar, Lord, we lay
   The first-fruits of Thy blessing;
By Thee the souls of men are fed
   With gifts of grace supernal;
Thou who dost give us earthly bread,
   Give us the bread eternal.

3 We bear the burden of the day,
   And often toil seems dreary;
But labor ends with sunset ray,
   And rest comes for the weary;

May we, the angel-reaping o'er,
   Stand at the last accepted,
Christ's golden sheaves for evermore
   To garners bright elected.

4 O blessed is that land of God,
   Where saints abide for ever;
Where golden fields spread far and
   Where flows the crystal river; [broad,
The strains of all its holy throng
   With ours to-day are blending;
Thrice blessed is that harvest-song
   Which never hath an ending.

W. C. Dix, 1864

529 7s. 6L.

Ludv. M. Lindeman, 1812—87

For the beau-ty of the earth, For the glo - ry of the skies,

For the love which from our birth O - ver and a-round us lies;

Lord of all, to Thee we raise This our grate-ful psalm of praise.

2 For the wonder of each hour
Of the day and of the night:
Hill and vale, and tree and flower,
Sun and moon and stars of light;
Lord of all, to Thee we raise
This our grateful psalm of praise.

3 For the joy of human love,
Brother, sister, parent, child;
Friends on earth, and friends above,
Pleasures pure and undefiled;
Lord of all, to Thee we raise
This our grateful psalm of praise.

4 For Thy Church that evermore
Lifts her holy hands above,
Offering up on every shore
Her pure sacrifice of love;
Lord of all, to Thee we raise
This our grateful psalm of praise.

F. S. Pierpont. 1864

Thanksgiving Day

530 7, 6. 8L.

L. Mason, 1823

Sing to the Lord of har-vest, Sing songs of love and praise;

With joy-ful hearts and voic-es Your Hal-le-lu-jahs raise:

By Him the roll-ing sea-sons In fruit-ful or-der move.

Sing to the Lord of har-vest A song of hap-py love.

2 By Him the clouds drop fatness,
  The deserts bloom and spring;
The hills leap up in gladness,
  The valleys laugh and sing.
He filleth with His fullness
  All things with large increase,
He crowns the year with goodness,
  With plenty and with peace.

3 Bring to His sacred altar
  The gifts His goodness gave,
The golden sheaves of harvest,
  The souls He died to save:

Your hearts lay down before Him,
  When at His feet we fall,
And with your lives adore Him,
  Who gave His life for all.

4 To God, the gracious Father
  Who made us "very good":
To Christ, who, when we wandered,
  Restored us with His blood:
And to the Holy Spirit,
  Who doth upon us pour
His blessèd dews and sunshine,
  Be praise for evermore.

J. S. B. Monsell, 1866

Various Occasions

7s. 6L.

Ludv. M. Lindeman, 1812—87

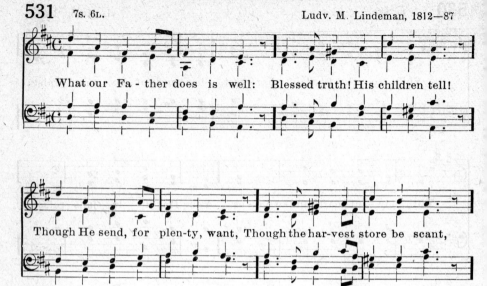

What our Fa - ther does is well: Blessed truth! His children tell!

Though He send, for plen-ty, want, Though the har-vest store be scant,

Yet we rest up - on His love, Seek-ing bet - ter things a - bove.

2 What our Father does is well:
Shall the willful heart rebel,
If a blessing He withhold
In the field, or in the fold?
Is He not Himself to be
All our store eternally?

3 What our Father does is well:
Though He sadden hill and dell,
Upward yet our praises rise
For the strength His word supplies,
He has called us sons of God;
Can we murmur at His rod?

4 What our Father does is well:
May the thought within us dwell;
Though nor milk nor honey flow
In our barren Canaan now,
God can save us in our need,
God can bless us, God can feed.

5 Therefore unto Him we raise
Hymns of glory, songs of praise;
To the Father and the Son
And the Spirit, Three in One,
Honor, might, and glory be,
Now and through eternity.

B. Schmolck, 1720

Thanksgiving Day

532 7s. 8l.

J. Hinze, 1678

Come, ye thank-ful peo-ple, come, Raise the song of har-vest home:

All is safe-ly gath-ered in, Ere the win-ter storms be-gin;

God, our Mak-er, doth pro-vide For our wants to be sup-plied;

Come to God's own tem-ple, come, Raise the song of har-vest home.

2 All the world is God's own field,
Fruit unto His praise to yield;
Wheat and tares together sown,
Unto joy or sorrow grown:
First the blade, and then the ear,
Then the full corn shall appear:
Lord of harvest, grant that we
Wholesome grain and pure may be.

3 For the Lord our God shall come,
And shall take His harvest home;
From His field shall in that day
All offenses purge away;

Give His angels charge at last
In the fire the tares to cast,
But the fruitful ears to store
In His garner evermore.

4 Even so, Lord, quickly come,
To Thy final harvest home!
Gather Thou Thy people in,
Free from sorrow, free from sin;
There for ever purified,
In Thy presence to abide:
Come, with all Thine angels, come,
Raise the glorious harvest home!

H. Alford, 1844

533 7, 6. 8L.

Lowell Mason, 1841

O love di-vine and gold-en, Mys-terious depth and height,
To thee the world be-hold-en, Looks up for life and light;
O love di-vine and gen-tle, The bless-er and the blest,
Be-neath thy care pa-ren-tal The world lies down in rest.

2 O love divine and tender,
   That through our homes dost move,
Veiled in the softened splendor
   Of holy household love.
A throne without thy blessing
   Were labor without rest,
And cottages possessing
   Thy blessedness, are blest.

3 God bless these hands, united;
   God bless these hearts made one!
Unsevered and unblighted
   May they through life go on,—
Here in earth's home preparing
   For the bright home above,
And there forever sharing
   Its joy where God is love.

J. S. B. Monsell, 1862

Marriage and the Home

534   7, 6. 8L.

John Stainer, 1840—1901

O Fa - ther all cre - at - ing, Whose wis-dom, love, and power

First bound two lives to - geth - er   In   E-den's pri-mal   hour,

To - day   to these Thy chil-dren Thine earliest gifts re - new,—

A   home by Thee made hap - py,   A   love by Thee kept true.

2 O Savior, guest most bounteous
　　Of old in Galilee,
　Vouchsafe today Thy presence
　　With these who call on Thee;
　Their store of earthly gladness
　　Transform to heavenly wine,
　And teach them, in the tasting,
　　To know the gift is Thine.

3 O Spirit of the Father,
　　Breathe on them from above,
　So mighty in Thy pureness,
　　So tender in Thy love;

That guarded by Thy presence,
　From sin and strife kept free,
Their lives may own Thy guidance,
　Their hearts be ruled by Thee.

4 Except Thou build it, Father,
　　The house is built in vain;
　Except Thou, Savior, bless it,
　　The joy will turn to pain;
　But naught can break the marriage
　　Of hearts in Thee made one,
　And love Thy Spirit hallows
　　Is endless love begun.

J. Ellerton. 1876

535 7, 6. 8L.

F. Mendelssohn

Crown with Thy ben - e - dic - tion This cov - e - nant of love;

And make this hal - lowed un - ion Fore - taste of heaven a - bove:

Let pure and per - fect glad - ness, Let pure and per - fect rest,

And peace that knows no sad - ness, Thy presence, Lord, at - test.

2 As once in Eden's springtime,
   As once at Cana's feast,
So consecrate this bridal—
   Be Thou its guest and priest!
With sunshine wreathe the altar,
   Chase every cloud away,
Nor let their voices falter
   Who plight their troth today.

3 God bless the bride and bridegroom,
   And fill with joy their life;
Keep them, through all its changes,
   True husband, faithful wife!

If Thou wilt smile upon them,
   They shall not need the sun;
This thought their hearts rejoicing—
   Henceforth, not twain but one.

4 With Thy great love befriend them,
   The love that casts out fear;
And make a rainbow round them
   For every falling tear:
Till, all their sheaves well-garnered,
   Heaven's harvest home they raise,
Where love, that knows no ending,
   Inspires more perfect praise.

J. B. Greenwood, b. 1828

Marriage and the Home

536 8, 6. 8L   H. J. Gauntlett, 1805—76

Lord, who at Ca - na's wedding feast Didst as a guest ap - pear,

Thou dear - er far than earth-ly guest, Vouch - safe Thy pres-ence here;

For ho - ly Thou in - deed dost prove The mar-riage vow to be,

Proclaim -ing it a type of love Between the Church and Thee.

2 The holiest vow that man can make,
  The golden thread in life,
The bond that none may dare to break,
  That bindeth man and wife;
Which, blessed by Thee, whate'er betides,
  No evil shall destroy,
Through care-worn days each care divides,
  And doubles every joy.

3 On those, who now before Thee kneel,
  O Lord, Thy blessing pour,
That each may wake the other's zeal
  To love Thee more and more;
O grant them here in peace to live,
  In purity and love,
And, this world leaving, to receive
  A crown of life above.
                                    Adelaide Thrupp, 1853

537   11, 10, 11, 10.

O hap-py home, where Thou art loved the dear-est,

Thou lov-ing Friend and Sav-ior of our race,

And where a-mong the guests there nev-er com-eth

One who can hold such high and hon-ored place!

2 O happy home, where two in heart united
In holy faith, and blessed hope, are one,
Whom death a little while alone divideth
And cannot end the union here begun!

3 O happy home, whose little ones are given
Early to Thee, in humble faith and prayer,
To Thee, their friend, who from the heights of heaven
Guides them, and guards with more than mother's care!

4 O happy home, where each one serves Thee, lowly,
Whatever his appointed work may be,
Till every common task seems great and holy,
When it is done, O Lord, as unto Thee!

Marriage and the Home

5 O happy home, where Thou art not forgotten,
　When joy is overflowing, full and free;
　O happy home, where every wounded spirit
　Is brought, Physician, Comforter, to Thee,—

6 Until at last, when earth's day's work is ended,
　All meet Thee in the blessed home above,
　From whence Thou camest, where Thou hast ascended,
　Thy everlasting home of peace and love!

C. J. P. Spitta, 1833

538　11, 10. 4L.　　　　　　　　　　　　Arr. fr. J. Barnby, 1889

O perfect Love, all hu-man thought transcend-ing, Low-ly we
kneel in prayer be-fore Thy throne, That theirs may be the
love that knows no end - ing, Whom Thou for - ev -er-more dost join in one.

2 O perfect Life, be Thou their full assurance
　Of tender charity and steadfast faith,
　Of patient hope, and quiet, brave endurance,
　With childlike trust that fears nor pain nor death.

3 Grant them the joy which brightens earthly sorrow;
　Grant them the peace which calms all earthly strife,
　And to life's day the glorious unknown morrow
　That dawns upon eternal love and life.

Dorothy F. Bloomfield, 1883

Family Prayer

539 L. M.

F. Barthélémon, 1741—1808

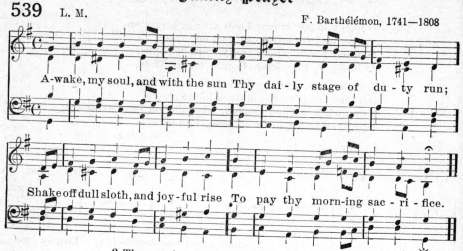

A-wake, my soul, and with the sun Thy dai-ly stage of du-ty run;

Shake off dull sloth, and joy-ful rise To pay thy morn-ing sac-ri-fice.

2 Thy precious time misspent, redeem;
   Each present day thy last esteem;
   Improve thy talent with due care,
   For the great day thyself prepare.

3 Wake, and lift up thyself, my heart,
   And with the angels bear thy part,
   Who all night long, unwearied, sing,
   High praise to the eternal King.

4 All praise to Thee, who safe hast kept,
   And hast refreshed me while I slept.
   Grant, Lord, when I from death shall wake,
   I may of endless light partake.

5 Lord, I my vows to Thee renew;
   Disperse my sins, as morning dew;
   Guard my first springs of thought and will;
   And with Thyself my spirit fill.

6 Direct, control, suggest this day,
   All I design, or do, or say;
   That all my powers, with all their might,
   In Thy sole glory may unite.

T. Ken. 1695

540 7s. 4L.

R. Redhead, 1852

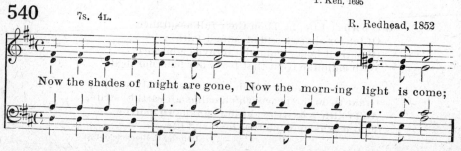

Now the shades of night are gone, Now the morn-ing light is come;

Morning

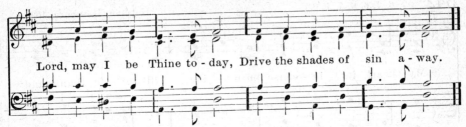

Lord, may I be Thine to-day, Drive the shades of sin a-way.

2 Fill my soul, O Christ, with light,
  Banish doubt and cleanse my sight,
  In Thy service, Lord, today,
  Help me labor, help me pray.

3 Keep my haughty passions bound;
  Save me from my foes around;

Going out and coming in,
Keep me safe from every sin.

4 When my work of life is past,
  O receive me then at last!
  Night of sin will be no more,
  When I reach the heavenly shore.

Anon, 1799

541 L. M.

S. Webbe, 1782

Now that the day-light fills the sky, We lift our hearts to God on high,

That He, in all we do or say, Would keep us free from harm to-day;

2 Would guard our hearts and tongues from strife,
  From anger's din would hide our life,
  From all ill sights would turn our eyes
  Would close our ears from vanities;

3 Would keep our inmost conscience pure,
  Our souls from folly would secure,
  Would bid us check the pride of sense
  With due and holy abstinence;

4 So we, when this new day is gone
  And night in turn is drawing on,
  With conscience by the world unstained,
  Shall praise His name for victory gained.

Anon., (Latin) 5th Century

Family Prayer

542 7, 6, 7, 6, 6, 7, 7, 6.

German, Hamburg, 1598

My heart its in-cense burn — ing, I'll of-fer thanks and praise, Now, with re-turn of morn — ing, And through all fu-ture days; I'll praise Thee on Thy throne, Great Source of ev-ery bless — ing, My song to Thee ad-dress — ing Through Christ, Thy on-ly Son.

Morning

2 Thy mercy claims my praises!
  This kept me through the night;
  And now from sleep it raises,
  To greet the dawning light.
  This, too, it is that hath
  My many sins forgiven,
  Which, in the face of heaven,
  So oft provoked Thy wrath.

3 In mercy still direct me
  Throughout the coming day:
  From Satan's wiles protect me,
  From sin, and from dismay:

Defend from fire and storm,
  From want and every weakness,
  From sorrow and from sickness,
  From sudden death's alarm.

4 Let angels keep their stations,
  Nor cease their guard of me,
  Averting all temptations
  Which draw my soul from Thee!
  Thy shield hold Thou above!
  Then nothing shall distress me,
  To duty I'll address me,
  Rejoicing in Thy love.

(German) Anon., 1592

543 7s. 6L. Ludv. M Lindeman, 1812—87

Christ, whose glo-ry fills the skies, Christ, the true, the on-ly light,

Sun of righteous-ness, a-rise, Triumph o'er the shades of night:

Day-spring from on high, be near; Day-star, in my heart ap-pear.

2 Dark and cheerless is the morn,
  Unaccompanied by Thee;
  Joyless is the day's return,
  Till Thy mercy's beams I see;
  Till Thou inward light impart,
  Glad my eyes and warm my heart.

3 Visit, then, this soul of mine;
  Pierce the gloom of sin and grief;
  Fill me, radiancy divine;
  Scatter all my unbelief:
  More and more Thyself display,
  Shining to the perfect day.

C. Wesley, 1740

Family Prayer

544   8, 7, 8, 7, 7, 7.

J. Chr. Bach, 1693

God, who mad-est earth and heav-en, Fa-ther, Son, and Ho-ly Ghost,

Who the day and night hast giv-en, Sun and moon and star-ry host,

All things wake at Thy command, Held in be-ing by Thy hand.

2 God, I thank Thee, in Thy keeping,
  Safely have I slumbered here;
Thou hast guarded me while sleeping
  From all danger, pain, and fear;
And the cunning of my foe
Hath not wrought my overthrow.

3 Let the night of sin that shrouded
  All my life, with this depart;
Shine on me with beams unclouded:
  Jesus, in Thy loving heart
Are my help and hope alone,
For the evil I have done.

4 Help me as the morn is breaking,
  In the spirit to arise,
So from careless sloth awaking,
  That when o'er the aged skies
Shall the morn of doom appear,
I may see it, free from fear.

5 Lead me, and forsake me never,
　Guide my wanderings by Thy word:
As Thou hast been, be Thou ever
　My defense, my refuge, Lord.
Never safe except with Thee,
Thou my faithful guardian be!

6 O my God, I now commend me
　Wholly to Thy mighty hand:
All the powers that Thou dost lend me
　Let me use at Thy command;
Thou my boast, my strength divine,
Keep me with Thee, I am Thine.

7 Thus afresh with each new morning
　Save me from the power of sin,
Hourly let me feel Thy warning
　Ruling, prompting all within,
Till my final rest be come,
And Thine angel bear me home.

H. Albert, 1643

545　L. M.

D. Vetter, 1713

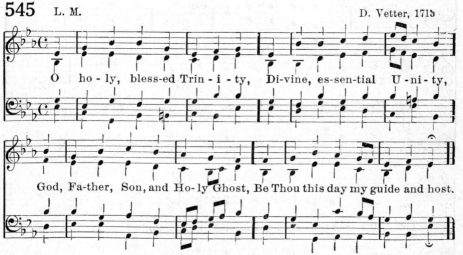

O ho-ly, bless-ed Trin-i-ty, Di-vine, es-sen-tial U-ni-ty,

God, Fa-ther, Son, and Ho-ly Ghost, Be Thou this day my guide and host.

2 My soul and body keep from harm,
O'er all I have extend Thine arm,
That Satan may not cause distress,
Nor bring me shame and wretchedness.

3 The Father's love shield me this day,
The Son's pure wisdom cheer my way,
The Holy Spirit's light divine
Illume my heart's benighted shrine.

4 My Maker, strengthen Thou my heart,
O my Redeemer, help impart,
Blest Comforter, keep at my side,
That faith and love in me abide.

5 Lord, bless and keep Thou me as Thine!
Lord, make Thy face upon me shine!
Lord, lift Thy countenance on me,
And give me peace—sweet peace from Thee.

M. Behm, 1593

Family Prayer

546   10, 4, 10, 10, 10.   J. B. Dykes, 1823—1876

Lead, kindly Light, a-mid th'encircling gloom, Lead Thou me on!

The night is dark, and I am far from home, Lead Thou me on!

Keep Thou my feet! I do not ask to see......

The dis - tant scene; one step e - nough for me.

2 I was not ever thus, nor prayed that Thou
     Shouldst lead me on;
I loved to choose and see my path, but now
     Lead Thou me on!
I loved the garish day; and spite of fears,
Pride ruled my will: remember not past years.

3 So long Thy power has blest me, sure it still
     Will lead me on
O'er moor and fen, o'er crag and torrent, till
     The night is gone;
And with the morn those angel faces smile,
Which I have loved long since, and lost awhile.

Morning

4 Meantime along the narrow rugged path,
     Thyself hast trod,
Lead, Savior, lead me home in childlike faith,
     Home to my God,
To rest forever after earthly strife
In the calm light of everlasting life.

J. H. Newman 1833
V. 4. E. H Bickersteth, 1876

547   8, 4, 7, 8, 4, 7.   H. Hiles, 1865

Come, my soul, thou must be wak-ing! Now is break-ing
O'er the earth an-oth-er day; Come to Him who made the
splen-dor, See thou ren-der All thy fee-ble strength can pay.

2 Gladly hail the sun returning:
     Ready burning
Be the incense of thy powers;
For the night is safely ended;
     God hath tended
With His care thy helpless hours.

3 Pray that He may prosper ever
     Each endeavor,
When thy aim is good and true;
But that He may ever thwart thee
     And convert thee,
When thou evil wouldst pursue.

4 Only God's free gift abuse not,
     Light refuse not,
But His Spirit's voice obey;
Thou with Him shalt dwell, beholding
     Light enfolding
All things in unclouded day.

5 Glory, honor, exaltation,
     Adoration,
Be to the eternal One;
To the Father, Son, and Spirit,
     Laud and merit,
While unending ages run.

F. R. L. von Canitz, 1700

548   7, 8, 7, 8, 7, 3.

J. A. Freylinghausen, 1704

Dayspring of e - ter - ni - ty, Brightness of the Fa-ther's glo - ry,

Dawn on us that we may see Clouds and darkness flee be - fore Thee;

Drive a - far, with conquering might, All our night.

2 Let Thy grace, like morning dew,
   Fall on hearts in Thee confiding;
Thy sweet comfort, ever new,
   Fill our souls with strength abiding,
And Thy quickening eyes behold
   Thy dear fold.

3 Give the flame of love, to burn
   Till the bands of sin it breaketh,—
Till, at each new day's return,
   Purer light my soul awaketh:
O ere twilight come, let me
   Rise to Thee.

4 Thou who hast gone up on high,
   Grant that, when Thy trumpet soundeth,
When with glory, in the sky,
   Thee Thy cloud of saints surroundeth,—
We may stand among Thine own,
   Round Thy throne.

5 Light us to the golden shore,
   O Thou rising Sun of morning!
Lead where tears shall flow no more,
   Where all sighs to songs are turning,
Where Thy glory sheds alway
   Perfect day.

Chr. K. von Rosenroth, 1684

Morning

11, 10. 4L.   Frantz Abt, 1819—85

Still, still with Thee, when pur-ple morning break-eth,

When the bird wak - eth, and the shad-ows flee;

Fair - er than morn - ing, love - lier than the day - light,

Dawns the sweet conscious-ness, I am...... with Thee!

2 Alone with Thee, amid the mystic shadows,
   The solemn hush of nature newly born;
 Alone with Thee, in breathless adoration,
   In the calm dew and freshness of the morn.

3 When sinks the soul, subdued by toil, to slumber,
   Its closing eye looks up to Thee in prayer;
 Sweet the repose beneath Thy wings o'ershading,
   But sweeter still, to wake and find Thee there.

4 So shall it be at last, in that bright morning,
   When the soul waketh, and life's shadows flee;
 O in that hour, fairer than daylight dawning,
   Shall rise the glorious thought, I am with Thee!

Mrs. H. B. Stowe, 1855

Family Prayer

550 8s. 6l.

F. J. Haydn, 1732—1809

When, stream-ing from the east-ern skies, The morn-ing light sa-lutes mine eyes, O Sun of righteous-ness di-vine, On me with beams of mer-cy shine; Chase the dark clouds of guilt a-way, And turn my dark-ness in-to day.

2 As every day Thy mercy spares,
Will bring its trials and its cares,
O Savior, till my life shall end,
Be Thou my counselor and friend!
Teach me Thy precepts all divine,
And be Thy great example mine.

3 When each day's scenes and labors
close,
And wearied nature seeks repose,
With pardoning mercy richly blest,

Guard me, my Savior, while I rest;
And as each morning sun shall rise,
O lead me onward to the skies!

4 And at my life's last setting sun,
My conflicts o'er, my labors done,
Jesus, Thy heavenly radiance shed,
To cheer and bless my dying bed;
Then from death's gloom my spirit
raise,
To see Thy face and sing Thy praise.

W. Shrubsole, 1813

Evening

551   7, 7, 6, 7, 7, 8.   Heinrich Isaac, 1490

Now rest be-neath night's shad - ow   The woodland, field, and meadow,

The world in slum-ber lies;   But thou, my heart, a - wake thee, To

prayer and song be - take   thee, Let praise to thy Cre - a - tor rise.

2 To rest the body hasteth,
    Aside its garments casteth—
       Types of mortality;
    These I put off, and ponder
    How Christ shall give me yonder
       A robe of glorious majesty.

3 Ye weary limbs, now rest you,
    For toil hath sore oppressed you,
       And quiet sleep ye crave;
    A sleep shall once o'ertake you
    From which no man can wake you,
       In your last, narrow bed—the grave.

4 Lord Jesus, who dost love me,
    O spread Thy wings above me,
       And shield me from alarm!
    Though Satan would devour me,
    Let angel-guards sing o'er me:
       This child of God shall meet no harm.

5 My loved ones, rest securely,
    For God this night will surely
       From perils guard your heads;
    Sweet slumbers may He send you,
    And bid His hosts attend you,
       And through the night watch o'er your beds.

                                  P. Gerhardt, 1648

552 10s. 4L.

W. H. Monk, 1861

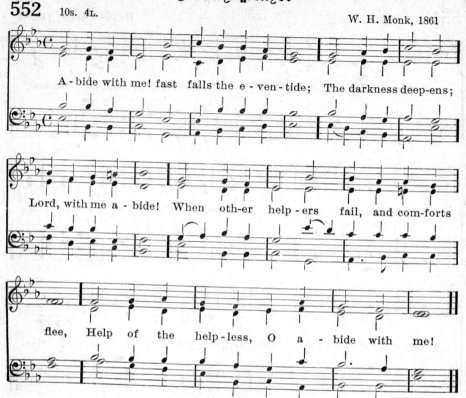

A-bide with me! fast falls the e-ven-tide; The darkness deep-ens; Lord, with me a-bide! When oth-er help-ers fail, and com-forts flee, Help of the help-less, O a-bide with me!

2 Swift to its close ebbs out life's little day;
Earth's joys grow dim, its glories pass away;
Change and decay in all around I see;
O Thou who changest not, abide with me!

3 Not a brief glance, I beg, a passing word,
But as Thou dwell'st with Thy disciples, Lord,
Familiar, condescending, patient, free,
Come, not to sojourn, but abide with me.

4 Come, not in terrors as the King of kings,
But kind and good, with healing on Thy wings;
Tears for all woes, a heart for every plea;
O Friend of sinners, thus abide with me!

5 Thou on my head in early youth didst smile,
And, though rebellious and perverse meanwhile,
Thou hast not left me, oft as I left Thee:
On to the close, O Lord, abide with me!

6 I need Thy presence every passing hour;
What but Thy grace can foil the tempter's power?
Who like Thyself my guide and stay can be?
Through cloud and sunshine, O abide with me!

Evening

7 I fear no foe, with Thee at hand to bless;
  Ills have no weight, and tears no bitterness.
  Where is death's sting? where, grave, thy victory?
  I triumph still, if Thou abide with me!

8 Hold Thou Thy cross before my closing eyes,
  Shine through the gloom and point me to the skies,
  Heaven's morning breaks, and earth's vain shadows flee;
  In life, in death, O Lord, abide with me!

H. F. Lyte, 1847

553 8, 8, 8, 4.

J. B. Dykes, 1823—76

The radiant morn hath passed a-way, And spent too soon her gold-en store;

The shad-ows of de-part-ing day Creep on once more.

2 Our life is but an autumn day,
  Its glorious noon how quickly past!
  Lead us, O Christ, Thou living way,
  Safe home at last.

3 O by Thy soul-inspiring grace
  Uplift our hearts to realms on high;
  Help us to look to that bright place
  Beyond the sky,

4 Where light and life and joy and peace
  In undivided empire reign,
  And thronging angels never cease
  Their deathless strain;

5 Where saints are clothed in spotless white,
  And evening shadows never fall,
  Where Thou, eternal Light of light,
  Art Lord of all.

G. Thring, 1864

Family Prayer

554 5, 11, 11, 11, 11, 5, 5. Norwegian Folk-Tune

The sun has gone down, And peace has de-scend-ed on country and town; The song-birds in si-lence have flown to their nest, And flow-ers are clos-ing their pe-tals in rest; So clos-es my heart to an-noy-ance and care, In hom-age and prayer, In hom-age and prayer.

2 I praise for this day
The Father in heaven, who prospered my way,
Who shielded from danger, protected from harm,
Promoted my labor, and strengthened my arm;
For hours that passed lightly as birds on the wing,
‖:Thanksgiving I bring.:‖

3 Forgive me, O Lord,
My sins and transgressions in deed and in word!
Thou knowest my heart and my innermost thought,
The words I have spoken, the deeds I have wrought,
My errors and failings I deeply regret,
‖:Forgive and forget!:‖

Evening

4 I ask for no more;
My light I extinguish and fasten the door,
And seeking my chamber, betake me to rest,
Assured that my slumber this night will be blest,
I fondly confide to Thy care and control
‖:My body and soul.:‖

S. O Bruun, 1695

555   7, 6, 7, 6, 8, 8.

A. H. Brown, 1862

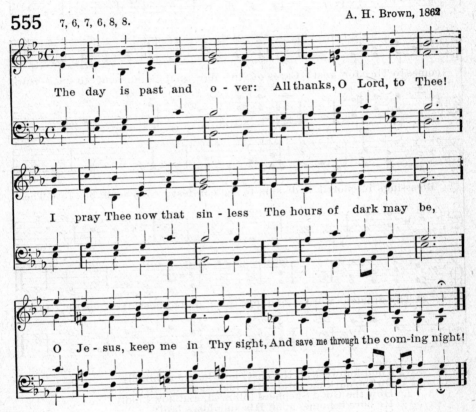

The day is past and o - ver: All thanks, O Lord, to Thee!

I pray Thee now that sin - less The hours of dark may be,

O Je - sus, keep me in Thy sight, And save me through the com-ing night!

2 The toils of day are over;
   I lift my heart to Thee;
And ask that free from peril
   The hours of dark may be,
O Jesus, make their darkness light,
And guard me through the coming night!

3 Be Thou my soul's preserver,
   O God! for Thou dost know
How many are the perils
   Through which I have to go.
Lover of men, O hear my call,
And guard and save me from them all!

Anatolius, ca. 800

Family Prayer

556 11, 10, 11, 10, 10, 10.

J. Barnby, 1865—96

Thou knowest, Lord, the wea-ri-ness and sor-row Of the sad heart that comes to Thee for rest; Cares of to-day and bur-dens of to-mor-row, Bless-ings im-plored and sins to be con-fest; We come be-fore Thee at Thy gracious word, And lay them at Thy feet, Thou knowest, Lord.

2 Thou knowest all the past; how long and blindly
On the dark mountains the lost wanderer strayed;
How the Good Shepherd followed, and how kindly
He bore it home, upon His shoulders laid;
He healed the bleeding wounds and soothed the pain,
And brought back life, and hope, and strength again.

3 Thou knowest all the present; each temptation,
Each toilsome duty, each foreboding fear;
All to each one assigned, of tribulation,
Or to belovèd ones, than self more dear;
All pensive memories, as we journey on,
Longings for vanished smiles and voices gone.

4 Thou knowest all the future; gleams of gladness
By stormy clouds so quickly overcast,
Hours of sweet fellowship and parting sadness,
And the dark river to be crossed at last.
O what could hope and confidence afford
To tread the path, but this: Thou knowest, Lord?

Evening

5 Thou knowest, not alone as God all-knowing;
   As man, our mortal weakness Thou hast proved;
   On earth with purest sympathies o'erflowing,
   O Savior, Thou hast wept, and Thou hast loved;
   And love and sorrow still to Thee may come,
   And find a hiding place, a rest, a home.

6 Therefore we come, Thy gentle call obeying,
   And lay our sins and sorrows at Thy feet,
   On everlasting strength our weakness staying,
   Clothed in Thy robe of righteousness complete:
   Then rising and refreshed, we leave Thy throne,
   And follow on to know as we are known.

Jane Borthwick, 1859

557 L. M. German

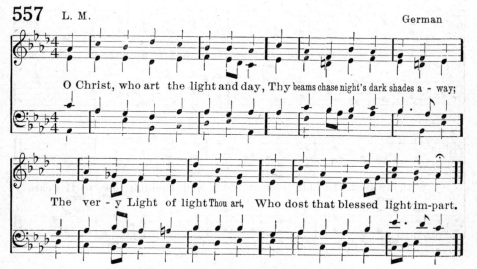

O Christ, who art the light and day, Thy beams chase night's dark shades a-way;

The ver-y Light of light Thou art, Who dost that blessed light im-part.

2 All-holy Lord, to Thee we bend,
   Thy servants through this night defend,
   And grant us calm repose in Thee,
   A quiet night from perils free.

3 Let not dull sleep the soul oppress,
   Nor secret foe the heart possess.
   Nor Satan's wiles the flesh allure,
   And make us in Thy sight impure.

4 Light slumbers let our eyelids take,
   The heart to Thee be still awake;
   And Thy right hand protection be
   To those who love and trust in Thee.

5 O Lord, our strong defense, be nigh;
   Bid all the powers of darkness fly;
   Preserve and watch o'er us for good,
   Whom Thou hast purchased with Thy blood.

6 Remember us, dear Lord, we pray,
   Whilst burdened in the flesh we stay;
   Thou only canst the soul defend;
   Be with us, Savior, to the end.

Anon., Latin, 8th Century

Family Prayer

558 8, 8, 7, 8, 8, 7.

Zinck's Koralbog, 1801

Darkness o'er the earth is stealing— In my lone-ly chamber kneeling,

I will say my evening prayer, Longing for a clos-er un-ion,

With my God I hold commun-ion And com-mit me to His care.

2 Yes, it is a blessed favor
   To commune with Thee, my Savior,
       Filled with hope and faith sincere;
   Cheer my heart, my burden lighten—
   May Thy word my pathway brighten,
       To my prayer incline Thine ear!

3 Thee, my God, I fain would follow,
   Love and honor, but how shallow
       And inconstant is my love!
   Spread the veil of mercy over
   All my sins, my errors cover
       With compassion from above!

4 Let Thine eye be vigil keeping
   Over me while I am sleeping.
       And my waking moments heed;
   May Thy love be unabated,
   Be with those who are elated,
       And with those who are in need!

Evening

5 Help the wanderer, cold and weary,
  On the highway dark and dreary—
    May he find an open door!
  Those who on the stormy ocean
  Ply their trade 'mid wild commotion—
    Guide them safely to the shore!

6 Hear the sick who are imploring
  Thee for aid, their health restoring,
    To the dying comfort bring!
  Christ, who bore our sin and sorrow,
  Grant them that the dawning morrow
    Come with healing on its wing.

7 When at last the shadows darken,
  Come and to my prayer, O hearken,
    Set us all from bondage free;
  Then, beyond this vale of sorrow,
  There shall dawn a brighter morrow,
    When Thy face in heaven we see.

M. B. Landstad, 1855

559 8, 7. 4L.   John B. Dykes, 1823—76

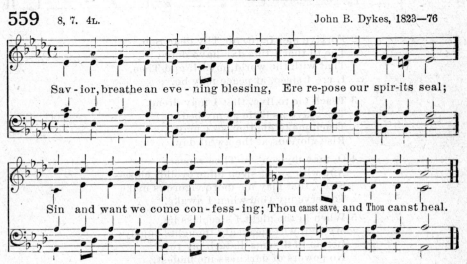

Sav-ior, breathe an eve-ning blessing, Ere re-pose our spir-its seal;
Sin and want we come con-fess-ing; Thou canst save, and Thou canst heal.

2 Though destruction walk around us,
    Though the arrow past us fly,
  Angel-guards from Thee surround us;
    We are safe if Thou art nigh.

3 Though the night be dark and dreary,
    Darkness cannot hide from Thee;
  Thou art He who, never weary,
    Watchest where Thy people be.

4 Should swift death this night o'ertake us,
    And our couch become our tomb,
  May the morn in heaven awake us,
    Clad in bright and deathless bloom.

James Edmeston, 1820

Family Prayer

560 L. M.

Thomas Tallis, 1515—85

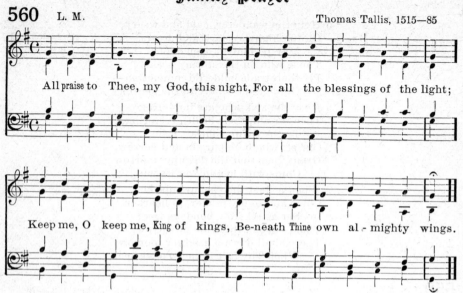

All praise to Thee, my God, this night, For all the blessings of the light;

Keep me, O keep me, King of kings, Be-neath Thine own al - mighty wings.

2 Forgive me, Lord, for Thy dear Son,
The ill that I this day have done;
That with the world, myself and Thee,
I, ere I sleep, at peace may be.

3 Teach me to live, that I may dread
The grave as little as my bed;
Teach me to die that so I may
Rise glorious at the awful day.

4 O may my soul on Thee repose,
And with sweet sleep mine eyelids close—
Sleep, that may me more vigorous make
To serve my God when I awake.

5 When in the night I sleepless lie,
My soul with heavenly thoughts supply;
Let no ill dreams disturb my rest,
No powers of darkness me molest.

T. Ken, 1693

561 7s. 4L.

Arr. fr. C. M. von Weber, 1826

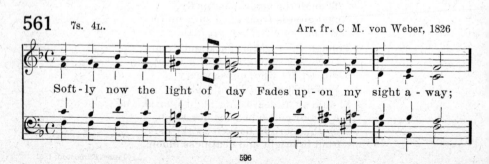

Soft - ly now the light of day Fades up - on my sight a - way;

Evening

Free from care, from la-bor free, Lord, I would commune with Thee.

2 Thou, whose all-pervading eye
   Naught escapes, without, within,
   Pardon each infirmity,
   Open fault, and secret sin.

3 Soon, for me, the light of day
   Shall forever pass away;
   Then, from sin and sorrow free,
   Take me, Lord, to dwell with Thee.

4 Thou who, sinless, yet hast known
   All of man's infirmity:
   Then, from Thine eternal throne,
   Jesus, look with pitying eye.

G. W. Doane, 1824

562   6, 5, 6, 5.   J. Barnby, 1868

Now the day is o-ver, Night is drawing nigh;
Shadows of the eve-ning Steal a-cross the sky.
eve-ning Steal a-cross the sky.

2 Jesus, give the weary
   Calm and sweet repose;
   With Thy tenderest blessing
   May our eyelids close.

3 Comfort every sufferer
   Watching late in pain;
   Those who plan some evil
   From their sins restrain.

4 Through the long night-watches,
   May Thine angels spread
   Their white wings above me,
   Watching round my bed.

5 When the morning wakens,
   Then may I arise
   Pure and fresh, and sinless
   In Thy holy eyes.

Baring-Gould, 1865

Family Prayer

563 8, 7, 8, 7, 7, 7.

A. P. Berggreen, 1849

Through the day Thy love hath spared us, Now we lay us down to rest; Through the si - lent watch-es guard us, Let no foe our peace mo - lest: Je - sus, Thou our guardian be; Sweet it is to trust in Thee.

2 Pilgrims here on earth, and strangers,
Dwelling in the midst of foes,
Us and ours preserve from dangers:
In Thine arms may we repose;
And when life's brief day is past,
Rest with Thee in heaven at last.

T. Kelly, 1806

Evening

564 6, 4, 6, 6.

J. H. Hopkins, 1872

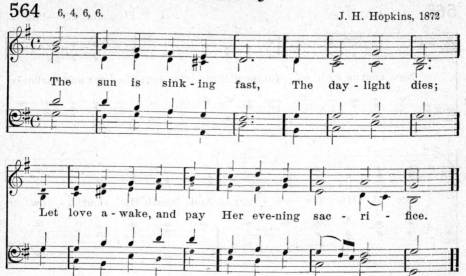

The sun is sink-ing fast, The day-light dies;

Let love a-wake, and pay Her eve-ning sac - ri - fice.

2 As Christ upon the cross
    His head inclined,
And to His Father's hand
    His parting soul resigned;

3 So now herself my soul
    Would wholly give
Into His sacred charge,
    In whom all spirits live;

4 So now beneath His eye
    Would calmly rest,
Without a wish or thought
    Abiding in the breast,

5 Save that His will be done,
    Whate'er betide,
Dead to herself, and dead
    In Him to all beside.

6 Thus would I live; yet now
    Not I, but He,
In all His power and love
    Henceforth alive in me.

7 One sacred Trinity,
    One Lord divine;
May I be ever His,
    And He for ever mine.

Anon. (Latin)

Family Prayer

565   11, 11, 11, 5.

F. F. Flemming, 1778—1813

Now God be with us, for the night is clos-ing; The light and darkness are of His dis-pos-ing; And 'neath His shad - ow here to rest we yield us, For He will shield us.

2 Let evil thoughts and spirits flee before us;
Till morning cometh, watch, O Father, o'er us;
In soul and body Thou from harm defend us,
    Thine angels send us.

3 Let pious thoughts be ours when sleep o'ertakes us;
Our earliest thoughts be Thine when morning wakes us;
All day serve Thee, in all that we are doing
    Thy praise pursuing.

4 Through Thy Beloved soothe the sick and weeping,
And bid the captive lose his griefs in sleeping;
Widows and orphans, we to Thee commend them,
    Do Thou befriend them.

5 We have no refuge, none on earth to aid us;
Save Thee, O Father, who Thine own hast made us;
But Thy dear presence will not leave them lonely
    Who seek Thee only.

6 Father, Thy name be praised, Thy kingdom given;
Thy will be done on earth, as 'tis in heaven;
Give daily bread; forgive our sins; deliver
    Us now and ever.

P. Herbert. 1566

Evening

566 L. M.

German, 1775

Sun of my soul, Thou Sav - ior dear, It is not night if Thou be near; O may no earth - born cloud a - rise To hide Thee from Thy ser - vant's eyes.

2 When the soft dews of kindly sleep
My weary eyelids gently steep,
Be my last thought, how sweet to rest
For ever on my Savior's breast.

3 Abide with me from morn till eve,
For without Thee I cannot live;
Abide with me when night is nigh,
For without Thee I dare not die.

4 If some poor wandering child of Thine
Have spurned today the voice divine,
Now, Lord, the gracious work begin;
Let him no more lie down in sin.

5 Watch by the sick; enrich the poor
With blessings from Thy boundless store;
Be every mourner's sleep tonight,
Like infants' slumbers, pure and light.

6 Come near and bless us when we wake,
Ere through the world our way we take,
Till in the ocean of Thy love
We lose ourselves in heaven above.

J. Keble, 1820

Family Prayer

567 7, 6. 8L.   J. B. Dykes, 1823—76

The hours of day are o - ver, The eve-ning calls us home;

Once more to Thee, O Fa - ther, With thankful hearts we come;

For all Thy count-less bless - ings We praise Thy ho - ly name,

And own Thy love un - chang - ing, Through days and years the same.

2 For this, O Lord, we bless Thee,
   For this we thank Thee most:
The cleansing of the sinful,
   The saving of the lost;
The Teacher ever present,
   The Friend for ever nigh,
The home prepared by Jesus
   For us above the sky.

3 Lord, gather all Thy children
   To meet Thee there at last,
Where earthly tasks are ended,
   And earthly days are past;
With all our loved ones round us
   In that eternal home,
Where death no more shall part us,
   And night shall never come.

                                        J. Ellerton, 1858

Grace Before and After Meat

568 L. M.   L. Bourgeois, 1551

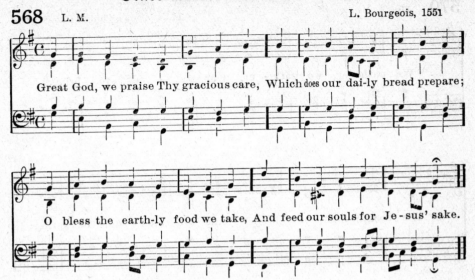

Great God, we praise Thy gracious care, Which does our dai-ly bread prepare;

O bless the earth-ly food we take, And feed our souls for Je-sus' sake.

2 We thank Thee, Lord, for this our food,
For life and health, and every good:
May manna to our souls be given,
The Bread of life, sent down from heaven.

J. Cennick, 1741

569 L. M.   German, 1605

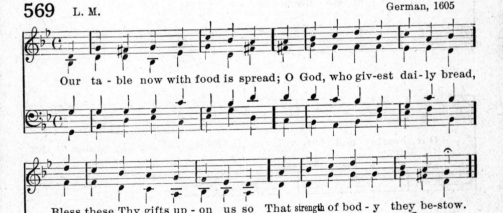

Our ta-ble now with food is spread; O God, who giv-est dai-ly bread,

Bless these Thy gifts up-on us so That strength of bod-y they be-stow.

2 O feed the hungry, God of love,
Who sigh for bread to Heaven above;
Give to our land prosperity,
And bless the earth, the sky, the sea!

3 Defend and bless our government,
And give us all a mind content!
O grant our souls the heavenly food
Which Jesus purchased with His blood.

T. Kingo, 1689

570   11s. 5L.

F. J. Wade's Cantus Diversi, **1751**

We gath-er, we gath-er, dear Je - sus, to bring

The breath-ings of love 'mid the blos-soms of spring;

Our Mak-er Re - deem - er, we grate-ful-ly raise

Our hearts and our voic-es in hymn - ing Thy praise, Our

hearts and our voic - es in hymn-ing Thy praise.

Children's Service

2 When stooping to earth from the brightness of heaven,
Thy blood for our ransom so freely was given,
Thou deignedst to listen while children adored,
‖: With joyful Hosannas, the blest of the Lord.:‖

3 Those arms, which embraced little children of old,
Still love to encircle the lambs of the fold;
That grace which inviteth the wandering home,
‖:Hath never forbidden the youngest to come.:‖

4 Hosanna! Hosanna! Great Teacher, we raise
Our hearts and our voices in hymning Thy praise;
For precept and promise so graciously given,
‖:For blessings of earth, and for glories of heaven.:‖

Anon.

571 8, 7. 6L

Erik K. Hoff, b. 1832

Sav-ior, like a shep-herd lead us, Much we need Thy tenderest care:

In Thy pleas-ant pastures feed us, For our use Thy folds prepare;

Bless-ed Je-sus, Bless-ed Je-sus, Thou hast bought us, Thine we are.

2 Thou hast promised to receive us,
  Poor and sinful though we be;
Thou hast mercy to relieve us,
  Grace to cleanse, and power to free;
Blessed Jesus, Blessed Jesus,
  Let us early turn to Thee.

3 Early let us seek Thy favor,
  Early let us do Thy will;
Blessed Lord and only Savior,
  With Thy love our bosoms fill;
Blessed Jesus, Blessed Jesus,
  Thou hast loved us, love us still.

Anon. ca. 1836

Children's Service

572   10, 4, 10, 4, 10, 10.   Charles H. Purday, 1799—1885

Je - sus, who call - edst lit-tle ones to Thee, To Thee I come;

O take my hand in Thine, and speak to me, And lead me home;

Lest from the path of life my feet should stray,

And Sa - tan prowl - ing make Thy lamb his prey.

2 I love to think that Thou with holy feet
     My path hast trod;
  Along life's common lanes and dusty street
     Hast walked with God;
  On Mary's bosom drawn an infant's breath,
  And served Thy parents dear at Nazareth.

Children's Service

3 O gentle Jesus, make this heart of mine,
  So full of sin,
  As holy, harmless, undefiled, as Thine,
  And dwell therein;
  Then God my Father I, like Thee, shall know,
  And grow in wisdom as in strength I grow.

4 To Thee, my Savior, then, with morning light
  Glad songs I'll raise,
  My saddest hours and darkest shall be bright
  With silent praise;
  And should my work or play my thoughts employ,
  Thy will shall be my law, Thy love my joy.

C. E. Mudie, 1872

573 C. M.

Arr. from C. G. Gläser, 1828
By L. Mason, 1839

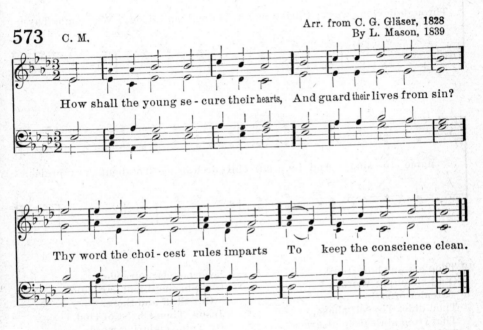

How shall the young se - cure their hearts, And guard their lives from sin?

Thy word the choi - cest rules imparts To keep the conscience clean.

2 'Tis, like the sun, a heavenly light,
  That guides us all the day;
And through the dangers of the night
  A lamp to lead our way.

3 The starry heavens Thy rule obey,
  The earth maintains her place;
And these Thy servants, night and day,
  Thy skill and power express.

4 But still Thy law and gospel, Lord,
  Have lessons more divine;
Not earth stands firmer than Thy word,
  Nor stars so nobly shine.

5 Thy word is everlasting truth:
  How pure is every page!
That holy book shall guide our youth,
  And well support our age.

I. Watts, 1719

Children's Service

6, 6, 4, 6, 6, 6, 4.

L. Mason, 1832

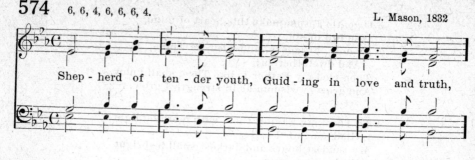

Shep-herd of ten-der youth, Guid-ing in love and truth,

Through devious ways; Christ our tri-umph-ant King, We come Thy

name to sing, And here our chil-dren bring To shout Thy praise.

2 Thou art our holy Lord,
   O all-subduing Word,
      Healer of strife;
   Thou didst Thyself abase,
   That from sin's deep disgrace
   Thou mightest save our race,
      And give us life.

3 Thou art the great High Priest;
   Thou hast prepared the feast
      Of holy love:
   And in our mortal pain,
   None call on Thee in vain;
   Help Thou dost not disdain,
      Help from above.

4 Ever be near our side,
   Our Shepherd and our Guide,
      Our Staff and Song;
   Jesus, Thou Christ of God,
   By Thine enduring word,
   Lead us where Thou hast trod,
      Make our faith strong.

5 So now, until we die,
   Sound we Thy praises high,
      And joyful sing;
   Let all the holy throng
   Who to Thy Church belong,
   Unite and swell the song
      To Christ our King!

Clement of Alexandria, ca. 220

575   8, 7. 6L.

Erik K. Hoff, b. 1832

Gracious Sav-ior, gen-tle Shep-herd, Children all are dear to Thee;

Gathered with Thine arms, and car-ried In Thy bos-om may we be;

Sweetly, fond-ly, safe-ly tend-ed, From all want and dan-ger free.

2 Tender Shepherd, never leave us
    From Thy fold to go astray;
By Thy look of love directed,
    May we walk the narrow way;
Thus direct us, and protect us,
    Lest we fall an easy prey.

3 Cleanse our hearts from sinful folly,
    In the stream Thy love supplied,
Mingled stream of blood and water,
    Flowing from Thy wounded side;
And to heavenly pastures lead us,
    Where Thine own still waters glide.

4 Let Thy holy word instruct us;
    Guide us daily by its light;
Let Thy love and grace constrain us
    To approve whate'er is right,
Take Thine easy yoke, and wear it,
    Strengthened with Thy heavenly might.

5 Taught to lisp the holy praises
    Which on earth Thy children sing,
Both with lips and hearts unfeigned,
    May we our thank-offerings bring;
Then with all the saints in glory
    Join to praise our Lord and King.

Jane E. Leeson, 1842

Children's Service

5, 5, 7, 5, 5, 8.

German, 1842

Beau - ti - ful Sav - ior! King of cre - a - tion!

Son of God and Son of Man! Tru - ly I'd love Thee,

Tru - ly I'd serve Thee, Light of my soul, my joy, my crown!

2 Fair are the meadows,
  Fairer the woodlands,
Robed in flowers of blooming spring;
  Jesus is fairer;
  Jesus is purer;
He makes our sorrowing spirit sing.

3 Fair is the sunshine,
  Fairer the moonlight
And the sparkling stars on high;
  Jesus shines brighter,
  Jesus shines purer,
Than all the angels in the sky.

4 Beautiful Savior!
  Lord of the nations!
Son of God and Son of Man!
  Glory and honor,
  Praise, adoration,
Now and for evermore be Thine!

Anon. (German) 1677 and 1842

Children's Service

577 7, 6. 8L L. Mason, 1823

When, His sal - va - tion bring-ing, To Zi - on Je - sus came,
The chil - dren all stood sing - ing Ho - san - na to His name.
Nor did their zeal of - fend Him, But as He rode a - long
He let them still at - tend Him, And smiled to hear their song.

2 And since the Lord retaineth
   His love for children still,
Though now as king He reigneth
   On Zion's heavenly hill;
We'll flock around His banner,
   Who sits upon the throne,
And cry aloud, "Hosanna
   To David's royal Son!"

3 For should we fail proclaiming
   Our great Redeemer's praise,
The stones, our silence shaming,
   Might well Hosanna raise.
But shall we only render
   The tribute of our words?
No; while our hearts are tender,
   They, too, shall be the Lord's.

J. King, 1830

Children's Service

578   8, 7. 8L.   From a Gregorian Chant by L. Mason, 1839

Heavenly Fa-ther, send Thy blessing   On Thy children gathered here;

May they all, Thy name con-fess-ing,   Be to Thee for ev-er dear;

May they be like Joseph, lov-ing,   Du-ti-ful, and chaste, and pure;

And their faith, like Da-vid, prov-ing,   Steadfast un-to death en-dure.

2 Holy Savior, who in meekness
  Didst vouchsafe a child to be,
Guide their steps and help their weak-
    ness,
  Bless and make them like to Thee;
Bear Thy lambs, when they are weary,
  In Thine arms, and at Thy breast;
Through life's desert, dry and dreary,
  Bring them to Thy heavenly rest.

3 Spread Thy golden pinions o'er them,
  Holy Spirit, from above,
Guide them, lead them, go before
    them,
  Give them peace, and joy, and love;
Thy true temples, Holy Spirit,
  May they with Thy glory shine,
And immortal bliss inherit,
  And forevermore be Thine.

Chr. Wordsworth, 1863

Preparation for Death

579 9, 8, 9, 8, 8, 8. German, Hamburg, 1690

Who knows how near my life's ex-pend-ed? Time flies, and death is hast-ing on, How soon, my term of tri-al end-ed, Death may be here and life be gone. My God, for Je-sus' sake, I pray Thy peace may bless my dy-ing day.

2 My many sins! O veil them over
With merits of Thy dying Son!
I here Thy richest grace discover,
Here find I peace, and here alone;
My God, for Jesus' sake, I pray
Thy peace may bless my dying day.

3 His bleeding wounds give me assurance
That Thy free mercy will abide;
Here strength I find for death's endurance,

And hope for all I need beside:
My God, for Jesus' sake, I pray
Thy peace may bless my dying day.

4 Naught shall my soul from Jesus sever,
Nor life, nor death; things high nor low;
I take Him as my Lord forever,
My future trust, as He is now;
My God, for Jesus' sake, I pray
Thy peace may bless my dying day.

613   Emilie Juliane of Schwartzburg-Rudolstadt, 1886

580

11s. 4L.

I would not live al - way; I ask not to stay

Where storm aft - er storm ris - es dark o'er the way;

The few lu - rid morn - ings that dawn on us here

Are e - nough for life's woes, full e - nough for its cheer.

2 I would not live alway, thus fettered by sin,
Temptation without, and corruption within;
E'en the rapture of pardon is mingled with fears,
And the cup of thanksgiving with penitent tears.

Preparation for Death

3 I would not live alway; no, welcome the tomb:
  Since Jesus hath lain there, I dread not its gloom;
  There sweet be my rest, till He bid me arise
  To hail Him in triumph descending the skies.

4 Who, who would live alway, away from his God;
  Away from yon heaven, that blissful abode,
  Where the rivers of pleasure flow o'er the bright plains,
  And the noontide of glory eternally reigns?

5 Where the saints of all ages in harmony meet,
  Their Savior and brethren transported to greet,
  While the anthems of rapture unceasingly roll,
  And the smile of the Lord is the feast of the soul.

W. A. Muhlenberg, 1826

581 9, 8, 9, 8, 8, 8.   Georg Neumark, 1622—81

To Thee, O Lord, I yield my spir-it, Who break'st in love this mortal chain;

My life I but from Thee in-her-it, And death becomes my chiefest gain

In Thee I live, in Thee I die, Content, for Thou art ev-er nigh.

L. R. Senfft von Pilsach, 1715

The Last Things

582   8, 7, 8, 7, 8, 8, 7.

J. Wolff, 1569

When my last hour is close at hand, Lord Je-sus Christ, at-tend me;

Be-side my bed, my Sav-ior, stand, To com-fort, help, de-fend me:

In-to Thy hands I will com-mend My trembling soul at

my last end,— How safe in Thy sweet keep - ing!

2 Countless as sands upon the shore,
   My sins are thronging round me;
But though they grieve and wound
      me sore,
   They cannot yet confound me;
My sins are numberless, I know,
But o'er them all Thy blood doth flow,
   Thy wounds and death uphold me.

3 Lord, Thou hast joined my soul to
      Thine,
   In bonds no power can sever;
Grafted in Thee, the living vine,
   I shall be Thine for ever:
Lord, when I die, I die to Thee,
Thy precious death hath won for me
   A life that never endeth.

4 Since Thou hast risen from the grave,
   The grave cannot detain me;
"Christ died,"—"Christ rose again"
      to save,
   These words shall still sustain me;
For where Thou art, there I shall be,
That I may ever live with Thee:
   This is my joy in dying.

5 To Thee, Lord Jesus Christ, I will
   With arms outstretched betake me;
I sleep in Thee—so sound—so still,
   No mortal man can wake me!
For Jesus Christ, Gods Son, I wait
To open me the heavenly gate,
   Which leads to life eternal.

N. Hermann, 1562

Preparation for Death

583 7, 6. 4L.

Melchior Vulpius, 1609

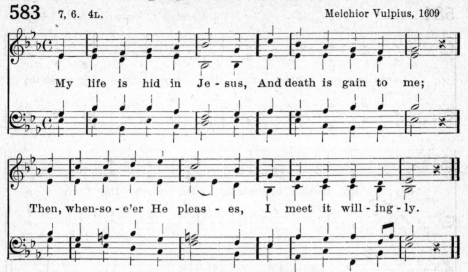

My life is hid in Je - sus, And death is gain to me;

Then, when-so - e'er He pleas - es, I meet it will - ing - ly.

2 For Christ, my Lord and brother,
  I leave this world so dim,
And gladly seek that other,
  Where I shall be with Him.

3 My woes are nearly over,
  Though long and dark the road;
My sin His merits cover,
  And I have peace with God.

4 Lord, when my powers are failing
  My breath comes heavily,
And words are unavailing,
  O hear my sighs to Thee!

5 When mind and thought, O Savior,
  Are flickering, like a light,
That to and fro doth waver,
  Ere 'tis extinguished quite;

6 In that last hour, O grant me
  To slumber soft and still,
No doubts to vex or haunt me,
  Safe anchored on Thy will;

7 And so to Thee still cleaving
  Through all death's agony,
To fall asleep believing,
  And wake in heaven with Thee.

8 Amen! Thou Christ, my Savior,
  Wilt grant this unto me:
Thy Spirit lead me ever,
  That I fare happily.

Anon., German, 1609

The Last Things

J. Clauders's "Psalmodia Nova," 1630

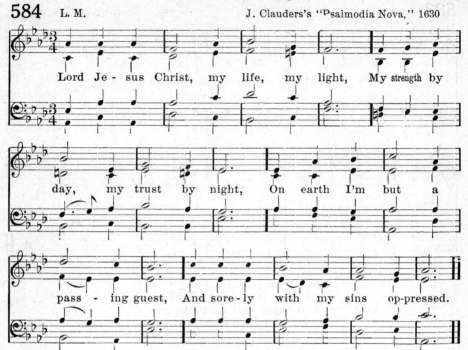

Lord Je-sus Christ, my life, my light, My strength by
day, my trust by night, On earth I'm but a
pass - ing guest, And sore-ly with my sins op-pressed.

2 Far off I see my fatherland,
   Where through Thy grace I hope to stand,
   But ere I reach that paradise,
   A weary way before me lies.

3 My heart sinks at the journey's length,
   My wasted flesh has little strength,
   Only my soul still cries in me,
   Lord, fetch me home, take me to Thee!

4 O let Thy sufferings give me power
   To meet the last and darkest hour;
   Thy cross the staff whereon I lean,
   My couch the grave where Thou hast been.

5 Since Thou hast died, the pure, the just,
   I take my homeward way in trust,
   The gates of heaven, Lord, open wide,
   When here I may no more abide.

6 And when the last great day is come,
   And Thou, our Judge, shalt speak the doom,
   Let me with joy behold the light,
   And set me then upon Thy right.

7 Renew this wasted flesh of mine,
   That like the sun it there may shine,
   Among the angels pure and bright,
   Yea, like Thyself in glorious light.

8 Ah, then I have my heart's desire,
   When singing with the angels' choir,
   Among the ransomed of Thy grace,
   For ever I behold Thy face!

M. Behm, 1610

Preparation for Death

585 8s. 6L.   Schumann's Gesangbuch, 1539

O Lord, my God, I cry to Thee! In my dis-tress Thou
help-est me. To Thee my-self I now com-mend: O
swift-ly now Thine an-gel send To guide me home and
cheer my heart, Since Thou dost call me to de-part.

2 O Jesus Christ, Thou Lamb of God,
  Once slain to take away our load;
  Now let Thy cross, Thine agony,
  Avail to save and solace me;
  Thy death to open heaven, and there
  Bid me the joy of angels share.

3 O Holy Spirit, at the end,
  Sweet Comforter, be Thou my friend;
  When death and hell assail me sore,
  Leave me, O leave me nevermore,
  But bear me safely through the strife,
  As Thou hast promised, into life!

N. Selnecker, 1572

The Last Things

586 8s. 6L.

W. H. Monk, 1861

My God, I know that I must die: My mor-tal life is passing hence; On earth I neith-er hope nor try To find a last-ing res-i-dence. Then teach me by Thy heaven-ly grace With joy and peace my death to face.

2 My God, I know not when I die;
  What is the moment or the hour,
How soon the clay may broken lie,
  How quickly pass away the flower.
Then may Thy child prepared be
Through time to meet eternity.

3 My God, I know not how I die;
  For death has many ways to come,
In dark mysterious agony,
  Or gently as a sleep to some.
Just as Thou wilt, if but it be
To bring me, blessed Lord, to Thee!

4 My God, I know not where I die,
  Where is my grave, beneath what strand:
Yet from its gloom I do rely
  To be delivered by Thy hand.
Content I take what spot is mine,
Since all the earth, my Lord, is Thine.

5 My gracious God, when I must die,
  O bear my happy soul above,
With Christ, my Lord, eternally
  To share Thy glory and Thy love.
Then comes it right and well to me
When, where, and how my death shall be.

B Schmolck, 1700

Preparation for Death

Schumann's Gesangbuch, 1539

Lord Je-sus Christ, true man and God, Who bor-est anguish, scorn, the rod, And diedst at last up-on the tree, To bring Thy Fa-ther's grace to me: I pray Thee, through that bit-ter woe, Let me, a sin-ner, mer-cy know.

2 When comes the hour of failing breath,
And I must wrestle, Lord, with death,
When from my sight all fades away,
And when my tongue no more can say,
And when mine ears no more can hear,
And when my heart is racked with fear:

3 When all my mind is darkened o'er,
And human help can do no more;
Then come, Lord Jesus! come with speed,
And help me in my hour of need;
Lead me from this dark vale beneath,
And shorten then the pangs of death.

4 Joyful my resurrection be,
Thou in the judgment plead for me,
And hide my sins, Lord, from Thy face,
And give me life, of Thy rich grace!
I trust Thee utterly, my Lord,
For Thou hast promised in Thy word!

5 Dear Lord, forgive us all our guilt;
Help us to wait until Thou wilt
That we depart; and let our faith
Be brave, and conquer e'en in death;
Firm resting on Thy sacred word,
Until we sleep in Thee, our Lord.

P. Eber, 1565.

588 7, 8, 7, 8, 7, 7. Swedish

Go and let my grave be made— Tired and wea-ry now with straying,
Farewell to the earth I've said, Heav-en's call to peace o-bey-ing:
Calls me now the hap-py rest Of the an-gels ev-er blest.

2 Therefore, earth, farewell I say,
  False the hopes from which we borrow!
Let me now in peace away—
  E'en thy very joy is sorrow;
Fleeting is thy beauty's glow,
Vain deceit and empty show!

3 Fare ye well, beloved friends!
  Ye whose tears so fast are flowing;
God for all will make amends,
  For our griefs are His bestowing:
Mourn not joys that e'en endure,
Heavenly joys alone are sure.

4 Weep not—lo! my Savior there,
  Mercy to my soul revealing;
I, too, have obtained a share
  In His heart's deep wounds so healing,
Whence the holy fountain streamed
Which this sinful world redeemed.

5 Weep not—my Redeemer lives—
  High above dark earth ascending,
Hope her heavenly comfort gives;
  Faith stands by, her shield extending;
Love eternal whispers near,
"Child of God, no longer fear."

E. M. Arndt, 1818

Burial and Resurrection

589   8, 7, 8, 7, 6, 6, 8, 8.   Freylinghausen's Gesangbuch, 1704

From place to place the Christian goes, By many a tempest driven,
At last the haven of repose He safely finds in heaven.
God, after life's alarms, Receives him in His arms.
He dies, as in the mold the grain, To yield its golden fruit again.

2 And sure thy parting has been blessed,
  Bless'd be thy life's example!
Thou spirit, calmly gone to rest,
  And thou, its mouldering temple.
    O soul, thy Savior's near!
    The morning star shines clear;
And you, ye members, softly sleep
Beneath love's shadow still and deep.

3 We wait with glad and patient hope
  The glorious revelation,
While He this pilgrim dress folds up
  In holy preservation.
    O happy souls who rest
    In Jesus' arms and breast.
Love leads us all our path aright,
Through such a depth to such a height

N. L. von Zinzendorf, 1735

The Last Things

590   8, 9, 8, 8, 9, 8, 6, 6, 4, 4, 4, 8.

Ph. Nicolai, 1599

Bless - ed are the heirs of heav - en, The dead, who die
in Christ for - giv - en, They from their la - bors have release; Saith the Spir - it: they are rest - ing,
No sting of death is them mo - lest - ing, For
they have found the home of peace; In peace they sweetly rest,

Burial and Resurrection

For - ev - er they are blest, Hal - le - lu - jah! Be-

fore God's throne   to His dear Son   Do follow them their works well done.

2 Glory, honor and thanksgiving,
Be unto God the ever-living,
  And to the Lamb for sinners slain!
Ransomed host that now victorious
Have won the crown of life all glorious,
  Extol the Lamb, enthroned to reign!
    For us Himself He gave,
    He sank into the grave,
      He is risen!
He went before, death's pathway o'er,
We follow to the heavenly shore.

3 Sun nor moon their light are casting
Where God in glory everlasting
  Dispels the gloomy shades of night;
Now the wished-for day appeareth,
O blessed sight, our souls it cheereth,
  The Lamb is now our sun and light!
    No more we weep or moan,
    The former things are gone,
      Hallelujah!
Death's shades now flee, we rise to see
The dayspring of eternity.

F. G. Klopstock, 1758

591 5, 6. 10L.   Zinck's Koralbog, 1801

Life's day is end - ed, The bat - tle fought and won; With joy un - blend - ed I greet the set of sun. My soul, now rest thee For - ev - er, tired of earth; At last di-

Burial and Resurrection

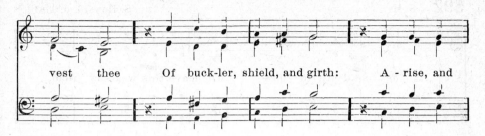

vest   thee   Of   buck-ler, shield, and girth: A - rise, and

haste   thee   To   heaven-ly   glo - ries   forth.

2 My pathway, leading
   Through realms of tears and pain,
I see receding,
   And ne'er shall tread again.
Life's stern endeavor,
   That set my soul aglow,
So that I never
   A moment's rest did know,
Shall cease forever,
   And God the prize bestow.

3 My shield remaineth,
   The warfare now is o'er;
My heart maintaineth
   Its trust in God secure.
I hard contended
   For faith both day and night;
The foe intended
   To break its saving might,
But now hath ended
   That tempter's losing fight.

4 Hence Christ in heaven
   Did me a crown prepare,
Which shall be given
   Not only me to wear,
But whomsoever,

The lowliest and the best,
Who doth endeavor
   To serve his Savior blest,
And so forever
   Shall be his worthy guest.

5 Now, world, I leave thee,
   And bid a last farewell,
Content, believe me,
   Hence in the grave to dwell.
Let flesh that faileth
   Return again to clay,
Where woe prevaileth,
   With trials day by day,
What now assaileth
   I meet without dismay.

6 All praise and honor,
   Now and forevermore,
Be our Atoner,
   That for us death He bore;
Him, bleeding, dying,
   Who kept me at His right,
When days were trying,
   I hold before my sight;
In His wounds lying
   At rest, I bid good night.

H. A. Brorson, 1742

The Last Things

592 S. M.

S. Howard, d. 1782

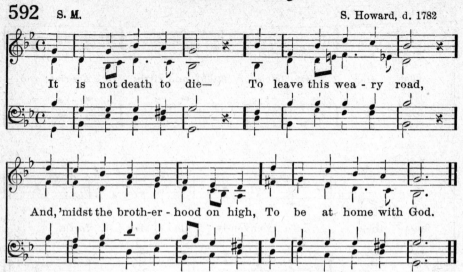

It is not death to die—
To leave this wea-ry road,

And, 'midst the broth-er-hood on high, To be at home with God.

2 It is not death to close
   The eye long dimmed with tears,
   And wake in glorious repose
   To spend eternal years.

3 It is not death to bear
   The wrench that sets us free
   From dungeon chain, to breathe the
   Of boundless liberty.   [air

4 It is not death to fling
   Aside this sinful dust,
   And rise on strong exulting wing,
   To live among the just.

5 Jesus, Thou Prince of life,
   Thy chosen cannot die;
   Like Thee, they conquer in the strife,
   To reign with Thee on high.

H. A. César Malan, 1832

593 L. M.

W. Knapp, 1698—1768

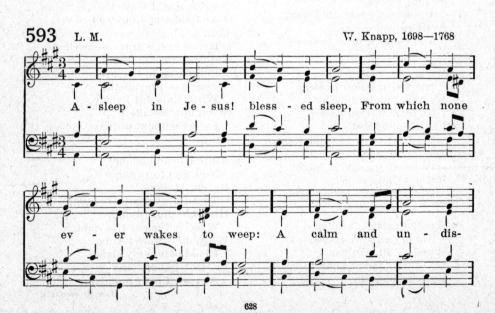

A-sleep in Je-sus! bless-ed sleep, From which none

ev-er wakes to weep: A calm and un-dis-

Burial and Resurrection

turbed re - pose, Un - brok - en by the last of foes.

2 Asleep in Jesus! O how sweet
To be for such a slumber meet;
With holy confidence to sing
That death has lost his venomed sting.

3 Asleep in Jesus! peaceful rest,
Whose waking is supremely blest:

No fear, no woe, shall dim that hour
That manifests the Savior's power.

4 Asleep in Jesus! O for me
May such a blissful refuge be!
Securely shall my ashes lie,
And wait the summons from on high.

Margaret Mackay, 1832

594 L. M.

Nicolaus Herman, d. 1561

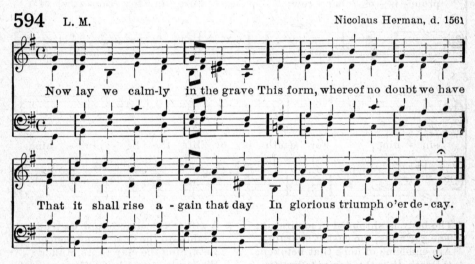

Now lay we calm-ly in the grave This form, whereof no doubt we have

That it shall rise a - gain that day In glorious triumph o'er de - cay.

2 And so to earth again we trust
What came from dust, and turns to dust,
And from the dust shall surely rise
When the last trumpet fills the skies.

3 His soul is living now in God,
Whose grace his pardon hath bestowed,
Who through His Son redeemed him here
From bondage unto sin and fear.

4 His trials and his griefs are past;
A blessed end is his at last;
He bore Christ's yoke, and did His will,
And, though he died, he liveth still.

5 He lives where none can mourn and weep,

And calmly shall this body sleep
Till God shall death himself destroy,
And raise it into glorious joy.

6 He suffered pain and grief below;
Christ heals him now from all his woe;
For him hath endless joy begun;
He shines in glory like the sun.

7 Then let us leave him to his rest,
And homeward turn, for he is blest;
And we must well our souls prepare,
When death shall come, to meet him there.

8 So help us, Christ, our hope in loss;
Thou hast redeemed us by Thy cross
From endless death and misery;
We praise, we bless, we worship Thee

M. Weisse, 1531

The Last Things

595   9s. 4L.   4th Century? 1542

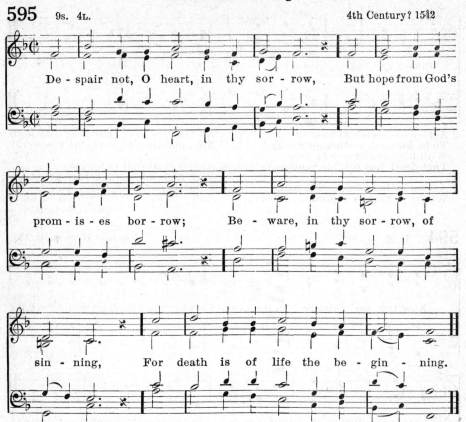

De - spair not, O heart, in thy sor - row, But hope from God's
prom - is - es bor - row; Be - ware, in thy sor - row, of
sin - ning, For death is of life the be - gin - ning.

2 The body is shrouded in mourning;
The garlands, the casket adorning,
Are emblems of hope that betoken,
O Death, that thy power is broken.

3 A dearly beloved one hath left us;
God hath in His wisdom bereft us;
But He will not leave us forsaken,—
We know that the dead shall awaken.

4 When dawneth the glorious morrow,
This body, that we view with sorrow,
A glorified form shall be given,
Restored to its spirit in heaven.

5 The seed that in springtime is planted,
Is hid in the ground; but, if granted
A measure of sushine and showers,
Will spring into fruitage and flowers.

6 A gift to the churchyard we tender,
As dust to the dust we surrender;
Returning the clay to its Maker,
We lay it to rest in God's acre.

7 A soul in that body abided,
A soul that in Jesus confided,
A soul that hath longed for salvation,
And now hath found hope's consum-
    mation.

8 O earth, we consign to thy keeping
This body with sorrow and weeping;
In peace to await resurrection,
When it shall arise in perfection.

9 O Christ, our souls' Maker and Lover;
When time and earth's travail are over,
Thou closest the grave's mournful
    story,
And callest Thine own to Thy glory.

A. C. Prudentius, ca. 413
P. Hegelund. 1586

Burial and Resurrection

596 10, 10, 5, 10.

J. Crüger, 1649

O how blest are ye whose toils are end - ed!
Who, through death, have un - to God as - cend - ed! Ye have a-
ris - en From the cares which keep us still in pris - - on.

2 We are still as in a dungeon living,
   Still oppressed with sorrow and misgiving;
          Our undertakings
   Are but toils and troubles and heart-breakings.

3 Ye, meanwhile, are in your chambers sleeping,
   Quiet, and set free from all your weeping;
          No cross or sadness
   There can hinder your untroubled gladness.

4 Christ has wiped away your tears forever;
   Ye have that for which we still endeavor.
          To you are chanted
   Songs that ne'er to mortal ears were granted.

5 Ah! who would then not depart with gladness,
   To inherit heaven for earthly sadness?
          Who here would languish
   Longer in bewailing and in anguish?

6 Come, O Christ, and loose the chains that bind us!
   Lead us forth, and cast this world behind us!
          With Thee, th' Anointed.
   Finds the soul its joy and rest appointed.

S. Dack, 1635

The Last Things

597 7, 6, 7, 6, 7, 6, 7, 4.

Chrétien D'Urhan, 1834

The sands of time are sink-ing, The dawn of heav-en breaks,

The sum-mer morn I've sighed for, The fair, sweet morn a-wakes.

O dark hath been the mid-night, But day-spring is at hand,

And glo-ry, glo-ry dwell-eth In Im-man-uel's land.

2 O Christ, He is the fountain,
   The deep, sweet well of love!
The streams of earth I've tasted;
   More deep I'll drink above.
There, to an ocean fullness
   His mercy doth expand,
And glory, glory dwelleth
   In Immanuel's land.

3 With mercy and with judgment
   My web of time He wove,
And aye the dews of sorrow
   Were lustered with His love:

I'll bless the hand that guided,
   I'll bless the heart that planned
When throned where glory dwelleth
   In Immanuel's land.

4 The bride eyes not her garment,
   But her dear bridegroom's face;
I will not gaze at glory,
   But on my King of grace;
Not at the crown He giveth,
   But on His piercèd hand;
The Lamb is all the glory
   Of Immanuel's land.

Annie R. Cousin, 1857

632

Burial and Resurrection

598 4, 6. 8L.

J. Barnby, 1869

Sleep thy last sleep, Free from care and sor-row; Rest, where none weep,
Till th' e-ter-nal mor-row; Though dark waves roll O'er the si-lent
riv-er, Thy faint-ing soul Je-sus can de-liv-er.

2 Life's dream is past,
    All its sin and sadness;
Brightly at last
    Dawns a day of gladness:
Under the sod,
    Earth, receive our treasure,
To rest in God,
    Waiting all His pleasure.

3 Though we may mourn
    Those in life the dearest,
They shall return,
    Christ, when Thou appearest:
Soon shall Thy voice
    Comfort those now weeping,
Bidding rejoice
    All in Jesus sleeping.

E. A. Dayman, 1868

The Last Things

599   7, 8, 7, 8, 7, 7.   Lüneburgisches Gesangbuch, 1686

Ten - der Shep - herd, Thou hast stilled Now Thy
lit - tle lamb's brief weep - ing; Ah, how peace - ful, pale, and
mild, In its nar - row bed 'tis sleep - ing! And no sigh of
an - guish sore Heaves that lit - tle bos - om more.

2 In this world of pain and care,
   Lord, Thou wouldst no longer leave
To Thy heavenly meadows fair   [it;
   Lovingly Thou dost receive it.
Clothed in robes of spotless white,
Now it dwells with Thee in light.

3 O Lord Jesus, grant that we
   There may live where it is living,
And the blissful pastures see
   That its heavenly food are giving;
Then the gain of death we'll prove,
Though Thou take what most we love.

J. W. Meinhold, 1835

634

Burial of Children

600 7, 7, 6, 7, 7, 8.   Heinrich Isaac, 1490

Praise God, this hour of sor - row Shall bring a bright-er mor - row:
I go to Par-a - dise. My moth-er dear and fa - ther, When
round my grave you gath - er, Lay me to rest with songs of praise.

2 What better can befall me
Than that the Lord doth call me
    From hence, where sin holds sway?
Who is on earth a stranger
Must ever be in danger,
    Till God hath closed life's fleeting day.

3 God takes His own from anguish
And pain, in which they languish
    Within this vale of tears,
And gives them to inherit
The crown that Christ did merit:
    The joy of heaven's eternal years.

4 I was on earth your treasure;
When now I know but pleasure
    Ye weep in bitter woe;
Believe, whate'er betideth,
God's love in all abideth,
    And soon your tears shall cease to
        flow.

5 Our days the Lord appointeth,
He woundeth and anointeth,
    He knoweth all things well.
No evil He effected,

No good He e'er neglected,
    And all His works His glory tell.

6 When ye shall see me nearing
The throne of God, appearing
    Adorned and crowned a bride,
My palms of victory swinging,
'Midst Hallelujahs ringing,
    In beauteous grace the Lamb be-
        side:

7 Ye both shall rue the sadness
That made you weep, and gladness
    E'er in your hearts shall reign.
Who follows where God guideth,
And takes what He provideth,
    Shall know surcease from all his
        pain.

8 Farewell, I now must leave you;
The grief this day doth give you
    Soon others, too, shall bear.
Be ye to God commended;
In heaven all woe is ended,
    And we shall meet in glory there.

J. Heermann, 1634
H. A. Brorson, 1714.

The Last Things

601 8, 8, 8.

Ludv. M. Lindeman, 1812—87

1 Day of wrath! that day of mourning! See ful-filled the prophet's warn-ing,
2 O what fear man's bos-om rendeth, When from heaven the Judge de-scend-eth,

Heaven and earth in ash-es burn - ing! 3. Wondrous sound the trumpet flingeth,
On whose sentence all de - pend - eth! 4. Death is struck, and nature quaking,

Through earth's sepulchers it ringeth, All be-fore the throne it bring - eth.
All cre - a - tion is a - wak-ing, To its Judge an an-swer mak - - ing.

5 Lo, the Book, exactly worded,
Wherein all hath been recorded!
Thence shall judgment be awarded.

6 When the Judge His seat attaineth,
And each hidden deed arraigneth,
Nothing unavenged remaineth.

7 What shall I, frail man, be pleading?
Who for me be interceding,
When the just are mercy needing?

8 King of majesty tremendous,
Who dost free salvation send us,
Fount of pity, then befriend us!

9 Think, good Jesus! my salvation
Caused Thy wondrous incarnation,
Leave me not to reprobation!

10 Faint and weary Thou hast sought
me,
On the cross of suffering bought me:
Shall such grace in vain be brought
me?

11 Righteous Judge! for sin's pollution
Grant Thy gift of absolution,
Ere that day of retribution.

12 Guilty, now I pour my moaning,
All my shame with anguish owning:
Spare, O God, Thy suppliant groan-
ing!

13 Thou the sinful woman savedst;
Thou the dying thief forgavest;
And to me a hope vouchsafest.

14 Worthless are my prayers and sigh-
ing,
Yet, good Lord, in grace complying,
Rescue me from fires undying!

15 With Thy favored sheep O place me!
Nor among the goats abase me;
But to Thy right hand upraise me.

16 While the wicked are confounded,
Doomed to flames of woe unbounded,
Call me, with Thy saints surrounded.

Christ's Second Coming

17 Bows my heart in meek submission, Strewn with ash - es of con - tri - tion;

Help me in my last con - di - - tion! -tion! 18 Ah, that day of

tears and mourning! From the dust of earth re - turn - ing, Man for judgment

must pre - pare him: 19 Spare, O God, in mer - cy spare him! Lord, all-

pity - ing, Je - sus blest, Grant them Thine e - ter - nal rest!

Thomas of Selano, 13th Century

The Last Things

602　7, 6. 6L.　　　　　　　　　　　　M. Teschner, 1613

Re - joice, re - joice, be - liev - ers, And let your lights ap - pear!

The eve - ning is ad - vanc - ing, And dark - er night is near.

The Bridegroom is a - ris - ing, And soon He draw-eth nigh;

Up, pray, and watch and wres - tle; At mid-night comes the cry!

2 The watchers on the mountain
  Proclaim the Bridegroom near;
Go meet Him as He cometh,
  With Hallelujahs clear.
The marriage-feast is waiting,
  The gates wide open stand;
Up, up, ye heirs of glory;
  The Bridegroom is at hand!

3 Ye saints, who here in patience
  Your cross and sufferings bore,
Shall live and reign for ever,
  When sorrow is no more.

Around the throne of glory
  The Lamb ye shall behold,
In triumph cast before Him
  Your diadems of gold!

4 Our hope and expectation,
  O Jesus, now appear;
Arise, Thou Sun so longed for,
  O'er this benighted sphere!
With hearts and hands uplifted,
  We plead, O Lord, to see
The day of earth's redemption,
  That brings us unto Thee!

L. Laurenti. 1700

Christ's Second Coming

603 8, 7, 8, 7, 8, 7, 7.

Severus Gastorius, 1675

O Son of God, we wait for Thee, We long for Thine ap - pear - ing,
We know Thou sit-test on the throne, And we Thy name are bear - ing.
Who trusts in Thee, may joy - ful be, And see Thee, Lord, de-
scend - ing To bring us bliss un - end - ing.

2 We wait for Thee, 'mid toil and pain,
In weariness and sighing;
But glad that Thou our guilt hast borne,
And cancelled it by dying.
Hence, cheerfully may we with Thee
Take up our cross and bear it,
Till we relief inherit.

3 We wait for Thee; here Thou hast won
Our hearts to hope and duty;
But while our spirits feel Thee near,
Our eyes would see Thy beauty;
We fain would be at rest with Thee
In peace and joy supernal,
In glorious life eternal.

4 We wait for Thee; soon Thou wilt come,
The time is swiftly nearing;
In this we also do rejoice,
And long for Thine appearing,
O bliss 'twill be when Thee we see,
Homeward Thy people bringing,
With transport and with singing!

Philip F. Hiller. 1767

The Last Things

604 8, 7, 8, 7, 8, 8, 7. Joseph Klug, Wittenberg, 1535

Great God, what do I see and hear! The end of things cre-
at - ed! The Judge of man-kind doth ap - pear, On clouds of glo - ry
seat - ed; The trum - pet sounds; the graves re - store The
dead which they con-tained be - fore; Pre - pare, my soul, to meet Him.

2 The dead in Christ shall first arise,
  At the last trumpet's sounding.
Caught up to meet Him in the skies,
  With joy their Lord surrounding;
No gloomy fears their souls dismay;
His presence sheds eternal day
  On those prepared to meet Him.

3 But sinners, filled with guilty fears,
  Behold His wrath prevailing,
For they shall rise and find their tears
  And sighs are unavailing;

The day of grace is past and gone;
They trembling stand before the throne,
  All unprepared to meet Him.

4 O Christ, who diedst and yet dost live,
  To me impart Thy merit:
My pardon seal, my sins forgive,
  And cleanse me by Thy Spirit.
Beneath Thy cross I view the day
When heaven and earth shall pass
  away,
  And thus prepare to meet Thee.

V. I. Anon., 1802. W. B Collier, 1812.
Alt. by T. Cotteril, and others.

Christ's Second Coming

605
8, 8, 8, 4.

R. N. Quaile

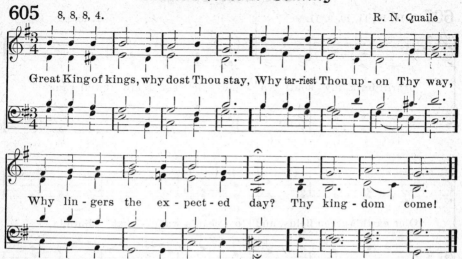

Great King of kings, why dost Thou stay, Why tar-riest Thou up-on Thy way,

Why lin-gers the ex-pect-ed day? Thy king-dom come!

2 Life in its fullness is with Thee,
Life in its holy liberty;
From death and chains this world set
  free;
Thy kingdom come!

3 Earth is still waiting for the day,
When old things shall have passed
  away,

And all be clad in new array:
  Thy kingdom come!

4 O King of glory, King of peace,
Bid all these storms and tumults
  cease,
Bring in Thy reign of righteousness;
Thy kingdom come!

H. Bonar, 1868

606
L. M.

German, 1543

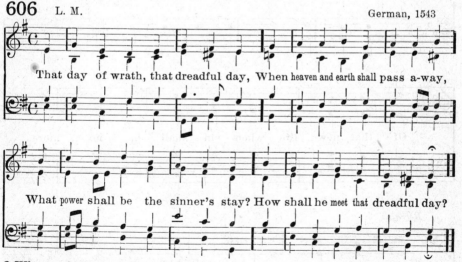

That day of wrath, that dreadful day, When heaven and earth shall pass a-way,

What power shall be the sinner's stay? How shall he meet that dreadful day?

2 When, shriveling like a parched
  scroll,
The flaming heavens together roll;
When louder yet, and yet more dread,
Resounds the trump that wakes the
  dead;

3 O on that day, that wrathful day,
When man to judgment wakes from
  clay,
Be Thou, O Christ, the sinner's stay,
Though heaven and earth shall pass
  away.

Thomas of Celano, 13th Century.
Tr. by Sir Walter Scott, 1805.

The Last Things

11, 10, 11, 10, 9, 11.

J. Barnby, 1868

Hark! hark, my soul! An - gel - ic songs are swell - ing

O'er earth's green fields, and o - cean's wave - beat shore;

How sweet the truth those bless - ed strains are tell - ing

Of that new life when sin shall be no more.

Refrain.

An - gels of Je - sus, An - gels of light,

The Heavenly Home

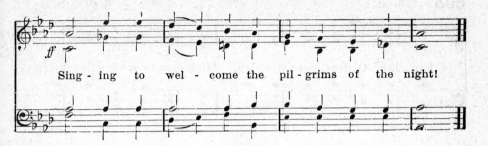

Sing - ing to wel - come the pil - grims of the night!

2 Onward we go, for still we hear them singing,
'Come, weary souls, for Jesus bids you come;'
And through the dark, its echoes sweetly ringing,
The music of the gospel leads us home.
Angels of Jesus, Angels of light,
Singing to welcome the pilgrims of the night.

3 Far, far away, like bells at evening pealing,
The voice of Jesus sounds o'er land and sea,
And laden souls by thousands meekly stealing,
Kind Shepherd, turn their weary steps to Thee.
Angels of Jesus, Angels of light,
Singing to welcome the pilgrims of the night.

4 Rest comes at length: though life be long and dreary,
The day must dawn, and darksome night be past;
Faith's journeys end in welcome to the weary,
And heaven, the heart's true home, will come at last.
Angels of Jesus, Angels of light,
Singing to welcome the pilgrims of the night.

5 Angels, sing on! your faithful watches keeping;
Sing us sweet fragments of the songs above;
Till morning's joy shall end the night of weeping,
And life's long shadows break in cloudless love.
Angels of Jesus, Angels of light,
Singing to welcome the pilgrims of the night.

Frederick W. Faber, 1854

The Last Things

7, 6. 8L.

A. R. Gaul, 1837—

For thee, O dear, dear coun-try, Mine eyes their vig - ils keep;

For ver - y love, be - hold - ing Thy hap - py name, they weep.

The men - tion of thy glo - ry Is unc-tion to the breast,

And med - i - cine in sick - ness, And love, and life, and rest.

2 O one, O only mansion!
  O Paradise of joy!
Where tears are ever banished,
  And smiles have no alloy;
The Lamb is all thy splendor;
  The Crucified thy praise;
His laud and benediction
  Thy ransomed people raise.

3 With jasper glow thy bulwarks,
  Thy streets with emeralds blaze;
The sardius and the topaz
  Unite in thee their rays;
Thine ageless walls are bounded
  With amethyst unpriced;
The saints build up thy fabric,
  The corner-stone is Christ.

The Heavenly Home

4 Thou hast no shore, fair ocean!
  Thou hast no time, bright day!
Dear fountain of refreshment
  To pilgrims far away!
Upon the Rock of Ages
  They raise thy holy tower;
Thine is the victor's laurel,
  And thine the golden dower.

5 O sweet and blessed country,
  The home of God's elect!
O sweet and blessed country
  That eager hearts expect!
Jesus, in mercy bring us
  To that dear land of rest;
Who art, with God the Father
  And Spirit, ever blest.

Bernard of Cluny, ca. 1145

609 C. M.

H. S. Irons, 1861

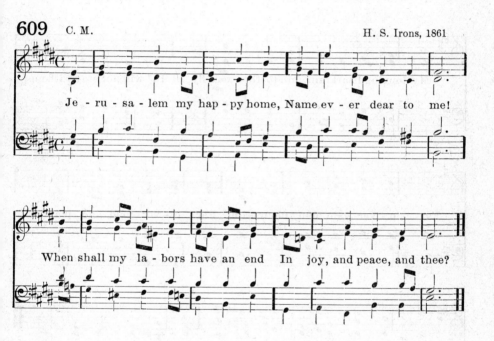

Je - ru - sa - lem my hap - py home, Name ev - er dear to me!

When shall my la - bors have an end In joy, and peace, and thee?

2 When shall these eyes thy heaven-
    built walls
  And pearly gates behold?
Thy bulwarks with salvation strong,
  And streets of shining gold?

3 O when, thou city of my God,
  Shall I thy courts ascend,
Where evermore the angels sing,
  Where sabbaths have no end?

4 There happier bowers than Eden's
    Nor sin nor sorrow know; [bloom.
Blest seats! through rude and stormy
    scenes
  I onward press to you.

5 Why should I shrink from pain and
    woe,
  Or feel at death dismay?
I've Canaan's goodly land in view,
  And realms of endless day.

6 Apostles, martyrs, prophets there
  Around my Savior stand;
And soon my friends in Christ below
  Will join the glorious band.

7 Jerusalem, my happy home!
  My soul still pants for thee;
Then shall my labors have an end,
  When I thy joy shall see.

Anon., 16th or 17th Century
Joseph Bromhead, 1795

The Last Things

610 10, 6, 10, 6, 7, 6, 7, 6.   M. Frank, 1580—1639

Je - ru - sa - lem, thou cit - y fair and high, Would God I were in thee!

My longing heart fain, fain to thee would fly,   It will not stay with me;

Far o - ver vale and mount-ain, Far o - ver field and plain,

It hastes to seek its fount - ain, And quit this world of pain.

2 O happy day, and yet far happier hour,
  When wilt thou come at last?
When fearless to my Father's love
    and power,
  Whose promise standeth fast,
My soul I gladly render,
  For surely will His hand
Lead her with guidance tender
  To heaven, her fatherland.

3 A moment's space, and gently, won-
    drously,
  Released from earthly ties,
The fiery car shall bear her up to Thee
  Through all these lower skies,
To yonder shining regions,
  While down to meet her come
The blessed angel legions,
  And bid her welcome home.

The Heavenly Home

4 O Zion, hail! Bright city, now un-
    fold
  The gates of grace to me!
How many a time I longed for thee of
    old,
  Ere yet I was set free
From yon dark life of sadness,
  Yon world of shadowy nought,
And God had given the gladness,
  The heritage I sought.

5 Innumerous choirs before the shin-
    ing throne
  Their joyful anthems raise,
Till heaven's glad halls are echoing
    with the tone
  Of that great hymn of praise,
And all its host rejoices,
  And all its blessed throng
Unite their myriad voices
  In one eternal song!

J. M. Meyfart, 1626

611   C. M.

C. E. F. Weyse, 1837

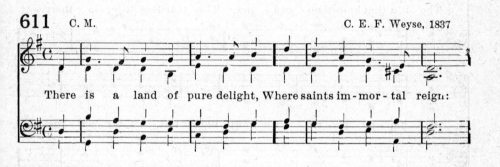

There is a land of pure delight, Where saints im-mor-tal reign:

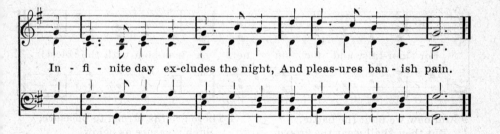

In-fi-nite day ex-cludes the night, And pleas-ures ban-ish pain.

2 There everlasting spring abides,
  With never-withering flowers;
Death, like a narrow sea, divides
  That heavenly land from ours.

3 Sweet fields beyond the swelling
    flood,
  Stand dressed in living green;
So to the Jews old Canaan stood,
  While Jordan rolled between.

4 But timorous mortals start and shrink
  To cross this narrow sea,

And linger trembling on the brink,
  And fear to launch away.

5 O could we make our doubts remove,
  Those gloomy doubts that rise,
And see the Canaan that we love,
  With faith's illumined eyes:

6 Could we but climb where Moses
  And view the landscape o'er, [stood,
Not Jordan's stream, nor deaths cold
    flood
  Should fright us from the shore.

I. Watts, 1707

The Last Things

612 7, 6. 8L.

S. S. Wesley, 1810—76

Brief life is here our por - tion; Brief sor-row, short-lived care;

The life that knows no end - ing, The tear-less life, is there.

O hap - py re - tri - bu - tion! Short toil, e - ter - nal rest;

For mor-tals, and for sin - ners A man-sion with the blest!

2 And now we fight the battle,
  But then shall wear the crown
Of full and everlasting
  And passionless renown;
And now we watch and struggle,
  And now we live in hope,
And Zion in her anguish
  With Babylon must cope;

3 But He whom now we trust in
  Shall then be seen and known;
And they that know and see Him
  Shall have Him for their own.
The morning shall awaken,
  The shadows shall decay,
And each true-hearted servant
  Shall shine as doth the day.

4 There grief is turned to pleasure,
  Such pleasure as below
No human voice can utter,
  No human heart can know.
There God, our king and portion,
  In fulness of His grace,
Shall we behold for ever,
  And worship face to face.

5 O sweet and blessed country,
  The home of God's elect!
O sweet and blessed country
  That eager hearts expect!
Jesus, in mercy bring us
  To that dear land of rest;
Who art, with God the Father
  And Spirit, ever blest.

Bernard of Cluny, ca. 1145

The Heavenly Home

613 10, 6, 10, 6, 7, 6, 7, 6.

M. Frank, 1580—1639

True Light, that lightest all in heaven and earth, Light us Thou Light di-vine;

Children Thou mad'st us by a sec-ond birth, Chil-dren, O Lord, of Thine;

Heirs of a life un-dy-ing, The hid-den life a-bove,

Strong on Thy strength re-ly-ing, Safe in a Fa-ther's love.

2 The earth, erewhile so oft bedewed
    with tears,
  Shall be, like man, new-born;
The heavens— unrolled through un-
    imagined years—
  Be bright with endless morn;
No room is there for sorrow,
  Toil, trouble, want, or care,
None anxious for the morrow,—
  There is no morrow there.

3 Light there, eternal light and life
    shall reign
  O'er all without, within;
No stricken soul e'er bow beneath the
    pain

Of unforgotten sin;
The day shall have no ending,
  No night its shadows cast,
All present gladness blending
  With gladness in the past.

4 We darkly now, as in a mirror, see
  These wondrous worlds on high;
Help us, O Lord, to live our life in
    Thee,
  The life that cannot die;
Till heavenward ever soaring,
  By Thy redeeming grace,
Before Thy throne adoring
  We see Thee face to face.

G. Thring, 1888

The Last Things

7, 6. 8L.

A. Ewing, 1830—95

Je - ru - sa - lem the gold - en, With milk and hon - ey blest,

Be - neath thy con - tem - pla - tion Sink heart and voice op - prest,

I know not, O I know not, What joys a - wait us there,

What ra - dian - cy of glo - ry, What bliss be - yond com-pare.

2 They stand, those halls of Zion,
   All jubilant with song,
And bright with many an angel,
   And all the martyr throng;
The Prince is ever in them,
   The daylight is serene,
The pastures of the blessed
   Are decked in glorious sheen.

3 There is the throne of David;
   And there, from care released,
The shout of them that triumph,
   The song of them that feast;

And they who with their leader
   Have conquered in the fight,
For ever and for ever
   Are clad in robes of white.

4 O sweet and blessed country,
   The home of God's elect!
O sweet and blessed country
   That eager hearts expect!
Jesus, in mercy bring us
   To that dear land of rest;
Who art, witn God the Father
   And Spirit, ever blest.

650   Bernard of Cluny, ca. 1145

The Heavenly Home

615 6s. 8l.

John Stainer, 1875

There is a bless-ed home Be - yond this land of woe,

Where tri - als nev - er come, Nor tears of sor - row flow;

Where faith is lost in sight, And pa - tient hope is crowned,

And ev - er - last - ing light Its glo - ry throws a - round.

2 There is a land of peace,
  Good angels know it well;
Glad songs that never cease
  Within its portals swell;
Around its glorious throne
  Ten thousand saints adore
Christ, with the Father One,
  And Spirit, evermore.

3 O joy all joys beyond,
  To see the Lamb who died,
And count each sacred wound
  In hands, and feet, and side;

To give to Him the praise
  Of every triumph won,
And sing through endless days
  The great things He hath done!

4 Look up, ye saints of God,
  Nor fear to tread below
The path your Savior trod
  Of daily toil and woe:
Wait but a little while
  In uncomplaining love,
His own most gracious smile
  Shall welcome you above.

Sir Henry W. Baker, 1861

The Last Things

616 8, 6, 8, 6, 6, 6, 6, 6.

J. Barnby, 1866

O Par - a-dise, O Par - a-dise, Who doth not crave for rest,

Who would not seek the hap - py land Where they that loved are blest?

Where loy - al hearts and true

Where loy - - - al hearts and true Stand ev - er in the light,

All rap - ture through and through, In God's most ho - ly sight.

2 O Paradise, O Paradise,
 The world is growing old;
Who would not be at rest and free
 Where love is never cold?
Where loyal hearts and true, etc.

3 O Paradise, O Paradise,
 'Tis weary waiting here:
I long to be where Jesus is,
 To feel, to see Him near;
Where loyal hearts and true, etc.

4 O Paradise, O Paradise,
 I long to sin no more,
I long to be as pure on earth

As on thy spotless shore;
Where loyal hearts and true, etc.

5 O Paradise, O Paradise,
 We shall not wait for long;
E'en now the loving ear may catch
 Faint fragments of thy song;
Where loyal hearts and true, etc.

6 Lord Jesus, King of Paradise,
 O keep me in Thy love,
And guide me to that happy land
 Of perfect rest above;
Where loyal hearts and true, etc.

Frederick W. Faber, 1862

The Heavenly Home

Ten thou-sand times ten thou-sand, In sparkling rai-ment bright,

The ar-mies of the ransomed saints Throng up the steeps of light:

'Tis fin-ished! all is fin-ished, Their fight with death and sin:

Fling o-pen wide the gold-en gates, And let the vic-tors in.

2 What rush of Hallelujahs
  Fills all the earth and sky!
What ringing of a thousand harps
  Bespeaks the triumph nigh!
O day for which creation
  And all its tribes were made;
O joy, for all its former woes
  A thousand-fold repaid!

3 O then what raptured greetings
  On Canaan's happy shore;
What knitting severed friendships
  up,
  Where partings are no more!

Then eyes with joy shall sparkle
  That brimmed with tears of late;
Orphans no longer fatherless,
  Nor widows desolate.

4 Bring near Thy great salvation,
  Thou Lamb for sinners slain;
Fill up the roll of Thine elect,
  Then take Thy power and reign:
Appear, Desire of nations,
  Thine exiles long for home:
Show in the heavens Thy promised
  sign;
  Thou Prince and Savior, come!

Henry Alford, 1867

The Heavenly Home

618 S. M.

Arr. fr. R. Schumann, 1810—56

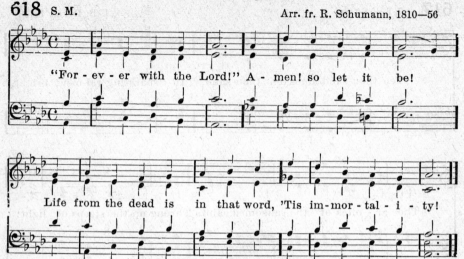

"For - ev - er with the Lord!" A - men! so let it be!

Life from the dead is in that word, 'Tis im - mor - tal - i - ty!

2 Here, in the body pent,
    Absent from Him I roam,
  Yet nightly pitch my moving tent
    A day's march nearer home.

3 My Father's house on high,
    Home of my soul, how near,
  At times, to faith's foreseeing eye,
    Thy golden gates appear!

4 Ah! then my spirit faints
    To reach the land I love,
  The bright inheritance of saints,
    Jerusalem above!

5 "Forever with the Lord!"
    Father, if 'tis Thy will,
  The promise of that faithful word
    E'en here to me fulfill.

6 Be Thou at my right hand,
    Then can I never fail;
  Uphold Thou me, and I shall stand;
    Fight, and I must prevail.

7 So when my latest breath
    Shall rend the veil in twain,
  By death I shall escape from death,
    And life eternal gain.

8 Knowing as I am known,
    How shall I love that word,
  And oft repeat, before the throne,
    "Forever with the Lord!"

J. Montgomery, 1835

Doxologies

1   S. M.

To God, the Father, Son,
  And Spirit, ever blest,
The One in Three, the Three in One,
  Be endless praise addressed.

2   C. M.

To Father, Son, and Holy Ghost,
  The God whom we adore,
Be glory, as it was, is now,
  And shall be evermore.

3   8, 7, 8, 7, 8, 8, 7.

Now to the holy Three in One,
  Who o'er creation reigneth,
Be everlasting honor done,
  To whom all praise pertaineth.
All blessing be to God Most High,
  All glory to His majesty,
Who all the world sustaineth.

4   L. M.

To Father, Son, and Holy Ghost,
  The God whom earth and heaven adore
Be glory, as it was of old,
Is now, and shall be evermore.

5   L. M.

Praise God, from whom all blessings
      flow!
Praise Him, all creatures here below!
Praise Him, above, ye heavenly host!
Praise Father, Son, and Holy Ghost!

6   7, 6. 4L.

To Father, Son, and Spirit,
  Eternal One in Three,
As was, and is forever,
  All praise and glory be.

7   6, 6, 4, 6, 6, 6, 4.

To God the Father, Son,
And Spirit, Three in One,
  All praise be given:
Crown Him in every song,
To Him our hearts belong,
Let all His praise prolong,
  On earth, in heaven.

8   8s. 6L.

Praise the name of God most high,
Praise Him, all below the sky,
Praise Him, all ye heavenly host,
Father, Son, and Holy Ghost:
As through countless ages past,
Evermore His praise shall last.

9   7s. 4L.

Holy Father, Holy Son,
Holy Spirit, Three in One!
Glory, as of old, to Thee,
Now, and evermore shall be.

10   7, 6. 8L.

To God the ever-glorious,
  The Father, and the Son,
And Spirit all-victorious,
  Thrice holy Three in One;
The God of our salvation,
  Whom earth and heaven adore,
Praise, glory, adoration,
  Be now and evermore.

11   8, 7. 4L.

Praise the Father, earth and heaven,
  Praise the Son, the Spirit praise,
As it was, and is, be given
  Glory through eternal days.

12   8, 7. 8L.

Praise the God of all creation:
  Praise the Father's boundless love;
Praise the Lamb, our expiation,
  Priest and King enthroned above,
Praise the fountain of salvation,
  Him by whom our spirits live;
Undivided adoration
  To the One Jehovah give.

13   8, 7, 8, 7, 4, 7.

Great Jehovah! we adore Thee,
  God the Father, God the Son,
God the Spirit, joined in glory
  On the same eternal throne;
    Endless praises
  To Jehovah, Three in One.

14   10s. 4L.

And now to God the Father, God the
      Son,
And God the Spirit ever Three in One,
Be praise from all on earth and all in
      heaven,
As was, and is, and ever shall be given.

Appendix

I. (18) 8, 7, 8, 7, 8, 8, 7.   *Older Form.*   J. Klug, Wittenberg, 1535

O Ho - ly Spir-it, grant us grace That we our Lord and Sav - ior

In faith and fer-vent love embrace, And tru - ly serve Him ev - er,

So that when death is draw-ing nigh, We to His o - pen

wounds may fly, And find in them sal - va - tion.

2 Help us that we Thy saving word
  In faithful hearts may treasure;
Let e'er that bread of life afford
  New grace in richest measure;
Yea, let us die to every sin,
  For heaven create us new within,
That fruits of faith may flourish.

3 And when our earthly race is run,
  Death's bitter hour impending,
Then may Thy work in us begun,
  Continue till life's ending;
Until we gladly may commend
  Our souls into our Savior's hand,
To rest in peace eternal.

B. Ringwaldt, 1581
S. Jonassön, 1693

656

Appendix

II. (53) 8, 7, 8, 7, 7, 7, 8, 8.

Older Form.

Composed or adapted by L. Bourgeois, 1851

Praise to Thee and ad-o-ra-tion, Blessed Je-sus, Son of God,

Who, to serve Thine own cre-a-tion, Didst par-take of flesh and blood;

Teach me that I nev-er may From Thy fold or pastures stray,

But with zeal and joy ex-ceed-ing Fol-low where Thy steps are leading.

2 Let me never, Lord, forsake Thee,
E'en though bitter pain and strife
On my way shall overtake me;
But may I through all my life
Walk in fervent love to Thee,
In all woes for comfort flee
To Thy birth, Thy death and passion;
Till I see Thy full salvation.

T. Kingo, 1689

Appendix

O Je - sus, our sal - va - tion, Low at Thy cross we lie:

Lord, in Thy great com-pas - sion, Hear our be - wail - ing cry.

We come to Thee with mourn - ing, We come to Thee in

woe; With con - trite hearts re - turn-ing, And tears that o - ver - flow.

2 O gracious Intercessor!
　O Priest within the veil,
Plead for each lost transgressor
　The blood that cannot fail.
We spread our sins before Thee,
　We tell them one by one:
O, for Thy name's great glory,
　Forgive all we have done.

3 O, by Thy cross and passion,
　Thy tears and agony,
And crown of cruel fashion,
　And death on Calvary;

By all that untold suffering,
　Endured by Thee alone;
O Priest, O spotless Offering,
　Plead, for Thou didst atone!

4 And in these hearts now broken
　Re-enter Thou and reign,
And say, by that dear token,
　We are absolved again.
And build us up, and guide us,
　And guard us day by day;
And in Thy presence hide us,
　And take our sins away.

James Hamilton, 1867

Appendix

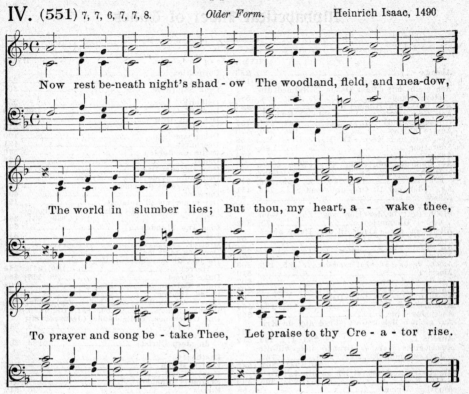

Now rest be-neath night's shad - ow The woodland, field, and mea-dow,

The world in slumber lies; But thou, my heart, a - wake thee,

To prayer and song be - take Thee,   Let praise to thy Cre - a - tor rise.

2 To rest the body hasteth,
  Aside its garments casteth—
    Types of mortality;
  These I put off, and ponder
  How Christ shall give me yonder
    A robe of glorious majesty.

3 Ye weary limbs, now rest you,
  For toil hath sore oppressed you,
    And quiet sleep ye crave;
  A sleep shall once o'ertake you
  From which no man can wake you,
    In your last, narrow bed—the grave.

4 Lord Jesus, who dost love me,
  O spread Thy wings above me,
    And shield me from alarm!
  Though Satan would devour me:
  Let angel-guards sing o'er me:
    This child of God shall meet no harm.

5 My loved ones, rest securely,
  For God this night will surely,
    From perils guard your heads;
  Sweet slumbers may He send you,
  And bid His hosts attend you,
    And through the night watch o'er your beds.

P. Gerhardt, 1648

Alphabetical Index of Tunes

Alphabetical Index of Tunes

Alphabetical Index of Tunes

Metrical Index of Tunes

Metrical Index of Tunes

Metrical Index of Tunes

Metrical Index of Tunes

Metrical Index of Tunes

Index of Subjects

This index does not contain references that may be found conveniently in the Table of Contents.

Abiding in Christ, 30, 57, 109, 351, 353, 437, 482.
Activity and Zeal, 254, 256, 257, 283.
Affliction, 217, 218, 240, 242, 271, 503, 516, 524.
Angels, 24, 122, 269, 542.
Atonement, 301, 306, 309, 314, 316, 318, 483.
Beginning of Service, 33—45. Also the following: 32, 73, 134, 135, 260, 355, 374, 375, 376, 382, 426.
Benevolence, 274, 449, 450, 452, 500.
Brotherly Love, 397, 405, 406, 407, 412, 451.
Children's Services, 570—578. Also the following: 105, 110, 111, 107, 146, 178, 179, 458.
Church of Christ, 78—89. Also the following: 47, 116, 132, 134, 245, 253, 424, 427 525.
Close of Service, 46—59. Also the following: 31, 75, 136, 137, 138, 140, 261.
Communion of Saints, 78, 86, 397, 405, 406, 407, 412, 468, 495.
Confession of Faith, 71, 76.
Confession of Sin, 96—104. Also the following: 273, 400, 441, 442, 497, 499, 522, 523.
Consecration, 94, 105, 107, 111, 227, 299, 398, 410.
Conversion, 356, 389, 390, 401, 402, 404.
Creation, 3, 8, 28.
Cross and Comfort, 237, 267, 277, 284, 342, 453, 465, 466, 503, 516, 517, 524, 553.
Eternal Life, 341, 492, 493, 513, 590, 592, 612, 618.
Faith, 27, 81, 163, 243, 244, 377, 390.
Following Christ, 91, 257, 338, 372, 394, 408, 475.
God — Almighty, 5, 12, 60, 385.
God — Eternal, 1, 61, 64.
God — Holy, 62, 72, 74.
God — Loving, 68, 434, 436, 448, 459, 476.
God — Merciful, 9, 20, 28, 450, 478.
Gospel, The, 123, 135, 171, 251. See Invitation.
Grace, 15, 28, 268, 276, 344, 414, 434, 440, 442.
Heaven, 607—618. Also the following: 52, 239, 250, 252, 263.
Heavenly Mind, 58, 248, 298, 354, 409, 462.
Holiness, 246, 279, 444, 469, 500, 501.
Holy Ghost, — Our Comforter, 39, 235, 374, 380, 381, 382.
Holy Ghost, — Our Guide, 26, 266, 354, 375, 376, 383.
Holy Ghost, — Our Teacher, 18, 125, 358, 426, 498.
Hope, 236, 237, 252, 373, 487, 509.
Humility, 276, 310, 408, 469.
Invitation, 159, 173, 393, 401, 411, 413, 433, 435, 438, 486.
Jesus Christ, — Our Atoner, 96, 98, 262, 265.
Jesus Christ, — Our Example, 30, 225, 279, 392, 394.
Jesus Christ, — Our High Priest, 267, 319, 321, 357, 477.
Jesus Christ, — Our King, 6, 117, 168, 292. See also Hymns for Advent and Ascension.
Jesus Christ, — Our Light, 33, 219, 220, 221, 223, 224, 259, 444.
Jesus Christ, — Our Redeemer, 66, 174, 307, 373, 432.
Jesus Christ, — Our Righteousness, 22, 27, 236, 396, 415.
Jesus Christ, — Our Savior, 208, 211, 231, 278, 417.
Jesus Christ, — Our Shepherd, 300, 343, 345, 346, 403, 420, 525, 571, 575.
Jesus Christ, — Our Teacher, 221, 228. 279.
Judgment, 601, 604, 606.
Justification, 27, 205, 393, 404, 415, 439, 447.

Index of Subjects

Kingdom of Christ, see Church of.   Also the following: 80, 89.
Law of God, 205, 416, 425, 455.
Lord's Day, 38, 40, 42, 471.
Love of God, 434.   See also Christmas Hymns.
Love to God and the Savior, 50, 154, 169, 295, 347, 393, 398, 419, 474.
Missions, 112—127.   Also the following: 29, 221, 223.
Obedience to God, 121, 216, 238, 413.
Patience, 233, 467, 475, 487.
Peace and Joy, 396, 418, 419, 480.
Perseverance and Faithfulness, 18, 165, 246, 372, 413, 487.
Pilgrimage, 86, 285, 286, 451, 458, 462, 468, 504, 505, 507.
Praise and Prayer, 1—32.   Also the following: 42, 43, 44, 63, 65, 74, 341, 358, 359,
    360, 364, 385, 443, 446, 488, 545.
Providence, 212, 230, 284, 345, 421, 422, 454, 460.
Redemption, 281, 297, 373, 404, 456.
Regeneration, 99, 295, 386, 479.
Repentance, 273, 305, 388, 400, 402, 441, 484.
Resignation, See Submission.
Resurrection, 588—600.   Also the following: 465, 506, 509, 513.   See also Hymns
    for Easter.
Salvation, 25, 81, 205, 411, 526.
Sanctification, 254, 266, 297, 353, 392, 457, 476.
Second Coming of Christ, 601—606.   Also the following: 166, 172, 496, 508, 510, 511.
Submission, 215, 216, 233, 238, 370, 473, 481, 531.
Temperance, 283, 425, 500.
Temptation, 280, 282, 304, 430.
Thanksgiving, 10, 11, 19, 24, 31, 443, 529.
Trials and Conflicts, 240, 255, 271, 428, 464, 521.
Trust in God, 84, 85, 226, 237, 272, 284, 349, 350, 384.
Victory, 87, 270, 493. 494.
Warfare, 87, 258, 270, 489, 490, 491.
Watchfulness, 269, 429, 430, 485, 508, 510, 512.
Word of God, 134—140.   Also the following: 46, 245, 251, 260, 261, 427, 573.

Index of First Lines

The names of the translators are given in this index.

_____

Index of First Lines

Index of First Lines

Index of First Lines

Index of First Lines

Index of First Lines

Index of First Lines

Index of First Lines

Index of First Lines

Index of First Lines